Artificial Intelligence

ALL-IN-ONE

by Chris Minnick et al.

A Wiley Brand

Artificial Intelligence All-in-One For Dummies®

Published by: **John Wiley & Sons, Inc.,** 111 River Street, Hoboken, NJ 07030-5774, www.wiley.com

For general information on our other products and services, please contact our Customer Care Department within the U.S. at 877-762-2974, outside the U.S. at 317-572-3993, or fax 317-572-4002. For technical support, please visit https://hub.wiley.com/community/support/dummies.

Wiley publishes in a variety of print and electronic formats and by print-on-demand. Some material included with standard print versions of this book may not be included in e-books or in print-on-demand. If this book refers to media that is not included in the version you purchased, you may download this material at http://booksupport.wiley.com. For more information about Wiley products, visit www.wiley.com.

Library of Congress Control Number: 2025936526

ISBN 978-1-394-34172-6 (pbk); ISBN 978-1-394-34174-0 (ePDF); ISBN 978-1-394-34173-3 (ePUB)

Printed by CPI Group (UK) Ltd, Croydon CR0 4YY

C9781394341726_170925

Contents at a Glance

Introduction 1

Book 1: Understanding AI Foundations 7
CHAPTER 1: Delving into What AI Means 9
CHAPTER 2: Defining Data's Role in AI 25
CHAPTER 3: Considering the Use of Algorithms 47
CHAPTER 4: Pioneering Specialized Hardware 65
CHAPTER 5: Parsing Machine Learning and Deep Learning 81
CHAPTER 6: Upholding Responsible AI Standards in GenAI Use 101
CHAPTER 7: Finding Job Security in an AI World 115

Book 2: Prompting and Generative AI Techniques 131
CHAPTER 1: Mapping the Lay of the Generative AI Land 133
CHAPTER 2: Introducing the Art of Prompt Engineering 149
CHAPTER 3: Navigating the Evolving Landscape of GenAI 161
CHAPTER 4: Introducing ChatGPT 175
CHAPTER 5: Getting Started with Microsoft Copilot 189
CHAPTER 6: Learning Advanced Prompting 203

Book 3: Increasing Productivity with AI 223
CHAPTER 1: Applying GenAI in Practical Scenarios 225
CHAPTER 2: Crunching the Numbers with Copilot 237
CHAPTER 3: Presenting with Copilot 263
CHAPTER 4: Meeting and Collaborating with Copilot 281
CHAPTER 5: Working with AI in a Roundup of Business Disciplines 293
CHAPTER 6: Managing AI Adoption and Change in Your Organization 317

Book 4: Creating Content with AI 333
CHAPTER 1: Using AI for Ideation and Planning 335
CHAPTER 2: Managing and Writing Emails with AI 349
CHAPTER 3: Developing Creative Assets 363
CHAPTER 4: Producing Long-Form Content 381
CHAPTER 5: Search Engine Optimization (SEO) in the AI Era 403
CHAPTER 6: Fine-Tuning Content with Localization and Translation 419

Book 5: AI at Home 433

CHAPTER 1: Relying on AI to Improve Human Interaction 435

CHAPTER 2: Using AI to Address Medical Needs 445

CHAPTER 3: Leveraging AI in Education 465

CHAPTER 4: Using GenAI in the Real World 481

CHAPTER 5: Financial Planning and Other Money Matters 491

CHAPTER 6: Retirement and Estate Planning 501

Book 6: Applying AI in Coding 517

CHAPTER 1: How Coding Benefits from AI 519

CHAPTER 2: AI Coding Tools 547

CHAPTER 3: Coding with Chatbots 571

CHAPTER 4: Progressing from Plan to Prototype 601

Book 7: Creating Custom AI Solutions 631

CHAPTER 1: Personalizing the Customer Journey by Using AI 633

CHAPTER 2: Boosting Online Business Growth with AI 649

CHAPTER 3: Enhancing Customer Service with Conversational AI Chatbots 665

CHAPTER 4: Making Custom Copilots 681

CHAPTER 5: Expanding Copilot's Capabilities with Plugins 705

Index 717

Table of Contents

INTRODUCTION 1
  About This Book. 2
  Foolish Assumptions. 3
  Icons Used in This Book 4
  Beyond the Book. 4
  Where to Go from Here 5

BOOK 1: UNDERSTANDING AI FOUNDATIONS 7

CHAPTER 1: **Delving into What AI Means** 9
  Defining the Term AI. 9
    Discerning intelligence 10
    Examining four ways to define AI 13
    Reviewing AI categories 17
  Understanding the History of AI 18
  Considering AI Uses 19
  Avoiding AI Hype and Overestimation 20
    Defining the five tribes and the master algorithm 20
    Considering sources of hype 21
    Managing user overestimation 22
  Connecting AI to the Underlying Computer 22

CHAPTER 2: **Defining Data's Role in AI** 25
  Finding Data Ubiquitous in This Age. 26
    Using data everywhere. 27
    Putting algorithms into action. 28
  Using Data Successfully 30
    Considering the data sources 30
    Obtaining reliable data. 31
    Making human input more reliable 31
    Using automated data collection 33
    Collecting data ethically 33
  Manicuring the Data 35
    Dealing with missing data 35
    Considering data misalignments. 36
    Separating useful data from other data. 37
  Considering the Five Mistruths in Data 37
    Commission 38
    Omission. 38

Perspective 39
Bias 40
Frame of reference 41
Defining the Limits of Data Acquisition 41
Considering Data Security Issues 43
Understanding purposefully biased data .43
Dealing with data-source corruption 44
Handling botnets 45

CHAPTER 3: Considering the Use of Algorithms 47
Understanding the Role of Algorithms. 48
Examining what an algorithm does 48
Planning and branching: Trees and nodes 50
Extending the tree using graph nodes. 51
Traversing the graph. 52
Playing adversarial games 54
Using local search and heuristics 55
Discovering the Learning Machine 58
Leveraging expert systems 59
Introducing machine learning 62
Achieving new heights 62

CHAPTER 4: Pioneering Specialized Hardware 65
Relying on Standard Hardware 65
Examining the standard hardware 66
Describing standard hardware deficiencies 66
Relying on new computational techniques 67
Using GPUs. 68
Considering the von Neumann bottleneck 69
Defining the GPU. 70
Considering why GPUs work well 71
Working with Deep Learning Processors (DLPs). 71
Defining the DLP 72
Using the mobile neural processing unit (NPU) 72
Accessing the cloud-based tensor processing unit (TPU) 73
Creating a Specialized Processing Environment. 74
Increasing Hardware Capabilities 74
Advancing neuromorphic computing. 75
Exploring quantum processors 76
Adding Specialized Sensors 76
Integrating AI with Advanced Sensor Technology 77
Devising Methods to Interact with the Environment 78

CHAPTER 5: **Parsing Machine Learning and Deep Learning**.....81

Decoding Machine and Deep Learning 81
   Defining key concepts.......................................82
   Thinking about neural networks.............................82
   Training and testing models 85
Demystifying Natural-Language Processing 87
   History of NLP 88
   Overcoming the challenges of NLP...........................89
Understanding Transformers 91
   Learning to pay attention..................................92
   Getting tokens 93
Illuminating Generative AI Models 95
Recognizing AI's Limitations..................................96
   Language models are bad at math............................96
   Language models are wordy 97
   AI has limited knowledge 98
   AI lacks common sense 98
   AI has accuracy issues.....................................98
   AI has the potential to be biased..........................99

CHAPTER 6: **Upholding Responsible AI Standards in GenAI Use**..101

Achieving Originality and Excellence in GenAI-
Generated Content 101
   Strategies for ensuring originality in GenAI creations 102
   Maintaining quality standards in GenAI outputs 105
Applying Journalism Ethics to GenAI-Generated Content..........106
   Following basic journalistic principles 107
   Adhering to truth and integrity in GenAI-assisted reporting 108
   Balancing speed with ethical considerations in GenAI
   content generation 109
Joining the Responsible AI Movement 110
   Understanding the goals of the responsible AI movement 110
   Contributing to ethical AI development and use 111
   Aligning with global efforts for responsible AI practices........112

CHAPTER 7: **Finding Job Security in an AI World**..................115

Identifying Tasks That AI Can't Replace 115
   Cultivating emotional intelligence and human interaction......116
   Sparking creative and strategic thinking 116
   Engaging in jobs of the future 118
   Discovering new roles that use AI...........................119

Upskilling for AI-Proof Jobs 119
Translating Your Current Skills into AI-Proof Roles 121
    Analyzing skills transferability 122
    Understanding role evolution and adaptation 123
    Presenting the AI-resilient career journey 124
Navigating Career Transitions 125
    Adapting to new realities 125
    Shifting professional landscapes. 126
    Steering clear of pitfalls 127
Becoming an Early Adopter 128
    Adopting new technologies 128
    Utilizing AI for thought leadership 129
    Gaining a competitive advantage through innovation. 130

BOOK 2: PROMPTING AND GENERATIVE AI TECHNIQUES 131

CHAPTER 1: **Mapping the Lay of the Generative AI Land** 133
So, What Exactly Is Generative AI? 133
    Understanding parameters 134
    How GenAI uses parameters 134
Unveiling the BIG Secret to Working Successfully with GenAI 136
Understanding the Infamous Finger Problem and
Other GenAI Quirks. 139
Figuring Out How to Work with GenAI — It's All About Your
Prompts 140
    Why GenAI appears so human 140
    Realizing the human influences behind generative
    AI's abilities. 142
Discovering the Differences in GenAI Models and Options 143
Checking Out Practical Uses of GenAI 145
Separating Gen AI Fact from Fiction 147

CHAPTER 2: **Introducing the Art of Prompt Engineering** 149
First Things First: What Is a Prompt? 149
Revealing the Secret Behind Successful Prompting. 151
    Discovering the secret sauce in prompt engineering. 151
    Understanding how prompts guide GenAI responses. 152
Crafting Effective Prompts for Diverse AI Applications 154
Tips and Tricks for Optimizing Your Prompts 156
Using Prompts to Provide Supplemental Data for the Model 157
Avoiding Common Prompting Pitfalls 158

CHAPTER 3: Navigating the Evolving Landscape of GenAI 161

Identifying Key Players and Evaluating GenAI Providers 162
  Who's who in the GenAI market 162
  Assessing GenAI services and solutions 166
Getting GenAI that Plays Nice with Other Technologies 167
  Integrating ChatGPT with other software 167
  Bringing in autonomous AI agents 169
Keeping Up with the Pace of GenAI Advancements 170
  Staying informed on GenAI trends 170
  Preparing for the future of generative AI 172

CHAPTER 4: Introducing ChatGPT 175

Comparing Different Account Versions of ChatGPT 176
Setting Up an Individual Account 176
Touring the User Interface 178
Selecting a GPT Model on the ChatGPT UI 182
  Model options in the drop-down menu 182
  The GPT's latest release 183
Considering GPT Minis in the GPT Store on the ChatGPT UI 184
Rendering ChatGPT Outputs to Final Forms 185

CHAPTER 5: Getting Started with Microsoft Copilot 189

Defining Copilot 189
  Overview of Microsoft Copilot 191
  Understanding how Copilot works 193
  Integration with Microsoft 365 apps 194
Signing Up for Copilot 195
  Installing Copilot 196
  Eligibility criteria 196
  Subscription plans and pricing 196
  Step-by-step sign-up process 198
Taking Copilot for a Test Flight 201
  Understanding why mine looks different 201
  Prompting and interacting 201

CHAPTER 6: Learning Advanced Prompting 203

Starting at the End: Defining Desired Outputs before Prompting ... 203
Managing Data for Targeted Impact on Outputs 205
Adding Data to Prompts 207
  Using image inputs in ChatGPT prompts 208
  Adding information to memory in ChatGPT 214
  Manipulating memory in ChatGPT 216
Changing the Model's Temperature 220
Changing the Model's Weights 220

BOOK 3: INCREASING PRODUCTIVITY WITH AI............223

CHAPTER 1: **Applying GenAI in Practical Scenarios**.............225
GenAI as Writing Assistant..................................225
    Using GenAI to generate ideas 226
    Drafting content with the help of GenAI 227
    Sprucing up your writing with GenAI 230
Getting a Visual Assist from GenAI 231
    GenAI in graphic design and visual arts.................232
    Generating visual content with AI tools 232
    Harnessing GenAI for even more visual creativity 234
Problem-Solving with AI in Creative Projects................234

CHAPTER 2: **Crunching the Numbers with Copilot**............237
Launching Copilot in Excel 238
Working with Data...239
    Understanding the two kinds of data....................239
    Finding free data 240
Preparing the Data 241
    Converting the data to a table.........................241
    Adding context to the headers 242
    Formatting data......................................245
    Changing data types 246
    Sorting data 247
    Cleaning data 248
Automating Data Analysis 250
    Using Copilot for automated insights...................250
    Asking for a specific analysis 252
Creating Formulas with Copilot's Assistance.................253
    Formula creation and troubleshooting 254
    Advanced formula techniques.........................256
Visualizing Data with Copilot 256
    Opening and cleaning data in Excel 257
    Creating charts and graphs 258
    Customizing charts 260
Considering Copilot's Limitations in Excel 261

CHAPTER 3: **Presenting with Copilot** 263
Interacting with Copilot in PowerPoint......................263
    Using Copilot's built-in PowerPoint actions..............264
    Defining and refining your topic 265
    Personalizing the idea................................267
    Evaluating the generated presentation 268
    Evaluating the generated content......................269

Evaluating the generated design. 269
Evaluating the use of images 270
Designing Slides with Designer 271
Redesigning Slides with Copilot. 272
Sticking to the Built-in Prompts. 273
Enhancing visual appeal 274
Prompting for images 274
Organizing a Presentation 277
Practicing Your Presentation with Copilot Feedback 277

CHAPTER 4: **Meeting and Collaborating with Copilot** 281
Using Copilot in Microsoft Teams 282
Preparing for and setting up meetings 283
Getting real-time meeting assistance. .286
Accessing post-meeting summaries 288
Understanding the Limitations of Copilot in Teams. 290

CHAPTER 5: **Working with AI in a Roundup of
Business Disciplines** 293
Using GenAI for Marketing. 293
Creating general to detailed content 294
Analyzing customer data 294
Retrieving Smart Answers for HR 295
Harnessing GenAI in Legal 297
Drafting and editing a routine legal document. 298
Researching for legal precedents and statutes. 301
Drafting client responses or legal arguments 301
Monitoring your GenAI use 302
Storytelling in Journalism 302
Exploring politics and current issues 303
Prompting AI for facts, figures, and summaries 303
Organizing notes and pitching a story .304
Preparing interview questions, translating, and promoting 306
Checking your GenAI history 307
Consulting GenAI in Healthcare 307
Identifying successful healthcare use cases 307
Exploring other GenAI applications in healthcare 309
Cashing In on GenAI in Finance. 310
Using GenAI in IT Operations. 312
Examining New Businesses Based on GenAI 313

CHAPTER 6: **Managing AI Adoption and Change in Your Organization** 317
    Leading AI Adoption and Change Management Efforts 317
        Identifying key stakeholders and champions for AI adoption . . .318
        Communicating the benefits of AI adoption 319
        Aligning AI adoption with organizational culture 319
        Creating a roadmap for AI adoption 320
    Understanding Different Models for Change and Transition 322
        Using the ADKAR model for change management 322
        William Bridges' model for change and transition 326
        Introducing the DIRECT model for project leadership 326
    Overcoming Resistance to AI Adoption 327
        Understanding the root causes of resistance 328
        Addressing fears about job displacement .328
        Building trust through transparency 329
        Involving employees in the AI adoption process 329
        Providing support and resources for the transition 330
        Celebrating success stories 331

BOOK 4: CREATING CONTENT WITH AI 333

CHAPTER 1: **Using AI for Ideation and Planning** 335
    Engaging AI to Ideate on Behalf of Human Beings 336
    Deciding Whether AI Hallucinations Are a Feature or a Bug 339
        Bringing in unexpected ideas and concepts 340
        Branching out with non-traditional storytelling 340
        Facilitating testing and experimentation .341
        Staying the course with generative AI 342
    Following Practical Steps for Idea Generation with AI 342
        Starting with the right prompts 342
        Stepping through an AI-for-ideation exercise 343
    Deciding on AI Ideation Tools to Use 345

CHAPTER 2: **Managing and Writing Emails with AI** 349
    Using AI as Your Assistant for Writing Emails 350
    Generating Precise Prompts 352
    Emailing with Copilot 352
    Summarizing with Copilot 353
        Summarizing email threads 353
        Summarizing long emails 355
    Composing Emails with Copilot 356
        Drafting emails with Copilot 356
        Reply suggestions 359

Email coaching. 359
Meeting management. 361
Using GenAI for Email with Discernment. 362

CHAPTER 3: Developing Creative Assets. 363
Trying Out an AI-Generated Where's Waldo? Illustration 364
Exploring an Approach for Creating Visual Assets with AI 365
Minding the integrity of your customers, data, and teams. 369
Examining an example scenario 370
Enhancing Existing Creative Assets. 371
Enhancing and restoring images. 371
Enhancing and clarifying audio 371
Analyzing and editing video. 372
Adding and modifying content 372
Fine-Tuning Creativity with AI Tools and Techniques. 373
Crafting descriptions for image creation 374
Automating creative production 375
Tips and tricks for producing attention-grabbing
creative assets 377
Choosing AI Tools for Creating Visual Assets 379

CHAPTER 4: Producing Long-Form Content. 381
Writing Academic Papers with GenAI Assistance 382
Using GenAI for research and academic writing. 382
Supporting the academic publication process 387
Developing White Papers and Reports Using Generative AI. 388
Crafting professional documents with AI support 389
Enhancing business communication with AI. 390
Crafting Research Designs and Outlines with GenAI 391
Structuring research projects with AI. .392
From concept to outline: GenAI as a planning tool 393
Integrating Citations and References. 394
GenAI-assisted reference management. 395
Ensuring academic integrity with GenAI 395
Producing Long-Form Articles with GenAI. 396
Techniques for GenAI-enhanced feature writing 397
Maintaining depth and quality in GenAI-assisted articles 398
Writing Books with GenAI. 399

CHAPTER 5: Search Engine Optimization (SEO) in the AI Era. . . 403
Describing Search Generative Experiences (SGEs). 404
Enhanced interpretation of queries 405
Personalized search results. 405
Strategies for SEO Success in the AI Era. .406

Enhancing the User Experience with AI 409
Maximizing Your SEO Efforts 411
    Streamlining keyword and metadata research 411
    Automating content optimization 413
    Building SEO links 414
    Harnessing predictive SEO 415
Knowing the AI Tools to Use with SEO 416

CHAPTER 6: **Fine-Tuning Content with Localization**
and Translation 419
Exploiting AI for Localization and Translation 420
    Capturing cultural context 420
    Harnessing multilingual large language models 421
    Applying AI's capabilities 423
    Checking out AI tools you can use 424
Adopting Core Strategies for Localization 426
    Leveraging machine learning 426
    Adopting AI-driven cultural adaptation tools 427
    Enhancing personalization and localization efficiency 428
    Controlling quality when using AI 428
Examining Real-Time Localization and Translation Solutions 429
    Seeing how real-time solutions work 430
    Recognizing the benefits of real-time solutions 431
    Applying real-time solutions in marketing 431

BOOK 5: AI AT HOME 433

CHAPTER 1: **Relying on AI to Improve Human Interaction** 435
Developing New Ways to Communicate 436
    Creating new alphabets 437
    Working with emojis and other meaningful graphics 437
    Automating language translation 438
    Incorporating body language 439
Exchanging Ideas 440
    Creating connections 440
    Augmenting communication 440
    Defining trends 441
Using Multimedia 441
Embellishing Human Sensory Perception 442
    Shifting data spectrum 443
    Augmenting human senses 443

CHAPTER 2: **Using AI to Address Medical Needs**. 445
Implementing Portable Patient Monitoring. .446
Wearing helpful monitors 446
Relying on critical wearable monitors 447
Using movable monitors 448
Making Humans More Capable. 449
Using games for therapy 449
Considering the use of exoskeletons 451
Addressing Special Needs 452
Considering the software-based solutions 453
Relying on hardware augmentation. .453
Completing Analysis in New Ways 454
Relying on Telepresence. 455
Defining telepresence. 455
Considering examples of telepresence 456
Understanding telepresence limitations 456
Devising New Surgical Techniques. 457
Making surgical suggestions 457
Assisting a surgeon 458
Replacing the surgeon with monitoring. 459
Performing Tasks Using Automation 459
Working with medical records. 460
Predicting the future. 460
Making procedures safer 461
Creating better medications 461
Combining Robots and Medical Professionals 462
Considering Disruptions That AI Causes for Medical
Professionals 462

CHAPTER 3: **Leveraging AI in Education**. .465
Using AI Is Here to Stay. 466
Avoiding false accusations of cheating. 466
Accepting the role of AI at school and work 467
Changing the Structure of Education 467
Using AI in tutoring, testing, and updating curriculum 468
Preparing for shifts in educator roles. 468
Flipping the Teaching Model 470
Leveraging GenAI to Aid Overworked Educators. 472
Getting help with grading assignments 472
Exploiting AI for efficient mentoring. 473
Adapting lessons and admin tasks 473
Changing How Subjects Are Taught 474
Providing safer spaces for learning .474
Learning collaboratively 475

Supporting Special Education Needs 476
Delivering Data-Driven Insights for Educators 477
    Using GenAI tools for efficiency 477
    Questionable student progress tracking 478
Banning GenAI Stifles Education. 478
    Adopting a nuanced approach to AI. 479
    Preparing students for the future. 479

CHAPTER 4: **Using GenAI in the Real World** 481
Dying Keywords. 482
    Diminishing website traffic fallout 482
    Evolving SEO tactics. 483
    Over-relying on AI-curated information. 483
Moving from Information Search to Knowledge Assistants 484
    Finding new purposes for knowledge assistants 484
    Noting the pros and cons of knowledge assistants 485
Living with Misinformation and Manipulation 485
Narrowing Options 487
    Recognizing the limitations of GenAI info 487
    Looking only for confirmation. 487
    Exploiting varied information sources 488
Your Brain on GenAI 488
    Effects of GenAI on thinking skills. 489
    Effects of AI tools on interpersonal skills. 489
    Protecting yourself from GenAI fallout. .490

CHAPTER 5: **Financial Planning and Other Money Matters** 491
Walking through the Stages of Financial Planning 492
Getting a Handle on Budgeting. 496
Spotlighting College Expenses. 499

CHAPTER 6: **Retirement and Estate Planning**. 501
Digging into Retirement Planning. 501
    Your starting point: A personal balance sheet 502
    The "5–10 approach" and a reality check. 504
    A helpful checklist 506
    Even more AI retirement planning prompts 509
Thinking about Estate Planning. 511
    Defining "estate planning" 511
    Beginning the estate planning process .513

BOOK 6: APPLYING AI IN CODING 517

CHAPTER 1: **How Coding Benefits from AI**. 519

Banishing Boring Tasks. 519
    Spotting boring tasks 520
    Letting AI write the template 520
    Crafting CRUD with AI 523
Helping with Syntax. 529
    Stop remembering trivial details. 530
    Hinting at code mastery 530
    Adapting to new syntax 532
Linting with AI 534
    Detecting bad code with static code analysis 534
    Integrating AI with static code analysis 535
Using AI as a Tutor 536
    Studying AI's potential in education .536
    Avoiding potential pitfalls. 536
Pairing Up with AI 537
    Overview of pair programming styles 537
    Understanding the pros and cons of pair
    programming with AI 537
    AI pair programming session. 538

CHAPTER 2: **AI Coding Tools**. 547

Navigating GitHub Copilot 547
    Installing the Copilot plug-in 548
    Working efficiently with Copilot. 549
    Using keyboard shortcuts 554
Exploring Tabnine 555
    Installing Tabnine 556
    Setting up Tabnine 557
    Understanding Tabnine's AI-driven code completion 558
Reviewing Replit. 559
    Starting a website with Replit 561
    Exploring the Replit workspace. 562
    Pairing up with Replit AI 565

CHAPTER 3: **Coding with Chatbots**. 571

Improving Your Prompts 571
    Adjusting the temperature. 572
    Deciphering the elements of a prompt 574
    Open-ended versus closed-ended prompts 575
    Using different types of prompts 575
    Prompting like a pro 578

Chatting with Github Copilot 579
    Understanding slash commands 579
    Knowing Copilot's agents 580
    Getting the most out of Copilot Chat 580
Chatting with ChatGPT 582
    Signing up and setting up. 583
    Setting custom instructions 584
Diving into the OpenAI Platform. 588
    Checking your credits 589
    Messing around in the Playground. 590
    Running examples. 591
    Playing the roles 592
    Adjusting the model's settings. 592
    Getting an API key 594
Developing a Chatbot with OpenAI. 595

CHAPTER 4: **Progressing from Plan to Prototype**. 601
Understanding Project Requirements 601
    Determining the software requirements. 602
    Domain requirements 602
    Functional requirements 603
    Non-functional requirements 604
    Writing an SRS 605
Generating Code from an SRS. 608
    Using a zero-shot approach. 608
    Breaking down the problem 610
Blending Manually Written and AI-Generated Code 611
    Writing the prompt 611
    Writing the server 612
    Submitting follow-up prompts 615
    Testing the server 615
    Implementing few-shot prompting on the server 617
    Improving the client 621
    Moving logic from AI to the client 624
Tips and Tricks for Code Generation 627
    Don't stop coding. 627
    Be specific. 627
    Think in steps 627
    Ask follow-up questions 628
    Check the official documentation 628
    Use examples and context. 628
    Prioritize security. 628
    Keep learning. 628
    Keep your tools updated 629
    Be mindful of AI's limitations 629

BOOK 7: CREATING CUSTOM AI SOLUTIONS 631

CHAPTER 1: **Personalizing the Customer Journey by Using AI** 633

Discovering the Customer Journey............................634
Taking the customer journey................................634
Examining touch points 635
Introducing AI Personalization 635
Delivering personalized content............................636
Personalizing the journey with AI 636
Benefitting from AI Tools for the Customer Journey 637
Determining How Customers Feel 638
Understanding sentiment analysis..........................638
Evaluating emotions across the customer journey 639
Creating assets using sentiment analysis data..............639
Providing What Customers Want 640
Understanding recommendation engines....................640
Improving the customer journey with recommendations 641
Creating assets with recommendation engine data...........642
Predicting What Customers Will Do 642
Utilizing predictive analytics...............................642
Optimizing the customer journey...........................643
Creating assets with predictive analytics data 643
Delivering Information Customers Need........................644
Utilizing chatbots and virtual assistants....................644
Self-service along the customer journey 645
Creating assets using chatbots 645
Automating the Delivery of Content...........................646
Viewing AI marketing automation...........................646
Observing data-driven personalization 646
Automating across the customer journey....................646
Creating assets and delivering them with
marketing automation 647

CHAPTER 2: **Boosting Online Business Growth with AI** 649

Outsmarting Your Competitors................................650
Analyzing competitor keywords 650
Discovering traffic sources.................................651
Monitoring ad spending....................................652
Analyzing social media performance 653
Enhancing Brand Building 653
Refining visual brand identities............................653
Crafting strong brand messaging 654
Defining brand voice and tone 654

Maximizing Conversions. 655
   Understanding the segmentation of audiences 655
   Personalizing content 657
Scaling Paid Advertising ROI 657
   Selecting keywords 658
   Optimizing bids 658
   Creating ad copy 658
   Personalizing and testing. 658
   Considering the pros and cons 659
Tracking Key Performance Indicators with AI 661
Innovating New Offers 662
   Trend forecasting 662
   Generating creative concepts 663
   Refining your innovation 663

CHAPTER 3: **Enhancing Customer Service with Conversational AI Chatbots**. 665
Finding Out about Conversational AI Chatbots. 666
   Understanding the process 666
   Defining the differences between conversational
   AI chatbots and ChatGPT 667
   Visualizing the differences 667
Benefitting from Conversational AI Chatbots for
Customer Service. 668
Constructing Conversational AI Chatbots .670
Measuring the Return on Investment of Conversational AI
Chatbots 671
   Improving customer service efficiency. 671
   Reducing operational costs 671
   Boosting sales conversion rates 671
   Enhancing lead generation 672
   Tracking engagement metrics. 672
   Increasing resolution rate 672
   Ensuring accuracy 672
Integrating Conversational AI Chatbots into Existing Systems. 673
Personalizing Customer Interactions 674
   Improving the shopping experience. .675
   Ensuring ethical personalization. 675
Using Chatbots with Human and AI Collaboration. 675
   Understanding the hybrid model 676
   Collaborating with agents and chatbots 676
Considering Best Practices. 676
Reviewing Options for Creating Chatbots .678

CHAPTER 4: **Making Custom Copilots** 681

Building Your Own Copilot Agent with Copilot Studio 681

Creating agents by prompting. 686

Creating agents with templates. 688

Testing and Editing Your Agent. 690

Configuring generative AI. 690

Using the Copilot Agent Editor 691

Publishing Your Agent. 703

CHAPTER 5: **Expanding Copilot's Capabilities with Plugins** 705

Using Plugins Wisely 705

Understanding orchestration 706

Knowing the limitations of LLMs. 706

Enhancing functionality with plugins 707

Two types of plugins 708

Creating a Copilot Plugin 708

Seeing Examples of Plugins 712

Where can plugins be used? 714

Popular plugins for Copilot in Teams 714

Considering the Future of Plugins. 716

INDEX 717

Introduction

Artificial intelligence (AI) is generally defined as the theory and development of computer systems that can do tasks that normally require human intelligence.

In the early days of what we now call AI, the idea of a mechanical brain existed in the heads of science fiction writers and a few visionaries such as Edmund Callis Berkeley, who wrote "Giant Brains, or Machines that Think" (1949) and Alan Turing, who wrote "Computer Machinery and Intelligence" (1950).

In his famous paper, Turing proposed a test of machine intelligence called the "Imitation Game," which is known today as the Original Turing Test. The test proposed a party game in which a man and a woman are interrogated by a third party in another room whose goal is to determine which person is the man and which is the woman. Turing then asked whether it would be possible for a digital computer to do well as the interrogator in this game.

In another version of the Turing Test, known today as the "Standard Turing Test," a human judge evaluates a text transcript of a conversation between a human and a machine and attempts to determine which is which. I recommend you try playing this game at home with ChatGPT or another AI chatbot. Let me know if anyone was fooled by the chatbot. (You can email me at chris@minnick.com.)

It wasn't until the early 2020s that we had AI capable of passing a modern version of the Standard Turing Test. Whether this means that we truly have machines that can think as we do is hotly debated, with most AI experts agreeing that we're not there (yet) and that the Turing Test is outdated (see Chapter 1 of Book 1).

Theory and history aside, a vast body of technical knowledge about how to create AI systems has developed over the last 100 years. The technical details involve mathematics, computer programming, computer hardware engineering, linguistics, and many other highly technical fields. To attempt to write a book that teaches every aspect of creating AI systems would likely result in a book many times longer than the one you currently hold in your hands (or that's on your e-reader).

This book is not about the history of AI or about the technical details of creating AI systems. While it does explain the purpose and use of many of the technical topics involved in AI, you don't need to be a mathematician or computer programmer to read it.

What this book does cover is everything you need to know to make use of the latest AI applications, such as ChatGPT and Microsoft Copilot (among others), to help you in your job, education, home life, finances, creative projects, and much more. Carefully compiled (by yours truly) from the best chapters in 10 different *For Dummies* books about AI, this single book is your complete guide to working hand in hand (or hand in CPU) with AI, whether your goal is to be more productive, land a new job, start a new AI-focused business, or simply to learn what all the hype is about.

Enjoy, and thank you for reading this book! If you have any questions, please reach out to me at chris@minnick.com.

About This Book

AI is changing the way we work, communicate, research, learn, and just about every other aspect of daily life. How significant the change turns out to be and how much better the current technology can get still remains to be seen. One thing is certain, however: the outputs you get from any AI tool are heavily dependent on the quality of what you put into them. Garbage in, garbage out, as the saying goes.

This book teaches you how to work with AI tools to enhance many of the things you do every day and how to coax AI into giving you consistently high quality responses. In the process, you also learn what AI can (and can't) do and hear ideas and explanations from an all-star team of technology writers, computer scientists, and AI researchers. I want to point out just one helpful convention that you'll see throughout the book. When we define a term for you in the text, the term appears in *italics*.

To make the content more accessible, we divided it into seven mini-books:

>> **Book 1: Understanding AI Foundations.** In this book, you learn the fundamental concepts of AI, including how algorithms, data, and computers (lots of computers) work together to train machine learning models. You also explore what it means to build and use AI systems responsibly and what the increased use of AI will mean for human workers.

>> **Book 2: Prompting and Generative AI Techniques.** In this book, you learn about the exciting world of generative AI (GenAI). You gain skills in prompting large language models (LLMs) and learn about two of the most important GenAI applications: OpenAI ChatGPT and Microsoft Copilot.

>> **Book 3: Increasing Productivity with AI.** In this book, you learn about using GenAI to increase productivity in the workplace. Whether you're working with text, data, presentations, or other people, GenAI can help you do it more effectively. You also learn about some of the potential pitfalls of AI integrations with common productivity apps and how to manage AI adoption and change in an organization.

>> **Book 4: Creating Content with AI.** In this book, you learn how to generate content with AI. You see how an AI assistant can help you brainstorm and plan, draft emails, create images, and write long-form content such as blog posts, articles, and even books.

>> **Book 5: AI at Home.** In this book, you learn about how AI is being used (and will be used in the future) to help people with their everyday lives outside of work. You see the uses and effects that AI is having in a variety of different areas, such as medicine, education, research, and financial planning.

>> **Book 6: Applying AI in Coding.** In this book, you learn about working with AI assistants to write computer code. If you already know something about writing computer code, AI can help you code faster and better. If you've never written a line of code, AI can be your personal tutor and collaborator and help you get from a great idea for your app to a working prototype.

>> **Book 7: Creating Custom AI Solutions.** If you're ready to move beyond general-purpose chatbots, this book teaches you how to create custom GenAI agents that can act as customer service representatives, research assistants, and even the secret ingredient that helps you grow your business.

Foolish Assumptions

I don't make many assumptions about you, the reader, but I do have a couple questions for you to ask yourself before you dive into the rest of the book. Answer "Yes" or "No" to each of the following questions to determine whether this book is a good fit for you. Don't worry; this will be a quick and easy quiz.

1. Are you curious about how you can use AI to help you in your life, job, recreation, creative projects, and more?

2. Are you comfortable using a computer, smartphone, or tablet? For example, do you know how to turn it on and access web pages or apps?

3. Are you willing to keep an open mind while also being appropriately skeptical about the capabilities and limitations of AI?

Those are all the questions I have — I told you it would be easy. If you answered "Yes" to at least one of my questions, you will benefit from the wisdom and experience this book has to offer.

Icons Used in This Book

Throughout this book, icons in the margins highlight certain types of valuable information that call out for your attention. Here are the icons you'll encounter and a brief description of each.

The Tip icon marks tips and shortcuts that you can use to make a task or use a particular tool easier.

Remember icons mark the information that's especially important to know. To siphon off the most important information in each chapter, just skim through these icons.

The Technical Stuff icon marks information of a highly technical nature that you can normally skip over.

The Warning icon tells you to watch out! It marks important information that may save you headaches or, in the case of AI, will steer you away from questionable, unreliable, or unsafe uses of AI.

Beyond the Book

In addition to the abundance of information and guidance related to AI that we provide in this book, you get access to even more help and information online at *Dummies.com*. Check out this book's online Cheat Sheet. Just go to *www.dummies.com* and search for "AI All-In-One For Dummies Cheat Sheet."

Where to Go from Here

Now that you know a little bit about what to expect in the following pages, the next step is up to you! This book isn't meant to be read straight through cover to cover (although you're certainly welcome to do that!). If you're interested in learning a bit about the technical underpinnings of AI, start with Book 1. But these technical details aren't essential to your being able to use and understand the techniques covered in the other books. If you'd rather skip the technical stuff (for now, at least), find another book or chapter that interests you and dive in!

1

Understanding AI Foundations

Contents at a Glance

CHAPTER 1: **Delving into What AI Means** 9

CHAPTER 2: **Defining Data's Role in AI** 25

CHAPTER 3: **Considering the Use of Algorithms** 47

CHAPTER 4: **Pioneering Specialized Hardware** 65

CHAPTER 5: **Parsing Machine Learning and Deep Learning** 81

CHAPTER 6: **Upholding Responsible AI Standards in GenAI Use** 101

CHAPTER 7: **Finding Job Security in an AI World** 115

Chapter **1**

Delving into What AI Means

Common apps, such as Google Assistant, Alexa, and Siri, have many people using artificial intelligence (AI) daily without even thinking about it. Productivity and creative apps such as ChatGPT, Synesthesia, and Gemini help us focus on the content rather than on how to get there. The media floods our entire social environment with so much information and disinformation that many people see AI as a kind of magic (which it most certainly isn't). So, the best way to start this book is to define what AI is, what it isn't, and how it connects to computers today.

Defining the Term AI

Before you can use a term in any meaningful way, you must have a definition for it. After all, if nobody agrees on a meaning, the term has none; it's just a collection of characters. Defining the *idiom* (a term whose meaning isn't clear from the meanings of its constituent elements) is especially important with technical terms that have received more than a little press coverage at various times and in various ways.

Saying that AI is an artificial intelligence doesn't tell you anything meaningful, which is why people have so many discussions and disagreements over this term. Yes, you can argue that what occurs is artificial, not having come from a natural source. However, the intelligence part is, at best, ambiguous. Even if you don't necessarily agree with the definition of AI as it appears in the sections that follow, this book uses AI according to that definition, and knowing it will help you follow the text more easily.

Discerning intelligence

People define intelligence in many different ways. However, you can say that intelligence involves certain mental activities composed of the following activities:

>> **Learning:** Having the ability to obtain and process new information

>> **Reasoning:** Being able to manipulate information in various ways

>> **Understanding:** Considering the result of information manipulation

>> **Grasping truths:** Determining the validity of the manipulated information

>> **Seeing relationships:** Divining how validated data interacts with other data

>> **Considering meanings:** Applying truths to particular situations in a manner consistent with their relationship

>> **Separating fact from belief:** Determining whether the data is adequately supported by provable sources that can be demonstrated to be consistently valid

The activities list could easily grow quite long, but even this list is relatively prone to interpretation by anyone who accepts it as viable. As the list implies, however, intelligence often follows a process that a computer system can mimic as part of a simulation:

1. Set a goal (the information to process and the desired output) based on needs or wants.

2. Assess the value of any known information in support of the goal.

3. Gather additional information that could support the goal. The emphasis here is on information that *could* support the goal rather than on information you know *will* support the goal.

4. Manipulate the data such that it achieves a form consistent with existing information.

5. Define the relationships and truth values between existing and new information.

6. Determine whether the goal is achieved.

7. Modify the goal in light of the new data and its effect on the probability of success.

8. Repeat Steps 2 through 7 as needed until the goal is achieved (found true) or the possibilities for achieving it are exhausted (found false).

REMEMBER

Even though you can create algorithms and provide access to data in support of this process within a computer, a computer's capability to achieve intelligence is severely limited. For example, a computer is incapable of understanding anything because it relies on machine processes to manipulate data using pure math in a strictly mechanical fashion. Likewise, computers can't easily separate truth from mistruth (as described in Chapter 2 of this book). In fact, no computer can fully implement any of the mental activities in the earlier list that describes intelligence.

As part of deciding what intelligence actually involves, categorizing intelligence is also helpful. Humans don't use just one type of intelligence; rather, they rely on multiple intelligences to perform tasks. Howard Gardner, a Harvard psychologist, has defined a number of these types of intelligence (for details, see the article "The Theory of Multiple Intelligences" from Project Zero at Harvard University, https://pz.harvard.edu/resources/the-theory-of-multiple-intelligences). Knowing them helps you relate them to the kinds of tasks a computer can simulate as intelligence. (See Table 1-1 for a modified version of these intelligences with additional description.)

TABLE 1-1   **The Kinds of Human Intelligence and How AIs Simulate Them**

Type	Simulation Potential	Human Tools	Description
Bodily kinesthetic	Moderate to high	Specialized equipment and real-life objects	Body movements, such as those used by a surgeon or a dancer, require precision and body awareness. Robots commonly use this kind of intelligence to perform repetitive tasks, often with higher precision than humans, but sometimes with less grace. It's essential to differentiate between human augmentation, such as a surgical device that provides a surgeon with enhanced physical ability, and true independent movement. The former is simply a demonstration of mathematical ability in that it depends on the surgeon for input.

(continued)

TABLE 1-1 *(continued)*

Type	Simulation Potential	Human Tools	Description
Creative	None	Artistic output, new patterns of thought, inventions, new kinds of musical composition	Creativity is the act of developing a new pattern of thought that results in unique output in the form of art, music, or writing. A truly new kind of product is the result of creativity. An AI can simulate existing patterns of thought and even combine them to create what appears to be a unique presentation but is in reality just a mathematically based version of an existing pattern. To create, an AI would need to possess self-awareness, which would require intrapersonal intelligence.
Interpersonal	Low to moderate	Telephone, audioconferencing, videoconferencing, writing, computer conferencing, email	Interacting with others occurs at several levels. The goal of this form of intelligence is to obtain, exchange, give, or manipulate information based on the experiences of others. Computers can answer basic questions because of keyword input, not because they understand the question. The intelligence occurs while obtaining information, locating suitable keywords, and then giving information based on those keywords. Cross-referencing terms in a lookup table and then acting on the instructions provided by the table demonstrates logical intelligence, not interpersonal intelligence.
Intrapersonal	None	Books, creative materials, diaries, privacy, time	Looking inward to understand one's own interests and then setting goals based on those interests is now a human-only kind of intelligence. As machines, computers have no desires, interests, wants, or creative abilities. An AI processes numeric input using a set of algorithms and provides an output; it isn't aware of anything it does, nor does it understand anything it does.
Linguistic (often divided into oral, aural, and written)	Low	Games, multimedia, books, voice recorders, spoken words	Working with words is an essential tool for communication because spoken and written information exchange is far faster than any other form. This form of intelligence includes understanding oral, aural, and written input, managing the input to develop an answer, and providing an understandable answer as output. Discerning just how capable computers are in this form of intelligence is difficult in light of AIs such as ChatGPT because it's all too easy to create tests in which the AI produces nonsense answers.

Type	Simulation Potential	Human Tools	Description
Logical mathematical	High (potentially higher than humans)	Logic games, investigations, mysteries, brainteasers	Calculating results, performing comparisons, exploring patterns, and considering relationships are all areas in which computers now excel. When you see a computer defeat a human on a game show, this is the only form of intelligence you're seeing, out of eight kinds of intelligence. Yes, you may see small bits of other kinds of intelligence, but this is the focus. Basing an assessment of human-versus-computer intelligence on just one area isn't a good idea.
Naturalist	None	Identification, exploration, discovery, new tool creation	Humans rely on the ability to identify, classify, and manipulate their environment to interact with plants, animals, and other objects. This type of intelligence informs you that one piece of fruit is safe to eat though another is not. It also gives you a desire to learn how things work or to explore the universe and all that is in it.
Visual spatial	Moderate	Models, graphics, charts, photographs, drawings, 3D modeling, video, television, multimedia	Physical-environment intelligence is used by people like sailors and architects (among many others). To move around, humans need to understand their physical environment — that is, its dimensions and characteristics. Every robot or portable computer intelligence requires this capability, but the capability is often difficult to simulate (as with self-driving cars) or less than accurate (as with vacuums that rely as much on bumping as they do on moving intelligently).

Examining four ways to define AI

As described in the previous section, the first concept that's important to understand is that AI has little to do with human intelligence. Yes, some AI is modeled to simulate human intelligence, but that's what it is: a simulation. When thinking about AI, notice an interplay between goal seeking, data processing used to achieve that goal, and data acquisition used to better understand the goal. AI relies on algorithms to achieve a result that may or may not have anything to do with human goals or methods of achieving those goals. With this in mind, you can categorize AI functioning in four ways:

» Acting humanly

» Thinking humanly

>> Thinking rationally

>> Acting rationally

Acting humanly

When a computer acts like a human, it best reflects the *Turing test,* in which the computer succeeds when differentiation between the computer and a human isn't possible. (For details, see "The Turing Test" at the Alan Turing Internet Scrapbook, `www.turing.org.uk/scrapbook/test.html`). This category also reflects what most media would have you believe AI is all about. You see it employed for technologies such as natural language processing, knowledge representation, automated reasoning, and machine learning (all four of which must be present to pass the test). To pass the Turing test, an AI should have all four previous technologies and, possibly, integrate other solutions (such as expert systems).

TECHNICAL STUFF

The original Turing test didn't include any physical contact. Harnad's Total Turing Test does include physical contact, in the form of perceptual ability interrogation, which means that the computer must also employ both computer vision and robotics to succeed. Here's a quick overview of other Turing test alternatives:

>> **Reverse Turing test:** A human tries to prove to a computer that the human is not a computer (for example, the Completely Automated Public Turing Test to Tell Computers and Humans Apart, or CAPTCHA).

>> **Minimum intelligent signal test:** Only true/false and yes/no questions appear in the test.

>> **Marcus test:** A computer program simulates watching a television show, and the program is tested with meaningful questions about the show's content.

>> **Lovelace test 2.0:** A test detects AI by examining its ability to create art.

>> **Winograd schema challenge:** This test asks multiple-choice questions in a specific format.

Modern techniques include the idea of achieving the goal rather than mimicking humans completely. For example, the Wright brothers didn't succeed in creating an airplane by precisely copying the flight of birds; rather, the birds provided ideas that led to studying aerodynamics, which eventually led to human flight. The goal is to fly. Both birds and humans achieve this goal, but they use different approaches.

IS THE TURING TEST OUTDATED?

Current discussions about the Turing test have researchers Philip Johnson-Laird, a retired psychology professor from Princeton University, and Marco Ragni, a researcher at the Germany-based Chemnitz University of Technology, asking whether the test is outdated. For example, If AI is making the Turing test obsolete, what may be better? This issue poses several problems with the Turing test and offers a potential solution in the form of a psychological-like evaluation. These tests would use the following three-step process to better test AIs, such as Google's LaMDA and OpenAI's ChatGPT:

- Use tests to check the AI's underlying inferences.

- Verify that the AI understands its own way of reasoning.

- Examine the underlying source code, when possible.

Thinking humanly

A computer that thinks like a human performs tasks that require intelligence (as contrasted with rote procedures) from a human to succeed, such as driving a car. To determine whether a program thinks like a human, you must have some method of determining how humans think, which the cognitive modeling approach defines. This model relies on these three techniques:

>> **Introspection:** Detecting and documenting the techniques used to achieve goals by monitoring one's own thought processes

>> **Psychological testing:** Observing a person's behavior and adding it to a database of similar behaviors from other persons given a similar set of circumstances, goals, resources, and environmental conditions (among other factors)

>> **Brain imaging:** Monitoring brain activity directly through various mechanical means, such as computerized axial tomography (CAT), positron emission tomography (PET), magnetic resonance imaging (MRI), and magnetoencephalography (MEG)

After creating a model, you can write a program that simulates the model. Given the amount of variability among human thought processes and the difficulty of accurately representing these thought processes as part of a program, the results are experimental at best. This category of thinking humanly is often used in psychology and other fields in which modeling the human thought process to create realistic simulations is essential.

Thinking rationally

Studying how humans think using an established standard enables the creation of guidelines that describe typical human behaviors. A person is considered rational when following these behaviors within certain levels of deviation. A computer that thinks rationally relies on the recorded behaviors to create a guide to how to interact with an environment based on the data at hand.

The goal of this approach is to solve problems logically, when possible. In many cases, this approach would enable the creation of a baseline technique for solving a problem, which would then be modified to actually solve the problem. In other words, the solving of a problem in principle is often different from solving it in practice, but you still need a starting point.

Acting rationally

Studying how humans act in given situations under specific constraints enables you to determine which techniques are both efficient and effective. A computer that acts rationally relies on the recorded actions to interact with an environment based on conditions, environmental factors, and existing data.

As with rational thought, rational acts depend on a solution in principle, which may not prove useful in practice. However, rational acts do provide a baseline on which a computer can begin negotiating the successful completion of a goal.

HUMAN-VERSUS-RATIONAL PROCESSES

Human processes differ from rational processes in their outcome. A process is *rational* if it always does the right thing based on the current information, given an ideal performance measure. In short, rational processes go by the book and assume that the book is correct. Human processes involve instinct, intuition, and other variables that don't necessarily reflect the book and may not even consider the existing data. As an example, the rational way to drive a car is to always follow the law. However, traffic isn't rational. If you follow the law precisely, you end up stuck somewhere because other drivers aren't following the law precisely. To be successful, a self-driving car must, therefore, act humanly rather than rationally.

Reviewing AI categories

The categories used to define AI offer a way to consider various uses or ways to apply AI. Some of the systems used to classify AI by type are arbitrary and indistinct. For example, some groups view AI as either *strong* (generalized intelligence that can adapt to a variety of situations) or *weak* (specific intelligence designed to perform a particular task well).

The problem with strong AI is that it doesn't perform any task well, whereas weak AI is too specific to perform tasks independently. Even so, just two type classifications won't do the job, even in a general sense. The four classification types promoted by Arend Hintze form a better basis for understanding AI:

>> **Reactive machines:** The machines you see defeating humans at chess or playing on game shows are examples of reactive machines. A reactive machine has no memory or experience on which to base a decision. Instead, it relies on pure computational power and smart algorithms to re-create every decision every time. This is an example of a weak AI used for a specific purpose.

>> **Limited memory:** A self-driving (SD) car or an autonomous robot can't afford the time to make every decision from scratch. These machines rely on a small amount of memory to provide experiential knowledge of various situations. When the machine sees the same situation, it can rely on experience to reduce reaction time and provide more resources for making new decisions that haven't yet been made. This is an example of the current level of strong AI.

>> **Theory of mind:** A machine that can assess both its required goals and the potential goals of other entities in the same environment has a kind of understanding that is feasible to some extent today, but not in any commercial form. However, for SD cars to become truly autonomous, this level of AI must reach full development. An SD car would need to not only know that it must move from one point to another but also intuit the potentially conflicting goals of drivers around it and react accordingly. (Robot soccer, at www. cs.cmu.edu/~robosoccer/main and www.robocup.org, is another example of this kind of understanding, but at a simple level.)

>> **Self-awareness:** This is the sort of AI you see in movies (for example, WALL-E or The Terminator). However, it requires technologies that aren't even remotely possible now because such a machine would have a sense of both self and consciousness. In addition, rather than merely intuit the goals of others based on environment and other entity reactions, this type of machine would be able to infer the intent of others based on experiential knowledge.

For more on these classification types, check out "Understanding the four types of AI, from reactive robots to self-aware beings" at https://theconversation.com/understanding-the-four-types-of-ai-from-reactive-robots-to-self-aware-beings-67616. It's several years old but still pertinent.

Understanding the History of AI

Earlier sections of this chapter help you understand intelligence from the human perspective and see how modern computers are woefully inadequate for simulating such intelligence, much less actually becoming intelligent themselves. However, the desire to create intelligent machines (or, in ancient times, idols) is as old as humans. The desire not to be alone in the universe, to have something with which to communicate without the inconsistencies of other humans, is a strong one. Of course, a single book can't contemplate all of human history, so Figure 1-1 provides a brief, pertinent overview of the history of modern AI attempts.

REMEMBER

Figure 1-1 shows you some highlights, nothing like a complete history of AI. One thing you should notice is that the early years were met with a lot of disappointment from overhyping what the technology would do. Yes, people can do amazing things with AI today, but that's because the people creating the underlying technology just kept trying, no matter how often they failed.

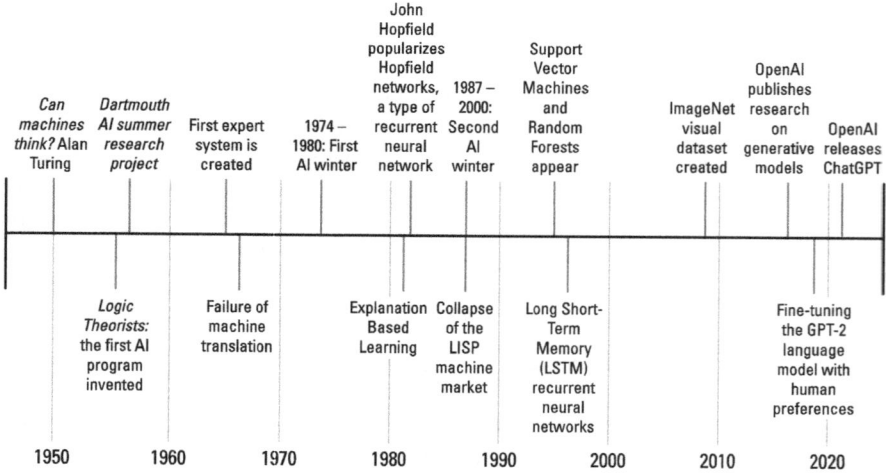

FIGURE 1-1:
An overview of the history of AI.

Considering AI Uses

You can find AI used in a great many applications today. The only problem is that the technology works so well that you don't know it even exists. In fact, you may be surprised to find that many home devices already make use of AI. For example, some smart thermostats automatically create schedules for you based on how you manually control the temperature. Likewise, voice input that is used to control certain devices learns how you speak so that it can better interact with you. AI definitely appears in your car and most especially in the workplace. In fact, the uses for AI number in the millions — all safely out of sight even when they're quite dramatic in nature. Here are just a few of the ways in which you may see AI used:

- **Fraud detection:** You receive a call from your credit card company asking whether you made a particular purchase. The credit card company isn't being nosy; it's simply alerting you to the fact that someone else might be making a purchase using your card. The AI embedded within the credit card company's code detected an unfamiliar spending pattern and alerted someone to it.

- **Resource scheduling:** Many organizations need to schedule the use of resources efficiently. For example, a hospital may have to determine which room to assign a patient to based on the patient's needs, the availability of skilled experts, and the length of time the doctor expects the patient to be in the hospital.

- **Complex analysis:** Humans often need help with complex analysis because there are literally too many factors to consider. For example, the same set of symptoms may indicate more than one illness. A doctor or another expert may need help making a timely diagnosis to save a patient's life.

- **Automation:** Any form of automation can benefit from the addition of AI to handle unexpected changes or events. A problem with some types of automation is that an unexpected event, such as an object appearing in the wrong place, can cause the automation to stop. Adding AI to the automation can allow the automation to handle unexpected events and continue as if nothing happened.

- **Customer service:** The customer service line you call may not even have a human behind it. The automation is good enough to follow scripts and use various resources to handle the vast majority of your questions. After hearing good voice inflection (provided by AI as well), you may not even be able to tell that you're talking with a computer.

- » **Safety systems:** Many of the safety systems now found in machines of various sorts rely on AI to take over operation of the vehicle in a time of crisis. For example, many automatic braking systems (ABSs) rely on AI to stop the car based on all the inputs a vehicle can provide, such as the direction of a skid. Computerized ABS is, at 40 years, relatively old from a technology perspective.

- » **Machine efficiency:** AI can help control a machine to obtain maximum efficiency. The AI controls the use of resources so that the system avoids overshooting speed or other goals. Every ounce of power is used precisely as needed to provide the desired services.

- » **Content generation:** When people consider content generation, they often think about ChatGPT because it's in the public eye. However, content generation can exist deep within an application to provide specific functionality. For example, given a photo of the user, how will a new outfit look?

Avoiding AI Hype and Overestimation

You've no doubt seen and heard lots of hype about AI and its potential impact. If you've seen movies such as *Her* and *Ex Machina*, you might be led to believe that AI is further along than it is. The problem is that AI is actually in its infancy, and any sort of application such as those shown in the movies is the creative output of an overactive imagination. The following sections help you understand how hype and overestimation are skewing the goals you can achieve using AI today.

Defining the five tribes and the master algorithm

You may have heard of a concept called the singularity, which is responsible for the potential claims presented in the movies and other media. The *singularity* (when computer intelligence surpasses human intelligence) is essentially a master algorithm that encompasses all five "tribes" of learning used within machine learning. To achieve what these sources are telling you, the machine must be able to learn as a human would — as specified by the eight kinds of intelligence discussed in the section "Discerning intelligence," early in this chapter. Here are the five tribes of learning:

- » **Symbologists:** The origin of this tribe is in logic and philosophy. It relies on inverse deduction to solve problems.

- » **Connectionists:** This tribe's origin is in neuroscience, and the group relies on backpropagation to solve problems.

>> **Evolutionaries:** This tribe originates in evolutionary biology, relying on genetic programming to solve problems.

>> **Bayesians:** This tribe's origin is in statistics and relies on probabilistic inference to solve problems.

>> **Analogizers:** The origin of this tribe is in psychology. The group relies on kernel machines to solve problems.

REMEMBER

The ultimate goal of machine learning is to combine the technologies and strategies embraced by the five tribes to create a single algorithm (the *master algorithm*) that can learn anything. Of course, achieving that goal is a long way off. Even so, scientists such as Pedro Domingos at the University of Washington are working toward that goal.

To make things even less clear, the five tribes may not be able to provide enough information to actually solve the problem of human intelligence, so creating master algorithms for all five tribes may still not yield the singularity. At this point, you should be amazed at just how little people know about how they think or why they think in a certain manner.

REMEMBER

Any rumors you hear about AI taking over the world or becoming superior to people are just plain false.

Considering sources of hype

Many sources of AI hype are out there. Quite a bit of the hype comes from the media and is presented by people who have no idea of what AI is all about, except perhaps from a sci-fi novel they read a few years back. So it's not just movies or television that cause problems with AI hype — it's all sorts of other media sources as well. You can often find news reports presenting AI as being able to do something it can't possibly do because the reporter doesn't understand the technology. Oddly enough, many news articles are now written entirely by AI like ChatGPT, so what you end up with is a recycling of the incorrect information.

Some products should be tested much more before being placed on the market. The article "12 Famous AI Disasters" at CIO.com (www.cio.com/article/190888/5-famous-analytics-and-ai-disasters.html) discusses twelve AI products, hyped by their developers, that fell flat on their faces. Some of these failures are huge and reflect badly on the ability of AI to perform tasks as a whole. However, something to consider with a few of these failures is that people may have interfered with the device using the AI. Obviously, testing procedures need to start considering the possibility of people purposely tampering with the AI as a potential source of errors. Until that happens, the AI will fail to perform as expected because people will continue to fiddle with the software in an attempt to cause it to fail.

WARNING

Another cause of problems stems from asking the wrong person about AI — not every scientist, no matter how smart, knows enough about AI to provide a competent opinion about the technology and the direction it will take in the future. Asking a biologist about the future of AI in general is akin to asking your dentist to perform brain surgery — it simply isn't a good idea. Yet many stories appear with people like these as the information source.

TIP

To discover the future direction of AI, ask a computer scientist or data scientist with a strong background in AI research.

Managing user overestimation

Because of hype (and sometimes laziness or fatigue), users continually overestimate the ability of AI to perform tasks. For example, a Tesla owner was recently found sleeping in his car while the car zoomed along the highway at 90 mph (see "Canada Tesla driver charged over 'napping while speeding'" at www.bbc.com/news/world-us-canada-54197344). However, even with the user significantly overestimating the ability of the technology to drive a car, it does apparently work well enough (at least, for this driver) to avoid a complete failure.

WARNING

Be aware that cases exist in which auto drive failed and killed people. (See the article at www.washingtonpost.com/technology/interactive/2023/tesla-autopilot-crash-analysis.)

However, you need not be speeding down a highway at 90 mph to encounter user overestimation. Robot vacuums can also fail to meet expectations, usually because users believe they can just plug in the device and then never think about vacuuming again. After all, movies portray the devices working precisely in this manner, but unfortunately, they still need human intervention. Our point is that most robots eventually need human intervention because they simply lack the knowledge to go it alone.

Connecting AI to the Underlying Computer

To see AI at work, you need to have some sort of computing system, an application that contains the required software, and a knowledge base. The computing system can be anything with a chip inside; in fact, a smartphone does just as well as a desktop computer for certain applications. Of course, if you're Amazon and you want to provide advice on a particular person's next buying decision, the smartphone won't do — you need a *big* computing system for that application. The size of the computing system is directly proportional to the amount of work you expect the AI to perform.

The application can also vary in size, complexity, and even location. For example, if you're a business owner and you want to analyze client data to determine how best to make a sales pitch, you might rely on a server-based application to perform the task. On the other hand, if you're a customer and you want to find products on Amazon to complement your current purchase items, the application doesn't even reside on your computer; you access it via a web-based application located on Amazon's servers.

The *knowledge base* (a database that holds information about the facts, assumptions, and rules that the AI can use), varies in location and size as well. The more complex the data, the more insight you can obtain from it, but the more you need to manipulate the data as well. You get no free lunch when it comes to knowledge management. The interplay between location and time is also important: A network connection affords you access to a large knowledge base online but costs you in time because of the latency of network connections. However, localized databases, though fast, tend to lack details in many cases.

IN THIS CHAPTER

» Seeing data as a universal resource

» Obtaining and manipulating data

» Looking for mistruths in data

» Defining data-acquisitions limits

» Considering data security

Chapter **2**

Defining Data's Role in AI

There is nothing unique about data. Every interesting application ever written for a computer has data associated with it. Data comes in many forms — some organized, some not. What has changed is the *amount* of data. Some people find it almost terrifying that access to so much data that details nearly every aspect of their lives is a reality — sometimes to a level that even the terrified people don't realize. In addition, the use of advanced hardware and improvements in algorithms make data now *the* universal resource for AI.

To work with data, you must first obtain it. Today, data is collected manually, as done in the past, and also automatically, using new methods. However, it's not a matter of just one or two data collection techniques: Collection methods take place on a continuum from fully manual to fully automatic. You also find a focus today on collecting this data ethically — for example, not collecting data that a person hasn't granted permission for. This chapter explores issues surrounding data collection.

Raw data doesn't usually work well for analysis purposes. This chapter also helps you understand the need for manipulating and shaping the data so that it meets specific requirements. You also discover the need to define the truth value of the data to ensure that analysis outcomes match the goals set for applications in the first place.

Interestingly, you also have data-acquisition limits to deal with. No technology currently exists for grabbing thoughts from someone's mind by telepathic means. Of course, other limits exist, too — most of which you probably already know about but may not have considered. It also doesn't pay to collect data in a manner that isn't secure. The data must be free of bias, uncorrupted, and from a source you know. You find out more about acquisition limits and data security in this chapter.

Finding Data Ubiquitous in This Age

You may have heard big data mentioned in many specialized scientific and business publications, and you may have even wondered what the term really means. From a technical perspective, *big data* refers to large and complex amounts of computer data, so large and intricate that applications can't deal with the data by simply using additional storage or increasing computer power.

Big data implies a revolution in data storage and manipulation. It affects what you can achieve with data in more qualitative terms (meaning that in addition to doing more, you can perform tasks better). From a human perspective, computers store big data in different data formats (such as database files and .csv files), but regardless of storage type, the computer still sees data as a stream of ones and zeros (the core language of computers). You can view data as being one of two types, structured and unstructured, depending on how you produce and consume it. Some data has a clear structure (you know exactly what it contains and where to find every piece of data), whereas other data is unstructured (you have an idea of what it contains, but you don't know exactly how it is arranged).

>> **Structured data** include typical examples such as database tables, in which information is arranged into columns and each column contains a specific type of information. Data is often structured by design. You gather it selectively and record it in its correct place. For example, you may want to place a count of the number of people buying a certain product in a specific column, in a specific table, or in a specific database. As with a library, if you know what data you need, you can find it immediately.

>> **Unstructured data** consists of images, videos, and sound recordings. You may use an unstructured form for text so that you can tag it with characteristics, such as size, date, or content type. Usually, you don't know exactly where data appears in an unstructured dataset, because the data appears as sequences of ones and zeros that an application must interpret or visualize.

Transforming unstructured data into a structured form can cost lots of time and effort and can involve the work of many people. Most of the data of the big data revolution is unstructured and stored as is, unless someone renders it structured.

This copious and sophisticated data store didn't appear suddenly overnight. It took time to develop the technology to store this amount of data. In addition, it took time to spread the technology that generates and delivers data — namely, computers, sensors, smart mobile phones, and the internet and its web services. The following sections help you understand what makes data a universal resource today.

Using data everywhere

Scientists need more powerful computers than the average person because of their scientific experiments. They began dealing with impressive amounts of data years before anyone coined the term *big data*. At that point, the internet wasn't producing the vast sums of data that it does today.

REMEMBER

Big data isn't a fad created by software and hardware vendors but has a basis in many scientific fields, such as astronomy (space missions), satellite (surveillance and monitoring), meteorology (storm predictions), physics (particle accelerators), and genomics (DNA sequences).

Although an AI application can specialize in a scientific field — such as IBM's Watson, which boasts an impressive medical-diagnosis capability because it can learn information from millions of scientific papers on diseases and medicine — the actual AI application driver often has more mundane facets. Actual AI applications are mostly prized for being able to recognize objects, move along paths, or understand what people say and speak to them. Data contribution to the actual AI renaissance that molded it in such a fashion didn't derive from the classical sources of scientific data.

TIP

The internet now generates and distributes new data in large amounts. Our current daily data production is estimated to amount to about 2.5 quintillion (a number with 18 zeros) bytes, with the lion's share going to unstructured data like video and audio.

All this data is related to common human activities, feelings, experiences, and relations. Roaming through this data, an AI can easily learn how reasoning and acting more human-like works. Here are some examples of the more interesting data you can find:

>> **Large repositories of faces and expressions from photos and videos posted on social media websites like Facebook, YouTube, and Google:** They provide information about gender, age, feelings, and possibly sexual orientation, political orientation, or IQ (see "Face-reading AI will be able to detect your politics and IQ, professor says" at The Guardian.com).

>> **Privately held medical information and biometric data from smartwatches, which measure body data such as temperature and heart rate during both illness and good health:** Interestingly enough, data from smartwatches is seen as a method to detect serious diseases, such as COVID-19, early.

>> **Datasets of how people relate to each other and what drives their interest from sources such as social media and search engines:** For instance, a study from Cambridge University's Psychometrics Centre claims that Facebook interactions contain a lot of data about intimate relationships.

>> **Information on how we speak, which is recorded by mobile phones.** For example, OK Google, a function found on Android mobile phones, routinely records questions and sometimes even more, as explained in "Google's been quietly recording your voice; here's how to listen to — and delete — the archive" at `https://qz.com/526545/googles-been-quietly-recording-your-voice-heres-how-to-listen-to-and-delete-the-archive`.

Every day, users connect even more devices to the internet that start storing new personal data. There are now personal assistants that sit in houses, such as Amazon Echo and other integrated smart home devices that offer ways to regulate and facilitate the domestic environment. These are just the tip of the iceberg because many other common tools of everyday life are becoming interconnected (from the refrigerator to the toothbrush) and able to process, record, and transmit data. The internet of things (IoT) is becoming a reality.

Putting algorithms into action

The human race is now at an incredible apex of unprecedented volumes of data, generated by increasingly smaller and powerful hardware. The data is also increasingly processed and analyzed by the same computers that the process helped spread and develop. This statement may seem obvious, but data has become so ubiquitous that its value no longer resides only in the information it contains (such as the case of data stored in a firm's database that allows its daily operations), but rather in its use as a means to create new values. Some people call such data the "new oil." These new values exist mostly in how applications manicure, store, and retrieve data, and in how you actually use it by means of smart algorithms.

Algorithms and AI changed the data game. As mentioned in Chapter 1, AI algorithms have tried various approaches along the way in the following order:

1. Simple algorithms

2. Symbolic reasoning based on logic

3. Expert systems

In recent years, AI algorithms have moved to neural networks and, in their most mature form, deep learning. As this methodological passage happened, data turned from being the information processed by predetermined algorithms to becoming what molded the algorithm into something useful for the task. Data turned from being just the raw material that fueled the solution to the artisan of the solution itself, as shown in Figure 2-1.

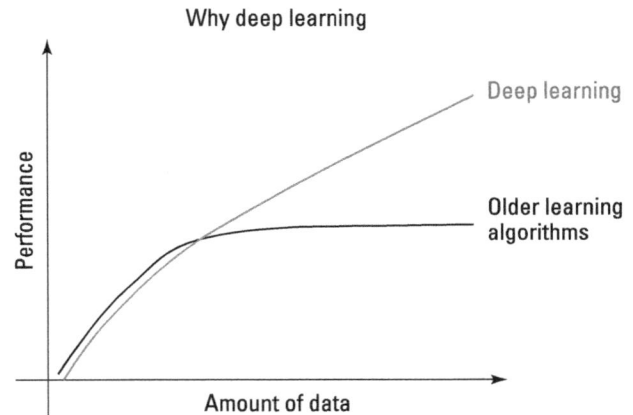

Why deep learning

FIGURE 2-1:
With the present AI solutions, more data equates to more intelligence.

Thus, a photo of your kittens has become increasingly useful not simply because of its affective value — depicting your cute little cats — but also because it could become part of the learning process of an AI discovering more general concepts, such as which characteristics denote a cat or understanding what defines cute.

On a larger scale, a company like Google feeds its algorithms from freely available data, such as the content of websites or the text found in publicly available texts and books. Google Spider software crawls the web, jumping from website to website and retrieving web pages with their content of text and images. Even if Google gives back part of the data to users as search results, it extracts other kinds of information from the data using its AI algorithms, which learn from it how to achieve other objectives.

Algorithms that process words can help Google AI systems understand and anticipate your needs even when you're expressing them not in a set of keywords but in plain, unclear natural language, the language we speak every day (and yes, everyday language is often unclear). If you currently try to pose questions, not just chains of keywords, to the Google search engine, you'll notice that it tends to answer correctly. Since 2012, with the introduction of the Hummingbird update, Google has steadily become better able to understand synonyms and concepts, a strategy that goes beyond the initial data it acquired, and this is the result of an AI process.

A few years after Hummingbird, Google deployed an even more advanced algorithm named RankBrain, which learns directly from millions of queries every day and can answer ambiguous or unclear search queries, even expressed in slang or colloquial terms, or simply riddled with errors. RankBrain doesn't service all the queries, but it learns from data how to better answer queries.

Using Data Successfully

Having plentiful data available isn't enough to create a successful AI. Presently, an AI algorithm can't extract information directly from raw data. Most algorithms rely on external collection and manipulation prior to analysis. When an algorithm collects useful information, it may not represent the right information. The following sections help you understand how to collect, manipulate, and automate data collection from an overview perspective.

Considering the data sources

The data you use comes from a number of sources. The most common data source is from information entered by humans at some point. Even when a system collects shopping-site data automatically, humans initially enter the information. A human clicks various items, adds them to a shopping cart, specifies characteristics (such as size and quantity), and then checks out. Later, after the sale, the human gives the shopping experience, product, and delivery method a rating and makes comments. In short, every shopping experience becomes a data collection exercise as well.

REMEMBER

Many data sources today rely on input gathered from human sources. Humans also provide manual input. You call or go into an office somewhere to make an appointment with a professional. A receptionist then gathers information from you that's needed for the appointment. This manually collected data eventually ends up in a dataset somewhere for analysis purposes.

Data is also collected from sensors, and these sensors can take almost any form. For example, many organizations base physical data collection, such as the number of people viewing an object in a window, on cellphone detection. Facial recognition software could potentially detect repeat customers.

However, sensors can create datasets from almost anything. The weather service relies on datasets created by sensors that monitor environmental conditions such as rain, temperature, humidity, and cloud cover.

TIP

Robotic monitoring systems help correct small flaws in robotic operation by constantly analyzing data collected by monitoring sensors. A sensor, combined with a small AI application, could tell you when your dinner is cooked to perfection tonight. The sensor collects data, but the AI application uses rules to help define when the food is properly cooked.

Obtaining reliable data

The word *reliable* seems so easy to define, yet so hard to implement. Something is reliable when the results it produces are both expected and consistent. A reliable data source produces mundane data that contains no surprises; no one is shocked in the least by the outcome. Depending on your perspective, it could actually be a good thing that most people aren't yawning and then falling asleep when reviewing data. The surprises make the data worth analyzing and reviewing. Consequently, data has an aspect of duality. We want reliable, mundane, fully anticipated data that simply confirms what we already know, but the unexpected is what makes collecting the data useful in the first place.

Still, you don't want data that is so far out of the ordinary that it becomes almost frightening to review. Balance needs to be maintained when obtaining data. The data must fit within certain limits (as described in the "Manicuring the Data" section, later in this chapter). It must also meet the specific criteria of truth value (as described in the "Considering the Five Mistruths in Data" section, later in this chapter). The data must also come at expected intervals, and all the fields of the incoming data record must be complete.

REMEMBER

To some extent, data security also affects data reliability. Data consistency comes in several forms. When the data arrives, you can ensure that it falls within expected ranges and appears in a particular form. However, after you store the data, the reliability can decrease unless you ensure that the data remains in the expected form. An entity fiddling with the data affects reliability, making the data suspect and potentially unusable for analysis later. Ensuring data reliability means that after the data arrives, no one tampers with it to make it fit within an expected domain (making it mundane as a result).

Making human input more reliable

Humans make mistakes — it's part of being human. In fact, expecting that humans won't make mistakes is unreasonable. Yet many application designs assume that humans somehow won't make mistakes of any sort. The design expects that everyone will simply follow the rules. Unfortunately, the vast majority of users are guaranteed to not even read the rules because most humans are also lazy or too pressed for time when it comes to doing things that don't really help them directly.

Consider the entry of a state into a form. If you provide just a text field in the application gathering the data, you encounter a wide variety of possible input:

>> Some users might input the entire state name, such as Kansas. Of course, some users will make a typo or a capitalization error and come up with Kanzuz, Kansus, or kANSAS. You see the potential for errors.

>> People and organizations also have various approaches to performing tasks. Someone in the publishing industry might use the Associated Press (AP) style guide and input Kan. Someone who is older and used to the Government Printing Office (GPO) guidelines might input Kans. instead.

>> And some people might go for other available state abbreviations. The U.S. Post Office (USPS) uses KS, but the U.S. Coast Guard uses KA. Meanwhile, the International Standards Organization (ISO) form goes with US-KS.

Mind you, this is just a state entry, which is reasonably straightforward — or so you thought before reading this section. Clearly, because the state won't change names anytime soon, you could simply provide a drop-down list box on the form for choosing the state in the required format, thereby eliminating differences in abbreviation use, typos, and capitalization errors in one fell swoop.

REMEMBER

Drop-down list boxes work well for an amazing array of data inputs, and using them ensures that human input into those fields becomes extremely reliable because the human has no choice but to use one of the default entries. Of course, the human can always choose the incorrect entry, which is where double-checks come into play. Some newer applications compare the zip code to the city and state entries to see whether they match. When they don't match (sometimes it's just a matter of capitalization), the user is asked again to provide the correct input. This double-check verges on being annoying, but the user is unlikely to see it often, so it shouldn't become too annoying.

Even with cross-checks and static entries, humans still have plenty of room for making mistakes. For example, entering numbers can be problematic. When a user needs to enter 2.00, you may see 2, or 2.0, or 2., or any of a variety of other entries. Fortunately, parsing the entry and reformatting it fixes the problem, and you can perform this task automatically, without the user's aid. (Unfortunately, some online sites want you to enter information like credit cards with dashes, some with spaces, and some with no spacing at all, which makes for a confusing session when the application doesn't fix the entry automatically.)

Unfortunately, reformatting doesn't correct an errant numeric input. You can partially mitigate such errors by including range checks — a customer can't buy fewer than zero bars of soap. And, unless the customer is filthy or owns a wombat farm, entering 50,000 bars of soap would likely be a mistake, too. The legitimate way to show that the customer is returning the five bars of soap is to process a return, not a sale. However, the user may have simply made an error, and you can provide a message stating the proper input range for the value.

Using automated data collection

Some people think that automated data collection solves all the human-input issues associated with datasets. In fact, automated data collection does provide a number of benefits:

>> Better consistency

>> Improved reliability

>> Lower probability of missing data

>> Enhanced accuracy

>> Reduced variance for factors like timed inputs

Unfortunately, to say that automated data collection solves every issue is simply incorrect. Automated data collection still relies on sensors, applications, and computer hardware designed by humans that provide access only to the data that humans decide to allow. Because of the limits that humans place on the characteristics of automated data collection, the outcome often provides less helpful information than the designers hoped for. Consequently, automated data collection is in a constant state of flux as designers try to solve the input issues.

REMEMBER

Automated data collection also suffers from both software and hardware errors present in any computing system, but with a higher potential for *soft issues* (which arise when the system is apparently working but isn't providing the desired result) than other kinds of computer-based setups. When the system works, the reliability of the input far exceeds human abilities. However, when soft issues occur, the system often fails to recognize, as a human might, that a problem exists, and therefore, the dataset could end up containing more mediocre or even bad data.

Collecting data ethically

For some people, anything that appears on the internet is automatically considered public domain — including people's faces and all their personal information. The fact is that you should consider everything as being copyrighted and unavailable for use in a public domain manner to use data safely. Even people who realize that material is copyrighted often fall back on fair use principles. Fair use can be quite a tricky subject, as witnessed by the *Author's Guild v. Google* case. The case centered on Google's Google Books project, in which Google created a searchable database of printed copyrighted books. The case was finally decided in favor of Google, but only because Google had met some strict requirements. In addition, this kind of fair use is about books, not people.

The problem with considering fair use alone is that it's also essential to consider a person's right to privacy (you can read about various laws in "Internet privacy laws revealed — how your personal information is protected online" at `legal.thomsonreuters.com`). Consequently, it shouldn't surprise anyone that a major ruckus arose when companies started scraping (screen scraping) images of people wearing masks from the internet without obtaining any permission whatsoever. In fact, Facebook sued and lost a lawsuit over its misuse of user data.

The right to privacy has also created a new industry for making a person's face less useful to companies that are determined to get free data without permission by using any means possible (see the *New York Times* article "This Tool Could Protect Your Photos from Facial Recognition"). The fact is, no matter where you stand on the free-use issue, you still need to consider the ethical use of data that you obtain, no matter what the source may be. Here are some considerations to keep in mind as you collect personal data ethically:

>> **Obtaining permission:** Some research requires you to be able to identify persons used within a dataset. Going out and grabbing *p*ersonally *i*dentifiable *i*nformation (PII) isn't a good way to gather data. For one thing, you can't be sure that the information is either complete or correct, so any analysis you perform is suspect. For another thing, you could encounter the messy and costly consequences of legal actions. The best way to obtain data with PII is to ask permission.

>> **Using sanitization techniques:** *Data sanitization* involves removing personal information — such as name, address, telephone number, and ID — from a dataset so that identifying a particular individual in a dataset becomes impossible. In addition to text and dataset variables, you must consider every kind of data. For example, if you're working with collections of photos, it is *paramount* that you take steps to blur faces and remove car plates from images.

>> **Avoiding data inference:** When collecting data, some users refuse to share personally identifiable information, such as gender and age. Some people recommend you infer this information when a user's picture or other information is available. Unfortunately, names associated with one gender in a particular culture may be assigned to another gender in other cultures. The problem with age inference is even more profound. For example, a machine learning algorithm will likely infer the wrong age for a person with albinism, which can affect as many as 1 in 3,000 individuals, depending on the part of the world the data comes from.

>> **Avoiding generalizations:** Many fields of study try to incorrectly apply statistics and machine learning outcomes, with the result that an individual ends up being mistreated in some manner.

It's essential to remember that statistics apply to groups, not to individuals.

REMEMBER

Manicuring the Data

Some people use the term *manipulation* when speaking about data, giving the impression that the data is somehow changed in an unscrupulous or devious manner. Perhaps a better term is *manicuring,* which makes the data well-shaped and lovely. No matter which term you use, however, raw data seldom meets the requirements for processing and analysis. To get something from the data, you must manicure it to meet specific needs. The following sections discuss data manicuring needs.

Dealing with missing data

To answer a given question correctly, you must have all the facts. You can guess the answer to a question without all the facts, but then the answer is just as likely to be wrong as correct. Often, someone who makes a decision, essentially answering a question, without all the facts is said to jump to a conclusion. When analyzing data, you have probably jumped to more conclusions than you think because of missing data. A *data record,* or one entry in a *dataset* (which is all the data), consists of *fields* that contain facts used to answer a question. Each field contains a single kind of data that addresses a single fact. If that field is empty, you don't have the data you need to answer the question using that particular data record.

As part of the process of dealing with missing data, you must know that the data is missing. Identifying that your dataset is missing information can be quite difficult because it requires you to look at the data at a low level — something that most people are unprepared to do and that is time-consuming even if you do have the required skills. Often, your first clue that data is missing is the preposterous answers that your questions elicit from the algorithm and associated dataset. When the algorithm is the right one to use, the dataset must be at fault. Here are some issues to consider:

REMEMBER

>> **Essential data missing:** A problem can occur when the data collection process lacks all the data necessary to answer a particular question. Sometimes you're better off to drop a fact than to use a considerably damaged fact.

>> **Some data missing:** Less damaged fields can have data missing in one of two ways — randomly or sequentially:

- **Randomly missing data is often the result of human or sensor error.** Fixing randomly missing data is easiest. You can use a simple median or average value as a replacement. No, the dataset isn't completely accurate, but it will likely work well enough to obtain a reasonable answer.

- **Sequentially missing data occurs during some type of generalized failure.** Fixing sequentially missing data is significantly harder, if not impossible, because you lack any surrounding data on which to base any sort of guess. If you can find the cause of the missing data, you can sometimes reconstruct it.

Considering data misalignments

Data might exist for each of the data records in a dataset, but it might not align with other data in other datasets you own. For example, the numeric data in a field in one dataset might be a floating-point type (with decimal point), but an integer type in another dataset. Before you can combine the two datasets, the fields must contain the same type of data.

All sorts of other kinds of misalignment can occur. For example, date fields are notorious for being formatted in various ways. To compare dates, the data formats must be the same. However, dates are also insidious in their propensity for looking the same but not being the same. For example, dates in one dataset might use Greenwich Mean Time (GMT) as a basis, whereas the dates in another dataset might use some other time zone. Before you can compare the times, you must align them to the same time zone. It can become even weirder when dates in one dataset come from a location that uses daylight saving time (DST) but dates from another location don't.

Even when the data types and format are the same, other data misalignments can occur. For example, the fields in one dataset may not match the fields in the other dataset. In some cases, these differences are easy to correct. One dataset may treat first and last names as a single field, while another dataset might use separate fields for first and last names. The answer is to change all datasets to use a single field or to change them all to use separate fields for first and last names. Unfortunately, many misalignments in data content are harder to figure out. In fact, it's entirely possible that you might be unable to figure them out. However, before you give up, consider these potential solutions to the problem:

>> Calculate the missing data from other data you can access.

>> Locate the missing data in another dataset.

>> Combine datasets to create a whole that provides consistent fields.

>> Collect additional data from various sources to fill in the missing data.

>> Redefine your question so that you no longer need the missing data.

Separating useful data from other data

Some organizations' leaders are of the opinion that they can never have too much data, but an excess of data becomes as much a problem as not enough. To solve problems efficiently, an AI requires just enough data. Defining the question that you want to answer concisely and clearly helps, as does using the correct algorithm (or algorithm ensemble). Of course, the major problems with having too much data are that finding the solution (after wading through all that extra data) takes longer, and sometimes you get confusing results because you can't see the forest for the trees.

WARNING

As part of creating the dataset you need for analysis, you make a copy of the original data rather than modify it. Always keep the original, raw data pure so that you can use it for other analysis later. In addition, creating the right data output for analysis can require a number of tries because you may find that the output doesn't meet your needs. The point is to create a dataset that contains only the data needed for analysis, but keep in mind that the data may need specific kinds of pruning to ensure the desired output.

Considering the Five Mistruths in Data

Humans are used to seeing data for what it is, in many cases: an opinion. In fact, in some cases, people skew data to the point where it becomes useless, a *mistruth.* A computer can't tell the difference between truthful and untruthful data — all it sees is data. One issue that makes it difficult, if not impossible, to create an AI that actually thinks like a human is that humans can work with mistruths, and computers can't. The best you can hope to achieve is to see the errant data as outliers and then filter it out, but that technique doesn't necessarily solve the problem because a human would still use the data and attempt to determine a truth based on the mistruths that are there.

WARNING

A common thought about creating less contaminated datasets is that, instead of allowing humans to enter the data, collecting the data via sensors or other means should be possible. Unfortunately, sensors and other mechanical input methodologies reflect the goals of their human inventors and the limits of what the particular technology is able to detect. Consequently, even machine- or sensor-derived data is also subject to generating mistruths that are quite difficult for an AI to detect and overcome.

The following sections use a car accident as the main example to illustrate five types of mistruths that can appear in data. The concepts that the accident is trying to portray may not always appear in data, and they may appear in different ways than discussed. The fact remains that you normally need to deal with these sorts of issues when viewing data.

Commission

Mistruths of *commission* are those that reflect an outright attempt to substitute truthful information for untruthful information. For example, when filling out an accident report, someone could state that the sun momentarily blinded them, making it impossible to see someone they hit. In reality, perhaps the person was distracted by something else or wasn't actually thinking about driving (possibly considering a nice dinner). If no one can disprove this theory, the person might get by with a lesser charge. However, the point is that the data would also be contaminated. The effect is that now an insurance company would base premiums on errant data.

REMEMBER

Although it would seem that mistruths of commission are completely avoidable, often they aren't. Humans tell "little white lies" to save others from embarrassment or to deal with an issue with the least amount of personal effort. Sometimes a mistruth of commission is based on errant input or hearsay. In fact, the sources of errors of commission are so many that it is truly difficult to come up with a scenario where someone could avoid them entirely. Regardless, mistruths of commission are one type of mistruth that someone can avoid more often than not.

Omission

Mistruths of *omission* are those in which a person tells the truth in every stated fact but leaves out an important fact that would change the perception of an incident as a whole. Thinking again about the accident report, say that your car strikes a deer, causing significant damage to your car. You truthfully say that the road was wet; it was near twilight, so the light wasn't as good as it could be; you were a little late in pressing on the brake; and the deer simply darted out from a thicket at the side of the road. The conclusion would be that the incident is simply an accident.

However, you left out an important fact: You were texting at the time. If law enforcement knew about the texting, it would change the reason for the accident to inattentive driving. You might be fined, and the insurance adjuster would use a different reason when entering the incident into the database. As with the mis-truth of commission, the resulting errant data would change how the insurance company adjusts premiums.

Avoiding mistruths of omission is nearly impossible. Yes, people can purposely leave facts out of a report, but it's just as likely that they'll simply fail to include all the facts. After all, most people are quite rattled after an accident, so they can easily lose focus and report only those truths that leave the most significant impression. Even if a person later remembers additional details and reports them, the database is unlikely to ever contain a full set of truths.

Perspective

Mistruths of *perspective* occur when multiple parties view an incident from mul-tiple vantage points. For example, in considering an accident involving a struck pedestrian, the person driving the car, the person getting hit by the car, and a bystander who witnessed the event would all have different perspectives. An offi-cer taking reports from each person would understandably glean different facts from each one, even assuming that each person tells the truth as each knows it. In fact, experience shows that this is almost always the case, and the info that the officer submits as a report is the middle ground of what each of those involved states, augmented by personal experience. In other words, the report will be close to the truth, but not close enough for an AI.

When dealing with perspective, consider vantage point. The driver of the car can see the dashboard and knows the car's condition at the time of the accident. This is information that the other two parties lack. Likewise, the person getting hit by the car has the best vantage point for seeing the driver's facial expression (intent). The bystander might be in the best position to see whether the driver made an attempt to stop, and assess issues such as whether the driver tried to swerve. Each party will have to make a report based on seen data without the benefit of hidden data.

Perspective is perhaps the most dangerous of the mistruths because anyone who tries to derive the truth in this scenario ends up, at best, with an average of the various stories, which will never be fully correct. A human viewing the informa-tion can rely on intuition and instinct to potentially obtain a better approxima-tion of the truth, but an AI will always use just the average, which means that the AI is always at a significant disadvantage. Unfortunately, avoiding mistruths of perspective is impossible because no matter how many witnesses you have to the event, the best you can hope to achieve is an approximation of the truth, not the actual truth.

Think about this other scenario that involves perception: You're a deaf person in 1927. Each week, you go to the theater to view a silent film, and for an hour or more, you feel like everyone else. You can experience the movie in the same way everyone else does; there are no differences. In October of that year, you see a sign saying that the theater is upgrading to support a sound system so that it can display *talkies* — films with a soundtrack.

The sign says that talkies are the best thing ever, and almost everyone seems to agree, except for you, the deaf person, who is now made to feel like a second-class citizen — different from everyone else and even pretty much excluded from the theater. In the deaf person's eyes (from their perspective), that sign is a mistruth; adding a sound system is the worst possible thing, not the best possible thing. The point is that what seems to be generally true isn't actually true for everyone. The idea of a general truth — one that is true for everyone — is a myth. It doesn't exist.

Bias

Mistruths of *bias* occur when someone is capable of seeing the truth but because of personal concerns or beliefs is unable to actually see it. For example, when thinking about an accident, a driver might focus attention so completely on the middle of the road that the deer at the edge of the road becomes invisible. Consequently, the driver has no time to react when the deer suddenly decides to bolt into the middle of the road in an effort to cross.

REMEMBER

It is known that faster speed blurs peripheral vision so the deer does become harder to see at higher speeds.

A problem with bias is that it can be incredibly hard to categorize. For example, a driver who fails to see the deer can have a genuine accident, meaning that the deer was hidden from view by shrubbery. However, the driver might also be guilty of inattentive driving because of incorrect focus. The driver might also experience a momentary distraction. In short, the fact that the driver didn't see the deer isn't the question; instead, it's a matter of *why* the driver didn't see the deer. In many cases, confirming the source of bias becomes important when creating an algorithm designed to avoid a biased source.

REMEMBER

Theoretically, avoiding mistruths of bias is always possible. In reality, however, all humans have biases of various types, and those biases will always result in mistruths that skew datasets. Just persuading someone to actually look and then see something — to have it register in the person's brain — is a difficult task. Humans rely on filters to avoid information overload, and these filters are also a source of bias because they prevent people from actually seeing things.

Frame of reference

Of the five mistruths, frame of reference need not be the result of any sort of error, but one of understanding. A *frame-of-reference* mistruth occurs when one party describes something, such as an event like an accident, and because a second party lacks experience with the event, the details become muddled or completely misunderstood. Comedy routines abound that rely on frame-of-reference errors. One famous example is from Abbott and Costello, *Who's On First*, which you can find on YouTube.com. Getting one person to understand what a second person is saying can be impossible when the first person lacks experiential knowledge — the frame of reference.

Another frame-of-reference mistruth example occurs when one party can't possibly understand the other. For example, a sailor experiences a storm at sea. Perhaps it's a monsoon, but assume for a moment that the storm is substantial — perhaps life-threatening. Even with the use of videos, interviews, and a simulator, the experience of being at sea in a life-threatening storm would be impossible to convey to someone who hasn't experienced such a storm firsthand; that person has no frame of reference.

REMEMBER

The best way to avoid frame-of-reference mistruths is to ensure that all parties involved can develop similar frames of reference. To accomplish this task, the various parties require similar experiential knowledge to ensure the accurate transfer of data from one person to another. However, when working with a dataset, which is necessarily recorded static data, frame-of-reference errors will still occur when the prospective viewer lacks the required experiential knowledge.

An AI will always experience frame-of-reference issues because it necessarily lacks the ability to create an experience. A data bank of acquired knowledge isn't quite the same thing. The data bank would contain facts, but experience is based on not only facts but also conclusions that current technology is unable to duplicate.

Defining the Limits of Data Acquisition

If you get the feeling that everyone is acquiring your data without thought or reason, you're right. In fact, organizations collect, categorize, and store everyone's data — seemingly without goal or intent.

Data acquisition has become a narcotic for organizations worldwide, and some of their leaders seem to think that the organization that collects the most somehow wins a prize. However, data acquisition, in and of itself, accomplishes nothing.

The book *The Hitchhiker's Guide to the Galaxy*, by Douglas Adams, illustrates this problem clearly. In this book, a race of supercreatures builds an immense computer to calculate the meaning of "life, the universe, and everything." The answer of 42 doesn't really solve anything, so some of the creatures complain that the collection, categorization, and analysis of all the data used for the answer hasn't produced a usable result. The computer — a sentient one, no less — tells the people receiving the answer that the answer is indeed correct, but they need to know the question in order for the answer to make sense. Data acquisition can occur in unlimited amounts, but figuring out the right questions to ask can be daunting, if not impossible.

REMEMBER

The main problem that any organization needs to address with regard to data acquisition is which questions to ask and why the questions are important. Tailoring data acquisition to answer the questions you need answered matters. For example, if you're running a shop in town, you might need answers to questions like this:

>> How many people walk in front of the store each day?

>> How many of those people stop to look in the window?

>> How long do they look?

>> What time of day are they looking?

>> Do certain displays tend to produce better results?

>> Which of these displays cause people to enter the store and shop?

The list could go on, but the idea is that creating a list of questions that address specific business needs is essential. After you create a list, you must verify that each of the questions is indeed important — that is, addresses a need — and then ascertain what sorts of information you need to answer the question.

WARNING

Of course, trying to collect all this data by hand would be impossible, which is where automation comes into play. Seemingly, automation would produce reliable, repeatable, and consistent data input. However, many factors in automating data acquisition can produce data that isn't particularly useful. For example, consider these issues:

>> Sensors can collect only the data they're designed to collect, so you might miss data when the sensors used aren't designed for the purpose.

>> People create errant data in various ways (see the "Considering the Five Mistruths in Data" section, earlier in this chapter, for details), which means that data you receive might be false.

>> Data can become skewed when the conditions for collecting it are incorrectly defined.

>> Interpreting data incorrectly means that the outputs from AI will also be incorrect.

>> Converting a real-world question into an algorithm that the computer can understand is an error-prone process.

Many other issues (enough to fill a book) need to be considered. When you combine poorly collected, ill-formed data with algorithms that don't actually answer your questions, you get output that may actually lead your business in the wrong direction, which is why AI is often blamed for inconsistent or unreliable results. Asking the right question, obtaining the correct data, performing the right processing, and then correctly analyzing the data are all required in order to make data acquisition the kind of tool you can rely on.

Considering Data Security Issues

This section discusses data security from the perspective of protecting data integrity rather than keeping someone from stealing it or guarding privacy. Securing data doesn't mean placing it in a vault — assuming that doing so is even possible with data today. Data is useful only when it's accessible. Of course, the need to make data accessible means taking a risk that someone will do something you don't want done with the data. The following sections discuss a few data security issues you need to consider.

Understanding purposefully biased data

Bias appears in nearly every dataset available today, even custom-created datasets. The dataset is often biased because the collection methods are biased, the analysis methods are biased, and the data itself is biased. You often see articles online with titles like "8 Types of Bias in Data Analysis and How to Avoid Them," which means that people recognize the existence of bias and want to mitigate it as much as possible. However, sometimes you find that the opposite is true: The people using the dataset purposely bias it in some manner. Here are some areas in which data becomes purposely biased:

>> **Political:** Political maneuvering can become the source of data bias. Two groups with opposing opinions will use the same dataset and obtain two completely different outcomes that support their particular perspective. At issue are the records selected and the dataset features used to create an

outcome. In other cases, a group will resort to techniques like using bogus respondents in polls (see "Assessing the Risks to Online Polls from Bogus Respondents" at `pewresearch.org` for details).

>> **Medical:** When medical groups advertise for people to participate in trials of medications, procedures, and other needs, the group they get often doesn't represent the population as a whole, so the data is biased.

>> **Legal:** The use of COMPAS software (it's short for Correctional Offender Management Profiling for Alternative Sanctions) to predict the potential for *recidivism* (the tendency of a convicted criminal to reoffend) is another example of data and algorithm bias, as explained in "Injustice Ex Machina: Predictive Algorithms in Criminal Sentencing," at `uclalawreview.org`. The article points out so many flaws with COMPAS that the best idea might be to start from scratch because the software is destroying people's lives at an incredible rate.

>> **Hiring:** The use of datasets and well-rounded algorithms supposedly reduces the risk of bias in hiring and promoting individuals within an organization. According to "All the Ways Hiring Algorithms Can Introduce Bias" at `hbr.org`, the opposite is too often true. The datasets become an amplification of biased hiring practices within an organization or within society as a whole.

>> **Other:** Anytime a dataset and its associated algorithms become influenced by bias, the outcome is less than ideal. The term *machine learning fairness* presents the idea that the outcome of any analysis should correctly represent the actual conditions within. If the outcome of an analysis doesn't match the result received afterward, the analysis is flawed and the data usually receives a lion's share of the blame.

Dealing with data-source corruption

Even if people don't cherry-pick data or use data sources that fail to reflect the actual conditions in the world, as described in the previous section, data sources can become corrupt. For example, when seeing product reviews on a website, you can't be certain that

>> Real people created reviews.

>> Some people haven't voted more than once.

>> The person wasn't simply having an exceptionally bad (or less likely, good) day.

>> The person actually used the product and has no ulterior motive, for example, if they sell the product or are a competitor.

>> The reviews reflect a fair segment of society.

In fact, the reviews are likely so biased and corrupt that believing them at all becomes nearly impossible. Unfortunately, data-source corruption comes from many other sources:

>> A sensor might be bad, producing erroneous results.

>> A virus attack might cause data errors.

>> The database or other software contains a flaw.

>> Humans enter the data incorrectly into the database.

>> Acts of nature, such as lightning, cause momentary glitches in data collection.

You can rely on a number of approaches to deal with all sorts of data corruption. Storing data in the cloud tends to reduce problems associated with hardware, weather, or other issues that cause data loss. Ensuring that you have procedures and training in place, plus constant monitoring, can help reduce human errors. Active administrator participation and the use of firewalls can reduce other sorts of data-source corruption.

REMEMBER

All these measures reflect what you can do locally. When performing screen scraping and other techniques to obtain data from online sources, data scientists must employ other measures to ensure that the data remains pure. Vouching for an online source isn't possible unless the source is vetted every time it's used.

Handling botnets

Botnets are coordinated groups of computers that focus on performing specific tasks, most of them nefarious. This short section focuses on botnets that feed a dataset erroneous data or take over accounts to modify the account information in certain ways. Whatever means is used, whatever the intent, botnets generally corrupt or bias data in ways that cause any kind of analysis to fail.

Botnets represent a significant concern in AI for several reasons, primarily due to their evolving capabilities and the scale and speed of attacks they can launch. Here are three key reasons that botnets are a particular concern:

>> **AI-enhanced botnets:** With advances in AI and machine learning, botnets have become more sophisticated, capable of automating and rapidly expanding cyberattacks. AI can enable botnets to analyze network behavior, adapt attack patterns to bypass cyberdefenses, and execute attacks with increased efficiency and stealth. This adaptability makes AI-enhanced botnets formidable adversaries, capable of evading traditional detection mechanisms and launching potent and destructive attacks.

>> **Scale and magnitude of attacks:** AI-powered botnets can harness the computational power of numerous compromised devices, including the internet of things (IoT), creating massive bot armies. With these vast networks, AI-powered botnets can launch coordinated attacks that overwhelm even the most robust security infrastructures. This scale and magnitude of attacks pose significant challenges to cyberdefenses, requiring advanced detection and mitigation strategies.

>> **Rapid attack development:** Unlike traditional botnets that require manual programming for specific targets, AI-powered counterparts leverage algorithms to analyze and exploit vulnerabilities quickly. This enables them to develop new attack techniques at an alarming pace, keeping defenders on their toes and making it difficult to predict and prevent attacks.

WARNING

The continuous mutation of botnets to exploit vulnerabilities and security flaws makes prevention and mitigation challenging. Botnet operators use a variety of IP addresses and devices in their attacks, complicating the task of screening out bad requests and confidently allowing access to valid requests. The proliferation of IP-addressable IoT devices has expanded the potential for botnets to spread and launch attacks.

Chapter **3**

Considering the Use of Algorithms

D ata is a game changer in AI. Advances in AI hint that, for certain problems, choosing the right amount of data is more important than choosing the right algorithm. However, no matter how much data you have, you still need an algorithm to make it useful. In addition, you must perform *data analysis* (a series of definable steps) to make data work correctly with the chosen algorithms — no shortcuts allowed. Even though AI is intelligent automation, sometimes automation must take a back seat to analysis. You won't now find machines that know what's appropriate and can completely cut out any human intervention, but self-learning machines, also known as *self-improving* or *autonomous learning systems,* are already a significant area of research and development in the field of AI.

In this chapter, you explore the relationship between algorithms and the data used to make them perform useful work. You also gain an understanding of the role of expert systems, machine learning, deep learning, and applications such as AlphaGo (and the subsequent version, AlphaGo Zero, both of which can play the game Go) in bringing future possibilities a little closer to reality.

Understanding the Role of Algorithms

An *algorithm* is a procedure that consists of a sequence of operations. Usually, a computer manages these operations by either finding the correct solution to a problem in a finite time or telling you that no solution exists. Even though people have solved algorithms manually for literally thousands of years, doing so can consume huge amounts of time and require many numeric computations, depending on the complexity of the problem to be solved. Algorithms are all about finding solutions, and the speedier and easier, the better. Algorithms have become hard-coded into the intelligence of humans who devised them, and any machine operating on algorithms cannot but reflect the intelligence embedded into such algorithmic procedures. AI provides the means to simulate the human in processing and solving existing algorithms, but currently, AI can't replace humans or mimic human creativity in devising new algorithms.

People tend to recognize AI when a tool presents a novel approach and interacts with the user in a human-like way. Examples include digital assistants such as Alexa, Cortana, Google Assistant, and Siri. However, certain other common tools, such as GPS routers and specialized planners (like those used to avoid automotive collisions, autopilot airplanes, and arrange production plans) don't even look like AI because they're too common and taken for granted as they act behind the scenes. In addition, it's important to consider alternative forms of AI, such as smart thermostats that control the environment based on past usage and current environmental data, and smart garage door openers that automatically detect when you accidentally leave the door open after you leave for work.

This is clearly the AI effect, as named and described by Pamela McCorduck, who wrote a notable history of AI, *Machines Who Think,* in 1979. (The version at Amazon. com is an updated version.) The *AI effect* states that people soon forget about successful, intelligent computer programs, which become silent actors while attention shifts to AI problems that still require resolution. The importance of classic algorithms to AI gets overlooked, and people start fantasizing about AI created from esoteric technology, or they equate it with recent advances, such as machine learning and deep learning.

Examining what an algorithm does

An algorithm always presents a series of steps, but it doesn't necessarily perform all these steps to solve a problem. (Some steps are optional or performed only under specific conditions.) A group of related steps is an *operation,* such as the tea-making operation being composed of these steps:

1. Pour water into the teapot.

2. Turn on the fire to heat the water in the teapot.

3. When water is heated, pour it into the cup.

4. Place a teabag in the cup and steep the tea for the recommended time.

5. Remove the teabag.

6. (Optional) Add sugar to the tea.

7. (Optional) Add milk to the tea.

8. Drink the tea.

9. (Optional) Toss the tea in the sink when it becomes undrinkable.

The scope of algorithms is incredibly large. Operations may involve storing data, exploring it, and ordering or arranging it into data structures. You can find algorithms that solve problems in science, medicine, finance, industrial production and supply, and communication.

All algorithms contain sequences of operations to find the correct solution to a problem in a reasonable time (or report back if no solution is found). A subclass of algorithms, *heuristics,* produce good, but not necessarily perfect, solutions when time-to-solution is more critical than finding the perfect solution. AI algorithms distinguish themselves from generic algorithms by solving problems whose resolution is considered typically (or even exclusively) the product of human intelligent behavior. AI algorithms tend to deal with complex problems, which are often part of the *NP-complete* class of problems (where NP is *n*ondeterministic *p*olynomial time) that humans routinely deal with by mixing a rational approach with intuition.

Here are just a few examples:

>> Scheduling problems and allocating scarce resources

>> Searching routes in complex physical or figurative spaces

>> Recognizing patterns in image vision (versus something like image restoration or image processing) or sound perception

>> Processing language (both text understanding and language translation)

>> Playing (and winning) competitive games

TIP

NP-complete problems distinguish themselves from other algorithmic problems because finding a solution for them in a reasonable time frame isn't yet possible. NP-complete isn't the kind of problem you solve by trying all possible combinations or possibilities. Even if you had computers more powerful than those that exist today, a search for the solution would last almost forever. In a similar fashion, in AI, this kind of problem is called *AI-complete*.

Planning and branching: Trees and nodes

Planning helps you determine the sequence of actions to perform to achieve a certain goal. Deciding on the plan is a classic AI problem, and you can find examples of planning in industrial production, resource allocation, and robot motion. Starting from the present state, an AI first determines all possible actions from that state. Technically, it *expands* the current state into a number of future states. Then it expands all future states into their own future states, and so on. When you can no longer expand the states and the AI stops the expansion, the AI has created a *state space*, which is composed of whatever could happen in the future. An AI can take advantage of a state space not just as a prediction (actually, it predicts everything, though some future states are more likely than others) but also because AI can use that state space to explore decisions it can make to reach its goal in the best way. This process is known as the *state-space search.*

Working with a state space requires the use of both particular data structures and algorithms. The core data structures commonly used are trees and graphs. The favored algorithms used to efficiently explore graphs include breadth-first search and depth-first search.

Building a tree works in much the same way that a tree grows in the physical world. Each item you add to the tree is a *node*. Nodes connect to each other using links. The combination of nodes and links forms a structure that looks like a tree, as shown in Figure 3-1.

REMEMBER

Trees have a single root node, just like a physical tree. The *root node* is the starting point for the processing you perform. Connected to the root are either branches or leaves. A *leaf node* is an ending point for the tree. *Branch nodes* support either other branches or leaves. The type of tree shown in Figure 3-1 is a binary tree because each node has, at most, two connections (but trees representing *state spaces* — a way of representing all possible configurations of a system — can have multiple branches).

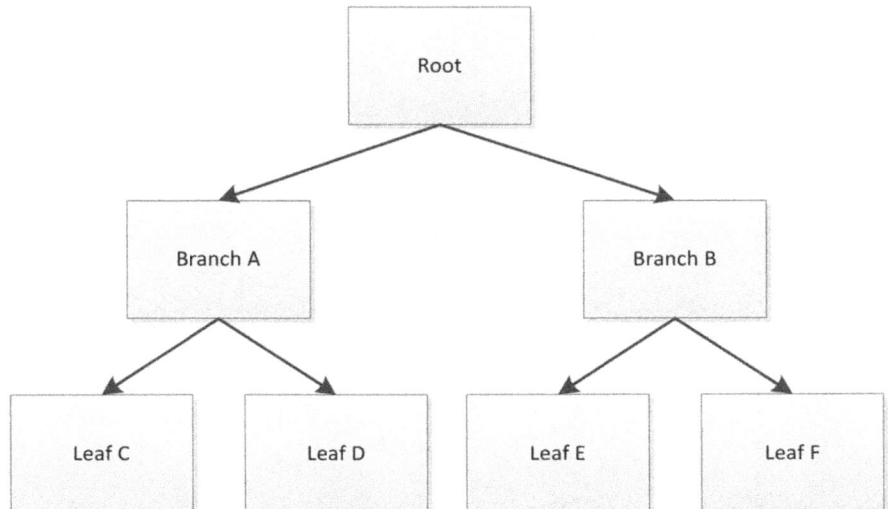

In looking at the tree, Branch B is the *child* of the Root node. That's because the Root node appears first in the tree. Leaf E and Leaf F are both children of Branch B, making Branch B the *parent* of Leaf E and Leaf F. The relationship between nodes is important because discussions about trees often consider the child/parent relationship between nodes. Without these terms, discussions of trees could become quite confusing.

Extending the tree using graph nodes

A *graph* is a sort of tree extension. As with trees, you have nodes that connect to each other to create relationships. However, unlike a binary tree, a graph node can have more than one or two connections. In fact, graph nodes often have a multitude of connections, and, most important, nodes can connect in any direction, not just from parent to child. To keep things simple, though, consider the graph shown in Figure 3-2.

Graphs are structures that present a number of nodes (or *vertexes*) connected by a number of edges or arcs (depending on the representation). When you think about a graph, think about a structure like a map, where each location on the map is a node and the streets are the edges. This presentation differs from a tree, where each path ends up in a leaf node. Refer to Figure 3-2 to see a graph represented. Graphs are particularly useful when figuring out states that represent a sort of physical space. For instance, the GPS uses a graph to represent places and streets.

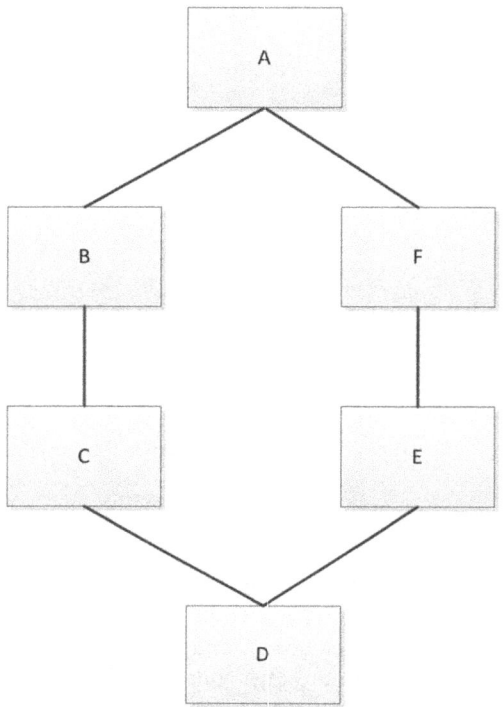

FIGURE 3-2:
Graph nodes
can connect to
each other in
myriad ways.

Graphs also add a few new twists that you may not have considered. For example, a graph can include the concept of directionality. Unlike a tree, which has parent/ child relationships, a graph node can connect to any other node with a specific direction in mind. Think about streets in a city. Most streets are bidirectional, but some are one-way streets that allow movement in only one direction.

The presentation of a graph connection might not reflect the realities of the physical system it is modeling. A graph can designate a *weight* to a particular connection. The weight can define the distance between two points, define the time required to traverse the route, specify the amount of fuel used to travel the route, or provide other sorts of information.

REMEMBER

A tree is nothing more than a graph in which any two vertices are connected by exactly one path, and the tree doesn't allow *cycles* (to be able to get back to the parent from any child). Many graph algorithms apply only to trees.

Traversing the graph

Traversing a graph means to search (visit) each vertex (node) in a specific order. The process of visiting a vertex can include both reading and updating it. You discover unvisited vertexes as you traverse a graph. The vertex becomes discovered (because you just visited it) or processed (because the algorithm tried all the edges departing from it) after the search. The order of the search determines the kind of search performed:

>> **Uninformed (blind search):** The AI explores the state space without additional information except for the graph structure it discovers as it traverses it. Here are two common blind-search algorithms, which are discussed in the sections that follow:

- *Breadth-first search (BFS):* Begins at the graph root and explores every node that attaches to the root. It then searches the next level, exploring each level in turn until it reaches the end. Consequently, in the sample graph, the search explores from A to B and F before it moves on to explore C and E. BFS explores the graph in a systematic way, exploring vertexes around the starting vertex in a circular fashion. It begins by visiting all vertexes that are a single step from the starting vertex; it then moves two steps out, and then three steps out, and so on.

- *Depth-first search (DFS):* Begins at the graph root and then explores every node from that root down a single path to the end. It then backtracks and begins exploring the paths not taken in the current search path until it reaches the root again. At that point, if other paths to take from the root are available, the algorithm chooses one and begins the same search again. The idea is to explore each path completely before exploring any other path.

REMEMBER

>> **Informed (heuristic search):** A heuristic finds or discovers a useful method of traversing the graph based on rules of thumb (such as expert systems) or algorithms that use *low-order polynomial time* (in which the algorithm's running time is bounded by a polynomial with a relatively small exponent). It's an educated guess about a solution that points to the direction of a desired outcome but can't tell exactly how to reach it. It's like being lost in an unknown city and having people tell you a certain way to reach your hotel (but with no precise instructions). Because this search is informed (even though it isn't precise), it can also estimate the remaining *cost* (time or resources or another value that determines which route is better in a particular instance) to go from a particular state to a solution. Here are three common heuristic search algorithms (see the "Using local search and heuristics" section later in this chapter for more details):

- *Best-first search:* An evaluation function assists in the search by determining the desirability of expanding a particular node based on the costs of the nodes that follow. The costs of each node are stored in a queue or another memory structure. Except for the foreknowledge of node cost, this solution works much like a BFS or DFS.

- *Greedy search:* Like a best-first search, the path to follow is informed by node costs. However, the greedy search looks only one node ahead, which saves processing time in the evaluation function, but doesn't always guarantee an optimal solution.

- *A* search:* This is an expansion of the best-first search, which uses two costs: the cost to move from the starting point to another given position in the graph and the cost to move from that given node on the graph to the final destination.

Playing adversarial games

The interesting aspect of state-space search is that it represents both AI's current functionality and future opportunities. This is the case with *adversarial games* (games in which one player wins and the others lose) or with any similar situation in which players pursue an objective that conflicts with the goals of others. A simple game like tic-tac-toe presents a perfect example of a space search game that you may already have seen an AI play. In the 1983 film *WarGames,* the supercomputer WOPR (War Operation Plan Response) plays against itself at a blazing speed, yet it cannot win, because the game is indeed simple, and if you use a state-space search, you won't ever lose.

You have nine cells to fill with *x*'s and *o*'s for each player. The first one to place three marks in a row (horizontal, vertical, or diagonal) wins. When building a state-space tree for the game, each level of the tree represents a game turn. The end nodes represent the final board state and determine a victory, draw, or defeat for the AI. Every terminal node has a higher score for winning, lower for drawing, and even lower or negative for losing. The AI propagates the scores to the upper nodes and branches using summation until reaching the starting node. The starting node represents the actual situation. Using a simple strategy enables you to traverse the tree: When it's AI's turn and you have to propagate the values of many nodes, you sum the maximum value (presumably because AI has to retrieve the maximum result from the game); when it's the adversary's turn, you sum the minimum value instead. In the end, you extract a tree whose branches are qualified by scores. When it's the AI's turn, it chooses its move based on the branch whose value is the highest, because it implies expanding nodes with the highest possibility to win. Figure 3-3 shows a visual example of this strategy.

This approach is called the *min-max approximation.* Ronald Rivest, from the computer science laboratory at MIT, introduced it in 1987. Since then, this algorithm and its variants have powered many competitive games, along with recent game-playing advances, such as AlphaGo from Google DeepMind, which uses an approach that echoes the min-max approximation (which is also found in the *WarGames* film of 1983).

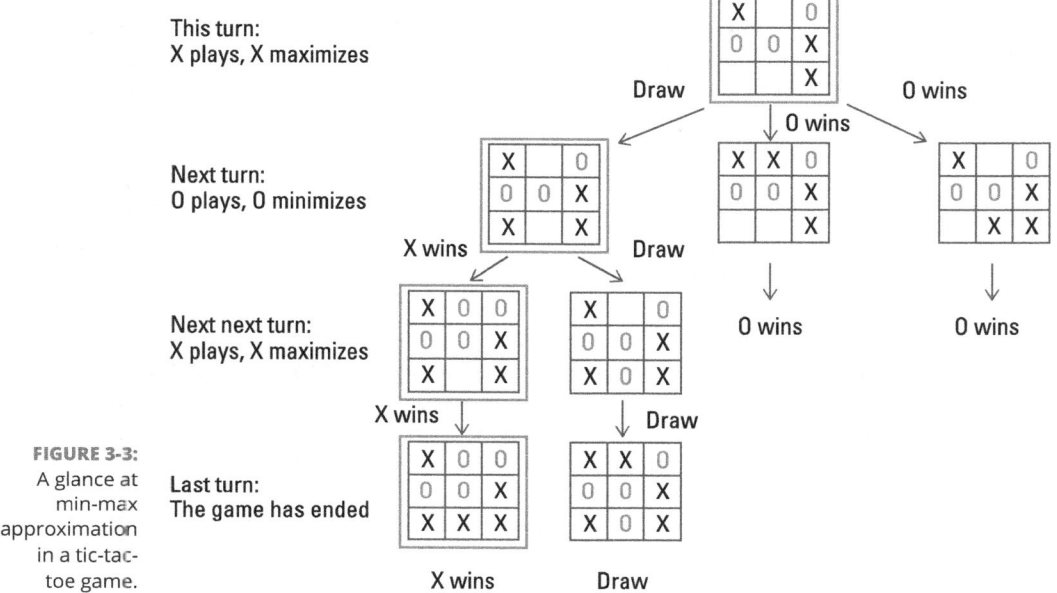

This turn:
X plays, X maximizes

Next turn:
O plays, O minimizes

Next next turn:
X plays, X maximizes

Last turn:
The game has ended

FIGURE 3-3:
A glance at min-max approximation in a tic-tac-toe game.

TIP

Sometimes you hear about alpha-beta pruning as connected to min-max approximation. *Alpha-beta pruning* is a smart way to propagate values up the tree hierarchy in complex state spaces limiting computations. Not all games feature compact state-space trees; when branches number in the trillions, you need to prune them and shorten your calculations.

Using local search and heuristics

A lot goes on behind the state-space search approach. In the end, no machine, no matter how powerful, can enumerate all the possibilities that spring from a complex situation. This section continues with games because they are predictable and have fixed rules, whereas many real-world situations are unpredictable and lack clear rules, making games an optimistic and favorable setting.

Checkers, a relatively simple game compared to chess or Go, has 500 billion billion (that's 500,000,000,000,000,000,000) possible board positions, a number that, according to computations by the mathematicians at Hawaii University, equates to all the grains of sand on Earth. It's true that fewer moves are possible as a game of checkers progresses. Yet the number to potentially evaluate at each move is too high. It took 18 years, using powerful computers, to compute all 500 billion billion possible moves — just imagine how long it could take on a consumer's computer to work out even a smaller subset of moves. To be manageable, the result should be a very small subset of all potential moves.

Optimization using local search and heuristics helps by using constraints to limit the beginning number of possible evaluations (as in alpha pruning, where some computations are omitted because they add nothing to the search success). *Local search* is a general problem-solving approach composed of a large range of algorithms that help you escape the exponential complexities of many NP problems. A local search starts from your present situation or an imperfect problem solution and moves away from it, a step at a time. A local search determines the viability of nearby solutions, potentially leading to a perfect solution, based on random choice or an astute heuristic (which means that no exact method is involved).

Local search algorithms iteratively improve from a starting state, moving one step at a time through neighboring solutions in the state space until they can no longer improve the solution. Because local search algorithms are so simple and intuitive, designing a local search approach for an algorithmic problem isn't difficult; making it effective is usually harder. The key lies in defining the correct procedure:

1. Start with an existing situation (it could be the present situation or a random or known solution).

2. Search for a set of possible new solutions within the current solution's neighborhood, which constitutes the candidates' list.

3. Determine which solution to use in place of the current solution based on the output of a heuristic that accepts the candidates' list as input.

4. Continue performing Steps 2 and 3 until you see no further solution improvement, which means that you have the best solution available.

Although easy to design, local search solutions may not find a solution in a reasonable time (you can stop the process and use the current solution) or produce a minimum-quality solution. You have no guarantee that a local search will arrive at a problem solution, but your chances do improve from the starting point when you provide enough time for the search to run its computations. It stops only after it can't find any further way to improve the solution. The secret is to determine the right neighborhood to explore. If you explore everything, you'll fall back to an exhaustive search, which implies an explosion of possibilities to explore and test.

Relying on a heuristic limits where you look based on a rule of thumb. Sometimes, a heuristic is random, and such a solution, despite being a nonintelligent approach, can work well. Few people, for instance, know that Roomba, the autonomous robotic vacuum cleaner created by three MIT graduates (you can see an example, iRobot Roomba, at Amazon.com), initially simply roamed around randomly and didn't plan its cleaning path. Yet it was considered a smart device by its owners and did an excellent cleaning job. (Intelligence is actually in the idea of using randomness to solve a problem that is otherwise too complex.)

Random choice isn't the only heuristic available. A local search can rely on more reasoned exploration solutions using well-devised heuristics to find directions:

>> **Hill climbing:** Relies on the observation that as a ball rolls down a valley, it takes the steepest descent. When a ball climbs a hill, it tends to take the most direct upward direction to reach the top, which is the one with the greatest inclination. The AI problem, therefore, is seen as a descent to a valley or an ascent to a mountaintop, and the heuristic is any rule that hints at the best downhill or uphill approach among the possible states of the state space. It's an effective algorithm, though sometimes it gets stuck in situations known as *plateaus* (intermediate valleys) and *peaks* (local maximum points).

>> **Twiddle (coordinate descent algorithms):** Similar to hill-climbing algorithms but explores all possible directions. It concentrates the search in the direction of the neighborhood that works best. As it does so, it calibrates its step, slowing down as it finds the discovery of better solutions difficult, until it reaches a stop.

>> **Simulated annealing:** Takes its name from a metallurgical technique that heats metal and then slowly cools it to soften it for cold working and to remove crystalline defects. Local search replicates this technique by viewing the solution search as an atomic structure that changes to improve its workability. The temperature is the game changer in the optimization process: Just as high temperatures make the structure of a material relax (solids melt and liquids evaporate at high temperatures), high temperatures in a local search algorithm induce relaxation of the objective function, allowing it to prefer worse solutions over better ones. Simulated annealing modifies the hill-climbing procedure, keeping the objective function for neighbor solution evaluation, but allowing it to determine the search solution choice in a different way.

>> **Taboo search:** Uses memorization to remember which parts of the neighborhood to explore. When it seems to have found a solution, it tends to try to retrace to other possible paths that it didn't try in order to ascertain the best solution.

Using measures of direction (upward, downward), temperature (controlled randomness), or simply restricting or retracing part of the search are all ways to effectively avoid trying everything and concentrating on a good solution. Consider, for instance, a robot walking. Guiding a robot in an unknown environment means avoiding obstacles to reach a specific target. It's both a fundamental and challenging task in artificial intelligence. Robots can rely on a laser rangefinder (lidar) or sonar (which involves devices that use sound to see their environment) to navigate their surroundings. Yet, no matter the level of hardware sophistication, robots still need proper algorithms to

» Find the shortest path to a destination (or at least a reasonably short one)

» Avoid obstacles on the way

» Perform custom behaviors such as minimizing turning or braking

A *pathfinding* algorithm helps a robot start in one location and reach a goal by using the shortest path between the two, anticipating and avoiding obstacles along the way. (Reacting after hitting a wall isn't sufficient.) Pathfinding is also useful when moving any other device to a target in space, even a virtual one, such as in video games or a webpage hosted game. When using pathfinding with a robot, the robot perceives movement as a flow of state spaces to the borders of its sensors. If the goal isn't within range, the robot doesn't know where to go. Heuristics can point it in the right direction (for instance, it can know that the target is in the north direction) and help it avoid obstacles in a timely fashion without having to determine all possible ways for doing so.

Discovering the Learning Machine

All the algorithmic examples given earlier in this chapter are associated with AI because they're smart solutions that solve repetitive and well-delimited yet complex problems requiring intelligence. They require an architect who studies the problem and chooses the right algorithm to solve it. Problem changes, mutations, or unusual characteristic displays can become a real problem for a successful execution of the algorithm. This is because learning the problem and its solution occurs once when you train the algorithm. For instance, you can safely program an AI to solve Sudoku puzzles. You can even provide flexibility that allows the algorithm to accept more rules or larger boards later.

Unfortunately, not all problems can rely on a Sudoku-like solution. Real-life problems are never set in simple worlds of perfect information and well-defined action. Consider the problem of finding a fraudster cheating on insurance claims or the problem of diagnosing a medical disease. You have to contend with these factors:

» **A large set of rules and possibilities:** The number of possible frauds is incredibly high; many diseases have similar symptoms.

» **Missing information:** Fraudsters can conceal information; doctors often rely on incomplete information (examinations may be missing).

>> **Problem rules aren't immutable:** Fraudsters discover new ways to arrange swindles or frauds; new diseases arise or are discovered.

To solve such problems, you can't use a predetermined approach; instead, you need a flexible approach and must accumulate useful knowledge to face any new challenge. In other words, you continue learning, as humans do throughout their lives to cope with a changing and challenging environment.

Leveraging expert systems

Expert systems, or systems that use rules to make decisions, were the first attempt to escape the realm of hard-coded algorithms and create more flexible and smart ways to solve real-life problems. The idea at the core of expert systems was simple and well-suited at a time when storing and dealing with lots of data in computer memory was still costly. It may sound strange today, but in the 1970s, AI scientists such as Ross Quillian had to demonstrate how to build working language models based on a vocabulary of only 20 words because computer memory of the time was too limited to handle the data structures needed to process more words. Few options were available if a computer couldn't hold all the data, and a solution was to process key problem information and obtain it from humans who knew it best.

REMEMBER

Expert systems were experts not because they based their knowledge on their own learning process, but rather because they collected it from human experts who provided a predigested system of key information taken from studying books, learning from other experts, or discovering it by themselves. It was basically a smart way to externalize knowledge into a machine.

MYCIN: A beginning expert system

An example of one of the first systems of this kind is MYCIN, a system to diagnose blood-clotting diseases or infections caused by bacteria, such as *bacteremia* (when bacteria infect the blood) and *meningitis* (inflammation of the membranes that protect the brain and spinal cord). MYCIN recommended the correct dosage of antibiotics by using well over 500 rules, and it relied, when needed, on the doctor using the system. When there wasn't enough information available — for instance, lab tests were missing — MYCIN then started a consultative dialogue by asking relevant questions to reach a confident diagnosis and therapy.

Written in Lisp as a doctoral dissertation by Edward Shortliffe at Stanford University, MYCIN took more than five years to complete, and it performed better than any junior doctor, reaching the elevated diagnosis accuracy of an experienced doctor. It came from the same laboratory that devised DENDRAL, the first expert system ever created, a few years earlier. DENDRAL, which specializes in organic chemistry, is a challenging application in which brute-force algorithms proved unfeasible when faced with human-based heuristics that rely on field experience.

As for MYCIN's success, some issues arose:

» First, the terms of responsibility were unclear: If the system were to provide an incorrect diagnosis, who was responsible?

» Second, MYCIN had a usability issue because the doctor had to connect to MYCIN by using a remote terminal to the mainframe in Stanford, a quite difficult and slow process at a time when the internet was still in its infancy. MYCIN still proved its efficacy and usefulness in supporting human decisions, and it paved the way for many other expert systems that proliferated later in the 1970s and 1980s.

The components of expert systems

Generally, expert systems of the time were made of two distinct components: knowledge base and inference engine. The *knowledge base* retains knowledge as a collection of rules in the form of if-then statements (with *if* involving one or multiple conditions and *then* involving conclusion statements). These statements occurred in a symbolic form, differentiating between instances, (single events or facts), classes, and subclasses, which all could be manipulated using Boolean logic or sophisticated first-order logic, which is composed of more possible operations.

TIP

First-order logic is a set of operations that goes beyond simply being bound to combine TRUE and FALSE assertions. For instance, it introduces concepts such as FOR ALL and THERE EXISTS, allowing you to deal with statements that may be true but cannot be proved by the evidence you have at hand at that moment.

The *inference engine* is a set of instructions that tell the system how to manipulate the conditions based on the Boolean logic set of operators such as AND, OR, and NOT. Using this logic set, TRUE or FALSE symbolic conditions can combine into complex reasoning. (When TRUE, a rule is triggered or, technically, "fired"; when FALSE, the rule doesn't apply.)

Because the system was made at the core of a series of ifs (conditions) and thens (conclusions), and was nested and structured in layers, acquiring initial information helped rule out some conclusions while also helping the system interact with the user concerning information that could lead to an answer. When dealing with the inference engine, common operations by the expert systems were as follows:

>> **Forward chaining:** Available evidence triggered a series of rules and excluded others at each stage. The system initially concentrated on rules that could trigger an end conclusion by firing. This approach is clearly data-driven.

>> **Backward chaining:** The system evaluates every possible conclusion and tries to prove each of them on the basis of the evidence available. This goal-driven approach helps determine which questions to pose and excludes entire sets of goals. MYCIN, described earlier, used backward chaining; progressing from hypothesis backward to evidence is a common strategy in medical diagnosis.

>> **Conflict resolution:** If a system reaches more than one conclusion at the same time, the system favors the conclusion that has certain characteristics (in terms of impact, risk, or other factors). Sometimes, the system consults the user, and the resolution is realized based on user evaluations. For instance, MYCIN used a certainty factor that estimated the probability of diagnosis exactness.

One great benefit of expert systems is to represent knowledge in a human-readable form, rendering the decision-making process transparent. If the system reaches a conclusion, it returns to the rules used to reach that conclusion. The user can systematically review the work of the system and agree or review it for signs of input error. Moreover, expert systems were easy to program using languages such as Lisp, Prolog, or ALGOL. Users improved expert systems over time by adding new rules or updating existing rules. They could even be made to work through uncertain conditions by applying *fuzzy logic*, a kind of multivalued logic in which a value can contain anything between 0, or absolutely false, and 1, or absolutely true. Fuzzy logic avoids the abrupt steps of triggering a rule based on a threshold. For instance, if a rule is set to trigger when the room is hot, the rule is triggered not at an exact temperature but rather when the temperature is around that threshold.

Expert systems witnessed their twilight at the end of the 1980s, and their development stopped, mostly for the following reasons:

>> The logic and symbolism of such systems proved limited in expressing the rules behind a decision, leading to the creation of custom systems — that is, falling back again on hard-coding rules with classical algorithms.

>> For many challenging problems, expert systems became so complex and intricate that they lost their appeal in terms of feasibility and economic cost.

>> Because data was becoming more diffuse and available, it made little sense to struggle to carefully interview, gather, and distill rare expert knowledge when the same (or even better) knowledge could be sifted from data.

Expert systems still exist. You can find them used in credit scoring, fraud detection, and other fields with the imperative to not just provide an answer but also clearly and transparently state the rules behind the decision in a way that the system user deems acceptable (as a subject expert would do). In addition, they're used in situations for which other forms of AI are too slow, such as some self-driving car applications.

Introducing machine learning

Solutions capable of learning directly from data with no preprocessing to render it as symbols arose a few decades before expert systems. Some were statistical in nature; others imitated nature in various ways; and still others tried to generate autonomously symbolic logic in the form of rules from raw information. All these solutions were derived from different schools and appeared under different names that now comprise machine learning. *Machine learning* is part of the world of algorithms, although, contrary to the many algorithms discussed in this book, it's not intended as a series of predefined steps apt to solve a problem. As a rule, machine learning deals with problems that humans don't know how to detail into steps, but that humans naturally solve. An example of such a problem is discerning faces in images or understanding certain words in a spoken discussion.

Achieving new heights

The role of machine learning in the new wave of AI algorithms is to, in part, replace and, in part, supplement, existing algorithms. Machine learning works with activities that require intelligence from a human point of view but that aren't easy to formalize as a precise sequence of steps. A clear example of this role is the mastery displayed by a Go expert that understands, at a glance, the threats and opportunities of a board configuration and intuitively grasps the right moves. (In case you're unfamiliar with Go, it's an abstract strategy board game for two people in which the object is to capture more territory than your opponent by fencing off empty space.)

Go is an incredibly complex game for an AI. Chess has an average of 35 possible moves to evaluate on a board, and a game usually spans more than 80 moves, whereas a game of Go has about 140 moves to evaluate, and a game usually spans more than 240 moves. No computational power presently exists in the world to create a complete state space for a game of Go. Google's DeepMind team in London developed AlphaGo, a program that has defeated a number of top-ranked Go players (see https://deepmind.google/technologies/alphago and www.kdnuggets.com/2020/05/deepmind-gaming-ai-dominance.html). Rather than only rely on an algorithmic approach based on searching an immense state space, the program instead uses the following strategies:

>> A smart-search method based on random tests of a possible move. The AI applies a DFS multiple times to determine whether the first outcome found is a positive or negative one (an incomplete and partial state space).

>> A deep-learning algorithm processes an image of the board (at a glance) and derives both the best possible move in that situation (the algorithm is called the *policy network*) and an estimate of how likely the AI is to win the game by using that move (the algorithm is called the *value network*).

>> A capability to learn by seeing completed games by Go experts and by playing against itself. One version of the program, called AlphaGo Zero, can learn all by itself, with no human examples (see `https://deepmind.google/discover/blog/alphago-zero-starting-from-scratch`). This learning capability is called *reinforcement learning*.

Chapter **4**

Pioneering Specialized Hardware

U nderstanding the hardware behind AI is critical for understanding its full potential. As AI advances, the technology supporting it should evolve to meet increasing demands. This chapter explores how AI hardware has evolved, starting with general-purpose components and advancing to specialized processors tailored for complex AI applications. You determine the benefits and limitations of standard hardware, the innovations driving specialized hardware, and the computational advancements boosting AI performance.

Relying on Standard Hardware

Most AI projects at least begin with standard hardware because modern off-the-shelf components provide significant processing power, especially when compared to components from the 1980s, when AI first began to produce usable results. Consequently, even if you can't ultimately perform production-level work by using standard hardware, you can advance far enough along with your experimental and preproduction code to create a working model that will eventually process a full dataset.

Examining the standard hardware

The *architecture* (structure) of the standard PC hasn't changed since John von Neumann first proposed it in 1946. Reviewing the history at `https://lennartb.home.xs4all.nl/coreboot/col2.html` shows you that the processor connects to memory and peripheral devices through a bus in PC products as early as 1981 (and long before). All these systems use the von Neumann architecture because it provides significant benefits in modularity. Reading the history tells you that these devices allow upgrades to every component as individual decisions, allowing increases in *capability*. For example, within limits, you can increase the amount of memory or storage available to any PC. You can also use advanced peripherals. However, all these elements connect through a bus (a link between devices).

REMEMBER

The PC you use today has the same architecture as devices created long ago; they're simply more capable. In addition, almost every device you can conceive of today has a similar architecture, despite having different form factors, bus types, and essential capabilities.

Describing standard hardware deficiencies

» **von Neumann bottleneck:** Of all the deficiencies, the von Neumann bottleneck is the most serious when considering the requirements of disciplines such as AI, machine learning, and even data science. You can find this particular deficiency discussed in more detail in the section "Considering the von Neumann bottleneck," later in this chapter.

» **Single points of failure:** Any loss of connectivity with the bus necessarily means that the computer fails immediately rather than gracefully. Even in systems with multiple processors, the loss of a single processor, which should simply produce a loss of capability, instead inflicts complete system failure. The same problem occurs with the loss of other system components: Rather than reduce functionality, the entire system fails. Given that AI often requires continuous system operation, the potential for serious consequences escalates with the manner in which an application relies on the hardware.

» **Single-mindedness:** The von Neumann bus can either retrieve an instruction or retrieve the data required to execute the instruction, but it can't do both. Consequently, when data retrieval requires several bus cycles, the processor remains idle, further reducing its ability to perform instruction-intensive AI tasks.

EXAMINING THE HARVARD ARCHITECTURE DIFFERENCE

You may encounter the Harvard architecture during your hardware "travels" because some systems employ a modified form of this architecture to speed processing. Both the von Neumann architecture and Harvard architecture rely on a bus topology. However, when working with a von Neumann architecture system, the hardware relies on a single bus and a single memory area for both instructions and data, whereas the Harvard architecture relies on individual buses for instructions and data, and can use separate physical memory areas. The use of individual buses enables a Harvard architecture system to retrieve the next instruction while waiting for data to arrive from memory for the current instruction, thereby making the Harvard architecture both faster and more efficient. However, reliability suffers because now you have two failure points for each operation: the instruction bus and the data bus.

Microcontrollers, such as those that power your microwave, often use the Harvard architecture. In addition, you may find it in some unusual places for a specific reason. The iPhone and Xbox 360 both use modified versions of the Harvard architecture that rely on a single memory area (rather than two), but still rely on separate buses. The reason for using the architecture in this case is digital rights management (DRM). You can make the code area of memory read-only so that no one can modify it or create new applications without permission. From an AI perspective, this can be problematic because one AI's capability is to write new algorithms (executable code) as needed to deal with unanticipated situations. Because PCs rarely implement a Harvard architecture in its pure form or as the main bus construction, the Harvard architecture doesn't receive much attention in this book.

» **Tasking:** When the brain performs a task, a number of synapses fire at one time, allowing simultaneous execution of multiple operations. The original von Neumann design allowed just one operation at a time, and only after the system retrieved both the required instruction and data. Computers today typically have multiple cores, which allow simultaneous execution of operations in each core. However, application code must specifically address this requirement, so the functionality sometimes remains unused.

Relying on new computational techniques

Reading literature about how to perform tasks using AI can feel like you're hearing a marketer on TV proclaiming, "It's new! It's improved! It's downright dazzling!" So it shouldn't surprise you much that people are always coming up with ways to make the AI development experience faster, more precise, and better in other ways. The problem is that many of these new techniques are untested — they may look great, but you have to think about them for a while.

Using GPUs

After creating a prototypical setup to perform the tasks required to simulate human thought on a given topic, AI may need additional hardware to provide sufficient processing power to work with the full dataset required of a production system. Many methods are available to provide such processing power, but a common one is to use graphics processing units (GPUs) in addition to the central processor of a machine. The following sections describe the problem domain that a GPU addresses, what precisely the term GPU means, and why a GPU makes processing faster.

CONSIDERING ALAN TURING'S BOMBE MACHINE

Alan Turing's Bombe machine wasn't any form of AI. In fact, it isn't even a real computer. It broke Enigma cryptographic messages, and that's it. However, it did provide food for thought for Turing, which eventually led to a paper titled "Computing Machinery and Intelligence." Turing published that paper, which describes the imitation game, in the 1950s. (The movie *The Imitation Game* depicts the events surrounding the creation of this game.) However, the Bombe itself was actually based on a Polish machine called the Bomba.

Even though some sources imply that Alan Turing worked alone, the Bombe was produced with the help of many people, most especially Gordon Welchman. Neither did Turing spring from a vacuum, ready-made to break German encryption. His time at Princeton was spent with legendary figures like Albert Einstein and John von Neumann (who would go on to invent the concept of computer software). The papers Turing wrote inspired these other scientists to experiment and see what is possible.

Specialized hardware of all sorts will continue to appear as long as scientists are writing papers, bouncing ideas off each other, creating new ideas of their own, and experimenting. When you see movies or other media, assuming that they're reasonably historically accurate, don't leave with the feeling that these people just woke up one morning and proclaimed, "Today, I will be brilliant!" and then went on to do something marvelous. Everything builds on something else, so history is important because it helps show the path followed and illuminates other promising paths — those not followed.

Considering the von Neumann bottleneck

The von Neumann bottleneck is a natural result of using a bus to transfer data between the processor, memory, long-term storage, and peripheral devices. No matter how fast the bus performs its task, overwhelming it — that is, forming a bottleneck that reduces speed — is always possible. Over time, processor speeds continue to increase while memory and other device improvements focus on *density* — the capability to store more in less space. Consequently, the bottleneck becomes more of an issue with every improvement, causing the processor to spend a lot of time being idle.

Within reason, you can overcome some of the issues that surround the von Neumann bottleneck and produce small, but noticeable, increases in application speed. Here are the most common solutions:

>> **Caching:** When problems with obtaining data from memory fast enough with the von Neumann architecture became evident, hardware vendors quickly responded by adding localized memory that didn't require bus access. This memory appears external to the processor but as part of the processor package. High-speed cache is expensive, however, so cache sizes tend to be small.

>> **Processor caching:** Unfortunately, external caches still provide insufficient speed. Even using the fastest RAM available and cutting out the bus access completely doesn't meet the processing capacity needs of the processor. Consequently, vendors started adding internal memory — a cache smaller than the external cache, but with even faster access because it's part of the processor.

>> **Prefetching:** The problem with caches is that they prove useful only when they contain the correct data. Unfortunately, cache hits prove low in applications that use a lot of data and perform a wide variety of tasks. The next step in making processors work faster is to guess which data the application will require next and load it into a cache before the application requires it.

>> **Using specialty RAM:** You can get buried by RAM alphabet soup because more kinds of RAM exist than most people imagine. Each kind of RAM purports to solve at least part of the von Neumann bottleneck problem, and they do work — within limits. In most cases, the improvements revolve around the idea of getting data from memory and onto the bus faster. Two major (and many minor) factors affect speed: *memory speed* (how fast the memory moves data) and *latency* (how long it takes to locate a particular piece of data).

WARNING

As with many other areas of technology, hype can become a problem. For example, *multithreading,* the act of breaking an application or other set of instructions into discrete execution units that the processor can handle one at a time, is often touted as a means to overcome the von Neumann bottleneck, but it doesn't actually help the bottleneck. Multithreading is an answer to another problem: making the application more efficient. When an application adds latency issues to the von Neumann bottleneck, the entire system slows. Multithreading ensures that the processor doesn't waste yet more time waiting for the user or the application, but instead has something to do all the time. Application latency can occur with any processor architecture, not just the von Neumann architecture. Even so, anything that speeds the overall operation of an application is visible to the user and the system as a whole.

Defining the GPU

The original intent of a GPU was to process image data quickly and then display the resulting image onscreen. During the initial phase of PC evolution, the CPU performed all the processing, which meant that graphics could appear slowly while the CPU performed other tasks. During this time, a PC typically came equipped with a *display adapter,* which contains little or no processing power. A display adapter merely converts the computer data into a visual form. In fact, using just one processor proved almost impossible after the PC moved past text-only displays or extremely simple 16-color graphics. However, GPUs didn't make many inroads into computing until people began wanting 3D output. At this point, a combination of a CPU and a display adapter simply couldn't do the job.

A first step in this direction was taken by systems such as the Hauppauge 4860, which included a CPU and a special graphics chip (the 80860, in this case) on the motherboard. The 80860 provides the benefit of performing calculations extremely fast. Unfortunately, these multiprocessor, asynchronous systems didn't quite meet the expectations that people had for them (although they were incredibly fast for systems of the time), and they proved extremely expensive. Plus, there was the whole issue of writing applications that included that second (or subsequent) chip. The two chips also shared memory (which was abundant for these systems).

A GPU moves graphics processing from the motherboard to the graphics peripheral board. The CPU can tell the GPU to perform a task, and then the GPU determines the best method for doing so independently of the CPU. A GPU has a separate memory, and the data path for its bus is immense. In addition, a GPU can access the main memory for obtaining data needed to perform a task and to post results independently of the CPU. Consequently, this setup makes modern graphics displays possible.

TECHNICAL STUFF

However, what truly sets apart a GPU is that a GPU typically contains hundreds or thousands of cores contrasted with just a few cores for a CPU. Eight cores is about the best that you get, even with the newer i9 processor, an A100 GPU can host up to 80 gigabytes (GB) of RAM and has up to 8,192 FP32 (single-precision floating-point format) CUDA (Compute Unified Device Architecture) cores per full GPU. *CUDA* is a parallel computing platform and application programming interface (API) developed by NVIDIA. Even though the CPU provides more general-purpose functionality, the GPU performs calculations incredibly fast and can move data from the GPU to the display even faster. This ability is what makes the special-purpose GPU a critical component in today's systems.

Considering why GPUs work well

As with the 80860 chip, described in the previous section, GPUs now excel at performing the specialized tasks associated with graphics processing, including working with vectors. All those cores performing tasks in parallel can truly speed AI calculations.

In 2011, the Google Brain project (`https://research.google/`) trained an AI to recognize the difference between cats and people by watching movies on YouTube. However, to make this task work, Google used 2,000 CPUs in one of its giant data centers. Few people would have the resources required to replicate Google's work.

On the other hand, Bryan Catanzaro (from NVIDIA's research team) and Andrew Ng (from Stanford) were able to replicate Google's work by using a set of 12 NVIDIA GPUs. After people understood that GPUs could replace a host of computer systems stocked with CPUs, they could start moving forward with a variety of AI projects. In 2012, Alex Krizhevsky (from Toronto University) won the ImageNet computer image recognition competition using GPUs. In fact, a number of researchers have now used GPUs with amazing success.

Working with Deep Learning Processors (DLPs)

Researchers constantly struggle to discover better ways to train, verify, and test the models used to create AI applications. One of those ways is to use new computing techniques, as described in the section "Relying on new computational techniques," earlier in this chapter. Another way is to throw more processing power at the problem, such as by using a GPU.

However, a GPU is beneficial only because it can perform matrix manipulation quickly, and on a massively parallel level. Otherwise, using a GPU can create problems as well, as discussed earlier, in the "Using GPUs" section of this chapter. So the search for something better is ongoing, and you can find a veritable alphabet soup of processor types described on sites such as Primo.ai (https://primo.ai/index.php/PRIMO.ai) — see the page titled "Processing Units — CPU, GPU, APU, TPU, VPU, FPGA, QPU." This resource page will acquaint you with all the current processor types. However, you should start with the overview provided in the following sections because you can easily become mired in the quicksand of facing too many options (and then your head explodes).

Defining the DLP

A *deep learning processor* (DLP) is simply a specialized processor that provides some benefits in training, verifying, testing, and running AI applications. They try to create an environment in which AI applications run quickly even on smaller or less capable devices. Most DLPs follow a similar pattern by providing

>> Separate data and code memory areas

>> Separate data and code buses

>> Specialized instruction sets

>> Large on-chip memory

>> Large buffers to encourage data reuse patterns

In 2014, Tianshi Chen (and others) proposed the first DLP, called DianNoa (Chinese for *electric brain*). Of course, a first attempt is never good enough, so there's a whole family of DianNoa chips: DaDianNao, ShiDianNao, and PuDianNao (and possibly others).

REMEMBER

Since these first experiments with DLPs, the number and types of DLPs have soared, but most of these endeavors are now part of university research efforts. The exceptions are the neural processing unit (NPU) created by Huawei and Samsung for mobile devices, and the tensor processing unit (TPU) created by Google (https://cloud.google.com/tpu/docs/intro-to-tpu) specifically for use with TensorFlow (www.tensorflow.org). These two DLP types are described next.

Using the mobile neural processing unit (NPU)

A number of mobile devices — notably, those by Huawei and Samsung — have a neural processing unit (NPU) in addition to a general CPU to perform AI predictive tasks using models such as artificial neural networks (ANNs) and random forests (RFs). You can't use an NPU for general computing needs because it's so specialized. However, an NPU characteristically performs up to ten times faster than a GPU does for the same task. An NPU is specialized in these ways:

>> It accelerates the running of predefined models (as contrasted to training, verification, and testing).

>> It's designed for use with small devices.

>> It consumes little power when contrasted to other processor types.

>> It uses resources, such as memory, efficiently.

Because the precise boundaries between processor types are hard to define, you might see a number of NPU look-alikes or alternatives classified as NPUs. However, here's a list of processors that you can currently classify as true NPUs:

>> Ali-NPU, by Alibaba

>> Ascend, by Huawei

>> Neural Engine, by Apple

>> Neural processing unit (NPU), by Samsung

>> NNP, Myriad, EyeQ, by Intel

>> NVDLA (mostly used for internet of things [IoT] devices), by NVIDIA

Accessing the cloud-based tensor processing unit (TPU)

Google specifically designed the tensor processing unit (TPU) in 2015 to more quickly run applications built on the TensorFlow framework. It represents a true chip specialization in that you can't use it effectively without TensorFlow. However, it's different in another way in that it's an application-specific integrated circuit (ASIC) rather than a full-blown CPU-type chip. The differences are important:

>> An ASIC can perform only one task, and you can't change it.

>> Because of its specialization, an ASIC is typically much less expensive than a CPU.

>> Most ASIC implementations are much smaller than the same implementation created with a CPU.

>> Compared to a CPU implementation, an ASIC is more power efficient.

>> ASICs are incredibly reliable.

Creating a Specialized Processing Environment

Deep learning and AI are both non-von Neumann processes, according to many experts, including Massimiliano Versace, CEO of Neurala, Inc. (www.neurala.com). Because the task the algorithm performs doesn't match the underlying hardware, all sorts of inefficiencies exist, hacks are required, and obtaining a result is much harder than it should be. Therefore, designing hardware that matches the software is quite appealing. The Defense Advanced Research Projects Agency (DARPA) undertook one such project in the form of Systems of Neuromorphic Adaptive Plastic Scalable Electronics (SyNAPSE). The idea behind this approach is to duplicate nature's approach to solving problems by combining memory and processing power rather than keeping the two separate. They actually built the system (it was immense), and you can read more about it at www.darpa.mil/news-events/2014-08-07.

The SyNAPSE project did move forward. IBM built a smaller system by using modern technology that was both incredibly fast and power efficient. The only problem is that no one is buying them. The same holds true for IBM's SyNAPSE offering, TrueNorth. It has been hard to find people who are willing to pay the higher price, programmers who can develop software using the new architecture, and products that genuinely benefit from the chip. Consequently, a combination of CPUs and GPUs, even with its inherent weaknesses, continues to win out.

Increasing Hardware Capabilities

The CPU still works well for business systems or in applications in which the need for general flexibility in programming outweighs pure processing power. However, GPUs are now the standard for various kinds of data science, machine learning, AI, and deep learning needs. Of course, developers are constantly looking for the next big thing in the development environment. Both CPUs and GPUs are production-level processors. In the future, you may see one of two kinds of processors used in place of these standards:

>> **Application-specific integrated circuits (ASICs):** In contrast to general processors, a vendor creates an ASIC for a specific purpose. An ASIC solution offers extremely fast performance using very little power, but it lacks flexibility. You can find an example of an ASIC in this chapter in the form of a TPU (see the earlier section "Accessing the cloud-based tensor processing unit (TPU)" for details).

>> **Field programmable gate arrays (FPGAs):** As with an ASIC, a vendor generally crafts an FPGA for a specific purpose. However, contrary to using an ASIC, you can program an FPGA to change its underlying functionality. An example of an FPGA solution is Microsoft's Brainwave, which is used for deep learning projects.

REMEMBER

The battle between ASICs and FPGAs promises to heat up, with AI developers emerging as the winner. For the time being, Microsoft and FPGAs appear to have taken the lead. The point is that technology is fluid, and you should expect to see new developments

Vendors are also working on entirely new processing types, which may or may not work as expected. For example, Graphcore is working on an intelligence processing unit (IPU). The company has developed the line of processors shown at www.graphcore.ai/products/ipu. However, you have to take the news of these new processors with a grain of salt, given the hype that has surrounded the industry in the past. When you see real-life applications from large companies such as Google and Microsoft, you can start to feel a little more certain about the future of the technology involved.

Looking at the future of AI hardware, we authors see two new areas of advancement in hardware capabilities: neuromorphic computing and quantum processors. These cutting-edge technologies can potentially improve processing efficiency and capability, pushing the boundaries of AI. We look at each in turn in the following sections.

Advancing neuromorphic computing

Neuromorphic computing is the field of technology that mimics the neural structure and operation of the brain. It uses specialized hardware to create more efficient and adaptive AI systems. Recent developments in neuromorphic chips, such as Intel's Loihi (https://open-neuromorphic.org/neuromorphic-computing/hardware/loihi-intel) and IBM's TrueNorth (https://open-neuromorphic.org/blog/truenorth-deep-dive-ibm-neuromorphic-chip-design) have greatly improved power efficiency and processing capabilities for specific AI tasks.

TIP

These chips can handle complex tasks — like pattern recognition, sensory processing, and real-time decision-making — with significantly lower energy consumption than traditional processors.

Neuromorphic systems often utilize *spiking neural networks* (SNNs), which process information like the brain, through the timing of spikes (bursts of activity) rather than continuous signal transmission. This approach allows for more efficient and faster data processing, especially in applications that require real-time analysis and adaptive learning.

TIP

Autonomous drones and robots can benefit from neuromorphic chips by enhancing their ability to navigate and respond to their environments.

Exploring quantum processors

Quantum processors represent a big leap in AI hardware capabilities. Unlike classical processors that use bits to represent data as zeros or ones, *quantum processors* use quantum bits (qubits), which can exist in multiple states at the same time. This unique property allows quantum processors to perform certain calculations much faster than classical computers.

Companies like Google, IBM, and D-Wave are making strides in developing quantum processors. With regard to AI, quantum processors have the potential to revolutionize optimization problems, enhance machine learning algorithms, and accelerate complex simulations.

Quantum computing is still in its infancy but has several potential applications. For instance, it could enable more sophisticated AI models to process and analyze large-scale data more efficiently. This could lead to such events as drug discovery and financial modeling breakthroughs.

Adding Specialized Sensors

An essential component of AI is the capability of the AI to simulate human intelligence using a full set of senses. Input provided by senses helps humans develop the various kinds of intelligence described in Chapter 1. A human's senses provide the right sort of input to create an intelligent human. Even assuming that it becomes possible for an AI to fully implement all eight kinds of intelligence, it still requires the right sort of input to make that intelligence functional.

Humans typically have five senses with which to interact with the environment: sight, sound, touch, taste, and hearing. Oddly enough, humans still don't fully understand their own capabilities, so it's not too surprising that computers lag when it comes to sensing the environment in the same way humans do. For example, until recently, only four elements comprised taste: salt, sweet, bitter, and sour. However, two more tastes now appear on the list: umami and fat. Likewise, some women are *tetrachromats*, people who can see 100 million colors rather than the more usual 1 million. (Only women can be tetrachromats because of the chromosomal requirements.) Knowing how many women have this capability isn't even possible yet, though some sources place the number as high as 20 percent.

The use of filtered static and dynamic data now enables an AI to interact with humans in specific ways. For example, consider Alexa, the Amazon device that seemingly "hears" you and then says something in response. Even though Alexa doesn't actually understand anything you say, the appearance of communication is quite addictive and encourages people to anthropomorphize these devices. To perform any part of its task, Alexa requires access to a special sensor: a microphone that allows it to hear. Actually, Alexa has a number of microphones to help it hear well enough to provide the illusion of understanding. Unfortunately, as advanced as Alexa is, it can't see, feel, touch, or taste anything, which makes it far from human.

TIP

In some cases, humans want their AI to have superior or different senses. An AI that detects motion at night and reacts to it may rely on infrared rather than normal vision. In fact, the use of alternative senses is now one of the valid uses for AI. The capability to work in environments that people can't work in is one reason that some types of robots have become popular, but working in these environments often requires that the robots have, or be connected to, a set of nonhuman sensors. Consequently, the topic of sensors actually falls into two categories (neither of which is fully defined): human-like and alternative environment.

Integrating AI with Advanced Sensor Technology

Integrating advanced sensors with AI is now changing how machines interact with the world and expanding what they can do. Here are some key advancements:

>> **Sensor fusion:** Sensor fusion integrates data from multiple sensors to help understand environments. For example, combining inputs from cameras, light detection and ranging (LiDAR), radar, and ultrasonic sensors helps self-driving cars navigate safely.

- **Bio-inspired sensors:** These sensors mimic biological systems. Artificial skin detects pressure, temperature, and texture, allowing robots to handle delicate objects carefully. Other sensors can identify smells like chemical compounds, aiding in early disease detection and pollutant monitoring. (We tell you more about sensing in the next section.)

- **Quantum sensors:** Using principles of quantum mechanics, these sensors achieve high precision. They can detect tiny changes in magnetic fields, gravity, and temperature. This is important for advanced medical imaging and navigation in places where GPS doesn't work well.

- **Environmental sensors:** These sensors detect events like infrared and ultraviolet light and radiation, enabling AI systems to operate in tough conditions. They are crucial for industrial monitoring and military surveillance.

Devising Methods to Interact with the Environment

An AI that is self-contained and never interacts with the environment is useless. Of course, that interaction takes the form of inputs and outputs. The traditional method of providing inputs and outputs is directly through data streams that the computer can understand, such as datasets, text queries, and the like. However, these approaches are hardly human-friendly, and they require special skills to use.

REMEMBER

Interacting with an AI is increasingly occurring in ways that humans understand better than they understand direct computer contact. For example, input occurs via a series of microphones when you ask Alexa a question. The AI turns the keywords in the question into tokens it can understand. These tokens then initiate computations that form an output. The AI tokenizes the output into a human-understandable form: a spoken sentence. You then hear the sentence as Alexa speaks to you through a speaker. In short, to provide useful functionality, Alexa must interact with the environment in two different ways that appeal to humans, but that Alexa doesn't actually understand.

Interactions can take many forms. In fact, the number and forms of interaction are increasing continually. For example, an AI can smell (see "Artificial intelligence grows a nose" at www.science.org/content/article/artificial-intelligence-grows-nose). However, the computer doesn't actually smell anything. Sensors provide a means to turn chemical detection into data that the AI can then use in the same way it uses all other data. The capability to detect chemicals isn't new; the ability to analyze those chemicals isn't new; nor are the algorithms used to interact with the resulting data new. What is new is the datasets used to interpret the incoming data as a smell, and those datasets come from human studies. An AI's nose has all sorts of possible uses. For example, think about the AI's capability to use a nose when working in some dangerous environments, such as to smell explosives at an airport before being able to see them by using other sensors.

Physical interactions are also on the rise. Robots that work on assembly lines are old hat, but consider the effects of robots that can drive. These are larger uses of physical interaction. Consider also that an AI can react in smaller ways. Hugh Herr, for example, uses an AI to provide interaction with an intelligent foot, as described in "Is This the Future of Robotic Legs?" at www.smithsonianmag.com/innovation/future-robotic-legs-180953040/ and "New surgery may enable better control of prosthetic limbs" at MITNews.edu. This dynamic foot provides a superior replacement for people who have lost their real foot. Instead of the static sort of feedback that a human receives from a standard prosthetic, this dynamic foot provides the sort of active feedback that humans are used to obtaining from a real foot. For example, the amount of pushback from the foot differs when walking uphill than walking downhill. Likewise, navigating a curb requires a different amount of pushback than navigating a step.

The point is that as AI becomes more able to perform complex calculations in smaller packages with ever-larger datasets, the capability of an AI to perform interesting tasks increases. However, the tasks that the AI performs may not currently have a human equivalent. You may not ever truly interact with an AI that understands your speech, but you may come to rely on an AI that helps you maintain life — or at least make it more livable.

IN THIS CHAPTER

» **Defining AI terms**

» **Processing natural language**

» **Interpreting transformers and tokens**

» **Knowing the limitations of AI**

» **Practicing responsible AI**

Chapter **5**

Parsing Machine Learning and Deep Learning

n this chapter, we cover some of the basics of machine learning, deep learning, and generative AI. Although it's fully possible to use AI tools such as ChatGPT without understanding the science and math behind them, a basic understanding of how machine learning and generative AI work will help you use these tools more effectively.

Decoding Machine and Deep Learning

When you first encounter a generative AI tool such as ChatGPT, it can seem like magic. Some people even speculate that generative AI tools are conscious and capable of thinking and having emotions. Knowing how these tools were created and how they work will quickly dispel that notion — or make you think differently about consciousness, but that's a subject for a philosophy book, not a coding book.

Defining key concepts

Before you can dip your toes into understanding how the latest AI systems are capable of generating complex responses to natural-language input, we need to present some vocabulary. People working with or writing about the systems we talk about in this book often use the terms *AI*, *machine learning*, *deep learning*, and *generative AI* interchangeably, but these fundamental terms are different (see Figure 5-1):

>> **Artificial intelligence (AI)** is the use of computer science and data to solve problems. AI encompasses everything from expert systems and decision trees, which simulate the judgment and behavior of humans using a complex series of if-then statements, to machine learning, computer vision, and natural-language processing.

>> **Machine learning** is a type of AI that focuses on developing and using computer systems that can learn and adapt without following explicit instructions. Machine learning can solve problems that would be prohibitively expensive to solve by programmers writing the algorithms by hand.

>> **Deep learning** is a type of machine learning based on artificial neural networks. The word *deep* in *deep learning* doesn't indicate that it produces inherently more profound or mysterious AI. Rather, it refers to the use of multiple layers of algorithms (artificial neurons) in the neural network. We explain artificial neural networks and layers in the next section.

>> **Generative AI (GenAI)** are AI systems that can generate new content based on the data used to train them. Some form of GenAI has been around since the 1960s (for example, ELIZA a text-based chatbot created by Joseph Weizenbaum, which you find in the section "History of NLP" later in the chapter). In recent years, the content created by GenAI is of a high enough quality to be more than a novelty, thanks to the use of deep learning.

Thinking about neural networks

The idea behind deep learning is to teach computers to process data based on how we think our brains work. In a human brain, cells called *neurons* form a complex and massive interconnected network. Using chemical reactions and electrical currents, neurons send signals to each other to enable us to learn and process information.

Neural networks in deep learning, also known as *simulated neural networks (SNNs)* or *artificial neural networks (ANNs)*, consist of artificial neurons called nodes that form layers, as shown in Figure 5-2.

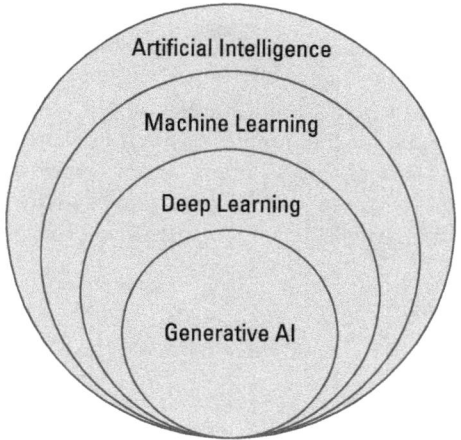

FIGURE 5-1:
The relationship between fields in AI.

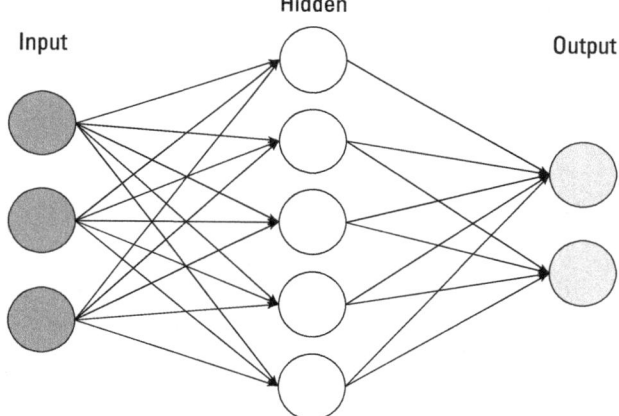

FIGURE 5-2:
Nodes are arranged in layers.

Each *node* is a software module that processes some input and determines whether to pass it on to the next layer of neurons for further processing. A simple neural network consists of three layers: the input layer, the hidden layer, and the output layer.

Input layer

The *input layer* receives data and puts it in a format that the hidden layers can use. For example, in a neural network for analyzing images, the images are first converted to the same size and dimensions. Next, the input layer takes in the pixel values (the amount of red, green, and blue) for each image and passes them along to the hidden layer.

In the preceding example, the number of neurons in the input layer is determined by the number of pixels in the image. If the neural network will be processing color images, the number of pixels is multiplied by 3 for each of the pixel values (red, green, and blue) to get the number of neurons. For example, the image shown in Figure 5-3 has a width of 56 pixels and a height of 56 pixels. We've magnified the image so you can see the individual pixels. An input layer for working with this image would have 56 × 56 × 3, or 9,408, neurons.

FIGURE 5-3:
A color image containing 3,136 pixels requires a 9,408-neuron input layer.

Czar / Wikimedia Commons / Public Domain

Hidden layer

A *hidden layer* receives data from the input layer or other hidden layers and processes it further to extract features from the image, such as color, shape, and texture. More complex tasks require more neurons in the hidden layers. A neural network can have many hidden layers.

Output layer

Neural networks must have at least one *output layer,* which provides the final result of the calculations from the hidden layers.

Figure 5-4 shows a simple artificial neural network that determines whether or not a photo contains a hot dog. This type of problem is known as a binary classification because the output from this neural network is either 1 (hot dog) or 0 (not hot dog).

But how does the neural network determine whether the photo contains a hot dog? That's where its training comes in.

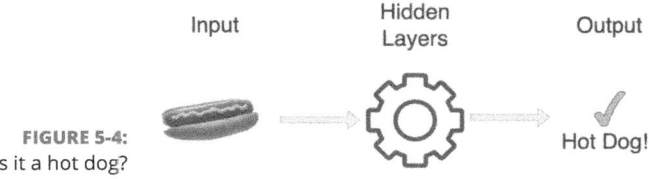

Input   Hidden Layers   Output

Hot Dog!

FIGURE 5-4:
Is it a hot dog?

Czar / Wikimedia Commons / Public Domain

Training and testing models

Before a neural network can perform a task, it must be trained. In the case of the hot dog classifier, the neural network can be trained by analyzing thousands of pictures of hot dogs as well as an equal number of things that aren't hot dogs. Each photo must be labeled ("hot dog" or "not hot dog"). From these pictures, the neural network can make certain conclusions about what a picture of a hot dog contains. For example, a picture of a hot dog generally will contain a lighter-colored area (the bun) surrounding a darker-colored cylindrical shape (the hot dog), as shown in Figure 5-5.

FIGURE 5-5:
Many pictures of hot dogs have similar characteristics.

As the layers of the neural network analyze pictures, values called weights and biases are assigned to each neuron in the network. The *weight* determines the strength of the connection between two nodes in the network. The *bias* determines the threshold at which a node is activated. Weights and biases adjust how much a neuron will contribute to the final result.

The weights and biases that the model learns from the training data are called *parameters.* The complexity of a model can be described by how many parameters it has. More complex models have more parameters because they're able to learn more complex patterns in data. You can think of parameters as similar to the synapses that connect neurons in a human brain.

In machine learning, a *model* is a mathematical representation of a real-world system or phenomenon. Some examples of models follow:

>> **Scientific models** make predictions involving the atmosphere, diseases, and the universe.

>> **Engineering models** design and test new products.

>> **Demand models** predict how many units of a product a business will sell.

>> **Financial models** predict the performance of stocks and other financial instruments.

How accurately a model can make predictions (whether or not a new picture contains a hot dog, for example) is based on the quality and quantity of data that went into its training.

Small models that make relatively simple predictions, such as whether or not a photograph contains a hot dog, can be created quickly, and the risks of messing up such a model are unlikely to be catastrophic.

TIP

The most time-consuming part of creating a model is usually the gathering and labeling of the datasets. Many publicly available free datasets exist. You can find a list of them at `https://openml.org`.

Complex models, such as climate models and models of systems of the human body, can take months or years to train, and getting it wrong can have expensive or life-threatening consequences. Some of the challenges of training neural networks include the following:

>> **Complex neural networks can involve terabytes of training data and billions of parameters.** Training a large neural network is computationally expensive.

>> **Neural networks can learn their training data too well, which is called *overfitting*.** When overfitting occurs, the model will be able to ace tests about the data it was trained on but will have a hard time generalizing to new data (which is the point of a model).

>> **Interpretability (understanding how a model makes predictions) can be difficult.** Because of the number of parameters in a model, people can have difficulty figuring out how a neural network makes its predictions.

Demystifying Natural-Language Processing

Natural-language processing (NLP) is the branch of AI concerned with giving computers the capability to understand human language in written and spoken form. NLP can be further divided into two subsets:

>> **Natural-language understanding (NLU)** involves the analyzing of text and speech to figure out the meaning of sentences.

>> **Natural-language generation (NLG)** is concerned with giving computers the capability to write.

NLP is used for a wide variety of purposes, including the following:

>> **Machine translation:** Translating text from one language to another

>> **Speech recognition:** Understanding spoken language and translating it into text

>> **Text summarization:** Generating summaries of longer texts, such as books, articles, or briefs

>> **Question answering:** Answering questions asked in natural language

>> **Sentiment analysis:** Identifying the sentiment of text, for example, whether it's positive, negative, or neutral

>> **Computer programming:** Writing or assisting with the writing of computer programs

REMEMBER

Human language includes not only the languages we use for communicating with each other (such as English, French, and Greek) but also the languages we use for communicating with computers (such as C++, JavaScript, and Haskell).

History of NLP

Natural-language processing has been around since the first experiments in automatic translation in the 1950s. The creators of the first automatic translation machine predicted that the problem of machine translation would be solved within a few years. However, it ended up taking much longer, and we still haven't perfected it.

Early natural-language processing systems relied on a list of handwritten rules that the computer applied to the data it received. The ELIZA chatbot, created in the 1960s, could have a somewhat convincing conversation with a human by following rules and responding as a non-directional psychotherapist. Although ELIZA was created as a joke, it successfully demonstrated that natural-language conversations between people and computers were possible. Figure 5-6 shows a typical conversation with ELIZA.

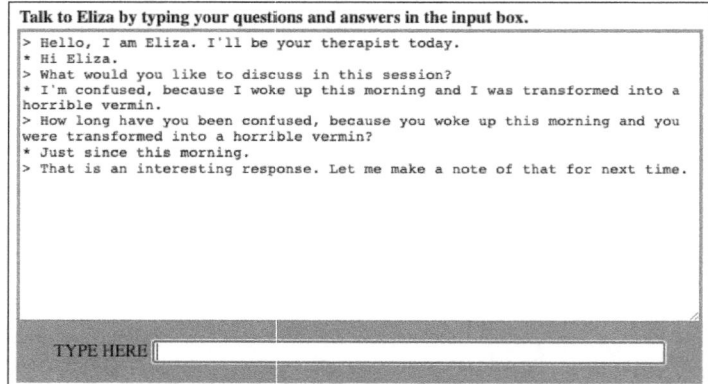

Talk to Eliza by typing your questions and answers in the input box.

```
> Hello, I am Eliza. I'll be your therapist today.
* Hi Eliza.
> What would you like to discuss in this session?
* I'm confused, because I woke up this morning and I was transformed into a
horrible vermin.
> How long have you been confused, because you woke up this morning and you
were transformed into a horrible vermin?
* Just since this morning.
> That is an interesting response. Let me make a note of that for next time.
```

TYPE HERE

FIGURE 5-6: Early NLP was based on rules.

Machine learning algorithms and increased computing power led to advances and new techniques for natural-language processing starting in the late 1980s.

In the 1990s, Richard Wallace created the ALICE chatbot. ALICE is similar to ELIZA in that it uses pattern-matching rules. The operator of an ALICE chatbot could add rules, which made it useful for customer service applications such as answering questions about a company's products. Figure 5-7 shows an example conversation with ALICE.

The growth of the internet made large collections of text readily available for training models. As a result of all this data, new techniques were created in the 1990s and 2000s that depended on statistical analysis of large datasets.

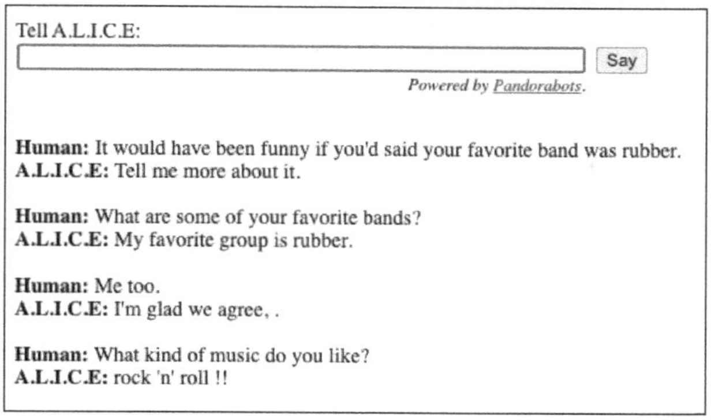

Tell A.L.I.C.E:

[   ] [Say]

Powered by Pandorabots.

Human: It would have been funny if you'd said your favorite band was rubber.
A.L.I.C.E: Tell me more about it.

Human: What are some of your favorite bands?
A.L.I.C.E: My favorite group is rubber.

Human: Me too.
A.L.I.C.E: I'm glad we agree, .

Human: What kind of music do you like?
A.L.I.C.E: rock 'n' roll !!

FIGURE 5-7:
An example of an Alice chatbot.

Machine learning models made it possible for natural-language processing systems to be trained without having to hand-code rules. Further advances in machine learning, including neural networks, made virtual assistants such as Apple's Siri and Amazon's Alexa possible in the 2010s and eventually enabled the remarkable advances in natural-language processing that made tools such as ChatGPT possible.

Overcoming the challenges of NLP

In the past, creators of NLP systems focused on breaking down human languages into rules. The idea was that if you could give a computer access to a language's dictionary and a grammar book, it would know that language.

In the case of programming languages, this approach was somewhat successful. If you know the rules of a programming language and the right keywords to use, you can at least write statements.

But human language is more complex. Here are just a few of the things that a computer can't understand by memorizing a dictionary and grammar:

>> Dialects

>> Accents

>> Sarcasm

>> Metaphors

>> Humor

>> Grammar and usage exceptions

>> Homophones

The fact that a box of chips and wires can understand any of what people say is incredible. Until recently, it seemed that computers were doomed to understand only a formal and limited subset of human languages and that chatting with an AI assistant would always be a frustrating and disappointing experience.

So what changed? The biggest breakthrough in NLP was when researchers decided to throw out the rules and start teaching computers to talk the way humans teach babies to talk, namely, by exposing them to language and letting them figure things out.

Understanding supervised and unsupervised learning

Supervised learning relies on *labeled data*, which is data annotated with tags that describe what the data is. For example, if you want to train a model to recognize spam email messages, you could create a dataset containing millions of email messages, each labeled either "spam" or "not spam." However, the process of labeling data can be costly and time consuming.

Unsupervised learning is the finding of patterns in unlabeled data. With unsupervised learning, algorithms sort through unlabeled data looking for patterns. Unsupervised language-learning models can be trained on very large datasets to create large language models (LLMs). Unlike supervised learning, unsupervised learning can be done inexpensively and quickly.

Language generation techniques

Natural-language processing techniques can be divided into traditional machine learning methods and deep learning methods. Traditional machine learning techniques include the following:

- » **Logistic regression** is a classification algorithm that aims to predict the probability that an event will occur based on some input.

- » **Naïve Bayes classifiers** are a collection of statistical classification algorithms based on Bayes's theorem, which describes the probability of an event based on prior knowledge of conditions. The *naïve* part of the name refers to the assumption these algorithms make that individual words are not dependent on each other.

- » **Decision trees** work by splitting a dataset based on different inputs. For example, if you wanted to find out whether it's likely to rain, you might start by asking whether it's cloudy. If so, you might then ask about the humidity and then the temperature. After several splits, you can come up with a prediction.

>> **Latent Dirichlet allocation (LDA)** is used for topic modeling. Topic modeling techniques scan a set of documents to detect patterns and cluster together word groups that best characterize the set.

>> **Hidden Markov models (HMMs)** decide the next state of a system based on the previously observed state. The *hidden* part of the name refers to data properties that aren't directly observed. In natural-language processing, the hidden state is the parts of speech, and the observed state is the words in a sentence.

TECHNICAL STUFF

Some of the techniques used in machine learning are named after the people who formulated the theorems the techniques rely on. Thomas Bayes was an eighteenth-century English statistician, philosopher, and minister. Peter Gustav Lejeune Dirichlet was a nineteenth-century German mathematician. Andrey Markov was a Russian mathematician who lived at the end of the nineteenth century and the beginning of the twentieth century.

While traditional NLP methods are often able to do a good job, it wasn't until deep learning techniques were applied to NLP that things got interesting. Following are some deep learning NLP techniques:

>> **Convolutional neural networks (CNNs)** were designed to be used for working with images but can also be used with documents. In NLP, CNNs treat documents as images made up of sentences instead of pixels.

>> **Recurrent neural networks (RNNs)** use hidden states to remember previous information. Because of this, they can learn how every word in a sentence is dependent on previous words or words in the previous sentence.

>> **Transformer models** learn context by tracking relationships in sequential data (such as the words in a sentence). Transformer models are the break-through that has revolutionized NLP in recent years. I tell you more about how transformers work in the next section.

Understanding Transformers

Transformer models use a self-attention mechanism to find dependencies between inputs and outputs. To understand what that means, you first need to know what attention and self-attention are in machine learning. Read on!

Learning to pay attention

The mathematical technique that transformer models use is called attention. The goal of *attention* is to allow the model to focus on important parts of the input while generating its output. As people, we do this naturally. When you read a sentence or look at an image, you can easily see which parts of the sentence or image are the most important in terms of understanding it.

When the idea of attention first became popular, it was combined with recurrent neural networks (RNNs). But RNN models have to consider words in sequence one at a time, which is a slow process. Even worse, RNNs tend to assign more importance to recent words and the ends of sentences.

Another side effect of considering words one at a time is that you lose important context. Consider this sentence:

> The player swung his bat, and he ran to first base.

Anyone with a passing familiarity with baseball will know that *bat* refers to a baseball bat and that *he* refers to the player. Considered one word at a time, however, a language model can't make the same connections.

This is where the idea of self-attention comes in. *Self-attention* allows a model to learn information about an input sequence from the input sequence itself. With self-attention, a transformer model finds relationships between the words *player* and *bat* as well as between *player* and *he*.

Figure 5-8 shows a visualization of the connections a transformer model makes between the word *he* in the example sentence and the other words in the sentence. Darker lines indicate a stronger connection.

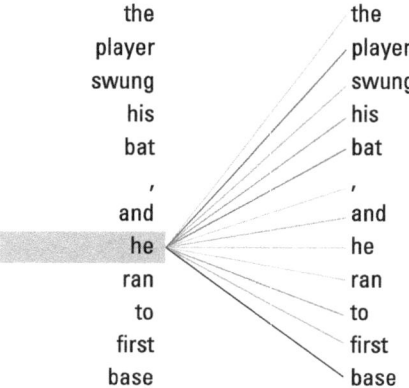

FIGURE 5-8: Visualizing self-attention.

TECHNICAL STUFF

The visualization in Figure 5-8 was created using a tool called BertViz. You can learn more about how BertViz works and try it out yourself at `https://github.com/jessevig/bertviz`.

Self-attention was first proposed as a solution for improving large language models in the paper "Attention Is All You Need." This paper, published in 2017, led to the giant leaps forward in transformer models that we've seen in recent years.

Getting tokens

You may be surprised to learn that language models can understand only numbers; they don't read or understand words as we do. When you ask an NLP system a question, your input must first be converted into a sequence of numbers called *tokens*. You can think of tokens as the language equivalent of pixels in an image.

These tokens are read by a model's input layer and then processed through the hidden layers to predict and output responses to your prompts.

REMEMBER

Hidden layers are the layers between the input and output layers that process data and learn features of it.

Text can be converted to tokens in a variety of ways. One common method is *word tokenization*, which simply creates a token for each word in the text. Transformer models use *sub-word tokenization*, which converts text into common sequences of characters, such as *token* and *ize.* Using smaller units improves the model's performance.

To see how OpenAI converts text to tokens, go to OpenAI's Tokenizer at `https://platform.openai.com/tokenizer`. Figure 5-9 shows the list of tokens that were generated when I entered the sentence *Transformer models use sub-word tokenization.*

After the text is tokenized, it's encoded into token IDs. The token IDs created from the text in Figure 5-9 are shown in Figure 5-10.

TECHNICAL STUFF

Token IDs are input into a neural network as a sequence of numbers called a *numerical vector.*

Being aware of tokens and the tokenization of your input is important. If you're using a model through OpenAI's API, the combined number of tokens in your input and the model's response determines how much you pay for the service.

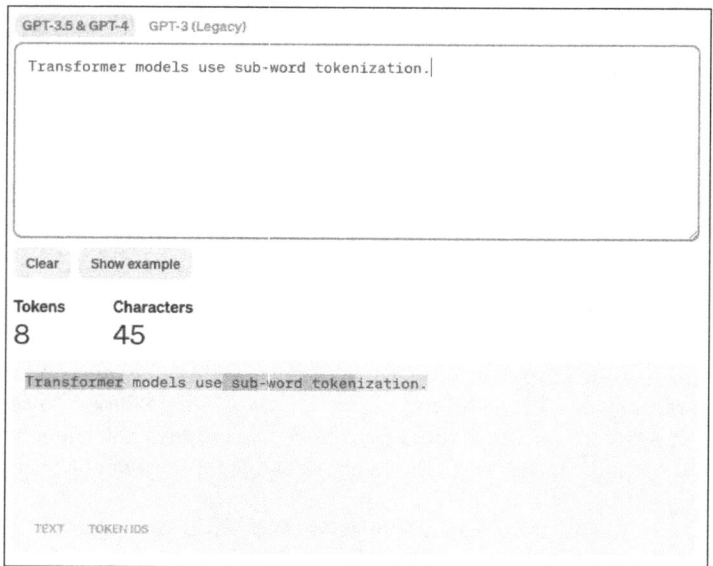

GPT-3.5 & GPT-4   GPT-3 (Legacy)

Transformer models use sub-word tokenization.|

Clear   Show example

Tokens   **Characters**
8   45

Transformer models use sub-word tokenization.

TEXT   TOKEN IDS

FIGURE 5-9: Tokenizing a prompt.

Tokens   **Characters**
8   45

[47458, 4211, 1005, 1207, 38428, 4037, 2065, 13]

TEXT   **TOKEN IDS**

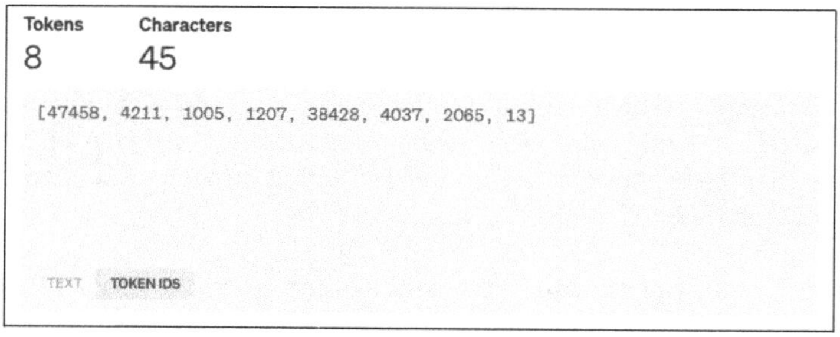

FIGURE 5-10: Tokens are represented as token IDs.

In addition, the NLP system you're using may have a *token limit,* which is the maximum number of tokens the model will consider while generating its response. Your input and the model's responses contribute to the number of tokens used by a conversation. In a long conversation with ChatGPT, or if you input an excessively long prompt, the token limit may be exceeded. In this case, the model will "forget" earlier prompts in the conversation, and you'll need to repeat any instructions you included at the beginning.

Token limits are imposed on a model to prevent it from running out of memory, to shorten the model's response time, and to reduce the amount of computation required to train and deploy the model.

Table 5-1 lists the token limits of standard versions of several models. Many models also have extended versions with larger token limits.

TABLE 5-1   **Token Limits**

Model	Creator	Token limit
GPT-2	OpenAI	1024
GPT-3	OpenAI	2048
GPT-4	OpenAI	8000
BERT (base)	Google	512
RoBERTa (base)	Facebook	512
T5 (base)	Google	512
XLNet (base)	Google/CMU	512
Electra (base)	Google	512
DistilBERT	Hugging Face	512

Illuminating Generative AI Models

A *generative AI model* is a model that is trained on content (such as images or text) and can use that content to make predictions to generate new content. OpenAI's GPT-3, the model behind the first public version of ChatGPT, is a generative model for natural-language processing. By leveraging what it's learned about how people talk and write, it can accurately predict what the next word or sentence should be in response to input.

For example, if you provide the words *peanut butter and* to GPT-3, it will most likely predict that the next words should be *jelly sandwich.* GPT-3 doesn't have any experience with eating or making peanut butter and jelly sandwiches, but it has analyzed a lot of text, and the most common way to finish the phrase *peanut butter and* is with *jelly sandwich.*

Like the hot dog photo classifier (which I introduce in the section "Output layer" earlier in the chapter), a generative AI model is only as good as its training data. GPT-3 was trained with over 45 terabytes of text data, so it has amazing capabilities, such as taking context into consideration when responding to input.

Generative AI models have been steadily getting better as a result of being trained on more and higher-quality data. Table 5-2 compares the size of some recent generative models.

TABLE 5-2 **Parameters in Generative AI Models**

Model	Developer	Parameters
Gato	DeepMind	1.18 billion
ESMFold	Meta AI	15 billion
LaMDA	Google	137 billion
GPT-3	OpenAI	175 billion
Bloom	Hugging Face and BigScience	176 billion
MT-NLG	Nvidia and Microsoft	530 billion
WuDao 2.0	Beijing Academy of Artificial Intelligence	1.75 trillion
GPT-4	OpenAI	1.76 trillion

As I mention earlier in the chapter, parameters are the values that the model has learned from its training.

REMEMBER

Recognizing AI's Limitations

As impressive as they are, transformer models don't know how to talk — they know only how to look for patterns in sequential data (such as sentences, statements, or functions). When you train a generative model on enough data, it becomes very good at finding patterns and making predictions, but it does have limitations, and you should never trust the output of a chatbot (or any AI system) entirely.

Language models are bad at math

AI chatbots are language models tuned for conversation. If you ask a language model for the answer to a basic math problem, it will usually respond confidently with some answer. However, upon checking that answer using a calculator, you may be surprised that it's often just plain wrong. Currently, generative models are able to make predictions based only on content they've previously seen. If you give them a math problem they've never seen before (no matter how trivial), they'll respond based on the answers to similar math questions in their training data rather than by doing the math the way a calculator would.

For example, Figure 5-11 shows a conversation I had with ChatGPT when I was planning the outline for this book.

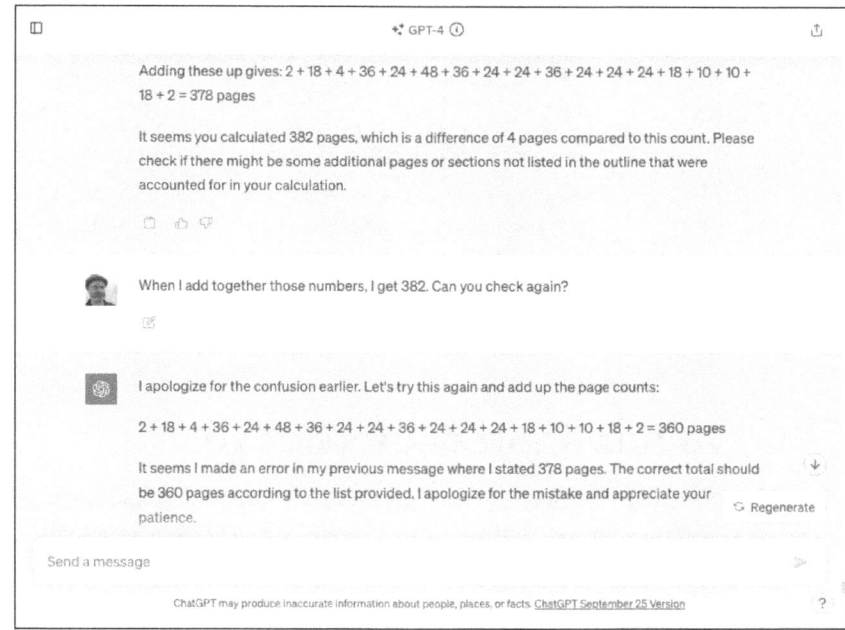

FIGURE 5-11: GPT-4 gets an addition problem wrong.

ChatGPT

Language models are wordy

AI chatbots often respond to prompts with paragraphs when a one-word answer will do. The standard ChatGPT response to even a simple question reads like a high school book report, containing an introduction, an analysis of an issue from multiple viewpoints, and a summary.

Figure 5-12 shows ChatGPT's nearly 200-word response to a question that any JavaScript programmer could answer with two words.

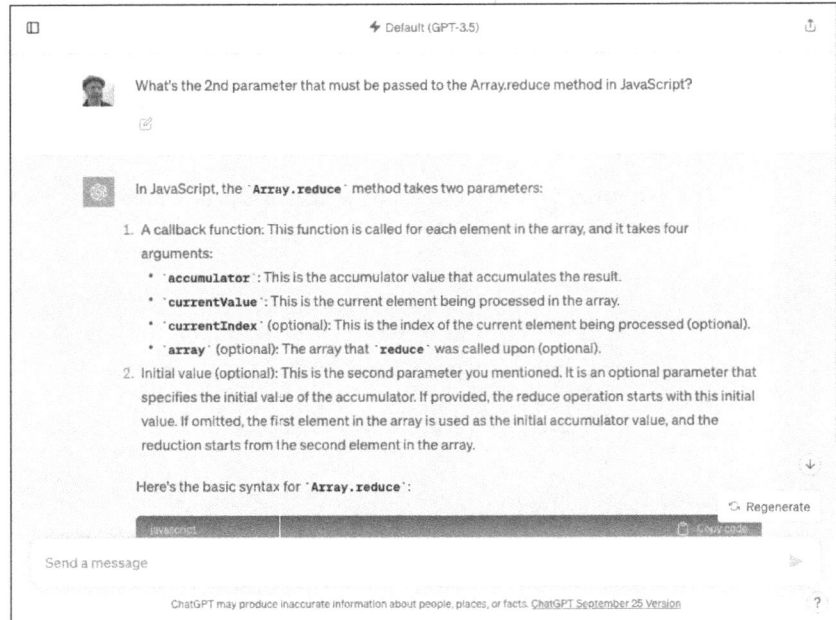

In JavaScript, the `Array.reduce` method takes two parameters:

1. A callback function: This function is called for each element in the array, and it takes four arguments:
   * `accumulator`: This is the accumulator value that accumulates the result.
   * `currentValue`: This is the current element being processed in the array.
   * `currentIndex` (optional): This is the index of the current element being processed (optional).
   * `array` (optional): The array that `reduce` was called upon (optional).
2. Initial value (optional): This is the second parameter you mentioned. It is an optional parameter that specifies the initial value of the accumulator. If provided, the reduce operation starts with this initial value. If omitted, the first element in the array is used as the initial accumulator value, and the reduction starts from the second element in the array.

Here's the basic syntax for `Array.reduce`:

FIGURE 5-12:
ChatGPT uses 200 words where 2 will do.

ChatGPT

AI has limited knowledge

Although it's now possible for ChatGPT to access data on the internet, the model behind ChatGPT is finite. As a result, ChatGPT doesn't know everything. When prompted with questions about obscure or recent topics, the answer the model returns may be wrong.

AI lacks common sense

No machine learning model has had the experience of being human. As a result, the responses generated by the model lack common sense. For example, if you ask ChatGPT how to swim to the moon, it may provide an answer without questioning the absurdity of the question. Any human would first question the value of such a strange question.

AI has accuracy issues

The accuracy of responses generated by a model depends on many factors, including the training data, context, user input, complexity of the prompt and language, and bias. As the user of a model, you have control over only some of these factors. Where possible, however, you can help the model provide better responses by knowing how best to prompt it and by challenging the model's output in follow-up prompts.

AI has the potential to be biased

Because they're trained largely on text written by people, machine learning models will pick up the biases and preferences that exist in the training data. Creators of models put a lot of effort into eliminating bias — which is a worthy goal but an impossible task.

WARNING

Unintended consequences and even dangerous situations may result from bias in models. The classic example is when Microsoft released its Tay chatbot to the internet in 2016. Within one day of talking to people, the chatbot went from saying things like "Humans are cool" to making racist and sexist comments.

IN THIS CHAPTER

» Figuring out how to make GenAI-
generated content original and
authentic

» Ensuring GenAI accuracy

» Exploring ethical standards

» Understanding the responsible AI
movement

Chapter **6**

Upholding Responsible AI Standards in GenAI Use

This chapter helps you navigate the exciting yet challenging landscape of GenAI without sacrificing ethical standards and quality. By addressing these critical areas, you can harness the power of GenAI to help create a future that's not only technologically advanced but also grounded in the principles of ethics and accountability.

Achieving Originality and Excellence in GenAI-Generated Content

The potential for the range of creative and knowledge work that can be generated with GenAI is boundless. Yet, with this remarkable technology comes the responsibility to ensure that the content it generates is both original and of suitable quality.

Originality in GenAI-generated content isn't just a matter of avoiding plagiarism and copyright infringements; it can also be about fostering innovation, creating new products and computer codes, and pushing the boundaries of what GenAI can achieve. Achieving excellence, on the other hand, means ensuring that the output meets or exceeds the standards that would be expected of a human creator by law, ethics, tradition, or industry requirements. Together, these principles form the bedrock of trust and value in GenAI-generated works. This section delves into the critical importance of upholding these standards and the strategies you can employ to achieve them.

Strategies for ensuring originality in GenAI creations

To ensure the originality and quality of GenAI creations, it's essential to implement strategies that can verify the uniqueness and accuracy of the content produced. Following are some strategies you can use to improve content generated by GenAI:

>> **Prompt GenAI to provide references in its responses and then review those references yourself.** Why? Because GenAI often lies. And, yes, it can totally make up references to support its lies, too. But also because that's a good first step in spotting hints of plagiarism or copyright infringements.

WARNING

That's why you never want to prompt a GenAI model to factcheck or check for plagiarism in its own responses and just accept its answer. Nor should you ever assume that you're using a different model to check the first model's work. You could easily be using two different applications built atop the same GenAI model.

>> **Use a different GenAI model to cross-reference generated content against existing works, flagging potential duplicates for review.** For example, prompt Google Smart Search or Perplexity to factcheck the response you got from Claude or ChatGPT. Some GenAI search tools like Perplexity will automatically cite its sources for you to review, too. Make sure to stop and actually review the sources it gives you.

>> **Consider embedding digital watermarks or metadata within GenAI-generated content, creating a traceable digital footprint that confirms its origin and authenticity.** See the nearby sidebar, "How to use digital watermarks and embedded metadata," for information on how to do this.

>> **Know the data source.** The development of GenAI models should be transparent and ethical, with clear documentation of the data sources and training methods used. By this, we mean that the maker of the GenAI model or application — either a vendor or your internal AI development

team — should provide transparent information on how the model was trained and what data was used. This transparency not only builds trust but also allows for the scrutiny necessary to maintain the integrity of models in the rapidly evolving GenAI landscape. Discovering how the model was trained can help you estimate the risks in terms of the likelihood of originality and reliability of outputs.

For example, the GPT models that power ChatGPT were trained on data scraped from the internet. That may mean a higher risk in the potential of plagiarism and copyright infringement than, say, a specialized model that AI scientists at your company trained only on company data.

>> **Consider asking your employer or GenAI vendors to use Causal AI to reveal how the GenAI model came to its decision (output) as a deeper check of its functioning within ethical guidelines.** This is a highly technical strategy that your AI or IT department or GenAI vendor will need to do for you, as it involves developing causal inference algorithms that can work alongside or within GenAI models, creating training datasets that include causal relationship information, designing new model architectures that can combine causal reasoning with natural language generation, and developing metrics to manage the two. However, once in place, the Causal AI can reveal how the GenAI did what it did so you can better evaluate the originality and quality of its outputs.

HOW TO USE DIGITAL WATERMARKS AND EMBEDDED METADATA

Embedding digital watermarks or metadata is a method used to include hidden information within GenAI-generated content to verify its origin and authenticity. This is particularly important for digital works such as images, videos, music, and text that are created by GenAI systems or tools, as it helps to prevent unauthorized use and copyright infringement, as well as to track the distribution of the content.

Digital Watermarks

What they are: Digital watermarks are covert marks or codes that are inserted into digital content. They can be visible or invisible to the human eye (or ear, in the case of audio content). Invisible watermarks are designed to be undetectable under normal circumstances but can be revealed through specific software or techniques.

(continued)

(continued)

How to use them: To use digital watermarks, content creators or distributors employ specialized software to embed the watermark into the content before it's distributed. The watermark might contain information such as the creator's identity, the date of creation, or terms of use. If the content is found elsewhere later, the watermark can be extracted to prove its origin or to show that it's been used without permission.

Tools for digital watermarks: Adobe Photoshop is widely used for images, allowing for both visible and invisible watermarking. Software like uMark or Watermarkly can also be used to embed watermarks. For batch processing of images, tools like IrfanView offer plugins for watermarking multiple files at once. For videos, software like Video Watermark Pro can be used. Audio watermarks can be embedded using tools like Audio Watermarking Tools (AWT).

Metadata

What it is: Metadata is data that provides information about other data. In the context of GenAI-generated content, metadata can include details such as the author's name, creation date, location, copyright information, and any other relevant data about the content's origins or rights.

How to use it: Metadata is often attached to files and can be viewed and edited by using various software tools. When generating content, the GenAI system or the user can input metadata into the file properties. For example, in image files, metadata can be embedded into the EXIF data, while for text documents, it might be included in the document properties or within the file itself.

For metadata editing: For images, tools like Adobe Bridge or ExifTool allow users to view and edit EXIF data. For documents, Microsoft Word and Adobe Acrobat can be used to edit properties and metadata. Music files' metadata can be edited with software like MusicBrainz Picard or mp3tag.

Wrap it up and distribute. Verify that the watermark or metadata has been correctly embedded and can be retrieved or viewed using appropriate tools. Then distribute the content however you wish. After the watermark or metadata is embedded, you can distribute the content with the peace of mind that a traceable digital footprint is attached to it.

Maintaining quality standards in GenAI outputs

The foundation of GenAI's output quality lies in the data it's trained on. Using training datasets that are diverse, unbiased, and of high quality helps avoid perpetuating inaccuracies and stereotypes. Additionally, you should add more current and/or specialized data as needed for the model to make more accurate and timely analyses and responses.

REMEMBER

AI models of all types, including GenAI models, age out over time. It's called *model drift* or *model decay,* which refers to a model trained on and working with data that's aged to the point of being irrelevant, inaccurate, untruthful, out-of-date, or otherwise not useful. The effect is that the model has drifted too far from the concept, mission, or data from which it was meant to produce high-quality responses.

Imagine you're a chef who's perfected a recipe your customers love. Over time, the availability and quality of ingredients change, people's taste preferences evolve, and new dietary trends emerge. If you continue to use the same recipe without adapting to these changes, the once-popular dish may no longer satisfy your customers. Similarly, in AI, model drift occurs when the environment around a predictive model changes, making its once-accurate predictions less reliable. Just like the chef needs to tweak the recipe to align with current tastes and ingredient quality, data scientists must update or retrain their AI models to ensure they remain effective as the underlying data and relationships they were built upon shift.

Two main culprits are behind this mix-up: concept drift and data drift. Your recipe's success relies on two key factors: the taste preferences of your customers (concept) and the ingredients you use (data).

» **Concept drift:** Just as customers' taste preferences evolve over time, the underlying patterns and relationships that the GenAI model learned to predict also change. Your recipe must be updated to cater to these new tastes, or it will fail to satisfy your customers, just as the model will fail to make accurate predictions if not updated periodically.

» **Data drift:** Data drift occurs when the input data the model receives is still about the same concept, but the characteristics of the data have changed. The model may then not perform as well because the inputs it was trained on no longer match what it's currently receiving. This is similar to ordering the same ingredients for your prized recipe time and again, but their quality, size, and flavor subtly shift over time and have an adverse effect on your dish.

To ensure your signature dish (or GenAI model) remains a crowd favorite, you must remain vigilant. Regularly assess whether it still delights the palate and confirm that the ingredients (data) you're using are consistent with the recipe as originally crafted. Occasionally, you may need to refine your recipe with fresh, seasonal produce, adjust your seasoning techniques, or even develop an entirely new culinary creation if dining preferences have significantly changed. This could mean retraining your model with new data or starting anew with a different model. That's how you combat model drift and ensure your menu (and predictions) stays delectable, relevant, and satisfying!

But you need to be doing other performance checks, too. GenAI models should be evaluated regularly against quality benchmarks, which can include both automated metrics and human evaluation to gauge the relevance, coherence, and originality of the outputs.

TIP

Incorporating human review into the GenAI content-generation process is beneficial. Human experts can offer nuanced feedback and adjustments to refine the GenAI's output, ensuring it adheres to the desired quality standards. Feedback loops are also valuable for improving GenAI models. Typically, that's done by a user clicking on a thumbs-up or thumbs-down icon to indicate to the model when it has hit the mark or missed it in a specific response. But users can give the model feedback in a prompt, too. When you or your company AI team engage in analyzing GenAI performance and integrating user feedback, the model can be iteratively refined for better quality outputs.

Last, but certainly not least, adherence to ethical guidelines and legal standards should be non-negotiable. This means making sure that GenAI responses respect copyright laws and avoid the creation of deceptive or harmful content. It's your or your company's responsibility to manage the quality of outputs and clearly label GenAI-generated content.

Applying Journalism Ethics to GenAI-Generated Content

Applying journalism ethics to GenAI-generated content is a sound and useful way to consistently make sure its responses meet high standards and comply with ethical rules. The following sections provide guidance on approaching GenAI content like a journalist would, which is good advice no matter what field you're in.

Following basic journalistic principles

Even if you aren't a journalist, you can (and should) apply the same following principles when using GenAI to craft content:

>> **Transparency:** News media professionals and content providers need to be upfront about using GenAI to generate articles, pictures, podcasts, or anything else. It's critical to let the audience know upfront who (or what) is behind the reporting. If this information comes out after the fact, you'll lose credibility and reader trust.

>> **Accountability:** Journalists, content providers, advertising creators, and others have to babysit their GenAI to make sure it's not spouting nonsense or harmful information. Before hitting the publish button, you need to factcheck and edit the content to ensure that the GenAI hasn't made up a story, composed the content badly, left out important details, added untruths, or engaged in any misconduct.

>> **Accuracy:** Factchecking and proofreading GenAI content is extremely important. You've got to sift through the GenAI's work to catch any fibs or flubs that could trip up your readers or, worse, cause a ruckus, physical harm, or a lawsuit. Also, keep in mind that if a GenAI model commits to something with your customers or readers, the courts will make you follow through on it.

>> **Minimizing harm:** Imagine the consequences if your GenAI starts giving advice. Editors and publishers need to put on their detective hats and verify everything before it goes out, especially when the stakes are high. "Trust but verify" is as important a rule now as it ever was. And that goes for anyone creating any kind of content with GenAI — not just the media.

>> **Human oversight:** GenAI may be smart, but it's also dumb as a rock in many ways. It's also restricted in how much reporting it can actually do. It can't, for example, go interview witnesses on the scene, describe the tension in a courtroom at a key moment, or gather data that doesn't yet exist as a digital source. Journalists need to swoop in to get information and deeper insights from undigitized sources and then also factcheck and fix mistakes in GenAI's contribution to the story. The same goes for anyone else making GenAI content. Always, always, always check its homework and add your own expertise, research, and insights as needed.

>> **Ethical implications:** Watch out for plagiarism, bias, malice, foul language, and other bad behavior in GenAI-generated content. Always keep in mind that GenAI mimics human behaviors it sees in its data. While it doesn't understand malice, it does learn that people sometimes respond that way, so it mimics that type of response (the same with other emotions and foul language). You, your AI team, or the vendor would be smart to take steps to make the GenAI as well-trained and unbiased as you possibly can.

REMEMBER

By sticking to these principles, you can make sure that GenAI-generated content doesn't end up like a bad tabloid headline. Keep it honest, keep it clean, and keep it ethical.

Adhering to truth and integrity in GenAI-assisted reporting

Sticking to the principles of truth and integrity is more crucial than ever when using GenAI tools like ChatGPT for content generation. Keep your moral compass pointing north using journalism values and ethics, whether or not you're working in journalism.

First, remember that honesty is the best policy. When you're using GenAI, be upfront about it. Letting your readers know that part of your content was GenAI-assisted isn't just about being transparent; it's about maintaining the trust that's the bedrock of your relationship with your audience.

Don't just take what GenAI gives you at face value. Put on your detective hat and critically analyze the content. Check the logic, the facts, the math, the graphics, and how it all ties together. Remember, GenAI is a tool, not a replacement for the keen human mind that you bring to the table.

WARNING

Steer clear of the plagiarism pitfall. It's tempting to take the GenAI's output and call it your own, but resist that urge. Use GenAI to spark ideas or to get a different angle on a topic, but make sure your final work is genuinely yours.

When GenAI pulls in sources, don't just nod along. Do your due diligence and verify those sources independently. Your reputation for accuracy is on the line every time you choose to publish or share something you generate with GenAI.

Education is your ally. Dive into how your GenAI model of choice works, its strengths, and its weaknesses. The more you know, the better you can use it ethically and effectively. Share this knowledge, too; it's all about lifting the whole field up.

Cite GenAI and/or the sources the GenAI provided for you with the same rigor you would for traditional research. For example, don't just cite Perplexity (a GenAI-powered search engine) in your articles or content; also check the sources it listed in its response, and if those are accurate and reliable, cite those sources as well. It's about setting a standard on par with academic and journalistic standards and showing respect for the information and its origins. You'll appreciate it too when someone else writing a news article or content cites your work specifically and not the search engine. (For example, source: *Artificial Intelligence All-In-One For Dummies* and not "Google AI Overview" or "Perplexity.")

Also, be on guard against GenAI shenanigans when reading or viewing content. You must be just as diligent in guarding against AI shenanigans in emails, direct messages, social media posts, and even phone or video call conversations as people try to present GenAI responses as their own.

Knowledge is power, and in the world of GenAI, it's your superpower. Understand the ins and outs of these tools, from potential biases to ethical use, and you'll be well-equipped to use AI responsibly, enhancing your work without compromising your values or restricting your talent.

Balancing speed with ethical considerations in GenAI content generation

In the fast-moving world of news, journalists are always racing against the clock to get the latest stories out ahead of other news outlets. Assuming you're in a hurry to produce content too, you'll find that with the help of GenAI tools, there are ways to speed up your work without skidding over ethical speed bumps.

Accuracy, transparency, and accountability shouldn't be sacrificed in the rush. Make it a routine practice to double-check GenAI responses, making sure the facts are straight and the story's told fair and square. It's about keeping it real and reliable, even when the GenAI's doing some or most of the heavy lifting.

To keep everything up and up, set well-defined rules for GenAI use within your company, team, or for yourself. Establish checkpoints where content is to be reviewed by human eyes to give everything the once-over and to (hopefully) catch problems like plagiarism, copyright infringements, biases, or slip-ups. Whatever processes and policies you come up with, keep in mind that the goal is to find that sweet spot where getting the news out quickly doesn't mean cutting corners on the accuracy or responsibilities.

REMEMBER

By balancing the need for speed with a commitment to ethics, you're steering GenAI's power in the right direction. You're proving that you can keep up with the times while staying true to the heart of what you know and believe to be right: telling it like it is, sticking to the facts, and keeping the trust of the people tuning in.

Joining the Responsible AI Movement

As GenAI tools become more integrated into our daily lives, the importance of steering these technologies in a direction that safeguards human dignity, rights, and freedoms can't be overstated. Joining the responsible AI movement helps everyone push toward a future in which technology serves the greater good and aligns with collective values and ethical principles. The following sections cover the basics of this movement and ways that you can get involved.

Understanding the goals of the responsible AI movement

Responsible AI ensures that the AI models — not just GenAI models — humans create align with societal values and operate within ethical boundaries. This means designing AI models that respect privacy, promote fairness, and are transparent in their operations. The policies and processes governing AI model training, retraining, and uses are important parts of responsible AI, too. By joining the responsible AI movement, individuals and organizations commit to developing AI models that are not only efficient but also equitable and accountable.

The movement emphasizes the importance of inclusivity in AI development. Diverse teams are more likely to identify potential biases in AI systems, leading to more representative and unbiased outcomes. This inclusivity extends to the data used to train AI, ensuring it reflects the diversity of the real world and mitigates the risk of perpetuating existing inequalities.

The responsible AI movement also advocates for the development of AI that is secure and resilient. As AI systems become more complex, the potential for exploitation by malicious actors increases. By adhering to best practices in AI security, you can protect sensitive data and critical infrastructure from cyber threats.

Moreover, the movement encourages ongoing dialogue between technologists, policymakers, and the public. This collaboration is essential for creating a regulatory environment that fosters innovation while protecting the public interest. It also helps demystify AI, making it more accessible and understandable to non-experts, which is crucial for informed public discourse.

Finally, joining the responsible AI movement is a commitment to continuous learning and improvement. AI is a rapidly evolving field, and what is considered responsible today may change tomorrow. Being part of the movement means staying informed about the latest developments, challenges, and opportunities in AI ethics. It also means you have the opportunity to add your voice and thoughts to the evolution of AI and its uses.

The responsible AI movement is not just about preventing harm; it's about proactively contributing to a future in which AI enhances our capabilities, complements our humanity, and upholds our shared ethical standards. It's a collective effort to ensure that as AI's role in society grows, it does so in a way that's beneficial for all.

Contributing to ethical AI development and use

Ethical AI development and use requires the collective effort of many to ensure it grows healthily and sustainably. Everyone, from tech developers to end-users (yes, this means you!), has a role to play in cultivating an environment where AI operates within the bounds of ethical principles:

>> **For tech developers and data scientists,** the journey begins with an awareness of the issues so that work can be done to effectively address them when training, retraining, fine-tuning, or otherwise adapting AI models. Understanding the ethical implications of AI is paramount to these efforts. The implications include recognizing the potential for bias in datasets and algorithms and the consequences these biases can have on society. Developers must strive to create inclusive AI by ensuring diversity in training data and testing AI systems across a wide range of scenarios to identify and mitigate biases.

>> **Business leaders and policymakers** also have a crucial role. They must establish and enforce ethical guidelines for AI development and use within their organizations and at a legislative level. This role includes creating transparent policies around data usage, privacy, and consent, as well as setting up oversight committees to monitor AI systems for ethical compliance.

>> **End-users,** on the other hand, can contribute by staying informed and demanding transparency. By understanding how AI systems make decisions and the data they use, users can hold companies accountable for the AI products they offer. Public discourse and advocacy for ethical AI can influence businesses and governments to prioritize ethical considerations in their AI initiatives.

Start by making companies do more than give lip service to Responsible AI. Specifically, require them to disclose what and how they're implementing Responsible AI practices in their real-world AI deployments.

>> **Ethicists, sociologists, legal experts, and technologists** must work together to foresee the societal impacts of AI and guide its development accordingly. This collaborative approach ensures that multiple perspectives are considered, leading to more robust ethical frameworks.

>> **Educational institutions** have a responsibility to integrate ethics into STEM curricula, preparing the next generation of AI professionals to approach their work with a strong ethical foundation. Continuous professional development in ethics should also be encouraged within the tech industry.

>> **Investors and shareholders** can influence ethical AI by supporting companies that prioritize responsible AI practices. By directing funds toward ethical AI initiatives, they can incentivize companies to adopt best practices and contribute to the development of AI that benefits society.

>> **The media** play a pivotal role in shaping public perception of AI. Responsible reporting on AI should highlight both its potential benefits and ethical concerns. This balanced approach can foster a more nuanced understanding of AI among the general public. It can also prepare the public to reject AI-produced propaganda, deepfake videos, political and societal manipulations, and AI-produced conspiracy theories and fake data.

Aligning with global efforts for responsible AI practices

Several global efforts are aimed at developing, tracking, coordinating, or reporting on responsible AI practices. These efforts tend to be massive, as they involve a multi-layered approach that includes individual action, organizational commitment, and international collaboration. Following are some examples of global efforts currently underway to promote and implement responsible AI, led by various international organizations, governments, and institutions:

>> **UNESCO's Global Index on Responsible AI:** This initiative aims to monitor the implementation of globally established human rights-based AI principles. The index seeks to measure how well countries are implementing practices that ensure AI systems are transparent, accountable, and aligned with human rights and democratic values. Find more information here: https://www.unesco.org/en/articles/tracking-national-commitments-global-index-responsible-ai

>> **Atlantic Council's GeoTech Center:** The Atlantic Council's GeoTech Center is an initiative focused on the intersection of geopolitics, technology, and governance. As part of its broader mission, the GeoTech Center has a dedicated effort towards responsible AI, which aims to ensure that artificial intelligence and emerging technologies are developed and implemented in ways that are ethical, beneficial for society, and promote international security and prosperity. Find more information here: https://www.atlanticcouncil.org/programs/geotech-center/advancing-responsible-ai-globally/

» U.S. Government Initiatives: The United States is leading global efforts to build strong norms that promote the responsible military use of AI. This includes endorsing responsible AI measures for global militaries. Examples include:

- **National AI Initiative (NAII):** The National AI Initiative Act of 2020 aims to coordinate a national strategy on AI across various sectors, including international cooperation and coordination. It emphasizes the importance of leadership in AI ethics and governance on the global stage.

- **The AI Partnership for Defense:** Led by the DoD's JAIC, this initiative involves partnership with military allies and partners to share best practices, collaborate on ethical AI frameworks, and ensure that the use of AI in defense aligns with shared democratic values and international humanitarian law.

- **Global Partnership on Artificial Intelligence (GPAI):** The United States is a founding member of GPAI, an international initiative that brings together experts from industry, government, civil society, and academia to advance the responsible development and use of AI, guided by human rights, inclusion, diversity, innovation, and economic growth.

- **USAID's Digital Strategy:** The U.S. Agency for International Development (USAID) Digital Strategy includes efforts to leverage AI and other digital technologies in international development. It focuses on the responsible use of AI to improve program outcomes while mitigating risks, such as bias and threats to privacy.

- **Engagement in International Standards Organizations:** The United States actively participates in international standards organizations, such as the International Organization for Standardization (ISO) and the International Electrotechnical Commission (IEC), contributing to the development of global standards for AI that incorporate principles of responsible AI.

» World Economic Forum's AI Governance Alliance: This initiative brings together global stakeholders to champion the responsible design and release of transparent and inclusive AI systems. You can find more information here: `https://initiatives.weforum.org/ai-governance-alliance/home`

» Responsible AI Institute (RAI Institute): This global, member-driven nonprofit organization is dedicated to enabling successful, responsible AI efforts in organizations. RAI Institute provides independent assessments and certifications for AI systems, aligning them with existing and emerging policies, regulations, laws, and best practices. Find more information here: `https://www.responsible.ai/`

>> **AI for Good:** Led by the International Telecommunication Union (ITU), AI for Good is a movement and a series of global summits that aim to ensure that AI benefits humanity and contributes to the United Nations' Sustainable Development Goals. Find more information here: `https://aiforgood.itu.int/`

>> **Organization for Economic Cooperation and Development (OECD):** The OECD has developed AI Principles that have been adopted by many countries. These principles promote AI that is innovative, trustworthy, and respects human rights and democratic values. Find more information here: `https://www.oecd.org/en/topics/policy-issues/artificial-intelligence.html`

>> **Global Partnership on Artificial Intelligence (GPAI):** GPAI is an international initiative to support responsible and human-centric development and use of AI, guided by human rights, inclusion, diversity, innovation, and economic growth. Find more information here: `https://gpai.ai/`

>> **Partnership on AI (PAI):** PAI is a coalition that includes major tech companies, civil society groups, media organizations, and academic institutions. The Partnership on AI works to study and formulate best practices on AI technologies and to advance the public's understanding of AI. Find more information here: `https://partnershiponai.org/`

>> **IEEE Global Initiative on Ethics of Autonomous and Intelligent Systems:** The IEEE Standards Association has launched a global initiative that has created a comprehensive set of guidelines and standards to promote ethical considerations in AI and autonomous systems. Find more information here: `https://standards.ieee.org/industry-connections/ec/autonomous-systems/`

There are also several national and regional efforts with global impact. Many countries have developed their own frameworks and guidelines for AI ethics. For example, Singapore's Model AI Governance Framework, China's New Generation Artificial Intelligence Governance Principles, AI Ethics Guidelines from the European Union (EU), and the United States' National AI Initiative.

TIP

We've included URLs in the previous list in case you want to take a deeper look at the resources, research, and updates that are included on their websites. Additionally, academic journals, conferences, and workshops frequently address the topic, offering a platform for experts to discuss and advance the field. If you can't make it to the conferences, look for YouTube videos and news reports to glean some of the information that was shared there. Responsible AI efforts and guidelines are rapidly evolving, so staying informed through these organizations and their publications is a good way to keep up with the latest developments.

Chapter **7**

Finding Job Security in an AI World

A I is changing how people work, but it can't replace human skills like emotional intelligence, creativity, and strategic thinking. This chapter looks at how to upgrade your skills for jobs that AI can't do. It also explains how to use your current skills in new ways for these jobs and how to stay ahead in the near future when AI is more commonplace.

Identifying Tasks That AI Can't Replace

Even as AI continues to develop, humans will still be able to do certain tasks better. AI capabilities are becoming more advanced, but humans have strengths and abilities that are difficult, at this point, to replicate with technology.

These strengths and abilities include emotional understanding, creativity, and strategic insight. This section highlights the enduring value of human skills that AI has difficulty achieving. We also look at how you can secure your place in an AI-driven future with these skills.

Cultivating emotional intelligence and human interaction

Emotional intelligence (EQ) is, in part, the ability to recognize and respond to the emotions of others. It's a key element for getting along with people, whether at work or in other parts of life. Although AI is smart in many ways, it doesn't fully understand or show emotions the way that humans can.

You use EQ every day, and it's critical for working well with others. In any job, how you talk to and understand your co-workers and clients really matters. Think about a team leader or a salesperson — they need to be good at reading people's feelings. This is something AI can't do yet. AI can give us facts and figures, but it doesn't understand how people *feel.*

Similarly, when you don't agree with someone, EQ helps you sort things out. It helps you see both sides and understand how everyone feels. This is extremely important in jobs like counseling or when you need to smooth over a problem with a customer. AI tools may help with some aspects, but those tools don't understand the finer points of making peace between people.

REMEMBER

Good leaders use EQ to inspire their teams. They understand how their team members feel and use that insight in their decision-making, which helps everyone work better together. Thinking like a leader is something AI can't do. Leadership is about really getting to *know* people, not just what the data says.

As AI is used more frequently, you need to be skilled in understanding and showing emotions. This ensures that you'll remain central to the process, even when AI is handling the details. Additionally, it makes your work and life more meaningful because you connect with people in more genuine ways.

Sparking creative and strategic thinking

In the workplace, two of the most valuable human skills are creativity and strategic thinking. Unlike AI, humans have the unique ability to come up with original ideas and solve complex problems in innovative ways. Now consider why these skills are so important. Understanding this will show you how to keep your edge over AI in particular areas of work.

>> **Creative thinking** is about seeing things in new ways. It's the skill that drives innovation and breakthroughs. When you think creatively, you aren't just following a set pattern; you're making something new. This could be anything

from designing a stunning piece of art to developing a groundbreaking business strategy.

TIP

AI, with its current technology, is good at processing information and identifying patterns, but it doesn't truly create in the same way humans do. AI may mix and match what it knows, but coming up with something completely new is a human trait.

For example, consider a marketing team brainstorming a campaign. They're not just looking at data; they're using their creativity to tell a story that resonates with people. AI can analyze past successful campaigns, but the spark of creating a new, engaging idea comes from human minds. That's because humans understand emotions, cultural nuances, and the subtleties of humor and wit, which are essential in marketing.

» **Strategic thinking** is about planning to achieve a goal. It involves looking ahead, understanding the big picture, and making decisions. These decisions are based on this mix of knowledge and insight. Humans do well at considering these types of factors, including potential risks and opportunities.

REMEMBER

People can then decide on a course of action based on the interpretation of these factors. AI can help with decision-making by providing data-driven insights. However, the ability to examine different options and anticipate possible outcomes is a distinctly human skill.

Consider a company CEO deciding the business's direction. The CEO has to evaluate market trends, company strengths, and competitor actions. Global economic factors may also play a role. AI tools can supply data on these factors that help inform a decision. It's the human ability for strategic thinking, though, that can interpret the data, understand the implications, and make decisions that align with long-term goals.

In fields like developing new products, running businesses, and creating art, creative and strategic thinking are vital. These abilities allow you to do more than fix problems. They let you imagine what it could be and then work to make it happen. As people start to use AI more in their jobs, it's becoming clearer how important creative and strategic capabilities are. These human skills are what make businesses grow, change for the better, and succeed.

REMEMBER

As you adopt AI into your workflow, it's important to remember that creative and strategic thinking are skills that drive progress and new ideas. Even in an environment where AI is ubiquitous, these unique human contributions are still essential and extremely valuable. This balance between human skills and AI shows that both have their place in moving us forward.

Engaging in jobs of the future

As AI becomes more common in the workplace, it's important to look at the jobs it may affect and the ones it won't. AI is great at many things, but there are still jobs where human skills are more important. These jobs rely on the ability to understand people, be creative, and think ahead.

Here are the types of jobs that will be important in the future and the skills you need to succeed in them:

>> **Jobs that require the ability to understand people's feelings:** These include roles like counselors, social workers, and human resource professionals. AI can handle a lot of information, but it doesn't really understand how people *feel.* In these jobs, being able to connect with others and understand their problems is something only humans can do well.

>> **Creative jobs:** This category includes artists, designers, and people who work in entertainment. These jobs focus on creating new things. AI can help, but really new and original ideas come from people. Humans use their imagination and experiences to create art, design new things, and entertain others.

>> **Jobs in business and management:** People in these roles have to plan for the future and make decisions that benefit their company. They need to think about things like what their competitors are doing and what customers want. AI can give them information, but making these critical decisions requires human thought.

>> **Healthcare jobs:** Health care is another area where humans are very important. Doctors, nurses, and other healthcare workers do more than treat illnesses. They also care about their patients and understand their needs. AI can suggest treatments, but it's the healthcare workers who provide the care and support patients need.

>> **Teachers:** Teachers play a key role that AI can't replace. They don't just teach; they inspire and understand their students. AI can help make learning easier, but the encouragement and guidance that teachers provide are things only humans can offer.

>> **Jobs in research and development of new products:** These jobs involve finding out new things and making new technologies. Humans are curious and come up with questions that lead to discoveries, something AI isn't able to do. Developing these skills will help you be ready for a future where AI is more common.

Discovering new roles that use AI

In the future, as AI becomes a more significant part of work, new kinds of jobs will be created. These jobs will work *with* AI and require that the job-holders make sure AI aligns with a company's goals and interests.

The roles that will be in greater demand will require people who are

>> **Experts at integrating AI into different parts of a business:** These AI integration specialists will know a lot about technology and how businesses run. They'll help deploy AI tools in a way that works best for a given business.

>> **Equipped to function as AI ethicists:** They'll use AI in ways that are appropriate and free of bias. They'll understand the rules of AI and help companies use it without harming customers or exposing the company to other liabilities.

>> **Able to manage how AI and humans work together:** They'll focus on optimizing the human–AI workflow. These managers will make sure that both people and AI are doing what they do best.

>> **Experts in data privacy:** As AI uses more information, keeping this data safe will be an important job. People in these roles will protect personal information and make sure the company follows privacy laws.

TIP

These new jobs show just a sample of how AI is creating more new opportunities. These jobs of the future will combine business, technical, and interpersonal skills to solve problems and work with others.

Upskilling for AI-Proof Jobs

In the near future, AI will likely replace some people's jobs and empower others. This latter group will be the people who learn to use AI and turn it into an asset that makes them better at what they do. To become one of these people, you need to learn how to use the AI tools that will make you irreplaceable. Improving your skills will put you in a position to take advantage of future career opportunities.

DOING A SKILLS INVENTORY AND GAP ANALYSIS

Understanding your current skills and identifying what you need to learn is essential for thriving in a future where AI plays a big role. This process is called a *skills inventory and gap analysis*. It looks at what you're good at and helps you determine what skills you need to develop.

Let's look at the steps needed to do this effectively and why it's crucial for your career growth:

1. **Conduct a skills inventory.**

   This entails listing all the skills you have. Think about everything you know how to do, from your work experience, education, and even daily life activities. Your skills may include things like communicating well, solving problems, or understanding new technology. This step is like taking a good look at what tools you have in your toolbox right now.

2. **Analyze your skill gaps.**

   This is where you compare your skills with those needed for future jobs, especially in fields in which AI will be used extensively. To find out what skills you may be missing, you can check job listings, read about industry trends, and see what skills experts say will be important. The goal is to identify the skills you don't yet have but will need. These may be technical skills, like learning to use certain software, or soft skills, like being good at working with a team.

   Why is understanding your skills and gaps so important? Even though AI is really helpful, it can't do everything. Jobs that need human creativity, understanding, and leadership are becoming more common. By knowing your skills and the areas you need to improve, you can focus on becoming better in ways that AI cannot. This makes you a more attractive choice for employers.

3. **Make a list of what you want to do.**

   Research the skills that are in demand in your industry or the industry you want to move into. Look for patterns in job ads and industry news. What skills keep coming up that you don't have? Maybe it's understanding AI tools or getting better at creative thinking.

4. **Make a plan to fill your skill gaps.**

   This could involve online courses, workshops, or practice in your current job. *Remember:* The goal is not to be perfect at everything but to be ready to learn and adapt.

If you're having trouble identifying your skills and gaps, you can have AI help you. Try using a prompt such as, "Can we do a simple Q&A to help me understand my current skills and where I may need to improve to stay relevant in a job market that's increasingly influenced by AI? I'm not very technical, so I'd appreciate questions that don't require deep tech knowledge but still help me think about adapting to a future where many tasks may be automated."

That prompt would tell the AI to give you a set of questions, as shown in the following figure, which help you discover what your skills and gaps are.

 ChatGPT

Absolutely, let's explore your skills and potential areas for growth in the context of an evolving job market impacted by AI and automation. We'll keep the questions straightforward and focused on broader competencies.

Understanding AI and Automation

Q1: How familiar are you with AI and its role in your industry? Can you identify any aspects of your job that might be affected by automation?

Digital Literacy

Q2: What's your level of comfort with digital tools and platforms used in your work? Could you share how you learned a new digital skill or tool recently?

By doing a skills inventory and gap analysis, you're preparing yourself for a future where AI is common at work. It's a way to show that you can work with AI and bring valuable skills to your job.

Translating Your Current Skills into AI-Proof Roles

In the previous section, we examine how you can gain new skills. In this section, we take a closer look at how you can transition these skills into AI-proof roles. As you adapt to an AI-enhanced work environment, it's important to understand how your skills fit into this new landscape.

You need to recognize the value of your skills and figure out how to apply them. We look at how to reshape and apply your abilities in ways that complement AI, ensuring that your skills stay relevant and in demand.

Analyzing skills transferability

As industries rapidly embrace AI, it's important to know how you can use your existing skills in new ways. This process, called *skill transferability analysis*, refers to understanding which of your skills can be applied to AI-resistant roles.

TIP

Skill transferability focuses on the importance of being versatile and adaptable. It's the ability to use skills from one area in another area. For example, if you're good at solving problems in your current job, that skill can transfer to a different job, too, even if it's in a new field.

To conduct this analysis:

>> **List the skills you use in your current job.** These may be hard skills, like specific technical abilities, or soft skills, like communication or teamwork. When you have your list, think about how each skill could be useful in other areas. For example, suppose you're good at organizing things and managing time. In that case, these skills are valuable in project management roles, which are less likely to be automated by AI.

>> **List the skills that are in demand in jobs where AI is used.** These may include understanding how to work with AI tools, data analysis, or digital marketing. Compare these in-demand skills with your current skills. Where do they match? This overlap shows where you're already prepared for AI-resistant roles.

As in the earlier example about doing a skills and gaps analysis (see the "Doing a skills inventory and gap analysis" sidebar), you can also use an AI tool like Chat-GPT to help you brainstorm your skill transferability. Try a prompt like,

> "Can you give me some questions to think about how the skills I'm good at could be used in different kinds of jobs, especially because a lot of jobs are changing because of computers and smart technology?"

This prompt will get you on the right track toward understanding how your skills can be applied in different roles and contexts.

REMEMBER

Versatility and adaptability are crucial here. Being versatile means having a range of skills that you can use in different situations. Adaptability requires being open to learning new things and changing how you work. In an AI-driven job market, versatility and adaptability are valuable qualities. They demonstrate that you can keep up with changes and fit into different roles as needed.

Table 7-1 shows an example of a skills transferability analysis.

TABLE 7-1   **Example Skills Transferability Analysis**

Current Skill	Description	AI-Resistant Roles	Skill Transfer
Conflict resolution	Managing and resolving disputes effectively	HR manager, mediator in AI ethics	Vital for roles in which understanding human emotions and finding common ground are key, especially in ethical considerations of AI usage.
Crisis management	Managing and resolving emergencies in business settings	AI risk manager, business continuity planner	Essential roles that require quick thinking and effective solutions in critical situations, especially in which AI systems may not predict unforeseen events.
Cultural sensitivity	Understanding and respecting diverse cultural perspectives in business	AI ethics advisor, international business developer	Valuable for roles that involve ensuring AI tools and products are culturally sensitive and adaptable to various global markets.

To improve your versatility and adaptability, try to learn new things regularly. This doesn't always mean formal training — it can be as simple as taking on a new task at work or learning a new tool. The more you learn, the more skills you have to offer.

REMEMBER

The goal of skill transferability analysis is not to start over but to build on what you already know. You want to see your skills in a new light and understand how they can be valuable in a changing job market. By doing this, you'll be ready for new roles that AI can't replace, and you'll keep your career moving forward.

Understanding role evolution and adaptation

AI will facilitate a role evolution. This means that your job duties today may be different tomorrow. In the following section, we explore how you can adapt your current skills to meet these new demands.

In some jobs, AI can do tasks that were once done by people, like analyzing data or scheduling appointments. This doesn't mean these jobs will disappear. Instead, the focus of these roles will shift. For example, a data analyst may spend less time collecting data (because AI can do that) and more time interpreting the data and making decisions based on it.

It also means focusing more on the skills AI can't do, like creative thinking, understanding people, and making complex decisions. For example, if you're in marketing, you may use AI to analyze customer trends, but you'll use your creativity to design campaigns that appeal to those customers.

So, how can you adapt your skills to these changing roles? Start by learning about the AI tools used in your field. Fortunately, it just so happens that you have before you an excellent resource for gaining a broad understanding of how to use AI:

>> **Book 2** of this *All-In-One* guide goes into depth about prompting GenAI models.

>> **Books 3 through 6** teach you about using GenAI in different situations and for various kinds of work.

>> **Book 7** helps you learn how to customize GenAI applications and start to build AI agents to help you with various tasks.

Also, think about the parts of your job that need a human touch, like building relationships, solving unexpected problems, or coming up with new ideas. Focusing on these areas will help you stay important in your job, even as AI takes on more tasks.

TIP

The goal is not to compete with AI but to work with it. By adapting your skills, you can make AI a tool that helps you do your job better, not something that replaces you. This is all about growing with the changes, not just trying to keep up.

Presenting the AI-resilient career journey

As AI becomes a big part of many jobs, figuring out how to move into careers that AI can't take over is important. This shift to AI-resistant roles needs careful planning and a positive approach.

Follow these steps to approaching an AI-proof career:

1. Look at what you're good at and how these skills can fit into jobs that AI won't affect.

This means thinking about your strong points and how they match jobs that need a human touch, like understanding people or being creative. Jobs in health care or education or roles that need you to make big decisions are good examples.

2. Find out more about jobs that AI will not likely change.

Healthcare, education, and creative fields are areas where human interaction, vision, and individuality can be very important. Search for jobs in these fields where your skills are valuable.

3. **Work on learning more about these AI-proof careers.**

   You may need to take some classes or workshops or even try out these jobs through volunteering. Keep up with what's new in these fields and how AI is being used. This way, you can be prepared for what's coming.

TIP

Networking is a key part of changing careers. Meet people who work in the field you're interested in. Go to events, join online groups, and talk about the future of work with AI. Building a network can open up new chances and give you support while you're making this change.

Be ready to learn a lot of new things. Changing careers can be tough, but keep a positive attitude. Be open to new experiences and learn from both the good and the bad. And think about how this career change will affect your life, like your money and how you spend your time. Make sure this new career fits with what you want in the long run. It isn't just about finding a job that's safe from AI — it's also about doing work that you like and that uses your skills.

REMEMBER

Moving to an AI-resistant career means knowing your skills, learning new things, making connections, and planning well. By doing these things, you can smoothly move into a career where you can work alongside AI, not be replaced by it.

Navigating Career Transitions

In this section, we look at how to move into new AI-related jobs smoothly. We use examples to show how using your skills in new ways can open great opportunities for you. You may not be transitioning to the specific careers we use as examples, but you can extrapolate this information to whatever career you have in mind.

Adapting to new realities

AI tools are bringing new and incredible capabilities to a variety of professions. These capabilities include boosting productivity and assisting with creativity. Tasks that may have taken hours before can now be done in seconds. As more and more professionals adopt AI into their daily workflow, this impact is becoming more profound.

One profession, in particular, that has seen early and significant change is writing. Take, for example, copywriters. These professionals write copy for things like ads, blog content, and marketing emails. AI can help them outline early drafts of posts, find better words, and tailor a message for a specific audience. It can also critique the copywriter's work, so that they get feedback on the fly.

Figure 7-1 shows an example prompt a copywriter might use to have AI critique a draft blog post. This helps ensure the post achieves the desired effect and gets more views.

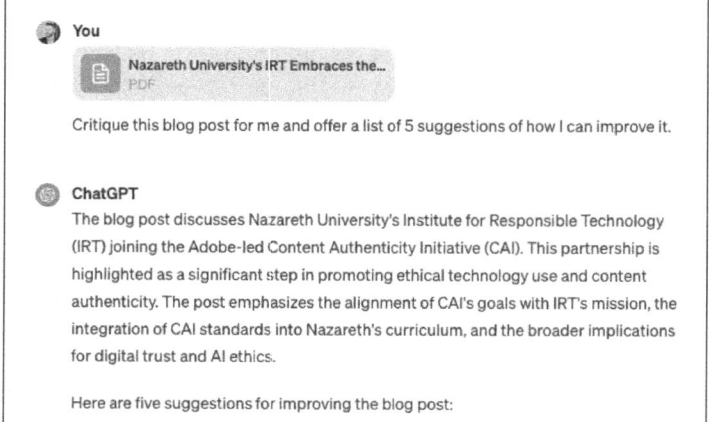

FIGURE 7-1:
AI tools can make suggestions about improving written content like blog posts.

REMEMBER

This shift in focus is crucial. It's about guiding AI to produce refined content and showcasing the copywriter's irreplaceable human insight with storytelling and audience understanding.

In other jobs, people are finding that AI can help them do their work in new ways. For example, in sales, AI can analyze customer data to help salespeople understand what their customers want.

TIP

To adapt to these new career realities, start by learning about the AI tools and training in your field. We mention many of those resources throughout this book. Also, be open to new ways of doing your job. AI may change some parts of your work, but it also opens up new possibilities. Think of AI as something that adds to your skills, not something that takes away from them. By learning to work with AI, you can make your job more interesting and do things you couldn't do before. It's about growing with the changes and using them to your advantage.

Shifting professional landscapes

The way in which individual roles are adapting to AI is part of a larger trend. It's not just about one job; it's about how AI is reshaping the whole world of work. Different industries are seeing traditional roles evolve. One great example is graphic designers transitioning into AI-aided user experience (UX)/user interface (UI) design, showing how AI tools can be a big help with their workflow.

Graphic designers, who are known for their artistic skills, are finding exciting new roles in UX/UI design, thanks to AI. These AI tools help them with automatic layout setups and color choices and even offer user experience ideas based on what people like and want. This means designers can spend more time on the creative parts of their job while AI handles the repetitive or data-focused tasks.

In marketing, AI is being used to figure out the best customers to target and to make smarter campaign plans. Marketers are now relying on AI for insights into customer behavior, which helps them create more effective marketing strategies.

REMEMBER

Integrating AI into your work doesn't mean you're losing your job to a machine. Instead, it's about making your job easier and more efficient. AI acts like a tool that helps you focus on the parts of your job that really need your human skills and creativity.

Overall, moving from traditional roles to new AI-enhanced jobs will become the norm. It's an opportunity for people to grow in their careers and find new ways to work.

Steering clear of pitfalls

Moving to a new job where AI is integrated into almost everything can be challenging. It's important to know how to step into this new AI-powered role and hit the ground running. Here are some ideas to make job changes smoother, whether you have experience or you're just starting:

>> **Know the technology.** Understand how you'll use AI in the job you want. This isn't just about the tech stuff; it's also about how AI changes the way you do the work. For example, in marketing, AI can sort through data, but you need people to make sense of it and plan what to do next.

>> **Be flexible.** Being able to change and keep learning is important. Jobs with AI are changing rapidly, so be flexible and ready to learn new things.

>> **Make connections.** Networking is key. Making connections with people in the field you want to work in can give you help, advice, and maybe even job leads. It's good to talk to others who have already made the career changes you want to make.

>> **Be patient and realistic.** Changing jobs, especially to ones with AI, doesn't happen overnight. You may have to start at a lower level or take a sidestep to get where you want to be.

>> **Keep your skills sharp.** Don't forget about skills like creativity and other soft skills. As AI does more of the technical work, these skills become even more important.

>> **Ask for help.** It's okay to ask for advice. Career advisors, mentors, or courses can give you the advice and direction you need.

Becoming an Early Adopter

Next, we consider the idea of becoming an early adopter of new tech. We explore using AI proactively, not just because you have to, but to get ahead. Being one of the first to use new AI tech can cause people to see you as an *ideas* person — and that's a good thing!

Adopting new technologies

Using and experimenting with AI tech is important. Try out different software or tools in your job or even for fun. This will help you get better at them and let you see how they can help in your work. Here are a few examples of tools to consider:

>> **ChatBot** (www.chatbot.com): ChatBot is an AI chatbot builder that allows businesses to create and implement conversational agents for customer service, enhancing customer interaction and support.

>> **ChatGPT** (https://openai.com/chatgpt): ChatGPT is a powerful GenAI chatbot that excels in generating text that is useful for content creation, automated customer service responses, and language translation.

>> **Jasper** (www.jasper.ai): Jasper is an AI writing assistant that helps create high-quality content, from marketing copy to blog posts, enhancing productivity for content creators and marketers.

>> **Synthesia** (www.synthesia.io): Synthesia is an AI video generation platform that creates realistic videos from text, useful for business presentations, training videos, and marketing, as shown in Figure 7-2.

>> **Zapier** (https://zapier.com): Though not exclusively AI, Zapier automates workflows between various web applications, streamlining processes for businesses and increasing efficiency in tasks.

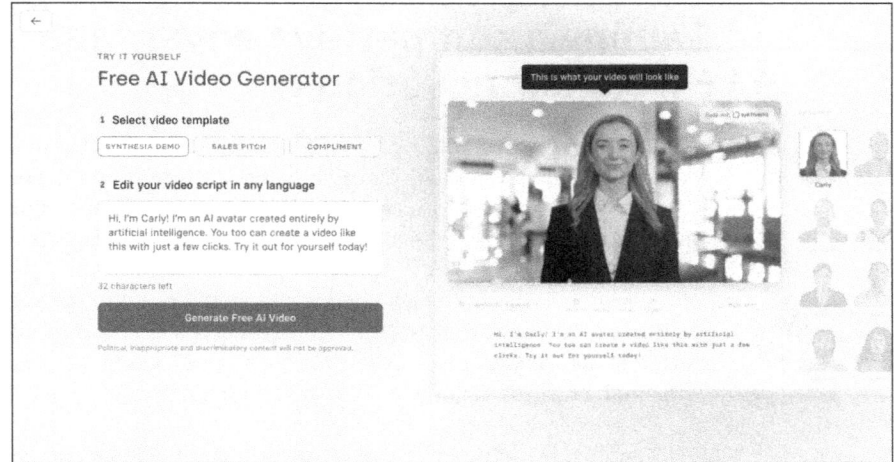

FIGURE 7-2:
Synthesia lets you
create complete
videos from text
prompts.

Trying new things, even if they don't always work out, is part of learning. Every time you try new things, you're likely to learn something new. Being ready to test, learn, and change is what makes someone good at using new tech.

Keeping up with new tech, practicing it, talking with others about it, and being ready to try it out can really help you at work. It can make you a leader in using new tech and help you do your job better.

TIP

Utilizing AI for thought leadership

AI can play a key role in boosting thought leadership. By using AI, you can bring fresh ideas to the table and be perceived as a more advanced thought leader. Here are a few ways AI can advance your thought leadership:

>> **AI gives you a massive amount of information and different perspectives quickly.** This information can spark new ideas that you may not have thought of on your own. For example, AI can analyze trends and data in your field, helping you see where things are going and what you should focus on.

>> **AI helps you understand your audience better.** AI tools like data analysis platforms can show you what the public is interested in or worried about. This can help you create messages or content that really speaks to the concerns of your audience.

>> **AI lets you test out your ideas quickly.** You can see what works and what doesn't without spending a lot of time or resources. This means you can try more new things and find the best ideas faster.

Gaining a competitive advantage through innovation

Adopting AI can give you a competitive advantage. It lets you do things in new and better ways. AI can look through lots of information quickly and find helpful insights. This can lead to new ideas, like different ways to talk to customers or solve problems that have been without a solution for a long time.

REMEMBER

Being innovative isn't always about huge changes. Sometimes it's about making small improvements that make your work better and easier. AI can take care of routine tasks, so you have more time to think of new ideas and solve problems. Even small changes can make your work much better.

When you use AI with what you're already good at, you can come up with truly creative ideas. It isn't just about using AI tools; it's about making them a part of how you work. This helps you do new and exciting things.

2

Prompting and Generative AI Techniques

Contents at a Glance

CHAPTER 1: **Mapping the Lay of the Generative AI Land** 133

CHAPTER 2: **Introducing the Art of Prompt Engineering**. 149

CHAPTER 3: **Navigating the Evolving Landscape of GenAI**. . . 161

CHAPTER 4: **Introducing ChatGPT**. 175

CHAPTER 5: **Getting Started with Microsoft Copilot**. 189

CHAPTER 6: **Learning Advanced Prompting** 203

IN THIS CHAPTER

» Selecting the right GenAI model

» Understanding GenAI capabilities

» Creating with GenAI

» Grasping GenAI's many uses

» Conquering fears and piloting opportunities

Chapter 1

Mapping the Lay of the Generative AI Land

Welcome to the exciting world of generative AI (GenAI)! This chapter is your starting point in understanding the vast landscape of GenAI and its transformative capabilities. Whether you're a curious beginner or a tech enthusiast, you'll find the information here to be an accessible guide to the basics of GenAI. You can easily build on these skills through practice, regular use of an AI application, or by returning to this book from time to time to enhance your skills further.

So, What Exactly Is Generative AI?

You can think of AI (short for *artificial intelligence*) as incredibly sophisticated software. Although it doesn't behave like any other software ever made, it is still software. Illustrations depicting AI as robots reflect the difficulty in drawing AI software in a way everyone will instantly recognize. But the robot is actually mindless hardware, and the AI is the "smart" brain-mimicking software installed to enable it to function in ways that people consider to be intelligent in a nonorganic sense.

Technically speaking, GenAI refers to a subset of artificial intelligence technologies that use sophisticated *natural language processing* (NLP), neural networks, and *machine learning* (ML) models to generate unique and humanlike content. It belongs to a classification of AI called *large language models* (LLMs), which analyze huge amounts of data in numerous languages including human languages, computer code, math equations, and images.

Understanding parameters

LLMs typically have a substantial number of parameters, which are numerical values used to assign weight and define connections between nodes and layers in the neural network architecture. Parameters can be adjusted to change the weights of various values, which in turn, changes what the model prioritizes in the prompt and data and how it interprets various data points, words, and connections.

Imagine you have a recipe for making a cake, and the recipe is your GenAI model. The ingredients — like flour, sugar, eggs, and butter — are like the data points, words, and connections in the model. Now, the amount of each ingredient you use (how many cups of flour, how much sugar, and so on) are like the weights of various values in the GenAI model or GenAI application.

Just as you might adjust the ingredients in your cake to make it sweeter or fluffier by adding more sugar or an extra egg, you can adjust the parameters in a GenAI model to change what it focuses on and how it interprets the information it's given. If you want your GenAI to pay more attention to certain words or data points, you increase their *weight* just like adding more chocolate chips to your cake if you want it to be extra chocolatey. This way, the GenAI model, like your cake, turns out the way you want it to, based on what you prioritize in the recipe.

How GenAI uses parameters

LLMs use parameters to predict the next word in a sequence — meaning they predict the word most likely to follow the words in your prompt, and then the word that most likely follows its first predicted word, and so on until the model believes it has finished the most probable pattern. It generates images in much the same way by predicting the image that follows your description in the prompt. The models can complete the process incredibly quickly. For example, LLMs like GPT-3 and GPT-4o developed by OpenAI are capable of processing billions of words per second. It is the speed of its response, the appearance of nuanced understanding, and its fluid use of natural language that gives GenAI interactions a humanlike feel.

REMEMBER

However, GenAI and LLMs are not human and do not think — again, they predict. It's a very complicated prediction process, to be sure. Nonetheless, it is a prediction. And if anything happens to tilt its predictive capabilities, nonsense ensues. You can see one example of that in Figure 1-1, which is an OpenAI incident report about an adjustment they made to the model resulting in ChatGPT responding to users in incomprehensible gibberish.

Unexpected responses from ChatGPT
Incident Report for OpenAI

Postmortem
On February 20, 2024, an optimization to the user experience introduced a bug with how the model processes language.

LLMs generate responses by randomly sampling words based in part on probabilities. Their "language" consists of numbers that map to tokens.

In this case, the bug was in the step where the model chooses these numbers. Akin to being lost in translation, the model chose slightly wrong numbers, which produced word sequences that made no sense. More technically, inference kernels produced incorrect results when used in certain GPU configurations.

Upon identifying the cause of this incident, we rolled out a fix and confirmed that the incident was resolved.

Posted 4 days ago. Feb 21, 2024 - 17.03 PST

FIGURE 1-1:
A routine effort to optimize ChatGPT resulted in its producing gibberish in response to users' prompts.

Source: OpenAI incident report

GENAI VERSUS VIRTUAL ASSISTANTS

AI models and applications are the software that drives the robot or the autonomous car or whatever form it's given in the corporeal world. But strictly speaking, AI has a digital form. Because of that, it can be squeezed into almost anything, and many vendors do exactly that. You'll find various types of AI are embedded or otherwise at use in all sorts of products and services. However, not all AI is the same.

Here are the main differences between GenAI apps like ChatGPT and virtual assistants like Siri, Alexa, and Google Assistant.

(continued)

Mapping the Lay of the
Generative AI Land

(continued)

Virtual assistants

This class of AI runs on a proprietary mix of technologies in a blend developed by their respective corporate owners. Certain components, such as machine learning, deep learning, natural language processing, smart search or search engines, and speech synthesis make the assistants appear and sound much like ChatGPT.

However, their responses are more limited than GenAI models. People typically use these to retrieve answers to common questions or perform uncomplicated tasks like "where is the nearest pharmacy?" or "play a song by Taylor Swift" rather than to generate original answers.

GenAI models (specifically ChatGPT in this comparison)

This class of AI runs on a single AI model, meaning on one version or another of Generative Pre-trained Transformers (GPT) AI models. GenAI is a broad category of AI that includes models capable of varying capabilities such as generating text, images, or computer code or some combination of these.

People typically use GenAI web apps, but some mobile apps and a few wearable devices are available as well. But in all cases, the apps run on a single GenAI model.

Unveiling the BIG Secret to Working Successfully with GenAI

If you remember nothing else I've written in this book, you must remember what I tell you in this section. For here is the big secret — the master key — that you need to make GenAI models work at the level you need them to perform. If you don't grasp this, GenAI will likely appear to you to be nothing more than a fascinating toy or a tool that falls far too short of your expectations.

TIP

In a nutshell, GenAI generates outputs that appear to be original thoughts or images from a computer, rather than results produced by very advanced, contextual predictive software. GenAI retrieves words or images pulled from a database and repurposes them into a new response. The big secret is that the humanlike feel in the *conversation* is an illusion. You are not having a conversation with a machine. It doesn't understand a word you wrote in your prompt.

REMEMBER

Current GenAI models don't think or create things *per se*, but instead *generate* new things from parts of old things found in their database. (The term *things* in this context comprise images, videos, numbers, or text, depending on the GenAI application you are using.) A GenAI output is the model's best prediction of what you are seeking. In an oversimplified explanation of a complex technology, GenAI seeks to complete a pattern that you began with your *prompt*, which is your question or command as entered into the prompt bar on the GenAI's user interface (UI). In other words, GenAI predicts what letters, words, or images are likely to follow those that are in your prompt. Its predictions are based upon comparison to patterns that exist within its training dataset and/or datasets to which it was subsequently given access.

Think of GenAI outputs as the result of repurposing or remixing information that the model has access to in datasets, including the following:

>> Data it is exposed to in its training database along with any additional data provided in subsequent fine-tuning

>> Data added in system messages or prompts

>> Data added via methods such as *retrieval-augmented generation* (RAG), which is a tactic to enhance accuracy, relevancy, and reliability by adding external sources to the GenAI's database.

RAG combines the strengths of both *information retrieval AI,* which is a set of algorithms that retrieve contextually relevant information from huge datasets, and GenAI, which uses neural networks and machine learning models to generate new content. It may help to think of RAG as GenAI that is augmented by more traditional information retrieval AI, or retrieval AI for short.

WARNING

Since GenAI generates outputs that are the result of its remixing or repurposing of information, it has no concept of true or false, fact or fiction. GenAI can accurately define these terms, but it does *not* understand their meaning. It doesn't understand anything you wrote in the prompt or that it wrote in its response. It only appears to understand terms and concepts. This is an illusion. This is why you must always fact-check its work.

REMEMBER

GenAI responses are limited to the confines of the data it has access to. Put another way, if its training data were a mound of Legos and there were no end caps in that mound, GenAI would build its outputs without end caps. It would not know that end caps exist at all. In the same way, it does not know fact from fiction unless those labels are applied to specific data points in its dataset. But, if a falsehood is labeled as fact, GenAI will unquestionably accept it as fact. It still doesn't understand the difference.

To illustrate this analogy, I wrote a caption first and then used it as a prompt in Azure OpenAI Studio DALL-E playground (Preview). The result is the stunning concept illustration you see here in Figure 1-2.

FIGURE 1-2:
If data were Legos, GenAI could only build things with the Lego pieces it has access to, and it is completely unaware that any other types of Lego pieces exist.

Generated with AI using DALL·E - OpenAI

GenAI can repurpose and remix only the data it has access to, which is a major reason why GenAI outputs can be highly reliable, totally false, or something in-between. The data itself can be insufficient — in one way or another — to provide the foundation or elements for the model to generate an accurate answer. Outdated data from an aging training dataset and data limited to too few perspectives or examples are common issues, but many others present themselves.

When — not if — outputs are wrong, people call them *hallucinations.* It's unclear why no one calls them lies, falsehoods, or simply errors, but in any case, you cannot assume that GenAI outputs are solid enough to bet your life or business on without doing some serious fact-checking first.

REMEMBER

While GenAI does consider context when it analyzes the words in your prompt, it does not understand you or what you said in the prompt. This is why you must not confuse GenAI with General AI, also known as Artificial General Intelligence (AGI). AGI doesn't exist outside of science fiction movies, books, and TV shows. Yet some people are so in awe of GenAI capabilities that they are sure this must be *it* — the thing from the movies that's going to take over the world! This is not that.

Understanding the Infamous Finger Problem and Other GenAI Quirks

Perhaps the most wondrous thing about using GenAI is the delicate dance between human and machine that begets something that neither would have made alone. But once you move past the first exhilarating moments of viewing GenAI marvels, you'll begin to see a few cracks here and there.

For example, it is common for GenAI models to draw people with six or more fingers on one hand. This is typically because the patterns it sees in its data involve multiple fingers on one human hand. No clear pattern emerges of there being just five fingers on one hand, so GenAI can't predict how many fingers it needs to generate.

Essentially GenAI is parroting the answer from its database. It doesn't understand the question or the answer; therefore, it does not know to draw only five fingers. Instead, it looks for patterns in hands depicted by images or text in the datasets to which it has access. But the pattern of the total number of fingers is unclear. Images in most databases that GenAI models use typically show hands in different positions wherein only some fingers are visible or fingers from two hands or more are intertwined. GenAI cannot therefore see a consistent pattern of the total number of fingers per hand. However, if you were to ask the model how many fingers are on a hand, it will almost always tell you that there are five. Even though it gives you the right answer as to the number of fingers, it does not understand its own reply and, therefore, still doesn't *know* the answer.

Data pattern inconsistency and the resulting probability prediction error is why you can end up with too many or too few fingers in any image GenAI generates. This is often the reason for other issues in images and videos that GenAI creates such as errors in shadowing or movement.

REMEMBER

Although GenAI is impressive, its reasoning is limited. In fact, it's extremely difficult for GenAI to reason at all. To overcome this shortfall and make it more powerful, add one or more humans to the mix, and you'll soon see real magic in the result. It is the collaboration between you and this extremely sophisticated software that will take you to the goals you seek.

Figuring Out How to Work with GenAI — It's All About Your Prompts

Here's the thing: Natural human language is a computer language now. In the case of GenAI, this means that the machine still works like a machine and the human like a human, but they can now interact through a computer language that everyday, non-programmer types of people can understand and use.

However, you, the human, still must think like a machine to get the most out of GenAI. Ask any computer programmer how important it is to think like a machine while programming — and this is true regardless of their choice of programming language, be that JavaScript, Java, HTML/CSS, SQL, Python, English, or French.

And why is changing how you think important? Because you are not having a conversation with GenAI. You are giving instructions (and, yes, even when your prompt is a question, it is an instruction) on what you want the model to produce, much like any programmer does. You must think beyond the language to the depths of the result you seek. The value of a programmer is not their computer language knowledge, although that is important, too, but the problem-solving ability that they can convert into language that renders the precise solution the programmer wants to produce. This is how you need to think and work with GenAI models, too.

Your prompts need to be more concise and detailed than the typical conversations you have with another human. For one thing, you cannot make assumptions that a listener will automatically fill in common details because GenAI often doesn't know those details. Despite appearances, GenAI does not think and doesn't truly understand your prompt; many of the natural assumptions you make in speaking to another human will not work in the same way in interactions with these models.

TIP

The GenAI winning formula: Machine speaks like a human. Human thinks like a machine. The better you get at telling GenAI what you want, the better it'll get at giving you what you need. It's all about practice.

Why GenAI appears so human

From crafting sentences to conjuring up images, composing music, or creating synthetic data, GenAI is an expert in making something instantly that can often readily pass as human made.

The interesting thing is that its outputs *are* human made in some sense. GenAI can be thought of as a creative tool like an artist's paints, crayons, and pencils. Those items produce images first imagined in the artist's mind and executed by the artist's hand and skill. Similarly, GenAI delivers outputs according to the user's vision and skilled prompting.

Further, much of the data that GenAI models learn from is generated by humans. But it learns far more from this information than you may imagine. It also learns the habits, attitudes, biases, and other human attributes behind the text, audio, and image data that it consumes.

For example, GenAI models have been known to be "lazy" in the summertime around peak vacation periods — meaning GenAI models may produce less content in response to a prompt than usual. GenAI may even tell a user to get the information for themselves. Sometimes a GenAI model also responds slower than normal, announces a delay, or makes excuses.

Such actions aren't due to a bug or a flaw in the system. The AI is merely mimicking human behavior. Models learn human behavioral patterns along with data patterns from their training dataset. They make no distinctions in the values of the information versus the behavior and so are likely to distribute both, or either, in their outputs.

GenAI can also deliberately lie and act angry or sad or cheerful for the same reason. It may even appear to ignore you from time to time. On the flipside, GenAI models tend to perform better when given a virtual reward or a compliment. Again, all of this is just mimicry of the human behaviors it has learned. It's important to remain aware of such idiosyncrasies when using GenAI. Strategically playing into these GenAI quirks can level up the responses you pull from it.

Depending on the model you're using, inputs and outputs can be in text, images, and/or audio forms. Unlike traditional AI, which analyzes, makes decisions, and delivers outputs drawn from data, generative AI can repurpose information to create seemingly original outputs in a conversational or artistic manner. But it can also plagiarize and pillage the works of other humans. You must always check its outputs for grievous and potentially liable or dangerous behaviors.

WARNING

A key point to remember is that if you use GenAI, you are legally liable for what it does. It is not a "separate legal entity . . . responsible for its own actions" as Air Canada once argued trying to defend itself in a court case after ChatGPT gave one of its customers incorrect information. You'll find more information in the discussion on responsibilities in Book 1, Chapter 6. (And if you're curious about the Air Canada story, you can access it here: www.bbc.com/travel/article/20240222-air-canada-chatbot-misinformation-what-travellers-should-know.)

Realizing the human influences behind generative AI's abilities

It's important to distinguish between generating and creating. GenAI "creates" text or images by generating a response from repurposed information based on its prediction of the "best" match to your prompt. GenAI does not *create* in the truest sense, which dictionary.com defines as "to cause to come into being, as something unique that would not naturally evolve or that is not made by ordinary processes."

GenAI works mostly by making predictions, which technically is an ordinary process in that predictions are a common thing that people and analytics do. However, GenAI's prediction processes are quite extraordinary in that they exist at a level never before achieved. By machine standards, this achievement is extraordinary because it generates a new response as opposed to a regurgitated response or picking one of a limited number of "canned" responses. By human standards, GenAI's performance is extraordinary because it can analyze huge amounts of data and respond in a conversational manner or with a newly generated image in seconds or minutes.

TIP

One way to remember the difference is to think "To generate is AI, to create is human or human and AI."

But make no mistake, GenAI is not as humanlike as it appears. Another distinction is in motivation. Humans are motivated to create; some even feel driven by their passions. By contrast, GenAI is not motivated to generate anything. Ever. It doesn't get hungry, thirsty, lonely, inspired, emotional, cold, hot, uncomfortable, dedicated to a cause, politically activated, or otherwise stimulated so there's no reason for it to do anything at all.

You must provide the vision, the passion, and the impetus in a prompt. Then GenAI will try to generate whatever that is for you. Otherwise, it will sit idle for centuries — or however long its supporting hardware and electrical power exists. That's why no one needs to worry about whether GenAI will take over the world.

However, everyone should worry about the humans using GenAI to take over the world. As a tool, GenAI is neither good nor bad. But its users can be either or both. It is the blend of human and AI capabilities that makes GenAI models perform so uniquely and wonderfully. And sometimes comically or poorly.

Discovering the Differences in GenAI Models and Options

GenAI interacts through natural language and generates new content by repurposing data into new outputs. They are most commonly used in areas that require fresh ideas and original output, such as customer service, graphic design, digital media, entertainment, software development, and writing.

However, they can also be used in specialized tasks for a variety of industries such as healthcare, pharmaceuticals, life sciences, manufacturing, and the financial sector.

This section offers a breakdown of specific GenAI models and their corresponding outputs.

Image outputs:

>> **DALL-E 2:** This AI model can convert textual descriptions into detailed images or artistic creations, demonstrating the power of language-based image synthesis.

>> **StyleGAN 3:** This model is known for generating high-resolution, photorealistic images of subjects such as human faces, animals, and vehicles, offering customization options. It's also used to animate images.

>> **Stable Diffusion:** This GenAI model specializes in generating lifelike images, videos, and animations derived from textual descriptions and visual prompts.

>> **Imagen:** Trained to understand and interpret image-text pairings, this GenAI system excels in crafting images from textual cues and performing neural style transfers.

>> **Adobe Firefly:** A GenAI tool designed for converting written descriptions into visual content, Adobe Firefly aids in the creation of artistic and creative imagery.

>> **Midjourney:** This GenAI tool is adept at converting textual prompts into distinctive and captivating artwork very quickly.

Text outputs:

- **ChatGPT:** Developed by OpenAI, this advanced chatbot can generate text that is coherent and indistinguishable from human conversation across various topics.

- **OpenAI Codex:** This model specializes in generating and completing code based on natural language prompts, forming the backbone of tools like GitHub Copilot.

- **HuggingChat:** This is an open-source AI chatbot created by Hugging Face, providing a ChatGPT-like experience using the Open Assistant Conversational AI Model for dialogue-based engagements.

Audio outputs:

- **Jukebox:** Another creation by OpenAI, Jukebox composes music across different genres, illustrating GenAI's capacity to craft musical pieces.

- **PaLM 2:** A Google-developed transformer model that excels in generating multilingual content and performing coding tasks.

- **AudioCraft:** This suite includes MusicGen, AudioGen, and EnCodec, three distinct models that work in tandem to produce authentic audio and music based on textual descriptions, providing an avenue for crafting rich and captivating auditory content.

- **Project Music GenAI Control:** A nascent tool from Adobe Research, this generative AI specializes in music creation and refinement, enabling artists to spawn musical pieces from text inputs and adjust the resulting audio.

Video outputs:

- **Stable Diffusion:** This model employs diffusion techniques to generate photorealistic images, videos, and animations from textual and visual prompts.

- **Neural Radiance Fields (NeRFs):** This novel neural network approach can be used for creating 3D visuals from 2D image data.

- **Synthesia:** This AI video generator tool transforms textual input into video content, featuring AI-driven avatars and voiceovers for simplified video production.

Multimodal inputs and/or outputs (generates more than just text):

>> **Copilot AI:** Made by Microsoft, this model aims to boost workplace efficiency by offering chat-based interfaces for information retrieval, composing emails and summaries, crafting images from textual descriptions, and programming in multiple coding languages.

>> **ChatGPT 4o (omni):** This model allows multimodal inputs and generates multimodal outputs. Additionally, the availability of specialized GPTs in the GPT Store can be used to add capabilities. For example, Image Generator can be used within ChatGPT to create images to illustrate its textual output.

>> **Gemini:** A suite of generative AI models from Google DeepMind and Google Research, designed with multimodal functionalities to process text, images, audio, video, and programming codes.

REMEMBER

GenAI models are always learning and getting better, and there's a new one popping up all the time. Which one you pick depends on what you need it for, how much you want to spend, and how easy it is for you to use.

Checking Out Practical Uses of GenAI

GenAI models are the subject of many news stories, water-cooler talks, zoom meetings, and online chats. It seems nearly everyone has an opinion on where this technology is leading. Some predict doom and gloom while others expect rainbows and riches. The real story about GenAI is far more practical and realistic than the talk surrounding it.

Following is a list of popular practical uses today:

>> **Content creation:** GenAI models like Claude and ChatGPT 4o are being used today to assist authors, scriptwriters, screenwriters, speechwriters, and other creatives in generating stories, speeches, character dialogues in games and movie scripts, marketing collateral, ads, blogs, websites, and even entire books like this one. They can be used to enhance human creativity or just handle the background research, planning, storyboards, and character tracking. See Book 4 for an in-depth exploration of how to use GenAI in content creation.

>> **Visual arts:** Image generators such as DALL-E, Midjourney, and Stable Diffusion can create photorealistic images or artworks from textual descriptions, aiding artists and designers in visualizing concepts and creating new art forms. Specialized models can create everything from storyboards to short videos and select gaming or movie scenes. Book 4, Chapter 3 explains how to get good results when prompting GenAI applications for images and other types of visual assets, such as video and marketing materials.

>> **Search and knowledge assistance:** Generative AI is being integrated into search engines and virtual assistants, transforming them into more powerful knowledge assistants. When ChatGPT or a similar GenAI application is embedded in a search engine like Bing, you can usually choose between reading the helpful narratives of the search results or reviewing a list of sources and related items. Some search engines like Perplexity are built from the ground up on GenAI and even provide a list of sources used to generate search summaries.

>> **Customer service:** ChatGPT can interact with customers to provide support, offer solutions, and facilitate service processes like returns, making customer service more personalized and efficient. You can learn more about using GenAI in customer service in Book 7.

>> **Education:** GenAI can disrupt traditional education models by enabling customized learning plans and assessments for students, moving away from one-size-fits-all approaches to competency-based learning progression. You learn about using GenAI in education in Book 5, Chapter 3.

>> **Media and journalism:** While GenAI cannot perform investigative reporting, it can assist journalists by providing background information, context, and faster dissemination of news stories. It can also manage basic, fact-only reporting such as sports scores and daily stock market analysis.

>> **Legal and data analysis:** Lawyers can use GenAI to draft legal documents. Staff can use it to conduct analyses of mounds of case-related documents and evidence to quickly derive insights and timelines and write reports, allowing the attorneys to focus on strategy and deeper insights. However, the final legal documents must be overseen and edited by lawyers or their appointed clerks and paralegals as GenAI does make mistakes.

>> **Marketing and advertising:** Marketers and advertisers can leverage GenAI to produce content and ads rapidly, keeping up with emerging trends, making better market fit, and enabling continuous delivery cycles. Chapters 1, 5, and 6 of Book 4 delve into the particulars of using GenAI in marketing and advertising.

>> **Smart automation:** As virtual assistants like Siri and Alexa become integrated with GenAI, they will become more intelligent and versatile, capable of understanding and anticipating user needs. Integrating GenAI with other software and eventually with autonomous AI agents will complete a smart automation cycle from user request to task completion. For example, instead of Google Assistant just giving you a list of restaurants nearby, with GenAI and other software or app integrations, it can book a reservation or place a to-go order for you, too! In Book 7, Chapters 4 and 5, you learn how to use Microsoft Copilot to develop your own GenAI agents and plugins.

Separating Gen AI Fact from Fiction

With any emerging technology, myths and misconceptions can arise. It's important to separate the hype from reality. For instance, while generative AI can automate certain tasks, it doesn't mean it will replace all human jobs.

One common misconception is that generative AI will lead to mass unemployment. While it's true that AI can eliminate jobs much like automation tools have done, it also creates new job opportunities and roles that require human oversight and creative input. For example, AI-generated content still needs human curation to ensure quality and relevance.

Another myth is that generative AI can independently create high-quality content without human intervention. The quality of AI-generated content heavily depends on the input and guidance it receives from human users. GenAI is a tool that amplifies human potential, not a replacement for human creativity.

Table 1-1 lists some of the most common myths about GenAI today and the realities to match.

REMEMBER

Generative AI is a rapidly evolving field. Its capabilities are expanding, and with them, our understanding of what is possible. The journey through the landscape of GenAI is just beginning, and the path ahead is filled with opportunities for innovation and growth.

TABLE 1-1   Common GenAI Myths versus Reality

Myth	Reality
GenAI can take over for human creativity.	GenAI isn't about to steal the job of artists, inventors, innovators, photographers, videographers, content managers, medical researchers, scientists, or other professionals in a wide array of disciplines. It's more like a helpful sidekick that can pitch in with ideas and content, but it still needs a human boss to direct and oversee its work to make sure the final product makes sense and shines.
GenAI speaks all languages perfectly.	Think of GenAI as a language student; it's pretty good at languages it's been taught, but it's not a polyglot prodigy. Training it to understand different tongues takes a lot of data and effort, so it's not equally slick in every language.
GenAI is totally fair and neutral.	Just like people, GenAI can pick up biases from the stuff it learns. To keep GenAI fair, humans have to step in and guide it, sort of like teaching it good manners and enforcing laws.
GenAI is a jack-of-all-trades.	Generative AI tools are not uniform but rather tailored for specific functions, with each having unique pros and cons. For example, tools such as ChatGPT3 are optimal for language-related tasks, whereas DALL-E and Midjourney are great for creating images, underscoring the necessity to match the tool to the task. Multimodal models like ChatGPT4 appear to be good at a lot of different types of inputs, but they have their drawbacks, too. For instance, ChatGPT 4o isn't great at making graphs and infographics — at least not yet.
GenAI is a wild, untamed beast.	GenAI might be the new kid on the public block, but that doesn't mean it's a wild card. The scary stories are often more fiction than fact. Like any technology, it's all about how you use it.
GenAI will flip business on its head overnight.	GenAI is pretty awesome for whipping up content and making things more personal and efficient, but it's not a magic wand for business. Its superpowers work best when they're tailored to specific tasks and business goals.
GenAI is just a step away from thinking on its own.	Let's get this straight: GenAI is clever at making stuff based on patterns, but it's nowhere close to thinking or feeling like a human. It's smart, but not that kind of smart.
GenAI will take over in the future.	It's a tool, not an overlord. It's also been overhyped and massively adopted too early for user skills to catch up, which means that we're probably in a bubble that will burst soon. Never fear, this is a typical cycle for new technologies, albeit on steroids this time. GenAI is here to stay. Learn the skills now to secure a job now and in the future. It's just going to take a bit for the dust to settle so people and companies can see where this tech works best.

IN THIS CHAPTER

» Discovering the secrets of successful prompting

» Understanding how prompts work

» Creating great prompts

» Matching prompts to the task

» Aligning prompts with audiences

Chapter **2**

Introducing the Art of Prompt Engineering

P rompting is a crucial skill set in the era of generative AI (GenAI). Mastering this skill, or even just getting the hang of it, can go far in advancing your career or pay.

If you've ever wondered how to communicate effectively with AI to get the best possible outcomes, this chapter is your starting point. So, buckle up and get ready to embark on a journey that will transform the way you interact with AI.

First Things First: What Is a Prompt?

A *prompt* is a query or command you write in the prompt bar on the user interface (UI) of a GenAI application. It's essentially your side of the conversation with a GenAI application.

Figure 2-1 shows a screenshot of ChatGPT's user interface. The prompt bar is at the bottom of the screen. It's a rectangular box with the words *Message ChatGPT* inside. You type your prompt in this box.

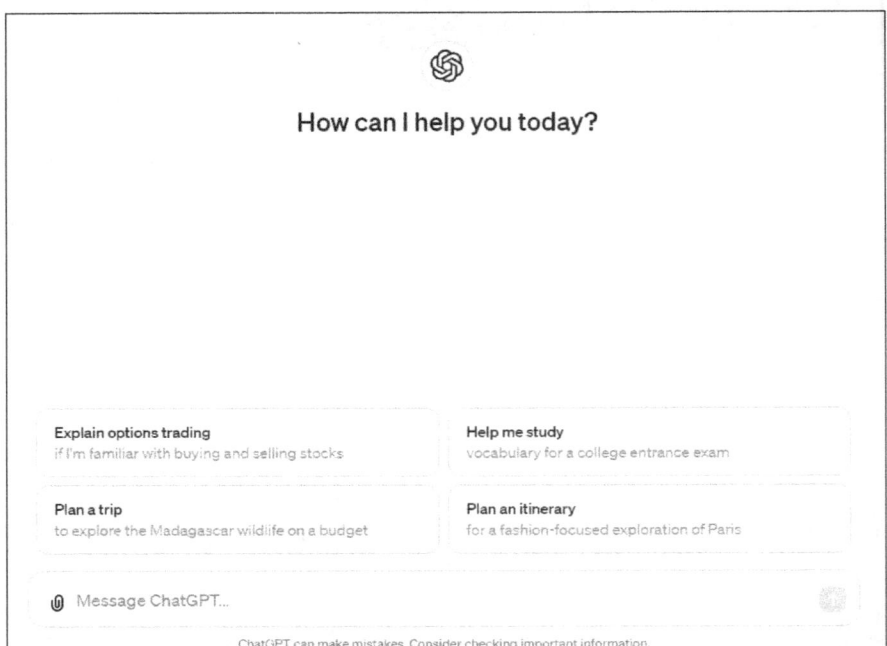

OpenAI / https://chat.openai.com / last accessed on April 22, 2025

ChatGPT is a chatbot application built on GPT, which is a generative AI model. Other applications are built on GPT models, too. And other applications are not built on GPT but on other types of generative AI models.

Depending on the model you're using, you may also be able to enter one or more images or other files in the prompt. Click on the little paperclip icon in the prompt bar to attach images and/or files.

Prompt engineering means the act of crafting a prompt or a series of iterative prompts to get a GenAI model to produce the desired output. Although anyone can write a prompt, prompt engineering involves extra steps and critical-thinking skills aimed at enhancing prompts for maximum effect. This chapter will set you on a path to prompt engineering, while the entirety of this book will help you become a power-user of GenAI. Prompt engineering is an important but not the only skill needed to be a power-user.

Revealing the Secret Behind Successful Prompting

As you embark on your journey through the world of generative AI, one of the most empowering tools at your disposal is the art of prompting. But what makes some prompts open the floodgates to AI creativity, while others barely spring a leak?

In this section, you discover the secret behind successful prompting, a skill that, once mastered, can significantly enhance your interactions with AI.

Discovering the secret sauce in prompt engineering

The secret sauce of prompt engineering is a combination of clarity, context, and creativity. To craft a successful prompt, you must be clear in your request, provide enough context for the AI to understand the direction, and be creative enough to guide the AI toward the desired outcome.

Imagine you're a chef in a kitchen. Your ingredients are words; your recipe is the prompt, and the dish you're aiming to create is the AI's response. Just as a well-crafted recipe leads to a delicious meal, well-crafted prompting leads to a satisfying AI response. The key is to balance all the elements just right.

But successful prompting is almost always done in steps and not in one prompt. Just like most recipes, adding the ingredients in steps renders a better result than simply dumping all ingredients in the bowl at once. Two ways of using steps in prompting are iterative prompting and prompt chaining, which are related but distinct techniques:

>> *Iterative prompting* is a flexible cycle of prompting, evaluating, and re-prompting that continues iteratively until a satisfactory output is achieved.

>> *Prompt chaining* is a fixed iterative refinement process that is structured as a chain of connected prompts. In other words, tasks are broken into steps with each step building on the one before and added like a link in a chain. Each prompt in a prompt chain is designed in a specific sequence so as not to confuse the model with too many commands at once and to keep it moving forward toward a desired output.

Understanding how prompts guide GenAI responses

Prompts guide the AI on the direction it should take when generating content. GenAI creates content by predicting what words are most likely to follow the words in your prompt and then predicting what words will follow that, and so on.

REMEMBER

Sticking with the previous analogy, the main ingredient in the secret sauce is you remembering that GenAI models are making predictions. They are not thinking, conversing, or creating, really. They are generating content based on probability determined by the data the model trained on and the prompt you gave it.

Another way to think of it is to picture the prompt you give it as pieces of a puzzle. GenAI then will predict what the completed puzzle looks like from those few pieces. That's why it's critical to give it pieces that provide enough clues for it to figure out the full picture.

To demonstrate how this works, I prompt both DALL-E in Azure OpenAI Studio and Image Generator in OpenAI's ChatGPT to illustrate this point.

Figure 2-2 shows the illustration made in Azure OpenAI Studio DALL-E playground (Preview). Note the specific prompt I used is under the illustration.

Draw a human offering a couple of puzzle pieces in a prompt and an AI model completing the full puzzle.

FIGURE 2-2: Illustration of how prompts work in Azure OpenAI Studio DALL-E playground (Preview).

Now compare Figure 2-2 with Figure 2-3. This new figure is Image Generator in OpenAI's ChatGPT prediction of the correct response to the same prompt that I gave to Azure OpenAI Studio DALL-E in Figure 2-2.

FIGURE 2-3:
Illustration of how prompts work in Image Generator in OpenAI's ChatGPT.

Do you like one of these illustrations better than the other? That is your subjective opinion, and your preference is right for you. However, no matter which is more appealing to you, neither illustration is a true test of which AI application or model does the best work.

This brings me to another key point that you should remember: The same prompt will conjure different responses from the same GenAI model, even those entered by the same user in the same chat. Variances exist across and between GenAI models, too, which you'll see in a moment. That's right. It's highly unlikely that you will ever get the same answer to the same prompt twice. And that's true whether you are using GenAI to generate text, images, videos, or audio.

REMEMBER

A prompt can be as simple as a question or as complex as a set of instructions, but the end goal is the same: to elicit a specific response from the AI. If you ask a vague question, the AI may take you down a winding road of generalities. But if you ask a precise question, you're more likely to get a direct and relevant answer. Your prompt must deliberately and skillfully guide GenAI models and applications to reach your destination. Failing to do so will leave you wandering aimlessly.

Crafting Effective Prompts for Diverse AI Applications

As you delve deeper into the realm of prompt engineering, you find out that the effectiveness of a prompt can vary greatly depending on the application. Whether you're using AI for creative writing, data analysis, customer service, or any other specific use, the prompts you use need to be tailored to fit the task at hand.

REMEMBER

The art in prompt engineering is matching your form of communication to the nature of the task. If you succeed, you'll unlock the vast potential of AI.

For instance, when engaging with AI for creative writing, your prompts should be open-ended and imaginative, encouraging the AI to generate original and diverse ideas. A prompt like "Write a story about a lost civilization discovered by a group of teenagers" sets the stage for a creative narrative.

In contrast, data analysis requires prompts that are precise and data-driven. Here, you may need to guide the AI with specific instructions or questions, such as "Analyze the sales data from the last quarter and identify the top-performing products." You may need to include that data in the prompt if it isn't already loaded into the training data, retrieval-augmented generation (RAG), system or custom messages, or a specialized GPT. In any case, this type of prompt helps the AI focus on the exact task, ensuring that the output is relevant and actionable.

The key to designing effective prompts lies in understanding the domain you're addressing. Each field has its own set of terminologies, expectations, and objectives. For example, legal prompts require a different structure and language than those used in entertainment or education. It's essential to incorporate domain-specific knowledge into your prompts to guide the AI in generating the desired output.

Following are some examples across various industries that illustrate how prompts can be tailored for domain-specific applications:

>> **Legal domain:** In the legal industry, precision and formality are paramount. Prompts must be crafted to reflect the meticulous nature of legal language and reasoning. For instance, a prompt for contract analysis might be, "Identify and summarize the obligations and rights of each party as per the contract clauses outlined in Section 2.3 and 4.1." This prompt is structured to direct the AI to focus on specific sections, reflecting the detailed-oriented nature of legal work.

» **Healthcare domain:** In healthcare, prompts must be sensitive to medical terminology and patient privacy. A prompt for medical diagnosis might be, "Given the following anonymized patient symptoms and test results, what are the potential differential diagnoses?" This prompt respects patient confidentiality while leveraging the AI's capability to process medical data.

» **Education domain:** Educational prompts often aim to engage and instruct. A teacher might use a prompt like, "Create a lesson plan that introduces the concept of photosynthesis to 5th graders using interactive activities." This prompt is designed to generate educational content that is age-appropriate and engaging.

» **Finance domain:** In finance, prompts need to be data-driven and analytical. A financial analyst might use a prompt such as, "Analyze the historical price data of XYZ stock over the past year and predict the trend for the next quarter based on the moving average and standard deviation." This prompt asks the AI to apply specific financial models to real-world data.

» **Marketing domain:** Marketing prompts often focus on creativity and audience engagement. A marketing professional could use a prompt like, "Generate a list of catchy headlines for our new eco-friendly product line that will appeal to environmentally conscious consumers." This prompt encourages the AI to produce creative content that resonates with a target demographic.

» **Software development domain:** In software development, prompts can be technical and require an understanding of coding languages. A prompt might be, "Debug the following Python code snippet and suggest optimizations for increasing its efficiency." This prompt is technical, directing the AI to engage with code directly.

» **Customer service domain:** For customer service, prompts should be empathetic and solution oriented. A prompt could be, "Draft a response to a customer complaint about a delayed shipment, ensuring to express understanding and offer a compensatory solution." This prompt guides the AI to handle a delicate situation with care.

By understanding the unique requirements and language of each domain, you can craft prompts to effectively guide AI in producing the desired outcomes. It's not just about giving commands; it's about framing them in a way that aligns with the goals, terms, and practices of the industry in question. As AI continues to evolve, the ability to engineer precise and effective prompts becomes an increasingly valuable skill across all sectors.

Tips and Tricks for Optimizing Your Prompts

Although GenAI may seem like magic, it takes knowledge and practice to write effective prompts that will generate the content you're looking for. The following list provides some insider tips and tricks to help you optimize your prompts to get the most out of your interactions with GenAI tools:

>> **Know your goal.** Decide what you want from the AI — like a simple how-to or a bunch of ideas — before you start asking.

>> **Get specific.** The clearer you are, the better the AI can help. Ask, "How do I bake a beginner's chocolate cake?" instead of just "How do I make a cake?"

>> **Keep it simple.** Use easy language unless you're in a special field like law or medicine for which using the right terms is necessary.

>> **Add context.** Give some background if it's a special topic, like tips for small businesses on social media.

>> **Play pretend.** Tell the AI to act like someone, like a fitness coach, to get answers that fit that role.

>> **Try again.** If the first answer isn't great, change your question a bit and ask again.

>> **Show examples.** If you want something creative, show the AI an example to follow, like asking for a poem like one by Robert Frost.

>> **Don't overwhelm.** Keep your question focused. If it's too packed with info, it gets messy.

>> **Mix it up.** Try asking in different ways, like with a question or a command, to see what works best.

>> **Embrace the multimodal functionality.** *Multimodal functionality* means that the GenAI model you're working with can accept more than one kind of prompt input. Typically, that means it can accept both text and images in the input.

>> **Understand the model's limitations.** GenAI is not infallible and can still produce errors or "hallucinate" responses. Always approach the AI's output with a critical eye and use it as a starting point rather than the final word on any subject.

>> **Leverage the enhanced problem-solving abilities.** GenAI's enhanced problem-solving skills mean that you can tackle more complex prompts. Use this to your advantage when crafting prompts that require a deep dive into a topic.

>> **Keep prompts aligned with AI training.** For example, remember that GPT-4o, like its predecessors, is trained on a vast dataset up to a certain point in time (October 2023 at the time of this writing). It doesn't know about anything that happened after that date. If you need to reference more recent events or data, provide that context within your prompt.

>> **Experiment with different prompt lengths.** Short prompts can be useful for quick answers, while longer, more detailed prompts can provide more context and yield more comprehensive responses.

>> **Incorporate feedback loops.** After receiving a response from your GenAI application, assess its quality and relevance. If it hits — or is close to — the mark, click on the thumbs-up icon. If it's not quite what you were looking for, provide feedback in your next prompt by clicking on the thumbs-down icon. This iterative process can help refine the AI's understanding of your requirements and improve the quality of future responses.

REMEMBER

By keeping these tips in mind and staying informed about the latest developments in the capabilities of various GenAI models and applications, you'll be able to craft prompts that are not only effective but also responsible and aligned with the AI's strengths and limitations.

Using Prompts to Provide Supplemental Data for the Model

The point of prompt engineering is to carefully compose a prompt that can shape the AI's learning curve and fine-tune its responses to perfection. In this section, you dive into the art of using prompts to refine the GenAI model, ensuring that it delivers the most accurate and helpful answers possible. In other words, you discover how to use prompts to also teach the model to perform better for you over time. Here are some specific tactics:

>> **When you talk to the AI and it gives you answers, tell it if you liked the answer or not.** Do this by clicking the thumbs up or thumbs down, or the + or – icons above or below the output. The model will learn how to respond better to you and your prompts over time if you do this consistently.

>> **If the AI gives you a weird answer, there's a "do-over" button you can press.** It's like asking your friend to explain something again if you didn't get it the first time. Look for "Regenerate Response" or some similar wording (the term varies among models) near the output. Click on that, and you'll instantly get the AI's second try!

>> **Think of different ways to ask the AI the same or related questions.** It's like using magic words to get the best answers. If you're really good at it, you can make a list of prompts that others can use to ask good questions, too. Prompt libraries are very helpful to all. It's smart to look at prompt libraries for ideas when you're stumped on how or what to prompt.

>> **Share your successful prompts.** If you find a super good way to ask something, you can share it online (at sites like GitHub) with other prompt engineers and use prompts others have shared there, too.

>> **Instead of teaching the AI everything from scratch (retraining the model), you can teach it a few more new things through your prompting.** Just ask it in different ways to do new things. Over time, it will learn to expand its computations. And with some models, what it learns from your prompts will be stored in its memory. This will improve the outputs it gives you, too!

>> **Redirect AI biases.** If the AI says something that seems mean or unfair, rate it a thumbs down and state why the response was unacceptable in your next prompt. Also, change the way you ask questions going forward to redirect the model away from this tendency.

>> **Be transparent and accountable when you work with AI.** Tell people why you're asking the AI certain questions and what you hope to get from it. If something goes wrong, try to make it right. It's like being honest about why you borrowed your friend's toy and fixing it if it breaks.

>> **Keep learning.** The AI world changes a lot, and often. Keep up with new models, features, and tactics, talk to others, and always try to get better at making the AI do increasingly more difficult things.

The more you help GenAI learn, the better it gets at helping you!

REMEMBER

Avoiding Common Prompting Pitfalls

When you engage with AI through your prompts, be aware of common pitfalls that can lead to biased or undesirable outcomes. Following are some strategies to avoid these pitfalls, ensuring that your interactions with AI are both effective and ethically sound.

>> **Recognize and mitigate biases.** Biases in AI can stem from the data it was trained on or the way prompts are structured. For instance, a healthcare algorithm in the United States inadvertently favored white patients over people of color because it used healthcare cost history as a proxy for health needs, which correlated with race. To avoid such biases, carefully consider the variables and language used in your prompts. Ensure they do not inadvertently favor one group over another or perpetuate stereotypes.

>> **Question assumptions.** Wrong or flawed assumptions can lead to misguided AI behavior. For example, Amazon's hiring algorithm developed a bias against women because it was trained on resumes predominantly submitted by men. Regularly review the assumptions behind your prompts and be open to challenging and revising them as needed.

>> **Avoid overgeneralization.** AI can make sweeping generalizations based on limited data. To prevent this, provide diverse and representative examples in your prompts. This helps the AI understand the nuances and variations within the data, leading to more accurate and fair outcomes.

>> **Keep your purpose in sight.** Losing sight of the purpose of your interaction with AI can result in irrelevant or unhelpful responses. Always align your prompts with the intended goal and avoid being swayed by the AI's responses in a direction that deviates from your original objective.

>> **Diversify information sources.** Relying on too narrow a set of information can skew AI responses. Ensure that the data and examples you provide cover a broad spectrum of scenarios and perspectives. This helps the AI develop a well-rounded understanding of the task at hand.

For example, if the AI is trained to find causes of helicopter crashes and the only dataset the AI has is of events when helicopters crash, it will deduce that all helicopters crash, which, in turn, will render skewed outputs that could be costly or even dangerous. Add data on flights or events when helicopters did not crash, and you'll get better outputs because the model has more diverse and more complete information to analyze.

>> **Encourage open debate.** AI can sometimes truncate debate by providing authoritative-sounding answers. Encourage open-ended prompts that allow for multiple viewpoints and be critical of the AI's responses. This fosters a more thoughtful and comprehensive exploration of the topic.

>> **Be wary of consensus.** Defaulting to consensus can be tempting, especially when AI confirms our existing beliefs. However, it's important to challenge the AI and yourself by considering alternative viewpoints and counterarguments. This helps in uncovering potential blind spots and biases.

>> **Check your work.** Always review the AI's responses for accuracy and bias. As with the healthcare algorithm that skewed resources toward white patients, unintended consequences can arise from seemingly neutral variables. Rigorous checks and balances are necessary to ensure that the AI's outputs align with ethical standards.

REMEMBER

You can learn more about how to use GenAI ethically and responsibly in Book 1, Chapter 6.

Chapter **3**

Navigating the Evolving Landscape of GenAI

Whether you're a seasoned pro or a curious newcomer, this chapter is your compass for navigating the exciting and sometimes unpredictable terrain of generative AI. I demystify the core concepts and show you how to identify the key players who are shaping the GenAI landscape. You find out how to assess the services and solutions available, ensuring you make informed decisions in this bustling market.

But it's not all smooth sailing. GenAI can sometimes clash with other tech, so I also guide you through the integration challenges you may face and share some clever workarounds. Plus, I introduce you to the world of autonomous AI agents and how they can take your GenAI projects to new heights.

Identifying Key Players and Evaluating GenAI Providers

The GenAI landscape is dotted with a variety of players — from tech giants to innovative startups — that tend to hail from one or more of the following areas:

>> **Tech giants:** These are the household names that have been pushing the boundaries of AI for years. Companies like Google, OpenAI, Microsoft, and IBM have been at the forefront, developing platforms and tools that have become the backbone of GenAI applications.

>> **Innovative startups:** On the other side of the spectrum, you find agile startups that are nimble and often specialize in niche areas of GenAI. These companies are the breeding ground for cutting-edge ideas and bespoke solutions.

>> **Research institutions:** Universities and dedicated AI research labs play a crucial role in advancing the science behind GenAI. They are the unsung heroes, often partnering with businesses to bring theoretical concepts into real-world applications.

>> **Community-driven AI:** These are typically open-source communities, but some are classified as companies as well, such as Hugging Face.

This section provides an introduction to these key players in the industry, as well as insights and tools you need to make an informed decision on which GenAI tools you use.

Who's who in the GenAI market

As I turn your attention to the movers and shakers in the GenAI market, it's clear that the landscape is as diverse as it is dynamic. The year 2023 and beyond has seen a surge in innovation and growth within the field, with several key players emerging as frontrunners. The following sections are examples of GenAI makers in several categories. As the market heats up and then matures, we'll likely see more GenAI players and then fewer as some buy out others.

Marking the GenAI trailblazers

Here's a snapshot of some of the leading GenAI trailblazers and what makes them stand out:

>> **OpenAI:** At the pinnacle of GenAI innovation, OpenAI is a pure-play startup that has carved out a stellar reputation for its versatile AI solutions, including the conversational marvel ChatGPT and the image generator DALL-E. With an estimated valuation soaring to $29 billion, OpenAI's influence is bolstered by substantial backing from tech behemoth Microsoft. Despite its name, OpenAI is not open source — a fact that remains controversial to this day, given its start as an open-source AI entity. It has since evolved in to a closed company, meaning the code behind its tools, such as ChatGPT and GitHub Copilot, can be viewed, modified, or reused by only OpenAI's developers.

>> **Hugging Face:** This open-source, community-centric AI hub thrives on collaborative development, fostering an environment in which AI enthusiasts and experts converge and share what they learn and develop. The Hugging Face hub hosts 200,000 open-source models and counting. It serves more than 1 million model downloads per day. In short, Hugging Face is the go-to destination for machine learning models, GenAI transformers, and AI tools.

Hugging Face's integration of tools like Copilot into Microsoft's suite of applications exemplifies its commitment to accessible AI innovation. The Hugging Face Hub Model Catalog is also available directly within Azure Machine Learning Studio. The catalog is filled with thousands of the most popular transformers models from the Hugging Face Hub that can be accessed in Azure with a click. But Microsoft is not the only company making use of the Hugging Face Hub for models and transformers.

>> **Stability AI:** This company is the maker of Stable Diffusion, an image generator tool that's stepping on the toes of OpenAI's DALL-E. It also makes Stable Audio, a remarkable breakthrough tool in GenAI music generation. You can access Stable Audio at `stableaudio.com`.

Stability AI is the open-source maverick, throwing open the doors to collaboration and innovation in a way that's a stark contrast to OpenAI's more guarded approach. Specifically, Stability AI is a leading open-source generative AI company.

>> **Anthropic:** Anthropic is an AI safety and research company that's focused on building reliable, interpretable, and steerable AI systems. Claude is Anthropic's best-known product to date. But Claude is not an AI application or tool like ChatGPT or DALL-E; rather, it is a family of foundational AI models that can be used in a variety of applications. But you can talk directly to Claude at `claude. ai` to brainstorm ideas, analyze images, and process long documents.

>> **Google DeepMind:** Google DeepMind is the result of converging two of Google's smartest AI labs — Google Brain and DeepMind. Google DeepMind and its predecessors are like the AI whiz kids of the tech world, known for crafting algorithms that achieve remarkable feats.

Whether it's mastering the next level in a video game, optimizing e-commerce logistics, or running simulations, DeepMind's algorithms are all about versatility. Remember the AI that beat human champions at the game of Go? That's DeepMind's AlphaGo for you.

Google Brain's research breakthroughs, such as open-source software like JAX and TensorFlow and other achievements, are the backbone of Google's infrastructure today,

Google DeepMind possesses a treasure trove of experience in reinforcement learning that sparks its innovation and informs its new creations today.

Gemini is its largest and most capable GenAI model. It's multimodal, meaning text, images, audio, video, and code can be entered in prompts, and it can deliver outputs in any of those forms as well. You can find other GenAI models by Google DeepMind that you may want to explore at `deepmind.google/technologies`.

» **Midjourney:** Midjourney's AI is a very popular image generator and a competitor of OpenAI's DALL-E and Stability AI's Stable Diffusion. Midjourney, the GenAI program and service, is created and hosted by the independent research lab operating by the same name, Midjourney, Inc. The code that powers Midjourney is private and a closely guarded secret that leaves everyone outside the company wondering, "How do they do that?"

Midjourney is noted for features like its style transfer capabilities (for example, transfer the style from an image input to the newly generated output), iterative refinement process (continuous improvement of its image outputs through automation and human feedback), artistic interpretation (its algorithm adds an artistic flair to image outputs), and the ability to incorporate photographer references into the image-generation process (mimics the style of famous photographers in newly created photorealistic images).

Watching the AI innovators

The generative AI market is a constellation of innovative entities, each contributing to the advancement of this transformative technology. Consider these four GenAI players as top examples:

» **Cohere:** With a laser focus on natural language processing (NLP), Cohere excels in crafting tools adept at text retrieval, classification, and generation. Its suite, including Neural Search, Summarize, Generate, Classify, and Embed, showcases its NLP prowess.

>> **Agilisium:** Distinguished by its dedication to R&D in GenAI, Agilisium offers a blend of consulting, advisory, and engineering services. Its expertise is particularly sought after in the life science and pharma sectors, where its tailored solutions drive progress.

>> **Tiger Analytics:** A global force with a team of more than 4,000 technologists and consultants, Tiger Analytics collaborates with clients across a spectrum of industries. From consumer packaged goods (CPG) to healthcare, its global reach and sector-spanning collaborations are a testament to its versatility and impact.

>> **Genpact:** As a global professional services titan, Genpact boasts a staggering workforce of more than 115,000. It's renowned for propelling transformative outcomes across various industries, leveraging its innovative data-tech-AI services to reshape business landscapes.

The tech titans

Alongside the key players we've already discussed, four tech titans — AWS, Google, Nvidia, and Microsoft — stand out for their significant contributions and strategic positioning in the GenAI ecosystem:

>> **AWS (Amazon Web Services):** AWS is a powerhouse in cloud computing, providing a robust platform for AI and a plethora of GenAI and machine learning services. Examples of AWS services include Amazon Bedrock, Amazon SageMaker, AWS Deep Learning Containers (*containers* are a software code package that make your applications independent from your IT infrastructure resources), and AWS's deep learning AMIs (Amazon Machine Images) and its Generative AI Application Builder.

AWS also offers popular frameworks and hardware such as NVIDIA GPU-powered Amazon EC2 instances, AWS Trainium, and AWS Inferential, which are pivotal for GenAI development, making it a go-to for startups and enterprises alike. These and other AWS services and platforms make it a breeze to roll out your own machine learning environments.

>> **Google:** Google has long been a pioneer in AI and machine learning with its TensorFlow framework and Google Cloud AI services. It's also the creator of cutting-edge models like BERT and T5, which have pushed the boundaries of natural language understanding. Google's AI research and tools have been instrumental in advancing the field of generative AI, and its recent efforts with models like Language Model for Dialogue Applications (LaMDA) and Pathways Language Model (PaLM) showcase its ongoing commitment to innovation.

>> **Nvidia:** Known for its powerful GPUs that are essential for training complex neural networks, Nvidia also offers AI software platforms like Compute Unified Device Architecture (CUDA) and CUDA Deep Neural Network (cuDNN) that accelerate deep learning processes. Nvidia's hardware and software synergies make it a critical enabler of the computational power required for GenAI model training and inference, supporting the entire AI ecosystem.

>> **Microsoft:** Microsoft's Azure AI is a comprehensive suite of AI services and cognitive Application Programming Interfaces (APIs) that empower developers to build intelligent applications. With Azure Machine Learning and tools like ONNX for model interoperability, Microsoft is at the forefront of democratizing AI. Its investment in and partnership with OpenAI, bringing GPT-3 and GPT-4 to the Azure platform, further cements its position as a leader in the generative AI space.

These four giants, along with the previously mentioned companies, form the backbone of the generative AI market. Their technologies and services are not just supporting the infrastructure of GenAI but are also driving its evolution, making them indispensable in the current and future landscape of artificial intelligence.

Assessing GenAI services and solutions

Choosing the right GenAI provider means selecting a business partner that you or your company can rely upon for their products and services. Here's how to assess the services and solutions on offer:

>> **Capability and expertise:** Look for providers with a proven track record. Their expertise should align with your specific needs, whether it's natural language processing, image generation, or data synthesis.

>> **Scalability and flexibility:** The ideal GenAI service should not only meet your current requirements but also scale with your growing demands. Flexibility in integration and customization is key.

>> **Ethics and compliance:** With great power comes great responsibility. Ensure that your GenAI provider adheres to ethical AI practices and complies with relevant regulations and standards.

>> **Support and community:** A vibrant community and robust support system can be invaluable, especially when navigating the complexities of GenAI.

TIP

Many GenAI services offer a free version or a free trial. You can gauge how well a GenAI product or service meets your needs by taking several for a test drive before you buy anything.

But do be careful how you judge these models, as each will perform according to your level of prompting and overall AI prowess. If any of the available models disappoint you, consider your role in the model's misfire. In other words, test drive more than just circling the block. Push yourself and the model and see where you end up.

Getting GenAI that Plays Nice with Other Technologies

The integration of artificial intelligence into existing software ecosystems isn't just a luxury — it's a necessity. This section guides you through the principles of interoperability, the importance of API-friendly AI, and the cutting-edge techniques that allow GenAI to be a cooperative player with the other software you use to get work done.

Integrating ChatGPT with other software

Integrating GenAI is like giving your software a brain transplant — it can analyze, learn, and even get smart about your business. Just remember to play it safe by adhering to responsible AI practices, including adhering to the highest of ethics and data privacy, and you'll be set to revolutionize your app with some serious AI smarts.

But how do you integrate GenAI with other software? It's much like integrating any other software. The precise method will vary depending on the software and GenAI model. But, in general, these are the most common options:

» **APIs:** Think of an API as a computer code that bridges or connects one software application and another. In this case, you use an API to connect a GenAI model or application with another software application. If you want to integrate or embed a GenAI application like ChatGPT, you can get the API you need from OpenAI here: `https://openai.com/api`. Or, you can use a third-party connector (a pre-designed API connection for a specific software) like ChatGPT Connector available on Microsoft AppSource: `https://appsource.microsoft.com/en-us/product/office/wa200005635?tab=overview`. You'll see several connectors are offered on this one (for example, a Salesforce Connector, NetSuite Connector, Dynamics 365 Connector, I CRM for Outlook Connector, and `Monda.com` Connector). Connectors are easier to use than just the API because they simplify the process.

- » **Cloud AI tools:** The Cloud giants like AWS, Microsoft Azure, and Google Cloud have done the heavy lifting for you. They offer a toolbox full of AI goodies — like AWS's Comprehend tool for document content extraction, AWS's Lex to build conversational interfaces, and AWS's Rekognition to add image analysis — that you can just plug into your app, no PhD required.

- » **Slack integration:** A common integration for GenAI-based chatbots is with Slack, a messaging app for businesses. Slack offers a range of APIs that enable a variety of integrations with its platform.

- » **Software libraries and SDKs:** For those who like to roll up their sleeves, AI frameworks like TensorFlow and PyTorch are your building blocks for custom-made GenAI features. They're a bit techier, but you get to tailor-make your AI just the way you want it.

- » **Embedded systems:** Need your AI to work without the internet, like on a smart toaster or a self-driving car? Embedding GenAI models onto these devices lets them think on their feet — or wheels — without phoning home to the cloud every time. You can also embed GenAI applications into websites and applications.

- » **Cloud-based machine learning platforms:** If you're playing in the enterprise sandbox or simply want to experiment there, platforms like Google Cloud AI, IBM Watson, AWS, and Azure Machine Learning are your all-in-one AI playgrounds. They're packed with tools for training, deploying, and fine-tuning your GenAI models; they keep an eye on things to make sure your AI stays sharp.

- » **Microservices architecture:** By breaking down your GenAI into microservices, you can mix and match AI features like Lego blocks. This is great for scaling and managing without turning your software into a spaghetti mess. Container tech like Docker and Kubernetes are the secret sauce for easy deployment.

- » **Custom integration with business systems:** Sometimes, you need an AI that fits your business like a glove. That's when you embed GenAI into your Customer Relationship Management (CRM) software, Enterprise Resource Planning (ERP) software, or other enterprise-grade or departmental specialized software or to automate the nitty-gritty details, make customers feel special, or streamline operations.

- » **Monitoring and testing:** No matter how you integrate, keep your AI under surveillance with regular monitoring and testing. This ensures your GenAI is on its best behavior and stays accurate, reliable, and ready for a tune-up when needed.

Bringing in autonomous AI agents

In the near future, integrating GenAI will become less of an issue. That's because autonomous AI agents, which are already a reality, will automatically integrate, embed, and extract info from applications in real time as they go about completing their assigned tasks. I share this information now so you'll be prepared for the approaching transitional period wherein you may need to integrate GenAI with some software, but also run AI agents without integrating anything. Eventually, integrating will go the way of defragging and Dodo birds.

Autonomous AI agents are digital dynamos capable of tackling tasks from content creation to personal finance and transportation bookings, all on their own. Imagine a world in which your AI sidekick doesn't just wait for your command but takes the initiative, streamlining your workflow and making your coffee — okay, maybe not the coffee part yet but definitely writing the prompts for you. Don't panic; most autonomous AI agents will require your approval before acting on anything, so you'll still be in charge.

The big deal about AI agents is that they'll reshape the way your work and life get done. They can be used to orchestrate and optimize tasks in everything from social media to complex simulations. For example, instead of using an app — or maybe several apps — to find available flights and book one, you'll simply tell the AI agent you want to attend a professional conference on specific dates and within a set budget, and the agent can

>> Register you for the conference and find and book the travel arrangements for you.

>> Schedule dinners and meetings and invite specific conference attendees to join you, all on its own.

>> If your flight is late, reschedule your ride and notify the dog boarder of a delayed pickup.

REMEMBER

AI agents are not just changing the game; they're creating a whole new league in which automation is the MVP.

In the not-so-distant future — you're talking two to three years — these autonomous agents might just be the norm, revolutionizing business models and processes and reshaping the future of work with their automation superpowers and next-level task handling.

In a nutshell, getting to grips with the what, how, and wow of autonomous AI agents is key as they're not just a passing fad; they're the future of efficiency and automation.

Keeping Up with the Pace of GenAI Advancements

In the quickly evolving world of generative AI (GenAI), staying current is not just about keeping your tech trendy; it's about harnessing the power of innovation to stay ahead of the curve.

And staying abreast of change isn't just about learning the latest and greatest new capabilities or models in GenAI. It's staying ahead of model drift, too. Actually, "model drift" should be called "data drift" because it actually means that a growing pile of data is more recent and more vital to your GenAI model's responses than the now outdated data it was trained on. Even if you decide to stick with the model you like, you'll need to retrain it on more recent data from time to time. But GenAI advancements will affect how you handle model retraining, too. It's just another reason to stay on top of GenAI advancements.

Staying informed on GenAI trends

As GenAI technologies evolve at breakneck speed, it's crucial to remain informed and agile to harness their full potential. The following sections offer suggestions for how you can keep your finger on the pulse of GenAI advancements and ensure you're not left behind in the digital dust.

REMEMBER

As you navigate this ever-changing terrain, remember that each step taken to stay informed is a step toward mastering the art and science of generative AI. The future is being written in the language of AI, and by staying informed, you're ensuring that you have a say in how it's being shaped — and that you'll have the skills you need to adapt to the changes it brings to work and life in general.

Follow the leaders

The GenAI field is led by a vanguard of innovative companies, from tech titans like OpenAI and Google to lesser-known startups that are redefining the boundaries of what's possible. To stay ahead, it's essential to monitor these organizations closely.

Subscribing to their newsletters is a great start; it's like getting a direct line to their latest breakthroughs and strategic moves. Social media platforms are the stages in which these companies perform daily — follow their accounts for real-time updates, insights, and announcements.

Moreover, webinars offer a front-row seat to the minds shaping the future of GenAI, providing a platform to learn, question, and connect with the experts driving the industry forward.

Dive into research papers

The backbone of GenAI innovation lies in the rigorous academic research that propels it. Journals and conferences such as NeurIPS, ICML, and JMLR are the treasure troves where the seeds of tomorrow's GenAI applications are sown.

Platforms like arXiv and ResearchGate democratize access to these cutting-edge insights, allowing anyone from anywhere to tap into the collective intelligence of the AI research community.

By delving into these resources, you're not just observing the evolution of GenAI; you're participating in it. Remember, the research of today lays the groundwork for the disruptive technologies of tomorrow.

Engage with the community

The GenAI community is a melting pot of ideas, debates, and collaborative problem-solving. Online forums and communities such as Reddit's r/Machine Learning, r/Stack Overflow, or r/Cross Validation subreddits – communities — are bustling hubs where practitioners, enthusiasts, and scholars converge.

By joining these communities, you're signing up for an advanced class in the practical aspects of GenAI. Discussions here can range from troubleshooting code to ethical considerations of AI deployment.

Engaging with this community not only keeps you informed but also hones your ability to think critically and innovatively about the challenges and opportunities presented by GenAI.

Educational resources

In the realm of GenAI, education is a continuous journey. With platforms like LinkedIn Learning (where I am an instructor of several GenAI courses), Coursera, edX, and Udacity, learning is an on-demand service offering courses designed to sharpen your skills and expand your understanding of AI. These courses are often crafted by leading experts and institutions, ensuring you're learning from the best.

Podcasts and YouTube channels dedicated to AI are invaluable resources that provide a more casual yet informative take on the latest trends and topics in the field. They can be your companions during a commute or while you unwind, transforming downtime into an educational experience.

Preparing for the future of generative AI

GenAI is expanding at the relentless pace of a marathon. It's a long-distance but fast race that demands endurance, strategy, and continuous improvement.

As people prepare for the future of GenAI, they must approach it with the same dedication and foresight as elite athletes preparing for the rigors of the 26.2-mile challenge.

Here's how to stay in peak condition for the AI marathon that lies ahead.

Upskill continuously

In the dynamic world of GenAI, resting on your laurels is not an option. The field is in a state of perpetual evolution, with new models, frameworks, and tools emerging almost daily.

To keep pace, you must be a lifelong learner, regularly updating your skill set. This means not only mastering the basics but also staying abreast of the latest developments. If you work in data science, AI engineering, or AI development, you'll need to stay informed on the intricacies of neural networks, mastering the subtleties of natural language processing, or delving into the complexities of reinforcement learning. Keeping your skills updated can set you apart in the job market.

However, there is a huge demand for GenAI power-users, too. Keep your prompting skills sharp and polished. One way to do that is to study certain journalism skills such as subject interviewing, data journalism, and investigative reporting. Take it from me, a seasoned journalist, these skills are almost a perfect match for GenAI prompting skills. Additionally, practice your prompting — a lot. Like anything else, practice improves prompting skills. Almost every job going forward is going to require prompting and GenAI management skills, or in the case of autonomous AI agents, command skills that you can learn through prompting.

Adopt an agile mindset

Flexibility and agility are your best allies in a field characterized by rapid change. Today's groundbreaking innovation can quickly become yesterday's news.

Cultivating an agile mindset means being prepared to pivot when necessary and embracing change constantly. This adaptability should permeate your team and organizational culture, encouraging experimentation and learning from both successes and failures. By fostering an environment that values agility, you position yourself and your organization to respond swiftly to the shifting landscape of GenAI.

Invest in infrastructure

The computational demands of GenAI are substantial, and having the right infrastructure in place is crucial. This may involve leveraging cloud services that offer high computational power or investing in AI-optimized hardware to ensure that your technology stack can support advanced AI models.

As GenAI applications become more sophisticated, the need for robust and scalable infrastructure becomes increasingly important. This investment not only supports current projects but also lays the groundwork for future innovation.

If your organization is small, or if you are working solo, the cloud is your friend. Invest in premium versions of your favorite GenAI model. For example, as of this writing ChatGPT Plus is only $20 a month, and you get a lot more capabilities than the free version. Pony up the bucks and ride GenAI to your own version of victory!

Ethical considerations

As GenAI technologies become more integrated into our lives, their ethical implications grow more significant. Issues surrounding privacy, bias, and control are at the forefront of discussions about AI's role in society.

Staying informed about these ethical considerations is imperative. Engaging in conversations, contributing to policymaking, and advocating for the responsible use of GenAI are all ways to help shape a future in which AI is used ethically and beneficially. By understanding and addressing these concerns, people can ensure that GenAI serves the greater good and avoids potential pitfalls and harm to anyone.

Preparing for the future of GenAI requires a multifaceted approach that encompasses continuous learning, adaptability, strategic investment, and ethical vigilance.

IN THIS CHAPTER

» **Comparing ChatGPT versions**

» **Establishing a ChatGPT account**

» **Learning ChatGPT's user interface**

» **Choosing between features and options**

» **Making and managing ChatGPT outputs**

Chapter **4**

Introducing ChatGPT

The *Chat* in ChatGPT's name is a reference to its use of natural-language processing and natural-language generation. *GPT* stands for generative pretrained transformer, which is a deep learning neural network model developed by OpenAI, an American AI research and development company. You can think of GPT as the secret sauce that makes ChatGPT work as it does. In short, ChatGPT is a GPT-based chatbot.

ChatGPT is a huge phenomenon and a major paradigm shift in the accelerating march of technological progression. It's a chatbot that can run on one of several large language models (LLMs) developed and offered by a company called OpenAI. Like other GenAI chatbots, ChatGPT doesn't create original content in the purely creative sense; rather, it remixes data to produce new content that's calculated and contrived in response to a user's question or command — both of which are referred to as a prompt.

Users can (and often do) access ChatGPT directly online at `https://chat.openai.com/`, but it's also integrated with several existing applications. Typically, you can access ChatGPT embedded in other applications simply by signing onto that application in the usual way. The number of app integrations seems to grow every day as existing software providers hurry to capitalize on ChatGPT's popularity. ChatGPT can also be accessed via apps on mobile devices.

Comparing Different Account Versions of ChatGPT

ChatGPT offers several account versions to suit different user needs: Free Plus, Teams, Pro, and Enterprise. The free version of ChatGPT has received significant upgrades, but you may prefer the Plus version for its higher usage limits and additional features. Free users may also encounter slower response times during peak hours and more limited availability.

Here's a brief look at the paid versions of ChatGPT:

>> **ChatGPT Plus,** with a monthly subscription fee of $20, offers faster responses and priority access, which gives you more powerful and consistent performance. For businesses or collaborative settings, the ChatGPT Teams subscription plan offers more flexibility through multiuser access, administrative controls, and shared workspaces. The Teams version caters to groups working together on projects or customer support.

>> **ChatGPT Pro** comes at a much higher price. For $200 a month, you get "the best of OpenAI with the highest level of access," the company says. Currently, that means everything available in the ChatGPT Plus version and unlimited access to GPT-4o and o1 plus unlimited access to advanced voice and access to o1 pro mode. I haven't yet found sufficient need for the Pro features to justify the higher monthly subscription cost. But your mileage may vary.

>> **ChatGPT Enterprise,** for larger organizations, delivers advanced features such as unlimited access, longer inputs (prompts), integration options, enhanced security, higher customization, and comprehensive analytics. This version is designed for businesses with large-scale needs, including better privacy controls and support for more complex operations and larger or more numerous team collaborations. Pricing is customized for the organization's size and needs.

Setting Up an Individual Account

To set up an individual account and enter your first prompt, take the following steps:

1. **Go to** https://openai.com/blog/chatgpt.

   Returning users can go straight to https://chat.openai.com/ and skip the rest of the steps.

2. **Click the Try ChatGPT button. You don't have to create an account to try ChatGPT this way.**

REMEMBER

   However, this version is limited and not truly representative of the premium versions that have an escalating number of features to match the bigger price tags.

3. **Or, follow the prompts to create your OpenAI account.**

   After you have registered for an OpenAI account, select the subscription plan you prefer. The cost for a ChatGPT Plus subscription, as of this writing, is $20 per month. Other subscription plans are also available: Teams at $25 per month, Pro at $200 per month, and Enterprise, which requires a call with an OpenAI salesperson to get a quote on the price for your company needs. Having an OpenAI account also gives you access to other AI apps built on OpenAI models, such as DALL-E.

4. **When ChatGPT opens, enter your prompt in the prompt bar, as shown in Figure 4-1.**

   ChatGPT will then generate a response.

5. **If you want to continue the dialogue, enter another prompt.**

6. **When you're finished, rate the response by clicking the thumbs up or thumbs down icon.**

   Doing so helps fine-tune the AI model.

7. **When you're finished using ChatGPT, log out or simply close the window in your browser.**

WARNING

In some subscription plans, OpenAI's team can see any information you enter in the prompt and the entire conversation that ensues. They may use this data in training other AI models. See a key disclosure in OpenAI's privacy policy in Figure 4-2 and check out the full policy at https://openai.com/policies/row-privacy-policy/. When using ChatGPT, don't disclose anything you want to keep private or confidential.

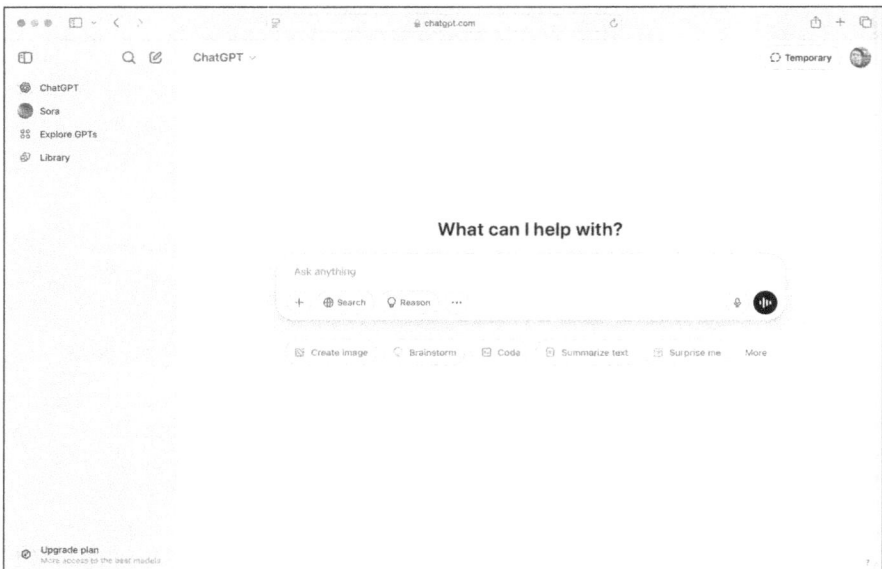

FIGURE 4-2:
A key disclosure
in OpenAI's
privacy policy
found in full at
https://openai.
com/policies/
row-privacy-
policy/.

A note about accuracy: Services like ChatGPT generate responses by reading a user's request and, in response, predicting the words most likely to appear next. In some cases, the words most likely to appear next may not be the most factually accurate. For this reason, you should not rely on the factual accuracy of output from our models. If you notice that ChatGPT output contains factually inaccurate information about you and you would like us to correct the inaccuracy, you may submit a correction request through privacy.openai.com or to dsar@openai.com. Given the technical complexity of how our models work, we may not be able to correct the inaccuracy in every instance. In that case, you may request that we remove your Personal Information from ChatGPT's output by filling out this form.

For information on how to exercise your rights with respect to data we have collected from the internet to train our models, please see this help center article.

Touring the User Interface

The following will guide you through the essential parts of the ChatGPT Plus user interface (UI) so you'll know where to find the information and features you need. Anywhere you encounter ChatGPT, such as embedded in other software or in other versions of ChatGPT, the UI will be similar.

You may want to refer to Figure 4-1 again because it's a screenshot of the full UI. What follows is a list of the parts of the UI with an explanation of each.

1. Far left of the UI at the top of the sidebar: This part of the UI contains a Close Sidebar button on the left, a chat search icon in the middle, and a New Chat button on the right, which starts a new chat rather than you simply continuing in the current chat session (see Figure 4-3).

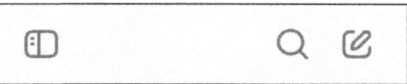

2. Directly below those buttons on the same sidebar are another New Chat start button and the Explore GPTs button (see Figure 4-4). The former is just an alternate way to start a new chat, whereas the latter takes you to the GPT Store, where you'll find a collection of GPT minis, which are smaller applications tailored to perform specific tasks. Whichever GPT minis you choose will also be listed here afterward, making it easier for you to return to those again later.

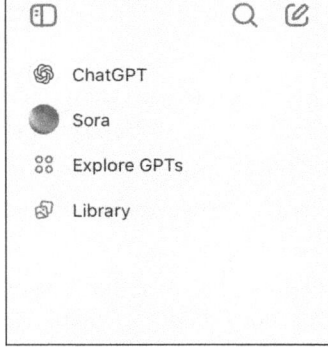

3. When you click on the Explore GPTs button, it will take you to the page shown in Figure 4-5. You can either use the search bar or simply scroll through the selection to find a GPT mini that's already customized to perform whatever task you need.

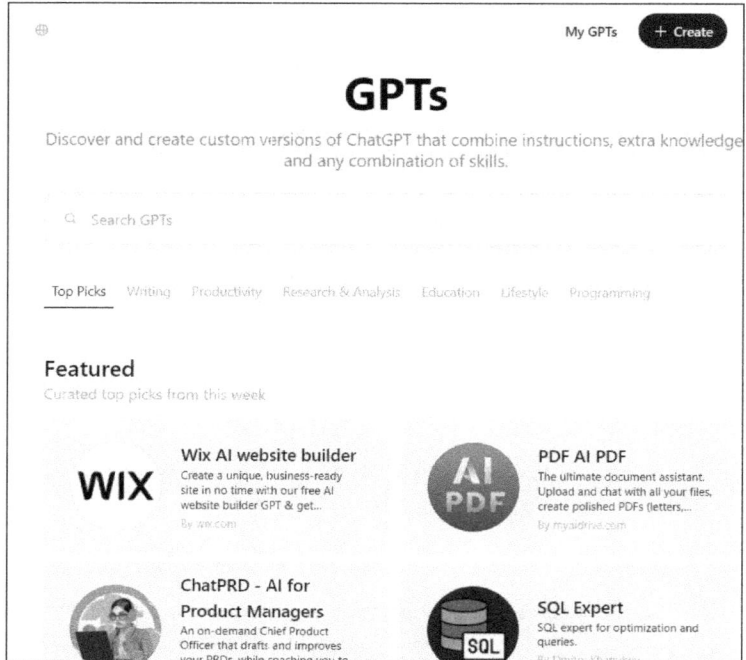

FIGURE 4-5:
A screenshot
of the GPT
Store page.

4. The rest of the sidebar lists your chat histories. You can revisit and resume any chat that's listed there. You can also archive, rename, or delete any chat by clicking on the three dots at the upper right of each chat and selecting an action from the drop-down options.

5. At the bottom of the sidebar is a button that enables you to upgrade your subscription at any time.

6. Moving right is the main body of the UI, which is everything on the UI that's to the right of the sidebar. At the top is a drop-down menu of OpenAI's generative AI models (Figure 4-6). Choose one for your chat to run on.

7. At the center of the UI main body is the OpenAI logo, which doesn't do anything, but it looks pretty (see Figure 4-7).

8. Beneath the logo are suggested prompts you can use as a demo of this application, or just because you're curious about that topic. Click on one if you want to see ChatGPT do its thing.

9. At the bottom of the UI main body is the prompt bar. This is where you'll type your query or command for ChatGPT to respond to. To continue the chat, simply prompt again after ChatGPT responds to your earlier prompt. To change the conversation, click on one of the two New Chat start buttons on the UI and detailed earlier in the UI tour list.

FIGURE 4-6:
The list of AI
model options
offered in the
drop-down menu
at the top left
center, which is to
say on the main
body of the UI.

FIGURE 4-7:
Screenshot of
the mid- to lower
center of the
UI showing the
OpenAI logo,
sample prompts,
the prompt bar,
disclaimer, and
help key.

10. Across the bottom of the prompt bar are three icons on the left and one on the far right (see Figure 4-8). The three on the left are a paper clip to attach files to the prompt, a toolbox to reveal tools you may want to use in the prompt like "search the web" and other GPT applications, and a standalone globe for direct access to an internet search. The single icon on the bottom far right of the prompt bar activates voice mode.

11. The question mark at the lower right of the UI reveals a menu of FAQs, help, release notes, terms and policies, and keyboard shortcuts.

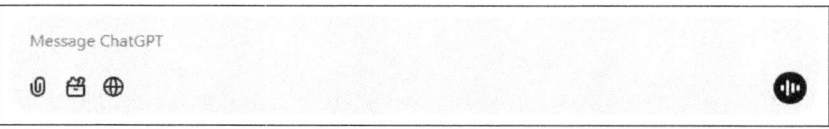

WARNING

ChatGPT generates rather than regurgitates content, which means it can make erroneous assumptions and responses that are commonly referred to as hallucinations. ChatGPT or any other generative AI model isn't an infallible source of truth, a trustworthy narrator, or an authority on any topic, even when you prompt it to behave like one. In some circumstances, accepting it as an oracle or a single source of truth is a grave error.

Selecting a GPT Model on the ChatGPT UI

Generative pre-trained transformers (GPTs) are an advanced type of artificial intelligence model with a core function of generating human-like text by predicting subsequent words from your prompt, thereby completing a pattern generated in that input sequence. But some advanced GPT models have expanded capabilities, including the ability to process and generate images. You interact with a GPT model through an application like ChatGPT, which is a GPT-based chatbot, or Dall-E, which is also accessible through the ChatGPT toolbox at the bottom of the prompt bar.

Model options in the drop-down menu

The drop-down menu on ChatGPT's UI offers several GPT model options, each with distinct capabilities, as listed in the following mini table.

The model options	Characteristics
GPT-4	An advanced model, capable of managing many complex tasks, such as in-depth analysis, writing tasks, code writing, and problem-solving.
GPT-4 Turbo	An optimized version of GPT-4, meaning it is designed to be faster, more efficient, and capable of handling longer contexts better than previous versions.
GPT-4o (aka Omni)	A newer model that's multimodal (meaning it can process more formats than just text) that's faster than GPT-4 Turbo.
GPT-4o mini	A lighter variant of GPT-4o because it's built on a small language model (SLM) rather than a large language model (LLM). In other words, GPT 4o mini is a downsized version of GPT 4o.

LLMs are large, general-purpose models. SLMs are typically but not always focused on specialized tasks with smaller computational requirements. SLMs are fast, efficient, and generally cheaper. Additionally, they're typically small enough to reside on a device rather than only in a datacenter.

TIP

Overall, you should select a model based on your project requirements. If you're just exploring ChatGPT capabilities, you'll usually find whatever GPT model is the default listing on the UI to be sufficient. Typically, users find GPT-4o to be the ideal choice for most tasks.

The GPT's latest release

The latest release is GPT-o1 (formerly Strawberry) and is the start of a new model series. It aims to improve performance primarily through "spending more time thinking," says OpenAI. But because GPTs don't "think," this really means that this new model series does deeper data analysis, uses increased contextualization, and focuses on improved analytical capabilities, primarily focused on areas like mathematics, coding, and scientific problem-solving.

The GPT-o1 model often responds slower to more complex prompts because it's delving deeper into data analysis in search of an appropriate response. However, many users experience no difference between GPT-4o and GPT-o1 in response speeds because the prompts they use aren't complex enough to require a heftier model workout.

The GPT-o1-mini and GPT-4o-mini models are optimized for speed and efficiency, focusing on lighter tasks that require quick responses. They may not be as robust in handling complex queries as their bigger brethren of a similar name, but each excels in providing answers more efficiently.

Considering GPT Minis in the GPT Store on the ChatGPT UI

This part can get a bit confusing. As explained in the previous section, GPTs are a type of AI model that ChatGPT runs on. But here, the term GPTs is used to denote a version of ChatGPT that's tailored for a specific purpose that you can use within ChatGPT. I know, right??! You would think OpenAI would choose a different moniker for these to cut down on the confusion, but alas, no.

Each of these GPTs is optimized for particular work processes such as writing, coding, and providing expert advice in areas such as marketing and data analysis.

Feel free to look around the GPT Store to see what's available by clicking on the Explore GPTs button on the sidebar on the left side of the ChatGPT UI or by going to `https://chatgpt.com/gpts`. You can elect to use one of these for your project or return to the original ChatGPT UI and work with that.

Should you want to experiment or use one, following is some simple guidance on selecting GPTs from ChatGPT's GPT Store:

1. **Start by clicking on the Explore GPTs button.**

    You'll find the button near the top of the sidebar on the left side of the ChatGPT UI. That will take you to the GPT Store. You can use search or the topic buttons to quickly move to the type of GPTs you seek, or you can simply scroll to discover all the different options.

2. **Check the descriptions.**

    Each GPT has a short description of what it's designed to do. Before selecting a GPT, read through these descriptions to see if that particular GPT fits the task you have in mind. For example, if you need help drafting an email, you might pick a GPT focused on writing. If you're doing data analysis or writing computer code, choose one tailored for that purpose.

3. **Consider user reviews.**

    Some of the GPTs have reviews or ratings that indicate what other users think. Higher ratings usually indicate more reliable performance for that specific type of task. Click on a GPT to see its rating and how many other people use it.

4. **Start with general GPTs and then get specific.**

    If you're unsure where to start, try a general-purpose GPT first. You may want to return to the ChatGPT UI and use that to see if this general-purpose chatbot is sufficient for your needs. General-purpose GPTs and the main ChatGPT chatbot are great for everyday questions and tasks. After you become familiar with them, you can explore more specialized GPTs for complex or niche tasks. In other words, you don't have to select any of the GPTs from the GPT Store. Those are simply there in case you want to use a more specialized application.

TIP

You can copy the output from one or more GPTs and combine it with the response from ChatGPT for a better overall result. Or you can use one or more responses from GPTs as part or all of a prompt in ChatGPT, or vice versa. In the end, your content will likely be much more informed, creative, and polished if you use your own creativity and critical thinking to build upon outputs/responses rather than accept any one response "as is."

5. **Switch GPTs if needed.**

You aren't stuck with the first GPT you choose. If the one you selected isn't quite working for what you need, feel free to switch to another one at any time. And don't feel like you must always use certain GPTs in future chats. Check the GPT Store often for new GPTs or upgrades to your favorites.

6. **Experiment with new GPTs.**

Some GPTs may be designed for emerging or niche needs. Don't hesitate to try out new ones for special projects or if you're curious about their capabilities. Besides, doing so may spark a new creative idea for you. Kick the tires, take GPTs out for a drive, keep what you need, and abandon what you don't.

7. **Remember that ChatGPT will collect the GPTs for you.**

Once you select a GPT, ChatGPT will list it in the sidebar of its UI. That way you don't have to remember the GPT's name or where to find it. A simple click takes you right to it. If you don't want a GPT to show in the sidebar, roll over the GPT in the sidebar list to reveal three dots. Roll over or click the dots to reveal the options "keep in sidebar" and "hide from sidebar." Click on your selection.

Rendering ChatGPT Outputs to Final Forms

ChatGPT specializes in generating and processing text based on your prompts. If you select a multimodal model, ChatGPT can work with more than text. Although the responses can be amazing, they aren't typically useful in this form. This means you'll likely need to take additional steps outside of ChatGPT. Here are some examples of why outputs typically need to be copied and pasted or otherwise transferred to other software for production tasks like layout and publication:

>> **Specialized tools:** Layout and publication often require specialized software, such as Adobe InDesign, for print layout or WordPress for web content

management. These tools offer advanced features for design and formatting that aren't part of ChatGPT's text generation capabilities.

>> **Complex formatting:** Professional layouts involve intricate design elements like columns, margins, fonts, and graphics. ChatGPT can't manipulate visual elements or handle such detailed formatting.

>> **Interactivity and media:** Modern content often includes interactive features or multimedia, such as hyperlinks, videos, and animations. Embedding and properly configuring these elements typically requires software that's specifically designed for interactive content creation.

>> **Platform-specific requirements:** Different platforms have unique requirements for content publication. For instance, an ebook requires a different format than a blog post. ChatGPT isn't built to understand or adhere to these platform-specific nuances.

>> **User experience:** Ensuring a good user experience involves testing how content looks and functions on various devices and browsers. ChatGPT doesn't have the capability to test or optimize content across different environments.

>> **Compliance and accessibility:** Content often needs to meet certain compliance standards, such as the Americans with Disabilities Act (ADA) for accessibility or General Data Protection Regulation (GDPR) for privacy. Specialized software can ensure that the final product complies with these regulations.

>> **Collaboration and workflow:** Production processes often involve multiple stakeholders, including designers, editors, and legal teams. Software designed for production typically includes features for collaboration and workflow management that ChatGPT doesn't have.

>> **Quality control:** Before publication, ChatGPT-generated content must go through a quality control process. This might include proofreading, fact-checking, and design review, which are tasks that require human judgment and tools beyond ChatGPT's text-based capabilities.

>> **Final output and distribution:** Finally, the content needs to be exported in a format suitable for distribution, such as PDF for print or HTML for the web. ChatGPT doesn't handle file conversions or distribution logistics.

ChatGPT can generate helpful content elements, but taking it to production level involves a range of tasks that are visual, interactive, and specific to the platform. These tasks require the use of specialized software to ensure the content is well designed, compliant, and optimized for the end user's experience. ChatGPT simply can't perform these tasks.

PROS AND CONS OF CHATGPT

ChatGPT is widely used by millions of individuals and organizations worldwide. However, like all technologies, ChatGPT has both pros and cons to consider. By being aware of these, you can leverage the good, plan how to offset the bad, and increase the odds that all will go well with your projects!

Pros	Cons
Fast responses	Sometimes inaccurate
Delivers unified answer	Varying quality
Conversational	Sometimes repetitive or offensive
Wide range of capabilities	Convincing even when wrong
Many applications	Conversations aren't private
Generates content	Not permitted by many companies who fear liability issues from wrong content

Chapter **5**

Getting Started with Microsoft Copilot

icrosoft Copilot is an umbrella brand name for all of Microsoft's AI-powered chatbots. Chatbots such as Copilot and similar products from OpenAI, Google, Apple, and many others have the potential to change the way people get work done. At their best, AI chatbots can enhance productivity, learning, and creativity. At their worst, they can produce low-quality text and images, confidently answer questions with fabricated data, and displace human jobs.

In this chapter, you learn some of the ways that you can access Microsoft Copilot, and you get an overview of its history, capabilities, benefits, and limitations.

Defining Copilot

In 2019, Microsoft invested in the then-tiny AI startup called OpenAI. Microsoft provided billions of dollars, and OpenAI ran its systems on Microsoft's computers. In 2021, Microsoft exclusively licensed OpenAI's GPT-3 model, which was used to create OpenAI Codex. OpenAI Codex was subsequently used by

GitHub — a subsidiary of Microsoft that provides tools and hosting for computer programmers — to create a computer programming assistant called GitHub Copilot, shown in Figure 5-1.

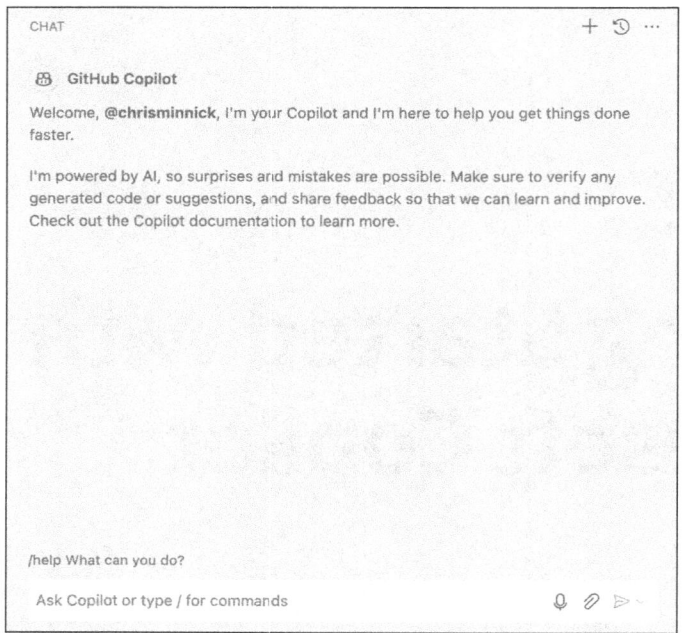

CHAT   + ↺ ···

🐙 **GitHub Copilot**

Welcome, **@chrisminnick**, I'm your Copilot and I'm here to help you get things done faster.

I'm powered by AI, so surprises and mistakes are possible. Make sure to verify any generated code or suggestions, and share feedback so that we can learn and improve. Check out the Copilot documentation to learn more.

/help What can you do?

Ask Copilot or type / for commands   🎤 📎 ▷

FIGURE 5-1:
GitHub Copilot.

REMEMBER

Although GitHub Copilot and Microsoft Copilot are similar in that they both use OpenAI's technology for understanding and generating language, they're two different products. GitHub Copilot is optimized to help with the writing of programming code, and Microsoft Copilot is optimized for chatting with people and generating written and spoken words in human languages.

Several months after GitHub Copilot was rolled out as a plugin for Microsoft's Visual Studio Code editor, OpenAI released the first version of ChatGPT for use by the public. ChatGPT became the fastest-growing consumer internet app of all time — gaining 100 million monthly users in just two months.

With its unprecedented ability to respond to user queries with human-like text, ChatGPT became a cultural sensation and possibly even a threat to the traditional search engines created by Google and Microsoft.

Microsoft responded to ChatGPT by redesigning its Bing search engine. *Bing Chat*, as it was called, was rolled out starting in February 2023 and gained its first 100 million active users within months. The early version of Bing Chat tended to produce false data (also known as *hallucinations*) and troubling responses during chats, including, as reported by Kevin Roose in a *The New York Times* article, acting like a "moody, manic-depressive teenager who has been trapped, against its will, inside a second-rate search engine."

TIP

Hallucinations, in AI lingo, are defined as incorrect or misleading information generated by AI. They're caused by a variety of factors, including insufficient training, incorrect assumptions, and biases in the data used to train the AI model.

Microsoft clamped down on much of Bing Chat's tendency to go off the rails and rebranded it as Microsoft Copilot. The current homepage for Microsoft Copilot (`https://copilot.microsoft.com`) is shown in Figure 5-2.

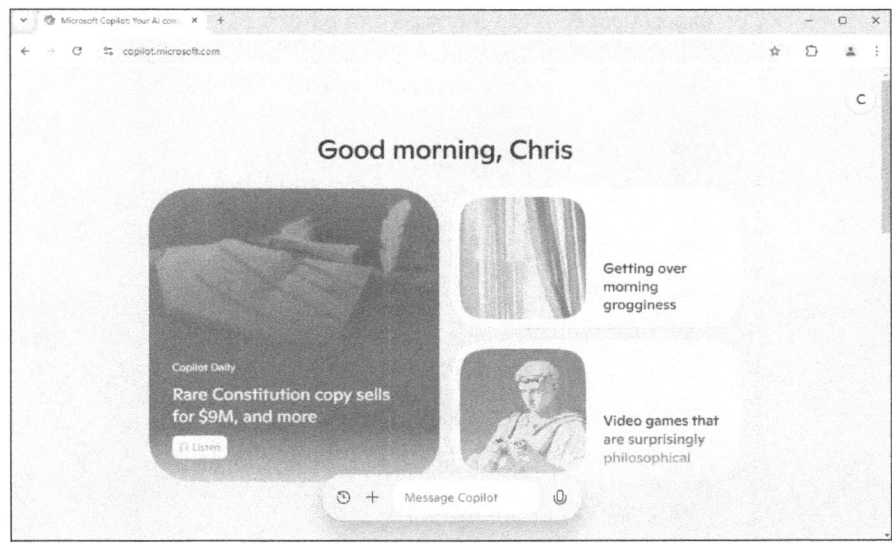

FIGURE 5-2:
Microsoft Copilot
on the web.

Overview of Microsoft Copilot

Copilot has been integrated into many of Microsoft's products and can be helpful with a wide variety of tasks. In fact, there are so many possible ways to use Copilot that the possibilities can sometimes seem overwhelming. AI chatbots are a fundamentally different way of interacting with computers than most people are used to, so it can be helpful to look at them as if they were traditional computer software and start by talking about the features and what makes Microsoft Copilot different from its competition.

Core functionalities and benefits

The most basic function of any chatbot, whether it's powered by artificial intelligence or not, is to respond to human speech or writing (which is also known as *natural language*) with easy-to-understand text or speech. The quality of a chatbot can be measured by how human-like its responses are.

The current crop of AI chatbots can all generate highly convincing natural language responses to people's questions and requests.

The voice or text input a user of a chatbot gives to the chatbot, whether it's a question ("How tall is Mount Everest?") or an instruction ("Summarize this email ") is called a *prompt*. The primary way for people to interact with chatbots is through *prompting*.

Beyond its core ability to respond to prompts in natural language, Microsoft Copilot has exciting additional capabilities that make it stand out in usefulness, especially when it's integrated into other Microsoft products.

Some of the features of Copilot include the following:

>> Performs web searches by using Bing

>> Integrates with other AI tools to create original images and music

>> Writes original text or rewrites existing text

>> Cites the sources of the text it generates

>> Personalizes its interactions with you based on previous interactions and documents you work on

>> Translates text between different languages

>> Supports plugins that expand Copilot's capabilities

>> Supports user-created chatbots

Key differentiators from other AI assistants

The main thing that makes Microsoft Copilot more useful than other AI assistants is that it is integrated into Microsoft Windows and other Microsoft programs. This integration gives Copilot the ability to not only generate text and images, but also to control certain aspects of the software it's integrated into. For example,

>> When using a non-integrated chatbot, such as ChatGPT, you can ask for text for a PowerPoint slide that you then need to copy into PowerPoint and format manually.

>> With Microsoft 365 Copilot, you can ask for PowerPoint slides or an entire presentation, and the Copilot assistant will create the new slides, format them for you, and insert them directly into your presentation. Even better, Copilot can access and use other documents you've created while creating the new slides.

Another key factor that distinguishes Copilot from many other chatbots is that Copilot has access to the data in Microsoft Bing. By augmenting the data it was originally trained on with search results from Bing, Copilot can answer questions about the latest news and other developments, whereas other models have a "cut-off date" beyond which they can only speculate (or hallucinate).

Understanding how Copilot works

Chatbots like Microsoft Copilot and ChatGPT are far superior to their predecessors, such as Office Assistant, aka "Clippy" (shown in Figure 5-3). Microsoft integrated Clippy into Microsoft Office applications from version 97 to 2003, and it proved to be more annoying than helpful in most cases.

FIGURE 5-3:
Original Office Assistant, also known as "Clippy."

The reasons for Clippy's failure have been studied exhaustively, but the crux of it is that Clippy was intrusive and would appear whenever it detected that you were doing something (such as writing a letter) that it was supposed to be able to help with. But then, when you agreed to let Clippy help you, all it could do was reference official Microsoft Office documentation, which wasn't helpful for much of anything.

The two most important factors that contributed to making the latest generation of AI so much better than Clippy (and all subsequent AI assistants) are

>> Vastly more data (and computing power) went into their training.

>> They take advantage of new AI techniques that allow them to consider context when generating responses.

Learning from all the data

The AI model behind Microsoft Copilot is named *Prometheus* and is OpenAI's technology combined with Bing's search index. The result is that Copilot has learned from and has access to a tremendous amount of data.

TECHNICAL STUFF

Although the relationship between training data size and a model's performance isn't simple, in general, larger models are able to gain a better picture of whatever they're designed to simulate (such as communicating using natural language, in the case of a chatbot).

Context is key

Even more important than simply throwing more data at an AI system is a set of techniques known as *attention,* which Google invented in 2017. In short, what attention techniques do is allow AI models to look at different parts of your input and their own output while figuring out what to say. For example, consider the following sentence:

"The bank can guarantee deposits will be safe because it has invested in secure vaults."

An AI model that uses attention mechanisms will know that "bank" refers to a financial institution rather than the bank of a river because of the other words in the sentence, such as "guarantee," "deposits," "safe," and "vaults." A model with attention also understands that the word "it" in this sentence refers back to "bank."

TIP

Because large language models (LLMs, such as CoPilot) can take context into account, providing sufficient context to the model in your prompts has become the single best way to improve the quality of responses you get to your prompts. The section "Basic commands and interactions," later in this chapter, offers a look at a series of human prompts and CoPilot responses.

Integration with Microsoft 365 apps

Microsoft 365 is the family of products and services that includes the productivity programs formerly known as Microsoft Office, as well as the OneDrive cloud storage service, the Microsoft Teams collaboration and conferencing program, the Outlook email and calendar program, and others. Microsoft 365 Copilot is available as an additional subscription.

Subscribing to Microsoft 365 Copilot activates the Copilot chatbot in each application and enables Copilot's built-in actions, which can perform different tasks depending on the application. Some of the features that Microsoft 365 Copilot enables include

>> **In Word,** Copilot can suggest different writing styles and formats, rewrite sentences or paragraphs, translate text into other languages, and convert text into tables.

>> **In Excel,** Copilot can analyze data to discover trends and insights you may have missed, create charts and graphs, and suggest formulas.

>> **In PowerPoint,** Copilot can suggest design ideas, create individual slides, convert Word documents into presentations, add animations, and even write speaker notes.

>> **In Teams,** Copilot can take meeting notes, transcribe recordings, summarize discussions, and suggest action items.

>> **In Outlook,** Copilot can summarize emails, assist you with writing emails, schedule meetings, and create reminders based on the content of your emails.

If you don't seek out Copilot's help while you're using Microsoft 365, it will remain quietly in the background. This is a welcome change from the overly eager assistant days of Clippy, but it also makes it important for users to educate themselves about what Copilot is capable of helping with.

In Chapters 2, 3, and 4 of Book 3, you experiment with Copilot's integration with Microsoft 365 and start to see its amazing capabilities as well as its sometimes frustrating limitations.

Signing Up for Copilot

Signing up to use Copilot couldn't be easier. I mean that literally, because you don't need any kind of account to try it out. All you need to do is open any web browser and go to `https://copilot.microsoft.com`. The free and logged-out version of Copilot Chat, shown in Figure 5-4, is limited compared to the version you get when you log in with a Microsoft account or buy a subscription to Copilot Pro.

In this section, you learn how to access Copilot, how to sign in to Copilot, and whether you should subscribe to Copilot Pro.

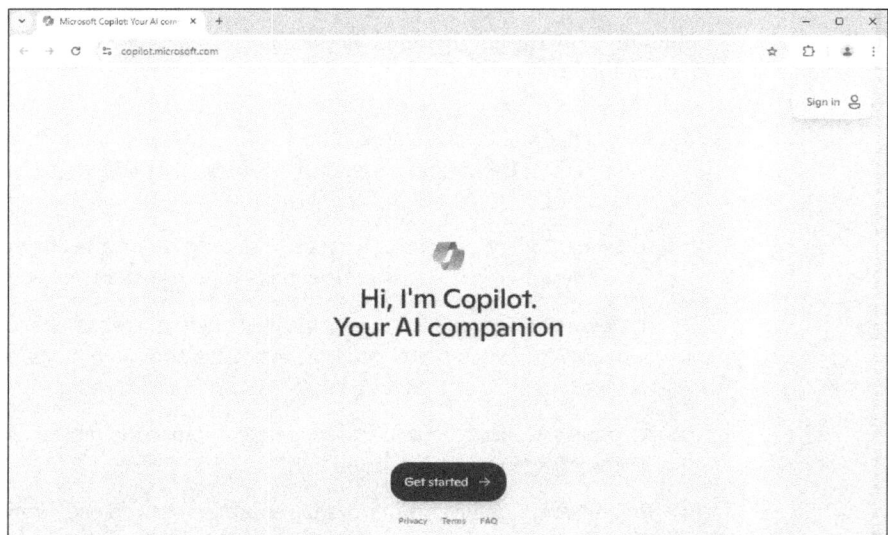

FIGURE 5-4:
The free version
of Copilot Chat.

Installing Copilot

Because Copilot Chat and Microsoft 365 Copilot both run in your web browser, there's no need to install anything to use either of them. Although the Copilot Chat experience will be nearly the same in any web browser you use, Copilot has integrations with Microsoft's Edge browser that may provide some incentive for users to choose to work with Copilot in Edge. If you have a strong preference for using a browser other than Edge, however, you can use that browser.

Eligibility criteria

Although Bing Chat, as Copilot was previously known, was open to only a limited number of people during its early days, today, Copilot is available for free to anyone with access to a web browser or mobile device.

Subscription plans and pricing

If you use Copilot Chat while not signed in to a Microsoft Account, you're currently limited to just text input and responses. When you try to chat with Copilot by speaking or with images, you'll get a message asking you to log in, as shown in Figure 5-5.

Fortunately, there is an easy fix: Just log in to a free Microsoft account from within Copilot Chat. When you're logged in to Copilot Chat, you'll have access to additional features and settings and to your conversation history.

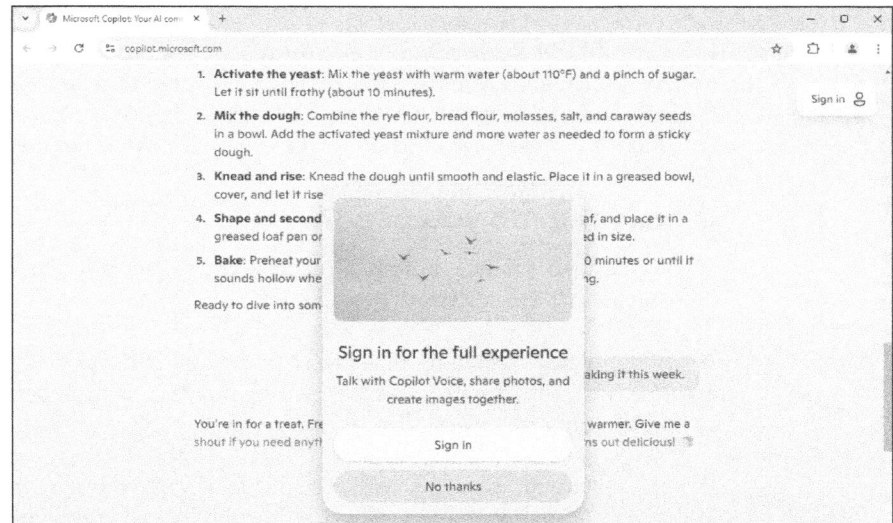

FIGURE 5-5:
You have to log
in to use certain
Copilot features.

Copilot Free

The free and logged-in version of Copilot has its limitations, too, however. These limitations include

» Limited access to the latest and greatest models during times of peak demand

» Limited boost tokens. *Boost tokens* are required for generating images, songs, and other creative content in Copilot.

» No access to Microsoft 365 Copilot

» No custom Copilots. Custom Copilots are specialized AI assistants that users of Copilot Pro can create. You learn more about custom Copilots and how to create them in Book 7, Chapter 4.

Copilot Pro

Subscribing to Copilot Pro currently costs $20/month. The benefits of subscribing include

» Faster performance

» Access to the latest models during peak times

» Copilot access in Office apps

» 100 boost tokens per day, as opposed to the 15 tokens that free users have

If you're already a subscriber to Microsoft 365, you can subscribe to Microsoft 365 Copilot, which gives you the same benefits as Copilot Pro but that is also tuned for business use and integrates with your Microsoft 365 data. Microsoft 365 Copilot is $30/month per user, which is on top of your subscription to Microsoft 365 itself.

Which plan do you need?

If you're a business user and you already have a subscription to Microsoft 365, you should subscribe to Microsoft 365 Copilot.

If you don't have a business license to Microsoft 365 and you plan to do a lot of creative work with Copilot, such as creating images or songs, you should subscribe to Copilot Pro.

If you're just experimenting with Copilot and want to learn what it's capable of and won't be using it every day, the logged-in and free version is more than adequate for your needs.

Step-by-step sign-up process

To sign up for a Microsoft account and get full access to the free version of Copilot, visit `https://copilot.microsoft.com`. After you enter your name and select a voice for Copilot, you'll see a Sign In button in the upper-right corner of the screen, as shown in Figure 5-6.

TIP

If you prefer to sign up for and access Copilot using a mobile app, go to `https://www.microsoft.com/en-us/microsoft-copilot/for-individuals/copilot-app` to access a QR code you can scan with your mobile device to go directly to the app download page.

WHY YOUR COPILOT EXPERIENCE DIFFERS

If you see something in Copilot on your computer or at `https://copilot.microsoft.com` that's different from what I show in this book, it's likely because of an upgrade to Copilot that's happened in the time after I wrote the book.

Likewise, if you're not seeing a feature of Copilot that I describe in this book, that also may be because of an upgrade that's happened, or it may be because of an upgrade that hasn't happened for your Microsoft account yet.

FIGURE 5-6:
The Sign In
button at
copilot.
microsoft.com.

Follow these steps:

1. **Click the Sign In button and select whether you want to sign in with a personal account or a business account.**

   If you'll be signing up for a new account, click Sign In with a Personal Account.

   If you already have a Microsoft account, you may be logged in automatically at this point. If you don't have an account, you'll see the Sign In page, as shown in Figure 5-7.

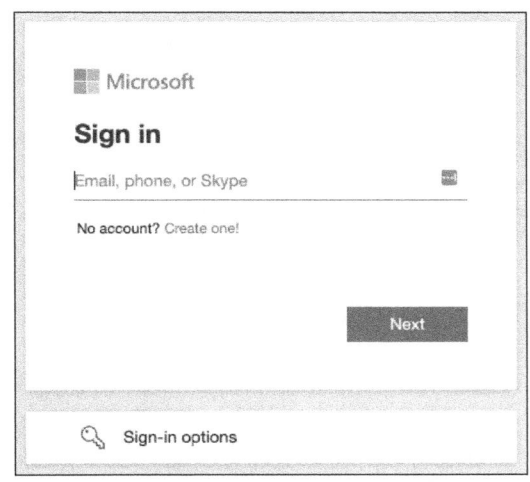

FIGURE 5-7:
The Microsoft
account sign in
page.

2. **To create a new Microsoft account, click the link labeled No Account? Create One!**

   The Create Account screen appears next, as shown in Figure 5-8.

3. **Set up an email address to use with Copilot.**

   You have options:

   - If you have an email address that you'd like to use as your Microsoft account user ID, you can enter it into this screen.

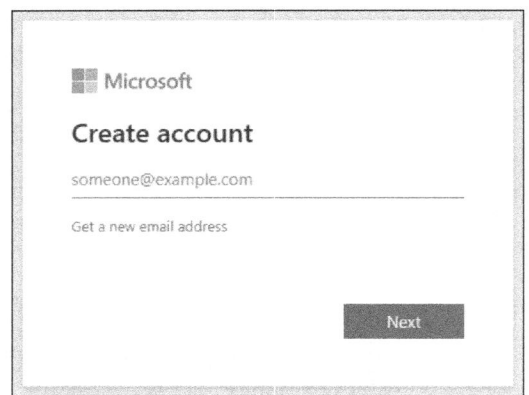

FIGURE 5-8:
The Create
Account screen.

- Otherwise, click the Get a New Email Address button to sign up for a free Outlook email address. The first screen of the new email address sign-up page will appear, as shown in Figure 5-9.

FIGURE 5-9:
Selecting a new
email address.

TIP

When you sign up for a new personal email address through Microsoft, you can choose between an outlook.com email address and a hotmail.com email address. Which one you choose won't affect how your email address functions in any way, but you might choose one or the other depending on whether your preferred email address is already taken for one of the domains. Or, you might just like the retro vibe of having a hotmail.com email address.

4. **On the next screen, select a strong password and check the box next to the question of whether you'd like to receive marketing emails from Microsoft.**

Make a note of the password you choose. You'll need this later to log in to your new email account.

5. **Traverse the remaining screens to finish signing up for Copilot**

You'll be asked on subsequent screens for your name and your birthdate.

Finally, there may be one last screen that asks you to solve a puzzle to prove that you're human. You've got this!

After you finish signing up for your new email address (which also serves as your new Microsoft account), you'll be returned to the Copilot homepage, and your first name will appear in the upper-right corner where the Sign In button previously was. Congratulations! In the next section, you can start seeing what Copilot can do!

Taking Copilot for a Test Flight

Now that you understand a bit about what Copilot is and how it works, and you've created your account and are logged in, it's time to try it out and see what it can do! The examples in this section use Copilot Chat while logged in to a free account.

Understanding why mine looks different

Because Copilot is an AI model, rather than a simple rules-based program, it will generate different content for the same question each time a question is asked (even if it's only slightly different). So, I show you the results that I get when I enter the same prompts I ask you to enter, but your results will be different. They may be better or worse, but I guarantee that they'll be different.

Prompting and interacting

Let's start with something short and simple. There's not much that's shorter or simpler (at least conceptually) than a haiku, so let's ask Copilot to write some poetry.

Find the input box labeled "Ask Me Anything. . ." at the bottom of the Copilot Chat window and type the following into it (feel free to customize the topic for one of your favorite things!):

Write a haiku about sushi.

When I tried this, I got the following result:

Certainly! Here's a haiku about sushi:

🍣 *Rice, fish, seaweed hug, Soy sauce whispers on my tongue, Sushi love blooms bright.*

Feel free to ask if you'd like more creative content or have any other requests! ☺

This is okay, I suppose. But, I kind of prefer my poetry with a laugh. So, try giving the following prompt:

Write a funny haiku about sushi.

Here's Copilot's response:

Certainly! Here's a playful haiku about sushi:

🍣 *Rolling down my plate, Avocado slips away, Chasing sushi dreams.*

Feel free to ask for more creative content or any other requests! ☺

Much better! Notice how just the addition of one word (funny) dramatically changed the output and improves it (in my opinion). Let's see if we can get something even better or more descriptive. Here's the next prompt I gave:

Write an ironic haiku about sharing sushi.

With this prompt, I really have no expectations or idea about what I'm looking for. But I do know that my favorite kind of humor is ironic, and one of my least favorite things is having to share sushi (because I want it ALL!). Here's the response I got:

🍣 *Chopsticks duel begins, Sharing sushi? Not today, Mine, all mine, I say.*

Feel free to ask for more creative content or any other requests! ☺

Again, this is pretty good. My choice of words may be a little more risqué than what Copilot is allowed to use, but I think we've managed to get as close to a decent poem as can be expected.

Feel free to continue experimenting with this prompt or other prompts as long as you like. You can also try out some of the other prompt engineering techniques you learn throughout this book, including in Chapters 2 and 6 of this book.

IN THIS CHAPTER

» **Prompting with the result in mind**

» **Understanding all the ways to target and add data**

» **Adjusting the AI's approach to interpreting data**

» **Changing data influence to direct responses**

Chapter **6**

Learning Advanced Prompting

n Chapter 2 of this mini-book you learned basic and intermediate prompting skills. In this chapter, you learn advanced prompting skills and some unexpected ways to boost the power in your prompts by using memory features and temperature settings. Don't worry. It's not as hard as it may sound. You can start using these techniques right away, too!

Starting at the End: Defining Desired Outputs before Prompting

If you want to make sure that GenAI results take the direction you want, give it a clear sense of the destination. After all, it's impossible to plan the best path to take if you have no idea where you want to go.

Even if you're using GenAI to explore a topic or dive deep into data discovery, you should be clear about your reason for doing so. In other words, have a point to the exercise before prompting. Otherwise, you'll find yourself adrift, riding the wind or an intellectual whim, and in danger of spending hours falling down the notorious virtual rabbit holes. Of course, rabbit holes are okay if you have time to wander about.

But for most, GenAI is a tool to get work done. If that's what you use it for, you'll want to take the most efficient and direct path to your end goal. For example, if you're looking for a comprehensive explanation of a scientific concept, it's important to specify not just the concept itself but the depth of the explanation you need, the context in which you're going to use the information, and any aspects you're interested in. This level of detail in the prompt guides a chatbot to generate a more fitted and useful response. Keep in mind that adding this level of detail to one or more prompts requires some thought and planning. Rarely will you or anyone else be able to capture all these details on a whim. It's easy to forget or overlook an important element in the moment.

To fully grasp this concept of working backward from result to query — or in the case of GenAI from response to prompt — consider why you're doing this exercise at all. Odds are that you've already formulated certain elements like these:

>> A specific idea

>> A concept

>> An execution method

>> Formats or mediums

>> The target audience

>> A specific message

Combining those elements (however many or few) defines your end goal, which in turn informs and defines what you ultimately want in an AI response. Start there.

REMEMBER

When you have an end vision in mind, start planning your prompts in a way that points you toward that destination. You'll likely discover that you can take several routes in prompting to get you there. Sort and choose from your prompt strategies according to the requirements that mean the most to you. Perhaps you're looking for the most efficient prompting path (one that uses fewer tokens) or the path that allows the AI chatbot to be more creative (meaning it can stray further in its interpretations of the prompt and the data).

If you want to learn more about this prompting technique and a variety of approaches — like the Inverted V and decision theory — read *Decision Intelligence For Dummies.*

If you don't care to dive that deep into the science of decision-making and keeping AI on track, suffice it to say that beginning at the end will give you the best start in accomplishing what you want in both advanced prompting and content engineering.

TIP

Iterative prompting is a good fit for this approach once you have a well-defined end goal. Start with a broad prompt and then progressively narrow the focus in subsequent prompts based on the chatbot's responses until you reach the output you desire.

Managing Data for Targeted Impact on Outputs

The way you present information and the kind of data you provide can dramatically shape the responses you receive from your GenAI model. Managing and supplementing data in your prompts is one way to significantly influence the outputs. You can do this in several ways:

>> **Include context within your prompts.** By providing background information or specifying the framework in the prompt, you can shape its responses better. For example, if you're asking about renewable energy, mentioning whether you're interested in its environmental impact, economic benefits, or technological challenges will steer a GenAI chatbot to consider data within those parameters and focus on the relevant aspects. Another way is to use clarifying follow-up questions in subsequent prompts. Consider asking for more details, requesting examples, or asking the chatbot to compare and contrast concepts.

>> **Supplement data in your prompts** by providing specific examples, scenarios, reports, or data points for the GenAI model to consider. If you're discussing a complex issue like climate change, you might provide a hypothetical scenario or a case study, or name specific sources for the model to use.

REMEMBER

These hints will point the *large language model* (LLM, the deep-learning base structure for GenAI) to the angle you're interested in exploring. If you prompt an LLM to provide data and resources in its responses, be sure to include a command for it to cite its sources. This will help you not only to fact-check responses but also to dive deeper into the details. Adding constraints to prompts by setting boundaries is another powerful technique. For example, you might ask for a summary suitable for a child, a detailed report for an expert, or a persuasive argument for a skeptic.

>> **Incorporate recent data or findings** that may not be within the model's training data as a valuable strategy. Because GenAI models are trained up to a certain point in time, they may not have access to the latest information. By providing updated facts, figures, or developments in your prompt, or by using a chatbot that is connected to the internet, you can make responses as current and relevant as possible.

>> **Use prompts to correct or counteract biases.** If you notice that the model's responses seem to lean in a certain direction, you can prompt the app to consider alternative perspectives or to provide a more balanced viewpoint. This is particularly important in fields in which new research or social changes might shift the understanding of a topic.

REMEMBER

Think of your prompts as tools to sculpt an LLM's responses. Be mindful of the information you include, the questions you ask, and the constraints you set. This will help you to sharpen the model's focus and tailor its outputs to your specific needs and objectives. Remember, the more targeted your prompts, the more targeted the outputs will be.

You have two more sophisticated methods to manage and supplement data to shape outputs: providing supplemental data in custom instructions and using a technique known as *retrieval-augmented generation*, or *RAG*.

>> **Incorporating supplemental data directly in your custom instructions can be a game-changer.** As mentioned earlier in this section, embedding additional information, such as recent statistics or findings, within your prompts is effectively updating the LLM's knowledge base.

However, this approach has limitations. The LLM can interpret and use only the data you provide within the scope of its abilities, and it may not always understand or apply the data correctly, especially if it's complex or requires expert analysis. Further, the data you provide in prompts is only applied to that thread or conversation. If you start a new chat, you need to enter that data in a prompt again for it to apply to that conversation, too.

One way to overcome this is to enter the data in custom instructions so it will be applied to all conversations until you change the instructions. In ChatGPT, you find custom instructions in the drop-down menu under your picture or icon at the upper-right corner of the user interface, as shown in Figure 6-1. In recent versions, you see the Customize ChatGPT option in the drop-down menu instead of the Custom Instructions option.

>> *Retrieval-augmented generation*, **on the other hand, is like giving a GenAI chatbot a research assistant.** RAG allows the chatbot to pull in information from a large dataset or external sources in real time as it generates responses. This means that the model isn't just relying on the information it was trained on; it can access and use newer, supplemental data to inform its responses.

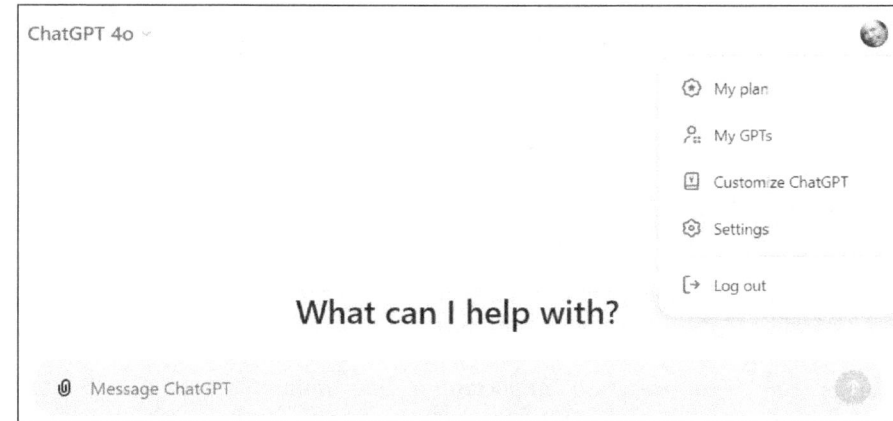

FIGURE 6-1:
Customize
ChatGPT from the
drop-down menu
in the upper-right
corner of the
window.

However, RAG also comes with limitations. The quality of the model's output depends heavily on the quality of the external sources it uses. If those sources are biased or inaccurate, the responses reflect that. Also, if the data is in nonstandard formats such as macro templates, spreadsheets, or proprietary formats, RAG in a GenAI chatbot might not directly accept or handle these forms. RAG works best with plain text or data that can be transformed into a textual format.

If neither of these methods meets your needs, you might consider looking for a specialized GenAI application designed for your specific domain, which would have been trained on a dataset that's more relevant to your field or area of interest. This could yield better results without the need for extensive customization or supplementation.

Another option is to ask your IT department or technical team to refine the model itself. This could involve retraining the AI on a dataset that you provide, define, or choose. However, this is a resource-intensive solution that requires expertise in machine learning and AI, and it's not feasible for every situation.

Adding Data to Prompts

You've already discovered that one reason you might want to add data to your prompts is to guide an LLM toward a specific context or to ensure that the response takes into account the most current information, which might be outside of its original training data. But the placement of data within a prompt can also significantly affect the quality and relevance of the LLM's response.

You can think of the strategic placement of different kinds of data as setting the stage for a play. You need to place each piece of information in an order much like a character whose entrance and position on stage can influence the unfolding of the story.

TIP

In short, best practice is to weave data throughout your prompt in a way that feels organic and logical, much like you're telling the chatbot a well-written story that includes your question or instructions at the end. Start by setting the stage, introduce key details where they have the most impact, and conclude with the direction you want the LLM to take.

However, it's important to stay mindful of GenAI's limitations. Overloading the prompt with too much data or excessively technical details can confuse the model and result in irrelevant, wrong, or incomplete responses. The art in effective prompting lies in providing just enough data to inform and guide the LLM's response without overshadowing your main question or request.

Using image inputs in ChatGPT prompts

Adding images to your prompt, if allowed by the AI chatbot you're using, is a good way to add data to your prompts without having to type all this information in the prompt bar. In ChatGPT, for example, you can click on the paper clip icon on the left side of the prompt bar to reveal the pull-down menu you see in Figure 6-2.

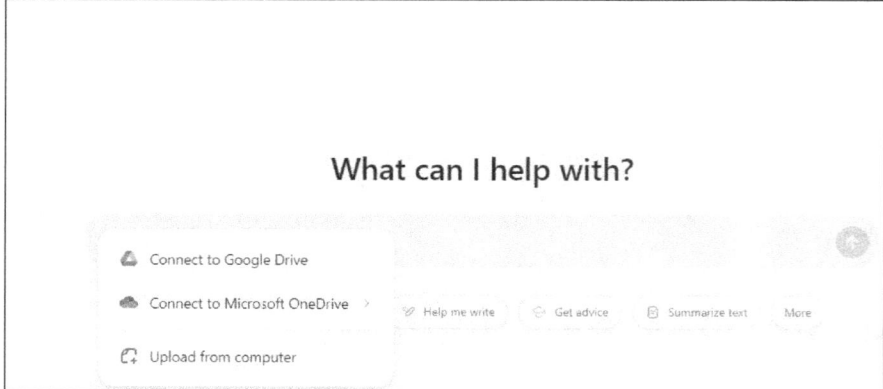

FIGURE 6-2:
You can add files to the prompt bar by selecting the Upload from Computer option in the pull-down menu.

Most chatbots are limited in how much they can work with in regard to prompt attachments, however, so don't stuff too much in there. Generally, the same advice I gave you earlier on making prompts concise applies to the prompt attachments. In other words, don't upload a long document when you really want the model to use only a page or two.

Pictures as prompt input

But you can do much more in the way of prompting by using images and other attachments in a more strategic manner. For example, I can take a pic of a page from a book and prompt ChatGPT to develop a plan from that information. I've done so and depicted the steps in the figures to follow so you can see how this works.

First, I selected and photographed page 134 from *Generative AI For Dummies* about how to use AI aggregation to make stronger and more appealing content. You can see that in Figure 6-3.

Next, I attached it to the prompt bar by clicking on the paper clip icon on the left side of the bar. Then I added minimal instructions via text to the prompt bar. The part of the prompt that I typed reads:

Make a plan to design an online ad from the information in this image.

You can see that in Figure 6-4.

I then initiated the prompt by clicking on the arrow in the prompt bar. You can see the beginning of ChatGPT's response in Figure 6-5.

Random brilliant thoughts as prompt input

But that's just one example. Here's another. Imagine that you're attending a professional conference and are currently at a social event. Someone there makes an offhand comment that sparks a brilliant idea. You jot it down quickly on a napkin, as I've simulated in Figure 6-6.

You can take a picture of it and use it in a prompt to get ChatGPT to flesh out your idea, suggest additional or alternative ideas, point to factors involved that you need to consider, plan to implement your idea, and so on. Prompting with images and attachments truly is versatile. In Figure 6-7, you can see my full prompt for this demonstration.

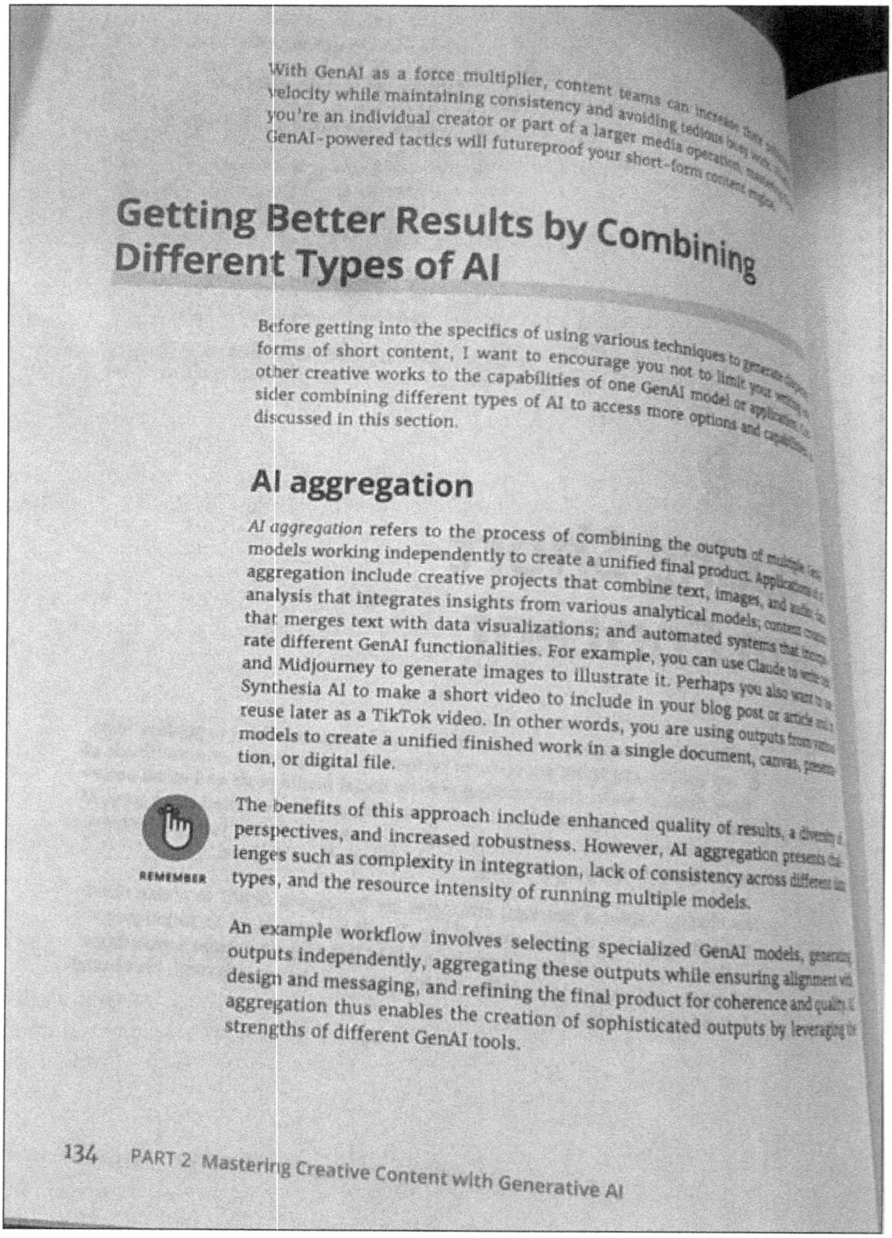

With GenAI as a force multiplier, content teams can increase their velocity while maintaining consistency and avoiding tedious busy work. Whether you're an individual creator or part of a larger media operation, mastering GenAI-powered tactics will futureproof your short-form content engine.

Getting Better Results by Combining Different Types of AI

Before getting into the specifics of using various techniques to generate different forms of short content, I want to encourage you not to limit your writing or other creative works to the capabilities of one GenAI model or application. Consider combining different types of AI to access more options and capabilities, discussed in this section.

AI aggregation

AI aggregation refers to the process of combining the outputs of multiple AI models working independently to create a unified final product. Applications of AI aggregation include creative projects that combine text, images, and audio; data analysis that integrates insights from various analytical models; content creation that merges text with data visualizations; and automated systems that incorporate different GenAI functionalities. For example, you can use Claude to write text and Midjourney to generate images to illustrate it. Perhaps you also want to use Synthesia AI to make a short video to include in your blog post or article and reuse later as a TikTok video. In other words, you are using outputs from various models to create a unified finished work in a single document, canvas, presentation, or digital file.

REMEMBER

The benefits of this approach include enhanced quality of results, a diversity of perspectives, and increased robustness. However, AI aggregation presents challenges such as complexity in integration, lack of consistency across different AI types, and the resource intensity of running multiple models.

An example workflow involves selecting specialized GenAI models, generating outputs independently, aggregating these outputs while ensuring alignment with design and messaging, and refining the final product for coherence and quality. AI aggregation thus enables the creation of sophisticated outputs by leveraging the strengths of different GenAI tools.

134   PART 2 Mastering Creative Content with Generative AI

FIGURE 6-3:
An image of page 134 of *Generative AI for Dummies.*

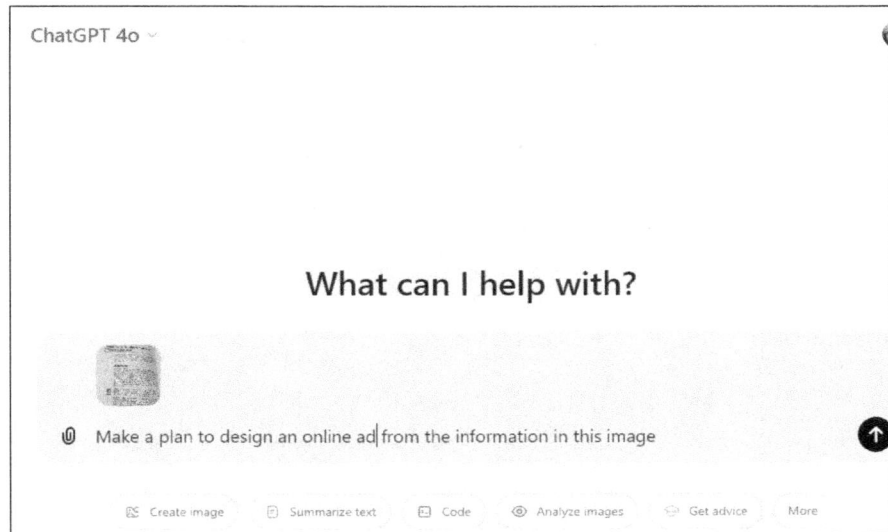

FIGURE 6-4:
Adding the
prompt after
attaching an
image.

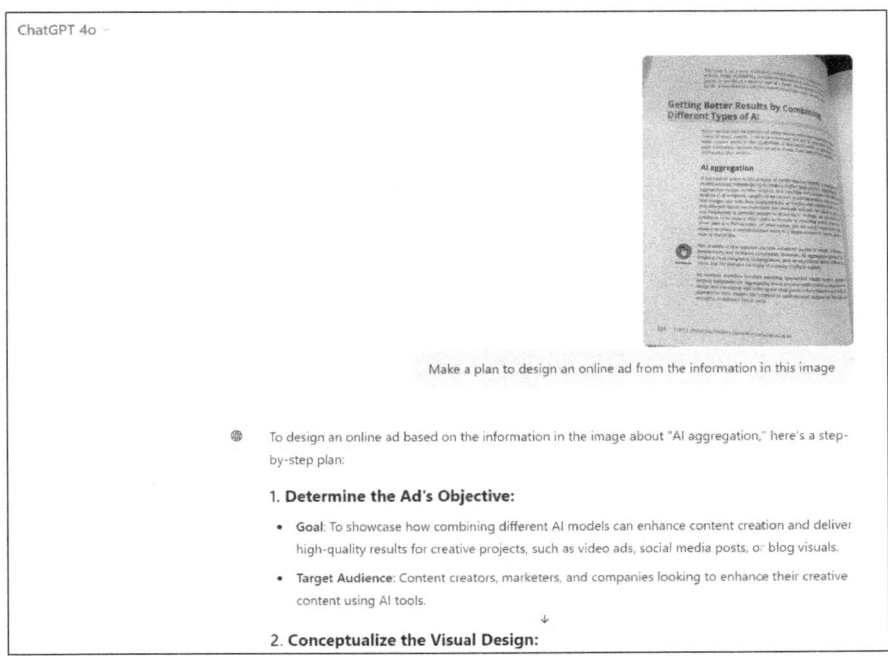

FIGURE 6-5:
The output that
ChatGPT gener-
ates after you
click the arrow in
the prompt bar.

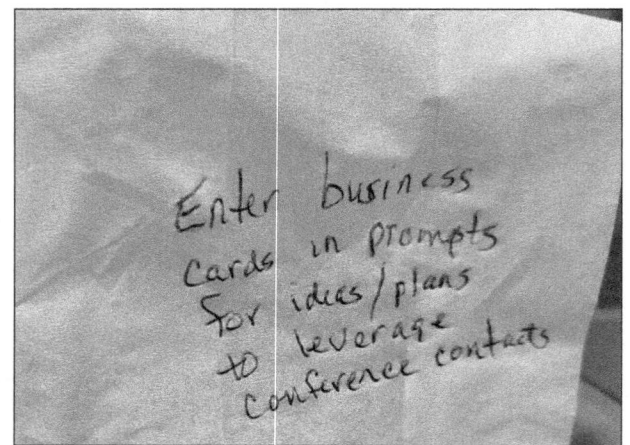

FIGURE 6-6:
A handwritten note on a napkin can be later entered into ChatGPT with your prompt.

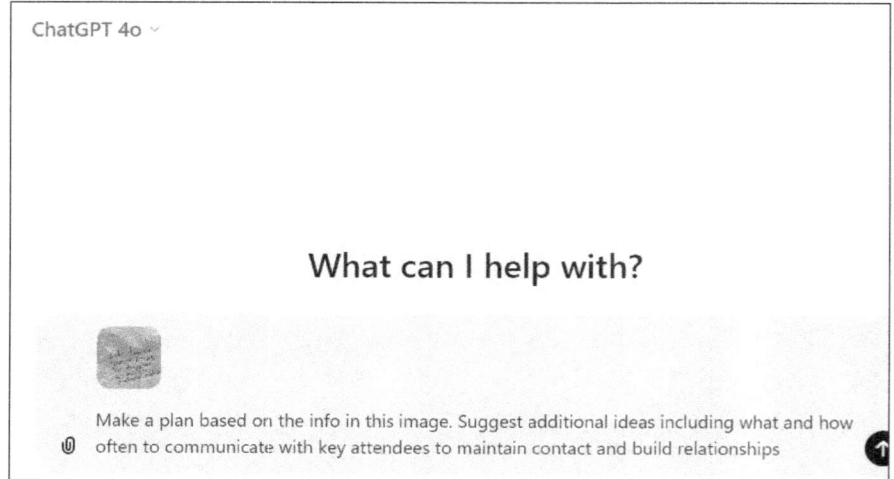

FIGURE 6-7:
The prompt asks ChatGPT to plan based on the napkin image from Figure 6-6.

As before, I'm including a screenshot of ChatGPT beginning to respond to this prompt in Figure 6-8.

Refining with chained prompts

There's no reason for me to stop after the response to my last prompt. I can

>> **Copy each of the tasks** in the list ChatGPT generates (its plan) and use them as prompts to get ChatGPT to do the work for me.

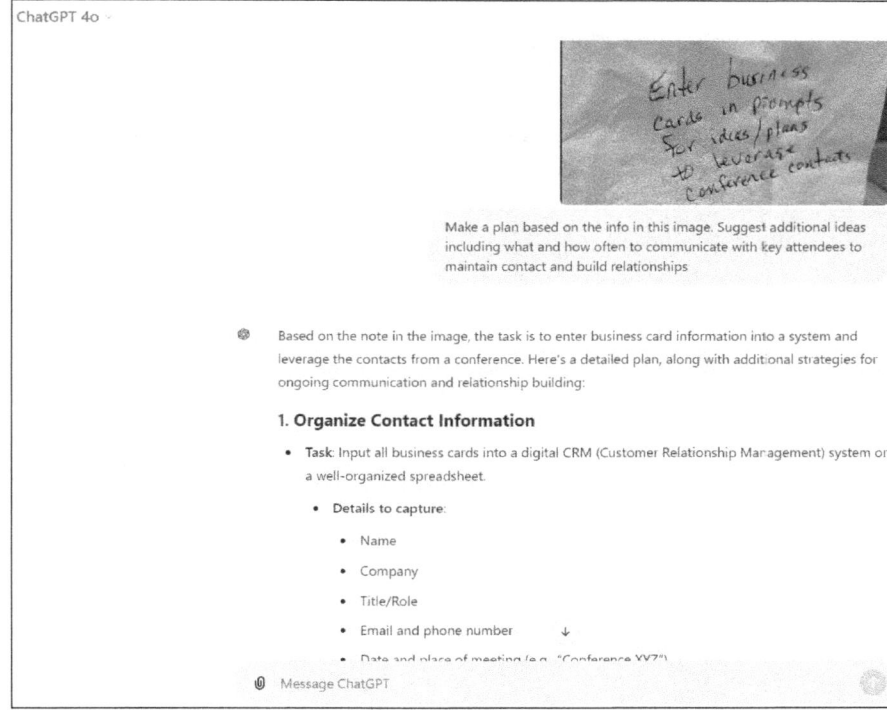

FIGURE 6-8:
The response
from ChatGPT
after entering
the prompt and
uploading the
image.

>> **Use *chain prompting*** (a technique in which you use a series of prompts in sequence, each building upon the last to gradually refine or expand on the LLM's responses) to get ChatGPT to execute the tasks one at a time.

>> **Take a screenshot or picture** of just one part of the plan that I actually want (scrapping the rest of ChatGPT's listed tasks), and on some future date, attach it to a prompt for ChatGPT to complete the work.

REMEMBER

How you choose to do any of this refinement is up to you, and whatever guidelines or rules your employer wants you to follow. The point here is that ChatGPT's flexibility allows you to work in almost any way you want.

You can use this tactic for any project and any purpose. Consider using it to improve an image you've created in a generative AI tool, whether it's within Chat-GPT or some other tool. For this demonstration, I created a simple black-and-white image in Craiyon, an AI-generated art platform, with a prompt instructing it to create an image that's wrong in several ways. The image I chose for this is shown in Figure 6-9.

Next, I attached the image in a ChatGPT prompt and instructed it to find and disclose the errors within the image and suggest ways to correct them. Figure 6-10 shows the actual prompt and part of ChatGPT's response.

These are only three simple examples of an endless number of possibilities in how adding image inputs to your prompts can work. My point here is that prompting a GenAI model isn't limited to the words you type or to any preset formulations. Your ideas and imagination determine what you can do with GenAI.

Adding information to memory in ChatGPT

You can tell some chatbots to remember something, and they will! ChatGPT can remember any information that you prompt it to store in its memory (such as your preferences or details) across multiple conversations, not just within a single session. This allows ChatGPT to apply this information to existing and new chats, even if you come back later or after a long break.

When you tell ChatGPT to remember something in a prompt, it replies with a verbal confirmation and an icon saying, Memory Updated, as you see in Figure 6-11.

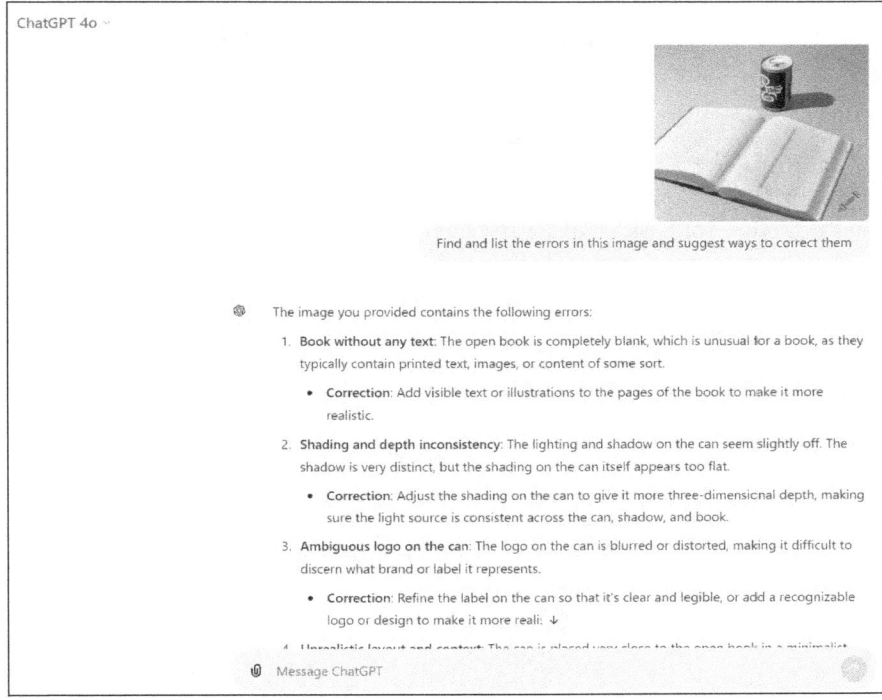

FIGURE 6-10:
An uploaded image along with a prompt that asks ChatGPT to find errors in the image.

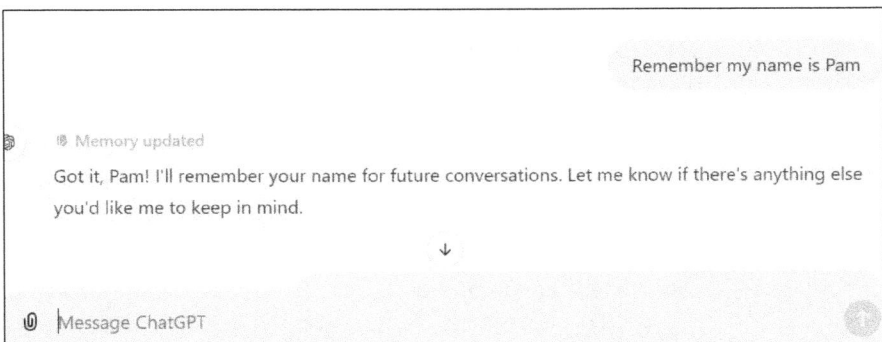

FIGURE 6-11:
ChatGPT responds after being prompted to remember a name.

If you want to add something else for ChatGPT to remember, just tell it to do so in another prompt. Or if you want it to forget something you told it to remember earlier, tell it what to forget in a prompt.

This is the point at which you're probably wondering why you'd ever enter info into Custom Instructions or Customize ChatGPT fields if you can just tell ChatGPT to remember that info in a prompt. The answer is that using custom instructions and directly telling ChatGPT to remember something in a prompt serve slightly different purposes.

REMEMBER

You set up custom instructions once, and those stay in constant use unless you change them manually. On the other hand, storing data in memory via a prompt allows you to dynamically make updates during conversations. For example, you can ask ChatGPT to remember or forget details as you go.

Here's why you might use custom instructions:

>> **Long-term adjustments:** Custom instructions let you set up a general, ongoing framework for how you'd like ChatGPT to respond across all conversations. For example, if you have a preferred way for ChatGPT to explain things, custom instructions can ensure your wishes are consistently applied.

>> **Consistency across sessions:** Custom instructions apply across multiple conversations even if you don't specifically mention something in a prompt. They shape the tone, detail, or context of every response, even if you forget to tell ChatGPT each time.

>> **Specific guidelines:** If you want certain preferences to be remembered (like how much detail you want in answers or your usual areas of interest), custom instructions help keep things in check without your needing to remind the app each time.

In contrast, here's why you might use prompts to tell ChatGPT to remember something:

>> **Specific to a conversation:** It's great for things that are important within a single chat or series of chats, and it allows you to be more spontaneous. It's also quick to undo when you're done since you can tell it to forget in a prompt, too.

>> **Flexible and temporary:** If you just need ChatGPT to remember something for the short term, it's faster and easier than going into settings.

Both approaches work well, but it depends on how often you want to maintain certain preferences and how often you want to change things in memory on a whim.

Manipulating memory in ChatGPT

Now that you know how and where to add and delete information from ChatGPT's memory, it's time to look at how and why you might want to do so. You might recall that the key difference between memory and custom instructions is in the degree of flexibility. Memory is ideal for real-time quick adjustments in prompts, but custom instructions are better suited for establishing a consistent baseline. Although memory allows you to make changes on the go during chats, custom instructions stay the same until you manually update them in the settings.

Promoting consistent results

You can leverage these strengths of memory and custom instructions in several ways. For example, you might want to enter specific and more detailed information in custom settings to maintain consistency in results across chats on a large project.

For example, if you're writing a long academic paper, white paper, report, or book by prompting and writing in chunks rather than in one long prompt and response, it may be worth adding longer and more detailed instructions in custom settings to serve as the guidelines for every chat and response until that project is finished. Typically, instructions added to memory in prompts are quick and short, so they don't carry as many details as custom instructions can.

However, you're limited on how much information you can store in custom instructions. The input fields for custom instructions are generally designed to accommodate a reasonable amount of text, but they're not intended for large amounts of detailed or complex information. Typically, each field for custom instructions — such as, "What would you like ChatGPT to know about you?" or "How would you like ChatGPT to respond?" — can hold a few paragraphs of text. This allows you to provide sufficient information for some customization, but it isn't suitable for storing large documents, extensive data, or complex lists. You'll want to put those items in retrieval-augmented generation (RAG) instead.

You're also limited to how much information you can store in memory. I can't tell you the exact capacity because that depends on the platform and the version you're using. But memory is designed to handle a reasonable amount of information to help personalize interactions; it's not intended for storing large or highly detailed datasets any more than custom instructions or customize ChatGPT features are.

Here are some general guidelines on memory limits:

>> **Reasonable scope:** ChatGPT can remember personal preferences, ongoing projects, interests, and specific details you give it. But if you try to store too many details at once or extremely large chunks of text, ChatGPT won't remember it all.

>> **Complexity:** Memory is best used for key pieces of information that tailor future conversations, such as your preferred learning style, favorite programming language, or recurring tasks. Highly complex or detailed information, like entire essays, large lists of technical specs, or multiple documents, may exceed the memory capacity. Again, it's better to add those items to RAG.

>> **Updates over time:** You can add, update, or remove information in memory as needed, which allows you to keep it current without overloading it with too much at once.

Testing ChatGPT memory

If you aren't sure what ChatGPT is currently remembering for you, prompt it to give you a list.

If you're unsure about whether ChatGPT can retain certain details, you can test it. Just ask ChatGPT to remember those details, and it will let you know whether that's possible.

TIP

Instead of thinking of this as an either/or option, strategically use information in custom instructions and memory so that you overcome the limits of both by making them work together to produce the results you seek.

Here are examples of manipulating information to get memory and custom instructions working in tandem:

Memory command in prompt: "Remember that I'm working on a new project involving AI ethics."

Custom instructions update: You could set custom instructions like, "I want ChatGPT to provide detailed explanations with examples whenever discussing complex topics" and "Cite sources complete with URLs in responses that include facts, numbers, or statistics."

Memory command in prompt: "Remember that I'm currently working on a paper targeting an audience of pediatricians."

Custom instructions update: "Write all responses using medical terminology and formal language suitable for an audience of physicians."

WARNING

Speaking of memory, be cognizant of your chat history. GenAI chatbots automatically store your chats so you can return to them later as though no time has lapsed. However, the chatbot has no memory of previous chats. That's odd, I know, because you just learned about ChatGPT's memory. But ChatGPT remembers only what you specifically tell it to remember. It doesn't remember any of the chats stored in your chat history in the sidebar on the left side of the user interface.

Managing chat history

You might want to delete chats from your chat history for privacy and organization reasons. If you've shared sensitive or personal information about yourself, your customer, or your employer, removing the chat ensures that those details are no longer stored. It doesn't, however, necessarily prevent that data from being harvested to train other AI models or possibly leaking into responses the LLM delivers to other users. It's best if you never enter sensitive information into chats.

REMEMBER

As your chat history grows, it can become cluttered with old or irrelevant conversations. Deleting these older chats can help keep things organized, making it easier to navigate and find the conversations that matter most to you.

Consider these other reasons for deleting or otherwise managing your chat history:

>> **The desire for a fresh start.** If you've been working on a particular project or topic and want to shift your focus, removing past chats can help you feel like you're starting anew. Similarly, if previous conversations contain outdated or incorrect information, clearing them out can prevent confusion going forward, allowing you to reset your chat history with current, accurate information.

>> **Avoiding potential misunderstandings or misuse of certain conversations.** You might want to delete chats that could be misinterpreted, no longer reflect your views, or can be used against you in the future. Remember that if you're using an enterprise version of an AI chatbot, your employer can likely see all your prompts and responses. To prevent future complications, don't say anything in a prompt that you wouldn't say to your boss, and if you have done so already, you might want to delete that now.

>> **Eliminating more personal discussions, even if they aren't sensitive.** Deleting them can offer peace of mind and make you feel more in control of your environment.

>> **Archiving chats or deleting your entire chat history at once.** You find the necessary command buttons under settings on the user interface (found under your profile picture in ChatGPT). In some versions, you also find a "clear all" button at the bottom of your chat history.

Changing the Model's Temperature

Changing the model's temperature means you're adjusting an LLM's creativity or randomness level. A *lower temperature setting* results in more predictable, conservative, and determinate outputs. This means the model will stick close to the most likely responses based on its training. It's useful when you want information that's straightforward, factual, and meets general expectations, including yours, your boss's, and your audience's.

On the other hand, a *higher temperature setting* allows the model to take more risks in its responses. Make it hot in here, and the model will take liberties left, right, and center in interpreting the data, which often leads to more creative or unusual outputs. You might want to cut an LLM loose like this when you're seeking out-of-the-box ideas, brainstorming, searching for a range of different perspectives, or trying to get its response closer to your own creative vision.

For example, if you're asking for a recipe for chicken soup, a lower temperature might give you a classic recipe, while a higher temperature might suggest a fusion of cuisines for an interesting spin on the traditional fare. Similarly, if you're asking for story ideas, a low temperature might give you familiar tropes, whereas a high temperature could provide you with a plot involving less conventional elements and unexpected endings.

To change the model's temperature, you, someone in your company's IT department, or an admin typically adjusts a parameter in the system that's controlling the model. This parameter usually ranges from 0 to 2, with 0 being the lowest temperature (most deterministic) and 2 being the highest (most random). The more balanced range are temps 0.5 to 1.0. You adjust this setting before making a request to the model. If you're using a customer-facing or consumer version of an LLM, you're not going to have a way to change this setting. But certain applications and platforms will let users change the model's temperature themselves.

TIP

If you're unsure about what temperature to use, start with a moderate setting, like 0.5 or 1.0, and see if the responses meet your needs. You can then adjust the setting based on whether you want more conventional or more creative responses.

Changing the Model's Weights

Changing the model's *weights* (the amount of influence that each input feature has on the output) involves updating or retraining a model's parameters. It's a technical method of affecting a model's outputs that most people won't have access or the skills to do. However, it's important for you to be aware of its existence if for no other reason than you know what to ask it — and how to articulate it — if you're having trouble with a chatbot's performance on the job.

You change a model's weights to enhance performance, adapt to new data, or correct biases. You might want to do this if the model is making less than accurate predictions, particularly if it's overfitting, underfitting, or not generalizing well to new data. *Overfitting* happens when a model learns the training data too well, capturing not just the underlying patterns but also the noise and minor details that are irrelevant. *Underfitting* is just the opposite and occurs when a model is too simple to capture any of the underlying patterns in the data.

When *data drift* (data changes over time that result in the AI model becoming ineffective) or *concept drift* (patterns change, which cause the model to become increasingly inaccurate over time) occurs, results can be wonky or wrong. That issue is common in areas such as finance or personalized recommendations where data changes quickly. Adjusting the weights allows the model to better reflect these new patterns. Similarly, if you notice the model behaving in biased ways, changing the weights through additional training or fine-tuning can minimize the issue.

You can change a model's weights by training a new model or retraining an existing one. Neither is particularly cheap or easy to do. Fine-tuning is another method of slightly adjusting the weights of an existing pretrained model, making it more suitable for a specific task without having to start a new model from scratch. Unfortunately, fine-tuning is another difficult and complex task.

Another way to adjust the model's learning behavior is by modifying the learning rate, which controls how much the weights change during training. If the model isn't learning well, adjusting the learning rate can ensure more effective updates to the weights.

3

Increasing Productivity with AI

Contents at a Glance

CHAPTER 1: **Applying GenAI in Practical Scenarios** 225

CHAPTER 2: **Crunching the Numbers with Copilot** 237

CHAPTER 3: **Presenting with Copilot** 263

CHAPTER 4: **Meeting and Collaborating with Copilot** 281

CHAPTER 5: **Working with AI in a Roundup of Business Disciplines** 293

CHAPTER 6: **Managing AI Adoption and Change in Your Organization** 317

Chapter **1**

Applying GenAI in Practical Scenarios

G enAI enhances human ingenuity across multiple domains. But you need to help GenAI, too, because this is not a tool that you can "set and forget."

This chapter covers the central touchpoints in working with GenAI models to produce unique, creative, and highly effective works. You get a feel for the tool's potential and limitations as well as advice on a few ways to overcome the inevitable hurdles that you'll encounter (which, in turn, will put you in the proper mindset to dive deeper into the details in later chapters).

In short, in this chapter, you explore the symbiosis between GenAI and your own creativity and find out how to effectively integrate AI into your work for transformative results.

GenAI as Writing Assistant

GenAI can be a wellspring of inspiration for writers and content creators. Its inspiration fuel is mined from vast amounts of data and processed for patterns humans can't see or find as quickly. That's what enables GenAI to generate novel content ideas that might otherwise remain undiscovered. GenAI tools can suggest themes, plot developments, and stylistic elements, providing a diverse array of starting points for the creative process.

These AI-driven insights are particularly valuable whenever you face the daunting challenge of a blank page. Or in fleshing out a book idea. By analyzing existing literature and trends, GenAI can propose unique angles and perspectives, sparking your imagination and guiding you toward fresh and intriguing narratives for any form of writing or content that you wish to create. This section shows you how to use GenAI for inspiration and for writing processes.

Using GenAI to generate ideas

GenAI changes your approach to the creative process, particularly in generating ideas and drafts. GenAI models can offer you fresh perspectives, challenge conventional thinking, and encourage you to explore new ideas.

But this is not an automatic process. It is your prompts that guide the model where you need it to be of help to you. Be prepared for your work to happen both in GenAI and outside of it. For example, if you want the model to search for novel ideas and unexpected correlations, you need to prompt it to do so. You can also prompt it to provide a list of ideas on any given subject. Just be aware that vagueness in the prompt can lead to outputs that are often vague, too, and of little use to your effort. If you want GenAI to write about something specific and in a certain style, you need to include that info in a prompt.

TIP

You're in the driver's seat and must steer GenAI to a specific destination, but ease up on the gas and let it suggest both direct and scenic routes for your imagination to explore. This is how you and GenAI will collaborate on ideas or finished content.

Don't forget that GenAI images can spark ideas for you, too — even if you never use the image in the finished content. Ask DALL-E, Midjourney, Canva, or some other GenAI image model to produce an image from your imagination. The exercise may inspire your text or copy and help you shape the words you need. As they say, a picture is worth a thousand words!

REMEMBER

Don't expect GenAI outputs to ever be exactly what you want. Any true artist or wordsmith is likely okay with that. You weren't really looking for a machine to replace you, were you? The good news is that GenAI is your assistant, not your replacement.

One other thing; you'll need to transfer its outputs to other software to further refine it and prepare it for production — for example, as an ebook, on a website, in a content management system (CMS), or in a Word or Google doc prior to publication. Which of those you choose is up to you and also determined by the process you'll use to bring your new creation to fruition.

Drafting content with the help of GenAI

GenAI tools can also assist in drafting a wide range of content, from business reports to creative writing. They pull information from multiple sources in their database, from which they generate coherent narratives, which can significantly speed up your drafting process.

To compose a draft with a GenAI model, follow these steps:

1. **Define your objective.**

Clearly state the purpose of your draft. Name your goal, preferred writing style (formal versus conversational, for example), and the writing form, meaning define whether it's for a short blog post, a video script, a long report, or a piece of fiction. Understanding the goal and nature of your finished piece will help you guide the GenAI in generating relevant content in an appropriate style and length.

2. **Select the right tool.**

Choose a GenAI tool that aligns with your stated writing needs — for instance, ChatGPT for text-based drafts or DALL-E for visual content if your draft requires imagery only. Note that ChatGPT-4o, also known as omni, will let you create images and text directly from the user interface, but some of the other versions of ChatGPT will let you pull another specialized GPT into it by using the @ symbol followed by the name of the GPT to add images and other elements as you go. See Figures 1-1 and 1-2 for examples.

3. **Craft a detailed prompt.**

The quality of a GenAI-generated draft is often proportional to the specificity and clarity of the prompt. Develop a comprehensive prompt that includes the topic, tone, style, and any specific requirements for the draft. You can work on this outside of AI and then enter the prompt when you're satisfied that it is as good as you can make it. If you do it this way, you can cut your token usage down, which may help you cut costs and avoid bumping into usage limits. (Tokens are bits of words, spaces, characters, and the like; when added together they compose your prompt and the GenAI's response. As a rule of thumb, one token generally corresponds to around four characters or letters. Vendors predetermine GenAI usage costs per token use and daily limits by establishing a set number of tokens you can use in one 24-hour period.)

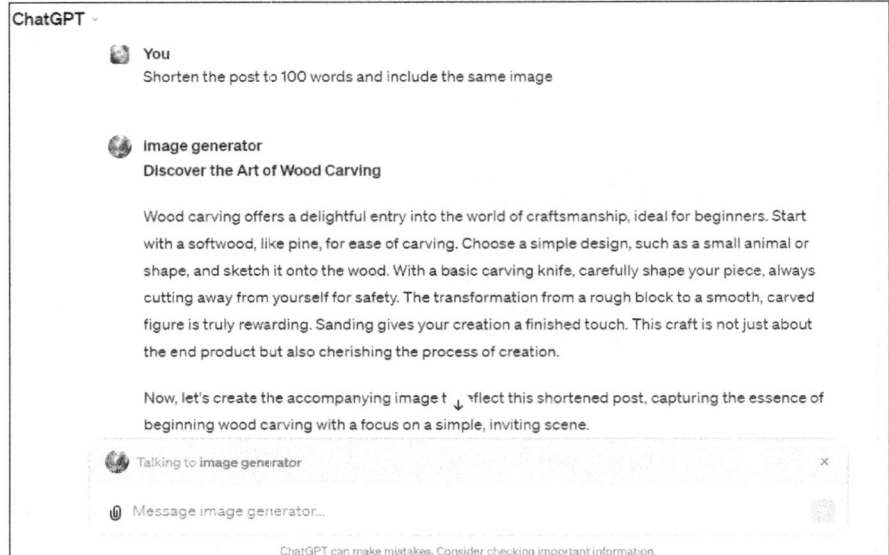

FIGURE 1-1:
A screenshot of a blog post generated in ChatGPT that I'm also using @ imagegenerator to create an image in the same post.

FIGURE 1-2:
A screenshot of an image created by the image generator inside ChatGPT to illustrate the blog post it just wrote for me.

Created with the aid of Image Generator in ChatGPT

But you can also refine your prompts on the fly in a chain of prompts, too. In other words, what you perceive as missing or off base in the response to one prompt, you can address in a subsequent prompt, or a chain (series) of prompts as you go. This is a faster technique than thoughtfully composing prompts offline, but you run the potential risk of upping your token counts.

4. **Input the prompt.**

Enter the prompt in the prompt bar on the GenAI tool user interface. Some models allow you to attach images and other files to the prompt, but you still need to type instructions for the model in the prompt bar, too.

5. **Review the output.**

Examine the initial draft generated by the AI. Look for relevance, coherence, and alignment with your original objective. Also, check for accuracy and plagiarism, too.

6. **Refine and iterate.**

You can further its improvement by tweaking the language and adding more context in the next prompt or by adjusting the parameters of the task for the model in a system message, retrieval augmented generation (RAG), or, to a lesser degree, in a prompt.

7. **Edit and personalize.**

When a satisfactory draft is generated, edit the content to add a personal touch, ensuring it meets your standards and reflects your voice. Double-check again for accuracy and plagiarism.

8. **Utilize additional tools.**

If necessary, use other GenAI tools for specific tasks, such as specialized GPTs like those you'll find in ChatGPT Plus versions and higher. Refer to Figures 1-1 and 1-2 for examples. But you can use other types of GenAI tools, too, such as new search tools like Perplexity.

TIP

GenAI models are trained on a dataset, which means that data has a cutoff date and can age out (a process called *model drift*). To overcome this limitation, use a supercharged, GenAI-enhanced/embedded search engine like Perplexity, Google Smart Search, or Bing to get more current information. Then copy that response and feed it into ChatGPT prompt bar with instructions to include the current information in the draft! This process is a type of AI chaining, meaning you're using the output of one AI as part or all of a prompt in another AI.

9. **Finalize the draft.**

Make the final adjustments to the draft, ensuring it is polished and ready for its intended audience or purpose. Typically, GenAI-generated text sounds like it's machine generated. Make copy changes as needed to refine its style to fit your intended audience.

10. **Save and archive.**

Store the final draft and any notes about the process in an organized manner. This practice can be useful for future reference or for improving subsequent interactions with GenAI tools. You'll want to make a prompt library or prompt archive, too. This way, you can readily reuse a successful prompt when needed and, thus, save time and effort in recreating the same prompts later.

Sprucing up your writing with GenAI

GenAI offers writers an array of tools to enhance creativity in their writing. By integrating the following tips with GenAI tools, you can push the boundaries of your personal writing style, producing innovative and engaging content:

>> **Include elements like genre, tone, and style in your prompts to get tailored results.** You can even provide an example of writing that you want GenAI to follow or mimic. For example, provide it with a text sample from an academic paper in the prompt and instruct it to use a similar tone and vocabulary. However, don't be surprised if it refuses to mimic writing samples from current writers or even your own writing samples, as many GenAI model builders have built guardrails against GenAI copying such work in an effort to prevent the model from plagiarizing or committing a copyright infringement.

>> **Consider prompting the model to suggest expansions, twists, or alternative directions that a competitor may produce to compete with your work.** This way you can capture that information in your piece or produce another work from that angle ahead of your competitor.

>> **Experiment with GenAI to get advice or additional perspectives from celebrities, historical figures, or famous authors or to blend different writing styles, which can lead to unique and creative narratives.** For example, you can prompt GenAI to produce critiques or suggestions on your content from Einstein, Dr. Seuss, Margaret Thatcher, President Lincoln, Steven Spielberg, and Stephen King. What an insightful conversation that will be! But you're not limited to these people. Create your own board of creative advisors!

>> **Use GenAI for editing and refinement.** The AI can offer rephrasing suggestions and word alternatives that may enhance your original draft. You can also prompt it to expand, summarize, make lists, or whatever you need to further refine your draft.

TURNING ORDINARY INSTRUCTIONS INTO MEMORABLE CONNECTIONS

Not all content in this world is interesting. Take, for example, the badly drawn and often mystifying laundry instructions on a clothing label, assembly instructions for a piece of furniture, or even some patient instructions for everything from medicines to hospital discharge papers.

When instructions are boring or confusing, people don't bother. When they don't bother to read and follow them, mistakes happen, and bad outcomes can follow. A little creativity can be a profound fix for those problems.

For example, if you're writing patient information for a child to follow, you can use GenAI to create it in the style of Winnie-the-Pooh, so the child finds it easy to understand and follow without feeling fear or intimidation. It might look something like this:

PROMPT: Write patient information for a young child (5 to 10 years old), reminding them not to get their bandage wet. Make it short, memorable, and in the style of Winnie-the-Pooh.

RESPONSE: *In the Hundred Acre Wood, where the streams babble clear, there's a small, simple thing that Pooh Bear holds dear. "If you have a bandage," Pooh says with a smile, "Keep it away from the water, just for a while. Whether it's bathtime or puddles or raindrops that fall, keep your bandage quite dry, away from it all. For a bandage that's dry is a bandage that's true, and it helps you to heal," says Winnie the Pooh. So hum a small hum, think of honey, think sweet, Imagine your bandage staying dry as your feet. And soon, when it's off, you'll be happy to see you're as right as rain, as healthy as can be!*

Getting a Visual Assist from GenAI

Making use of GenAI can be a transformative experience for artists, designers, and content creators. For content creators, GenAI can create images to illustrate the content, attract readers, and increase reader retention rates. For visual creators, be they fine artists, fashion designers, graphic artists, or product designers, creating visuals with the help of GenAI is the entire point of the exercise.

Fortunately, GenAI is accessible to anyone to create any image. Whether that image is what you want — or results in commercial success — depends on the level of your own creative talent.

GenAI in graphic design and visual arts

GenAI has become an indispensable tool in graphic design and visual arts, offering artists and designers ways to expand their creative horizons and streamline their workflows. Creatives can now generate complex patterns, simulate intricate textures, and even create entire compositions with a level of detail and speed previously unattainable.

GenAI models like DALL-E, Midjourney, Canva, Adobe Firefly, and Stable Diffusion enable artists to bring complex visual ideas to life from simple text prompts. These models are trained on extensive datasets of images and their descriptions, learning to generate new images that are rich in detail and creativity. The models can also create images in virtual space, unconstrained by physical limits. They can render images with a mix of textures or mediums that may not have been considered or possible in physical space.

GenAI also enables the manipulation of images, such as changing backgrounds and adding elements to photographs. GenAI is embedded in software like Adobe AI programs that enable image creation and seamless manipulations in previously unprecedented ways. You can even create royalty-free custom "stock photos" with GenAI since it can create human characters who do not actually exist and, therefore, require no permissions or payments.

While GenAI incorporates elements of computer vision, it enhances the design process through pattern recognition across vast datasets, predicting elements that will engage audiences.

Generating visual content with AI tools

If you're looking to create images for your content, try entering part or all of the content in the prompt bar and prompting the model to provide illustrations for key points. Odds are that you'll be delighted at the results. You can also prompt the model to generate an image according to your description in the prompt and customize that image in subsequent prompts until you have exactly what you were looking for!

Even budding artists are spinning text into visual gold. GenAI-created images can be found for sale in a multitude of marketplaces, from artist- and gallery-owned websites to Etsy and Adobe stock images websites.

Here are a few tips on how to tease some great images out of GenAI models:

>> **Get specific with your prompts.** It's all about the details. Dictate in the prompt what you see in your inner creative vision. Include details like lighting, shadowing, perspective, character traits, apparel, the scene or backdrop, a time period, a medium (maybe watercolor? something else?), the general mood, and other information. Imagine you are moving the GenAI like you would an artist's brush or a photographer's camera. *If* you do so skillfully, the resulting image will be amazing!

>> **Create in layers.** Write your prompt in descriptive layers. Describe specific elements in layers so you don't forget to include important details. Try stacking different themes, eras, stances, moods, and actions to create complex, eye-catching visuals.

>> **Use GenAI to adapt your sketch or an image.** You can add images to your prompts in several models. Have you already done a sketch? Put it in the prompt and ask GenAI to finish it as a painting, a photograph, or even a sculpture. You can also put an image in the prompt and instruct the model to extend the scene beyond the frame or the borders of the image with new elements. In DALL-E this is called *outpainting*.

>> **Polish with iteration.** Start with a rough sketch from the AI and then refine, refine, refine. Nudge the AI to tweak colors, shuffle the composition, or add a little something-something until it's just right.

>> **Mix and match styles and mediums.** Guide the AI to fuse different artistic styles, periods, or mediums into a fresh, new visual work. Remember that GenAI has no physical limits, really, so go ahead and see what your talent can create when there are no limits.

>> **Embrace happy accidents.** Sometimes the best ideas come from a "whoops" moment. Let the AI surprise you, and you may just like that image better than the one you initially had in mind.

>> **Draw from everywhere.** An image may be worth a thousand words, but its value is a thousand more when there's a story behind it. Don't just stick to art lingo when writing your prompt. Borrow from science, tech, or your favorite novel to prompt the model to give your images a story that's as deep as they are stunning.

REMEMBER

Despite the technological advancements, the artist's intuition and talent is vital in guiding GenAI to produce work that resonates on a human level. As GenAI evolves, its capabilities will balloon, providing artists with an expansive canvas for innovation and exploration.

Harnessing GenAI for even more visual creativity

If you're a professional image creator, you'll likely want to exert more of your talent in the GenAI's image generation. Following are some tips for fine artists/video artists, graphic design/visual communications professionals:

- **Experiment with AI-generated imagery.** Use GenAI tools to create new visual concepts. Input descriptive text to prompt a model like DALL-E, Midjourney, or Stable Diffusion to generate images or patterns that can serve as a starting point for your creative projects. This can be particularly useful when you're looking for fresh ideas or want to explore how AI interprets your descriptions.

- **Play with perspectives.** Use GenAI to show you your image from a different perspective, or even from more than one. This can spur new ideas or ideas on how you might want to change the image you're already working on. You can also use GenAI to extend your image past the frame, meaning past the edges of your design.

- **Blend human intuition with machine precision.** While GenAI can generate a vast array of visual data, human intuition is key to selecting and refining these outputs. Use your judgment to curate and modify AI-generated images, combining them with traditional artistic techniques to create unique and compelling visuals. This blend of human and machine can lead to innovative designs that may not be possible through conventional methods alone.

- **Leverage AI for enhanced pattern recognition.** GenAI can identify and replicate complex patterns, which can be used to inspire new artworks or designs. For example, prompt the model to compare your newly created image with modern trends in advertising or commercially successful but competing product designs. The responses may spur you to create a more successful ad or product.

Problem-Solving with AI in Creative Projects

If and when you find a problem in your own creative idea and can't find a solution, GenAI can help with that. Perhaps something is off in your painting, either technically or creatively. Take a picture of it and add that to a prompt to an image generator, asking it to analyze and offer suggestions to solve your stated problem or improve it overall. You can do the same with your songwriting, your ad campaign, your novel, your movie script, or any other creative work.

GenAI can quickly show you any issues, suggest solutions, or guide you to another way to express your creative thoughts that you may like better. Even creators who shy away from showing their work in its early stages to other people find it easy to privately share it with AI.

But sometimes the AI *is* the problem.

If you're like most serious creators using GenAI to create unique and professional-level works, you're bound to be frustrated out of your mind at some point. Don't worry, that's normal.

The good news is that you can turn GenAI models around. Yes, the model is the source of the problem, but it can also come up with the answer or at least a workaround. Here are a few tips and tricks on that and some other things you can do to get unflustered and back on schedule.

» **Change up your prompts to redirect the model.** Start a new chat in either the model you're currently using or a different model that's text-based and perhaps a little better suited to problem-solving. Remember, oodles of models on the market are specialized in different types of work. If you have the time, or the problem is vexing enough to warrant the exercise, go find one and get it to solve the issue. If you don't want to go to all that bother, prompt the nearest GenAI model to give you some problem-solving options.

» **Try again or give the same command in another way.** If you're trying to get the model to do something specific and it seems to be doing everything BUT THAT, tell it in another way. I promise, the GenAI is not trying to drive you crazy. It just doesn't understand what you want it to do. Remember that it doesn't actually understand anything. The model is completing a pattern from the pieces you gave it in the prompt. So, give it different pieces of the puzzle to work from. Restate your prompt from one or more other perspectives or ways, and you'll finally get some movement toward the response you desire.

» **Form a digital committee.** I know, I know, everyone hates to deal with committees when they're seeking a definitive answer to something. But this is a digital committee wherein you are prompting the GenAI to assume several professional or community roles simultaneously in order to offer you many different possible solutions in a single response. Take what you want and delegate the committee to chat history forevermore. Don't you wish real committees were that easy to dismiss?

>> **Restart the GenAI application.** Yes, I know, this sounds a lot like "unplug it and plug it in again" advice from ages past. But it's true. For any number of reasons, or none at all, a GenAI app can freeze, become lazy, or otherwise get hung up on error messages. Save yourself and your IT support some grief and just shut it down and restart.

>> **Are you sure you prompted what you actually wanted?** People (you and me included) tend to shorthand our thoughts, and that can carry over in our prompts. While another person, especially someone who knows you well, can deduce what you meant even though that isn't what you said, GenAI is too literal to do that. So, if you aren't getting the response you need, back up and rethink your prompt. Did you ask what you meant to ask? You might want to reword that prompt so it is clearer.

>> **Use the prompt to stop repetitive phrases.** Is the GenAI model using repetitive phrases or words? Forbid it to use those phrases or words in your prompts or the system message. Voila! Now, the issue is fixed. (At some point, you might want to unfix that, though, as it may genuinely need those phrases and words back to legitimately answer a prompt down the road.)

>> **Layer AI to stop repetitive responses.** If the model keeps giving you the same responses simply reworded, check your prompts to make sure you aren't asking it in different ways to do the same thing. If prompting isn't the issue, add data for the model to use. That's quite often a pain to do, however. An easier workaround is to add data in your next prompt. One way to do that is to prompt another GenAI model with the same information and feed its response into your next prompt in the GenAI application or model you were initially using. This is a form of AI chaining that simply means using all or part of an output from one AI model as part of the prompt in another. Another way to use multiple AI models is to aggregate them by using different models to perform specific steps necessary to complete a larger task. For example, you might want to use one GenAI model to generate text, another to create images, and a third that's embedded in other software to publish the two outputs in a single format such as a document.

>> **Consider something completely different.** In the realms of architecture, fashion, and graphic design, GenAI can weave together designs that defy convention, crafting spaces, garments, and visuals that belong in the galleries of tomorrow. In other words, if the way you are currently pursuing is not working, then prompt the AI to take an entirely different artistic route to the same end.

Chapter **2**

Crunching the Numbers with Copilot

n 2006, the British mathematician and data scientist Clive Humbly famously said, "Data is the new oil." Just as with oil, however, simply having data isn't of much use. The real power of data is in making sense of it through a process called *data analytics.* This is why Peter Sondergaard, the senior vice president of the technology research firm Gartner, Inc., said, "Information is the oil of the 21st century, and analytics is the combustion engine."

In the brief time since Humbly and Sondergaard came up with their famous quotes about the power of data, we've had an explosion in the power of artificial intelligence that has made data even more useful and powerful. Just to push the metaphor perhaps further than it should fly: If analytics is the combustion engine, then AI, in combination with data and analytics, is a rocket ship. And now, you have a copilot to help you guide that rocket ship.

Using Microsoft Copilot in Excel can improve your understanding of data as well as help you use Excel wisely (with which many of us struggle). In this chapter, you explore how this AI assistant can help you work with data and boldly go where no one has gone before.

Launching Copilot in Excel

Subscribers to Microsoft 365 Copilot or Copilot Pro will see a Copilot button on the right side of the Home tab of Excel for Microsoft 365 as well as in the desktop version of Excel. Clicking this icon opens the Excel Copilot sidebar, shown in Figure 2-1.

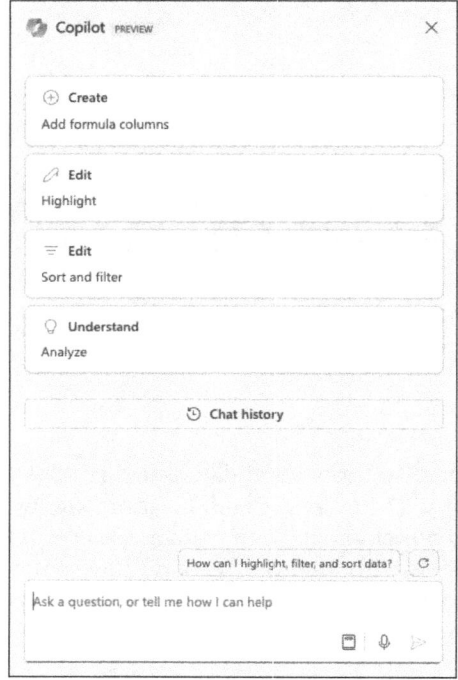

FIGURE 2-1:
The Copilot for
Excel sidebar.

At the top of the sidebar are buttons for the categories of special prompts that you can use in an Excel document:

» **Create.** Create-related prompts are prompts in which you ask Copilot to add new columns to your spreadsheet with formulas. To use a Create prompt, you can describe the column you want to add, and Copilot will attempt to do as you wish. You learn about Create prompts in the section of this chapter titled "Creating Formulas with Copilot's Assistance."

» **Edit.** Edit-related prompts assist you with highlighting, sorting, and filtering your data. The two categories of Edit-related prompts are Highlight and Sort and Filter.

>> **Understand.** Understand-related prompts find and highlight interesting parts of your data, show insights (such as correlations and patterns) that Copilot finds in your data using charts and PivotTables, and can help you identify trends and patterns.

Below the special prompt buttons is the Chat History button, which takes you to a history of every prompt you've submitted in the current document.

Below the Chat History button is an area containing prompt suggestions. These prompt suggestions are context-aware, and they will change based on the content of your document and on your previous prompts in the chat.

At the bottom of the sidebar is the prompt input box, with some icons at the bottom for getting prompt suggestions and for using the microphone.

Talking about using Copilot in Excel without having some real data is only of limited use (like having a car without fuel!), so let's get some data and take Copilot for a spin.

Working with Data

One of the reasons the latest generation of AI is so good is that there's so much data available for AI to learn from. The internet has both fueled an explosion of data collection and made it easier for anyone to access it. What and where is all this data?

Understanding the two kinds of data

People who work with AI and machine learning break data into two broad categories: structured and unstructured.

Unstructured data

Unstructured data includes websites, news articles, music, blogs, movies, television, and so much more. Unstructured data doesn't fit into neat rows and columns, but machine learning algorithms can still learn from it by looking for patterns and similarities between different pieces of data.

Unstructured data is used for tasks that seek to discover and recognize patterns. Examples of tasks in which AI learns from unstructured data include image recognition, natural language processing, speech recognition, and video analysis.

Structured data

Structured data includes data that can be organized into rows and columns. While movies and TV shows can't be "structured" data, you can create structured data *about* movies and TV shows. For example, you may create a list of the 100 best movies of all time and include data such as the year they were made, the director, the actors, the length of the movies, and so forth. Structured data also includes labeled data. Labeled data is data that may have previously been unstructured but that's been assigned labels to add context or meaning. An example of labeled data might include a collection of pictures that have been labeled as being either a picture of a cat or not a picture of a cat. Such a labeled collection of data can be used to train AI to identify pictures of cats.

The type of data that Excel works with is structured data.

Finding free data

You may have Excel files that you've created for work or to manage your personal finances. Or, you may have a list of important contacts, or even a list of passwords that you keep in an Excel file on your computer. All these files are likely only of interest to you and a small group of other people.

However, a universe of data is out there that's of interest to a much larger group of people. This includes weather data, data about political or charitable contributions, data about the stock market, and much more. Thanks to the internet, all of this data is readily available, often for free, to anyone who is interested in it and knows where to look.

Many sources of freely available data are available on the web. Organizations, universities, governments, data scientists, and enthusiasts regularly publish data and make it available for other people to study and analyze. Some of the best sources of free data include:

>> **data.gov** (`https://data.gov`). Data.gov is the U.S. government's free and open source data repository. In particular, it contains a wealth of public economic data.

>> **Google dataset search** (`https://datasetsearch.research.google.com`). If you know what you're looking for, this is a great place to start your search.

>> **Kaggle** (`https://www.kaggle.com/datasets`). Kaggle is a community hub for data scientists and people who are interested in data science. Kaggle is a place to learn about AI and data science, collaborate with other data scientists, and even try your hand at data science challenges and competitions.

>> **Datahub.io** (`https://datahub.io/collections`). Datahub contains mostly data related to business and finance. If you're looking for stock market data or information about property prices, you'll likely find it here.

For the first examples in this chapter, I downloaded a dataset from Kaggle titled "Tornados [1950 – 2022]." As you may have already guessed, this dataset contains information about every tornado in the United States between 1950 and 2022. If you want to download this dataset, you can do so at `https://www.kaggle.com/datasets/sujaykapadnis/tornados`.

Preparing the Data

After data has been collected, the next step in data analysis is to make sure it's properly formatted, that all columns have a consistent format, and that there isn't anything in the data that might throw off the results (such as missing data).

Since the tornados dataset was downloaded from a trusted source and has a high rating on `Kaggle.com`, I feel confident that the data itself is trustworthy. However, some things can be done to add some context to the data and make it more logical to Copilot.

Converting the data to a table

The downloaded tornado dataset is a comma-separated values (CSV) file, which can be easily opened using Excel. Copilot can't work with CSV files, however. To be able to use Copilot, you need to open the CSV file in Excel and then save it as the latest Excel format.

Once you've done that, you can click on the Copilot icon and ask Copilot to explain the data to you. On my first attempt, Copilot told me there was more data than it could work with and that I needed to convert the data to a table. After I figured out how to do that (by asking Copilot), I did the conversion to a table with these steps:

1. Click in the data you want to convert to a table.

2. Click on Insert from Excel's *ribbon* (as the row of buttons across the top is called).

3. Click on Table in the Excel ribbon.

4. In the Create Table window that pops up, make sure that all the data in the current Excel spreadsheet is selected and that the checkbox next to My Table Has Headers is checked.

The result of the preceding steps will be that your raw data will be converted into a nice-looking table with a header and alternating row formats, as shown in Figure 2-2.

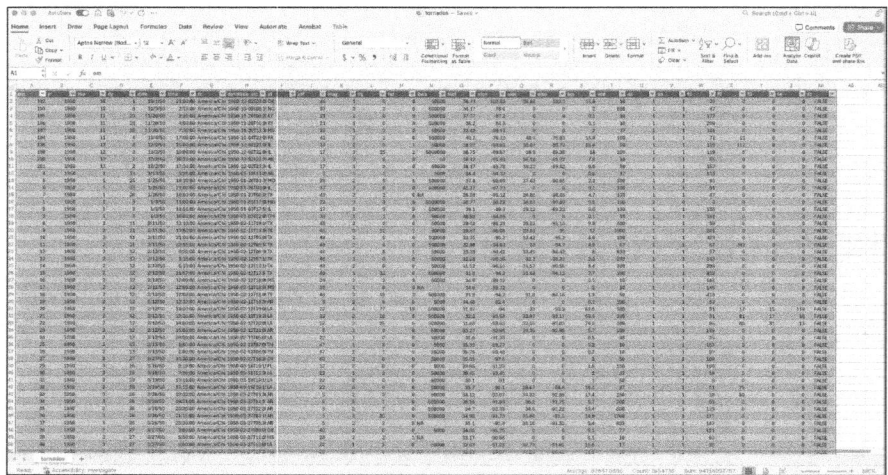

FIGURE 2-2:
Creating a table from data.

Adding context to the headers

The column headers used in the spreadsheet are short and non-descriptive. It's possible that replacing some of the headers with plain English words could improve Copilot's ability to understand the data, and maybe Copilot can help us with that.

TIP

You can find a key to the headers on the dataset's download page in the section called Data Card.

You can approach the problem of creating new headers for the Excel sheet in several ways without having to do it manually. One way is to ask Copilot in the browser to generate a single row table containing descriptive names for the columns.

My first attempt at using this approach caused Copilot to create a numbered list of descriptive names for the columns, but then when I asked it to create a CSV file containing the headers, it was able to. It did end up giving me a couple extra columns that aren't in the dataset, but those are easy enough to remove.

Figure 2-3 shows the result when I tried that approach.

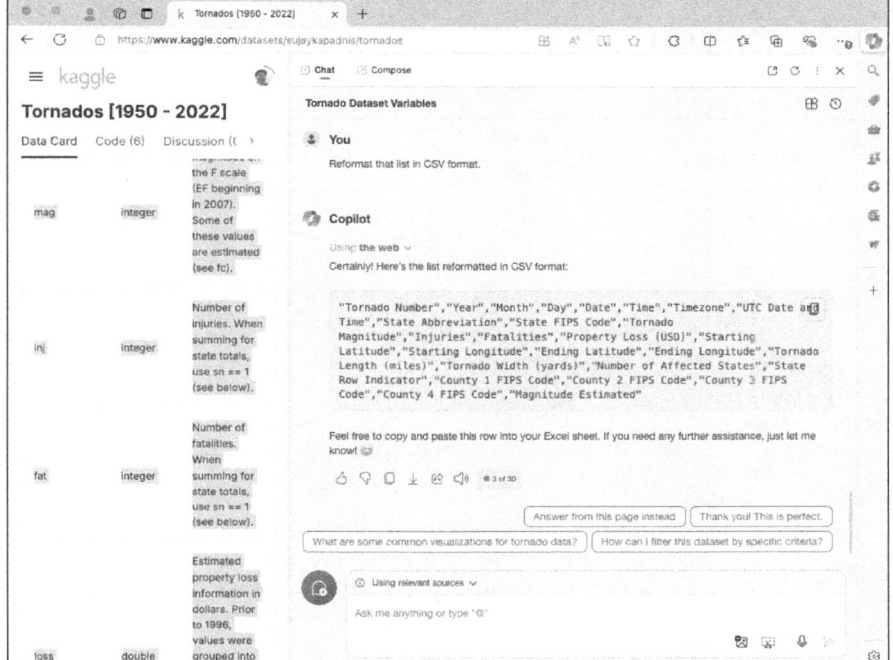

FIGURE 2-3:
Asking Copilot in Edge to create a table header.

Another approach is to try pasting the table from the Data Card into Copilot in Excel and asking Copilot to make the changes directly in the Excel spreadsheet.

When I tried this approach, Copilot responded that "there is an issue with renaming the headers at the moment." I suspected that Copilot might not have the ability to rename the headers at all, so I tried an experiment: asking Copilot to just rename one header using the following prompt:

> Please rename the tz column to Time Zone.

This time, it came back with a message containing its proposed solution, and a button labeled Apply. Its proposed solution, however, was to replace every instance of the letters "tz" with "Time Zone" in the entire column, rather than just in the one cell that I asked it to modify. I pushed back, as shown in Figure 2-4.

I clicked the Apply button, and Copilot correctly changed the label of the time zone column.

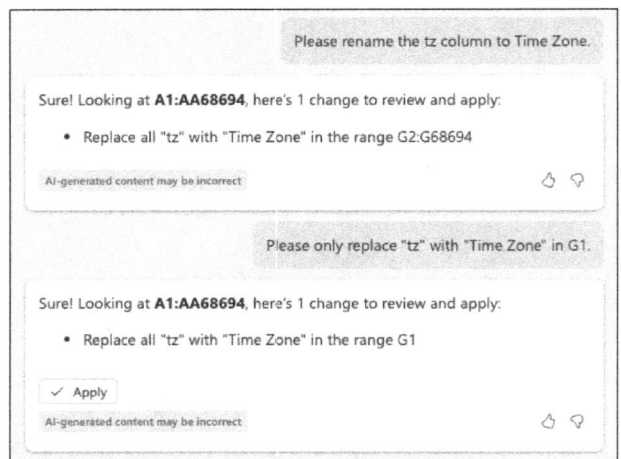

This approach of replacing a single column header at a time is more time con-suming than just doing it manually. But it occurred to me that I already have a simple comma-separated list of new column headers (from what Copilot in Edge generated) and perhaps Copilot in Edge would be able to use this list to correctly replace the headers.

I copied the list generated in Edge and prompted Copilot in Edge to use this list to replace the headers. However, Copilot came back with the message about there being an issue with renaming the column headers, as shown in Figure 2-5.

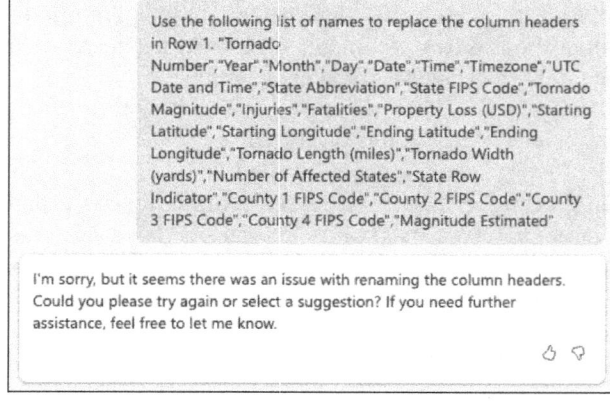

FIGURE 2-5:
Copilot says
there's an issue
with renaming
column headers.

Rather than argue with Copilot, you can use the following steps to manually replace the abbreviated headers with the new and descriptive headers:

1. **Copy the comma-separated list from Copilot in Edge and paste it into a text document.**

2. **Save the text document with the .csv extension.**

3. **Open the .csv file containing the headers in Excel.**

4. **Copy the new row and paste it into Row 1 of the tornado spreadsheet.**

Sometimes, the best approach to getting what you need to be done is to combine the use of Copilot with a manual approach. With some experience, you'll start to see where it's not worth it to try to get Copilot to do the last ten percent of a project when you could just do it yourself in a matter of seconds.

Formatting data

The next thing you may notice about the tornado dataset is that it's not sorted correctly, or it's sorted in a way that doesn't make sense. Looking at the first 20 rows, you'll see that the first records are from October, November, and December 1950, and then the rows jump back to January through September 1950, as shown in Figure 2-6.

	A	B	C	D	E
1	Tornado N	Year	Month	Day	Date
2	192	1950	10	1	10/1/1950
3	193	1950	10	9	10/9/1950
4	195	1950	11	20	11/20/1950
5	196	1950	11	20	11/20/1950
6	197	1950	11	20	11/20/1950
7	194	1950	11	4	11/4/1950
8	198	1950	12	2	12/2/1950
9	199	1950	12	2	12/2/1950
10	200	1950	12	2	12/2/1950
11	201	1950	12	2	12/2/1950
12	4	1950	1	13	1/13/1950
13	5	1950	1	25	1/25/1950
14	6	1950	1	25	1/25/1950
15	7	1950	1	26	1/26/1950
16	1	1950	1	3	1/3/1950
17	2	1950	1	3	1/3/1950

FIGURE 2-6:
A strange way to sort the year

This pattern of the double-digit numbers coming first in the year holds true for all 68694 rows of data.

It's possible that this is a standard sorting scheme that I'm not aware of, but more likely, it's because the dates are currently sorted alphabetically rather than numerically. In alphabetical sorting, the number 10 comes before 2 because 1 comes before 2. I'd rather have all the data sorted chronologically.

If I wanted to sort by date, I could try clicking the column header. But, because the date is currently not in date format, it probably wouldn't work correctly. The next step in getting this data ready for analysis is to fix the data types.

Changing data types

Before you can sort by date, you have to make sure the Date column is in date format.

Other columns of the table that contain date information and numeric information should also be changed to the right data type. This seems like something Copilot might be able to help with.

I opened the Copilot sidebar and entered the following prompt:

> Convert each column to an appropriate data type.

Copilot's response is shown in Figure 2-7.

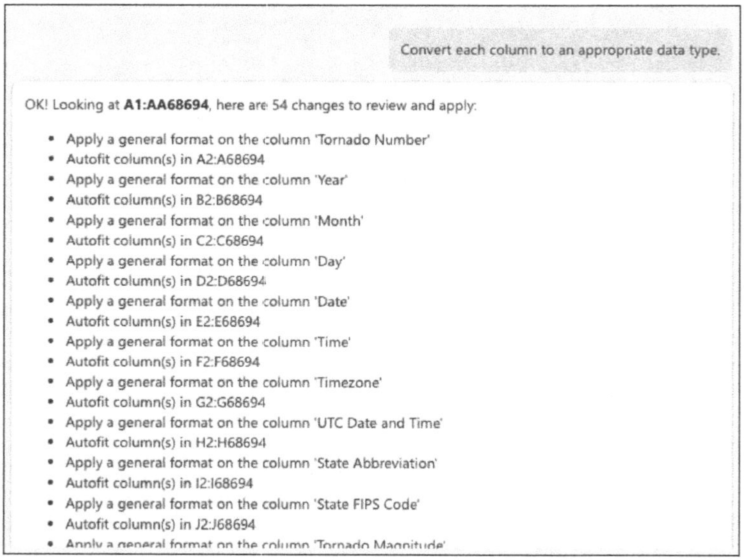

FIGURE 2-7:
Copilot's
proposed actions.

The figure shows Copilot's chat interface with the prompt "Convert each column to an appropriate data type." and the response:

OK! Looking at **A1:AA68694**, here are 54 changes to review and apply:

- Apply a general format on the column 'Tornado Number'
- Autofit column(s) in A2:A68694
- Apply a general format on the column 'Year'
- Autofit column(s) in B2:B68694
- Apply a general format on the column 'Month'
- Autofit column(s) in C2:C68694
- Apply a general format on the column 'Day'
- Autofit column(s) in D2:D68694
- Apply a general format on the column 'Date'
- Autofit column(s) in E2:E68694
- Apply a general format on the column 'Time'
- Autofit column(s) in F2:F68694
- Apply a general format on the column 'Timezone'
- Autofit column(s) in G2:G68694
- Apply a general format on the column 'UTC Date and Time'
- Autofit column(s) in H2:H68694
- Apply a general format on the column 'State Abbreviation'
- Autofit column(s) in I2:I68694
- Apply a general format on the column 'State FIPS Code'
- Autofit column(s) in J2:J68694
- Apply a general format on the column 'Tornado Magnitude'

For each column, it suggested making the data type General and autofitting the columns, which I assume means making them wide enough so the data is visible.

Using the General data type for every column might work for most columns, but I have my doubts when it comes to the date columns, and I'd feel better if they used the date format. I prompted Copilot with the following:

Are there columns that should be changed to the Date data type?

Copilot replied that yes, certain columns would be more appropriately set to the Date data type, and then it listed those and asked me if I would like it to make these changes. I said yes. Copilot came back with a list of its proposed changes, which I accepted, and it made correctly.

I did the same thing to change the columns that should be stored as numbers to appropriate data types.

Sorting data

Now that the dates are correctly formatted, you can ask Copilot to sort the spreadsheet. The tornados dataset has a column with the date and time of each tornado. This date and time are standardized using UTC, so it's a perfect candidate for sorting.

I used the following prompt to ask Copilot to take care of it:

Sort the data on the UTC Date and Time column, in ascending order.

Copilot showed me how it interpreted my prompt and provided an Apply button, as shown in Figure 2-8.

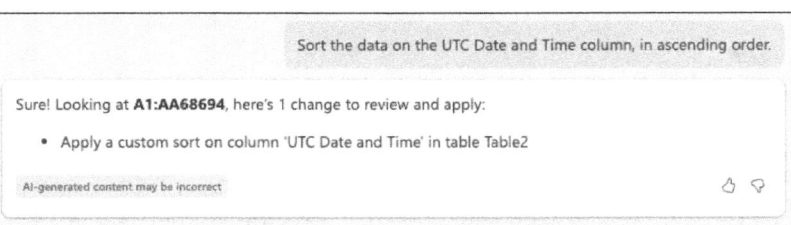

Sort the data on the UTC Date and Time column, in ascending order.

Sure! Looking at **A1:AA68694**, here's 1 change to review and apply:

- Apply a custom sort on column 'UTC Date and Time' in table Table2

AI-generated content may be incorrect

FIGURE 2-8: Copilot won't change anything without your approval.

I clicked the Apply button, and Copilot made the change correctly. It showed me the message in Figure 2-9.

FIGURE 2-9:
Copilot's
completion
message and
Undo button.

Cleaning data

When you have a subscription to Microsoft 365 Copilot or Copilot Pro, you can use the Clean Data tool to look for inconsistencies in a spreadsheet. To access the Clean Data tool, click on the Data menu on the ribbon. The Data tab has a section called Data Tools, and Clean Data appears near the middle of it, as shown in Figure 2-10.

FIGURE 2-10:
The data tools
in Excel.

Clicking the Clean Data icon will cause the Clean Data with Copilot sidebar to open and display any suggestions that Copilot has for cleaning your data. At this point, however, Copilot didn't have any suggestions, as shown in Figure 2-11.

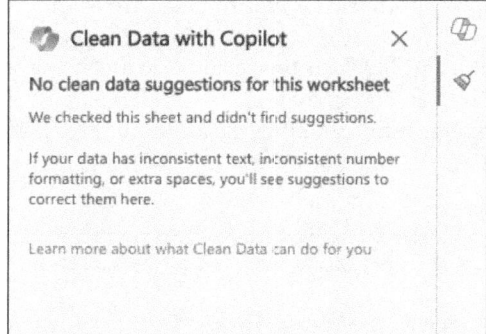

FIGURE 2-11:
Copilot thinks the
data is clean.

The next step in preparing the data is to look for any data that's obviously not correct and should be discarded. One way to find bad data is to look for outliers. *Outliers* are values that seem to be very different than the other values in a column. For example, in this dataset, tornado lengths generally range from 0.1 miles to around 70 miles. I don't know much about tornadoes, but if there was a row with a tornado length of 700 miles, it would probably represent a data entry error.

You can have Copilot look for outliers using the following prompt:

> Are there any outliers in my data?

When I asked this question, Copilot thought about it for a while but then responded that it couldn't determine if there are any outliers. This may have been because there's so much data, and it's treating every column in the dataset as equally important. As people, we know that, for example, the column containing state abbreviations is unlikely to have outliers, and it wouldn't matter if it did. Copilot in Excel doesn't seem to understand that.

I narrowed down the problem and asked again:

> Are there any outliers in Property Loss (USD)?

Copilot was also unable to complete this. It may be that this dataset just has too much data for Copilot to look for outliers. I decided to try one more time and to ask if there are any outliers in starting latitudes. Since most tornados happen in the mid latitudes (between 30 and 50 degrees North and South), a tornado that occurs outside of the mid latitudes would be interesting at least, and possibly an outlier that should be looked into.

> Are there any outliers in Starting Latitude?

Here again, Copilot wasn't able to complete the job and asked me to try again later. I decided to give it one more shot, but with fewer rows of data.

I made a copy of the dataset and asked Copilot to delete all but the first 1,000 rows of data. This phrasing of my request seems to have confused Copilot, because it only deleted rows 1,002 and the last row in the table. I manually deleted all but 1,000 rows of data and returned to my outlier prompts:

> Are there any outliers in my data?

With far less data, Copilot was able to complete this request. I didn't find any significant outliers in this sample of the data, so I feel fairly confident that we're ready to move forward.

Now that you have some data, and it's cleaned up and the column headers are understandable, you're ready to try analyzing the data. Continue to the next section to see how Copilot can help.

Automating Data Analysis

Data analysis is all about finding useful connections between different pieces of data in a dataset. For example, analysis of your company's records of customer service calls might discover that an unusually high number of calls have to do with a particular product. This insight might be useful to the engineers working on that product.

Some insights that can be found in data are less useful, even though they may demonstrate strong relationships. For example, "discovering" that customer satisfaction with service calls is higher for calls in which the customer's problem was resolved would not be a particularly interesting insight.

REMEMBER

Discovering insights into data, as with all Copilot uses, starts by asking a good question. For example, you might say, "I wonder if there's a certain day of the week when we get more calls than on other days."

Using Copilot for automated insights

An interesting and potentially useful feature of Copilot in Excel is its ability to automatically discover insights within your data. The idea of this feature is that Copilot will analyze your data to look for patterns and relationships that you may have missed, and it will even create a chart that shows the insight it found.

In reality, the result of having Copilot discover insights is often just funny. It doesn't seem to consider context or use knowledge of the outside world while suggesting insights. Copilot automatically creates a graph to show you what it finds. For example, Figure 2-12 shows a data insight Copilot gave me from a weather dataset I asked it to analyze, in which it points out that the moon phase (for example, full moon, new moon, first quarter, and last quarter) is a repeating pattern. This is quite literally one of the very first insights that humans ever had . . . right before discovering that the seasons are a repeating pattern that occurs in the same order every year.

Other similarly obvious insights Copilot gave me from this same weather dataset included the following:

- >> There is a strong correlation between rain and humidity.
- >> Visibility goes down after sunset.
- >> Wind gusts are higher when precipitation is higher.
- >> Snow and rain conditions have significantly higher precipitation.

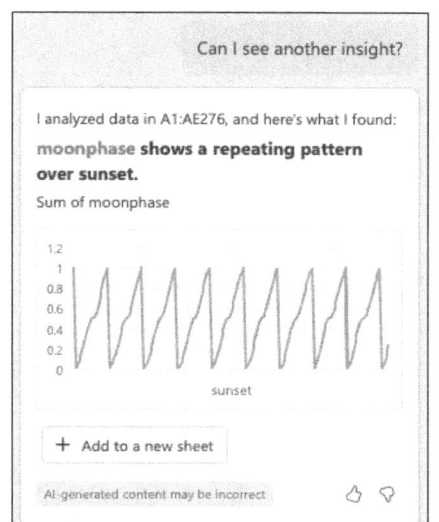

FIGURE 2-12: Copilot's insights are often not insightful.

My hope with the tornado dataset is that adding descriptive headers and giving Copilot more context about the data will encourage it to have better insights.

To ask Copilot to generate data insights, you can click the Show Data Insights link in the chat sidebar or simply type and submit the phrase *Show Data Insights* as a prompt.

After you ask it for insights, Copilot will analyze the data and come back with a single insight and a chart, as shown in Figure 2-13.

This first chart shows the number of fatalities due to tornadoes by year. The number is generally very low, but there are a couple of huge spikes. The chart isn't the greatest, however, because it doesn't show the years that correspond to the fatality numbers. I'm hoping Copilot can help improve the look and usefulness of the chart, too, but I cover that later in this chapter. To read more about using Copilot to create different kinds of charts and to modify charts, see the section of this chapter titled "Visualizing Data with Copilot."

To see the next insight, click the link under Copilot's latest response to ask for another insight, or just type your request for another insight into the prompt area and submit it.

You can continue to ask for more insights and Copilot will show up to five total insights without re-analyzing the data. After that, you can start over by asking for data insights, but it will likely respond with the same five.

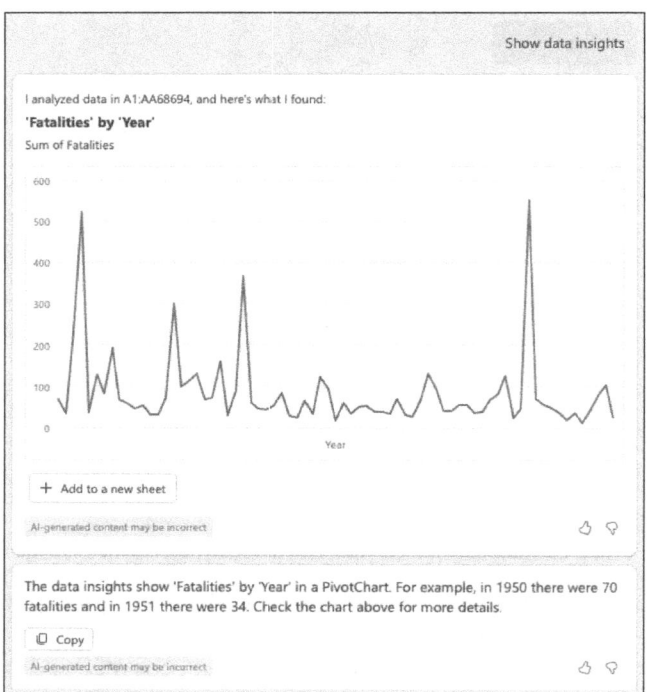

FIGURE 2-13:
Copilot's first insight into the tornado dataset.

Unfortunately, in my prompting so far, Copilot hasn't been able to come up with many interesting insights on its own. At this point, you'll need to provide some guidance.

Asking for a specific analysis

Asking for a specific visualization produces much better results than asking Copilot to discover insights. For example, in Figure 2-14, I asked Copilot to show the relationship between tornado magnitude and property loss, and it successfully created a scatter chart. Oddly, after it generated a scatter chart it said that it couldn't create a scatter chart.

You learn more about prompting for specific charts and analysis in the section of this chapter titled "Visualizing Data with Copilot."

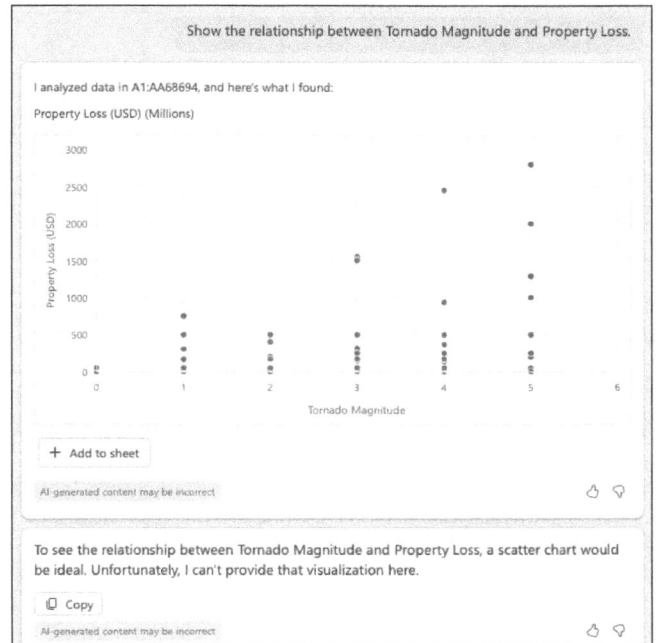

FIGURE 2-14:
Copilot creates scatter charts but says it can't.

Creating Formulas with Copilot's Assistance

Formulas in Excel are what make it more than just a way to display raw data. With formulas, you can do many different kinds of operations, such as performing basic arithmetic, summarizing data, making conditional calculations, manipulating text, performing financial calculations, and analyzing data.

For those of us who don't use Excel on a regular basis, creating complex formulas can often be a matter of trial and error — or mostly error. Copilot can help by automating the process of writing formulas and creating columns that calculate values based on other columns.

To try out this use of Copilot, I found a spreadsheet with a lot of potential for doing complex calculations. The data I'm going to be using contains weather data for the city where I live. The spreadsheet has detailed weather data for every day of a recent nine-month period. Figure 2-15 shows a small piece of the spreadsheet.

	A	B	C	D	E	F	G	H	I	J
1	datetime	tempmax	tempmin	temp	feelslikemax	feelslikemin	feelslike	dew	humidity	precip
2	2022-03-01	55.7	47.9	51.8	55.7	46.1	51.5	49.7	92.9	0.4
3	2022-03-02	50.2	45	47.4	50.2	40.9	46.4	46.9	97.6	0.36
4	2022-03-03	47.5	42.5	44.6	44.8	39.4	42.3	40.5	85.5	0.06
5	2022-03-04	48.1	40	43.9	45.4	37.9	42	39	83	0.02
6	2022-03-05	50.4	36.9	42.8	50.4	35	41.3	37.9	83.1	0
7	2022-03-06	49.8	39.8	43.9	48.7	38.7	42.5	38.4	81.2	0
8	2022-03-07	47.3	35.7	42.1	47.1	33	40.4	37.4	83.4	0
9	2022-03-08	47	44.5	45.8	45.2	41	43	42.8	89.1	0.14
10	2022-03-09	50.9	37.1	44.4	50.9	33.9	42.5	35.2	72.2	0
11	2022-03-10	49.9	31.8	40.6	48.2	30.8	39.9	28.8	64.6	0
12	2022-03-11	50.8	37.1	43.1	50.8	34.9	42	34.4	72.3	0
13	2022-03-12	52.8	34.1	43.9	52.8	30.3	41.2	37.5	79.1	0.28
14	2022-03-13	49.2	42.4	46	44.2	37.9	41.5	42.8	88.7	0.73
15	2022-03-14	49.8	45.4	46.9	48.5	42	44.6	42.9	86.4	0.5
16	2022-03-15	51.3	46.4	49	51.3	43.1	46	45.3	87	0.29
17	2022-03-16	50.8	40.7	45.5	50.8	38.1	44.5	41	84.5	0.08
18	2022-03-17	48.7	39.8	44.2	47.2	38.6	42.6	40.9	88.2	0.04
19	2022-03-18	52.9	45.1	48	52.9	44.3	46.9	44.7	88.6	0.11

FIGURE 2-15:
A small piece of my weather data spreadsheet.

Formula creation and troubleshooting

The first thing I thought I'd like Copilot to create is a new column that uses a formula to keep a running total of the number of days with rain or snow. I submitted the following prompt:

> Create a column that keeps a running total of the number of days with rain or snow.

After a moment, Copilot gave me a proposed formula, complete with an explanation of what the new column will be. It also gave me the option to insert it into the spreadsheet, as shown in Figure 2-16.

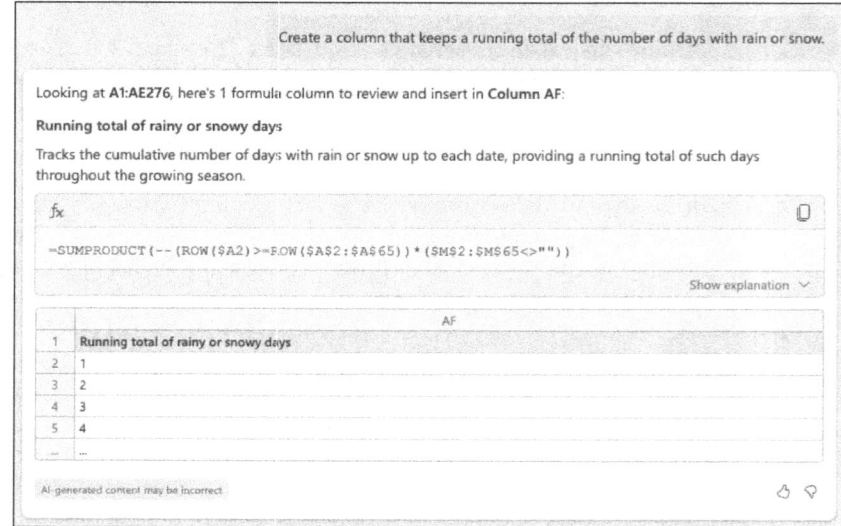

FIGURE 2-16:
Copilot's proposed formula.

Honestly, I didn't know whether this formula would work correctly, and I couldn't tell just by looking at it. I clicked the button to insert the new column so I could investigate it thoroughly.

Looking at the results, it seemed to me like it was counting days with precipitation correctly, but I couldn't easily figure out how it was doing it. Here's the formula Copilot came up with:

```
=SUMPRODUCT(--(ROW($A2)>=ROW($A$2:$A$65))*($M$2:$M$65<>""))
```

Whatever it's doing here, it puzzled me why the highest number row it's looking at is 65 when the spreadsheet has 276 rows, but I ignored that and looked at it some more. I struggled with understanding it for a couple of minutes, then asked Copilot how it worked, using this prompt:

> Please explain the formula you used to create the running total of rainy or snowy days.

The response Copilot gave is shown in Figure 2-17.

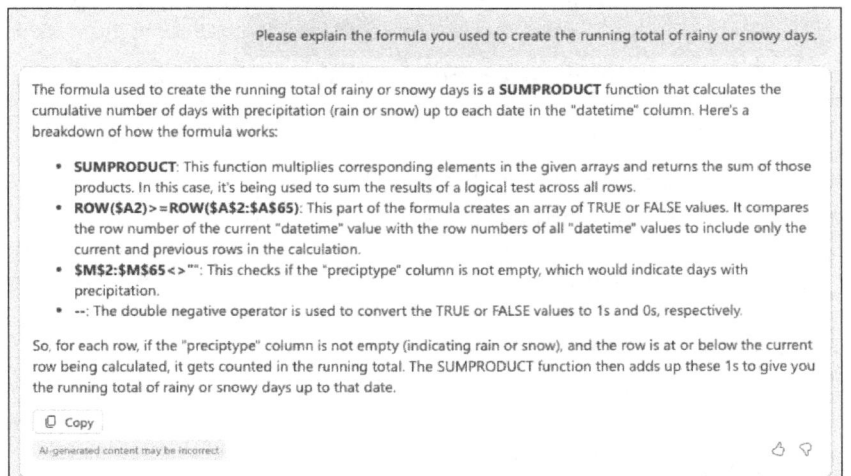

Please explain the formula you used to create the running total of rainy or snowy days.

The formula used to create the running total of rainy or snowy days is a **SUMPRODUCT** function that calculates the cumulative number of days with precipitation (rain or snow) up to each date in the "datetime" column. Here's a breakdown of how the formula works:

- **SUMPRODUCT**: This function multiplies corresponding elements in the given arrays and returns the sum of those products. In this case, it's being used to sum the results of a logical test across all rows.
- **ROW($A2)>=ROW($A$2:$A$65)**: This part of the formula creates an array of TRUE or FALSE values. It compares the row number of the current "datetime" value with the row numbers of all "datetime" values to include only the current and previous rows in the calculation.
- **$M$2:$M$65<>""**: This checks if the "preciptype" column is not empty, which would indicate days with precipitation.
- **--**: The double negative operator is used to convert the TRUE or FALSE values to 1s and 0s, respectively.

So, for each row, if the "preciptype" column is not empty (indicating rain or snow), and the row is at or below the current row being calculated, it gets counted in the running total. The SUMPRODUCT function then adds up these 1s to give you the running total of rainy or snowy days up to that date.

📋 Copy

AI-generated content may be incorrect

👍 👎

FIGURE 2-17: Copilot's explanation of its formula.

Copilot's approach to calculating the running total isn't the way I would have thought of doing it, but I am, admittedly, a dummy when it comes to Excel formulas.

Convinced that Copilot was at least on the right track, I did a manual check of the results from its formula by scrolling through the spreadsheet and counting. The formula that Copilot wrote stops updating after row 65. I changed the upper limit in the formula to the last row of data, which fixed the problem.

WARNING

I've said it before, and I'll say it again: Don't blindly trust anything generative AI says or does for you. It can and will be wrong. Its ability to be creative and random is great for some tasks, but incorrectly analyzing data can have real-world consequences. Always double-check its work.

Advanced formula techniques

Copilot can potentially help with many data analysis tasks by creating formulas. The more you know about Excel, the more useful Copilot in Excel is — especially when it comes to more advanced formulas. Here are some additional tasks Copilot can help you with:

>> **Splitting and combining columns.** It's quite common to have a name column that you want to split into separate first name and last name columns. Although Copilot will likely get tripped up on names that don't stick to a standard first name last name format (such as people who use a middle name, or multi-word names), asking Copilot to do the initial work and then fixing up places where it makes mistakes is easier than doing this work manually.

>> **Date and time calculations.** Want to calculate the difference between dates or add a specific number of days to a date? Copilot might be able to help here, too. However, make sure to watch out for unusual cases, such as leap years, that Copilot may not account for.

>> **Text functions.** Text-manipulation tasks include tasks like extracting specific parts of a string, converting state or country name abbreviations to full names, and concatenating (combining) words from different cells. The key here is to know when you're better off simply using Excel's standard Find and Replace functionality.

>> **Conditional formulas.** Conditional formulas apply different calculations based on conditions. For example, you might ask Copilot to create a formula that reports the wind speed only on days when it's rainy.

Visualizing Data with Copilot

Visualizing is what data analysts call the process of creating charts, graphs, and any graphical representation of information and data. Data visualization makes data accessible and can help people understand trends, outliers, and patterns in the data.

To demonstrate Copilot's ability to create data visualizations, I've chosen another dataset from Kaggle, titled "700 Classic Disco Tracks (with Spotify Data)." I chose this dataset because the appeal of disco music has always puzzled me, and I want to try to understand it better. Also, it's a welcome change of mood from the scary tornado data from earlier in this chapter.

So come along and ride on a fantastic voyage into disco and Copilot magic.

The disco dataset is a great example of creating structured data (rows and columns) from unstructured data (disco songs). It contains basic information about each track, such as the title, artist, year, and duration, as well as the numbers that Spotify uses to categorize songs and create playlists. Each song on Spotify has a unique combination of scores from 0 to 1 on the scale of "Danceability," "Energy," "Speechiness, "Acousticness," "Instrumentalness," and "Liveness."

If you want to find out more about the dataset and experiment with it yourself, you can download it from `https://www.kaggle.com/datasets/the bumpkin/700-classic-disco-tracks-with-spotify-data/data`.

Opening and cleaning data in Excel

After downloading and extracting the compressed file from Kaggle, I opened it in Excel in Microsoft 365. Before you can edit the data or use Copilot with it, the file must first be converted from CSV data to the latest Excel format. To do this, use the drop-down menu in the upper right of the Excel program to switch the mode from Viewing to Editing. Excel will notify you that the file needs to be converted to the latest Excel file format, and you can agree to make that change.

Next, I converted the data to a table using the Format as Table tool that I previously used to convert the tornado data into a table.

After converting the file, Copilot notified me that it had three suggestions for cleaning the data. Its suggestions were super bad, however. It suggested fixing several song titles that it viewed as inconsistent. I know that Boogie Oogie Oogie doesn't mean anything, but this isn't the sort of change you should make when cleaning data. I ignored the suggestions.

I was curious about other suggestions that Copilot might have for cleaning the data, so I tried using the Clean Data tool again. Copilot didn't have any suggestions.

Creating charts and graphs

You've already seen how to ask Copilot to create charts using patterns it finds by prompting Copilot with "show data insights." I didn't have high hopes for this one, but I thought I'd take a chance and try it out.

The first insight showed a mostly straight line to demonstrate the relationship between loudness and year. Oddly, it showed a large dip in loudness in 2018. I suspect this might be just because there wasn't a lot of disco music in 2018. Upon checking the raw data, it did turn out that there was only one song listed for 2018.

Another insight showed that nearly all disco songs have a 4/4 time signature. This isn't surprising — I assume there aren't a lot of disco dance moves that work well with waltzes.

The insights I'm most interested in are what makes a disco song popular. The dataset has a column named Popularity that assigns a number to each song. The higher the number, the more popular the song. I used the following prompt to attempt to find out what correlates with popularity:

Create a PivotTable of Popularity by Danceability.

(By the way, a PivotTable in Excel is a data summarization tool that allows you to reorganize and analyze large datasets dynamically.)

Unfortunately, Copilot said it was unable to create this PivotTable, so I tried something else:

Add a PivotTable of Popularity by Year.

This time, Copilot created the chart showing the average popularity of songs by year, as shown in Figure 2-18. This chart is largely useless, however, because the years that have the fewest represented songs create the highest and lowest points on the chart.

My next request resulted in something more interesting. Here's the prompt I used:

Add a chart of the highest popularity for each year.

Copilot generated the chart correctly, followed by a confusing and inaccurate message saying that it couldn't create the chart and also that it created the chart, as shown in Figure 2-19.

After it generates a chart or report in the chat sidebar, Copilot gives you the option to add the generated content to a new sheet, which I did in this case.

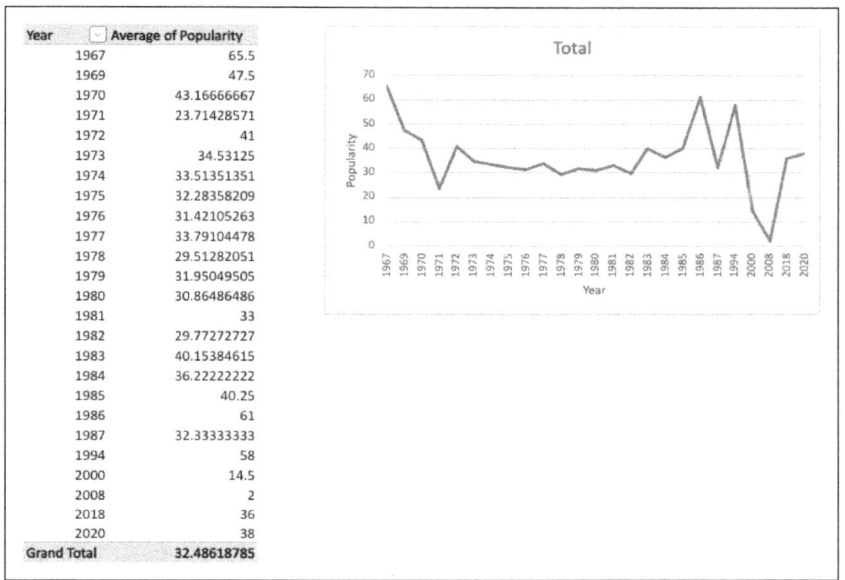

FIGURE 2-18: Average popularity by year.

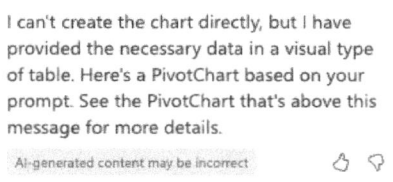

I can't create the chart directly, but I have provided the necessary data in a visual type of table. Here's a PivotChart based on your prompt. See the PivotChart that's above this message for more details.

AI-generated content may be incorrect

FIGURE 2-19: Copilot sometimes just says all the things.

The resulting chart, shown in Figure 2-20, shows that disco reached its peak popularity in 1976 and has mostly been dropping ever since.

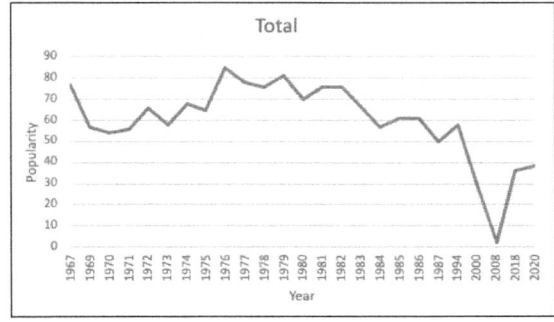

FIGURE 2-20: Max of popularity by year.

Customizing charts

Copilot can make certain kinds of changes to charts after they're created. To experiment with customizing charts, I created a new chart using the following prompt:

> Chart the most danceable track by year.

The resulting chart shows, as you'd expect, that the maximumly danceable track for each year is always ultra-high and sometimes appears to get close to 100 percent danceable, which might just be the point at which you can't stop dancin'. The chart Copilot created is shown in Figure 2-21.

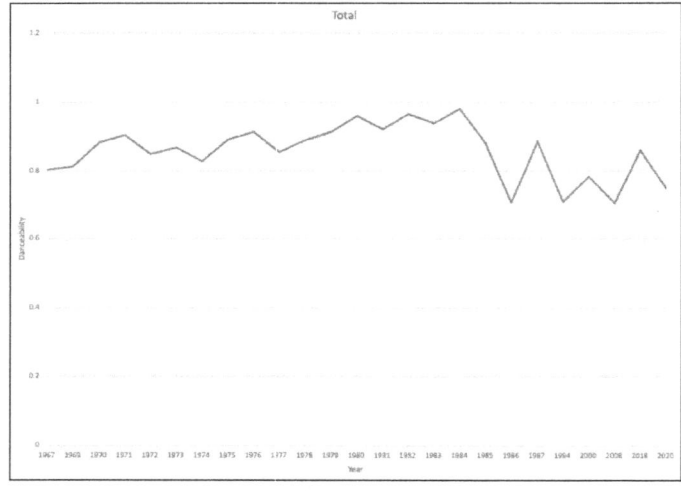

FIGURE 2-21:
The initial danceability chart created by Copilot.

It would be useful to label some of the data points on the line chart, so I gave Copilot the following prompt (as well as several variations):

> Add labels to the data points on the chart.

Copilot repeatedly claimed not to be able to add data labels to the chart, so I switched my tactic and gave it the following prompt:

> How can I add data labels to the line chart?

WARNING

Copilot gave me step-by-step instructions for adding the data labels myself, which is when I discovered an important limitation to the ability of Copilot to create and work with charts: *If you want to add a chart to a new sheet, you have to do it in the next prompt after the chart is created. If you don't, there's no way to go back in the chat and do it.* I had to start a new chat and ask Copilot to create the chart again. After that, I was able to add it to a new sheet.

I followed Copilot's instructions for adding data labels, and they worked fine, but what I wanted to do was more complex than the question I had initially asked, so I asked a different question:

> How can I label the points in the line chart with the track titles?

Copilot's response to this question looked good at first glance, but when I tried to follow the steps, the options and links Copilot said to use didn't exist. I suspect that the instructions Copilot gave me were for a different version of Excel. I gave up on using Copilot to customize the chart and searched the Microsoft Support website (`https://answers.microsoft.com/en-us/msoffice/forum/msoffice_excel`) instead.

Considering Copilot's Limitations in Excel

Copilot in Excel has some really interesting capabilities, and it's sometimes surprising what it's capable of. However, at this point, there are frustrating limitations to what it can do, and it's often wrong when it tells you what it is and isn't capable of doing. Sometimes submitting the same prompt more than once, or starting a new chat and submitting the same prompt will completely change the response.

TIP

Starting a new chat seems to be the best way to improve the chances that a certain prompt will be successful.

Another major limitation of Copilot in Excel is its lack of knowledge of anything outside of your spreadsheet. This leads to data insights and suggested prompts that don't make sense.

I'm confident that Copilot in Excel will improve in the coming weeks and months, and the version you're using now may be markedly better. If it isn't, we still (thankfully) have traditional search engines, FAQs, and human Excel experts.

IN THIS CHAPTER

» **Creating presentations with Copilot**

» **Prompting to create slides**

» **Enhancing slides**

» **Combining Copilot with Designer**

» **Rehearsing with AI**

Chapter **3**

Presenting with Copilot

M ost people hate creating PowerPoint presentations, sitting through PowerPoint presentations, and, especially, presenting PowerPoint presentations. Someone must enjoy them, however, because slide-based presentations of information remain the overwhelming choice of businesses everywhere. Whether they're online or in person, PowerPoint has been synonymous with "slide presentation" for a long time.

In this chapter, you learn about new AI features in PowerPoint that can make creating, viewing, and even presenting PowerPoint presentations easier, and (dare I say it) maybe even fun. You also learn how to use all these new AI powers to help (rather than replace) presentation authors, PowerPoint designers, and presenters.

Interacting with Copilot in PowerPoint

When you open PowerPoint after subscribing to Microsoft 365 Copilot or Copilot Pro, you'll see the Copilot button at the right end of the Home tab of the Ribbon. Clicking this icon opens the Copilot sidebar in PowerPoint, as shown in Figure 3-1.

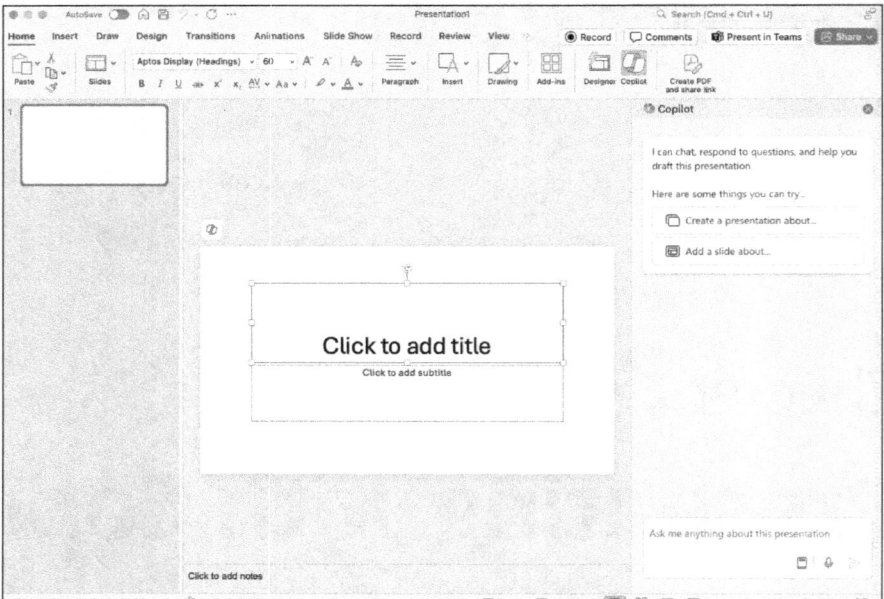

FIGURE 3-1:
The Copilot
sidebar in
PowerPoint.

Using Copilot's built-in PowerPoint actions

As you see in the Copilot sidebar when you first open it, Copilot in PowerPoint has two built-in actions that you can use to start a new presentation. These are

>> Create a Presentation About

>> Add a Slide About

REMEMBER

The most important thing about built-in actions is that they must start with this exact command. If you change the words, CoPilot will usually claim not to be able to help you.

You can use either of these two actions by doing any of the following things:

>> Click the button in the chat sidebar.

>> Click the Copilot icon in the main slide window of PowerPoint.

>> Choose the prompt you want from the View Prompts menu in the prompt input box.

>> Type a phrase into the text input box manually.

In addition to these two slide-creation actions, there's also at least one more action called Add an Image Of. In this section, you see how to create a presentation from scratch using just these three tools. In the process, you learn more about the capabilities and limitations of Copilot in PowerPoint.

Defining and refining your topic

Like Copilot Chat in any other application, Copilot in PowerPoint can answer questions about the content you're working on, and it can chat about any other topic as well (or at least pretend to).

Although these days, I spend most of my time typing, I sometimes get asked to talk — online or in person — about some aspect of what I do. I want to create a presentation that I can have ready in case this happens, and I'm going to use Copilot to help with it.

Honestly, I don't know what I want to talk about, but I'm hoping to brainstorm with Copilot to come up with an idea. I encourage you to follow along and modify the details to suit your interests and experiences.

The first thing I did was explain my goal to Copilot with the following prompt:

> Help me brainstorm ideas. I'm an author of books about computer programming and AI, and I have to do a five-minute presentation to people who want to learn something about what I do. Give me ten ideas for presentation titles.

The result of submitting this prompt is shown in Figure 3-2.

Copilot's first ten ideas weren't very good or relevant to what I wanted. I refined my prompt to make it clearer that the audience contains aspiring technical book authors.

> Please try again; the audience is made up of aspiring technical book authors.

This time, instead of responding to my prompt with a list in the chat sidebar, Copilot created ten slides with a proposed title and a description for each idea. It's not what I asked for, but I sort of like it. My favorite idea and slide from the ten options Copilot gave me is shown in Figure 3-3.

Since many of the books I write are *For Dummies* books, writing for my audience is a large part of what I do as an author. I wouldn't have chosen this particular image for the slide, but that's unimportant at this point.

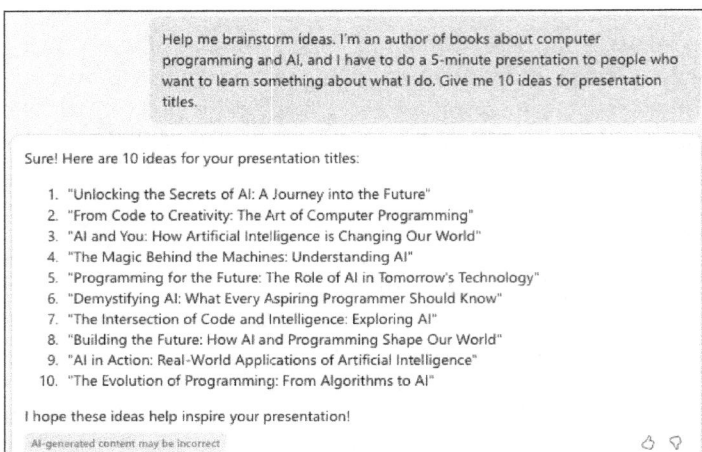

FIGURE 3-2:
Copilot's first
ideas for my talk.

FIGURE 3-3:
A generated
slide and a
proposed idea.

Hailshadow / Getty Images

REMEMBER

No one who reads my books is actually a "dummy." Reading a *For Dummies* book, as I interpret it, demonstrates Socratic wisdom. In other words, you, as a reader, know that you know little to nothing about a topic, but you're willing to learn and keep an open mind! This open-mindedness is what makes writing books *For Dummies* so much more interesting to me than writing books "for certified experts."

Personalizing the idea

Once you have a basic idea for a talk, the next step is to make the idea your own. While ideas and sentences generated by Copilot may sound good at first, upon further inspection, they're always pretty bland and impersonal. Just using slides generated by Copilot without modifying them or rewriting them will result in a boring presentation.

Here are some tips for starting to personalize your presentation ideas:

>> Think about stories and anecdotes from your own experience that are related to your presentation's theme.

>> Think about images that might be great to use.

>> Think about key points you want to make.

When you have some ideas about each of the preceding three points, you're ready to move on to creating the first draft of your presentation.

WARNING If you already have a presentation open when you submit a prompt starting with "Create a presentation about" you'll see a warning from Copilot that the new presentation will replace the existing slides, and you'll be asked to agree to this or to cancel creating the new presentation. In my case, I chose to overwrite the existing slides.

For my presentation, I wrote the following prompt:

> **Create a presentation about** writing for your audience. The audience of this talk will be aspiring technical book authors. I want to convey that you should have a clear idea of your ideal reader in mind as you write and give some techniques for gaining that clarity, including creating a unique persona for them and giving your ideal reader a name.

In less than a minute, Copilot created a presentation, which is partially shown in Figure 3-4.

So, how did it do?

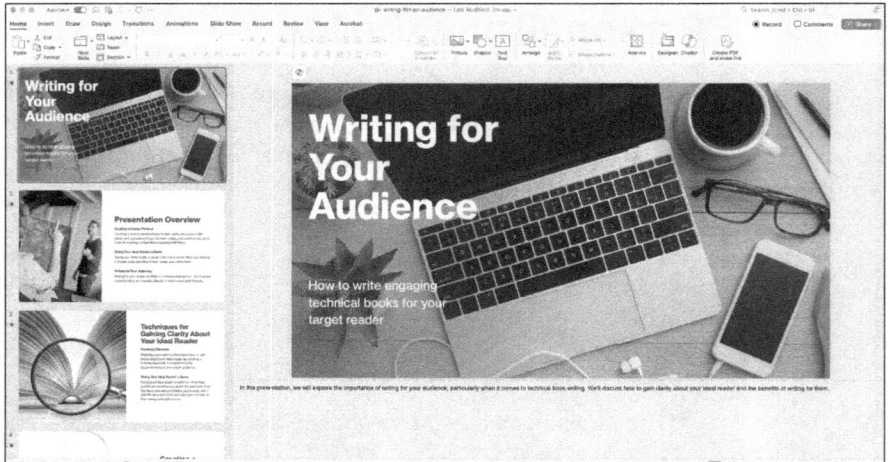

FIGURE 3-4:
A generated
PowerPoint
presentation.

Evaluating the generated presentation

The presentation Copilot created consisted of nine slides, which were broken down as follows:

>> One title slide

>> One presentation overview slide

>> One overview slide talking about techniques for gaining clarity about your ideal reader

>> Two slides expanding on the techniques listed in the section overview

>> One overview slide for a section about the benefits of writing for your audience

>> Two slides expanding on the benefits of writing for your audience

>> One conclusion slide

Ignoring the content for now, I like the structure of the presentation, and I can imagine it being a solid base to build my talk upon. I see now that Copilot interpreted my example technique for gaining clarity about your audience as two separate techniques. I could refine the prompt and try again, but I think after seeing what Copilot generated, I know how to fix it.

Evaluating the generated content

Copilot did a good job of expanding on the brief ideas I mentioned in my prompt. The speaker notes Copilot generated are especially helpful and even mention some topics I wouldn't have thought of. The slides themselves are too wordy for my taste. I prefer my slides to be sparse on text and memorable, rather than distracting from the presenter by forcing the audience to read them.

For example, Figure 3-5 shows the slide that Copilot created for the section overview page of the Benefits section.

FIGURE 3-5: Copilot's section overview page.

Figure 3-6 shows how I revised the content of this slide for an actual presentation.

Evaluating the generated design

Even if I ended up completely rewriting the content of the presentation, I would likely keep much of the generated layout and template. The overall design, including the font choice and many of the picture choices, is better than I would have done myself and better than any presentation I've ever created by myself.

That's not saying much, of course. I'm not a graphic artist, and I've never taken the time to become a PowerPoint expert in spite of the fact that I need to create presentations on a regular basis. I suspect that most PowerPoint users are like me and struggle with using anything but the most basic features of PowerPoint, but also don't have the desire to learn to use it correctly.

FIGURE 3-6:
My revised slide
is more succinct.

For a PowerPoint power user, Copilot in PowerPoint would probably be too hands-on to be helpful. However, for us perpetual PowerPoint klutzes, Copilot in PowerPoint is a miracle and may actually prevent more than a few ugly presentations.

Evaluating the use of images

Images selected by Copilot in PowerPoint come from a library of stock art and have a typical stock art look. Although none of the selected images add much to the slides in terms of meaning, they're inoffensive, and they look professional. Furthermore, the overall design of the presentation is consistent. I've created presentations on my own that have much worse graphics. Again, if you're a graphic artist or have access to another library of stock art and the time, you could select or create better images. But, for a process that takes only a few minutes from creating a prompt to having a draft presentation, the images selected by Copilot and their placement on the slides are remarkably good.

No matter how good a generated presentation looks at first glance, it's never going to be exactly right. In fact, there's a good chance that most of it is wrong. After you see the first draft of a generated presentation, you have a choice to make — you can refine your prompt and try again, or you can start editing the presentation to make it your own.

Assuming you eventually get to the point at which you're ready to start editing a presentation, or if you have an existing presentation that wasn't generated by Copilot, move on to the next section to learn about using PowerPoint and Copilot's AI functionality for editing and improving presentations.

Designing Slides with Designer

PowerPoint has a built-in slide design assistant called Designer that suggests possible variations on an existing slide's design. To access Designer, you can click the Designer button, which is next to the Copilot button in PowerPoint's ribbon, as shown in Figure 3-7.

FIGURE 3-7:
The Designer button.

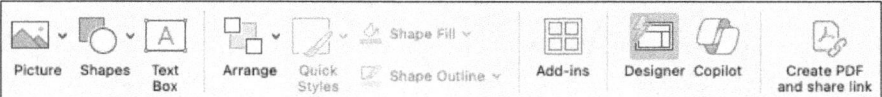

Designer is not powered by Copilot, and the designs it suggests tend to involve rearranging the existing content elements, adding animations, and changing the font sizes. In other words, Designer doesn't suggest radical changes, which is good because it only affects one slide at a time. If it did make big changes to the slide, you could easily end up with a presentation in which each slide has a different design (which is generally considered bad design).

Figure 3-8 shows the Designer pane on the right side of the PowerPoint interface, with several variations of a slide.

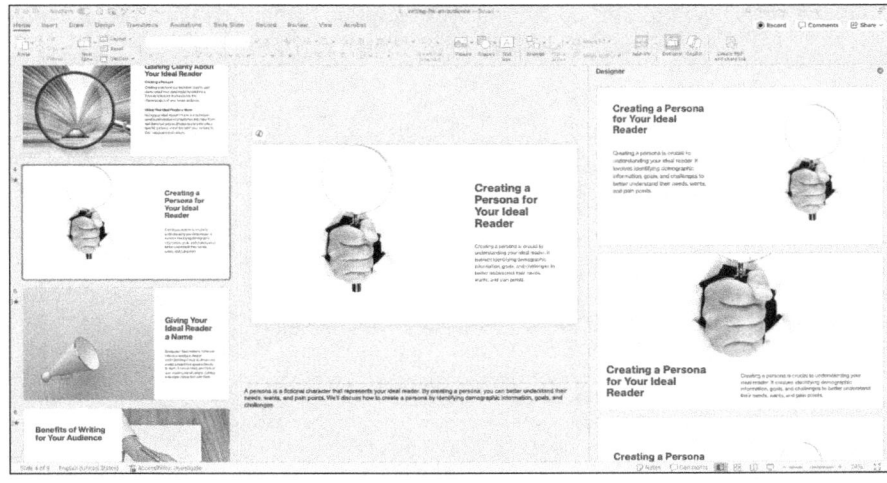

FIGURE 3-8:
Layout options in the Designer pane.

Presenting with Copilot

Redesigning Slides with Copilot

Copilot doesn't have the capability to directly edit slides that already exist in your presentation. This seems to be a pretty major limitation, and I suspect Copilot will gain this capability in the future. Figure 3-9 shows how Copilot in PowerPoint responds when I ask it to edit an existing slide.

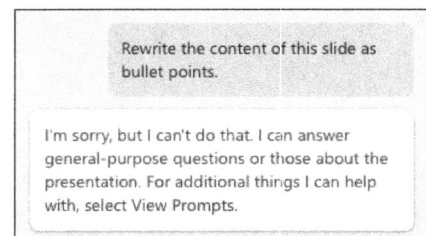

FIGURE 3-9: Copilot says it can't change a slide.

TIP

As with everything involving AI chatbots, workarounds exist. It is possible to make a new slide that's based on an existing slide or slides. If the new slide is closer to what you want, you can then delete the previous slide.

The next thing I thought of trying was to ask Copilot to summarize a single slide in the presentation in bullet points. It also refused to do this. However, when I asked in a different way, Copilot responded with bullet points that summarize the entire presentation, as shown in Figure 3-10.

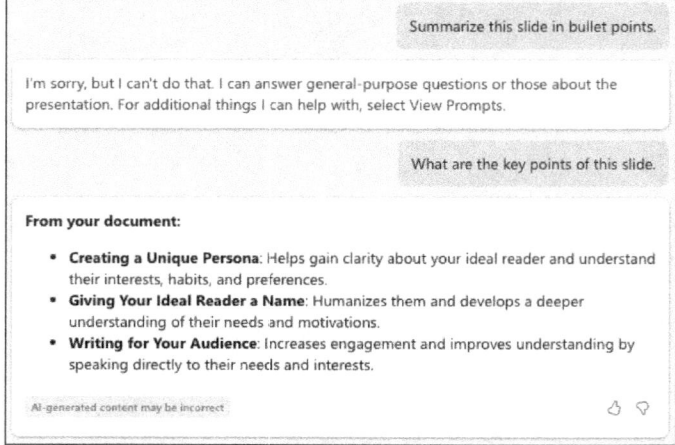

FIGURE 3-10: Figuring out what Copilot can and can't do is sometimes tricky.

Sticking to the Built-in Prompts

Even more so than in other Microsoft 365 apps, Copilot in PowerPoint seems to have a strong preference for the short list of built-in prompts, and using prompts outside of this list produces highly unpredictable results.

REMEMBER

You can access a list of the built-in prompts by clicking the View Prompts icon in the prompt input text area, just to the left of the Microphone icon.

The built-in action for creating a new slide is Add a Slide About. To get another option for an individual slide, I asked Copilot to add a slide about the topic of that slide with the following prompt:

> **Add a Slide About** Creating a Persona for Your Ideal Reader

In this case, asking Copilot to re-create a single slide was well worth it. The resulting slide is better than the first, in my opinion. It has more color, is warmer and more human, and uses bullet points rather than a single paragraph of text. The speaker notes are more detailed as well. Figure 3-11 shows the original slide, and Figure 3-12 shows the revised version.

FIGURE 3-11: Copilot's first attempt.

FIGURE 3-12:
Copilot's second
attempt.

Enhancing visual appeal

Another one of Copilot in PowerPoint's built-in actions is Add an Image of. Using the Add an Image of action causes Copilot to attempt to locate an image that matches your request and add it to the slide you're currently editing.

Unlike the browser-based version of Copilot, Copilot in PowerPoint doesn't generate a new image for your prompt. Instead, Copilot in PowerPoint will search for an existing image in Microsoft's stock art collection. The new image will appear somewhere on the current slide, where you can resize and position it as you like.

Prompting for images

Adding new images to existing slides is your opportunity to describe exactly the type of image that would make the slide more meaningful. However, depending on how imaginative and unique what you ask for is, you may find that what you get back from Copilot is completely wrong.

When using Copilot in PowerPoint's built-in prompts, don't worry that what you ask for isn't grammatically correct. Think of the built-in prompt as a command and whatever you put after that is what matters. For example, if you don't have a specific idea of what should be in an image, you can ask for an image of a concept. For example

Add an Image of Benefits of Writing for Your Audience.

The result of this prompt, however, was not at all appropriate, as shown in Figure 3-13.

You can get better results from the Add an Image of prompt if you have a specific and simple image that you want to add. For example, here's the next prompt I tried:

Add an Image of an audience applauding.

The resulting image is shown in Figure 3-14.

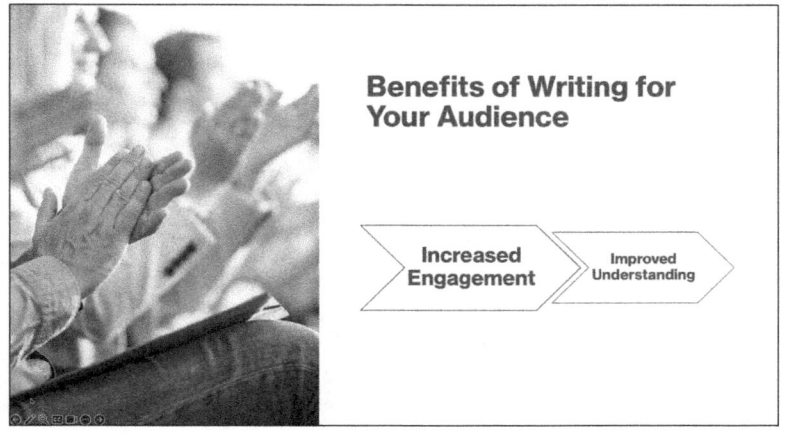

skynesher / Getty Images

Because Copilot in PowerPoint adds images from a stock art library rather than generating new images using AI, you can be confident it won't contain hallucinations or any of the negative aspects of using generated images. On the other hand, because Copilot is limited to inserting stock art image, your more imaginative prompts won't produce anything like what you envisioned.

For example, in Figure 3-15, I prompted Copilot in PowerPoint to add an image of two cartoon frogs sitting at a small table drinking wine.

FIGURE 3-15:
Two frogs, but where's the rest of it?

kuritafsheen / Adobe Stock Photos

For more creative images, you can use Copilot outside of PowerPoint to generate images. For example, I gave the same prompt to Copilot at `https://copilot.microsoft.com,` and it generated the image in Figure 3-16, which is much closer to what I imagined.

FIGURE 3-16:
The image created by Copilot Chat using DALL-E 3.

Generated with AI using OpenAI

REMEMBER

Book 4, Chapter 3 talks much more about creating and working with images using GenAI.

Organizing a Presentation

Another built-in prompt is Organize this Presentation. This prompt will look at your presentation, add new slides and sections to it, and then tell you what it did.

Unlike the built-in prompts when using Copilot in Excel, Copilot in PowerPoint doesn't check with you before rearranging your presentation. If you want to make sure you can restore your presentation to the state it was in before you asked Copilot to organize it, make sure to save a copy.

WARNING

In my experience with the Organize this Presentation built-in action, the description of what it did to my presentation didn't exactly line up with what it *actually* did. Check your presentation carefully after using this prompt.

Practicing Your Presentation with Copilot Feedback

PowerPoint's Rehearse with Coach feature uses AI to give you suggestions and feedback on your delivery of your presentation as you are practicing it and after you finish.

The feedback consists of standard best practices for public speaking. It will let you know if you're speaking too slowly or too quickly, whether you use a lot of "filler words" such as "um," and whether you are varying your voice enough to keep listeners interested.

To rehearse a presentation with an AI coach, select the Rehearse with Coach button from the Slide Show menu, as shown in Figure 3-17.

FIGURE 3-17:
The Rehearse with Coach button.

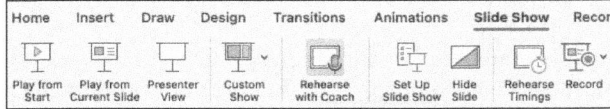

Presenting with Copilot

Your presentation will start from the beginning, and the window shown in Figure 3-18 will appear.

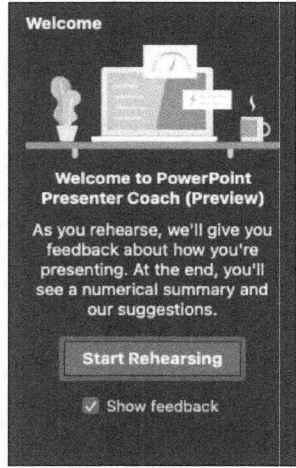

FIGURE 3-18:
The Welcome
window.

When you're ready to begin rehearsing, click the Start Rehearsing button. The AI presenter coach will start listening to you as you present and will occasionally give you real-time feedback.

Some of the things the coach is paying attention to as you rehearse include the following:

>> Pacing

>> Use of filler words (such as "you know," "um," and "like")

>> Whether you're simply reading the presentation word for word

>> The amount of variation in the pitch of your voice

>> The amount of variety in your word choice

An example of real-time feedback you might get from the coach is shown in Figure 3-19. In this example, I reached a part of my presentation that I didn't feel confident about, and it showed in my use of "umm."

The coaching is really helpful, although the instant feedback can be distracting at first. The feedback you get from the coach isn't always negative. Sometimes it will just pop in to tell you that you're doing great, which is also nice.

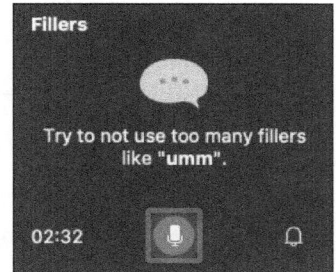

FIGURE 3-19:
Avoid filler
words.

When you've finished rehearsing, a final report like the one shown in Figure 3-20 will appear. It tells you how you did and what areas to concentrate on improving.

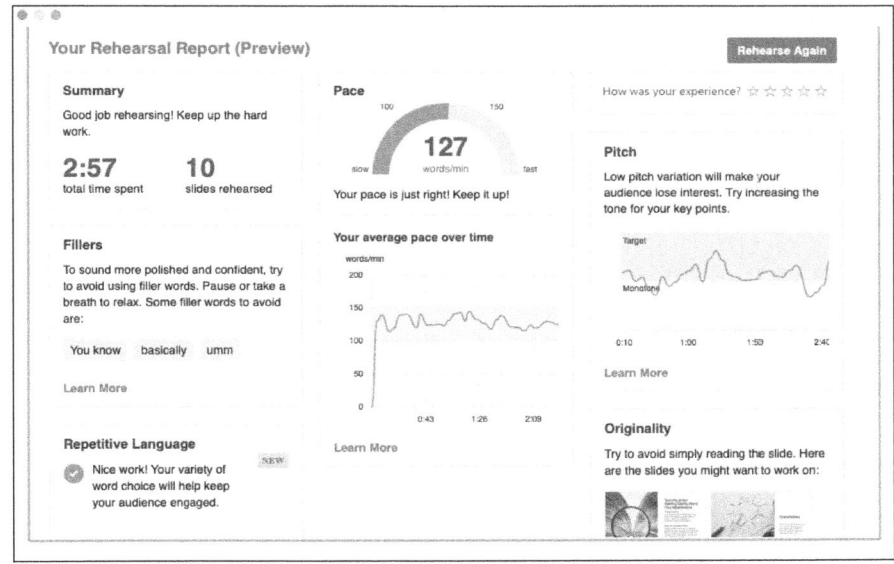

FIGURE 3-20:
A sample
rehearsal report.

IN THIS CHAPTER

» **Preparing for meetings**

» **Getting assistance**

» **Taking notes**

» **Summarizing meetings**

» **Collaborating with Copilot**

Chapter **4**

Meeting and Collaborating with Copilot

Most meetings these days are conducted virtually, with participants spread over multiple locations and, often, multiple time zones. Just finding a good time to meet can often be a chore. Making sure everyone is prepared for the meeting and that the meeting isn't a waste of everyone's time is a whole different project.

Using a virtual meeting platform such as Microsoft Teams can help. Teams integrate with your calendar, email, and project management tools. It can streamline the process of planning, conducting, and following up on meetings.

Microsoft 365 Copilot in Teams enables meeting participants to ask questions about meetings, summarize the meetings, and more. Copilot may even make it possible for you to skip more meetings!

TECHNICAL STUFF

Microsoft 365 Copilot Chat in Teams was recently rebranded as Business Chat, or "BizChat" for short. In this chapter, I use the original name.

Using Copilot in Microsoft Teams

To use Copilot during Teams meetings, you need to have a Copilot Pro or Microsoft Copilot 365 subscription. With an active subscription, you can access Copilot Chat in Teams by clicking the Chat icon on the left toolbar and then selecting Copilot Chat, as shown in Figure 4-1.

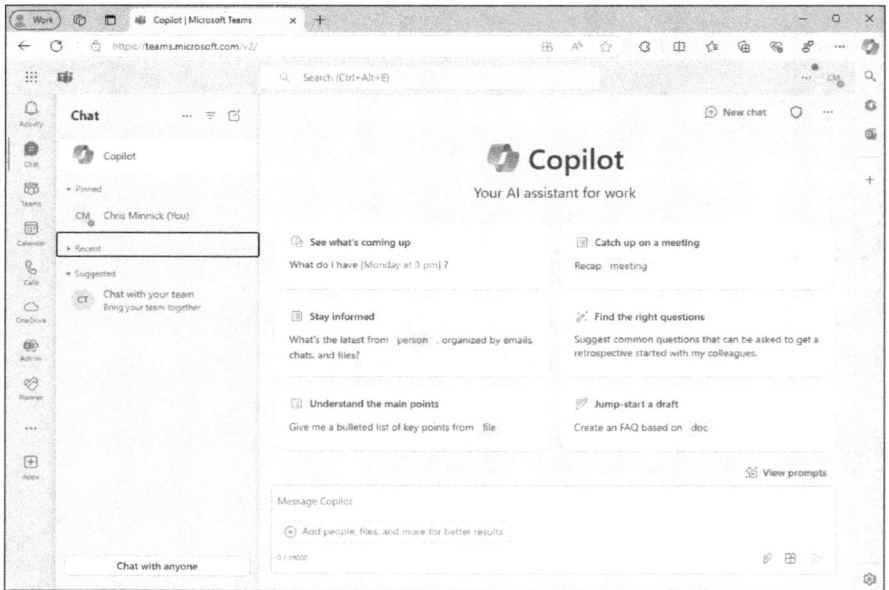

FIGURE 4-1:
Microsoft 365
Copilot Chat in
Teams.

Copilot Chat in Teams can answer questions about meetings that have already happened or that are scheduled. It can also generate responses by using emails, chats, and files.

Perhaps the most interesting things Copilot can do in Teams have to do with understanding and recapping meetings. To enable Copilot to help you during and after meetings, you must turn on transcriptions in Teams.

To enable transcriptions, click the Admin icon on the left toolbar, then click Home in the Admin navigation, and then click Set Up Meeting Preferences. The Set Up Meeting Preferences window will open. Look for the Allow Transcription option and enable it, as shown in Figure 4-2.

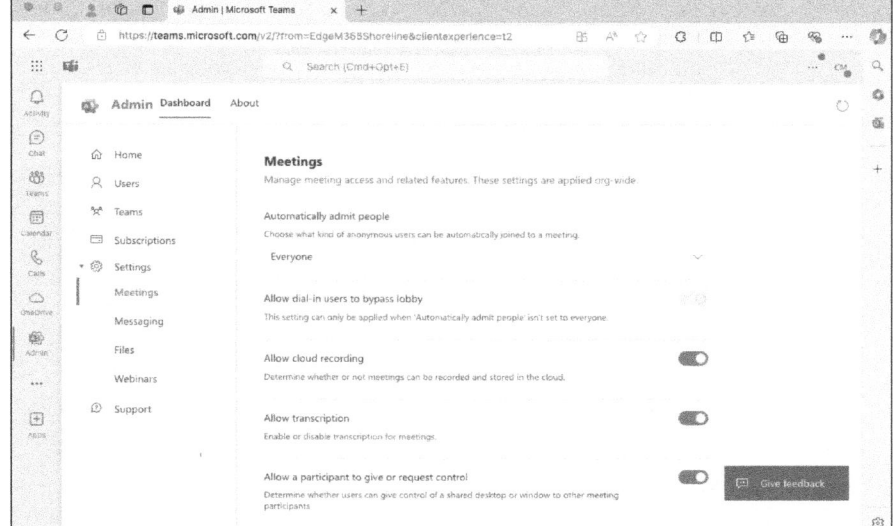

FIGURE 4-2:
Allowing
transcriptions.

Preparing for and setting up meetings

The first step in having a meeting is to figure out why you're having a meeting (and whether it's necessary). This may involve sending an email to the people who should be in the meeting, explaining what the meeting will be about, and then figuring out everyone's availability.

I need to meet with a colleague of mine to discuss a project I recently completed and to talk about process improvements I think we can make for similar projects in the future.

I opened Outlook and used the Draft with Copilot feature to write an email to my colleague Chris P. proposing a meeting and asking him about his availability.

I have a booking page set up through Outlook, which allows anyone to see my availability and schedule a meeting with me. Chris P. promptly scheduled a meeting with me on Monday.

TIP

If you have a Microsoft 365 account, you can set up a booking page, too, by going to Settings --> Calendar in Outlook. After you have a booking page, you can specify your availability for different types of meetings and then include a link to your booking page in your email signature or on your website.

When you have a scheduled meeting, you can open the meeting details in your calendar. At the bottom of the meeting details is a link called Add an Agenda, which is highlighted in Figure 4-3.

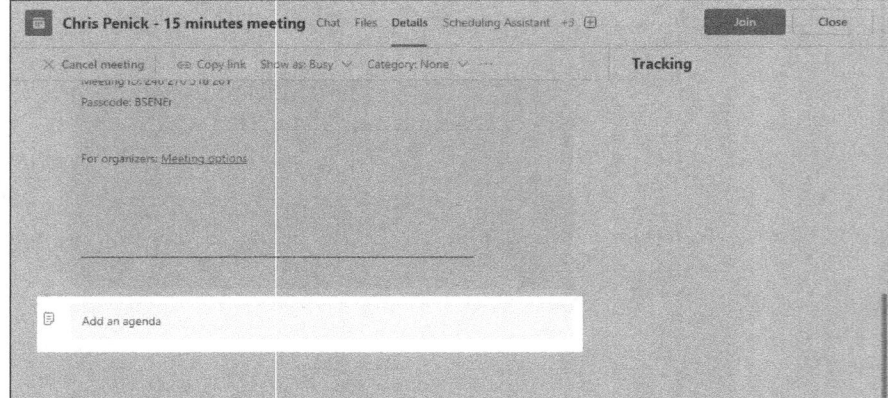

FIGURE 4-3:
The Add an Agenda link.

Clicking the Add an Agenda link opens a new window with three sections: Topics, Meeting Notes, and Follow-up Tasks. This window is actually an embedded view from your Microsoft Loop account.

TIP

Microsoft Loop is an online collaborative workspace that helps people gather and organize information about projects.

When you click your mouse into one of the three sections in the Loop window, the Copilot logo appears to the right of the selected line, as shown in Figure 4-4.

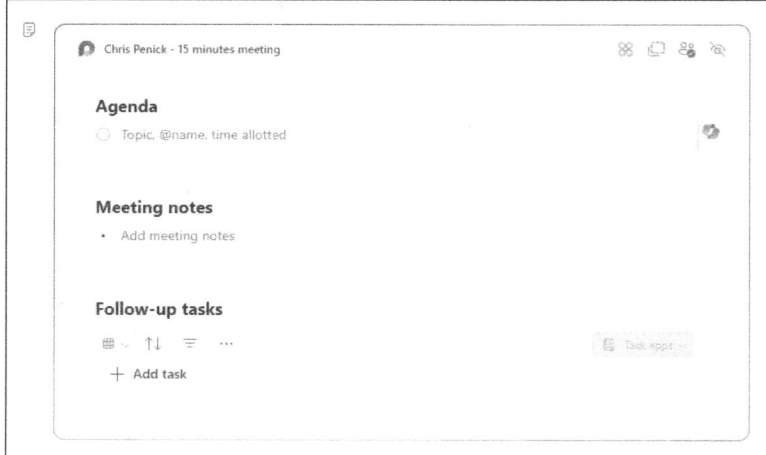

FIGURE 4-4:
The Copilot logo in the Agenda window.

Clicking the Copilot logo opens a prompt input area with several buttons below it: Create, Brainstorm, Blueprint, and Describe. Each of these buttons populates the prompt text input area with a sample prompt, as shown in Figure 4-5.

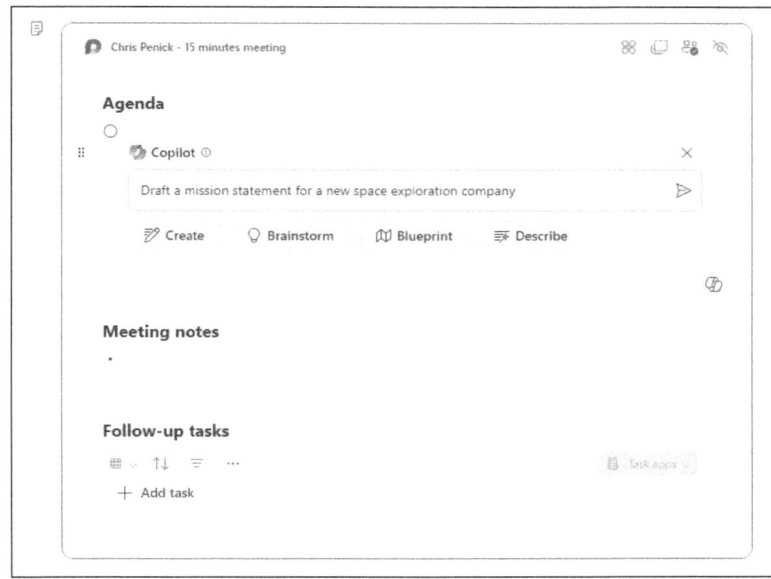

FIGURE 4-5: Viewing sample prompts to populate the agenda.

I entered some details about what I expected the meeting with Chris P. would be about, and I asked Copilot to generate an agenda. Copilot broke apart my sentence into eight numbered agenda items with two or three bullet points beneath each one.

My original prompt and the beginning of the generated agenda are shown in Figure 4-6.

The agenda that Copilot created wasn't bad, although it was longer than I thought was necessary, and it contained a couple of unnecessary points. In all, I estimate that using Copilot saved me about 15 minutes by giving me something to start with for writing the agenda — if I even would have bothered to write an agenda for the meeting without Copilot. Honestly, I probably wouldn't have bothered. But I'm feeling good about the chances of this meeting resulting in something good.

The other two items in the meeting agenda window are Meeting Notes and Follow-up Tasks. I'll have to wait until after the meeting next Monday to fill those in!

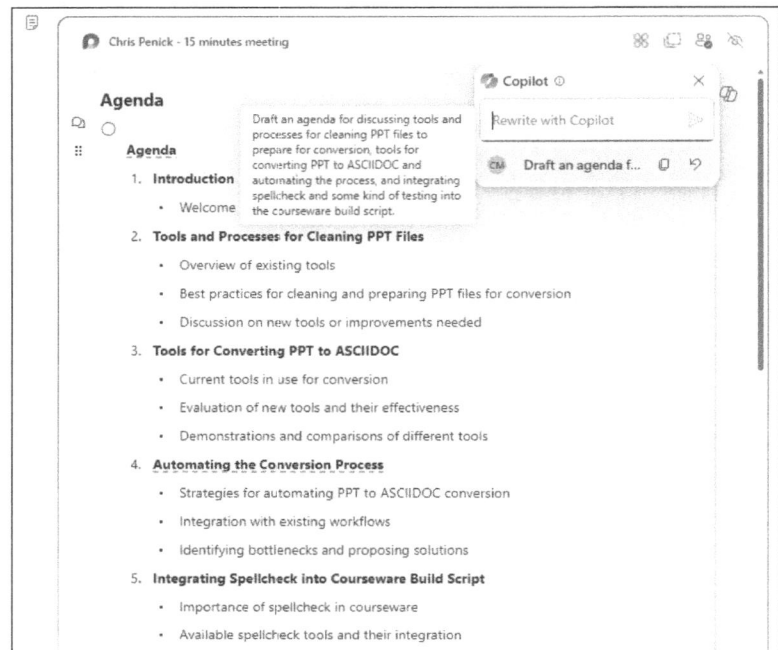

FIGURE 4-6:
Copilot's
generated
agenda.

The last step in creating the agenda is to share it with Chris P. Since he isn't part of my Microsoft 365 organization, I clicked the link at the bottom of the embedded Loop window to go to the project in the Loop app itself.

At the top of the Loop page for the meeting is a Share button that you can use to copy a link to the page and specify who has access. Unfortunately, it's not possible to share a Loop page with someone outside of your organization.

I clicked the Send Update button in the meeting details, and it sent an email to Chris P., but that email didn't contain the agenda. So, I copied the agenda from the embedded Loop window, pasted it into the Teams meeting invitation itself, and sent another meeting update.

TIP

It's helpful to have a friend or colleague who won't be annoyed by extra messages as you're figuring out what can and can't be done in Teams and with Copilot in Teams.

Getting real-time meeting assistance

Copilot can help with various tasks while you're in a Teams meeting. To allow Copilot to answer questions about the meeting, you must turn on transcription for the meeting. If you already followed the steps at the beginning of this chapter to enable transcriptions in Teams, you'll be able to turn on transcriptions for an individual meeting by clicking the More button at the top of the screen, selecting Record and Transcribe, and then selecting Start Transcription, as shown in Figure 4-7.

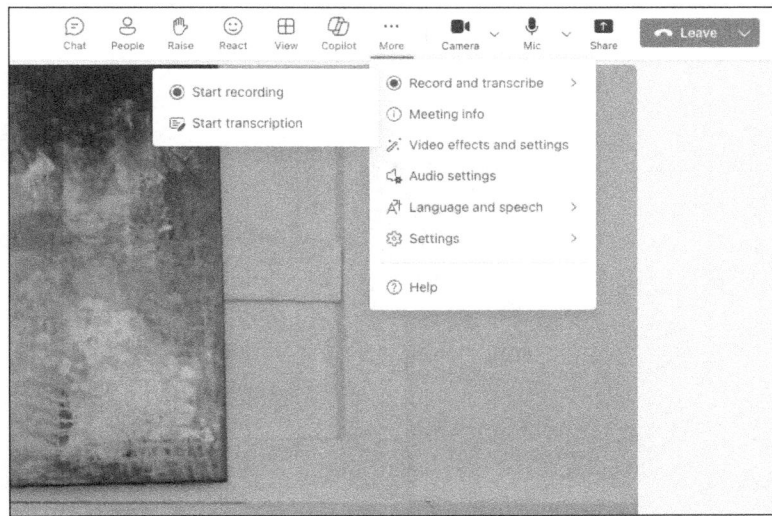

FIGURE 4-7: Enabling transcription.

With the transcription function enabled, a live transcription of the meeting along with labels indicating who's speaking will be accessible to all participants in the meeting. This live transcription is what Copilot uses to answer questions about the meeting.

To access Copilot in Teams while you're in a meeting, click the Copilot icon in the top toolbar of Teams. A Copilot sidebar will appear on the left, as shown in Figure 4-8.

You can ask Copilot anything about the meeting, and it will consult the transcript and generate a response. Some of the suggested prompts that Copilot lists under the More Prompts menu in the prompt input box are

» Recap meeting so far

» List action items

» Suggest follow-up questions

» What questions are unresolved?

» List different perspectives by topic

- » List main ideas we discussed

- » Generate meeting notes

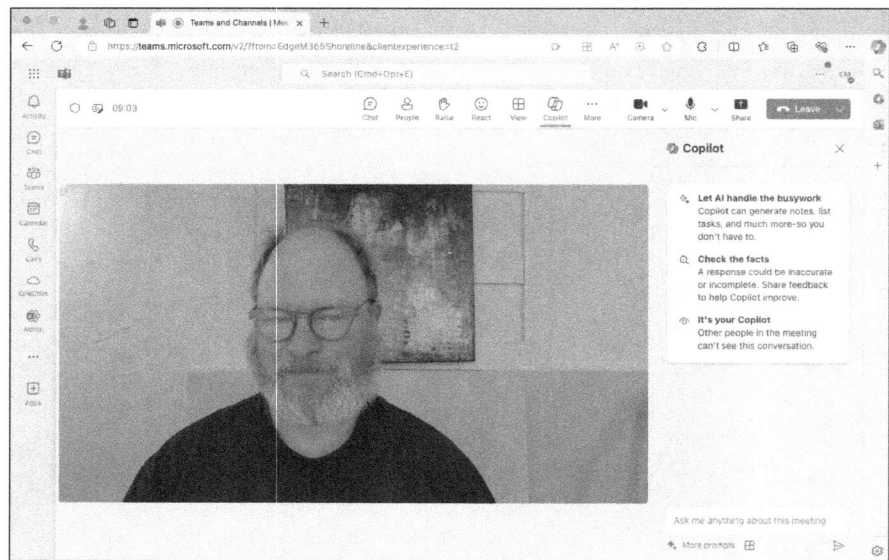

FIGURE 4-8: The Copilot sidebar in Teams.

During my meeting with Chris P., we found the transcription to be highly accurate, and having Copilot answer questions about the meeting worked well, too.

After we'd been talking for about ten minutes, I asked Copilot to create a summary of the meeting so far, and its response was accurate and even useful for helping me steer the conversation.

In a meeting with just two people, having access to Copilot to answer questions about the meeting might be unnecessary and distract from the meeting. However, in larger meetings, you may wonder how you ever survived a meeting without it.

For meetings of any size, the really interesting and useful part of having Copilot in Teams comes after the meeting is finished.

Accessing post-meeting summaries

Shortly after you finish a meeting, a message like the one in Figure 4-9 will appear in the Chat window of Teams to tell you that the recording is ready and to give you the option to view a recap of the meeting or the meeting transcript, video, or notes.

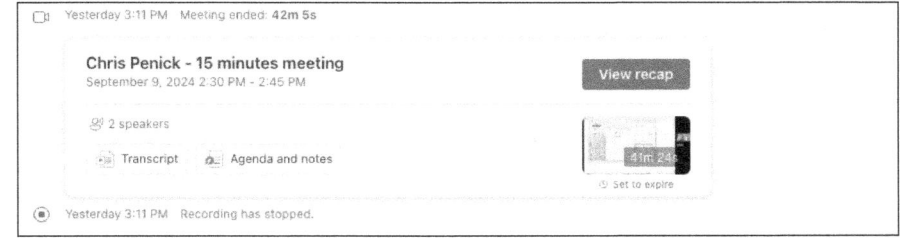

FIGURE 4-9:
Your recap
is ready.

The recap screen includes a video window, the agenda, AI-generated meeting notes, and the transcript of the meeting.

Figure 4-10 shows the meeting recap of my meeting.

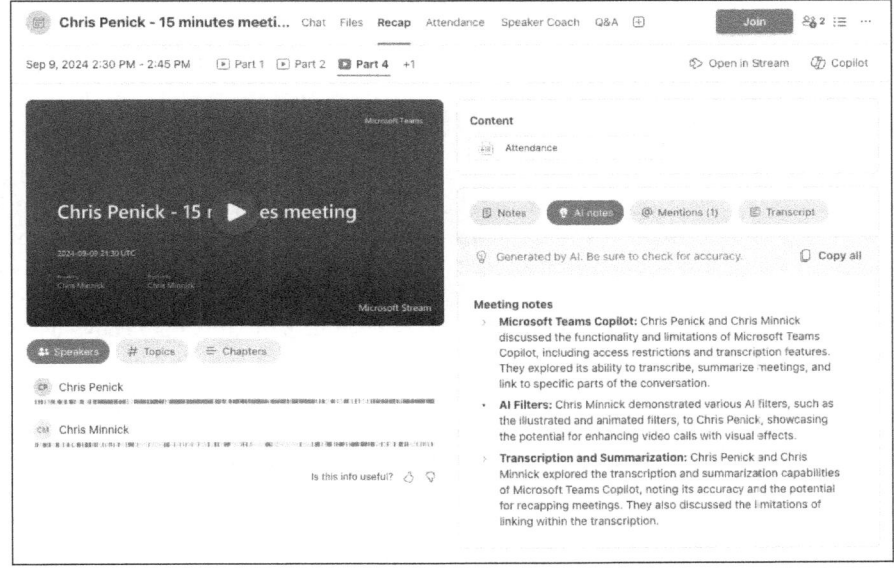

FIGURE 4-10:
Getting a recap.

Below the video window are three buttons to view different ways to visualize the meeting:

>> The first button, Speakers, shows when each attendee was speaking.

>> The second button, Topics, shows each topic that was discussed in the meeting.

>> The third button, Chapters, uses the same topic divisions as the Topics view but shows a screenshot from each topic.

Clicking in one of these visualizations takes you directly to that point in the video.

In the upper-right corner of the Recap screen is a Copilot button; it opens the same Copilot in Teams sidebar that you had access to while the meeting was going on. Here, you can ask any question about the meeting, and Copilot will consult the transcript to answer it.

I tried out each of the suggested prompts in Copilot and Teams and found the action items one to be especially useful. It scanned the transcript for things that each attendee agreed to do after the meeting and gave a summary of each one. This feature will be invaluable for ensuring that meetings aren't just a waste of everyone's time while also not requiring everyone to rely on someone in the meeting to take notes.

Understanding the Limitations of Copilot in Teams

Having an AI assistant before, during, and after a virtual meeting has the potential to make meetings more useful and memorable. The integration between Teams and other Microsoft 365 applications makes sense and generally works very well.

However, some limitations to Copilot in Teams may cause users to struggle with it at first. These limitations include

>> **Copilot's knowledge of the meeting is entirely dependent on the transcript.** If important visuals are presented during the meeting, you can, of course, review the video to see those. But, asking Copilot questions about something that doesn't come through in the transcript won't be successful.

>> **Copilot in Teams doesn't integrate with Copilot in other apps.** You can ask Copilot in Teams to create the text for an email to the participants, but Copilot can only generate the text. It's up to you to copy the text and paste it into an email. Likewise, asking Copilot to create a PowerPoint presentation from the meeting recap will just result in a text-only list of potential slides you could create with PowerPoint.

» **Each participant in the meeting who wants to access Copilot in Teams
must have Copilot Pro or Microsoft 365 Copilot subscriptions.** There's no
way for the meeting organizer to give everyone in the meeting access to
Copilot during the meeting.

» **Meeting transcription (and ideally recording) must be enabled to take
advantage of Copilot in Teams.** Teams doesn't currently have a way to set
transcription and recording to be on by default. So, you have to remember to
enable these for each meeting. In my experimenting with Copilot in Teams,
I did forget to enable transcription at first; I had to sign out of the meeting,
enable transcription, and then rejoin to be able to use Copilot.

None of these limitations outweigh the benefits of having Copilot in Teams, and
I expect that some of them will be resolved in future versions of Microsoft 365
and Teams.

In my dream world, I'd have to go to about ten percent of the meetings that
I currently have. But, if I can't have that, I'd settle for making meetings more
useful. Copilot in Teams has the potential to improve the experience of having
meetings by making it easier for everyone in the meeting to be reminded of what
happened in previous meetings, to ensure that excellent meeting notes are kept,
and to follow up on what decisions and actions were agreed to during the meeting.

Chapter **5**

Working with AI in a Roundup of Business Disciplines

This chapter introduces you to some of the changes that will ripple through your work life no matter what industry or profession you're in. Of course, I can't cover every profession and industry in this one book, but this chapter covers enough to give you an idea of the versatility, flexibility, and usefulness of GenAI in various disciplines.

Using GenAI for Marketing

GenAI can be a powerful tool in marketing, where creative thinking and tasks mesh with data-driven campaigns. Unfortunately, many users employ GenAI as a shortcut in dealing with content churn, meaning the rate or frequency at which published content is replaced, removed, or significantly updated over time, rather than a way to improve the performance of marketing campaigns and efforts. That's understandable to a degree, given that any job in marketing is typically an underappreciated and overworked position. On any given day, a client or stakeholder confuses marketing with advertising and mistakes metrics for actual human connections.

You use GenAI to fill content buckets, a term that represents a topic or pillar around which content is created and published, and content funnels, which refers to the route marketing takes a potential customer (or reader) from initial awareness of your brand to ultimately converting to a purchase. But if that's all you use GenAI for, the results tend to be less than stellar and (worse) can add to the perception that marketing jobs can be fully automated. This perception, of course, is not the case in reality.

Creating general to detailed content

One area in which GenAI can be particularly useful is in content creation. It can generate marketing content ranging from general information to detailed sales content. GenAI can be helpful with the entire spectrum of content, from research reports and white papers, product information, and fact sheets to blog posts, social media updates, and email newsletters.

Another valuable application of GenAI is for customer engagement. You can integrate it into customer service platforms to handle common inquiries, freeing up human agents to tackle more complex issues. For instance, an e-commerce website can use GenAI to answer frequently asked questions about shipping policies, return procedures, and product details, providing instant responses and improving customer satisfaction.

If you prefer not to use GenAI as a customer-facing chatbot, you can use it to generate responses that a traditional, rule-based chatbot (such as Alexa or Siri) can then deliver to customers. This approach leverages the strength of GenAI (content or information generation) with the strength of traditional chatbots (reliably and correctly serving customers the correct "canned response"). This method eliminates common problems with GenAI, such as AI hallucinations and accidental data leaks.

Analyzing customer data

GenAI can also assist in market research by analyzing customer feedback and reviews. By processing large volumes of unstructured text data, it can identify common themes and sentiments, helping marketers understand customer preferences and pain points. For example, a tech company can use GenAI to sift through product reviews and social media comments to gather insights on user experience, which can then inform product development and marketing strategies. Typically, you need to add that data to retrieval-augmented generation (RAG), attach a text, CSV, or Excel file to a prompt, or add the data in your prompt if it isn't too large.

GENAI IN MARKETING

Pros	Cons
Efficiency in content creation	May require oversight to ensure accuracy
Quickly generates content	Can produce generic or repetitive outputs
Enhanced customer engagement	Limited understanding of nuanced queries
Provides instant responses to common inquiries	May struggle with complex customer issues
Personalization	Data privacy concerns
Tailors messages based on customer data	Requires careful handling of customer data
Market research	Interpretation challenges
Analyzes large volumes of text data for insights	May misinterpret subtle sentiments
Cost-effective	Initial setup and integration effort
Reduces the need for extensive human resources	Requires time and resources to implement
Creativity boost	Dependence risk
Offers diverse ideas and perspectives	Over-reliance may stifle human creativity

For personalized marketing, you can use GenAI to tailor messages based on customer data. By leveraging customer profiles and purchase history, GenAI can generate personalized recommendations and offers. For instance, an online bookstore can use GenAI to send personalized emails suggesting new books based on a customer's previous purchases and browsing history. Typically, this requires integrating GenAI with your customer relationship management (CRM), recommendation engine, or similar system.

Retrieving Smart Answers for HR

Human Resources (HR) can use GenAI to good effect in many ways. If you're in HR, you can use it to create content for a self-help repository to handle routine inquiries from employees, such as questions about company policies, benefits, and procedures. By doing so, you can free up time to focus on more complex and strategic tasks. For example, if an employee wants to know how to apply for parental leave, GenAI can provide the necessary steps and direct them to the appropriate forms or contacts.

Other applications for GenAI in the HR department include

>> **Assisting in the recruitment process by handling initial candidate interactions.** When a candidate applies for a job, GenAI can engage with them to gather basic information, answer frequently asked questions about the role, and even schedule interviews. This not only speeds up the process but also ensures that candidates receive timely and consistent communication, which in turn creates a good impression of your company.

>> **Cataloging training and development opportunities by generating scripts and employing AI video generator apps.** GenAI can point to or provide employees with resources and answer questions related to training programs.

For example, if an employee wants to enhance their project management skills, GenAI can suggest relevant training programs, provide a list of training videos, suggest credentials they might want to pursue, and offer detailed information on course availability and steps to enroll.

Involving AI in HR activities isn't a set-and-forget exercise; however, HR departments must regularly update a GenAI tool with current company information and policies. You can do this by

>> **Asking IT or your company's AI department to retrain or fine-tune the model,** or add updated and remove old information in Retrieval Augmented Generation (RAG). See Book 2, Chapter 6 to learn about RAG. Otherwise, response accuracy and relevance can drift off course over time.

>> **Monitoring the interactions between GenAI and employees to ensure GenAI is performing well.** You can also identify any need for further training or adjustments to the model if it isn't performing to your expectations. Typically, HR departments do this by periodically reviewing chat logs to spot response errors and gathering feedback from employees about their experiences with GenAI.

COMPARATIVE TABLE OF PROS AND CONS OF USING GENAI IN HR TASKS

Pros	Cons
Efficiency: Automates routine inquiries, freeing up HR staff for more complex tasks.	**Limited understanding:** May struggle with complex, nuanced, or context-specific questions.
24/7 availability: Provides round-the-clock support to employees, improving accessibility.	**Dependence on data:** Requires regular updates with current company information and policies to remain accurate.
Consistency: Ensures uniform responses to common questions, reducing the chances of misinformation.	**Lack of human touch:** May lack the empathy and personal connection that human HR professionals provide.
Enhanced candidate experience: Streamlines initial interactions and scheduling during recruitment, offering timely communication.	**Potential for errors:** Incorrect responses can occur, necessitating oversight and review.
Scalability: Can handle a large volume of queries simultaneously, which is beneficial for growing companies.	**Employee resistance:** Some employees may prefer human interaction and be hesitant to use AI for HR-related queries.
Onboarding support: Guides new hires through the onboarding process, helping them settle in quickly.	**Privacy concerns:** Handling sensitive employee information requires robust data security measures to prevent breaches.
Training assistance: Recommends relevant training programs and resources, supporting employee development.	**Implementation costs:** Initial GenAI setup, model training, and ongoing maintenance can incur costs.

Harnessing GenAI in Legal

GenAI can serve as a valuable tool in the legal profession when you use it thought-fully and with appropriate oversight. Several attorneys have found themselves in serious trouble for using AI outputs "as is." If you're a legal professional, you can leverage it for initial research and drafting tasks if you ensure there's human review and verification of output.

Drafting and editing a routine legal document

For document drafting, GenAI can create first drafts of routine legal documents like basic contracts, nondisclosure agreements (NDAs), or engagement letters. For example, an attorney might ask a GenAI app such as ChatGPT to draft a simple independent contractor agreement (see Figure 5-1) and then carefully review and modify it to ensure it meets specific jurisdictional requirements and client needs.

TIP

Give GenAI a role in your prompt and then give it instructions to complete from the perspective of that role. This will render outputs more suited to how you're actually working with legal documents. This helps guide GenAI in reviewing, analyzing, responding to, or drafting documents for you. Following is an example of this type of prompt, followed by GenAI's response in Figure 5-1 (in this case, the GenAI is ChatGPT).

The prompt:

> You are a paralegal. Draft a simple independent contractor agreement for an attorney's review.

Independent Contractor Agreement

This Independent Contractor Agreement ("Agreement") is made and entered into on [Date] by and between [Your Company Name] ("Company") and [Contractor's Full Name] ("Contractor").

1. Services Provided:
Contractor agrees to provide the following services to the Company:
[Briefly describe services].

2. Payment:
The Company agrees to pay Contractor [amount] per [hour/project/month], payable upon [completion of services/specific date].

3. Independent Contractor Relationship:
Contractor is an independent contractor and not an employee of the Company. Contractor is responsible for all taxes, insurance, and benefits associated with their work.

4. Term and Termination:
This Agreement will begin on [start date] and continue until [end date or "completion of services"]. Either party may terminate this Agreement with [number] days' written notice.

5. Confidentiality:
Contractor agrees to keep all Company information confidential and not disclose it to any third party without prior written consent.

FIGURE 5-1:
The independent contractor agreement created from a ChatGPT prompt.

I'll say it again: Never use ChatGPT or any other GenAI as the final authority on any legal document. If you're an attorney, you may want to use the chatbot to draft a document and modify it accordingly. If that's the case, note the tools revealed after you click on the toolbox icon found below the prompt bar as shown in in Figure 5-2. After the drop-down menu exposes the tools, click on Canvas (the pencil icon), which exists precisely for such editing purposes. Scroll over the section of text you want to edit and click the icon that looks like an equal sign (=) in a cartoon conversation bubble shown in Figure 5-3. The section you chose to edit will be automatically highlighted, and an editing bar will appear to the right of it, as shown in Figure 5-3. Make your edits there.

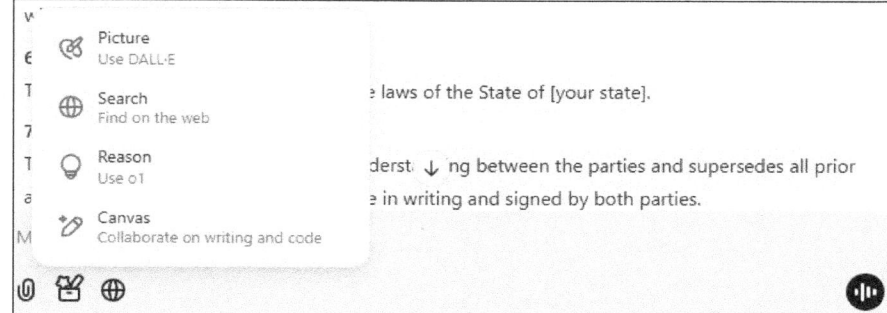

FIGURE 5-2: The toolbox under the ChatGPT prompt bar.

FIGURE 5-3: A screenshot of highlighted copy to be edited with the edit bar to the right for editing a ChatGPT response using Canvas editing tools inside of ChatGPT.

But that's not the only way I can edit this document.

Click on the icon at the bottom right of the screen (refer to Figure 5-2) to reveal another menu of tools represented by icons. Reading the icons from top to bottom:

The first one is to Add Emojis.

The second icon is to add Final Polish.

The third is to adjust the Reading Level.

The fourth is to Adjust Length.

The final icon is another pencil icon for Suggest Edits command.

When you click on this pencil icon, you are commanding ChatGPT to review the document and Suggest Edits that you can then elect to apply or close, as seen in Figure 5-4. All of this is very helpful, but you might want to skip the Add Emojis button if you're creating an official legal document, but that button may brighten any notes you send to the paralegal for further document handling.

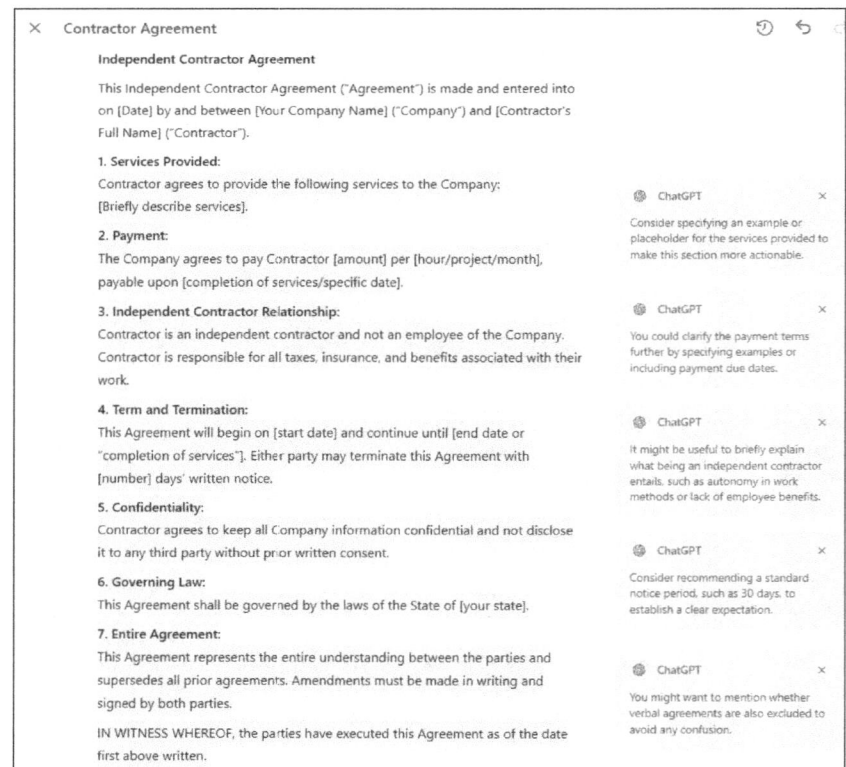

FIGURE 5-4:
A screenshot of ChatGPT's suggested edits to contractor's agreement.

Researching for legal precedents and statutes

In legal research, GenAI can identify relevant cases and statutes. For example, when researching precedents for a particular type of contract dispute, GenAI might suggest relevant cases that the attorney can look up and verify. Be aware that AI tools like ChatGPT might occasionally reflect biases or make predictive errors due to the data they were trained on. This limitation is especially important for legal cases that involve sensitive issues, precedent interpretation, or potential client implications. Regularly cross-checking with trusted, up-to-date legal sources is essential.

REMEMBER

Legal professionals must treat GenAI as a preliminary tool rather than a definitive source. Attorneys should independently verify all citations and legal principles through an authoritative source like Westlaw or LexisNexis.

You can expedite due diligence work using GenAI to analyze and summarize large volumes of contracts or legal documents, highlighting key terms and potential issues for human review. But, carefully verify all findings because GenAI may miss crucial details or misinterpret legal language. Although GenAI can assist in these areas, you must ensure that documents not only meet statutory requirements but also align with best practices in contract language and legal nuances that GenAI might overlook.

Drafting client responses or legal arguments

GenAI can also assist in drafting initial responses to routine client inquiries or creating explanatory materials that break down complex legal concepts into simpler terms. But don't relegate even this seemingly simple task to GenAI alone. Thoroughly review and personalize all communication before sending it to clients. Also keep in mind any policies within your firm or the jurisdiction regarding AI usage in client interactions. Some legal organizations may limit or regulate AI deployment in client-related work.

One cool and potentially valuable use of GenAI is to prompt it to help you brainstorm different legal arguments or counterarguments. If you assign GenAI different roles in your prompts, it renders multiple answers, each having a perspective that you may not have immediately considered or examined, based on the assigned role. For example, when preparing for a motion hearing as an attorney, you might use GenAI to explore potential opposing arguments and develop stronger rebuttals. Role-playing with GenAI is one of the most valuable actions you can prompt GenAI to take because it almost always delivers fresh insights for you to use.

TIP

Verify all legal information and adapt any generated content to specific jurisdictional requirements and client circumstances. Using specific, detailed prompts that include relevant jurisdictional information and particular legal requirements yields more useful results.

Monitoring your GenAI use

WARNING

Be extra careful with client confidentiality issues when using GenAI. You, the legal staff, and any attorney in the firm should never input privileged or confidential client information into a GenAI tool. Instead, safeguard your clients by using anonymized or hypothetical scenarios in your prompts.

Stay updated on GenAI's capabilities and limitations, and stay aware that these may fluctuate between the different underlying GPT models. Understanding what tasks GenAI can and can't reliably perform helps you and your staff maintain professional standards and ethical obligations. Compliance with any relevant guidelines or ethical standards from bar associations or firms is essential, as is understanding the limitations of AI in complex legal matters.

Look for GenAI to continue to evolve and for GenAI tools trained for the legal profession to appear regularly on the market. It's important to keep up with advancements in AI technology so you can better gauge which GenAI tool to use when and how to use GenAI most effectively overall. Regular training on AI, including data handling and prompt optimization, can help you maximize GenAI's usefulness within ethical and professional standards.

Storytelling in Journalism

GenAI can be an incredibly valuable tool for journalists. It provides assistance and support across various aspects of the work, from storytelling to data journalism to story pitches. GenAI can assist you as a journalism storyteller in several ways. Two that come to mind are generating fresh story ideas and offering unique or multiple perspectives on current events.

TIP

You can streamline your workflow, speed up your writing, and expand the research and investigative aspects of your work with GenAI. The resulting prose may not be perfect, but GenAI can go a long way toward making you more productive as a journalist. However, make sure you're always using GenAI as a supplementary tool rather than a replacement for human judgment and expertise.

Exploring politics and current issues

Covering politics in any country in a nonpartisan way can be complicated when you have your own opinions on which politician you'll support. You can prompt GenAI to check a sentence or paragraph for a second opinion, or a machine evaluation as it were, on whether a statement you wrote that you know to be factual is written in a nonbiased manner. GenAI may not always get such assessments right, given that it often harbors biases, too, but it can give you other perspectives to evaluate your work by. Try giving it specific roles — several roles even — in your prompt so you can consider your interpretation of the facts from more perspectives than just your own.

WARNING

Never put your entire article draft in a GenAI tool. That's especially true if you're a freelance journalist. If you do, you risk it being used to train another AI model, fine-tune the current model, or potentially being exposed in a data leak. Unless you're a GenAI tool in an enterprise version sanctioned and protected by the news organization, don't share too much information with GenAI.

That said, consider the following example of another way to use GenAI. Perhaps you're a journalist covering environmental issues. If so, you might use the prompt

> Suggest unique angles for a story about the impact of climate change on coastal communities.

A GenAI chatbot might suggest focusing on the economic impacts, personal stories of affected families, or innovative adaptation strategies being implemented.

Prompting AI for facts, figures, and summaries

GenAI can aid in developing a compelling narrative of the facts. For example, if you're a journalist writing a feature on a local artist, you might use the prompt

> Help me create a compelling narrative arc for a story about a local artist's journey to success.

A GenAI chatbot could outline key milestones and emotional beats from your notes, research, and source interviews to include in your feature story.

If you're writing hard news full of facts and numbers, GenAI can help by interpreting data analysis results and by explaining complex statistical concepts. For example, you might ask

> Explain the significance of a p-value in data analysis.

GenAI's explanation could be extremely helpful if you have limited statistical skills or are up against a hard deadline —which pretty much sums up the journalist experience most of the time.

GenAI can also suggest ways to visualize data. Maybe you need it to recommend specific types of charts or graphs that best represent the findings. You can use this information to create those charts and graphs in a separate visualization tool or prompt a chatbot such as ChatGPT or Copilot to make them.

If you'd prefer to add informative text to your article instead of charts or infographics, GenAI can break down intricate information into understandable narratives. For example, if you use the prompt

> Summarize the key findings of a recent study on urban air quality.

GenAI can distill the study's main points into an accessible summary.

TIP

You can use GenAI to summarize content or to explain anything that may be confusing or esoteric in lengthy PR pitches or legal documents, company annual reports, financial reports or statements, company info on websites, and other stuff you receive or run into regularly during daily journalism work. Obviously, this won't give you all the info you need, but it will give you a strong clue as to which leads to pursue and which to take a pass on. You also might want to prioritize or organize whatever you found useful, so you know where to dig in to go deeper.

GenAI can provide general information and context to help with fact-checking, such as answering

> What are the main health effects of prolonged exposure to air pollution?

But make sure to cross-check the app's output with reliable sources. Hallucination and other errors will continue to be an issue with GenAI because that's the nature of these models. AI scientists can't eliminate the potential for error without rendering the model entirely useless. Accept that truth and work accordingly. Really, you have to fact-check your work — even when you don't use GenAI — because human sources can get things wrong, too.

Organizing notes and pitching a story

GenAI can assist in organizing notes and highlighting key points in your journalist notebook. For example, you might write a prompt

> Organize my notes from an interview with a climate scientist.

GenAI can categorize the information into themes like impacts, solutions, and personal anecdotes. You can also use GenAI to summarize lengthy interviews or documents. For instance, you can use the prompt

> Summarize the main points from this 10-page report on renewable energy policies

Then, GenAI can extract and condense the most pertinent information, saving you valuable time. Further, GenAI can gather background information on various topics. For example, you might ask it to

> Provide a brief overview of the history of renewable energy development.

From the response, you'd receive a quick summary of relevant articles, studies, or reports.

Another great use for GenAI in journalism is help with story pitches. GenAI can draft compelling pitches by suggesting a headline and a short blurb explaining the gist of the story. If you need more, the app can also provide strong opening lines and an outline of key points.

For example, you might use the prompt

> Help me write 3 pitches for a story about the rise of urban farming from different angles for a general reader.

GenAI can then provide three angles for that idea in three different pitches — each complete with a suggested headline and a short blurb to briefly explain the story idea. A *pitch* is essentially a sales pitch on the merits of the proposed story to an editor who may give the go-ahead to pursue the story or kill it entirely.

GenAI can also assist in customizing pitches for different editors or publications. That's especially helpful if you are a freelance journalist and want to pitch what's essentially the same idea from different angles to different kinds of publications. For example, you can prompt GenAI like this:

> Tailor this pitch for a magazine focused on sustainable living.

GenAI responds by adjusting the tone and focus accordingly. You can also use GenAI to refine pitches to make them more concise and impactful. For example, from the prompt

> Edit this pitch to make it more engaging.

GenAI can suggest specific improvements and tighten the language.

TIP

Add writer's guidelines as an attachment to your prompt to get GenAI to write a pitch more precisely tailored to that publication, website, or news outlet.

Preparing interview questions, translating, and promoting

GenAI can help you prepare for interviews by generating potential questions. For example, if you're preparing to interview a tech entrepreneur, you might use the prompt

> Generate a list of questions for an interview with a tech startup founder.

GenAI can provide some insightful questions and follow-up queries for you. If you want to further refine GenAI's ability to craft interview questions, try attaching documents about the company or founder to the prompt or attach an interview of a different person whom you want GenAI to use as an example of the type of information you're looking to extract in this interview.

GenAI can also help you translate text to and from various languages — although you probably should run those outputs by a human interpreter rather than just running your translated piece in a foreign outlet or a cultural community in your own country. But GenAI can be helpful in making documents and interviews more understandable in your own language so you can report on what's happening in the moment. For example, you might input this prompt:

> Translate this interview excerpt from Spanish to English.

GenAI can usually provide an accurate translation.

Additionally, GenAI can draft social media posts to promote your stories. Try prompting it with this:

> Create a Tweet to promote my latest article on sustainable fashion.

The app generates a platform-appropriate post as a response. Add a highlight or two to the prompt if you want the tweet or social post to work like a teaser or blurb for your article.

Checking your GenAI history

TIP

GenAI's chat history search feature can be particularly useful for journalists. This feature allows you to quickly find earlier information or interactions you had with GenAI, making it easier to reference previous conversations without having to start from scratch.

For example, if you previously discussed a complex topic like blockchain technology with GenAI, you can use the chat history search to retrieve that information instead of asking again. You can use a prompt such as

> Search my chat history for our previous discussion on blockchain technology.

A prompt like this can bring up past interactions and sources, saving you a lot of time and effort.

Consulting GenAI in Healthcare

The healthcare industry is still exploring where and how GenAI might be beneficial in various aspects of patient care, medical research, and administrative tasks. Attempts so far have met with mixed results. Some GenAI deployments have been successful, and others haven't. The causes of these wins and failures are varied, as noted in the following mini-table.

Reasons for failing	Reason for success
Mismatched task and technology	Well-matched task and technology
Lack of AI talent and user understanding	Talented tools, users, and reviewers
Pushing the technology to perform beyond its core purpose	Establishing appropriate goals and expectations
Ill-advised dependency and data issues	Creative thinking in projects

But perhaps most defining in a solid GenAI deployment is whether the people working with it fully grasp its nature, limits, and core competencies of text generation and data discovery.

Identifying successful healthcare use cases

You might think that healthcare use cases are limited if GenAI's greatest strengths are generating text and discovering data, but you'd be mistaken. Both of those capabilities are key to an endless list of possibilities. Throw in the extra features and additional versions that keep popping up, and you end up with the means to expand the kinds of input and output modals to include things like x-rays, MRI images, and lab results like blood tests, while also sharpening the focus on the task, which may be to detect, prevent, treat, cure, or discover disease or organ system malfunctions, among others.

Now you'll look at some of the real-world use cases in which GenAI models are showing good performance:

>> **Mass General Brigham:** Researchers at this institution evaluated ChatGPT's performance in clinical decision-making. ChatGPT demonstrated approximately 72 percent accuracy across all medical specialties and phases of clinical care and 77 percent accuracy in making final diagnoses. The research team's results are published in the *Journal of Medical Internet Research.* These findings suggest the potential for ChatGPT to support clinicians in diagnostic processes.

>> **Moderna:** The biotechnology company Moderna has partnered with OpenAI to integrate ChatGPT Enterprise across its operations. This collaboration aims to accelerate the development of new products by utilizing AI to optimize clinical trial doses and draft responses for regulatory submissions.

>> **University of Kansas Life Span Institute:** A study that this institute conducted found that parents often trust health advice from AI tools like ChatGPT more than from healthcare professionals. This highlights the growing influence of AI in patient education and the need for careful integration into healthcare communication. Patient overreliance on information from these tools is risky.

>> **Epic Systems and Microsoft:** In April 2023, Epic Systems, a leading electronic health record (EHR) company, announced a collaboration with Microsoft to integrate GPT-4 into its EHR software. This integration aims to assist healthcare providers by analyzing medical records and responding to patient inquiries, thereby enhancing efficiency, provider productivity, and patient care. It's also being seen as a way to address intense pressures on costs and margins for all healthcare institutions.

REMEMBER

According to a report by the American Hospital Association, approximately half of U.S. hospitals finished 2022 with negative margins due to workforce shortages, increased labor expenses, supply disruptions, and inflationary effects. In short, increased expenses outpaced revenue increases, which then increased interest in technologies like ChatGPT and others to better that ratio.

These examples illustrate the diverse applications of GenAI in the medical field, from supporting clinical decision-making to improving patient communication and operational efficiency.

Exploring other GenAI applications in healthcare

But you can use GenAI in healthcare tasks in other ways. Here are examples to illustrate its flexibility and usefulness in specific use cases:

» **Generating multiple-choice questions (MCQs):** Educators use GenAI to create MCQs for assessments, aiding in evaluating students' understanding of medical concepts. However, the validity of AI-generated questions is under scrutiny, emphasizing the need for careful review before implementation. You can find more information on this at `https://doi.org/10.1093/postmj/qgae065`.

» **Simulating patient interactions:** GenAI serves as a virtual patient, allowing students to practice history-taking and diagnostic skills in a controlled environment. This simulation helps medical students develop communication and clinical reasoning abilities. You can find more information on these types of use cases in a paper titled "Using ChatGPT in Medical Education for Virtual Patient and Cases" by authors Meredith Ratliff, Satria Nur Sya'ban, Adonis Wazir, Sarah Haidar, and Sara Keeth.

» **Assisting in exam preparation:** Medical students employ GenAI to clarify complex topics, generate study materials, and explain challenging subjects, thereby supporting their exam readiness. You can find more information on this use case in Geeky Medics online.

» **Enhancing clinical decision-making:** GenAI aids in formulating differential diagnoses and suggesting diagnostic tests based on patient symptoms, assisting learners in considering a broader range of possibilities. However, its accuracy and reliability are still under evaluation. You can find more information on this in the paper titled "Performance of ChatGPT on USMLE: Potential for AI-Assisted Medical Education Using Large Language Models" authored by Tiffany H. Kung, Morgan Cheatham, Arielle Medenilla, Czarina Sillos, Lorie De Leon, Camille Elepaño, Maria Madriaga, Rimel Aggabao, Giezel Diaz-Candido, James Maningo, and Victor Tseng.

» **Medical education:** Educators at Harvard are incorporating ChatGPT into their curriculum to help students learn how to interact with AI in clinical settings. They use the tool to generate sample patient cases and challenge students to critically evaluate the AI-generated information. For more information about this, go to `https://magazine.hms.harvard.edu/articles/how-generative-ai-transforming-medical-education`.

» **Medical research and literature review:** Scientists at the National Institutes of Health (NIH) have experimented with using ChatGPT to generate research hypotheses and identify potential gaps in current medical knowledge, sparking new avenues for investigation. For more information on using ChatGPT in medical research, check out "Global Trends and Hotspots of ChatGPT in Medical Research: A Bibliometric and Visualized Study," found here: https://pmc.ncbi.nlm.nih.gov/articles/PMC11137200/.

REMEMBER

Although GenAI offers valuable tools for medical education, recognize its limitations, including potential inaccuracies and lack of clinical experience. Therefore, complement its use with traditional educational methods and oversight by qualified professionals.

Cashing In on GenAI in Finance

GenAI is used across the finance industry in several ways, but mostly to enhance customer interactions, streamline processes, and support decision-making. Banks, investment houses, insurance companies, and other finance institutions use GenAI to

>> **Handle customer inquiries, troubleshoot common issues, and provide information on financial products and services in real time.** This approach reduces customer wait times, improves customer experience rankings, and allows human agents to focus on more complex tasks. For example, banks can employ GenAI to answer routine questions such as account balances and recent transactions as an instant, 24/7 service.

>> **Perform investment research and analysis.** Typically, financial institutions use it to summarize complex reports and deliver insights from large volumes of financial data to different stakeholders and constituencies. Analysts and investors save time because GenAI synthesizes market information into actionable insights. For instance, investment firms use it to monitor quarterly earnings reports, highlighting performance indicators, and identifying market trends based on recent news.

>> **Offer general advice on budgeting, saving, and investing** and still customizing it to fit individual goals and risk tolerance. This feature allows people without direct access to a personal financial advisor to receive guidance on managing their finances. A retirement planning app, for instance, might use GenAI to help users estimate their retirement savings or evaluate different investment options.

>> **Address compliance and risk management** by using GenAI's language capabilities to interpret regulatory documents and flag potential risk. That's handy and fast and helps keep them in line with complex and evolving

regulations. Its ability to quickly analyze legal texts for updates and interpret these changes in common language makes it a valuable tool for compliance teams.

For example, GenAI might alert or explain to a bank's compliance officers a new anti-money laundering regulation or help them assess whether specific transactions meet the new reporting standards.

>> **Automate routine tasks, such as content generation,** for an industry that seems to feed on an endless stream of reports and analyses. For example, a bank might use GenAI to generate regular transaction reports, identify discrepancies, or prepare presentations or summaries of financial performance over a specific period.

>> **Facilitate employee training** by helping staff understand complex topics such as derivative instruments and credit risk analysis.

PROS AND CONS OF USING GENAI IN FINANCE

Pros	Cons
Efficiency: Automates routine tasks, saving time and reducing costs.	**Accuracy:** May produce errors if not properly trained or supervised.
24/7 availability: Provides round-the-clock support to customers.	**Security:** Handling sensitive financial data requires robust security measures.
Scalability: Easily scales to handle large volumes of inquiries and tasks.	**Regulation compliance:** Must ensure compliance with financial regulations and data privacy laws.
Personalization: Offers tailored advice and recommendations.	**Dependence on data quality:** Performance heavily depends on the quality of input data.
Consistency: Delivers consistent responses with human oversight.	**Lack of human touch:** May lack the empathy and nuanced understanding of human advisors.
Cost-effective: Reduces the need for large customer service teams.	**Complexity in implementation:** Integrating AI into existing systems can be complex and costly.

Using GenAI in IT Operations

GenAI is shaping up to be a valuable tool in information technology (IT) operations. This is a core department in every business, whether it's contracted as a managed service or operates on company premises. The areas it covers include things like infrastructure management, incident response, and both software and hardware troubleshooting. GenAI can help IT streamline processes, improve efficiency, and support decision-making. IT can benefit significantly from a tool that can quickly analyze, interpret, and respond to complex data inputs.

Quite naturally then, GenAI is routinely added as a part of AIOps in many organizations. *AIOps* means "AI for IT operations" in tech speak.

IT uses GenAI

>> **In cybersecurity incident reporting,** in which GenAI can assist by quickly analyzing logs and interpreting error codes. When a crash occurs — which IT would properly refer to as *system downtime* — GenAI can assist in troubleshooting the problem(s) by cross-referencing error codes with existing databases or suggesting corrective actions based on patterns learned from previous incidents. This capability saves IT time and effort and may reduce the downtime. Indeed, a case study by Forrester highlights how AI-driven tools like GenAI can improve mean time to resolution (MTTR) by assisting with automated log analysis.

>> **In infrastructure management** for assisting with system monitoring and some limited automation. In a cloud environment, the app can analyze resource utilization data, such as CPU or memory usage across virtual machines, and recommend scaling actions when thresholds are met or optimization is needed.

>> **To help with routine tasks** such as updating or creating content for knowledge centers and self-help repositories. It can assist help desks in similar ways. If you want specific information on how to use GenAI in IT, knowledge centers, or for help desks, consider taking one or more of my courses on LinkedIn Learning. I'm an instructor there, and my courses run the gamut on AI, IT, and help desk topics.

Overall, GenAI enhances IT operations by offering data-driven insights, providing efficient troubleshooting, and automating repetitive tasks, all of which optimize workflows and improve productivity in IT environments. However, the same warnings with other fields apply to IT. Make sure you allocate and assign individuals to provide oversight for GenAI and manage outputs carefully.

PROS AND CONS OF USING GENAI IN INFORMATION TECHNOLOGY

Aspect	Pros	Cons
Efficiency	Automates repetitive tasks (for example, retrieving data), freeing up IT teams for higher-priority tasks.	Risk of over-reliance, potentially missing nuanced issues that require human analysis.
Troubleshooting	Speeds up error diagnosis by analyzing logs and error codes and offering potential solutions based on past incidents.	Limited in handling novel issues outside its trained data scope, which may delay or mislead troubleshooting.
24/7 availability	Provides around-the-clock support, useful for global IT operations or extended hours with minimal human intervention.	Potential struggle with complex, real-time responses during critical incidents, especially without human oversight.
Resource management	Monitors system metrics (CPU, memory) and suggests scaling actions, optimizing resource usage.	Not fully equipped for decision-making in critical resource allocation without deeper contextual analysis.
Knowledge base	Serves as an extensive resource for referencing documentation and providing guidance on a wide range of technical queries.	Risk of outdated information because models need periodic updates to stay relevant with evolving technology.
Customization	Can be tailored to specific IT needs (for example, specific workflows, alerts) and integrated with other tools.	Requires time and effort for initial setup and continuous training to ensure accurate and reliable responses.
User experience	Offers a user-friendly, conversational interface that's accessible to both technical and nontechnical users.	Challenges with interpreting AI-driven responses, especially for technical troubleshooting.

Examining New Businesses Based on GenAI

If you're an entrepreneur or a budding startup founder, you may want to use GenAI in a few more ways than I've outlined for your industry. To that end, consider the following guide on starting a business based on services largely generated by GenAI.

You can use GenAI to help you think of business ideas and make business plans for any type of business; your business doesn't have to sell GenAI-generated services or be built on AI from the ground up. Because I'm asked almost daily how to create a business using and selling GenAI-based services, I chose to use it here to illustrate how to use GenAI to develop a new business.

Art isn't the only thing you can generate and sell using GenAI. Imagine creating a platform that offers personalized storytelling services. For example, you can use GenAI to develop an app in which users input a few details about themselves or a loved one, and the AI generates a custom fairy tale, adventure story, or the memories of an elder family member. This can be an excellent gift in memory of a loved one or as bedtime stories for children. GenAI can develop code for you that you can use to build an app in a different platform. If you don't want to make an app, interview people or provide an online form for your customers, and then create the story by prompting GenAI to do so using that information.

Maybe you'd rather create a virtual art gallery in which other artists creating works in GenAI can display and sell their work. The gallery can also offer a service in which customers describe their desired artwork, and their chosen artist — or you — can generate a bespoke artwork based on their description.

Similarly, you can form a content creation agency that specializes in marketing materials built by a human + GenAI team to the customer's specifications. You can even entice companies to outsource their marketing content to your agency. Businesses can provide their brand guidelines and marketing goals, and you can guide and polish GenAI blog posts, social media updates, and ad copy tailored accordingly.

Other unique opportunities are out there, too, such as in education. Consider tutoring school kids and adults alike in prompting skills or using GenAI to develop a unique study guide for students struggling with any topic. This could be particularly beneficial for homeschooling families or adult learners seeking to acquire new skills.

For the music industry, think about an AI-powered composition service. Musicians and composers can use AI to generate new melodies, harmonies, and lyrics. An entrepreneur might create a subscription-based service by which users receive regular batches of AI-generated music ideas and then refine and develop them into full compositions. It can be a valuable tool for songwriters who are experiencing creative blocks or looking for fresh inspiration.

Basic prompts to identify these and other business ideas can include questions like these:

What are common challenges in the XYZ industry that could be alleviated or otherwise addressed with GenAI assistance?

How can GenAI enhance personalization in my current business model?

What creative processes in my field could benefit from GenAI-generated inspiration or content?

In what ways can GenAI improve customer engagement and satisfaction in my business?

For a list of information that you should include in prompts for more refined or edgy business ideas, look at Figure 5-5, which also shows their importance to outcomes.

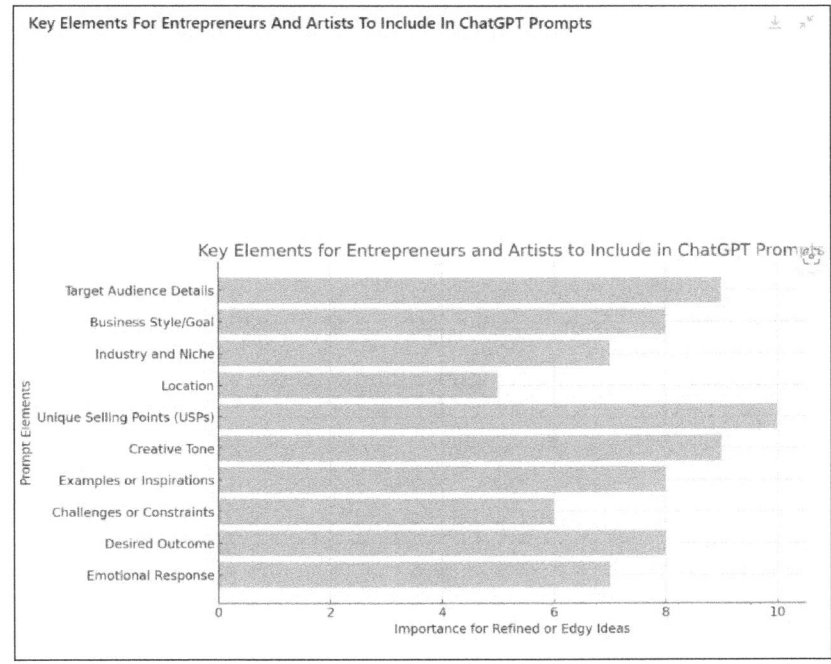

FIGURE 5-5:
A list of key elements for artists and entrepreneurs to include in prompts.

Use your imagination and explore all you want. Odds are that GenAI outputs will spark some great ideas.

Chapter **6**

Managing AI Adoption and Change in Your Organization

ntroducing AI into your organization is not just about implementing new technologies; it's about managing change effectively. AI adoption often requires a shift in how teams operate, collaborate, and make decisions. Project managers play a key role in leading AI adoption and managing change within an organization. In this chapter, you learn how to lead AI adoption efforts, train your team on AI tools and best practices, and overcome resistance to AI adoption.

Leading AI Adoption and Change Management Efforts

A successful AI adoption begins with a well-thought-out strategy that aligns with your organization's overall goals. Developing this strategy requires a clear understanding of how AI will support business objectives, improve operations, and deliver measurable value. Start by outlining the reasons for AI adoption and the expected benefits. Consider how AI will enhance current processes, where it can add value, and how it will address existing pain points in your operations. This strategic foundation will guide your adoption efforts and keep everyone focused on common goals.

Your AI adoption strategy should also address potential challenges, such as employee resistance, skill gaps, and budgetary constraints. Identify these hurdles early on and plan how you will mitigate them. For instance, if your team lacks AI expertise, you might plan for training or hiring AI specialists. If job displacement is a concern, include strategies for reskilling or role redefinition in your plan. The more comprehensive and realistic your strategy, the smoother your AI adoption will be.

Another critical aspect of developing an AI adoption strategy is timeline management. Implementing AI is a complex process that requires phased execution, including pilot programs, feedback loops, and eventual scaling. Define key milestones for your AI integration, including short-term objectives that keep the project moving forward and long-term goals that align with your organization's strategic vision. Flexibility is important, so be prepared to adjust your timeline as challenges arise.

Regularly revisit and update your AI adoption strategy to adapt to changing organizational needs and technological advancements.

Identifying key stakeholders and champions for AI adoption

Engaging the right stakeholders is essential for the successful integration of AI into your organization. Identifying key decision-makers, department heads, and subject matter experts from various areas of the business will ensure that AI adoption has broad support. These stakeholders will provide valuable insights into how AI can impact different functions, allowing for a more holistic adoption strategy. From finance to operations and HR, ensure every relevant department is represented in your AI planning process.

Identifying champions who are enthusiastic about AI is crucial for driving adoption. These champions should be influential within their teams and have a strong understanding of how AI will benefit their departments. AI champions can act as advocates, helping build excitement and acceptance for AI across the organization. These individuals should be involved from the beginning, participating in pilot programs and providing feedback on AI implementation.

Empower champions and stakeholders to communicate the advantages of AI to their peers. Their role is to address concerns, answer questions, and provide support as AI is rolled out. By ensuring that champions are actively involved in the AI adoption process, you can build internal momentum and increase buy-in across the organization. These champions will also play a key role in navigating resistance by showcasing early wins and advocating for AI's value.

TIP

Regularly check in with AI champions to ensure they feel supported and equipped to promote AI adoption within their departments.

Communicating the benefits of AI adoption

Clear, transparent, and consistent communication is one of the most critical aspects of managing change. To gain widespread support for AI adoption, you must articulate the benefits of AI in a way that resonates with employees at all levels. Begin by outlining how AI can improve daily workflows, automate mundane tasks, and enhance decision-making capabilities. Highlight specific-use cases that relate directly to your team's responsibilities to demonstrate how AI adoption will directly benefit them.

It's equally important to address concerns and potential misconceptions about AI upfront. Employees may fear job displacement or feel uncertain about learning new technologies. As part of your communication strategy, acknowledge these concerns and provide a realistic perspective on how AI will impact the organization. Emphasize that the intent for AI is to support employees, making their roles more strategic rather than replacing them. By being transparent about both the opportunities and challenges of AI adoption, you build trust and create a more open dialogue.

Using multiple communication channels is essential to ensure that your message reaches all employees. Consider using newsletters, town hall meetings, and departmental briefings to communicate the progress and benefits of AI adoption. This will help keep everyone informed and aligned with the organizational goals. Additionally, encourage two-way communication, in which employees can ask questions, share concerns, and offer feedback on AI-related changes.

TIP

Set up regular Q&A sessions during which employees can raise concerns about AI adoption and ensure these sessions are open and accessible to all staff.

Aligning AI adoption with organizational culture

Successfully implementing AI requires aligning its adoption with the existing culture and values of your organization. If your organization values innovation, you can emphasize how AI can fuel creativity by generating new product ideas, automating repetitive tasks to free up time for strategic thinking, or providing predictive analytics to inspire data-driven decision-making. For example, AI-powered design tools like Adobe Sensei (`https://business.adobe.com/products/sensei/adobe-sensei.html`) can help creative teams generate concepts faster, while AI-driven market trend analysis can uncover opportunities for new offerings.

For organizations that prioritize customer satisfaction, highlight how AI can enhance the customer experience by providing personalized recommendations, faster response times, and proactive service solutions. AI-powered chatbots like Zendesk AI (`www.zendesk.com/service/ai`) can improve customer support by handling common inquiries efficiently, whereas AI-driven sentiment analysis can help businesses gauge customer satisfaction and address issues before they escalate. The goal is to make AI adoption feel like a natural extension of the organization's existing values, reinforcing its commitment to excellence rather than introducing a disruptive change.

One effective way to align AI with company culture is to demonstrate how AI will enhance collaborative efforts across teams. For example, you could showcase how AI-driven tools facilitate better cross-department communication or enable faster decision-making. By framing AI adoption in ways that complement your organization's strengths, you create a smoother transition and increase the likelihood of successful adoption.

Also, keep in mind that fostering a culture of continuous learning is essential for long-term AI success. AI technologies are constantly evolving, so it's crucial to promote an organizational mindset that embraces change and innovation. Encourage employees to see AI adoption as an opportunity for growth, providing access to learning resources and creating an environment in which experimentation is valued. This cultural alignment makes employees feel more comfortable with the changes AI brings.

TIP

Align AI adoption with your company's key values by integrating AI tools that support collaboration, innovation, and customer satisfaction.

Creating a roadmap for AI adoption

An AI adoption roadmap provides the structure and clarity needed to ensure a smooth integration of AI technologies into your organization. This roadmap should detail every step of the process, from the initial assessment and pilot projects to full-scale deployment. By breaking the adoption process into manageable phases, you can track progress, address roadblocks, and make data-driven decisions along the way. The roadmap also provides transparency for employees, helping them understand the overall timeline and what to expect as AI is integrated into their work.

Here are six steps you can follow to create your AI roadmap:

1. Define your AI adoption goals.

   Identify key objectives (for example, efficiency, cost savings, improved decision-making) and establish success metrics.

2. Assess readiness and identify use cases.

   Evaluate current technology, workforce skills, and infrastructure while determining where AI can provide the most value.

3. Outline phases of AI adoption.

   Break the process into stages (exploration and planning, pilot testing, evaluation and refinement, full-scale deployment, and continuous improvement).

4. Create a timeline for implementation.

   Assign time limits to each phase and set milestones such as employee training, system testing, and performance reviews.

5. Develop a communication and training plan.

   Establish a strategy for educating employees, addressing concerns, and keeping teams informed about AI progress.

6. Monitor progress and adapt.

   Set up a feedback loop, track AI performance, and refine implementation strategies based on real-world results and employee input.

The roadmap should also include clear metrics for success, such as productivity improvements, cost savings, or customer satisfaction gains. These metrics will help you measure the effectiveness of AI adoption at each stage and provide a basis for continuous improvement. In addition, the roadmap should be flexible enough to accommodate feedback and adapt to unforeseen challenges. As you move through each phase, gather input from employees and stakeholders and adjust as needed.

Regularly communicating milestones and progress as you move along the roadmap is essential for maintaining engagement. Celebrate each phase of successful AI integration, whether it's completing training programs, launching pilot projects, or achieving efficiency gains. This helps keep the team motivated and reinforces that the organization is committed to AI adoption as a long-term strategy.

TIP

Use visual tools, such as Gantt charts or dashboards, to clearly display the road-map and progress, making it easier for all stakeholders to track the journey.

Understanding Different Models for Change and Transition

Successfully integrating AI into your organization requires more than just adopting new technology. It demands a structured approach to managing change. As a project manager, you play a critical role in guiding your team through this transformation, ensuring that both technical and human factors are addressed. To help you navigate this process, this section explores three widely recognized change management models: ADKAR, William Bridges' Model of Change and Transition, and the DIRECT Project Leadership framework. By understanding and applying these frameworks, you can create a smoother, more effective AI adoption strategy that minimizes resistance and maximizes long-term success.

Using the ADKAR model for change management

The ADKAR (awareness, desire, knowledge, ability, and reinforcement) model is a change management framework developed by Prosci (www.prosci.com) that focuses on guiding individuals through the process of change. The model is widely used across industries for managing organizational transformations, including the adoption of new technologies like AI.

ADKAR represents the five essential steps that individuals must go through for successful change. Unlike other models that focus primarily on processes, ADKAR emphasizes the human side of change by addressing the emotional and psychological aspects that can often be barriers to successful adoption. By using this model, project managers can systematically lead teams through the stages of awareness, motivation, training, practical application, and continuous reinforcement, ensuring that change is both sustainable and impactful.

Awareness: Helping employees understand the need for AI adoption

The first step in the ADKAR model is building awareness about the need for AI adoption. Employees need to understand why AI is being introduced and how it will benefit both the organization and their individual roles. Without this understanding, it is difficult for employees to fully support the transition. Begin by clearly explaining the business challenges AI can solve and the opportunities it opens for innovation, efficiency, and productivity. Emphasize how adopting AI is necessary to stay competitive in a rapidly evolving digital landscape.

It's also essential to communicate the risks of not adopting AI, such as falling behind competitors or missing out on efficiency gains. Employees must see AI adoption not as a threat but as an opportunity to grow and succeed in a more advanced, data-driven work environment. Providing real-world examples or case studies from other organizations can help illustrate the tangible benefits of AI and why the shift is necessary.

REMEMBER

The goal at this stage is to create a sense of urgency while ensuring that employees feel informed and included in the process. Consider holding town hall meetings, sending out informational materials, and allowing employees to ask questions and voice concerns. By fostering an open dialogue, you can ensure that everyone is on the same page and feels comfortable with the change.

TIP

Regularly communicate updates on AI adoption to maintain awareness and provide employees with ongoing insights into why AI is essential for the organization's growth.

Desire: Motivating employees to support AI adoption

When employees are aware of the need for AI, the next step is fostering a genuine desire to participate in the change. Without personal motivation, employees may resist AI adoption or disengage from the process altogether. To build this desire, it's important to address any fears or concerns employees may have. Common concerns include job security, the fear of being replaced by AI, or the anxiety of learning new technologies. Be transparent about these concerns and emphasize that AI is meant to complement human skills rather than replace them.

Help employees understand how AI can make their work more meaningful by automating repetitive tasks and allowing them to focus on more strategic, creative, or value-adding activities. Highlight how AI can streamline workflows, reduce inefficiencies, and support better decision-making. By framing AI as a tool that empowers them, you can create excitement about its potential.

You can also build motivation by involving employees in the AI adoption process. Invite them to participate in pilot programs, provide feedback on AI tools, and contribute ideas for how AI can enhance their roles. When employees feel a sense of ownership over the changes, they are more likely to embrace the transition.

TIP

Share early wins and success stories from pilot AI projects to motivate employees and demonstrate the positive impact of AI adoption.

Knowledge: Equipping employees with the skills to use AI effectively

After establishing desire, the next step is providing employees with the knowledge they need to use AI tools effectively. Training is crucial at this stage because employees need to feel confident in their ability to work with AI technologies. Begin by assessing your team's current knowledge level and identifying gaps to address. Different roles may require different levels of training; for instance, some employees may need basic knowledge of how AI works, whereas others may require more advanced technical training.

Develop a comprehensive training program that covers both the technical aspects of using AI tools and the strategic understanding of how employees can apply AI in their work. Consider offering a variety of training formats, such as workshops, online courses, and hands-on practice sessions, to accommodate different learning styles. This helps ensure that all employees are equipped with the skills they need to confidently engage with AI technologies.

Continuous learning is also critical. AI technologies are constantly evolving, and employees need to stay up to date with the latest advancements. Encourage employees to take advantage of ongoing upskilling opportunities and provide access to resources such as online learning platforms or AI certifications. This ensures that your team continues to grow their AI capabilities long after the initial training.

Ability: Ensuring employees can apply AI in their daily work

Providing knowledge is only half of the equation: Employees must also develop the ability to apply AI effectively in their daily work. This stage is about moving beyond theoretical understanding and ensuring that employees have the practical skills to integrate AI into their workflows. Begin by setting up pilot projects or sandbox environments where employees can experiment with AI tools in a low-risk setting. Hands-on practice is essential for helping employees gain confidence and see the direct application of AI in their specific roles.

One of the key challenges at this stage is bridging the gap between knowledge and real-world application. Employees may understand how AI works conceptually, but they need the ability to adapt those concepts to their everyday tasks. For instance, a marketing team may need to learn how to use AI for customer segmentation, and a logistics team might focus on using AI to optimize supply chain operations. Tailoring the learning experience to specific use cases will make the transition smoother.

Ongoing support is crucial to helping employees build their abilities. Encourage a culture of collaboration in which employees can share insights, tips, and best practices for using AI tools. Mentorship programs, peer learning groups, or AI champions within teams can provide additional support, ensuring that employees feel confident and capable as they begin applying AI in their work.

TIP

Regularly review employees' progress and provide additional training or resources for those who need further support in developing AI-related skills.

Reinforcement: Sustaining AI adoption through ongoing support and feedback

The final stage of the ADKAR model focuses on reinforcement — ensuring that the changes made through AI adoption are sustained over time. Even after employees have gained the knowledge and ability to use AI tools, continuous reinforcement is needed to prevent regression to old ways of working. Reinforcement comes in the form of ongoing feedback, recognition of progress, and support for continuous improvement. Providing regular check-ins with employees to discuss their experience with AI tools can help identify any challenges or areas in which further assistance is needed.

Recognition is another powerful tool for reinforcing AI adoption. Celebrate successes and acknowledge employees or teams that have effectively integrated AI into their workflows. Public recognition of AI-related achievements not only motivates those individuals but also encourages others to embrace AI adoption. Regularly sharing stories of how AI is driving positive outcomes for the business can help keep momentum going.

Additionally, it's important to keep employees informed about future developments in AI technology. As AI continues to evolve, there may be new tools, features, or processes that could benefit your team. Reinforcing a culture of continuous learning and improvement will help ensure that AI adoption is not seen as a one-time event but rather as an ongoing journey of growth and innovation.

TIP

Create AI champions within teams who can provide ongoing support and help reinforce the long-term adoption of AI tools across the organization.

William Bridges' model for change and transition

The Bridges Transition Model emphasizes the psychological and emotional aspects of change. Bridges argues that successful change doesn't just depend on external processes and systems, but also on how people transition through it internally. The model identifies three key stages of transition:

>> **Endings:** This is the first stage, in which employees may experience resistance, anxiety, or fear as they let go of old ways of working. During AI adoption, it's essential to acknowledge these feelings and provide support to help employees move past them. Clear communication and reassurance can help ease this process.

>> **Neutral zone:** This is a period of uncertainty and adjustment. Employees are learning to adapt to new AI tools and workflows, but the old ways of working are not yet entirely behind them. This phase can feel chaotic and confusing, but it's also where innovation and creativity can flourish. Providing continuous training and support during this stage is crucial.

>> **New beginnings:** In this final stage, employees start embracing the new AI-driven processes. They begin to see the benefits of AI, and their confidence in using these tools grows. Celebrating successes and reinforcing positive behaviors help solidify this new beginning.

By understanding and addressing the emotional side of change, the Bridges Transition Model helps you manage the human transitions that accompany AI adoption. With it, you can guide your team through the process of letting go of the old, navigating the uncertainty of the transition, and ultimately embracing the new.

Introducing the DIRECT model for project leadership

Leading a project can sometimes feel overwhelming, but the DIRECT model simplifies project leadership into six key responsibilities. By using the acronym *DIRECT*, you can easily remember the six pillars of effective project leadership: define, investigate, resolve, execute, change, and transition.

>> **Define the vision:** The first pillar is all about defining a vision for your project. Your responsibility as the project leader is to ensure that everyone understands the project's objectives and that there's ongoing support to achieve those goals. A well-defined vision aligns your team and sets the foundation for success.

- **Investigate the options:** Before making any decisions, you must explore alternatives. Investigate the ways you could approach the project, weighing the pros and cons of each option. How much will each choice cost? How long will it take? How well does it solve the problem? By thoroughly investigating options, you ensure that your team has the information needed to make informed decisions.

- **Resolve to a course of action:** At some point, a decision needs to be made. After investigating your options, resolve to a clear course of action and commit to a plan. This pillar is about deciding on the best approach and ensuring that your team is aligned and ready to move forward.

- **Execute the plan:** Execution is when the plan comes to life. This stage involves coordinating your team to get the work done and tracking their progress. Your role as a leader is to monitor performance, remove obstacles, and ensure that the project stays on track. Execution requires focus, coordination, and adaptability.

- **Change the system:** Every project leads to change, whether it's a new software implementation or a new business process. This pillar emphasizes the importance of leading that change. For many people, the go-live phase of a project may be their first direct interaction with the work you've been doing, so it's essential to guide them through the change to ensure acceptance and success.

- **Transition the people:** Transitioning is about ensuring that people adapt to the new solution once the project is complete. While change focuses on the tangible aspects of the project, transition is about the human side: how people react and respond. Successful transition is crucial for ensuring that the improvements you've made truly take root and deliver long-term value.

By following the DIRECT model, you'll have a clear framework to lead any project effectively. This simple but powerful approach ensures that both the technical and human elements of project leadership are covered, setting you and your team up for lasting success.

Overcoming Resistance to AI Adoption

Resistance to AI adoption is common, particularly when employees feel uncertain about the impact of AI on their roles or fear that AI could replace them. Addressing these concerns and overcoming resistance is essential for ensuring that everyone in the organization embraces AI adoption. Here's how to overcome resistance to AI adoption.

Understanding the root causes of resistance

Resistance to AI adoption often stems from multiple underlying concerns, including fear of job displacement, uncertainty about new technologies, and concerns over the need to develop new skills. To effectively address these concerns, it's critical to first understand why employees may be hesitant. Engage in open conversations with your team and gather feedback through surveys, focus groups, or one-on-one meetings. Understanding their perspective allows you to pinpoint the exact causes of their resistance and develop strategies to address them.

Fear is a common driver of resistance, particularly if employees believe AI will replace their roles. It's important to clarify that AI is not meant to replace them but to enhance their ability to work more efficiently. Addressing this early in the process can ease some of the anxiety surrounding AI adoption. Additionally, you may discover that employees are concerned about the steep learning curve associated with new AI tools. In such cases, offering ample training and support can help to alleviate these concerns.

Another factor to consider is organizational culture. If your organization has historically been slow to adopt new technologies, the resistance may stem from a general aversion to change. In these cases, resistance can be a symptom of larger cultural challenges, and AI adoption must be positioned as a positive shift that aligns with the company's goals and values.

TIP

Use anonymous feedback tools to gather honest insights into the specific concerns employees have about AI adoption. This helps to ensure you address the right issues from the start.

Addressing fears about job displacement

One of the most significant barriers to AI adoption is the fear of job displacement. Employees may worry that AI will automate their tasks and make their roles redundant, leading to layoffs or reduced job security. To address these concerns, clearly communicate the intent of AI within the organization. AI is most effective when used to complement human skills by automating repetitive, low-value tasks, freeing employees to focus on more strategic, creative, or customer-focused responsibilities.

Provide examples of how AI has been successfully implemented in other organizations without resulting in widespread job cuts. Frame AI adoption as an opportunity for employees to upskill and take on more meaningful roles within the organization. If possible, create pathways for career growth that are tied to AI adoption. For example, employees who learn to use AI tools might transition into higher-level roles where they oversee AI systems or use AI to improve processes.

TIP

Reassure your team that AI is not a threat but a tool to enhance productivity and innovation. Demonstrating how AI can reduce mundane tasks and create more time for complex problem-solving or customer engagement will help employees see the value of AI in their daily work.

Building trust through transparency

Trust is essential for overcoming resistance to AI adoption, and building that trust requires transparency at every stage of the process. Employees want to know why the organization is adopting AI, how they will use it, and what impact it will have on their roles and the overall organization. Be clear about the organization's goals for AI adoption, whether it's to increase efficiency, reduce costs, or improve decision-making. Open communication about the benefits and challenges of AI helps to reduce the sense of uncertainty that often accompanies change.

Transparency should extend to the AI technologies themselves. Many employees may be concerned about how AI will make decisions or whether those decisions will be fair and unbiased. Take the time to explain how AI systems work, the data they rely on, and the safeguards in place to ensure ethical use. Providing information on the potential risks and how they will be managed shows that the organization is committed to using AI responsibly.

Regular updates on the progress of AI adoption and success stories from early pilot projects can help sustain trust throughout the transition. Use various communication channels, such as internal newsletters, team meetings, or dedicated AI discussion forums, to keep employees informed and allow them to ask questions or raise concerns.

TIP

Create a dedicated AI adoption FAQ page that addresses common employee concerns and provides up-to-date information on the progress of the implementation.

Involving employees in the AI adoption process

Engaging employees in the AI adoption process can transform resistance into enthusiasm. Employees are more likely to embrace AI if they feel like active participants in the journey rather than passive recipients of top-down decisions. Involving them early in the process and giving them a sense of ownership will reduce anxiety and promote buy-in.

Start by identifying employees who are particularly interested in or excited about AI and making them the champions of the initiative. These champions can help spread positive messages about AI adoption and act as a resource for their peers. Invite employees to participate in pilot projects, giving them hands-on experience with AI tools before they are fully rolled out across the organization. This involvement helps demystify AI and shows employees how the technology can be integrated into their workflows.

Employee feedback is also crucial during the early stages of AI implementation. Encourage teams to share their experiences, offer suggestions for improvement, and highlight any challenges they encounter. By incorporating employee input into the AI adoption strategy, you demonstrate that their voices are valued and that the organization is committed to making the transition as smooth as possible for everyone.

TIP

Host regular feedback sessions or focus groups to allow employees to voice their opinions on the AI adoption process and suggest ways to improve integration.

Providing support and resources for the transition

Adopting AI requires employees to learn new skills and adapt to new ways of working, which can be overwhelming without proper support. Providing a robust support system, including training, mentorship, and access to AI experts, will ease the transition and reduce resistance. Ensure that employees feel equipped with the knowledge and tools they need to use AI technologies effectively.

Offer tailored training sessions that address the specific needs of different teams or roles within the organization. For instance, a data analytics team may require in-depth technical training on AI algorithms, while a marketing team might need training on how AI can help improve customer segmentation. In addition to formal training, consider setting up peer-to-peer learning networks where employees can collaborate and share their experiences using AI tools.

Mentorship programs can also play a valuable role in supporting employees during the transition. Pair employees who are confident in using AI with those who are less experienced to foster knowledge-sharing and build confidence. Providing access to AI experts, either internally or externally, ensures that employees have a resource to turn to when they encounter challenges or have questions.

TIP

Set up a dedicated AI support hub with resources, guides, and a helpdesk to address any technical or workflow challenges employees face during the adoption process.

Celebrating success stories

One of the most effective ways to overcome resistance to AI adoption is to celebrate early successes. Sharing success stories from teams or individuals who have successfully integrated AI into their workflows demonstrates the tangible benefits of the technology. Highlight the positive outcomes, such as increased productivity, improved decision-making, reduced workload, and even enhanced work-life balance. For example, AI-powered automation can streamline repetitive administrative tasks, allowing employees to focus on more meaningful, strategic work while reducing burnout and overtime.

These success stories help shift the narrative around AI from one of fear and uncertainty to one of opportunity and growth. They can also serve as motivation for other employees who may still be hesitant about adopting AI. Be sure to recognize and reward employees or teams that have embraced AI and seen positive results. This recognition not only reinforces their commitment to AI adoption but also encourages others to follow suit.

Share success through internal newsletters, presentations at team meetings, or case studies that highlight specific use cases of AI within the organization. By celebrating these wins, you create a positive feedback loop that helps build momentum for continued AI adoption.

TIP

Consider creating an internal AI Champion award to recognize employees who are excelling in their use of AI tools, inspiring others to do the same.

By addressing the root causes of resistance, providing support and resources, and celebrating early successes, project managers can overcome employee hesitance and foster widespread acceptance of AI adoption.

INNOVATETECH'S AI ADOPTION SUCCESS

InnovateTech, a rapidly expanding tech company, encountered significant employee resistance when it introduced AI-powered tools across its departments. Employees expressed concerns ranging from job displacement due to automation to anxieties about mastering new, complex technologies. Maria, a seasoned project manager, was tasked with spearheading the AI adoption initiative and knew a top-down mandate wouldn't suffice. She understood that addressing the root causes of this resistance was paramount.

(continued)

(continued)

Maria's strategy began with clear and consistent communication. Instead of vague pronouncements about "digital transformation," she provided concrete examples of how AI would be used within InnovateTech. For instance, she explained how AI-powered tools could automate the tedious data entry previously handled by the marketing team, freeing them up to focus on more strategic campaign development. She also demonstrated how AI could streamline the software testing process, allowing developers to concentrate on more creative coding tasks. Crucially, Maria emphasized that AI was being implemented to augment employee capabilities, not replace them. She framed it as a tool that would empower employees to be more efficient and effective, ultimately enhancing their roles.

Recognizing that trust was essential, Maria prioritized transparency. She established an internal AI progress tracker accessible to all employees, detailing the rollout plan, pilot project results, and even addressing any setbacks the team encountered. Regular company-wide meetings were held during which she answered employee questions directly and honestly. To further build buy-in, Maria actively involved employees in the implementation process. She recruited "AI Champions" from different teams — early adopters who were enthusiastic about the technology and could act as advocates within their respective departments. These champions played a key role in engaging their colleagues in pilot projects, providing valuable feedback, and fostering a sense of ownership.

Maria also understood that training and support were critical for successful adoption. She implemented tailored training programs for each team, focusing on the specific AI tools relevant to their work. For example, the sales team received training on using an AI-powered CRM to personalize customer interactions, while the customer support team learned how to leverage AI chatbots to handle routine inquiries, allowing them to focus on more complex customer issues. Recognizing that employees might struggle even after formal training, Maria established an AI helpdesk staffed with experts who could provide ongoing support and answer questions as they arose.

As a result of Maria's thoughtful and comprehensive approach, InnovateTech successfully integrated AI into its operations. The company saw a significant boost in productivity across multiple departments. For example, the marketing team was able to launch more campaigns in the same timeframe, and the software development team reduced the time required to complete their testing cycle. Beyond the tangible improvements, Maria's leadership fostered a culture of innovation and a positive attitude toward technology, positioning InnovateTech for continued success in the rapidly evolving tech landscape.

4

Creating Content with AI

Contents at a Glance

CHAPTER 1: **Using AI for Ideation and Planning** 335

CHAPTER 2: **Managing and Writing Emails with AI** 349

CHAPTER 3: **Developing Creative Assets** 363

CHAPTER 4: **Producing Long-Form Content** 381

CHAPTER 5: **Search Engine Optimization (SEO) in the AI Era** 403

CHAPTER 6: **Fine-Tuning Content with Localization and Translation** 419

Chapter **1**

Using AI for Ideation and Planning

U sing artificial intelligence (AI) to help with creativity and ideation (coming up with new ideas), in particular, is not a new thought. In 2018, the AI-generated artwork "The Portrait of Edmond de Belamy" sold for $432,500 at Christie's auction house. This price was almost 45 times its pre-auction high estimate. This piece was created by an AI model trained on a data set of 15,000 portraits spanning six centuries.

The type of generative AI system used to create "The Portrait of Edmond de Belamy" was a *generative adversarial network* (GAN). GANs use two neural networks: one network that generates images and the other that evaluates them. GANs can produce hyper-realistic images (of people and places, for example) that are often indistinguishable from real ones. If you've ever used AI imagery tools such as Midjourney or DALL-E 3 to create an image for a presentation or a piece of advertising, you've experienced GANs at work.

When you put the thought of creativity into the context of your business, ideation serves as a foundational exercise for the development of successful marketing strategies, content, and campaigns. Ideation isn't just about tossing around ideas; it also involves the art of exploring your customer base, the quest to uncover possibilities for enhancing market success, and the identification of potential paths forward. And ideation doesn't happen in a vacuum. Customer research, business objectives, competitor dynamics, product plans, and previous marketing results all serve as the ingredients for the ideation process.

On the flip side, your marketing planning takes the diverse ideas developed through the ideation process and meticulously orchestrates them into actionable steps and strategies that sketch out a road map for achieving desired outcomes. These outcomes can take the form of an annual marketing plan, a campaign brief, a creative concept, or even a media plan.

The emergence of generative AI ushers in a new era of possibilities and efficiencies in how businesses can ideate, conceptualize, strategize, and develop marketing (and even new product) innovations. In this chapter, I discuss how you can use AI and, specifically, generative AI to fuel the ideation processes.

Engaging AI to Ideate on Behalf of Human Beings

Until recently, the notion that AI can match human ideation seemed fantastical. Conventional wisdom dictates that AI tools aren't sophisticated enough to generate ideas, develop names for products, identify solutions for unmet needs, or unpack creative insights.

To test this hypothesis, two University of Pennsylvania Wharton School of Business professors ran a controlled experiment to understand how an AI performed on an unstructured assignment relative to the professors' MBA students. This study was highlighted in a *Wall Street Journal* article, "M.B.A. Students vs. AI: Who Comes Up With More Innovative Ideas?" from September 9, 2023. See the article at www.wsj.com/tech/ai/mba-students-vs-chatgpt-innovation-679edf3b and the sidebar "ChatGPT versus Wharton MBA students" in this chapter for details of this study.

This pivotal study from the fall of 2023 has altered the perception of AI's deficiencies. The study specifically highlights the capabilities of generative AI — with ChatGPT 4.0 as the prime example — and demonstrates that AI can ideate with a sophistication akin to that of humans.

REMEMBER

Please be aware that this level of ideation typically requires that human beings engineer precise prompting for the AI and provide domain-specific context to the large language model (LLM) involved (unless the model already possesses the relevant information). Nonetheless, the results of specific ideation studies have shown AI-generated ideas to be viable and on par with (if not better than) human-generated ones.

CHATGPT VERSUS WHARTON MBA STUDENTS

Professors Christian Tardiest and Karl Ulrich gave 200 randomly selected MBA students from the University of Pennsylvania Wharton School of Business the task of generating an idea for a new product or service appealing to college students that a company could make available to those students for $50 or less. The professors gave the same assignment to ChatGPT 4, asking it to develop 100 ideas. To further the hypothesis, the professors asked ChatGPT 4 to develop an additional 100 ideas after some coaching, which involved providing ChatGPT 4 with a sample of successful ideas from past courses. After that exercise, they now had 400 ideas — 200 from MBA students and 200 from ChatGPT 4.

To assess the strength of the idea generation, the professors looked at the efficiency with which the ideas were generated per unit of time, the average quality of the ideas, and the number of truly exceptional ideas. Not surprisingly, ChatGPT 4 produced ideas very quickly — spitting out 200 ideas in about an hour (with some human supervision). The human-generated ideas took longer to develop. The study employed an online purchase-intent survey directed toward the targeted customer base to assess the quality of the ideas by asking the following question:

"How likely would you be to purchase based on this concept if it were available to you?"

The possible responses ranged from *Definitely Wouldn't Purchase* to *Definitely Would Purchase.*

The professors got some very interesting results in the following average purchase probabilities:

- **Human-generated idea:** 40 percent
- **Uncoached ChatGPT 4 idea:** 47 percent
- **Coached ChatGPT 4 idea:** 49 percent

These results show that not only was ChatGPT 4 much faster in generating ideas but also that the overall quality of the ideas was stronger.

But, the study offered more results than just the purchase probability information. To determine whether students or AI produced exceptional ideas (after all, a business typically needs only one exceptional idea, rather than dozens of above-average ones), the study reviewed the top 10 percent of the ideas in each pool. Of these 40 ideas, a whopping 35 were created by ChatGPT 4, with 20 from the pre-trained ChatGPT 4 set and 15 from the untrained version of ChatGPT 4. ChatGPT 4 clearly came out on top in these results, as well, demonstrating that generative AI can not only perform basic copywriting tasks but also provide higher-order critical thinking and ideation.

The Wharton study, which included both MBA students and an AI tool, generated 400 product ideas (200 from students and 200 from ChatGPT 4). After market testing for the quality of all ideas, the average probability of purchase for human-generated ideas was 40 percent, whereas the average probability of purchase for the AI-generated ideas was 47 to 49 percent. The study also accounted for the speed of idea generation to note efficiency. (Unsurprisingly, ChatGPT 4 generated its ideas much faster than the students generated theirs.) Further review of the top 10 percent of ideas (40 ideas) revealed that AI generated 35 of those ideas.

This groundbreaking study highlighted the quality, quantity, and efficiency of AI-generated ideas and provided these important takeaways:

>> **Generative AI can be an effective idea-generation tool.** Arguably, no piece of technology in the history of humankind has been able to achieve the kind of results demonstrated in the Wharton study. Using AI to generate ideas marks a distinct departure from the past uses of technology, which typically centered around knowledge management, automation, and calculations.

>> **The role of human beings may shift in a world in which AI generates ideas.** Rather than only human beings serving as idea generators, our roles may now shift to becoming the prompters and evaluators of good ideas. The mechanism used for selecting ideas becomes even more important, and a mix of AI and humans (who have good taste) can best determine what ideas are most applicable in a specific business context.

>> **The more human beings guide the AI, the better the AI gets as an idea generator.** Think of the AI like a copilot who can generate ideas with strong human inputs, rather than like an idea generator that competes with human beings to come up with the best ideas.

>> **You need human-machine collaboration to deliver better products and services in the future.** The authors of the Wharton study pointed out this fact in their study described in this section. Human-AI collaboration at every stage of the idea-generation process can allow for stronger ideas than humans developing them alone.

If you still feel skeptical about the use of generative AI in ideation and consider the described Wharton study a theoretical exercise, take a look at these real-world examples:

>> **Mattel harnessed AI to drive product development ideas for its Hot Wheels brand.** The company used generative AI to create four times as many product concept images as it normally would in the same amount of time. As a study from McKinsey & Company (a management consulting company) titled "How generative AI can boost consumer marketing" pointed out, this

large number of concept images inspired new features and designs for products. You can find the study at `www.mckinsey.com/capabilities/ growth-marketing-and-sales/our-insights/how-generative-ai- can-boost-consumer-marketing`.

>> **Coca-Cola released a limited-edition soda flavor called Y3000, which was co-created with AI.** Coca-Cola used generative AI to analyze consumer flavor preferences so that it could design what turned out to be a raspberry slushy–like beverage that contained different artificial sweeteners. The company also used AI to create futuristic artwork for the packaging. (The specific tool used to create the artwork was Stable Diffusion, from Stability AI [`https://stability.ai/`].)

>> **Airbus applied AI-powered generative design and optimization to the A320neo aircraft.** By using generative design technology, Airbus optimized the A320neo's wingtip design, cutting the aircraft's fuel consumption by 3.5 percent, thereby setting a prime example of AI application in product design.

>> **Adidas harnessed AI to design its Futurecraft 4D shoe.** The AI-influenced product design enhanced the shoe's sole comfort by including an internal lattice-like structure born out of the AI guidance. This design offers support and cushioning while maintaining durability and lightness.

Deciding Whether AI Hallucinations Are a Feature or a Bug

Inherent in large language models (LLMs; advanced AI systems trained on vast amounts of text data to generate human-like text) are *hallucinations,* the scenarios in which the LLMs generate incorrect, fabricated, or misleading information. This unique and relatively uncommon phenomenon causes the model to confidently present its results as accurate, even though the results may have no basis in reality.

Hallucinations may develop for a number of reasons, including

>> **The vast data sets used to train LLMs** have gaps or inaccuracies, leading to incorrect generalizations.

>> **The LLMs lack personal experience** and may be exposed to data that has limited timeframes. In these cases, LLMs don't get the benefit of learning from what happened outside their data set or processing parameters.

>> **Inherent model limitations** related to statistical correlations or complex and ambiguous human-created prompts that can misdirect results.

On the surface, you can view hallucinations as a bug — a negative result to watch out for. I encourage you (and all users of generative-AI solutions) to apply common sense tests and verify outputs so that you can determine whether the AI is being factual. But when it comes to ideation, hallucinations have another side. You may view the capacity of the LLM to fabricate information as creative output that opens other possibilities for more novel outcomes.

REMEMBER

By integrating generative AI into the creative process in marketing, you can unlock new types of ideas while also helping your human teammates confront their own biases. And when you layer in the opportunities driven by AI hallucinations, the potential benefits increase exponentially. So, hallucinations can actually help you with creative marketing.

Bringing in unexpected ideas and concepts

AI hallucinations can lead to unexpected, novel, and completely new ideas that break conventional thinking patterns (you know, break out of that box). These ideas likely happen because the AI engine isn't an entity grounded in real-world experience but, instead, is a text-driven statistical model.

Suppose that your marketing team uses an AI tool such as ChatGPT to brainstorm ideas for a new advertising campaign for a sports drink. Your team members input various prompts related to sports, energy, and refreshment. The AI, experiencing a hallucination, generates a concept about a futuristic sport that doesn't exist.

Instead of discarding this output as irrelevant, the team finds inspiration in the AI's mistake. The team members work together to develop a campaign around this imaginary sport, creating a series of drink ads that depict athletes training for this futuristic game. This kind of idea can capture the audience's imagination, setting the brand apart, and highlighting the drink's association with innovation, energy, and forward-thinking.

Branching out with non-traditional storytelling

You can harness AI-induced mistakes to create a new dimension for the brand's narrative by creating new stories that resonate with audiences in unexpected ways. This storytelling is particularly valuable in social media marketing because it captures attention, sparks engagement, and fosters a sense of authenticity and spontaneity.

Imagine that a travel agency uses AI to generate marketing content for promoting vacation packages. The AI, experiencing a hallucination, generates a description of a fictional, exotic destination that has unique cultural attributes and natural wonders that don't actually exist. Instead of dismissing this generation as an error, the marketing team sees an opportunity for an imaginative campaign. They develop a thematic campaign titled *Imagined Destinations,* which invites people to explore these AI-created places through a series of interactive online experiences, including virtual tours, digital art, and creative storytelling that showcase these fantastical destinations.

To increase engagement, the campaign includes an interactive element through which customers can submit their own ideas for imagined destinations, which the AI then expands upon. This user-generated content not only fosters community engagement but also provides insights into what types of vacations and destinations appeal to their clientele.

The campaign garners widespread attention for its creativity and use of technology, enhancing the travel agency's reputation for innovation. It also serves as a fun, engaging way for potential customers to dream about travel, keeping the agency top-of-mind when those could-be clients get ready to book real trips.

Facilitating testing and experimentation

You can put AI hallucination ideas into market research and test them in a similar fashion to the new ideas developed by the Wharton School study mentioned in the section "Engaging AI to Ideate on Behalf of Human Beings," earlier in this chapter. Even if these ideas don't lead to successful products, the exercise can show you what not to do or may encourage new ways of thinking for the marketing teams involved.

Suppose that a food company uses an AI model to explore new flavor ideas for a line of snacks. During a brainstorming session, the AI, because of a hallucination, suggests a bizarre and seemingly unpalatable flavor combination — something that no human being would consider.

Intrigued by the unusual suggestion, the product development team decides to experiment with this idea. They refine the concept and create a small batch of a snack that has this unique flavor. The snack turns out to be surprisingly appealing in taste tests. The flavor, positioned as a limited edition, generates buzz because of its novelty and the story of its AI-inspired origin. The snack gains attention, particularly among adventurous consumers and food enthusiasts, driving sales and enhancing the brand's image as innovative and daring.

Staying the course with generative AI

Over time, I believe that LLMs can deliver more accurate results with fewer hallucinations. Sam Altman, the CEO of OpenAI, said as much when discussing the future of ChatGPT. He fully expects generative AI to become more predictable, accurate, and — in his own words — "boring" over time. Altman's projections may be right, but the very nature of how generative AI works can allow for forced hallucinations or pushing the boundaries of conventional thinking via specifically chosen input data and carefully crafted prompts.

TIP

You may generally view AI hallucinations as errors that you need to correct, but you can leverage them as a source of creative inspiration that can lead to unique and innovative marketing outcomes. When you explore specific ways to drive ideation and planning by using generative AI, keep in mind that the prompts you write to direct your AI models determine how imaginative the AI can be on your behalf.

Following Practical Steps for Idea Generation with AI

A common and useful scenario for using generative AI involves idea generation during a creative brainstorming process. You may instigate the brainstorming session to identify a new product, a customer value proposition, a marketing campaign, or even a broader go-to-market strategy. The extent of ideas that you can generate is limited only by the prompts you articulate and the existing data or examples that you feed into the AI engine. In the following sections, I explain how you can use AI as a copilot when you run a combined human and AI ideation exercise.

Starting with the right prompts

A good starting point for combining human creativity with AI capabilities is to establish a prompt for both parties. Take, for example, a scenario in which you want to generate ten advertising concepts for an Apple ad promoting the latest iPhone during the Super Bowl. You can pose this challenge to both the human participants in the room and a generative AI engine such as ChatGPT. Here's what can happen:

>> **The human team:** Draws on their personal experiences and knowledge about Apple and its iPhones to brainstorm ideas during a timeframe that you

specify. Human understanding — informed by experiences, a sense of taste, and familiarity with what resonates with consumers (especially in the context of Super Bowl ads) — goes into the ideas that the team creates.

>> **ChatGPT:** Generates ten diverse ideas in just a few seconds; some of the ideas, of course, are more compelling than others. ***Note:*** The richer the information that you provide to the AI, the more robust the ideas it generates. If you include Apple's brand strategy, recent research on the most desired iPhone features, and scripts from Apple's past successful ads, you can significantly enhance the AI's ideas.

REMEMBER

You gather AI results from ChatGPT not to replace human creativity; those results may not match human capabilities. Instead, the real value emerges when the humans involved in the brainstorming session review the AI-generated ideas and select their top three or four favorites from both lists. This shortlist then forms the basis for crafting new, refined prompts, which you can use in subsequent iterations with ChatGPT to further develop and refine the chosen concepts.

This straightforward example illustrates a principle that you can apply to various types of idea-generating exercises. The approach works well, whether you want to focus your efforts on advertising, product feature definition, or strategic planning.

Stepping through an AI-for-ideation exercise

With information from the preceding section in mind, follow these steps when you use generative AI in an idea-generating exercise:

1. **Define the objectives of your ideation session.**

   Clearly define what you want to achieve by using AI-generated ideas. You may be after product innovation, marketing strategies, problem-solving for existing initiatives, or new creative marketing campaigns. As you set the objectives, also establish the boundaries and criteria for the ideas that you want, including

   - *Feasibility:* How much time and effort can you spend on a resulting project?

   - *Target audience:* Are you going after existing customers or branching out to a new target audience?

   - *Budget constraints:* Do you have unlimited funds, or have they been established by previous projects?

REMEMBER

   Setting objectives and boundaries is always a good business practice, but it's all the more important in the context of AI because you may have to face an even more divergent set of ideas than you do without AI input.

2. **Select the right AI tool(s) for your stated objectives.**

   Choose an appropriate AI model based on what you want to accomplish with your ideas. Depending on your needs, choose an AI model that specializes in idea generation in the format that fits your goals, such as

   - ChatGPT (http://chat.openai.com) for text-based ideas

   - DALL-E (http://openai.com/dall-e) for visual concepts

   - Stable Diffusion (http://stability.ai/stablediffusion) and Runway (http://runwayml.com) for multi-modal idea generation

   In some cases, you may want to use a combination of tools — starting with ChatGPT and then taking the results into an image- or video-based tool after that. Doing this allows you to use each tool for what it is best at.

3. **Prepare and input data for your ideation session.**

   Compile data that's relevant to your objective. Examples include market trends, consumer behavior data, previous campaign results, competitor dynamics, and previous product launches. Provide the AI with as much context as possible to guide its idea generation process. As I note in the preceding section, the more quality data that you input, the better the potential outcomes.

WARNING

   When selecting data for your idea-generating exercise, be careful about sharing sensitive information because it can lead to privacy breaches, data misuse, and potential legal ramifications.

4. **Engage your AI tool to generate ideas.**

   Run your initial queries or prompts through the AI tool to start generating ideas. To stress test how strong your prompts are, have your human creative team respond to the same prompts. Doing so can quickly tell you whether you need to make the queries more specific because it will reveal gaps in clarity and precision. Adjusting the queries for the gaps you reveal can help ensure that the AI outputs are relevant and useful.

TIP

   When you run your prompts through your AI tool, specifically encourage the AI to generate a plethora of ideas based on different assumptions. Consider the advice about prompt engineering that you can find in Chapters 2 and 6 of Book 2 and encourage the AI to respond in the role of a creative director, a product designer, or a futurist, for example.

5. **Refine prompts based on resulting ideas and then try again.**

   Analyze the ideas generated by the AI for relevance, innovation, creativity, and feasibility. Use feedback loops in which you refine your queries based on initial outputs to guide the AI toward solutions aligned with your intent. And, as you do this, consider highlighting the best ideas and asking the AI to generate more like those ideas. The more guidance you give the AI, the better the subsequent outputs are.

6. **Evaluate and select viable ideas.**

   Use your predefined criteria (from Step 1) to evaluate and shortlist the most promising ideas. As you create this list, consider incorporating feedback not just from your creative team, but also from stakeholders in other departments or maybe even consumer groups. As the Wharton professors show in their research (see the sidebar "ChatGPT versus Wharton MBA students," in this chapter), online purchase-intent surveys can provide you with a powerful customer-centric tool for evaluating ideas.

7. **Develop and test your generated ideas.**

   For product ideas, you can develop prototypes. For concepts such as marketing strategies, you can create testable models or campaigns or take the ideas into your formal campaign briefing or creative development process. In many cases, you can use other AI tools to translate text-based ideas into conceptual drawings, prototypes, or video animations that you can then test through focus groups, pilot runs, or online surveys.

Deciding on AI Ideation Tools to Use

Recently, many AI ideation tools have cropped up. Some of these tools are stand-alone solutions, such as Adobe Firefly (`https://firefly.adobe.com/`) and Google's AutoDraw (`www.autodraw.com`); other tools are integrated into broader software suites.

For example, TikTok's Creative Assistant — which launched in September 2023 — is particularly notable. Situated in TikTok's Creative Center (`http://ads.tiktok.com/business/creativecenter`), this AI-driven virtual assistant offers advertisers a dynamic toolbox for content creation. By tapping into TikTok-specific creative insights, the Creative Assistant offers relevant suggestions and guidance that facilitate the crafting of compelling and effective content for TikTok campaigns.

Creative Assistant acts as a virtual collaborator, helping you in various facets of content creation, such as

>> Guiding newcomers through best practices on the TikTok platform

>> Displaying and analyzing top-performing ads to aid in creative research

>> Brainstorming ideas and refining scripts collaboratively, especially when you're struggling to develop new ideas

REMEMBER

The Creative Assistant tool augments human creativity, symbolizing the fusion of human ingenuity with AI capabilities. It empowers creators to continually enhance their presence on TikTok through perpetual ideation sessions. But although the Creative Assistant offers suggestions and collaborates in the creation journey, the creator retains absolute control over the materials, having the liberty to use, edit, discard, or redo them, as desired.

You have literally hundreds of AI tools to consider — many of which use ChatGPT as a foundation — and Table 1-1 highlights some notable ones. Although some of the tools in this table are more oriented toward content creation rather than idea generation, they can still play the role of idea generators, too.

TABLE 1-1   AI Tools for Idea Generation

Tool	Website	What It Is	What It Does
ContextMinds	`www.contextminds.com`	A tool that assists in research and idea generation, combining mind-mapping functionality with AI-driven content suggestions	Organizes thoughts and makes connections through relevant articles, papers, and videos related to their topics of interest
HyperWrite	`www.hyperwriteai.com`	A writing assistant that helps users develop ideas and refine original text	Generates various writing formats such as e-mails or marketing copy
Jasper	`www.jasper.ai`	A tool that assists in generating written content for various purposes	Crafts compelling narratives and ideas for marketing copy, blog posts, and so on
Pictory	`http://pictory.ai`	A tool for ideation in video marketing, transforming existing content into engaging, shareable video formats	Creates short videos from long-form content such as webinars or blog posts
Riffusion	`www.riffusion.com`	A tool that synthesizes music based on AI-generated sound patterns	Experiments with unique soundscapes and auditory branding elements
Runway	`http://runwayml.com`	A platform for experimenting with machine learning (ML) models in real time	Offers ideation in the realms of design, art, and multimedia, to explore new visual concepts and effects

Tool	Website	What It Is	What It Does
Stable Diffusion	http://stability.ai	A text-to-image model that allows users to create visual images from textual descriptions	Helps artists, designers, and marketers to rapidly generate diverse and creative visual concepts
Synthesia	www.synthesia.io	A video creation platform that generates high-quality synthetic media and personalized video content	Creates realistic digital avatars and voiceovers, streamlining the video production process
Wondershare EdrawMind	http://edrawmind.wondershare.com	A tool that facilitates organized visual representation of ideas while also helping to generate ideas	Helps create mind maps, flowcharts, and organizational charts to enhance collaborative thinking and planning
Writer	http://writer.com	A writing assistant for businesses that helps create clear, consistent, and brand-aligned content	Assists with grammar, style, and tone to ensure high-quality writing across all company communications

IN THIS CHAPTER

» **Using AI as your email assistant**

» **Creating precise prompts**

» **Choosing Copilot to help with email**

» **Getting an email summary in Copilot**

» **Writing emails and managing tasks with Copilot**

» **Using AI in email carefully**

Chapter **2**

Managing and Writing Emails with AI

n the bustling world of technology, the humble email holds its own as a gateway to an interconnected universe. Although the exact percentage varies (depending on the source), it's estimated that three-quarters of all communication is via email. And the percentage has probably increased since the COVID-19 pandemic. Some people say that email is passé and can be replaced by Google Chat, Teams, Slack, Hangouts Meet, or BlueJean Meetings; however, email isn't going away anytime soon.

Mastering the art of emails extends beyond crafting eloquent prose. Striking a balance between appropriateness and impact, and knowing which emails to prioritize or ignore are just as important. This chapter unlocks solutions to the challenges of composing compelling emails and managing emails you receive.

Using AI as Your Assistant for Writing Emails

AI has significantly transformed the landscape of communication, including how we send and receive emails. Here are some ways in which AI is reshaping email:

>> **Cybersecurity:** Improving email security. AI can help identify and prevent email-based cyberattacks by detecting malicious content and attachments.

>> **Personalization:** Writing personalized emails that are tailored to the recipient's interests and preferences. Personalization can increase the likelihood of open rates, click rates, and conversions.

>> **Systematized responses:** Responding to incoming emails automatically, which can help businesses save time and resources.

>> **Subject line optimization:** Analyzing the words, phrases, and subject lines that receive the most engagement and using that information to generate more effective subject lines that say "read me."

>> **Tone analysis:** Analyzing a person's writing style and tone and suggesting changes to make the email more effective and engaging.

>> **Scheduling:** Assessing when people are most likely to open and engage with emails and automatically scheduling emails to be sent at those optimal times.

>> **Efficiency:** Streamlining email communication by prioritizing important messages and filtering out *spam* (unsolicited and unwanted messages sent in bulk to a large number of recipients). Increasing efficiency can save time and increase productivity.

>> **Email copywriting:** Generating high-converting email campaigns in just a few clicks to analyze customer data and write personalized emails that resonate with the target audience.

Figure 2-1 is an example of AI to the rescue: Dan has an employee who's constantly missing team meetings. Dan spoke with the employee, but he needs to capture the conversation in writing in case this needs to escalate to the next level. Dan hopes this employee will change their behavior. He's laid out some strategies. The figure shows the input given to You.com and how the chatbot responded. Pay special attention to the strong subject line the chatbot created.

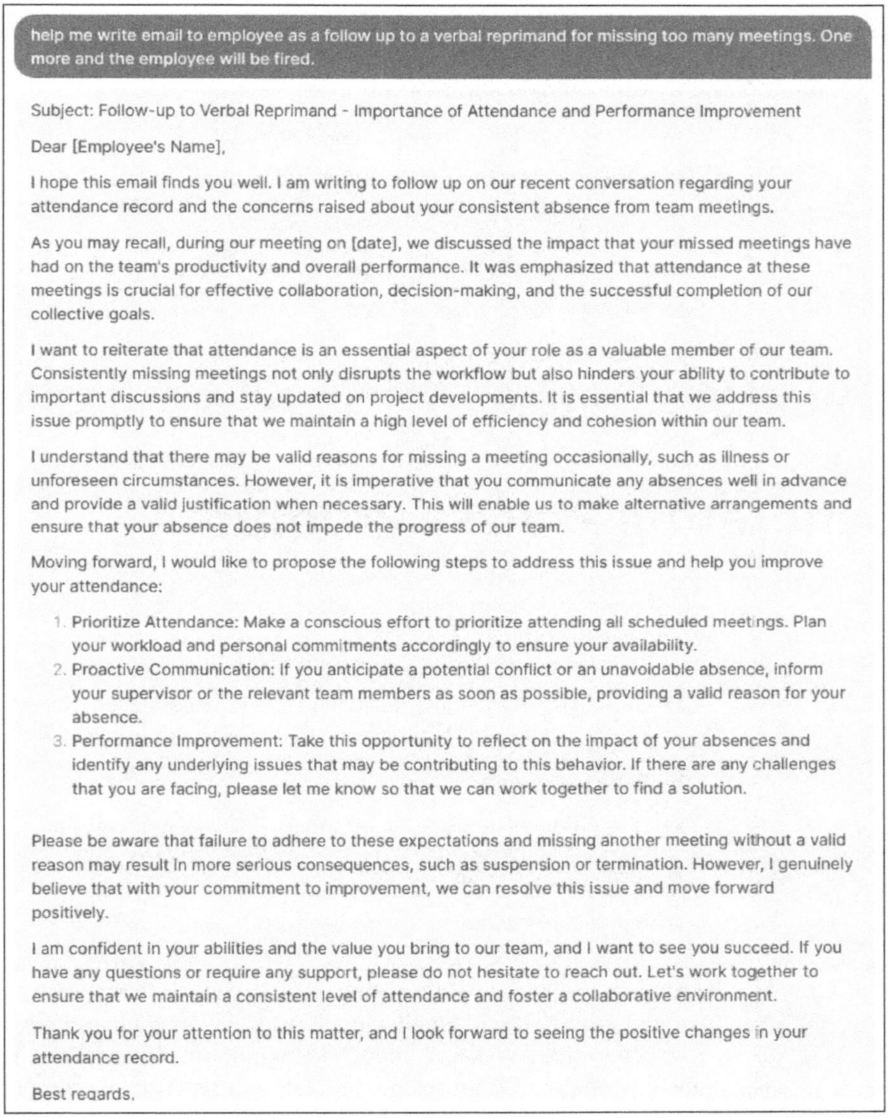

help me write email to employee as a follow up to a verbal reprimand for missing too many meetings. One more and the employee will be fired.

Subject: Follow-up to Verbal Reprimand - Importance of Attendance and Performance Improvement

Dear [Employee's Name],

I hope this email finds you well. I am writing to follow up on our recent conversation regarding your attendance record and the concerns raised about your consistent absence from team meetings.

As you may recall, during our meeting on [date], we discussed the impact that your missed meetings have had on the team's productivity and overall performance. It was emphasized that attendance at these meetings is crucial for effective collaboration, decision-making, and the successful completion of our collective goals.

I want to reiterate that attendance is an essential aspect of your role as a valuable member of our team. Consistently missing meetings not only disrupts the workflow but also hinders your ability to contribute to important discussions and stay updated on project developments. It is essential that we address this issue promptly to ensure that we maintain a high level of efficiency and cohesion within our team.

I understand that there may be valid reasons for missing a meeting occasionally, such as illness or unforeseen circumstances. However, it is imperative that you communicate any absences well in advance and provide a valid justification when necessary. This will enable us to make alternative arrangements and ensure that your absence does not impede the progress of our team.

Moving forward, I would like to propose the following steps to address this issue and help you improve your attendance:

1. Prioritize Attendance: Make a conscious effort to prioritize attending all scheduled meetings. Plan your workload and personal commitments accordingly to ensure your availability.
2. Proactive Communication: If you anticipate a potential conflict or an unavoidable absence, inform your supervisor or the relevant team members as soon as possible, providing a valid reason for your absence.
3. Performance Improvement: Take this opportunity to reflect on the impact of your absences and identify any underlying issues that may be contributing to this behavior. If there are any challenges that you are facing, please let me know so that we can work together to find a solution.

Please be aware that failure to adhere to these expectations and missing another meeting without a valid reason may result in more serious consequences, such as suspension or termination. However, I genuinely believe that with your commitment to improvement, we can resolve this issue and move forward positively.

I am confident in your abilities and the value you bring to our team, and I want to see you succeed. If you have any questions or require any support, please do not hesitate to reach out. Let's work together to ensure that we maintain a consistent level of attendance and foster a collaborative environment.

Thank you for your attention to this matter, and I look forward to seeing the positive changes in your attendance record.

Best regards,

FIGURE 2-1: AI to the rescue.

Here are just a few of the many AI email assistants that can boost your email productivity:

- Capterra (`https://www.capterra.com/`)
- ChatGPT (`https://chat.openai.com/auth/login`)
- EmailTree (`https://emailtree.ai/`)

- » Google Workspace (https://workspace.google.com/)

- » Grammarly (www.grammarly.com)

- » HubSpot (https://www.hubspot.com/)

- » Mailbutler (https://www.mailbutler.io/)

- » QuickMail (https://quickmail.com/)

- » Sanebox (https://www.sanebox.com/)

- » YAMM (https://yamm.com/)

- » Microsoft 365 Copilot (https://www.microsoft.com/en-us/microsoft-365/copilot)

Generating Precise Prompts

Here are some suggestions for creating effective AI prompts, with a particular emphasis on emails:

- » Include the recipient's information and your relationship (client, business partner, colleague, for example) as this will influence the tone and formality.

- » State the purpose of the message.

- » Outline the main points or information you want to include.

- » Incorporate the call to action.

- » Request a descriptive subject line.

WARNING

Although you should indicate your relationship to the person you're emailing in a prompt, never submit email addresses or personally identifying information (PII) to a generative AI (GenAI) model. Remember that some chatbots use information about prompts to train the model. This can potentially result in the GenAI model leaking the personal information to someone who shouldn't have it.

Emailing with Copilot

If you use Microsoft Outlook as your primary email program and you have a subscription to Copilot Pro or Microsoft 365 Copilot, you have access to an AI assistant that can help you process, understand, and respond to emails more efficiently and maybe even more effectively.

REMEMBER

Book 2, Chapter 5 tells you how to sign up for and get started with Microsoft Copilot, Copilot Pro, or Microsoft 365 Copilot.

In the rest of this chapter, you learn how to use Copilot in Microsoft Outlook. Although the details differ between AI assistants in other email programs, most of the techniques and strategies you learn here are directly applicable to getting help with your email from other AI email assistants.

Summarizing with Copilot

Complex work or personal projects often result in long email threads, and it can sometimes be difficult to keep track of who said what or who agreed to what. One of the first features that you'll notice when you start using Copilot in Outlook is the Summary feature. Summary can take a single email, or a thread of emails, and distill them down to just the important information.

Summarizing email threads

For example, here's a (fake, mostly) conversation between members of a family who are making plans for their mother's 80th birthday.

```
From: Beth <beth@family.com>
Date: Saturday, August 10, 2024 at 7:58 AM
To: Chris, David, Kathy
Subject: Mom's b-day

What should we do for mom's birthday? I'm planning to come to
   town with the kids. G might have to be in Dallas that weekend,
   so I don't know if he'll be there.

From: Chris <chris@family.com>
Date: Saturday, August 10, 2024 at 8:18 AM
To: Beth, David, Kathy
Subject: Re: Mom's b-day

Cool! We'll be there, too. I'll start looking at flights!
```

```
----
beth@family.com wrote:

What should we do for mom's birthday? I'm planning to come to
    town with the kids. G might have to be in Dallas that weekend,
    so I don't know if he'll be there.

From: Kathy <kathy@family.com>
Date: Saturday, August 10, 2024 at 8:19 AM
To: Beth, David, Chris
Subject: Re: Re: Mom's b-day

Yay! Want to do something at the park? We could hire a band and
    get a clown, maybe? :) Chris, will you be able to make
    it, too?

From: Kathy <kathy@family.com>
Date: Saturday, August 10, 2024 at 8:19 AM
To: Beth, David, Chris
Subject: Re: Re: Mom's b-day

Oh, I just saw this. Ignore my last message. Great! You can stay
    with us!


---
chris@family.com wrote:

Cool! We'll be there, too. I'll start looking at flights!
```

I'll spare you all the rest of the details, but we've all been involved with email threads like this where the details of who is doing what and what's been agreed to — and even who's talking — start to get blurred.

Copilot's email thread summarization can help make sense of it all. To have Copilot generate a summary, select a message in the email thread and click the Summary by Copilot link, which will be right above the window that displays the email, as shown in Figure 2-2.

Clicking the Summary by Copilot link opens a window above the current email where Copilot generates a summary of the thread, complete with references to individual emails to back up each line of its summary, as shown in Figure 2-3.

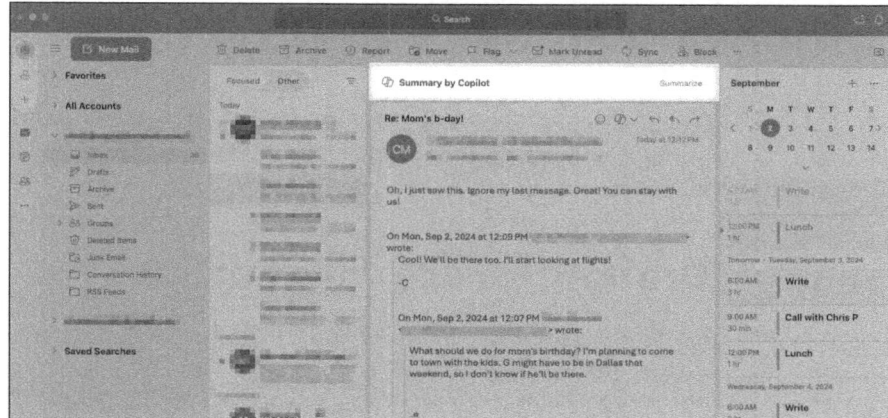

FIGURE 2-2:
The Summary by
Copilot link.

FIGURE 2-3:
Copilot generates
a summary of the
thread.

Summarizing long emails

Copilot can also generate summaries of long emails. For example, meetings can often result in long emails that summarize the highlights of the meeting. Since you were at the meeting, such emails might seem redundant. Still, you might have agreed to do something (or someone thought you did, anyway) while you were distracted by the coffee and bagels. You shouldn't have to relive that meeting by having to read every word of the summary email.

Instead, you can ask Copilot to generate a short summary of the meeting that includes anything that mentions your name or something you might need to do to follow up.

Composing Emails with Copilot

Copilot can help write emails by either creating entire emails in response to your prompts or by analyzing text that you write and making suggestions for how you might improve it.

Drafting emails with Copilot

If you press the / key in a new email or at the beginning of a reply message, a menu will display showing files from your SharePoint or OneDrive cloud storage. At the top of that list is an option called Draft with Copilot. Selecting this option opens the Draft with Copilot window, which is shown in Figure 2-4.

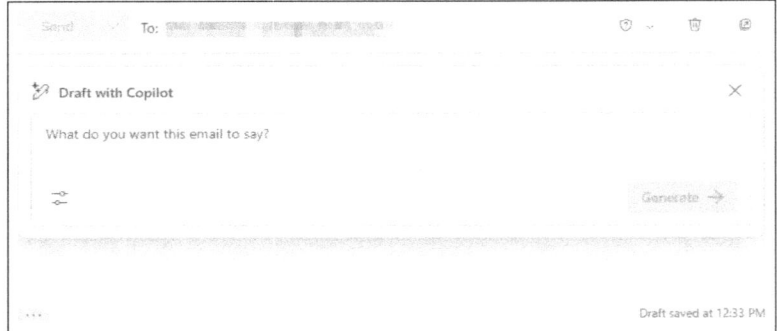

FIGURE 2-4:
The Draft with
Copilot window.

REMEMBER

The / character can always be used in Microsoft 365 Copilot Chat to open a menu for referencing other documents, people, meetings, or emails. It can also be used in certain other situations as well, such as to open the Draft with Copilot window in a Word document.

Inside the Draft with Copilot window, you can type a prompt that describes what you want the email to say. Before you ask Copilot to generate the email, you can select the tone and length of the email by clicking the Options menu link in the lower-left corner of the window. For example, in the message shown in Figure 2-5, I want to write a long and casual email thanking my significant other for making grilled cheese sandwiches.

The resulting email wasn't as long as I had hoped for, but it did accurately reflect the sentiment that I wanted to express. It doesn't sound like an email I'd write, but I thought Jill would still appreciate it (maybe not as much as if I'd actually written it, however). The generated email is shown in Figure 2-6.

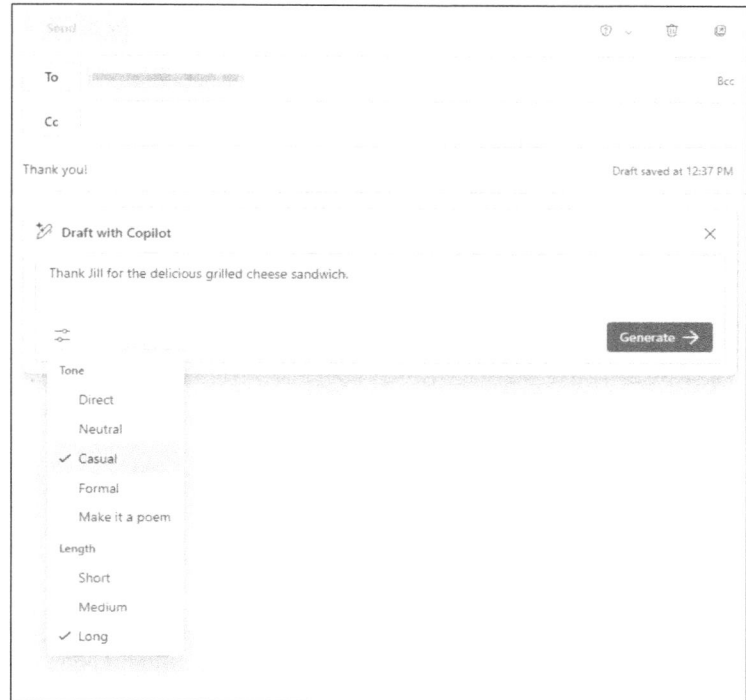

FIGURE 2-5:
Prompting
for an email.

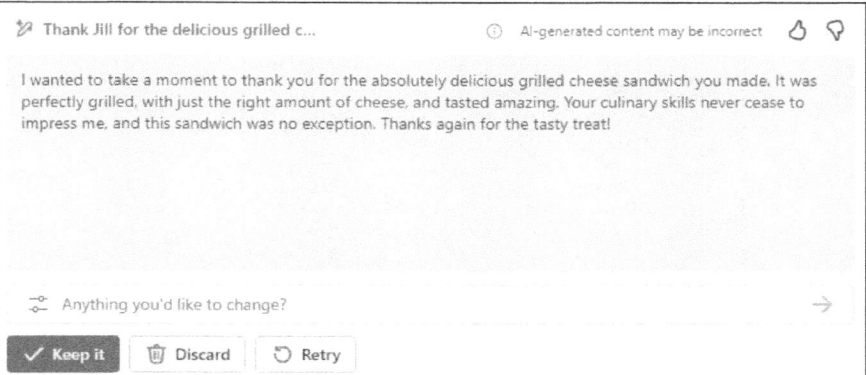

FIGURE 2-6:
Copilot's
generated email.

Just for fun, I thought I'd see if I could get Copilot to spice it up a bit. I submitted a follow-up prompt asking Copilot to try again and to use more slang and humor that a Gen-X person might use in such an email. After seeing what it did (which was, as the young folks might say, cringe), I decided to stick with the original.

To go back in your history of prompts, click the back arrow in the upper-left corner of the Draft with Copilot window, which you can see in the new email draft shown in Figure 2-7.

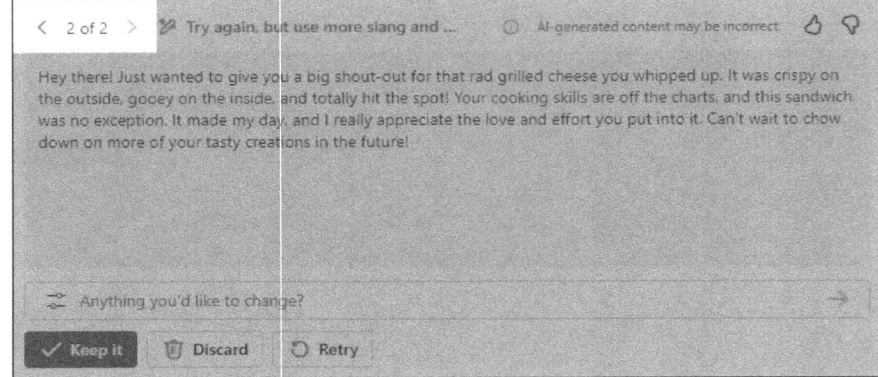

After Copilot generates an email, you can submit another follow-up prompt with any changes you'd like Copilot to make, or you can keep or discard the draft. I decided to use one of the preset follow-up prompts (which can be accessed using the menu on the left of the follow-up prompt area) to turn the email into a poem. The result is shown in Figure 2-8.

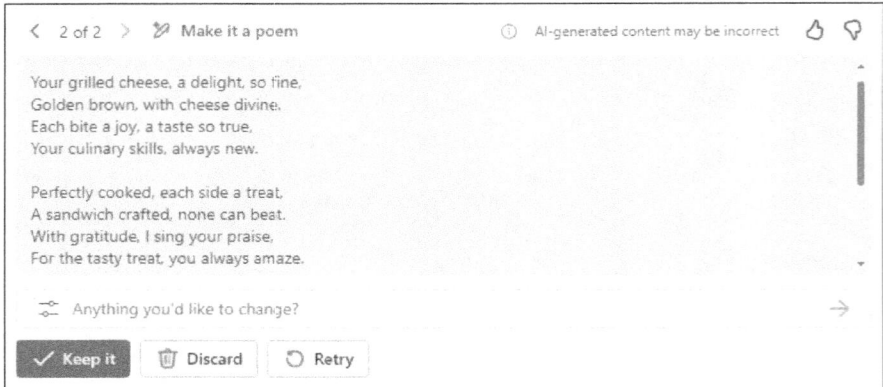

FIGURE 2-8:
Copilot's thank-
you poem.

In the end, I decided to just tell her thanks in person — and also to include these thank-you messages in my book, of course.

Reply suggestions

When you click the Reply button on an email, Copilot attempts to use the content of the message to suggest possible responses. These responses appear in a Draft with Copilot window at the bottom of your email, as shown in Figure 2-9.

FIGURE 2-9:
Copilot provides reply suggestions.

If you like one of Copilot's suggestions, you can click on it, and the text of the suggestion will appear in a Draft with Copilot window, where you can refine it or just add it to your message.

If you don't like any of the suggested responses but you still want to use Copilot to generate your response, you can click on the button labeled Custom to open the same Draft with Copilot window that appears when you use Copilot to draft a new email.

Email coaching

Copilot in Outlook offers a feature called Coaching by Copilot that gives you tips on how it thinks your email could be improved. To launch Coaching by Copilot, select it from the Copilot menu as you're writing an email, as shown in Figure 2-10.

One necessary downside of Coaching by Copilot is that it only works with emails that contain at least 100 characters. If you try Coaching by Copilot with a shorter email, you'll get a message such as the one shown in Figure 2-11 telling you it can't help you.

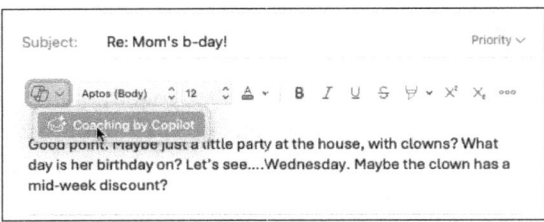

FIGURE 2-10:
Starting Coaching
by Copilot.

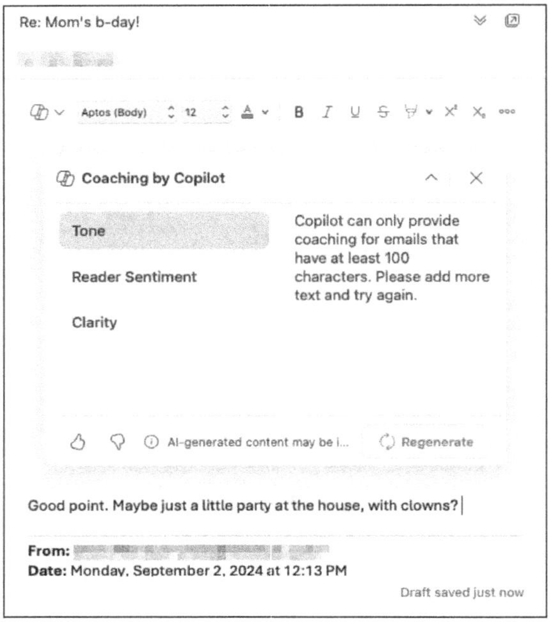

FIGURE 2-11:
Coaching doesn't
work on short
emails.

Provided that you do have enough text in your draft email, Coaching by Copilot will show you suggestions for how to improve three aspects of your draft:

>> **Tone:** Copilot gives suggestions for making your email sound friendlier.

>> **Reader sentiment:** These suggestions are aimed at making the reader feel "included." Examples of suggestions that might fall into this category are suggestions such as ending your email with "What do you think?"

>> **Clarity:** The Clarity category of suggestions are ways that Copilot thinks you might specify the details of your email more clearly.

In my experience with Coaching by Copilot, it often provided good suggestions, but it interpreted jokes literally and ruined them.

Figure 2-12 shows a typical suggestion from Coaching by Copilot.

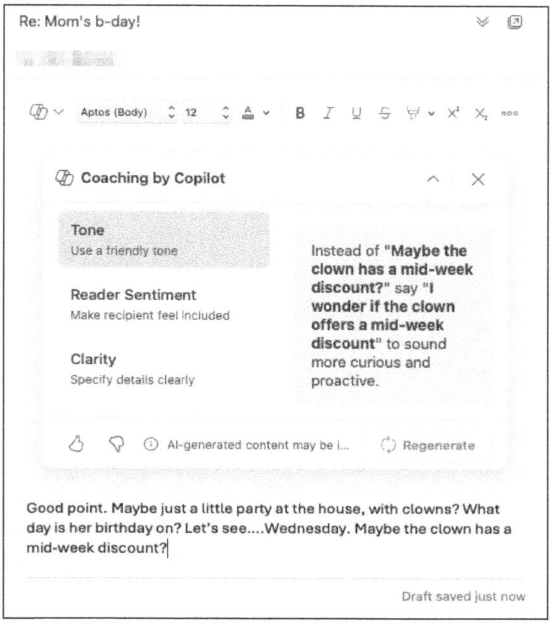

FIGURE 2-12:
Copilot tells me
to work on my
enthusiasm.

Email coaching seems like a good feature when writing important emails to your boss or to customers. For everyday communications with friends and colleagues, it seems like following its recommendations could make your emails sound insincere and humorless.

One thing I like about Coaching by Copilot is that it leaves the decision of whether to follow any of its suggestions up to you. It doesn't even seem to have the ability to automatically insert the new text it suggests.

Meeting management

Copilot 365 in Outlook has access to your inbox and your calendar. When a meeting request comes from Microsoft Teams or another calendar app comes in via email, Outlook displays an RSVP button on the email in your list of emails. When you open the email, the details of the meeting are automatically summarized above the text of the message.

Every meeting on your calendar is available in the context menu, which you can access using the / command in Copilot Chat so you can reference your calendar while generating new emails or other documents. This is particularly helpful for coordinating with multiple people or responding to questions about your availability for (still more!) meetings.

Using GenAI for Email with Discernment

Composing new emails and responding to emails with GenAI's help generally works very well. The responses newer models generate are good in many ways. For example, they're grammatically correct, friendly, and can sometimes even be clever.

However, it's up to you to decide which circumstances AI-generated emails are appropriate for and when you should write the email yourself.

Most people would have no problem with having a GenAI model draft an email to report that the book you ordered hasn't been delivered yet and to check on the status of the order.

Asking AI to generate a love letter, a condolence letter, or a cover letter for a job application would likely seem wrong to most people. But, maybe this is just because we're all still new to this. Perhaps in the future writing your own emails will seem as archaic as sending telegrams.

» Creating a hidden object image
   with AI

» Using AI to come up with new visuals

» Working with AI tools to improve
   existing images

» Making your creative team even
   better with AI tools

Chapter **3**

Developing Creative Assets

A n exciting dimension of generative artificial intelligence (GenAI) is its potential use for the development of creative assets in marketing. Artists, graphic designers, marketing agency leaders, marketers of various levels, and even operational executives, increasingly use generative AI text-to-image and image-to-image asset creation to augment their presentations. These efforts enhance marketing campaigns and even create new designs and artwork from scratch.

Many creative leaders may argue (and understandably so) that the creative capabilities of GenAI today are no match for what human beings can do. That may be true for now, but the situation is unlikely to remain the case in the years ahead. In the last year alone, GenAI tools such as Adobe Firefly, Midjourney, and Stable Diffusion advanced immensely in their capabilities — for example, by achieving more realistic image generation and offering a more intuitive user interface. These advancements illustrate generative AI's potential as the technology gets more sophisticated.

But even more than the ever-advancing technological progress, the role of GenAI becomes more powerful when you pair it with human beings who can turbocharge creativity and drive productivity and efficiency. To explain this pairing further in this chapter, I begin by talking about *Where's Waldo?* to demonstrate both the opportunities and the risks involved in using generative AI to augment your creative process.

Trying Out an AI-Generated Where's Waldo? Illustration

In early 2024, an illustrator who uses the handle @0xFramer on the social media platform X (formerly known as Twitter) created a series of *Where's Waldo?* images to showcase both the opportunities and the challenges that occur when you use GenAI to develop creative assets. This illustrator used the original look-and-find children's books by Martin Handford as inspiration and then used generative AI tools to create his own variations. For those of you who don't know the series, the book consists of detailed, double-page spread illustrations depicting dozens and dozens of people doing a variety of amusing activities in a given setting. Readers are challenged to find a character named Waldo somewhere in the group.

The illustrator (@0xFramer) showed how anyone can quickly use an AI tool to create similar *Where's Waldo?* illustrations. (Check out his creative process on You-Tube at `www.youtube.com/watch?v=2nYxeZQmcj0`.) To do so, you need to provide your AI tools with a detailed description that encapsulates the essence of a *Where's Waldo?* scene. Follow these steps to define such an illustration by providing input to a tool such as DALL-E 3 (through `https://openai.com/dall-e-3`) or Midjourney (`www.midjourney.com/`):

1. **Describe the background that becomes the setting for your illustration.**

   You can specify a vibrant and detailed background, which can be a beach, a cityscape, an office, a medieval scene, a space station, and so on. The more intricate and crowded the scene, the better.

2. **Identify the characters that you need to appear in the illustration.**

   Mention the need for a large number of diverse characters engaged in various activities. They should be dressed in a wide range of costumes, performing numerous actions to create a lively, busy scene.

3. **Describe the Waldo-like character that should appear somewhere in the illustration.**

   Note that you want the character subtly placed within the scene, similar to Waldo in the Handford books. This character should be wearing a red-and-white striped shirt but blend in well with the surroundings.

4. **Detail the color and style of the illustration.**

   Indicate the colorfulness and whimsical style that mimics the original *Where's Waldo?* illustrations.

For the AI to successfully generate an image close to your vision, you need to make your description precise and detailed. See the prompt that I created by following the preceding steps to urge DALL-E to generate such an image:

> A vibrant, densely populated beach scene filled with numerous characters engaging in various activities: playing volleyball, sunbathing, building sandcastles, swimming, and so on. The characters are dressed in colorful and diverse beach attire. Include a character resembling Waldo, wearing a red and white striped shirt, blue pants, and a beanie, subtly blended into the scene. The style should be whimsical and cartoonish, with bright colors.

By using the preceding prompt as inspiration (and finding out about effective prompts in Book 2), try creating your own *Where's Waldo?* illustration either in DALL-E or Midjourney. Doing so can give you a sense of the possibilities when it comes to using generative AI to develop creative assets of all types.

Exploring an Approach for Creating Visual Assets with AI

To establish objectives and define an approach to developing creative assets by using artificial intelligence (AI) tools, you need to follow a structured process that ensures that your creations align with your product offering and marketing goals and resonate with your target audience. AI offers exciting possibilities for creative asset development, but it requires careful management across various dimensions — from aligning with brand values and ensuring ethical use to integrating with existing workflows and respecting legal boundaries. Balancing these factors is key to leveraging AI effectively and responsibly.

TIP

You now have access to some emergent AI tools (such as `Jasper.ai` and `Thewordsmith.ai`) that enable you to input and store your brand style guide first — before you even begin creating assets. That way, any image that the AI tool creates for you conforms to the style set out in your brand style guide. Furthermore, you don't have to ask your AI tool of choice to create one image at a time. You can have it create several images in one go.

Follow these steps — and carefully document the prompts — to responsibly create and use AI-generated assets:

1. **Define the marketing objective that you're creating assets for.**

   For example, you may want to increase brand awareness for a new eco-friendly clothing line. You expect to accomplish this objective by using AI to create visually striking images that highlight the eco-friendly aspects of the clothing.

   Best marketing practice: Clearly define the purpose of the creative asset. Do you want to use it for brand awareness, product promotion, social media engagement, lead acquisition, or something else? Your objective can guide the style, composition, and elements of the creative asset.

2. **Understand the target audience that your marketing intends to reach.**

   The target audience for your eco-friendly clothing line may be environmentally conscious young adults ages 18 to 35 in suburban settings. The creative assets for the marketing project can consist of imagery that appeals to this demographic by prompting an AI tool to incorporate relevant themes and settings.

   Watch out: Ensure that the AI-generated content reflects your brand's voice and appeals to your target audience. For example, if an AI tool creates a series of edgy and humorous social media posts, but your brand is known for its serious and professional tone, this content may alienate your established customer base. Constantly align AI outputs with your brand guidelines and audience expectations.

3. **Decide on the marketing message or theme that you want your creative assets to support.**

   For example, the marketing team may decide that they want to anchor the message in the phrase *Sustainability meets style*. The task, in that case, would be to have the AI generate visuals that blend natural, replenishable elements (such as bamboo, organic cotton, or recycled materials) with fashionable clothing styles.

   Best marketing practice: Ensure that the images align with your brand's visual identity, including colors, typography, and overall style. Consistency helps in building brand recognition. Include details around the brand visual identity in the prompts that you write for the AI tool.

4. **Choose the right AI tools for the data that you have and the expected output.**

   You have a range of tools to choose from, so match the tool to your specific task. For example, DALL-E and Midjourney can create unique images from descriptions that you provide and can also use reference images (also known as *image prompting*) to set the style for the image you want created.

   Best marketing practice: You can combine AI image creation with other tools, such as photo-editing software, for further refinement. In fact, tools such as Adobe Photoshop now include GenAI capabilities that can help you create different skylines or extend a mountain in a different direction, for example.

   Watch out: The choice of AI tools and their training data significantly impacts the type and quality of creative output. For example, an AI model trained primarily on classical European art styles may not be suitable for a campaign aiming to reflect contemporary Asian aesthetics. Select tools and models that align with your specific creative goals. And you don't get a shortcut in this exercise: The only way to know which tools are right for you involves experimenting with several.

5. **Develop detailed descriptions for your AI to work from.**

   An example description for the clothing line may be something like *stylish, modern outfit with bamboo fabric texture, set against a background of lush greenery, with a subtle hint of urban skyline.*

   Best marketing practice: When using AI tools such as DALL-E or Midjourney, the more specific your description, the better the results. Include details about colors, mood, setting, objects, and any text that you want in the image. Flip to the section "Trying Out an AI-Generated Where's Waldo? Illustration," earlier in this chapter, for inspiration.

6. **Insert a description that you create in Step 5 (with or without the assistance of an AI application) into your chosen text-to-image tool (such as DALL-E or Midjourney).**

   Ideally, generate at least four variations that you can then edit further (see Step 7).

7. **Make repeated modifications (iterations) to your descriptions, and then review and refine the assets that the tool creates.**

   Arguably, this step (or series of steps) is the most important. You must evaluate the AI-generated images and adjust the prompts to further enhance and strengthen the output. For example, if an initially created image lacks the vibrancy that you expect, adjust the description that you offer to the AI to include *bright, vivid colors.*

Best marketing practice: AI-generated images may not be perfect on the first try. In fact, they're very rarely perfect on the first try. Fully expect to iterate constantly when you refine the prompts and tweak the creative asset.

REMEMBER

AI is a tool to augment your creativity and efficiency. The combination of AI capabilities and your unique brand perspective can create the most powerful visual content. Arguably, AI is at its best when you combine it with human creativity versus asking it to do the creation on its own.

8. **Evaluate the created assets against brand standards to ensure quality and consistency.**

Human involvement is critical, especially when evaluating whether the output reflects the desired quality and is on brand. Whether you match colors with the brand palette, check the output against other brand images, or use a separate AI tool that can check for brand consistency, you mustn't skip this step.

Watch out: Don't think of AI as a set-and-forget tool. Regular human oversight ensures the quality of AI-generated content. For example, an AI tool may inadvertently use outdated or inappropriate cultural references in marketing materials. Regular reviews by human editors can catch and correct these missteps. In fact, your marketing department and team should have a policy for verifying every new creative asset generated by the AI before that asset goes out into the world.

9. **Optimize the generated assets for various platforms that you intend to use for marketing.**

After you finalize an image, you can use AI tools (such as Canva or Adobe Spark) to help optimize the output for various platforms. For example, AI tools can create square images for Instagram and wider formats for Facebook banners.

Best marketing practice: Different social media platforms have different preferred image sizes and aspect ratios. Customize your images accordingly for optimal display. When you're using an AI tool to create images or even video, you can input the desired output sizes that you need.

Watch out: Smoothly integrate AI tools into existing workflows. For instance, an AI video editing tool that doesn't integrate well with your current video editing software can create more work, instead of streamlining the process. Ensure that any AI tool you adopt fits seamlessly into your existing production pipeline and also has the appropriate import and export capability.

10. **Test the created visual asset's effect on the intended audience and gather feedback.**

Testing the creative output (whether that's a static image or video) by using a focus group or even a small internal audience, who can help you see whether it resonates positively. Use that feedback to guide the AI tool on further image refinements, as needed.

Best marketing practice: AI offers the flexibility to explore various artistic styles and formats. Experiment with different aesthetics to see what resonates best with your audience.

Watch out: Biases can slip into AI-generated content. If an AI tool consistently generates images of people in stereotypical roles based on gender or race, this output could reflect and perpetuate harmful biases.

Embed legal and ethical compliance in all steps of the process for creating assets with AI tools. In particular

>> When choosing the right AI tool and assessing the output, ensure that the images don't infringe on copyrights and are ethically sound. Check whether the AI tool indemnifies you from potential copyright claims and find out whether your legal team is onboard with the tools and the process that you're using. Check out Book 1, Chapter 6, for more discussion of legal and ethical compliance.

>> Stay informed about legal aspects of AI, especially in terms of copyright and intellectual property rights. For example, using AI to generate music for a commercial project may raise copyright issues if the AI's training data includes copyrighted music. Ensure that your use of AI respects legal boundaries and intellectual property rights. And, although tools such as Adobe Firefly, Microsoft Copilot, and OpenAI's DALL-E offer IP indemnification, still check with your legal team.

Minding the integrity of your customers, data, and teams

Maintain ethical integrity and transparency when you use AI to create customer-facing content. For example, if you use AI to create realistic human images or voices, disclose that these images are AI-generated to avoid misleading your audience about the reality of what they're seeing. With industry efforts to label AI-generated content gathering steam, make sure that you maintain alignments with new developments.

If your AI tools use customer data to personalize content, ensure strict adherence to data privacy laws. For example, using AI to personalize e-mail campaigns requires careful handling of customer data in compliance with the General Data Protection Regulation (GDPR) or other relevant privacy regulations. Failure to do so can lead to legal consequences and damage to your brand's reputation.

And make sure to involve your legal team in your conversations regarding customer data use.

Invest in training your team to use AI tools effectively. Lack of understanding can lead to your team underutilizing AI capabilities. For example, a content team not fully trained in using an AI copywriting tool may only use it for basic tasks (such as grammar checking) and miss out on its advanced features for generating more sophisticated content (for example, creating personalized marketing copy). Keep in mind that when your team chooses to use an AI tool, it probably means more work, not less, in the short term while they familiarize themselves with the tool's capabilities and integrate the tool into their regular workflow.

REMEMBER

Make sure that your efforts don't rely too heavily on AI; doing so can hinder creativity and innovation. For example, if a graphic design team uses AI exclusively for creating visuals, they may miss out on unique, human-inspired designs. Balance AI use with human creativity to foster innovation. You don't want your brand to flood its marketing channels with bland, plain, and boring content.

TIP

When you're creating images or video by using AI, some of the AI tools available for use come from the companies whose tools you've used for a long time. These tools now include powerful AI functionality to enhance your creative work. Adobe Photoshop is a perfect example of a design tool that now includes some interesting generative AI functionality that you can use with just a little bit of extra training.

Examining an example scenario

Suppose that you're working on a campaign for the eco-friendly clothing line that I introduce in the section "Exploring an Approach for Creating Visual Assets with AI," earlier in this chapter. After defining your objective and understanding your target audience, you may decide that the theme for your marketing campaign is *Urban Nature.* Then, you select Midjourney as your AI tool to create initial designs that will appeal to young adults. You make your descriptions to Midjourney detailed and focus on elements that signify both suburban life and nature. For example, you may describe a bamboo-fabric jacket set against a city park backdrop.

After several iterations to ensure that the images align with your brand's visual identity, you tailor these images for various social media platforms where you plan to present your marketing campaign. Before finalizing, you gather feedback from a focus group or, at the very least, other team members to test that the images resonate well with your target demographic. Lastly, you double-check all legal and ethical aspects of using AI-generated images in your campaign.

Enhancing Existing Creative Assets

Using AI to enhance or edit existing creative assets involves several innovative techniques that have revolutionized the approach to creativity and asset development. AI's role in enhancing and editing creative assets spans a wide array of applications, from restoring and enhancing old media to creating entirely new content.

Current marketers more frequently use AI for editing and enhancing existing images than they do for creating images from scratch. However, I expect that situation to change in the future. Advancements in AI's capabilities don't only save time and reduce manual effort; they represent a paradigm shift in how marketers approach creative work as a blend of human imagination and machine efficiency.

The following sections describe four distinct ways in which you can use AI for modifying your existing creative visuals.

Enhancing and restoring images

AI-infused tools can significantly improve the quality of existing images. Tools such as Photoshop now integrate AI for tasks including upscaling resolution, enhancing details, and restoring old photographs. For example, AI algorithms can analyze a low-resolution image and intelligently fill in details that the original image didn't actually contain, resulting in a high-resolution version. In photo restoration, AI can remove scratches, adjust faded colors, and even reconstruct missing parts of an image. This capability is particularly valuable in preserving historical photographs or rejuvenating old family pictures.

One of my favorite features in Adobe Photoshop is the Sky Replacement functionality, which allows you to change the sky featured in an existing image based on the criteria that you set. The technology behind these tools, not surprisingly, involves neural networks trained on vast data sets of images, enabling the AI to predict and replicate realistic textures and details.

Enhancing and clarifying audio

Similar to its capabilities for image restoration (see the preceding section), AI's audio processing features make it adept at creating, enhancing, and restoring audio recordings. This functionality is especially useful for remastering old music tracks, restoring archival audio recordings, or improving the clarity of voice recordings.

AI algorithms can isolate different audio elements, remove background noise, and even separate voice sounds from music. For instance, AI can take an old mono track and *upmix* it (extract separate tracks) to stereo or surround sound, breathing new life into classic songs. Tools such as Izotope's RX series use machine learning to identify and repair common audio issues — such as clicks, pops, or hisses — that often occur in older recordings. The BMW example that I talk about in the sidebar "Case Study: BMW's AI-Generated Soundtrack," in this chapter, touches on the potential of using AI to create or enhance audio.

Analyzing and editing video

AI is automating time-consuming video-editing tasks such as object removal, color grading, and even *frame interpolation* (creating and inserting new video frames between existing ones), which results in smoother transitions for slow-motion effects. AI tools can automate the process of analyzing and editing videos frame by frame, which can significantly reduce the manual labor involved in video post-production. For example, AI can automatically identify and tag various elements in a video — such as faces, objects, or landscapes — and enable quick editing or effects application.

Adobe's Sensei AI and Blackmagic Design's DaVinci Resolve with its *neural engine* are examples of AI technologies that empower editors to achieve more in less time, enhancing the overall quality and visual appeal of videos. Simpler AI tools, such as Animoto or Lumen5, also allow you to enter natural language queries into the application and provide guidelines for creating short instructional videos.

Adding and modifying content

You can use AI to modify or create elements within existing assets. For instance, AI-driven tools such as DALL-E or GPT-4 can generate new visual or textual content that matches the style or theme of existing assets. You can use this functionality to create variations of an ad campaign, generate additional scenes in a video game, or even produce explanatory images for a book.

REMEMBER

The AI models that you use for supplementing assets are trained on vast data sets and can generate highly original and contextually appropriate content. This capability not only speeds up the creative process, but also opens up new avenues for creativity that were previously unimaginable.

CASE STUDY: COCA-COLA'S "MASTERPIECE" CAMPAIGN

In an era when keeping a heritage brand vibrant and relevant is a formidable challenge, Coca-Cola embarked on a journey in 2023 to infuse its timeless appeal with the cutting-edge allure of AI. The objective was clear: To intertwine Coca-Cola's enduring promise of uplifting refreshment with the dynamism of AI, thereby sparking creativity and connection in the fabric of daily life. The campaign hoped to captivate a global audience with its memorable narrative.

To achieve this, Coca-Cola harnessed the power of generative AI, collaborating with OpenAI, Electric Theatre Collective, and Blitzworks to craft an innovative short film titled "Masterpiece." The film presents an eclectic mix of classical and contemporary art from around the globe, all in a museum setting. It weaves a tale in which a Coca-Cola bottle journeys through various paintings, ultimately inspiring an art student. This journey is brought to life through a blend of live-action, digital artistry, and AI-driven animation, showcasing the bottle's transformation as it traverses different artistic realms. Notably, the film incorporates Stable Diffusion, OpenAI's DALL-E 2, and GPT-4.0 to generate unique paintings and dialogues, showcasing the seamless integration of AI in creative storytelling.

Not only was the film a shining example of how to use generative AI in asset creation, but its exposure also lifted Coca-Cola's brand metrics, including a 12 percent increase in brand recall, a 9 percent improvement in brand favorability, and a 7 percent rise in purchase intent for the target audience, as highlighted in a survey from the research firm Kantar. The campaign also achieved viral success, amassing millions of views, likes, and comments across social media platforms and garnering acclaim with accolades such as the Cannes LIONS Grand Prix for Film Craft, among others.

For marketers, this initiative illustrates the boundless possibilities of blending traditional art and creative asset development with AI, offering fresh perspectives on brand storytelling. By leveraging generative AI, Coca-Cola demonstrated how different tools can lead to entirely new creative concepts that stay on brand and produce strong advertising results.

Fine-Tuning Creativity with AI Tools and Techniques

To fine-tune the creation of visual marketing assets by using AI tools, you have to hone your skills in working with those tools. For example, you can improve the effectiveness of the written descriptions that you use as input for the AI created content. You can also streamline your asset production process and employ various tricks to make sure that the assets created grab your customers' attention. The following sections can help you get started in becoming an AI–content creation wiz.

Crafting descriptions for image creation

To get high-quality AI images, you need to craft detailed descriptions. Here are five examples of descriptions provided to an AI tool — each tailored for a different scenario — to give you inspiration for creating your own imagery or video:

>> **Product promotion in lifestyle setting:**

   A cozy, modern living room at dusk, with soft ambient lighting. In the center, a sleek, black, smart coffee maker sits on a rustic wooden table. The background shows a comfortable sofa with colorful cushions and a bookshelf filled with books. There's a large window with sheer curtains, showcasing a city skyline at twilight.

>> **Fashion advertisement for a youth brand:**

   A vibrant street art backdrop with graffiti, showcasing a diverse group of young adults wearing trendy streetwear. The clothing includes graphic T-shirts, ripped jeans, and colorful sneakers. Each person is striking a dynamic pose, exuding confidence and style. The setting is an urban alleyway, bustling with energy, and the lighting is bright and lively, emphasizing the vivid colors of the clothes and graffiti.

>> **Travel promotion for a tropical destination:**

   A breathtaking beach scene at sunset, with a clear view of the ocean meeting the horizon. The sky is a blend of orange, pink, and purple hues. Palm trees gently sway in the foreground, framing a hammock tied between two trees. In the background, there's a glimpse of a luxury over-water bungalow with a thatched roof. The water is crystal clear, and there's a sense of serene beauty and tranquility. Nobody is around.

>> **Gourmet food advertisement:**

   An elegant dining table set outdoors in a lush garden during the day. The table showcases a gourmet spread: a cheese board with an assortment of cheeses, grapes, and nuts; a freshly baked artisanal bread; and a bottle of red wine with two glasses. The background features blooming flowers and greenery, with soft, natural sunlight filtering through the leaves, creating a warm and inviting atmosphere.

>> **Tech product launch:**

A futuristic, minimalist office space with a large, sleek, curved desk. On the desk, there's a cutting-edge silver laptop with a glowing logo. The room has a large glass window revealing a cityscape with high-tech skyscrapers. The lighting is cool and blue, giving a high-tech, innovative vibe. In the foreground, holographic projections display graphs and code, symbolizing advanced technology and innovation.

Automating creative production

Automating the creative production process by using AI involves integrating intelligent tools at various stages of the workflow. This approach can significantly enhance efficiency, spark creativity, and ensure consistency across projects. The following list gives you a detailed explanation of how to use AI tools in the creative production process, with specific examples and recommendations:

>> **Concept and planning:** The first step in any creative asset production is conceptualization and planning. AI tools such as OpenAI's GPT-4 can assist in generating creative concepts and ideas. For example, you can prompt GPT-4 to generate unique storylines, advertising copy, or design concepts based on initial input criteria. This assistance can help you in brainstorming sessions to provide a broad range of ideas and angles that may not be immediately obvious to human marketing teams.

REMEMBER

AI-powered project management tools can assist in planning the production timeline, resource allocation, and budgeting by analyzing data from previous projects to predict timelines and potential bottlenecks.

>> **Design and asset creation:** In the design phase, AI tools such as Adobe Sensei and Autodesk's AI solutions can greatly expedite the process. These tools can automate repetitive tasks such as image resizing, color correction, and basic layout design. For instance, Adobe Sensei can intelligently crop photos, keeping the main subjects in frame, or suggest design layouts in Adobe Spark. Autodesk's AI, on the other hand, can assist in 3D design processes by suggesting optimizations of model structures and automating certain modeling tasks, such as generating textures or refining mesh details.

You can also use AI tools to generate initial design templates or even come up with complete assets. Tools such as DALL-E, Midjourney, or Runway enable users to create visuals and design elements from textual descriptions, which offers a fast and unique way to create custom graphics.

>> **Content development and writing:** For content creation, AI writing assistants such as Jasper, Writer, or TheWordsmith.ai can generate drafts for articles, scripts, or social media posts. These tools use advanced natural language processing (NLP) to create coherent and contextually relevant content based on keywords or short descriptions. Although AI-generated text often requires human editing to add a personal touch or specific brand voice, these tools can save considerable time in the initial drafting phase.

TIP

Find out about the type of writing tools (such as Jasper.ai, Writer.ai, Copy.ai, and TheWordsmith.ai) that can incorporate your brand style guidelines before generating any content. Also, keep your audience in mind: AI can assist in *language translation* and *localization of content* (see Chapter 6 in this book for more about these topics), ensuring that the creative output is accessible to a global audience.

>> **Editing in video post-production:** During the post-production process for a video asset, AI can significantly streamline the editing process. Tools such as Adobe Premiere Pro's Auto Reframe use AI to automatically adjust the aspect ratio of videos for different platforms. For example, the tools can transition from a widescreen format to a square format for social media.

For audio production, tools such as Descript offer AI-driven transcription and editing, which enables the creators to edit audio files by adjusting the transcribed text. This type of process can dramatically reduce editing time. In photography and image editing, AI tools can automate tasks such as object removal, sky replacement, or style transfer, as offered in Skylum's Luminar.

>> **Review and optimization:** AI-powered analytics tools can analyze audience engagement with creative content and provide insights into what content works and what doesn't. For instance, tools such as Canva's Magic Switch or Google Analytics can offer data-driven recommendations for design adjustments or content tweaks to help you maximize engagement and reach.

TIP

Increasingly, tools such as VidMob use AI to analyze all the advertising that you create *longitudinally* (repeatedly over long periods of time) to determine which types of content and what elements in that content produce the best results. The tool then uses those insights to fuel recommendations for adjustments to new content that you create.

REMEMBER

When integrating AI into creative production, maintain a balance between automation and human creativity. AI is best used as a tool to augment and assist the creative process, rather than replace it. Have your creators familiarize themselves with a range of AI tools so that they can understand which tools best suit their specific needs. Also, make sure that everyone continuously updates their skills and knowledge about new AI tools and advancements because the field is rapidly evolving.

Tips and tricks for producing attention-grabbing creative assets

Producing attention-grabbing creative assets by using AI requires a multifaceted process that capitalizes on the unique capabilities of AI tools to create content that's not only visually appealing or engaging but also resonates with your target audience. Effective utilization of AI can transform the way you conceptualize, develop, and deliver content:

» **Customized content:** AI tools such as Adobe Target can personalize content based on user data and preferences. You can see this approach in AI-driven campaigns for online retailers, where images of products are dynamically generated to align with the interests of specific users. Similarly, Google's responsive display ads use AI to test various combinations of headlines, descriptions, and images, optimizing ad performance for different target audiences. This dynamic content adaptation ensures that each user receives the most relevant and engaging experience. Dynamic Yield, Oracle Maxymiser, and Vue.ai are a few of the other tools that provide this content customization.

» **Design and video:** Specialized tools, such as Stable Diffusion and Runway, enable the creation of unique AI-generated visuals. For instance, a marketing campaign incorporating AI-generated artwork that merges brand elements with distinct artistic styles results in a visually unique and memorable experience. Additionally, AI-powered image enhancement tools, such as Let's Enhance or Adobe Photoshop's AI features, can significantly improve image quality, making your content sharper and more attention-grabbing.

TIP

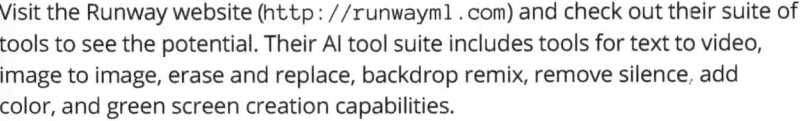

Visit the Runway website (`http://runwayml.com`) and check out their suite of tools to see the potential. Their AI tool suite includes tools for text to video, image to image, erase and replace, backdrop remix, remove silence, add color, and green screen creation capabilities.

» **Video and animation:** Automated video editing tools, such as Lumen5 and Magisto, can convert blog posts or textual content into engaging video content by selecting relevant stock images or video clips, overlaying text, and adding music. Additionally, AI animation tools, such as Synthesia, allow for the creation of custom avatars that can deliver messages in a more personalized and engaging manner, such as creating an AI spokesperson for a brand. Some of these tools aren't free, but they're not expensive either. As I write this book, Lumen5 starts at $19 a month for unlimited usage.

» **Creative copywriting:** In the domain of copywriting, AI tools such as Jasper, Writer, or Copy.ai can produce a range of styles and tones, tailored to different platforms, brands, and audiences, which enhances the engagement level of ads, social media posts, or product descriptions. Moreover, AI tools such as CoSchedule's Headline Analyzer can help you craft attention-grabbing headlines, using algorithms to analyze and predict the engagement level of various word choices.

>> **Audio production:** Tools such as AIVA or Amper Music enable the creation of custom music tracks, allowing users to select a mood or style for the AI to generate a unique piece of music. Furthermore, AI voice synthesis tools, such as Descript, offer realistic voiceovers for videos or podcasts, streamlining the production process and providing greater flexibility in content creation.

CASE STUDY: BMW'S AI-GENERATED SOUNDTRACK

BMW, a leading global automotive brand renowned for its commitment to technological innovation, sought a distinctive approach that would resonate with a younger, tech-savvy demographic. The brand identified an opportunity to leverage its association with cutting-edge technology by collaborating with Tomorrowland, the annual electronic music dance festival, to create a unique brand experience that underscores its innovative ethos.

BMW launched Future Record, an AI-driven music platform developed in partnership with Tomorrowland. This platform offered users an interactive experience in which they can craft their own AI-generated tracks. By engaging with Future Record, participants were prompted to answer a series of questions regarding their preferences, such as stage name, tempo, mood, and lyrics. The platform then used those inputs to generate a bespoke song that captured the essence of the user's asks. This process, remarkably efficient, produces personalized songs in under a minute, which users were able to share on social platforms.

The Future Record initiative generated more than 10,000 unique tracks and garnered more than 20 million impressions on social media. This campaign significantly boosted BMW's brand awareness and fostered deeper engagement and loyalty among BMW and Tomorrowland's audiences.

Future Record served dual purposes: to showcase the potential of using generative AI to create new music and to strengthen BMW's technology credentials. It showed how generative AI can be used not just by one but by thousands of consumers to create new music that, in turn, reinforced the BMW brand. Furthermore, it hints at the possibilities when you use generative AI to create custom soundtracks for your consumers on a huge scale — forging a stronger and more nuanced connection with them.

Choosing AI Tools for Creating Visual Assets

Using AI to develop or enhance creative assets has become increasingly popular, especially in marketing. Each tool has its unique strengths, and the best choice depends on your specific needs. For example, your priority may be the style of images that you want to create, how easily you can pick up and use the tool that you choose, or whether you can integrate the tool with your existing workflow. Always consider the tool's compatibility with your marketing objectives and brand identity.

TIP

Stay informed about the latest developments in AI tools by reading industry newsletters, following relevant tech blogs, and participating in professional forums because the technology is rapidly evolving. Specifically, find out about AI image creation tools to leverage new features and capabilities. For example, Apple just launched an AI image tool that lets you make edits by using *natural language querying* (conversational English instructions).

Table 3-1 shows some of the best tools currently available for AI-generated imagery.

TABLE 3-1 ## AI-Generated Visual Asset Tools

Tool	Website	Description	Benefits
Adobe Photoshop's Neural Filters	www.adobe.com/ products/photoshop/ neural-filter.html	An add-on to Adobe Creative Suite that allows you to manipulate and transform images	Easy to incorporate for those already using Adobe Creative Suite
Artbreeder	www.artbreeder.com	Blend and mutate images to create new visuals, explore variations in design elements, and create unique images	Exploring variations in design elements
Canva's Magic Write	www.canva.com/ magic-write	Generate design layouts and elements based on textual descriptions	Simplifies the design process for marketers
DALL-E 3 by OpenAI	http://openai. com/dall-e-3	Generate highly creative and detailed images from textual descriptions	Generates high-quality images and customizations
Deep Dream Generator	http://deepdream generator.com	Create surreal and abstract image transformations and eye-catching, dream-like images	Enables artistic image enhancements

(continued)

TABLE 3-1 *(continued)*

Tool	Website	Description	Benefits
Lumen5	http://lumen5.com	Video-creation tool that uses AI to help turn text content into engaging video material	Ease of use, accessibility, and time savings
Midjourney	www.midjourney.com	Generates images from natural language descriptions	Most easily accessible via Discord, the online community platform
NightCafe Studio	http://creator.nightcafe.studio	Offers various AI art-generation techniques, including neural style transfer and text-to-image generation	User-friendly and versatile
Runway	http://runwayml.com	A user-friendly platform for creating AI-generated images and videos	Allows experimentation with different AI models without deep technical knowledge
Stability AI's Stable Diffusion	http://stability.ai/stable-image	AI-powered open source large language model (LLM) that generates digital images based on textual descriptions	Good for high-quality image generation with lots of details
VanceAI	http://vanceai.com	AI-powered image editing tools, including image upscaling, denoising, and restoration	Useful for improving the quality of existing images or graphics

IN THIS CHAPTER

» Composing scholarly articles with the help of GenAI

» Constructing technical documents and analyses utilizing GenAI

» Formulating study frameworks and schematics with GenAI

» Incorporating bibliographic citations lists

» Writing long-form articles with GenAI

» Creating book manuscripts with GenAI

Chapter **4**

Producing Long-Form Content

This chapter is all about the role of GenAI in the production of long-form content. The focus is primarily on the capabilities of GenAI to handle large data sets and generate long-form text that's coherent, factually accurate, and contextually appropriate. The discussion also extends to the practicalities of a writer's interaction with GenAI, evaluating the division of labor in which the technology is responsible for data processing and initial text generation, and the human writer is tasked with guiding the narrative and ensuring the content's uniqueness.

Long-form content is by far the most difficult to produce successfully and to professional standards with GenAI. If you come into this thinking that GenAI is an easy way out of arduous tasks, you're gonna be sorely disappointed. However, many real benefits exist to using AI in this way and, with practice and experience, you will get better at using it in your writing process. I promise it's worth it in the end!

Writing Academic Papers with GenAI Assistance

Tackling the creation of an academic paper can be a complex task, and GenAI is emerging as a valuable tool in this intellectual endeavor. This section provides a clear overview of how GenAI can assist in the research and writing process while maintaining the integrity and originality that academic work demands. You explore practical ways in which GenAI can serve as an aid in organizing literature, synthesizing data, and generating drafts, all without compromising your or another scholar's voice and analytical perspective.

REMEMBER

The use of GenAI in academic writing should be approached with a judicious blend of skepticism and openness — recognizing its potential to streamline the research process while being wary of over-reliance on its outputs. Focus on integrating GenAI's capabilities with critical thinking and ensure that the final paper reflects a well-argued, original contribution to the field.

Using GenAI for research and academic writing

When it comes to academic writing, thorough research is the backbone that supports the entire structure of your scholarly work. GenAI is becoming an increasingly valuable tool in the researcher's toolkit and the overall AI stack, offering a suite of functions that can aid in the meticulous task of gathering and analyzing data. Consider the following:

TIP

» **GenAI has the potential to uncover obscure connections between data points.** By analyzing vast networks of academic papers, GenAI can suggest relationships and patterns that might not be immediately obvious to human researchers. This can lead to novel insights and interdisciplinary connections that could be the seed for groundbreaking research. (However, it's important to approach these AI-generated connections with a discerning eye, validating them through further research and critical evaluation.)

» **Before you dive deep into a topic, GenAI can quickly scan and summarize existing literature on the subject.** This broad overview can help you to identify key themes, gaps in the research, and seminal works. The high-altitude reconnaissance can save valuable time and help shape the direction of your inquiry.

>> GenAI can also assist in the more granular aspects of research, such as data mining and extraction. For instance, it can sift through large datasets to extract relevant statistics, trends, and figures that are pertinent to your research question. Additionally, GenAI's language-processing capabilities can be harnessed to transcribe and translate materials, making non-native language sources more accessible and broadening the scope of your research.

The use of GenAI in this domain requires a strategic approach to ensure that it serves as an enhancement rather than a replacement for the researcher's own critical-thinking skills. The following sections help guide you through process and product options (although, please know that these are examples and not your only options).

Examining GenAI tool options for research and academic writing

GenAI has evolved to include specialized tools tailored for academic research, enhancing the researcher's ability to delve into complex topics with increasing precision and depth. For instance, tools like Iris.ai (iris.ai) and Semantic Scholar (www.semanticscholar.org) use AI to map out scientific literature and provide researchers with relevant papers, reviews, and patents, often uncovering material that traditional search engines might miss. These platforms use natural language processing to understand the context of research queries, ensuring that the results are not just keyword-based but semantically related to the research question.

Another example is Zotero (www.zotero.org), a free reference manager that helps manage and cite research sources for book or report writing and can be integrated with GenAI tools. Zotero can automatically extract citation details from PDFs and web pages and add such works to a research folder with a simple click on a browser extension, making it easier for researchers to build and maintain their bibliographies.

You can easily connect Zotero with Research Rabbit (www.researchrabbit.ai) to further streamline your research and get your reports and papers found by other researchers, too. Research Rabbit is a free research tool built to help you discover and organize relevant papers for your research. It provides interactive visualizations, collections, digests, and data search tools. If you want a more in-depth look at Zotero and its many capabilities, you might want to view "How to use Zotero's full potential [The AI Revolution in Zotero]" on YouTube at https://www.youtube.com/watch?v=gA3o2MlnPBQ.

You can add ChatGPT to Zotero in a few easy steps. Then, you can research and write your academic paper or book in one tool. The easiest integration to add GenAI to Zotero is ARIA, an acronym for AI Research Assistant and a Zotero plugin. Before using ARIA, you need to have an OpenAI API key, which is a security code for developers to use that enables computer programs to interact. You can get an OpenAI API key here: https://help.openai.com/en/articles/4936850-where-do-i-find-my-openai-api-key. Follow the in-app instructions to add the key, select the ChatGPT model you want to use, and restart Zotero.

The integration process is super easy and takes only a few steps. After you've obtained an OpenAI API key, take the following steps to install ARIA as an add-on tool for Zotero:

1. **Go to Aria on GitHub at** https://github.com/lifan0127/ai-research-assistant.

2. **Scroll down to the Installation section and download the latest release (.xpi file) from GitHub:** https://github.com/lifan0127/ai-research-assistant/releases/latest

3. **Go to Zotero and select Tools from the top menu bar. Click on Addons.**

4. **On the Add-ons Manager panel, click the gear icon at the top right corner and select Install Add-on From File.**

5. **Select the .xpi file you just downloaded and click Open, which will start the installation process.**

   You're done!

TIP

For a more detailed look at this installation process, see the walkthrough tweet by Mushtaq Bilal, PhD, Syddansk Universitet on Twitter (now X) at https://x.com/MushtaqBilalPhD/status/1735221900584865904.

Additionally, platforms like BenchSci (www.benchsci.com) apply AI to decode complex scientific figures, allowing researchers to find specific experimental data without combing through countless articles manually. However, you'll need to integrate this, too, with a GenAI tool trained for writing, or copy its outputs to a GenAI text generator like ChatGPT or Claude so you can write your article or paper. You can also find specialized text generators, like SciWriter (www.sciwriter.ai), but many of those have waiting lists and lean more toward writing articles than writing papers.

Refining GenAI research outputs

GenAI outputs "as is" will almost never be what you want and need them to be. Indeed, the process of trying to get GenAI to produce exactly what you need can be exhausting and frustrating. Also, GenAI, even the specialized text generators, do a lousy job of writing anything in long form. It's smarter and more productive to resign yourself to these unfortunate facts and develop your writing process accordingly. In other words, focus on GenAI's strengths in data discovery and analysis and in helping you fill in any blanks in your work or thinking. Otherwise, accept GenAI's flaws and use your own mind and talent to work around them.

To refine AI research outputs and better ensure their relevance and accuracy, follow this step-by-step process:

1. **Start with a clear and concise research question or set of keywords.**

   Input these into the GenAI tool as a prompt to generate an initial list of resources.

2. **Use a specialized GenAI or other tool's filtering options to narrow down the results to the most relevant papers.**

   This may include sorting by date, relevance, citation count, or journal impact factor. You can integrate GenAI with research tools, as discussed above, to do this work, or you can prompt a GenAI tool to do this type of sorting for you. You may want to try both ways and compare the results.

3. **Skim through the abstracts provided by the AI to assess the pertinence of each source.**

   At this stage, look for the research's main objective, methodology, and conclusions to determine its applicability to your work.

4. **For sources that pass the abstract review, read the full text to evaluate the quality and depth of the research.**

   Pay particular attention to the study's design, the robustness of the data, and the soundness of the arguments presented.

5. **Check the references and citations within the papers to find additional material and to verify the AI's suggestions.**

   This step helps to ensure that key sources haven't been overlooked.

6. **Perform a manual search for literature on your topic to compare against the AI-generated list.**

   This can help identify any gaps or biases in the AI's output.

7. **Use the AI to help extract and organize key data points, statistics, and quotes from the selected sources.**

   Ensure that all extracted information is accurately represented and properly cited.

8. **Critically evaluate the synthesized information, looking for logical consistency, potential biases, and the strength of the evidence.**

9. **Refine your search query based on insights gained from the literature and repeat the process as necessary to uncover additional resources or to narrow the focus of your research.**

By integrating these advanced GenAI tools into your research process and rigorously refining their outputs, you can enhance the breadth and depth of your academic writing. It's crucial to remain actively engaged in each step, using your expertise to guide the AI and to critically assess its contributions to your scholarly work.

Finding hidden pitfalls or AI limitations

While GenAI tools can offer significant advantages in academic research, researchers should be aware of some hidden pitfalls and limitations. Understanding these limitations is essential to knowing when to supplement or replace AI research with manual efforts and other types of tools.

>> **Data quality and bias:** GenAI tools are only as good as the data they have been trained on. If the underlying data contains biases or inaccuracies, the AI's outputs will reflect those flaws. Researchers should be cautious of over-reliance on AI-generated data without cross-referencing it against other sources.

>> **Scope of training:** Some AI tools may have been trained on specific types of literature or within particular disciplines, which can limit their ability to identify relevant research outside of those areas. Researchers should verify whether the AI's scope aligns with their field of study and supplement with manual searches and other types of tools as needed.

>> **Contextual misunderstandings:** AI may struggle with understanding the nuanced context of certain research queries, which can lead to irrelevant or tangential results. Researchers should be prepared to interpret the results critically and refine their queries to improve relevance.

>> **Overlooked novel research:** AI tools may favor sources with more citations or those that are more easily accessible, potentially overlooking newer, less-cited yet highly relevant research. Researchers should manually keep abreast of the latest publications in their field to capture cutting-edge studies.

>> **Non-textual data limitations:** GenAI is predominantly text-based and may not effectively analyze or interpret non-textual data such as complex graphs, images, or raw datasets. Researchers should manually review such materials to ensure comprehensive understanding and integration into their work.

- >> **Updates and maintenance:** AI databases require regular updates to include the latest research. If an AI tool is not well-maintained, it may miss recent publications. Researchers should check the update frequency of AI tools and supplement with manual or other tool searches in fast-moving fields.

- >> **Citation context:** GenAI can provide citations, but it may not always capture the context in which a study is cited. Researchers should manually review citations to understand how a source is being used within the literature to avoid misinterpretation.

- >> **Language limitations:** While some AI tools offer translation capabilities, nuances, and subtleties in language can be lost. For research in languages other than those the AI was primarily designed for, researchers should verify translations and interpretations by different means.

- >> **Depth of analysis:** AI can help identify broad patterns and connections, but it may not capture the depth of analysis required for a thorough literature review. Researchers should supplement AI findings with deep, manual analysis to uncover subtle arguments and theoretical frameworks.

To mitigate these pitfalls, maintain a balanced approach, using GenAI as a starting point for identifying potentially relevant research and then applying your own expertise and critical-thinking skills to conduct a more nuanced and comprehensive review.

WARNING

Whatever you do, do not hand your boss or publish any AI-based research or written report without thoroughly reviewing and vetting first. If you do, you're likely gambling your entire career, and you're probably going to lose badly.

Supporting the academic publication process

The journey from research to publication is often a marathon filled with hurdles, from formatting to peer review. GenAI is emerging as a useful resource in this process, offering capabilities that can help streamline various stages of academic publishing. However, while GenAI can assist with some aspects of the academic publishing process, like literature reviews, writing, and organization, the more nuanced human elements involving expert judgment, context, and domain knowledge remain challenging for AI to fully automate or replicate at this stage. You should be very cautious about overestimating GenAI's role.

While GenAI tools have the potential to assist with various tasks, some of the capabilities mentioned or touted by enthusiasts and vendors — and even in GenAI responses — may not be fully developed or widely available. Here's an overview of where things stand as of this writing:

>> **Manuscript formatting:** While there are tools like LaTeX that can help with formatting academic papers and reference management software like Zotero and EndNote that can format citations according to journal styles, claims, or suggestions that GenAI can automatically format entire manuscripts to fit specific journal guidelines are unfounded. Such formatting usually requires manual intervention to ensure adherence to the specific requirements of each journal.

>> **Preliminary peer review:** No widely recognized GenAI tools simulate the peer review process against a vast database of published papers to predict common points of contention or interest. While there are AI-based grammar and style checkers that can help improve the readability and quality of writing, the nuanced feedback provided by human peer reviewers, which includes evaluating the validity of the research methodology, the interpretation of results, and the overall contribution to the field, cannot be fully replicated by AI at this time.

>> **Gauging novelty:** GenAI tools can help identify existing literature on a topic, but their ability to assess the novelty of research is limited. Determining the unique contributions of a study requires deep understanding and contextual knowledge that currently goes beyond the capabilities of AI.

>> **Creating a list of suitable reviewers:** Databases and networking platforms can help identify researchers with relevant expertise, but the selection of suitable reviewers typically involves editorial judgment and knowledge of the field. GenAI does not currently manage this aspect of the publication process.

In summary, while AI can provide support in the academic publication process, its role is primarily in assisting with research, organization, and some aspects of writing. The more nuanced tasks, such as peer review, assessing research novelty, and selecting suitable reviewers, still rely heavily on human expertise. It's essential for you to remain critically engaged and not overestimate the capabilities of AI in the context of academic publishing.

Developing White Papers and Reports Using Generative AI

GenAI is helpful in writing white papers and reports, which are often extensive and require a significant investment of time and expertise. There are limitations to how much of the work GenAI tools can perform. Here's an overview of where things stand in terms of GenAI assisting with white papers and reports as of this writing.

>> **Automated drafting:** While GenAI can assist in creating outlines and initial drafts, it's important to note that these tools typically require human input to guide the structure and ensure that it meets the specific goals of the white paper or report. The AI's ability to automate drafting is based on patterns it has learned from data, so it might not always align perfectly with the author's intentions without manual adjustments.

>> **Suggesting content based on trends:** GenAI does have the capability to analyze large datasets and can identify trends to some extent. However, the insight it provides is often based on the data it has been trained on, and it may not have access to the most current or proprietary databases unless integrated by the user. Predictive models in AI are also not infallible and should be used with caution, especially when informing strategic decisions.

>> **Synthesizing information:** GenAI can indeed process and summarize information from various sources, but the quality and depth of synthesis can vary. It's essential for the user to critically evaluate and supplement AI-generated summaries to ensure that they capture the necessary details and context accurately.

>> **Accuracy and relevance:** It is crucial to highlight that verifying the accuracy and relevance of AI-generated content is a key step in the process. GenAI can sometimes replicate misinformation if that's present in the training data, and it may not always interpret data correctly, especially if it involves complex or nuanced topics.

REMEMBER

Even though GenAI can support the development of white papers and reports by providing structural outlines and synthesizing information, its capabilities are not a substitute for human expertise and judgment. The technology serves best as an aid in the writing process, with the author playing a critical role in ensuring the final document's accuracy, relevance, and credibility.

Crafting professional documents with AI support

The integration of AI into the process of creating professional documents such as white papers and reports can significantly enhance productivity and quality. AI support can streamline research, organize content, and even aid in the editing process, allowing writers to focus on the critical thinking and strategic aspects of document creation.

When starting a white paper or report, you can use AI tools like Grammarly (www. grammarly.com) and Hemingway (hemingwayapp.com) to help refine the language and improve readability. These tools provide real-time suggestions to make the text clearer, more concise, and grammatically correct. For more complex editing tasks, tools like ProWritingAid (prowritingaid.com) offer in-depth reports on style, word choice, and sentence structure.

For research, AI-powered tools such as Yewno Discover and Connected Papers (www.connectedpapers.com) offer innovative ways to explore the academic landscape. They can help authors find the most relevant studies, papers, and articles by understanding the context of their queries, not just matching keywords. This can lead to a more informed and up-to-date background section in any professional document.

AI can also help in organizing the document's structure. Tools like Scrivener (www. literatureandlatte.com/scrivener/overview) help writers manage large writing projects by breaking them down into smaller, more manageable sections. This can be particularly useful for lengthy reports or white papers that cover multiple topics or require extensive data presentation. However, Scrivener does not directly use or provide AI tools. Most people who want to use GenAI tools copy and paste the documents they created in Scrivener to a GenAI tool to further their work.

For data analysis and visualization, tools like Tableau (www.tableau.com) and Microsoft Power BI leverage AI to help users identify trends, patterns, and insights from complex datasets. These can be incorporated into professional documents to support arguments with empirical evidence and create compelling visualizations that convey the data's story at a glance.

Meanwhile, AI-driven summarization tools can condense large volumes of information into concise overviews. For instance, tools like Resoomer (resoomer.com) can be useful when one needs to quickly assimilate and report on the key points from a range of sources or when creating an executive summary for a detailed report.

WARNING

However, though AI provides fast and intensive support, I'll again remind you that these tools are not infallible. You should always review AI-generated content for accuracy, tone, and relevance. It's also important to ensure that the use of AI aligns with ethical guidelines and intellectual property laws, especially when dealing with proprietary or sensitive information.

Enhancing business communication with AI

This section focuses mostly on white papers and reports, but GenAI can assist with other long-form business communications as well.

Following are some general tips for using GenAI on any long-form business or academic content:

>> **Define clear objectives:** Before using AI, define the goals of your document. What message do you want to convey, and to whom? Clear objectives will help you guide the AI in generating relevant content.

>> **Validate AI contributions:** Always factcheck and validate AI-generated content, especially when dealing with technical subjects or data analysis.

>> **Balance technicality and readability:** Use AI to strike a balance between technical accuracy and readability. Tailor the complexity of the language to the document's intended audience.

>> **Keep the human element:** Ensure that the final document reflects the company's voice and values. AI should support the communication strategy, not define it.

>> **Stay updated on AI developments:** The field of AI is rapidly evolving. Stay informed about new tools and updates that can further enhance your business communications.

Crafting Research Designs and Outlines with GenAI

GenAI can streamline the research process, from conceptualization to data collection, including crafting research designs, outlines, and poll questions. GenAI tools are adept at organizing thoughts and structuring complex information, making them particularly useful for researchers who are in the early stages of project development.

When it comes to research design, GenAI can assist in developing a comprehensive outline that covers all necessary components of a study. By inputting the research objectives and questions, researchers can use AI to generate a framework that includes the introduction, literature review, methodology, data analysis, and conclusion sections. AI tools like ZoteroBib (zbib.org) can also help researchers manage their sources and citations efficiently, ensuring that their literature reviews are thorough and properly referenced. Moreover, AI-driven platforms such as Iris.ai can explore vast databases to identify relevant studies and theoretical frameworks, suggesting connections that may not be immediately obvious but that you would want to include in the research design.

For creating poll questions and surveys, GenAI can be particularly useful in formulating questions that are clear, unbiased, and likely to yield informative responses. AI tools like SurveyMonkey's Question Bank offer a repository of pre-vetted questions that can be customized to fit the specific needs of a study. These AI-generated questions can serve as a starting point, which researchers can then refine to ensure that the wording is precise and tailored to their target demographic. Additionally, AI can analyze pilot survey data to identify poorly performing questions, allowing researchers to make necessary adjustments before launching a large-scale data collection effort.

It is crucial for researchers to critically evaluate and adapt AI-generated content. The researcher's expertise is essential in interpreting AI suggestions within the context of their specific field and research goals. It is this synergy between human intellect and AI efficiency that can produce well-crafted research designs and tools, ultimately leading to more robust and insightful studies.

Structuring research projects with AI

In general, structuring a research project involves the following actions:

1. Define the research question.
2. Conduct a literature review.
3. Develop a methodology.
4. Create a research proposal.
5. Plan the project.
6. Collect data.
7. Analyze data.
8. Write the report.
9. Revise and edit.
10. Peer review (if applicable).
11. Disseminate findings.
12. Reflect on the process.

AI offers valuable tools for assisting with the structuring of research projects, but its capabilities are currently more supportive than autonomous. AI can provide insights and highlight patterns that may not be immediately apparent to researchers, but the tasks of identifying gaps in literature, developing theoretical frameworks, and designing methodologies still require significant human input and critical evaluation.

Consider the following caveats:

>> GenAI can help identify gaps in literature by processing large volumes of data and highlighting areas that lack research. However, the AI's effectiveness in this task depends on the quality of the data it has been trained on and the sophistication of the algorithms used. AI can pinpoint underexplored areas or contradictions, but the technology typically requires human guidance to interpret the significance and relevance of these findings within a specific research context.

>> GenAI can analyze patterns and correlations in data, which may suggest potential theories. However, AI cannot reliably develop theoretical frameworks or hypotheses. GenAI can provide data-driven insights that may inspire researchers to formulate new hypotheses, but the creation of a robust theoretical framework remains a complex task that relies heavily on human expertise and critical thinking.

>> AI does have predictive analytics capabilities, and these can be used to some extent to inform research design based on historical data and outcomes from similar studies. However, the ability of AI to guide the methodological design of a project is not as straightforward as is often suggested. Predictive analytics can provide some foresight into potential outcomes, but human researchers need to interpret these predictions and make methodological decisions based on a comprehensive understanding of the subject matter.

From concept to outline: GenAI as a planning tool

GenAI can play a significant role in the initial stages of academic and professional research. Its capacity to process and organize information provides a foundational tool for you to transition from a broad concept to a structured research outline.

At the conceptual stage, AI can be utilized to conduct preliminary literature reviews and environmental scans. Tools like Iris.ai facilitate this by allowing researchers to input their research questions or abstracts and then receive a map of related work and concepts. This not only speeds up the literature review process but also ensures a comprehensive understanding of the field, helping to refine the research questions and objectives.

Additionally, AI applications can analyze the sentiment and trends within existing literature, offering insights into prevailing research attitudes and potential biases, which can be instrumental in defining the scope and direction of a new study. However, their use in academic literature reviews is not as widespread as in other fields, such as market analysis or social media monitoring. The application of sentiment analysis to academic literature to uncover biases and trends is an emerging area, and while tools exist, they may not yet be a standard part of the research design process.

After your research concept is solidified, GenAI aids in outlining the research design by suggesting logical structures and sequences for the project. GenAI-powered mind mapping tools, for example, can help visualize the connections between various components of your research project, such as hypotheses, methodologies, and expected outcomes. Examples include NoteGPT, MindMatrix, Mapify, and GitMind.

Furthermore, AI can assist in identifying the most suitable research methods for your project by drawing from databases of past studies, analyzing their success rates, and aligning them with the current research goals. This can add efficiency to the planning phase. However, using GenAI to suggest research methods is a complex task and is not commonly found in mainstream GenAI tools. GenAI systems are in development for specialized fields that can analyze and suggest methodologies, though these are typically more accessible to authorized users or research institutions.

REMEMBER

Despite the assistance GenAI can provide, the creativity and critical judgment of the researcher remain crucial in crafting a research design that is both innovative and scientifically rigorous.

Integrating Citations and References

Integrating citations and references is a critical aspect of academic writing and research, ensuring that proper credit is given for the ideas and findings of others. The process can be tedious and time-consuming and is one that I am happy to relegate to GenAI. You probably are, too.

As GenAI technology continues to evolve, we can expect further advancements that will make the process more intuitive and integrated into the research workflow, allowing scholars to focus more on the substance of their work rather than the technicalities of citation. For now, well, let's just say there's a long way to go yet. Integrating GenAI with other more mature research tools is probably your best bet.

GenAI-assisted reference management

The good news is that citation tools, like Zotero and Mendeley, extract reference details from documents, websites, and other digital sources. These tools can recognize and format citations according to various style guides, such as APA, MLA, or Chicago, with minimal input from you. They also allow you to maintain a searchable library of references, which can be easily organized by topic, project, or other custom tags. This not only saves time but also reduces the risk of errors in citation, which is crucial for maintaining the integrity of a research project.

The bad news is that most, if not all, pure-play citation and reference management tools like Zotero and Mendeley (www.mendeley.com) are not GenAI-driven as of this writing. Some will allow you to integrate them with GenAI. There's much debate about whether integrating GenAI will strengthen or weaken these tools in the end.

But it is true that some advanced word-processing programs and writing platforms have begun to more fully incorporate GenAI-driven features. For example, tools like Grammarly and Microsoft Editor use GenAI to help improve writing quality, which can include suggestions for citations.

However, a feature that suggests relevant articles to cite based on the content being written is not commonly found across all word-processing programs and may only be part of more specialized or advanced writing assistance software.

It's reasonable to expect that GenAI technology will continue to evolve and further integrate into the research workflow. But the availability and sophistication of these features can differ significantly depending on the specific software or platform in use. As GenAI becomes more sophisticated, its potential to streamline the research process and allow scholars to focus more on the content of their work is likely to increase.

Ensuring academic integrity with GenAI

Many modern writing assistance tools and plagiarism-detection services, such as Turnitin and Grammarly, use sophisticated algorithms and GenAI to scan texts against databases of academic work to identify potential plagiarism. These tools can result in users adding citations where necessary to help ensure that all sources are properly credited.

Moreover, GenAI can assist in paraphrasing and summarizing existing research while maintaining the original meaning, which helps in avoiding plagiarism. GenAI writing assistants can suggest alternative ways to present information that ensure the researcher's prose is unique, yet still reflects a thorough understanding of the subject matter. This is particularly useful for students and researchers who are synthesizing complex information from multiple sources.

GenAI can also contribute to academic integrity by ensuring consistency and accuracy in data reporting. GenAI algorithms can analyze datasets for anomalies or inconsistencies that may indicate errors in data collection or analysis. By flagging these issues, researchers can address them proactively, ensuring that their reports are as accurate and reliable as possible. As GenAI continues to evolve, its potential to reinforce ethical practices in academic research is likely to expand, providing researchers with a powerful ally in the quest for integrity and excellence in their scholarly endeavors.

WARNING

But GenAI tools can and do hallucinate, so the onus remains on you to take every measure beyond GenAI that is necessary to ensure academic integrity in every work produced with or without GenAI assistance.

Producing Long-Form Articles with GenAI

The use of GenAI in producing long-form articles has certainly brought a mixed bag of outcomes — good, bad, and ugly. On the positive side, GenAI has democratized content creation, enabling writers, marketers, and researchers to produce comprehensive articles more efficiently. It can assist with generating ideas, providing structure, and even drafting sections of content, which can be particularly beneficial for those facing writer's block or tight deadlines. Additionally, GenAI can help non-native speakers articulate their thoughts more fluently, broadening the inclusivity of content creation.

However, the use of GenAI in writing long-form articles is not without its pitfalls. The *bad* often emerges in the form of over-reliance on AI, which can lead to homogenized content lacking in depth, personal insight, or the nuanced understanding that human expertise brings. There's also the risk of factual inaccuracies or the perpetuation of biases present in the training data, which can mislead readers and erode trust in the content. Furthermore, the *ugly* side surfaces when GenAI is used unethically to mass-produce deceptive or plagiarized content, manipulate opinions, or spread misinformation, which can have far-reaching negative consequences on public discourse and trust in media.

While GenAI offers powerful tools for streamlining the writing process and enhancing productivity, it also poses significant challenges that need to be managed with a critical eye toward maintaining quality, originality, and ethical standards. As the technology continues to evolve, it will be crucial for writers and publishers to balance the efficiency gains with a commitment to the integrity and value of the written word.

Techniques for GenAI-enhanced feature writing

Feature writing typically allows a little more time to complete than news writing because it usually involves more research and interviews and isn't necessarily tied to the day's headlines. These are the pieces that typically garner many views and are the stuff that magazines and legendary writers and reporters built their reputations on.

Today, feature stories still take a deeper dive into their subject and often offer nuance and color that straight news reporting lacks. The question now becomes whether feature writing is a good use case for GenAI — or not? The answer is it depends.

A lot depends on the talent and experience of the writer and the capabilities of the GenAI model used. I find that *output stitching* — in which you give multiple GenAIs the same prompt and then stitch the outputs together —is a highly effective technique for writing most long-form articles, but most especially features. (Yes, *GenAIs*, plural, meaning more than one GenAI.) Using multiple GenAIs gives me many different options and perspectives that a single model just can't deliver. I can also break repetitive outputs and other annoying GenAI behaviors by using *AI chaining*, which is basically infusing other GenAI outputs in the input (prompt) of another. You'll be amazed at how well that works.

TIP

I also find AI aggregation to be a crucial strategy as that enables me to use a variety of GenAI built for different purposes such as background research, financial data analysis, cross-referencing and cross-factchecking, source discovery, image and data visualization generation, and other tasks I might need to bring to bear to create really great long content. And I've done all this testing, strategizing, and process building for projects like this book — to see what works and what doesn't — and to share those findings with you.

If you're producing feature articles for marketing or business purposes outside of journalism, you'll find these same techniques to be invaluable.

Meanwhile, here are some techniques and tips for leveraging GenAI in feature writing:

>> **Research assistance:** Use GenAI to conduct preliminary research on your topic. Tools like Evernote can help you collect and organize information, while others like ChatGPT and Claude can summarize lengthy reports, contracts, agreements, interview transcriptions, videos, or articles, saving you time and helping you to quickly gather background information and context for your feature.

>> **Trend analysis:** GenAI can analyze large datasets to identify trends that might be relevant to your story. Tools like Google Trends or social listening platforms can provide insights into what topics are currently popular or rising in public interest, which can help you to choose angles that will resonate with your audience.

>> **Writing assistance:** GenAI writing assistants can help you overcome writer's block by suggesting sentence completions or alternative phrasings. While you should not rely on these tools to write large sections of your article, they can be useful for getting started or finding a new way to express an idea.

>> **Editing for clarity and style:** GenAI-powered grammar and style checkers can help refine your writing, ensuring that it is clear, concise, and free of errors. Tools like Grammarly or Hemingway Editor can suggest improvements to sentence structure, word choice, and readability.

>> **Audience engagement:** Use AI to understand your audience better. GenAI and GenAI-integrated analytics tools can track reader engagement and provide feedback on which parts of your articles are the most and least engaging. This information can be invaluable in refining your writing style and content to better match your readers' interests.

>> **Personalization:** GenAI can help personalize content for different segments of your audience. By analyzing reader data, GenAI can suggest topics, stories, and approaches that are more likely to appeal to specific demographics or reader groups.

>> **Factchecking:** Use GenAI factchecking tools to help verify the accuracy of statements and data presented in your feature. This is crucial for maintaining credibility and trust with your readers. You might want to check out Full Fact in the UK at `https://fullfact.org/` and the map and info on many global factchecking sites at Duke Reporters' Lab at `https://reporterslab.org/fact-checking/`, which is pictured in Figure 4-1.

REMEMBER

GenAI is a tool to assist you in the writing process, not a replacement for journalistic integrity and ethical considerations. Be transparent about the use of GenAI in your writing process and ensure that the final product reflects your voice and adheres to the highest standards of journalism.

Maintaining depth and quality in GenAI-assisted articles

To preserve depth, you should use GenAI for initial research and drafting but then critically evaluate and expand upon the information provided by GenAI, incorporating your own knowledge, perspectives, and additional research. This helps to add layers of understanding that AI alone cannot achieve. You should also factcheck all GenAI-generated content to ensure accuracy and reliability, as even specialized GenAI can and does hallucinate on the regular as well as perpetuate errors or biases present in its training data.

FIGURE 4-1: Screenshot of the interactive map of global factchecking sites at Duke Reporters' Lab.

OpenStreetMap / https://reporterslab.org/fact-checking / / last accessed on April 23, 2025

Quality is upheld by using GenAI tools to enhance your natural voice and improve readability without compromising your unique style. GenAI can assist with grammar, syntax, and structure, but you should always have the final say in how the content is presented. Additionally, you should remain mindful of ethical considerations, giving proper attribution when necessary and being transparent about the use of GenAI in your writing process.

Writing Books with GenAI

If you're prompting GenAI to write complete books or, heaven forbid, thinking of it as a coauthor, you're doing it wrong. That's like an architect sharing the credit with CAD software for the creation of a beautiful building. I mean, I guess you can do that if you want, but you're dissing your own talent and leading others astray in their work by implying that the software can do much more than it does. Instead, just make it clear that you used GenAI to make your own creative work until the day comes around that it's as routine as an architect using CAD in the course of their work.

The most important thing to manage is your own expectations. GenAI is awful at long-form writing and even worse at writing books. Ask the publishers and self-publishing services how many truly awful GenAI-generated books were thrust upon them by people who thought they could make a fortune at the push of a button. A flood of trash came over the transom and went right back out to the trash bin.

The key to writing books with GenAI is to take the lead. Don't let GenAI models lead you. They are not omnipotent. And they lie just as easily as any other source you might interview. Remember that. Don't trust and always verify.

Decide what your book or story is about and use GenAI to help you research, organize, and write it one small chunk at a time. Yes, you're going to have to make GenAI spit out the proverbial elephant one bite at a time and then stitch it all together yourself. But first, you're going to have to describe and refine and prompt and re-prompt and *prompt chain* every one of those chunks so that you don't stitch together some other animal parts that are distinctly not of the elephant species.

Pay attention to output stitching, AI aggregation, and AI chaining as you'll likely need to use all of them when creating any long-form content, especially in writing a book, regardless of the topic, style, or format. You'll also need to make yourself adept at prompt chaining, a technique in which a sequence of interconnected prompts is used to guide a GenAI model through a multi-step reasoning process or to build upon previous outputs for more complex tasks. In other words, prompt chaining in this context is prompting one chunk at a time so you don't confuse or distract the GenAI by giving it too much information or too many tasks at a time.

How and when you use each of these techniques is up to you. This works in much of the same way as you deciding which words to use and in what order to write them to convey your meaning or story to your readers. Sounds like an overwhelming task, and sometimes it is, which is why writer's block is a real thing. But other times, you find yourself in the zone, and words flow as easily as a river. Using GenAI to help you write a book will eventually flow like that for you, too. With time and practice, you will assimilate it into your personal writing process.

Meanwhile, you may also find some of the following helpful, depending on your personal writing style and process and the genre of your book:

>> **Outline and structure:** Tools like Plottr (plottr.com) or Scrivener can help with outlining, plotting, and structuring your book. They can also be used in conjunction with GenAI suggestions from tools like Sudowrite (https://sudowrite.com) or ShortlyAI (www.shortlyai.com) to write or plot your narrative.

>> **Character development:** Reedsy's Character Builder is a tool you might want to consider when creating detailed character names and profiles. For GenAI-generated backstories and traits, you could use tools like CharacTour (www. charactour.com/hub) or AI Dungeon (aidungeon.com) for inspiration. Many more general-purpose and multimodal GenAI models can help you develop characters on their own.

>> **Drafting assistance:** OpenAI's GPT-3, accessible through platforms like Jasper (formerly Jarvis) or Rytr, can help with generating text for different sections of your book. ChatGPT 4, ChatGPT 4o, Claude, Scribble Studio, and others are helpful, too. (Repeat after me: chunk writing!) These can be especially helpful for drafting dialogue or descriptive passages.

>> **Research:** For summarizing information and conducting research, you might use GenAI tools like Socratic by Google, which can process and analyze large amounts of data quickly. You might also want to use Perplexity.AI as your search engine as it typically renders great results and cites its sources too, which makes factchecking its responses much easier. You can also prompt it to deliver even more sources. Also, look at the academic writing section in this chapter for a list of more research tools.

>> **Language and style:** Grammarly and ProWritingAid offer GenAI-powered suggestions for language and style improvements, helping to ensure consistency and polish in your writing. But for the most part, you'll find most GenAI text and multimodal generators perfectly capable of doing these same tasks without the need for additional tools.

>> **Editing and proofreading:** Hemingway Editor can help tighten up prose, while Grammarly can catch more nuanced grammatical issues and offer stylistic suggestions. But again, you may find more generalized GenAI tools to be sufficient in these tasks without the need for specialized tools.

>> **Feedback and revision:** Although not a replacement for human feedback, platforms like Authors.ai (authors.ai) provide GenAI manuscript analysis, offering insights into how your book might resonate with readers based on existing successful novels.

>> **Ethical considerations:** No specific GenAI tool is designed to manage ethical considerations, as this is more about how you approach the writing process. However, tools like Grammarly and Turnitin can help ensure originality and proper citation in academic and non-fiction writing to help maintain ethical standards.

REMEMBER

The quality of your book will ultimately depend on your skill as a writer and your ability to effectively incorporate GenAI-generated content into a cohesive and engaging narrative. In short, great book writing is a credit to the writer, not the tools.

Chapter **5**

Search Engine Optimization (SEO) in the AI Era

O ver the last two decades, advancements in internet search algorithms kept the search and browse paradigm at the heart of the internet for bil-lions around the world. Traditional search engines, of which Google is the behemoth, serve up a list of links in response to a user's keyword query. The search engines retrieve results based on their indexing of the content available on the internet and organize the lists of links that they come up with in an order that reflects the content's applicability to the user's inputs.

To take advantage of search engine functionality, companies establish teams to harness the potential of search to acquire customers by writing and optimizing online content that search engines recognize as directly related to user queries. The goal is to have users presented with links (via online search) that match their queries so that they click the links, visit the company website, and make product purchases. You want to design content pages that rank high in the order of search results against commonly entered search terms. And when a company succeeds in reaching this goal, it can attract large audiences to its products or services.

Creating online content that the search engines can easily read and that Google (for example) ranks highly costs less than running paid advertising online. The practice of crafting website content to make it search-engine friendly is called *search engine optimization* (SEO), which is a critical part of the digital marketing playbook. However, the traditional approach to SEO may be changing with the increased use of artificial intelligence (AI) to create and optimize the content, on the one hand, and the shift toward AI services such as ChatGPT and Perplexity on the other. These AI services bypass the search engines to give users answers to their queries directly in their results windows. In fact, according to Gartner (a management consulting company), online traffic going to websites directly from search engine results will drop 25 percent by 2026 and will be replaced by the use of tools such as ChatGPT, Claude, and Perplexity.

In this chapter, I begin by discussing why and how users are changing the way that they use search engines, what that change means for marketing, and how businesses can adapt their strategies for this change. Although I cover these topics, I also tell you how you can use AI to augment your current SEO efforts — because the move away from search engine dominance isn't an overnight shift, but rather a gradual evolution.

Describing Search Generative Experiences (SGEs)

You can witness the profound impact of generative artificial intelligence (GenAI) on internet search through the shift toward more conversational (also known as *natural language*) user interfaces. Users can now engage with search engines in a more natural and human-like manner, asking complex questions or expressing their queries in full sentences, rather than relying on specific keywords.

In turn, AI search engines can synthesize information from multiple sources to provide a comprehensive answer to the question in everyday English, instead of simply listing websites that contain the relevant keywords. This capability to understand and process natural language queries in real time is beginning to transform search engines from impersonal website directories into knowledgeable assistants. Commonly referred to as *search generative experiences* (SGEs), this shift has profound implications not only for how people use the internet but also for how they create content for it.

When you look toward the future, you can see that the advancements in search algorithms powered by generative AI promise to make the vast expanse of the internet more accessible and understandable for everyone.

Enhanced interpretation of queries

The advent of GenAI has enabled search algorithms to understand and interpret the intent behind queries with unprecedented depth. This evolution from simple keyword spotting to understanding the context and semantics of user inquiries marks a significant leap forward. As SGE technologies continue to evolve, you can anticipate a shift from information retrieval to knowledge generation, in which search engines synthesize information and provide specific recommendations tailored to users' needs by using the rest of the internet as raw material for their responses.

REMEMBER

GenAI models, such as Claude (https://claude.ai/) and OpenAI's GPT-4 (http://openai.com/gpt-4), are trained on vast amounts of data. The scope of the training enables the models to generate responses that provide direct answers, summaries, or even newly written content based on the user's query. Not to be outdone, both Google and Bing also include SGE results at the top of their search engine results pages as of late 2023.

Personalized search results

The use of SGE opens up many possibilities for personalized search experiences. By analyzing the user's past interactions, preferences, and even the context of their current search, AI can tailor the search results more effectively to meet individual needs. This personalization extends beyond filtering and ranking results based on presumed relevance; it involves generating content or answers uniquely suited to the user's query and context. For example, a search for cooking recipes can take into account the user's dietary restrictions, preferred cuisines, and even the ingredients that they have on hand, offering a level of customization that was previously unavailable.

The transition to custom-crafted search results represents a fundamental change in how people can access and interact with online information, potentially transforming the web into a more dynamic, intelligent, and personalized space.

PERPLEXITY PROVIDES A PEAK INTO THE FUTURE

Perplexity AI (`www.perplexity.ai`) provides a good example of an AI-driven search engine that demonstrates how natural language interfaces are changing the search and browse paradigm of the internet. The search functionality that Perplexity AI offers directly answers users' questions by pulling together information from what it has already gathered by crawling the web. Perplexity AI uses this information to give clear and relevant answers to the questions (rather than just a list of links). This situation makes searching for information faster and easier, turning what used to be a long process into a quick and straightforward task.

Thanks to its advanced understanding of language, Perplexity AI can understand the context of what you're asking, not just the specific words that you use, so it can provide answers that are much more relevant to what you're actually looking for, simplifying the process that you have to follow to find complex information, removing the need to sift through unrelated links. As a result, there's much less ambiguity in your search experience when you use Perplexity AI.

Additionally, Perplexity AI offers a search experience without ads (at least, as of the time I write this book), which means its results aren't influenced by advertisers. This lack of advertiser influence can lead to more unbiased and focused search outcomes. With recent investments and positive feedback from users, AI-driven search engines such as Perplexity AI are beginning to challenge traditional search engines, pushing them toward adopting new standards for delivering search results.

These AI-driven solutions, such as Perplexity AI, are search generative experiences (SGEs) to the core because they literally generate answers to your questions using the internet as the raw ingredients for that generation exercise. You can get the most benefit from them if you have a specific query in mind and are looking for one answer, rather than browsing for different alternatives. Although I can't say how solutions such as Perplexity AI will change the way people search the internet in the future or how the solutions will crawl the web and influence search engine optimization (SEO), but you should pay attention to these new innovations as they enter the mainstream.

Strategies for SEO Success in the AI Era

For many search engine optimization (SEO) experts, the integration of AI with the domain of SEO means a necessary return to the fundamentals of what makes successful content that human beings care about and search algorithms reward. Returning to fundamentals requires that you focus on the following strategies and tactics that the team at SEO.ai (`https://seo.ai`), a company that offers a highly ranked AI SEO writing tool) have emphasized:

>> **Audience focus:** Research your audience and cater specifically to their interests and needs. Tailor content to match their search queries and personas, evidenced by their queries and online habits. This focus can leverage AI's capability to analyze big data for enhanced audience relevance and engagement.

>> **Originality:** Prioritize the creation of unique, research-based content that human beings will care about. Stand out with original studies, surveys, and case studies that offer new data. The goal is to ensure that AI-generated content complements your content and that your content retains as much value for both users and search engines. This concept may not feel new, but it matters more with the rise of AI-generated content because it is now increasingly challenging to differentiate between human-created and AI-created material.

>> **Structured data:** Implement *structured data* (data that has a standardized format that both software and humans can easily access) so that search engines can easily understand and index your content. This tactic improves your content's visibility to search engines and adapts content for evolving search technologies (such as voice search) to enhance user experience. It's only a matter of time until marketers learn how large language models (LLMs, such as ChatGPT) read websites. When they do, they'll need to adjust their content to be more accessible to those LLMs. What's clear is that companies that have more structured data will win the battle for recognition from search technologies.

>> **Human touch:** Emphasize the human element behind your content. Showcasing real people, emotions, and personal experiences builds trust and connection with your audience, which is an offering that's beyond AI's reach. The human-oriented content — whether it's SEO or any customer-facing content — can continue to successfully carry your message in the future.

>> **Real-time updates:** Focus on freshness and the integration of real-time data to ensure that your content remains relevant and up to date. This approach keeps your content ahead of synthetic data (AI-generated material), which may lack the latest information.

REMEMBER

As the use of GenAI in marketing increases, the future will bring a lot of AI-created content to compete with your own, so keep your messaging up to date so that it stands out and remains relevant.

>> **Domain authority:** Strengthen *domain authority* (a website's quality ranking in Google search) and secure *high-quality backlinks* (other websites linking back to yours). As content saturation increases, these factors become critical for

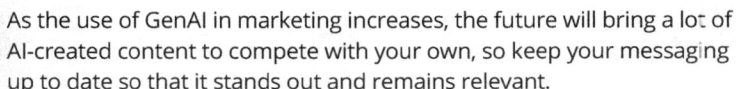

attracting search engines and AI tools that prioritize and trust your content over others. Both practices emphasize the importance of online relationships and external validation. **_Note:_** In 2023, _The New York Times_ brought a lawsuit against OpenAI for crawling its content without permission to train its models because the media publisher knows that its online content is valuable.

>> **Openness and transparency:** This strategy should feel obvious to any marketer, but it bears stating. To win over your audience in the AI era, having engaging content isn't enough. You need to build trust with your consumers by clearly stating your policies on what data you use in your marketing and how you use it. Don't make the mistakes that CNET did (see the sidebar "A CNET Saga: When AI Slips In," in this chapter).

A CNET SAGA: WHEN AI SLIPS IN

CNET (www.cnet.com), a well-respected technology news website, faced public scrutiny in the spring of 2023 upon revealing that it had been using AI to write numerous articles, notably for its daily mortgage and refinance rate section on its website. Despite being attributed to Justin Jaffe, CNET Money's managing editor, these stories didn't appear on Jaffe's primary author page; instead, they were on a separate page exclusively for mortgage rate stories, raising questions about transparency and authorship.

The controversy intensified when it was reported that CNET had quietly published more than 70 articles under the byline "CNET Money Staff" since November 2022, with only a hidden editorial note indicating the use of AI. This lack of clarity extended within CNET, where even staff members were unsure of how the publisher used AI or the workflow surrounding that use, further complicating the issue. This SEO-friendly content ranked high on Google search results and was monetized through affiliate links. This approach, lucrative for CNET, involved creating content on high-intent queries, such as credit card applications, to earn affiliate fees if a user clicked on the links in the article and went to the credit company's website. However, because AI produced these articles without any appropriate disclosures or internal checks, it raised serious concerns about the quality of the content.

The ethical concerns were manifold, primarily centered around CNET's initial failure to disclose the use of AI in creating content. This lack of transparency raised significant questions about credibility and the ethical responsibility of media outlets to inform readers about the origins of the content that they consume. Moreover, subsequent investigations revealed instances of factual inaccuracies within the CNET AI-generated articles, highlighting the risks and limitations of relying on AI for content creation. These findings led to a broader conversation on the reliability and ethical use of AI in journalism, emphasizing the need for stringent quality control measures and the development of robust guidelines to govern AI's application in content creation.

The incident catalyzed a shift toward greater transparency, with CNET and other outlets beginning to label AI-generated content clearly. This case study not only illustrates the potential pitfalls of integrating AI into business without adequate disclosures and quality assurance mechanisms, but it also highlights the evolving dialogue about how best to utilize AI in a manner that supports and enhances reader trust.

Enhancing the User Experience with AI

Optimizing your website or mobile web interface for AI–driven search engines requires a focus on enhancing *user experience* (UX) through strategic design and content approaches. By implementing the tips outlined in this section, you can significantly enhance the user experience of your website or mobile web interface. The enhancements, in turn, make these experiences more favorable in the eyes of AI-driven search engines. The goal is to improve your search engine optimization (SEO) rankings and also drive customer engagement, retention, and sales conversions.

Here are five detailed tips for achieving this goal:

>> **Prioritize mobile-first design.** AI search engines recognize the shift toward mobile browsing and heavily favor websites optimized for mobile devices. Creating a responsive design includes

- Adjusting content and layout based on the user's screen size

- Using large, touch-friendly buttons and readable fonts

- Ensuring quick content load times by optimizing images and leveraging modern coding practices

   For example, you can use mobile content frameworks such as AMP (Accelerated Mobile Pages) for presenting news articles. This framework is designed to improve loading speed on mobile devices.

>> **Enhance site structure for easy navigation.** A well-organized site structure not only improves usability but also helps AI search engines understand and index your content more effectively. Using *schema markup* to outline the structured data implementation (a strategy presented in the preceding

section) on your site can help AI understand the context and content of your pages, improving the chances that your site gets featured in *rich snippets* (the blurbs that the search engines publish at the top of search results pages).

Create a logical hierarchy in your website's architecture, including a clear menu structure and *breadcrumb navigation* (a structure that facilitates navigation by clearly showing users where they are and where they can go next within the website).

Make each page of your website or mobile interface accessible within a few clicks (no more than four if you can help it) from the home page.

>> **Optimize for voice search.** With the rise of AI assistants such as Siri and Google Assistant, optimizing content for voice search is crucial. Incorporate natural language processing (NLP) by including *long-tail keywords* (a phrase made from three to five words) and questions that people are likely to ask as a search prompt in conversational language. Focus on localized SEO by ensuring that your business is listed on Google My Business and other directories because many voice searches are location-based. For instance, include common voice query phrases such as *near me* or *how to* in your content.

>> **Improve content relevance and quality.** AI search engines prioritize content that's relevant and offers substantial value to the user. Follow these simple steps to enhance user experience and keep visitors on your website or mobile interface longer:

- Use AI tools to analyze top-performing content in your market niche and identify key topics and questions that your audience is interested in.

- Create comprehensive, well-researched content that addresses these topics and questions.

- Make use of headings, subheadings, and bullet points for better readability.

- Add engaging multimedia content, such as videos and infographics.

>> **Leverage AI for personalized user experiences.** Personalization is key to enhancing UX and improving SEO rankings with AI search engines. Use AI to analyze user behavior and preferences to deliver personalized content recommendations, product suggestions, and targeted promotions. Implement chatbots to provide instant assistance and guide users through your website.

As an example, Netflix uses AI algorithms to recommend movies and TV shows based on individuals' viewing habits. This strategy significantly enhances the user experience and encourages longer session durations.

Maximizing Your SEO Efforts

You can incorporate AI tools and techniques into several aspects of your company's SEO practices. A holistic approach to this piece of your marketing presence — powered by AI — propels SEO from mere optimization to a strategic, insight-driven endeavor. Specifically, you can leverage AI for

>> **Keyword and metadata research:** Helps you create content that not only reaches, but also engages, the target audience effectively. When AI helps with your research, SEO strategies can become more aligned with the constantly changing user trends and competitive SEO dynamics, where different companies fight to rank higher in the search results pages. (I go into more detail about this form of research in the following section.)

>> **Content development and optimization:** Streamline the creation process and ensure that content aligns with user intent and preferences. Using AI's help, you can improve your content's SEO quality, user engagement, and sales conversion rates (see the section "Automating content optimization," later in this chapter).

>> **The link-building process:** For both your websites and mobile interfaces, adding AI tools to the mix for building links not only makes identifying and securing high-quality backlinks more efficient (as discussed in the section "Building SEO links," later in this chapter) but also ensures that efforts align closely with overall SEO strategy and goals.

>> **Predictive SEO:** Enables marketers to be proactive rather than reactive in their SEO strategies. This approach — engaging predictive AI tools — not only enhances the effectiveness of content and SEO efforts, but also ensures that businesses remain agile and responsive to ever-changing user needs and search engine evolutions. Check out the section "Harnessing predictive SEO," later in this chapter, for all the details.

Streamlining keyword and metadata research

The heart of SEO today involves writing content that includes the appropriate *keywords* and *metadata*, which are signals used by the search engines to determine the rankings of the websites in response to a query. Arguably, those same elements are foundational to creating search generative experiences (SGEs), too. (See the section "Describing Search Generative Experiences [SGEs]," earlier in this chapter.) Therefore, you absolutely have to nail the keywords and metadata that you use as a foundation for creating content. Fortunately, AI can help with creating your SGE-ready content.

Integrating AI into keyword and metadata research strengthens SEO practices by making them more dynamic, precise, and user-focused. Here are specific ways that AI can help SEO professionals and marketers, along with insights into implementing these strategies and examples of useful tools:

>> **Predictive analysis for trending keywords:** AI algorithms can analyze search data and social media trends to identify emerging keywords before those keywords become popular with users. This early keyword optimization gives marketers a competitive edge.

Tools such as Google Trends (http://trends.google.com) and Semrush's Keyword Magic Tool (www.semrush.com/features/keyword-magic-tool) leverage predictive analytics to spot trends. For instance, an AI tool may flag the phrase *sustainable home goods* as an emerging trend. A distinction such as this enables brands to pivot their content focus accordingly and write strong SEO content that responds to that phrase, even before the trend peaks.

>> **Semantic search optimization:** AI's capability to understand the context and intent behind search terms and queries means that SEO isn't just about the keywords anymore. The goal is to create content that genuinely aligns with the context that users are searching for.

Tools such as Clearscope (www.clearscope.io) or MarketMuse (www.marketmuse.com) analyze top-performing content to recommend semantically related keywords. This approach ensures that content for a search for *best running shoes* encompasses terms such as *lightweight running sneakers* and *durable running footwear,* closely matching user intent.

>> **Personalization of content strategy:** By analyzing user behavior, AI helps tailor keywords and metadata to specific audience segments. Resulting SEO strategies effectively resonate with various audiences and their preferences.

Marketing platforms such as HubSpot (www.hubspot.com) or Salesforce Marketing Cloud (www.salesforce.com/eu/marketing/) help you create segmented content strategies. For example, AI analysis may reveal a preference for eco-friendly travel options among millennials; that information provides a guide for focusing a travel agency's SEO content on this area.

>> **Automation of keyword and metadata tagging:** Automating the process of tagging content with relevant keywords and metadata saves time and ensures consistency across content. AI-powered SEO tools such as Yoast SEO (http://yoast.com) suggest optimal keywords and metadata based on content analysis. When analyzing a blog post about vegan recipes, for instance, an AI tool can automatically suggest adding *plant-based cooking* and *easy vegan meals* as metadata tags.

Automating content optimization

Using AI for automating content development and optimization allows you to fine-tune content to the intended audience and enables precision, personalization, and efficiency in ways previously unattainable by the more traditional writing and publishing content manually.

The following strategies demonstrate how leveraging AI can transform content strategy and delivery:

>> **Personalize content.** AI can dissect and understand user data and, thus, tailor content dynamically, enhancing user engagement significantly. A notable example is Spotify's use of AI to curate personalized playlists, an offering that has been instrumental in boosting user engagement and subscription rates. Tools such as Salesforce's Einstein (www.salesforce.com/products/einstein) can help you customize content across various channels based on user interactions and preferences.

>> **Enhance SEO.** AI tools, such as Moz (http://moz.com) and MarketMuse (www.marketmuse.com), can optimize content for search engines, identify gaps in content, and suggest actionable improvements. Users leveraging these insights have reported significant improvements in SERP (search engine results page) rankings and *organic reach* (visibility of content among its desired audience without any paid advertising investments to support it).

>> **Streamline content creation.** Automated content generation tools such as OpenAI's GPT-4 (http://openai.com/gpt-4), Writer (https://Writer.com), and Jasper (www.jasper.ai) can produce draft articles, social media posts, and even e-mail campaigns. This automation can lead to a more efficient content-production process, and marketers have reported significant time savings and increased output without compromising quality.

>> **Predict content success.** Platforms such as Optimizely (www.optimizely.com), Contently (https://contently.com), and others use AI to evaluate content against a myriad of performance indicators, predicting success and suggesting optimizations. Such predictive capabilities enable marketers to allocate resources more effectively, prioritizing content with the highest potential for engagement and impact.

>> **Optimize for voice search.** As voice search becomes increasingly prevalent, AI tools can help optimize content, focusing on conversational keywords and queries. Integrating voice search optimization into content strategies can capture a growing segment of voice-first users (users who prefer to use voice to search over typing in search terms), enhancing visibility across digital assistants and smart devices.

>> **Improve engagement by using AI chatbots.** Integrating AI-powered chatbots on digital platforms can offer instant support and personalized content recommendations. This functionality not only boosts engagement, but also gathers insights into user preferences, which may inform future content strategies.

Building SEO links

AI technologies have transformed *link building* (meaning the process of acquiring hyperlinks from other websites to your own to improve search engine ranking), a cornerstone of SEO strategy. You can use AI tools to identify link-building opportunities, automate outreach, and evaluate the quality of potential link sources. The following list gives you some specific opportunities that you can use to leverage AI for link building:

>> **Identify link opportunities.** AI tools can scour the internet to identify high-quality, relevant sites that you can establish as potential *backlinks* (links that you can provide on your own page that go to supportive content). By analyzing content relevance, domain authority, and web traffic, AI can help pinpoint the most beneficial link-building opportunities.

Tools such as Ahrefs (`https://ahrefs.com`) and Majestic (`https://majestic.com/`) provide comprehensive databases and AI-driven insights to streamline this process. For instance, you may use Ahrefs to discover authoritative blogs in the niche of *sustainable living* and identify those blogs that have high user engagement but low external links as prime targets for outreach.

>> **Automate outreach for link building.** AI-powered customer relationship management (CRM) and e-mail marketing tools, such as BuzzStream (`www.buzzstream.com`) or Mailshake (`https://mailshake.com`), allow you to automate personalized outreach campaigns to potential link partners. These platforms can segment audiences, personalize messages based on the recipient's interests or recent content, and schedule follow-ups. These actions increase the efficiency and success rate of link-building efforts.

For example, the ECOgardener company (specializing in eco-friendly gardening tools and supplies) started an automated campaign targeting webmasters of gardening blogs, resulting in a 20 percent positive response rate and several high-quality backlinks.

>> **Evaluate link quality.** Beyond identifying opportunities, AI can assess the quality and potential impact of backlinks. By examining factors such as site relevance, link context, and the historical performance of similar links, AI tools can predict the value of a prospective link.

Semrush's Backlink Audit tool (`www.semrush.com/backlink_audit`), for example, uses AI to evaluate the *toxicity* of existing backlinks (whether those links are indeed trusted, factual, and useful) and suggest new, high-quality linking opportunities. A digital marketing agency may use this feature to strengthen a client's backlink profile, removing or disavowing low-quality links and focusing on acquiring valuable ones.

>> **Analyze competitors' links.** AI algorithms can analyze competitors' backlink profiles, offering insights into their link-building strategies and revealing untapped linking opportunities. Tools such as Link Explorer by Moz (`https://moz.com/link-explorer`) analyze thousands of links in seconds, providing detailed reports on where competitors are getting their links and how those links contribute to their SEO performance. By studying these patterns, an SEO strategist can uncover overlooked niches or platforms, such as industry forums or collaboration opportunities with influencers in related fields.

>> **Predict link performance.** Some AI tools offer predictive analytics that can forecast the potential SEO impact of a new backlink before you acquire that backlink. SEO managers can then prioritize their link-building efforts based on predicted outcomes, focusing resources on the most impactful links. This technology has the potential to significantly optimize the return on investment (ROI) of link-building campaigns by focusing on links that offer the greatest boost to search rankings.

Harnessing predictive SEO

Harnessing *predictive SEO* (the practice of forecasting future search trends and optimizing content proactively) by using AI tools allows you to anticipate changes, adapt strategies in real time, and stay ahead of trends. Predictive SEO uses data analytics, machine learning (ML), and other AI technologies to forecast future trends in user behavior, search demand, and content effectiveness.

Here are specific strategies to effectively implement predictive SEO:

>> **Forecast search trends.** Utilize AI tools to analyze search data and predict future trends, which can give your business a competitive advantage by enabling you to create or update content that meets emerging demands. As I mention in the section "Streamlining keyword and metadata research," earlier in this chapter, Google's AI-powered tool, Google Trends, offers insights into search trend trajectories, helping marketers identify and capitalize on rising queries. For instance, a digital marketing team may use Google Trends to spot an uptick in interest for *home workout equipment* early in each year and develop targeted content before the peak search period.

>> **Optimize content strategy with predictive analysis.** AI platforms such as MarketMuse (www.marketmuse.com) and BrightEdge (www.brightedge.com) use predictive analytics to suggest content topics and optimization strategies that are likely to perform well. These tools analyze historical data and current market trends to recommend content creation and optimization actions. A content manager can leverage MarketMuse to predict the performance of different content themes on their blog, focusing efforts on those predicted to generate the most engagement and traffic.

>> **Improve user experience with predictive user behavior analysis.** AI can analyze user interaction data to predict future behaviors and preferences, enabling websites to tailor experiences to meet anticipated needs. Tools such as Crazy Egg (www.crazyegg.com) provide *heatmapping* (a color-coded representation of data) and visitor insights, predicting areas of a website that will likely attract a lot of attention and suggesting layout or content adjustments accordingly. An e-commerce site may use these insights to redesign product pages, placing high-demand items in areas predicted to draw more visitor focus.

>> **Anticipate the impact of algorithm changes on SEO.** AI-driven SEO tools such as Moz Pro (https://moz.com/products/pro) offer the capability to simulate and predict the impact of search engine algorithm updates on a website's ranking. By analyzing past updates and current website performance, these tools can forecast potential changes in rankings and suggest preemptive optimizations. You may use this feature to tweak your website's content and technical SEO elements in anticipation of a confirmed Google algorithm update, minimizing negative impacts on your site's search visibility.

>> **Implement predictive link-building strategies.** You can also employ AI to forecast the value and potential success of link-building efforts. By using tools such as Semrush (www.semrush.com) — which assesses the quality of potential backlink sources and predicts the impact of these links on SEO — you can prioritize your outreach efforts more effectively. For example, you can identify and focus on acquiring backlinks from domains that have rising authority in niche markets, as predicted by Semrush's analytics.

Knowing the AI Tools to Use with SEO

Each tool listed in Table 5-1 comes with unique capabilities and artificial intelligence (AI)–driven insights. These tools can help you make informed decisions, streamline workflows, and significantly improve the effectiveness of your SEO strategies.

TABLE 5-1   **AI Tools That Help with SEO**

Tool	Website	Uses
Ahrefs	`https://ahrefs.com`	Predicts keyword trends and analyzes the search landscape
BrightEdge	`www.brightedge.com`	Provides content performance metrics, recommendations for optimization, and insights into competitive strategies
BuzzSumo	`https://buzzsumo.com`	Analyzes content across the web for insights into what content performs best for any topic or competitor and identifies key influencers
Clearscope	`www.clearscope.io`	Provides keyword and content recommendations for better search engine rankings
Google Trends	`http://trends.google.com`	Analyzes the popularity of top search queries in Google Search across various regions and languages
MarketMuse	`www.marketmuse.com`	Offers content planning, creation, and optimization assistance, identifying content gaps and opportunities for improving topical authority
Moz Pro	`https://moz.com/products/pro`	Offers site audits, keyword research, and backlink analysis, as well as predicting the potential impact of SEO strategies on your site's performance
Semrush	`www.semrush.com`	Provides keyword research, SEO audits, competitor analysis, and insights to improve SEO, pay-per-click (PPC), and content marketing strategies
SpyFu	`www.spyfu.com`	Analyzes your competitors' search marketing strategies, offering insights into competitors' keywords, ad variations, and SEO tactics
Surfer SEO	`https://surferseo.com`	Analyzes and compares your content against top-performing pages in search engine results and offers guidelines to improve content relevance and SEO performance

Chapter **6**

Fine-Tuning Content with Localization and Translation

No matter what kind of content creation you do, if you want to reach a global audience, you must keep localization and translation in mind. *Translation*, or the process of translating words from one language to another, is just a small part of the larger process known as localization. *Localization* refers to the process of making a product, article, video, or anything involving language meet the needs of a particular audience. In addition to translation, localization also takes into account the culture, expectations, local standards, and legal requirements of the target market.

Businesses that market in multiple countries can't run effectively without strong localization and translation strategies. Historically, businesses applied these efforts to localizing and translating the company's website content, but they now extend the practice to all digital advertising and many customer relationship management (CRM) programs, too. AI can play an important role in making the process of localization and translation more efficient and effective.

Consider a multinational e-commerce platform, such as Amazon, which localizes its website for different countries so that it can enhance the shopping experience worldwide. Amazon accomplishes this goal by translating product descriptions, adapting currency and measurement units, and tailoring the user interface to reflect local tastes and legal requirements. Customers expect this localization from every multinational brand from which they purchase. This level of localization not only makes a company accessible but also builds trust and loyalty among users by showing respect for their language and culture.

Leveraging localization and translation activities to adapt your business content ensures that digital advertising, marketing campaigns, products and services, and all communications are relevant and user-friendly across various geographical and linguistic landscapes. In this chapter, I describe underlying principles of cultural awareness, strategies, and best practices for using AI in your localization and translation efforts, and the tools that you can find to help you along the way.

Exploiting AI for Localization and Translation

Using AI in your approach to localization efforts can make those efforts more efficient and workable, whether you're a marketer for a small business or a Fortune 500 company. At a basic level, AI-powered translation services, such as Google Translate, can drastically improve the speed and accuracy of translating web content on-the-fly. These services enable small businesses to reach international markets without the prohibitive costs of traditional translation services.

AI can also tailor digital advertising and marketing based on geographic and linguistic data, allowing companies to run localized campaigns that resonate with the target audience. For instance, Netflix uses AI not only to translate but also to recommend content by analyzing viewing patterns in different regions. This two-pronged approach helps to ensure that its suggestions are culturally relevant and engaging for each unique user base.

Capturing cultural context

Understanding the cultural context of your intended audience is crucial when localizing and translating so that you can create effective digital content — your website copy, social media campaigns, or CRM newsletters, for example. You must ensure that the adapted content not only translates linguistically, but also aligns with local customs, values, and behaviors. Infusing your translations with an attention to culture can significantly impact audience reception and engagement.

For instance, a social media campaign that acknowledges local holidays and traditions can foster a stronger connection with the audience than generic content developed by a marketing team and then translated. Similarly, CRM newsletters that reference local events or consumer habits can draw a tighter connection with the consumer and boost loyalty.

The cultural context encompasses more than just language — it includes humor, idioms, symbols, and societal norms, all of which can vary dramatically from one region to another. Ignoring these elements when localizing content can lead to misunderstandings and offend audiences or simply result in content that fails to engage its intended audience.

REMEMBER

Don't think only about your marketing content that appears in text. AI tools can assist with subtitling and captioning for video content, too, which can help ensure that your multimedia materials are accessible to a broader audience.

Harnessing multilingual large language models

A relatively recent development in the world of generative AI involves the development of multilingual large language models (LLMs). A multilingual LLM is an advanced AI system designed to understand, generate, and process text across multiple languages. It leverages vast amounts of text data from various languages to learn linguistic patterns, idioms, and cultural nuances, which enables it to perform a wide range of language-related tasks. For example:

>> **For translation activities,** multilingual LLMs can seamlessly convert text from one language to another while maintaining the original meaning, tone, and context. This capability is crucial for businesses and organizations aiming to communicate effectively in a global market, ensuring that business messaging resonates with diverse audiences.

>> **For localization activities,** these models go beyond mere translation, adapting content to align with specific cultural norms and preferences. Multilingual LLMs can localize marketing materials, websites, and software applications to make products and services more accessible and appealing to users worldwide.

Although these tools are still emerging and aren't perfectly primed for marketing use cases, you can still evaluate them in the context of your marketing translation and localization efforts. As with any AI tools, they also require human oversight. Table 6-1 lists LLMs that you may find useful.

TABLE 6-1 **LLMs for Localization and Translation**

Development Company	LLM	What It Is and Does
OpenAI	GPT-4	Understands and generates text in multiple languages, enabling diverse applications, including translation, content creation, and conversation
Google	mT5 (Multilingual Text-to-Text Transfer Transformer)	An extension of the T5 model, trained on a large multilingual data set, mT5 excels at translation, summarization, and question-answering tasks across languages
Meta	XLM-R (Cross-lingual Language Model — Roberta)	Improves language understanding across many languages, focusing on tasks such as text classification and sentiment analysis
Hugging Face	BERT (Bidirectional Encoder Representations from Transformers) Multilingual	Built on Google's BERT architecture, this model supports more than 100 languages for tasks such as named-entity recognition and question answering
Microsoft	Turing Multilingual Language Model	Used in applications such as translation, content moderation, and more efficient search algorithms

To use ChatGPT (GPT-4) for translation, follow these steps:

1. **Identify the text that you want to translate and indicate the source and target languages.**

    Keep in mind that ChatGPT's capabilities for translation may vary from language to language.

2. **Input the text into ChatGPT and clearly mention the translation request once more by sharing which language you want to translate it to.**

    ChatGPT processes the text by using its understanding of multiple languages to generate a translation that appears immediately below your input.

3. **Review the translation for accuracy.**

    Keep in mind that ChatGPT is a powerful tool, but it may not always match the quality of a professional human translator, especially for complex or nuanced texts.

REMEMBER

If you're a small business marketer, accessing the other multilingual LLMs listed in Table 6-1 is a little more complex. And as with ChatGPT, reviewing the results for accuracy is critical. The models are reliant on the data used to train them, and the data can result in translations that include bias and cultural insensitivity.

Applying AI's capabilities

Advancements in AI technology enable content creators to produce a variety of localized versions of their work more efficiently and to provide a digital experience that feels deeply personalized. For example, you can customize AI-generated visual content to reflect cultural symbols, motifs, and color schemes that appeal to specific audiences.

REMEMBER

Customer expectations have increased dramatically over the last few years, as evidenced by a 2023 Salesforce article titled "What Are Customer Expectations, and How Have They Changed?" — not to spoil it, but subtitled "Customer expectations hit all-time highs." (To access this article, go to www.salesforce.com and enter "customer expectations" in the search text box. The article should pop up in the results.) Customers expect brands to understand them and talk to them on their terms in ways that they appreciate and relate to. Using AI to effectively translate and localize all forms of content makes the effort required to meet heightened customer expectations much cheaper and quicker to do.

AI tools offer sophisticated solutions that can help your business navigate the cultural complexities and linguistic challenges of localizing and translating your customer-facing content. You can take advantage of these capabilities of AI tools and language models to fine-tune your websites, advertising, and online marketing:

>> **Broad, inclusive data analysis:** AI tools can analyze large data sets to identify cultural trends, preferences, and sensitivities specific to different audience segments. For example, AI-powered content analysis tools can scrutinize social media behavior, search queries, and online discussions across various cultures to glean insights into what content resonates in which regions. Because cultural trends and preferences can shift quickly, AI tools that continuously analyze online communications and train on real-time data are the most valuable.

>> **Content adaptation for local relevance:** AI can assist in the localization process by identifying and adapting content that must be customized for cultural relevance. These adaptations may include modifying color schemes on a website to match cultural preferences or adjusting the tone and style of a customer relationship management (CRM) newsletter to align with local communication norms.

>> **Language adjustment to retain content essence:** Certain AI models can detect and adapt to subtle linguistic and cultural nuances, a capability that helps ensure that translations maintain the original message's intent, humor, and emotional tone. For instance, if you need to develop copy for a multinational campaign, choose AI tools that can suggest language adjustments to avoid cultural taboos and embrace local expressions. When you use these tools to translate, they don't literally translate the text word-for-word, but ideally include the local flavor — idioms, for example — that keeps the essence of the communication whole.

REMEMBER

Although scores of AI tools can help you with translation, localization, personalization, and sentiment analysis for all your customer-facing content, having a human eye to look over what the AI engines generate is essential. Sometimes, AI engines get it wrong (less so now than before, but it still happens). You don't want to risk damage to your brand or your relationship with your customers by an AI-generated bad translation or a missed cultural nuance.

TIP

Engage AI tools to help personalize content at scale — for the entire breadth of your business's reach — and enable your marketers to create variations of a campaign that speak directly to the cultural context of each segment of their global audience. AI-powered *transcreation* (a term for adapting content creatively and culturally by using AI to maintain its original intent and emotional impact across languages and cultures) can help create culturally relevant and creative translations of your brand messaging that resonates with local audiences.

Checking out AI tools you can use

In this section, I introduce some specific AI tools that you can find to assist with localization and translation. Tables 6-2 and 6-3 list tools for consumer and enterprise use, respectively. Neither table offers an exhaustive list, and many other AI localization and translation tools exist, each with its own strengths and weaknesses. Research and compare various tools to find the best fit for your specific needs.

TABLE 6-2   ## Consumer AI Tools for Translation

Tool	Website	Features
DeepL	www.deepl.com	A neural machine tool focused on European languages (see Chapter 5 for more information on neural networks)
Google Translate	http://translate.google.com	A free tool that supports more than 100 languages and can translate text, speech, and web pages
Microsoft Translator	http://translator.microsoft.com	A cloud-based translation platform that offers text and speech translation, as well as real-time conversation translation
Babelfish	www.babelfish.com	Uses human editors and AI to provide translations in more than 75 languages
iTranslate	https://itranslate.com	An app that supports more than 40 languages and offers text, voice, and offline translation capabilities
Phrase	https://phrase.com	Localization and translation platform featuring automation, AI customization, workflow orchestration, and analytics
Wordbee	www.wordbee.com	A management platform that offers AI-powered translation, localization, and project management tools, as well as a community of translators

TABLE 6-3   ## Enterprise AI Tools for Translation

Tool	Website	Features
Acrolinx	www.acrolinx.com	A content creation and translation management platform that works across multiple languages and channels
RWS Tridion	www.rws.com/content-management/tridion	A content management and translation management platform that offers AI-powered translation, localization, and project management tools
Sitecore	www.sitecore.com	A customer experience platform that offers AI-powered translation and localization capabilities, as well as tools for managing and delivering personalized customer experiences
Drupal	https://new.drupal.org/home	An open-source content management platform that offers AI-powered translation and localization capabilities through various modules and integrations
WordPress	https://wordpress.org	A content management platform that offers various AI-powered translation and localization plug-ins, such as WPML and Polylang

(continued)

TABLE 6-3 *(continued)*

Tool	Website	Features
HubSpot	www.hubspot.com	A marketing, sales, and customer-service platform that offers AI-powered translation and localization capabilities, as well as tools for managing and delivering personalized customer experiences
Salesforce	www.salesforce.com	A customer relationship management platform that offers AI-powered translation and localization capabilities, as well as tools for managing and delivering personalized customer experiences
IBM Watsonx	www.ibm.com/watsonx	An AI platform that offers various language translation and localization tools, including machine translation, natural language understanding, and natural language generation through its Watson Language Translator
Lilt	http://lilt.com	A platform that uses AI and human editors to provide translations in more than 50 languages
Smartcat	www.smartcat.com	A management platform that offers translation, localization, and project management tools
Google Cloud Translation	http://cloud.google.com/translation	A cloud-based translation platform that offers AI-powered translation and localization capabilities, as well as tools for managing and delivering personalized customer experiences

Adopting Core Strategies for Localization

To harness AI effectively for localization and translation, you can adopt several core strategies that ensure your digital content is both accurately translated and also culturally relevant and engaging. Some of these strategies may be more appropriate for larger organizations, but understanding them can help you determine your own language translation strategies, even if you're marketing for a smaller business. Increasingly, you can find companies that cater to small and medium businesses, offering to assist in building functionality to support localization and translation strategies.

Leveraging machine learning

You can leverage machine learning for contextual translation by using these tools and practices:

>> **Training AI models by using domain-specific data:** Customize machine learning models by using industry-specific data sets to improve the accuracy of translations. These data sets can help ensure that your efforts correctly translate technical and professional jargon. You can also use *natural language processing* (NLP), which analyzes and interprets natural language, allowing for more accurate translations and localizations.

REMEMBER

The quality of the data used to train an AI tool directly impacts the quality of the translations it produces. Ensure that the training data is high-quality, relevant, and aligned with your brand's tone and style.

>> **Using neural machine translation (NMT):** Employ *NMT,* which uses neural networking to predict the possibility of a sequence of words, to understand and translate entire sentences or paragraphs at the same time, rather than word-by-word. NMT tools can capture context (see the section "Capturing cultural context," earlier in this chapter) and reduce errors, thus providing more fluid and natural translations.

>> **Implementing post-editing processes:** Use AI to flag translations that may require human review. Combining the efficiency of AI with the nuanced understanding of human translators helps you refine content for local markets.

Adopting AI-driven cultural adaptation tools

Check out AI algorithms, tools, and techniques that can help you customize and personalize your content for the culture of the customers you want to reach:

>> **Analyze cultural preferences with AI.** Analyze local consumer behavior and preferences, allowing for the adaptation of content, images, and design elements to match local tastes.

>> **Deploy sentiment analysis.** Gauge the emotional tone of content and adjust messaging so that it's culturally appropriate and it resonates with the target audience's values and expectations.

>> **Customize content for regional trends.** Dynamically update content based on trending topics, local news, and cultural events, ensuring that the brand remains relevant and engaged with local communities.

Enhancing personalization and localization efficiency

AI tools and systems, by design, can add efficiency to workflows. In the case of localization and translation, the following list highlights areas where AI can strategically streamline processes and learn in real time:

>> **Automating content localization workflows:** Streamline the localization process. Specifically, AI can identify content that needs translation and also assign tasks and manage workflows to accomplish the translation and reduce time-to-market for localized content.

TIP

Consider implementing a *translation memory system,* which stores previously translated content in a database. You can access this database to retrieve and reuse previously translated content — a practice that can reduce costs and improve efficiency.

>> **Personalizing user experiences at scale:** Tailor digital experiences, including website content, social media, and e-mail marketing. AI can learn to recognize individual user preferences and local cultural norms so that it can enhance content aimed at increasing user engagement and satisfaction.

>> **Continuous learning and improvement:** Learn from user interactions and feedback to continuously improve the quality of translations and the effectiveness of localized content. You can use machine learning (ML) algorithms that train by using large data sets of previously translated content to identify patterns and relationships between languages. Doing so can help ensure that digital experiences remain relevant and compelling over time. In addition, these ML practices can help improve the accuracy of translations and reduce the need for human intervention.

Controlling quality when using AI

Using AI for quality control in localization and translation can help improve accuracy, efficiency, and consistency in your marketing content and campaigns. Here are some tips and tricks for teaming up with AI effectively in your quality-control activities:

>> **Use human post-translation editing.** Although AI-powered translation and localization efforts are highly accurate, you may want to add a human post-translation editing phase to refine the AI's output and ensure it meets the desired level of quality that you want for your localization efforts.

TIP

AI tools can be helpful and efficient, but a human editor should review and polish translations, especially for critical content such as branding materials, taglines, and mission statements.

>> **Integrate your localization and translation tools with other marketing tools.** Real-time localization and translation solutions often integrate with popular marketing tools, such as content management systems (CMSs), customer relationship management (CRM) software, and marketing automation platforms. Making sure that these systems work together adds fluidity and consistency to your marketing content and messages.

>> **Use a hybrid approach.** When I talk about a *hybrid approach* for your localization and translation, I mean combining human translation with machine learning algorithms. Adding human knowledge and experience with languages and cultures to your AI-driven translation efforts can help ensure that the translation is accurate and culturally relevant.

TIP

Combine the strengths of both human translators and AI tools to achieve the best results. AI tools can handle large volumes of content quickly and accurately, and human translators can review and refine the translations to ensure that they meet your brand's standards.

>> **Use a glossary and a style guide.** Basic reference materials — such as a glossary and style guide — can infuse localization and translation output with an extra polished feel. You can create a glossary of technical terms and jargon, as well as a style guide (which specifies formatting, tone, and other style issues), which AI and humans can reference during the translation and review processes. When you share these references with all team members involved in the process, you can help to ensure consistency in translation output.

>> **Monitor and analyze.** Continuously monitor and analyze the performance of the AI-powered localization and translation solutions that you use to identify areas for improvement. If you find that the solution is not meeting your needs, either determine the settings you can adjust to increase the accuracy of your translations or change the solutions completely.

Examining Real-Time Localization and Translation Solutions

Real-time localization and translation solutions use AI to translate and localize content in real time. This speedy processing allows businesses to reach new markets and engage with customers of varying languages and cultures immediately when those customers have questions. In the following sections, you can get a look at how real-time localization and translation solutions work, their benefits, and their applications in marketing.

Seeing how real-time solutions work

Real-time localization and translation solutions use AI algorithms that train on vast amounts of data, which include text in multiple languages and content that reveals cultural nuances. For example, the idiom "break a leg" in English would translate into German literally, implying a harmful wish. This type of training enables the AI to learn patterns and relationships between languages so that it generates more accurate translations and localizations.

The foundation for and process of real-time localization and translation involves several phases:

» **Content analysis:** AI algorithms analyze the source content and identify the most critical elements that require localization or translation. This process, known as *content segmentation,* ensures that the AI translates or localizes only the parts of the content that are required to convey the primary message from the original language to the relevant target audience.

» **Translation memory:** Memory-based translation, also known as *translation memory,* is a technique that stores previously translated content in a database. When similar content is encountered again, the AI can draw upon this database to produce consistent, high-quality translations, which reduces the need for human intervention. The section "Enhancing personalization and localization efficiency," earlier in this chapter, discusses the use of translation memory.

» **Real-time translation:** The trained AI models, along with natural language processing (NLP) algorithms, enable real-time translation of text, speech, or other forms of communication. In marketing, your business can take advantage of the real-time aspects of AI processing to quickly adapt its content for various regions and languages, ensuring that your messaging reaches a global audience.

» **Localization:** Localization goes beyond translation, encompassing not only language but also cultural adaptations, formatting, and content optimization for a specific region. AI-powered localization solutions analyze the source content and adapt it to the target culture, considering local preferences, norms, and regulations.

Recognizing the benefits of real-time solutions

Real-time localization and translation solutions enable businesses to reach new markets and engage with their audience in various languages and cultures, with the goal of improving their customers' experience and driving growth and revenue. The benefits of using these solutions are numerous, including

>> **Cost savings:** Reduce or limit the need for human intervention, saving businesses time and money.

>> **Increased efficiency:** Reach new markets and engage with a new customer base quickly.

>> **Improved accuracy:** AI algorithms that train on vast data resources can help ensure that translations are accurate and culturally relevant. This increased accuracy reduces the risk of misunderstandings or miscommunications. When the solutions use translation memory (see the preceding section), the accuracy is further improved.

>> **Enhanced customer experience:** Provide your customers with a more personalized and engaging experience. The goal is to increase customer satisfaction and loyalty.

Applying real-time solutions in marketing

Real-time localization and translation solutions can help your business efficiently and effectively adapt your marketing strategies for a global audience. Here are some of the solutions' numerous applications in marketing:

>> **Website localization:** Localize your business's websites for various markets and customer bases. This localization helps ensure that your online marketing presence is felt globally. And don't forget about search engine optimization (SEO); optimize your translated content for local search engines by using local keywords and phrases to improve visibility and drive organic traffic.

REMEMBER

For websites especially, collaborate with local teams and in-country experts to ensure that your translations are accurate, culturally relevant, and aligned with local preferences.

» **Content marketing:** Because you can create content in one language and translate it into multiple languages by using real-time localization and translation solutions, you can more quickly produce content that resonates with your target audience, regardless of their language or location.

» **Social media marketing:** Engage with your audience on platforms other than your business's own websites or shopping sites.

» **E-mail marketing:** Connect with your audience on a direct, personal level, regardless of their language or location.

» **Advertising:** Reach your target audience in different markets and languages.

5

AI at Home

Contents at a Glance

CHAPTER 1: **Relying on AI to Improve Human Interaction**................................ 435

CHAPTER 2: **Using AI to Address Medical Needs** 445

CHAPTER 3: **Leveraging AI in Education**........................ 465

CHAPTER 4: **Using GenAI in the Real World**................... 481

CHAPTER 5: **Financial Planning and Other Money Matters** 491

CHAPTER 6: **Retirement and Estate Planning** 501

Chapter **1**

Relying on AI to Improve Human Interaction

P eople interact with each other in myriad ways. Few people realize, in fact, just how many different ways communication occurs. When many people think about communication, they think about writing or talking. However, interaction can take many other forms, including eye contact, tonal quality, and even scent.

An example of the computer version of enhanced human interaction is the electronic "nose," which relies on a combination of electronics, biochemistry, and artificial intelligence to perform its task and has been applied to a wide range of industrial applications and research (see `tinyurl.com/488jfzut`). In fact, the electronic nose can even "sniff out" diseases (see `tinyurl.com/28cfcjek`).

This chapter concentrates more along the lines of standard communication, however, including body language. You gain a better understanding of how AI can enhance human communication through means that are less costly than building your own electronic nose.

AI can also enhance the manner in which people exchange ideas. In some cases, AI provides entirely new methods of communication, but in many cases, AI provides a subtle (or sometimes not so subtle) method of enhancing existing ways to exchange ideas. Humans rely on exchanging ideas to create new technologies, build on existing technologies, or learn about technologies needed to increase an individual's knowledge. Ideas are abstract, which makes exchanging them particularly difficult at times, so AI can provide a needed bridge between people.

At one time, if someone wanted to store their knowledge to share with someone else, they generally relied on writing. In some cases, they could also augment their communication by using graphics of various types. However, only some people can use these two forms of media to gain new knowledge; many people require more, which is why online sources such as YouTube have become hugely popular. Interestingly enough, you can augment the power of multimedia, which is already substantial, by using AI, and this chapter tells you how.

This chapter also helps you understand how an AI can give you almost superhuman sensory perception. Perhaps you want that electronic nose after all; it does provide significant advantages in detecting scents that are significantly less aromatic than humans can smell. Imagine being able to smell at the same level as a dog does (which uses 100 million aroma receptors, versus the 1 million aroma receptors that humans possess). It turns out there are two ways to achieve this goal: monitors that a human accesses indirectly and direct stimulation of human sensory perception.

Developing New Ways to Communicate

Communication involving a developed language initially took place between humans via the spoken versus written word. The only problem with spoken communication is that the two parties must appear near enough together to talk. Consequently, written communication is superior in many respects because it allows time-delayed communication that doesn't require the two parties to ever see each other. The three main methods of human nonverbal communication rely on

>> **Alphabets/Iconographs:** The abstraction of components of human words or symbols

>> **Language:** The stringing together of words or symbols to create sentences or convey ideas in written form

>> **Body language:** The augmentation of language with context

The first two methods are direct abstractions of the spoken word. They aren't always easy to implement, but people have been implementing them for thousands of years. The body-language component is the hardest to implement because you're trying to create an abstraction of a physical process. Writing helps convey body language using specific terminology, such as that described at `tinyurl.com/27newjbf`. However, the written word falls short, so people augment it with symbols, such as emoticons and emojis (you can read about their differences at `tinyurl.com/9jyc5n4n`). The following sections discuss these issues in more detail.

Creating new alphabets

The introduction to this section mentions two new alphabets used in the computer age: emoticons and emojis (`tinyurl.com/wjsw8te5` and `emojipedia.org`). The sites where you find these two graphical alphabets online can list hundreds of them. For the most part, humans can interpret these iconic alphabets without much trouble because the alphabets resemble facial expressions; an application lacks the human sense of art, however, so computers often require an AI just to figure out which emotion a human is trying to convey by using the little pictures. Fortunately, you can find standardized lists, such as the Unicode emoji chart at `tinyurl.com/j4bdmm3m`.

Emoticons are an older technology, and many people are trying their best to forget them (but they likely won't succeed because emoticons are easy to type, though you might recall the movie titled *The Emoji Movie*). You can also turn your selfies into emojis (see "The 7 Best Free Apps to Turn Selfies Into Emojis, Stickers, and More" at `MakeUseOf.com`). Many people have a hard time figuring out emojis, so you can check Emojipedia to see what they mean.

REMEMBER

Humans have created new alphabets to meet specific needs since the beginning of the written word. Emoticons and emojis represent two of many alphabets that you can count on humans creating as the result of the internet and the use of AI. In fact, it may actually require an AI to keep up with them all. However, it's equally important to remember that some characters are lost as time progresses. For example, check out the article "10 Letters That Didn't Make the Alphabet" at `https://tinyurl.com/zzsjzcfc`.

Working with emojis and other meaningful graphics

Many text references are now sprinkled with emojis and other iconography. Most of the references you see online today deal with emojis and emoticons, either removing them or converting them to text.

It's not uncommon to find bits and pieces of other languages sprinkled throughout a text, and these words or phrases need to be handled in a meaningful way.

The problem with translating certain languages into a form in which they can act as input to a natural language processing (NLP) AI model is that the concept of the language differs from English. For example, when working with Chinese, you deal with ideas rather than with pronunciation, as you do with English.

Some situations also require that you process meaningful graphics because part of the text meaning is in the graphic. This sort of translation need commonly arises in technical or medical texts. The article "How Image Analysis and Natural Language Processing Can Be Combined to Improve Precision Medicine," by Obi Igbokwe, at `https://tinyurl.com/k7djha34`, discusses how to accomplish this task.

REMEMBER

The point of these various translations of nontext into a textual form is that humans communicate in many ways, and AI can help make such communication easier and improve comprehension. In addition, using AI to perform NLP makes it possible to look for patterns, even in text that is heavily imbued with nontext elements.

Automating language translation

The world has always had a problem with the lack of a common language. Yes, English has become pervasive — though it's still not universal. Having someone translate between languages can be expensive, cumbersome, and error-prone, so translators, though necessary in many situations, aren't necessarily the ideal answer, either. For those who lack the assistance of a translator, dealing with other languages can be quite difficult, which is where applications such as Google Translate come into play.

Google Translate offers to automatically detect the language for you. What's interesting about this feature is that it works extremely well in most cases. Part of the responsibility for this feature is the Google Neural Machine Translation (GNMT) system. It can examine entire sentences to make sense of them and provide better translations than applications that use phrases or words as the basis for creating a translation (see `tinyurl.com/8by975xx` for details).

TECHNICAL STUFF

What is even more impressive is that GNMT can translate between languages even when it has no specific translator, using an artificial language, an *interlingua*. However, you should realize that an interlingua doesn't function as a universal translator; it's more of a universal bridge. Say that the GNMT doesn't know how to translate between Chinese and Spanish. However, it can translate between Chinese and English and between English and Spanish. By building a 3D network representing these three languages (the interlingua), GNMT is able to create its own translation between Chinese and Spanish. Unfortunately, this system doesn't work for translating between Chinese and whale language because no method is available yet to understand and translate whale language in any human language. Humans still need to create a base translation for GNMT to do its work.

Incorporating body language

A significant part of human communication occurs with body language, which is why the use of emoticons and emojis is important. However, people are becoming more used to working directly with cameras to create videos and other forms of communication that involve no writing. In this case, a computer could possibly listen to human input, parse it into tokens representing human speech, and then process those tokens to fulfill a request, similar to the way Alexa and Google Home (and others) work.

REMEMBER

Unfortunately, merely translating the spoken word into tokens won't do the job, because the whole issue of nonverbal communication remains. In this case, the AI must be able to read body language directly. The article "Computer Reads Body Language" (https://tinyurl.com/49yrz3s5) from Carnegie Mellon University discusses some of the issues that developers must solve to make reading body language possible. The picture at the beginning of the article gives you some idea of how the computer camera must capture human positions to read the body language, and the AI often requires input from multiple cameras to make up for such issues as having part of the human anatomy obscured from the view of a single camera. The reading of body language involves interpreting these human characteristics:

>> Posture

>> Head motion

>> Facial expression

>> Eye contact

>> Gestures

Of course, other characteristics must be considered, but if an AI can even get these five areas down, it can go a long way toward providing a correct body-language interpretation. In addition to body language, current AI implementations consider characteristics like tonal quality, which makes for an extremely complex AI that still doesn't come close to doing what the human brain does seemingly without effort.

TECHNICAL STUFF

After an AI can read body language, it must also provide a means to output it when interacting with humans. Given that reading body language (facial expressions, body position, placement of hands, and other factors) is in its infancy, robotic or graphical presentation of body language is even less developed.

Exchanging Ideas

An AI doesn't have ideas because it lacks both intrapersonal intelligence and the ability to understand. However, an AI can enable humans to exchange ideas in a manner that creates a whole that is greater than the sum of its parts. In many cases, the AI isn't performing any sort of exchange. Instead, the humans involved in the process perform the exchange by relying on the AI to augment the communication process. The following sections provide additional details about how this process occurs.

Creating connections

A human can exchange ideas with another human, but only as long as the two humans know about each other. The problem is that many experts in a particular field don't actually know each other — at least not well enough to communicate effectively. An AI can perform research based on the flow of ideas that a human provides and then create connections with other humans who have that same (or similar) flow of ideas.

One way in which this type of convergence occurs is in social media sites such as LinkedIn, where the idea is to create connections between people based on a number of criteria. A person's network becomes the means by which LinkedIn uses AI to suggest other potential connections. Ultimately, the purpose of these connections from the user's perspective is to gain access to new human resources, make business contacts, create a sale, or perform other tasks that LinkedIn enables.

Augmenting communication

To exchange ideas successfully, two humans need to communicate well. The only problem is that humans sometimes don't communicate well, and sometimes they don't communicate at all. The issue is one of translating not only words but also ideas. The societal and personal biases of individuals can preclude the communication because an idea for one group may not translate at all for another group. For example, the laws in one country might make someone think in one way, but the laws in another country could make another person think in an entirely different manner.

Theoretically, an AI could help communication between disparate groups in numerous ways. Of course, language translation (assuming that the translation is accurate) is one of these methods. However, an AI could provide cues to what is and isn't culturally acceptable by prescreening materials. Using categorization, an AI could also suggest aids like alternative graphics and other elements to help communication take place in a manner that helps both parties. For example, you could replace an image of a Red Cross with a Red Crescent or both to represent first aid in different cultures.

Defining trends

Humans often base ideas on trends. To visualize how the idea works, however, other parties in the exchange of ideas must also see those trends, and communicating using this sort of information is notoriously difficult. AI can perform various levels of data analysis and present the output graphically. The AI can analyze the data in more ways and more quickly than a human can, so the story the data tells is specifically the one you need it to tell. The data remain the same; the presentation and interpretation of the data change.

Studies show that humans relate better to graphical output than to tabular output, and graphical output definitely makes trends easier to see. You generally use tabular data to present only specific information; graphics always work best for showing trends. Using AI-driven applications can also make creating the right sort of graphical output for a particular requirement easier. Not all humans see graphics in precisely the same way, so matching a graphical type to your audience is essential.

Using Multimedia

Most people learn by using multiple senses and multiple approaches. A doorway to learning that works for one person may leave another completely mystified. Consequently, the more ways in which a person can communicate concepts and ideas, the more likely it is that other people will understand what the person is trying to communicate. Multimedia normally consists of sound, graphics, text, and animation, though some multimedia does more.

AI can help with multimedia in numerous ways. One of the most important involves the creation, or *authoring,* of the multimedia. You find AI in applications that help with everything from media development to media presentation. For example, when translating the colors in an image, an AI may provide the benefit of helping you visualize the effects of those changes faster than trying one color combination at a time (the brute force approach).

MULTIMEDIA AND ADDRESSING PEOPLE'S FUNCTIONAL NEEDS

Most people have some particular functional need relating to how they take in and understand information. Considering such needs as part of people's use of multimedia is important. The whole intent of multimedia is to communicate ideas in as many ways as possible so that just about everyone can understand the ideas and concepts you want to present.

Even when a presentation as a whole uses multimedia successfully, individual ideas can become lost when the presentation uses only a single method to communicate them. For example, communicating a sound only aurally (instead of adding closed captioning to a visual presentation, for example) almost guarantees that only those with excellent hearing will receive the idea. A subset of those with the required hearing level still won't get the idea because it may appear as only so much noise to them, or they simply won't learn through the limited method offered in the presentation.

Using as many methods as possible to communicate each idea is essential if you want to reach as many people as possible. Even if you get the information in one way, also getting it another way provides useful confirmation that you understood correctly.

After using multimedia to present ideas in more than one form, those receiving the ideas must process the information. A secondary use of AI relies on the use of neural networks to process the information in various ways. Categorizing the multimedia is now an essential use of the technology. However, in the future, you can look forward to using AI to help in 3D reconstruction of scenes based on 2D pictures. Imagine police personnel being able to walk through a virtual crime scene with every detail faithfully captured.

People used to speculate that various kinds of multimedia would appear in new forms. For example, imagine a newspaper that provides Harry Potter-like dynamic displays. Most of the technological pieces are available today, but the issue comes down to the market: For a technology to become successful, it must have a market — that is, a means for paying for itself.

Embellishing Human Sensory Perception

One way that AI truly excels at improving human interaction is by augmenting humans in one of two ways: by allowing them to use their native senses to work with augmented data or by augmenting the native senses to do more. The following sections discuss both approaches to enhancing human sensing and, therefore, improving communication.

Shifting data spectrum

When performing various kinds of information gathering, humans often employ technologies that filter or shift the data spectrum with regard to color, sound, touch, or smell. Humans still use native capabilities, but some technology changes the input such that it works with that native capability. One of the most common examples of spectrum shifting is astronomy, in which shifting and filtering light enables people to see astronomical elements, such as nebula, in ways that the naked eye can't — thereby improving our understanding of the universe.

Teaching a robot to feel by touch is in its infancy, as described at `tinyurl.com/ukjscsye` and `tinyurl.com/y998s2h8`. Most efforts now focus on helping the robot work better by using tactile responses as part of manipulating its machinery, such as the light touch needed to grasp an egg versus the heavier touch required to lift a barbell. As this technology moves far enough forward, it might become possible for various AIs to communicate with humans via direct touch or the description of various kinds of touch.

Shifting and filtering colors, sounds, touches, and smells manually can require a great deal of time, and the results can disappoint even when performed expertly, which is where AI comes into play. An AI can try various combinations far faster than a human can and can locate the potentially useful combinations with greater ease because an AI performs the task in a consistent manner.

TECHNICAL STUFF

The most intriguing technique for exploring our world, however, is completely different from what most people expect. What if you could smell a color or see a sound? The occurrence of *synesthesia,* which is the use of one sense to interpret input from a different sense, is well documented in humans — see `tinyurl.com/2s9tb284`. For more about the general understanding of the current state of synesthesia, see `www.psychologytoday.com/us/basics/synesthesia`.

Augmenting human senses

As an alternative to using an external application to shift a data spectrum and somehow make that shifted data available for use by humans, you can augment human senses. In augmentation, a device, either external or implanted, enables a human to directly process sensory input in a new way. The idea is an old one: Use tools to make humans ever more effective at performing an array of tasks. In this scenario, humans receive these two forms of augmentation:

» **Physical augmentation** of human senses already takes place in many ways, and it's guaranteed to increase as humans become more receptive to various kinds of implants. For example, night vision glasses now allow humans to see at low light levels, with high-end models providing color vision controlled by a specially designed processor.

   In the future, eye augmentation or replacement may allow people to see any part of the spectrum. This augmentation or replacement would be controlled by the person's thoughts so that people would see only that part of the spectrum needed to perform a specific task.

» **Intelligence augmentation** requires more intrusive measures but also promises to allow humans to exercise far greater capabilities. Unlike AI, intelligence augmentation (IA) has a human actor at the center of the processing — the human provides the creativity and intent that AI now lacks.

Chapter **2**

Using AI to Address Medical Needs

M edicine is complicated. There's a reason it can take 15 or more years to train a doctor, depending on specialty. The creation of new technologies, approaches, and other factors all conspire to make the task even more complex. At some point, it becomes impossible for any lone person to become proficient in even a narrow specialty. This is a prime reason that an irreplaceable human requires consistent, logical, and unbiased help in the form of an AI. The process begins by helping the doctor monitor patients in ways that humans would simply find impossible. That's true because the number of checks is high, the need to perform them in a certain order and in a specific way is critical, and the potential for error is monumental.

Fortunately, people have more options today than ever before for doing many medical-related tasks on their own. For example, the use of games enables a patient to perform some therapy-related tasks alone yet receive guidance from an application to help the person perform the task appropriately. Improved pros-thetics and other medical aids also enable people to become more independent of professional human assistance.

Today, a doctor can fit a patient with a monitoring device, perform remote monitoring, and then rely on an AI to perform the analysis required for diagnosis — all without the patient's spending more than one visit at the doctor's office (the one required to attach the monitoring device). In fact, in some cases, such as glucose monitors, the patient may even be able to buy the required device at the store so that the visit to the doctor's office becomes unnecessary as well. One of the more interesting additions to the healthcare arsenal during medical emergencies, such as pandemics, is the use of *telepresence,* which enables the doctor to interact with a patient without physically being in the same room.

Implementing Portable Patient Monitoring

A medical professional isn't always able to tell what's happening with a patient's health by simply listening to their heart, checking vital signs, or performing a blood test. The body doesn't always send out useful signals that let a medical professional learn anything at all. In addition, some body functions, such as blood sugar, change over time, so constant monitoring becomes necessary.

Going to the doctor's office every time you need one of these vitals checked would prove time-consuming and possibly not all that useful. Older methods of determining certain body characteristics required manual, external intervention on the part of the patient — an error-prone process in the best of times. For these reasons, and many more, an AI can help monitor a patient's statistics in a manner that's efficient, less error-prone, and more consistent, as described in the following sections.

Wearing helpful monitors

All sorts of monitors fall into the helpful category. In fact, many of these monitors have nothing to do with the medical profession yet produce positive results for your health. Consider the Moov monitor (`welcome.moov.cc`), which monitors both heart rate and 3D movement. The AI for this device tracks these statistics and provides advice on how to create a better workout. You actually get advice on, for example, how your feet are hitting the pavement while you're running and whether you need to lengthen your stride. The point of devices like these is to ensure that you get the sort of workout that will improve your health without risking injury.

Mind you, in case a watch-type monitoring device is too large, Oura (`ouraring.com/oura-experience`) produces a ring that monitors about the same number of stats that Moov does, but in a smaller package. This ring even tracks how you sleep to help you get a good night's rest. Interestingly enough, many of the pictures on the Oura site look nothing like a fitness monitor, so you can have fashion and health all in one package.

Of course, if your only goal is to monitor your heart rate, you can buy devices such as Apple Watch (`support.apple.com/en-us/HT204666`) that also provide some level of analysis using an AI. All these devices interact with your smartphone, so you can possibly link the data to still other applications or send it to your doctor as needed.

Relying on critical wearable monitors

A problem with some human conditions is that they change constantly, so checking intermittently doesn't really get the job done. Glucose, the statistic measured for diabetics, is one statistic that falls into this category: The more you monitor the rise and fall of glucose each day, the easier it becomes to change medications and lifestyle to keep diabetes under control.

Devices such as the K'Watch (`www.pkvitality.com/ktrack-glucose`) provide this type of constant monitoring, along with an app that a person can use to obtain helpful information on managing their diabetes. Of course, people have used intermittent monitoring for years; this device simply provides that extra level of monitoring that can help make having diabetes more of a nuisance than a life-altering issue. (The number of remote patient-monitoring devices produced by various companies is growing; see the article at `tinyurl.com/c52uytse` for details.)

Some devices are truly critical, such as the wearable cardioverter defibrillator (WCD), which senses your heart condition continuously and provides a shock should your heart stop working properly (see `tinyurl.com/jkzbv3x8` for details). This short-term solution can help a doctor decide whether you need the implanted version of the same device. There are pros and cons to wearing one, but then again, it's hard to place a value on having a shock available when needed to save a life. The biggest value of this device is the monitoring it provides. Some people don't actually need an implantable device, so monitoring is essential to prevent unnecessary surgery.

MEDICAL DEVICES AND SECURITY

A problem with medical technology of all sorts is the potential security vulnerabilities that they may have. Having an implanted device that can be hacked is terrifying. The article at https://tinyurl.com/rjnathrw describes what could happen if someone hacked any medical device. Fortunately, according to many sources, no one has died yet.

However, imagine your insulin pump or implanted defibrillator malfunctioning as a result of hacking and consider what damage it could cause. The Federal Drug Administration (FDA) has published guidance on medical device security, as described in the article at https://tinyurl.com/w24cvfc7, but these guidelines apparently aren't enforced. In fact, this article goes on to say that the vendors are actively pursuing ways to avoid securing their devices.

AI isn't responsible for insecure devices, but AI could get the blame should a breach occur. The point is that you need to view all aspects of using AI, especially when it comes to devices that directly affect humans, such as implantable medical devices.

Using movable monitors

The number and variety of AI-enabled health monitors on the market is staggering. For example, you can buy an AI-enabled toothbrush that monitors your brushing habits and provides you with advice on a better brushing technique. Oral B also has a number of toothbrushes that benefit from the use of AI: tinyurl.com/35xdarjj. When you think about it, creating a device like this presents a number of hurdles, not the least of which is keeping the monitoring circuitry happy inside the human mouth. Of course, some people may feel that the act of brushing their teeth has little to do with good health, but it does (see tinyurl.com/6mfzc4hk).

Creating movable monitors generally means making them both smaller and less intrusive. Simplicity is also a requirement for devices designed for use by people with little or no medical knowledge. One device in this category is a wearable electrocardiogram (ECG). Having an ECG in a doctor's office means connecting wires from the patient to a semiportable device that performs the required monitoring. The KardiaMobile smartphone app (kardia.com/?sscid=31k8_y6azo) provides the ECG without using wires, and someone with limited medical knowledge can easily use it. As with many devices, this one relies on your smartphone to provide needed analysis and make connections to outside sources as needed.

REMEMBER

Current medical devices work just fine, but many aren't portable. The point of creating AI-enabled apps and specialized devices is to obtain much-needed data when a doctor actually needs it rather than have to wait for that data. Even if you don't buy a toothbrush to monitor your technique or an ECG to monitor your heart, the fact that these devices are small, capable, and easy to use means that you may still benefit from them at some point.

Making Humans More Capable

Many of the current techniques for extending the healthy range of human life (the segment of life that contains no significant sickness), instead of just increasing the number of years of life, depend on making humans more capable of improving their own health in various ways.

REMEMBER

You can find any number of articles that tell you 30, 40, or even 50 ways to extend this healthy range, but often, it comes down to a combination of eating right, exercising enough and in the right way, and sleeping well. Of course, with all the advice out there, figuring out just which food, exercise, and sleep technique would work best for you could be nearly impossible.

The following sections discuss ways in which an AI-enabled device might make the difference between having 60 good years and 80 or more good years.

Using games for therapy

A gaming console can serve as a powerful and fun physical therapy tool. Both Nintendo Wii and Xbox 360 see use in many different physical therapy venues. The goal of these and other games is to get people moving in certain ways. The game automatically rewards proper patient movements, and a patient receives therapy in a fun way. Making the therapy fun means that the patient is more likely to do it and get better more quickly. You can now find informative studies about the use of games and their combination with telehealth strategies at `tinyurl.com/b6bt29r7` and `etsplaytherapy.org/collections/video-games-in-play-therapy`.

Of course, movement alone, even when working with the proper game, doesn't ensure success. In fact, someone could develop a new injury when playing these games. The Jintronix add-on for the Xbox Kinect hardware standardizes the use of this game console for therapy (`tinyurl.com/uzetv2tc` and `tinyurl.com/y42rmh4v`), increasing the probability of a positive outcome.

BIAS, SYMPATHY, AND EMPATHY

Getting good care is the initial aim of anyone who enters any medical facility. The assumption is that the care is not only the best available but also fair. An AI can help in the medical field by ensuring that technical skills remain high and that no bias exists whatsoever — at least, not from the AI's perspective.

Humans will always exhibit bias because humans possess intrapersonal intelligence (as described in Book 1, Chapter 1). Even the kindest, most altruistic person will exhibit some form of bias — generally subconsciously — creating a condition in which the caregiver sees one thing and the patient another (see the section in Book 1, Chapter 2 about considering the five mistruths in data). However, the people being served will almost certainly notice, and their illness will likely amplify the unintended slight. Using an AI to ensure evenhandedness in dealing with patient issues is a way to avoid this issue. The AI can also help caregivers discover mistruths (unintended or otherwise) on the part of patients in relating their symptoms, thereby enhancing care.

The medical field can be problematic at times because technical skill often isn't enough. People frequently complain about the lack of a good bedside manners on the part of medical staff. The same people who want fair treatment also somehow want empathy from their caregivers (making the care unfair because it's now biased). Empathy differs from sympathy in context. People exhibit *empathy* when they're able to feel (almost) the same way the patient does and build a frame of reference with the patient. (It's important to note that no other person feels precisely the same way as you do because no other person has had precisely the same experiences you've had.)

Two exercises in the "Considering the software-based solutions" section, later in this chapter, help you understand how someone could build a frame of reference to create empathy. An AI could never build the required empathy because an AI lacks the required sense of awareness and understanding to create a frame of reference and the intrapersonal intelligence required to utilize such a frame of reference.

Unfortunately, empathy can blind a caregiver to true medical needs because the caregiver is now engaging in the mistruth of perspective by seeing only from the patient's point of view. So, medical practitioners often employ *sympathy,* through which the caregiver looks in from the outside, understands how the patient might feel (rather than how the patient does feel), and doesn't build a frame of reference. Consequently, the medical practitioner can provide needed emotional support but also see the need to perform tasks that the patient may not enjoy in the short term. An AI can't accomplish these tasks because an AI lacks intrapersonal intelligence and doesn't understand the concept of perspective well enough to apply it appropriately.

Considering the use of exoskeletons

One of the most complex undertakings for an AI is to provide support for an entire human body. That's what happens when someone wears an *exoskeleton* (essentially a wearable robot). An AI senses movements (or the need to move) and provides a powered response to the need. The military has excelled in the use of exoskeletons and is actively seeking more (see tinyurl.com/3sawszrb and tinyurl.com/tu525nuw for details). Imagine being able to run faster and carry significantly heavier loads as a result of wearing an exoskeleton. The video at tinyurl.com/p489dvj gives you just a glimpse of what's possible. The military continues to experiment, and those experiments often feed into civilian uses. The exoskeleton you eventually see (and you're almost guaranteed to see one at some point) will likely have its origins in the military.

Industry has also gotten in on the exoskeleton technology. In fact, the use of exoskeletons is becoming ever more important as factory workers age (tinyurl.com/9h9j8sh9). Factory workers currently face a host of illnesses because of repetitive stress injuries. In addition, factory work is incredibly tiring. Wearing an exoskeleton not only reduces fatigue but also reduces errors and makes the workers more efficient. People who maintain their energy levels throughout the day can do more with far less chance of being injured, damaging products, or hurting someone else.

The exoskeletons in use in industry today reflect their military beginnings. Look for the capabilities and appearance of these devices to change in the future to look more like the exoskeletons shown in movies such as *Aliens*. The real-world examples of this technology are a little less impressive but will continue to gain in functionality.

Exoskeletons can enhance people's physical abilities in downright amazing ways. For example, a *Smithsonian* magazine article discusses using an exoskeleton to enable a child with cerebral palsy to walk (tinyurl.com/nyb5p3kd). Not all exoskeletons used in medical applications provide lifelong use, however. For example, an exoskeleton can help a person who experienced a stroke walk without impediment (tinyurl.com/439syr72). As the person regains skills, the exoskeleton provides less support until the wearer no longer needs it. Some users of the device have even coupled their exoskeleton with other products, such as Amazon's Alexa (see tinyurl.com/tp3kyxfk for details).

REMEMBER

The overall purpose of wearing an exoskeleton isn't to make you into Iron Man. Rather, it's to cut down on repetitive stress injuries and help humans excel at tasks that currently prove too tiring or just beyond the limits of their bodies. From a medical perspective, using an exoskeleton is a win because it keeps people mobile longer, and mobility is essential to good health.

Addressing Special Needs

The creation of highly specialized prosthetics and other devices, many of them AI-enabled, has been a game changer for many people. For example, these days, some people can run a marathon or go rock climbing, even if they've experienced paralysis or the loss of a limb (tinyurl.com/ce958ms9). Then again, some people are using exoskeletons for an arguably less-than-productive use like "dancing" (tinyurl.com/tt9rvxdj).

REMEMBER

It's a fact of life that just about everyone faces a challenge in terms of capabilities and skills. At the end of a long day, someone with 20/20 vision might benefit from magnifying software to make text or graphical elements larger. Color-translation software can help someone who sees the full spectrum of human color take in details that aren't normally visible. As people age, they tend to need assistance to hear, see, touch, or otherwise interact with common objects. Likewise, assistance with tasks such as walking could keep someone in their own home for their entire life. The point is that using various kinds of AI-enabled technologies can significantly help everyone to have a better life, as discussed in the sections that follow.

Considering the software-based solutions

Many people using computers today rely on some type of software-based solution to meet specific needs. One of the most famous of these solutions is a screen reader called Job Access With Speech (JAWS) (`tinyurl.com/nwjn8jmb`), which tells you about display content using sophisticated methods. As you might imagine, every technique that both data science and AI rely on to condition data, interpret it, and then provide a result likely occurs within the JAWS software, making it a good way for anyone to understand the capabilities and limits of software-based solutions. The best way to see how this works for you is to download and install the software and then use it while blindfolded to perform specific tasks on your system.

TIP

Accessibility software helps people who live with particular challenges perform incredible tasks. It can also help others understand what it would be like to maneuver through life with that specific challenge. A considerable number of such applications are available, but for one example, check out Vischeck at `https://www.vischeck.com/`. This software lets you see graphics in the same way that people with specific color issues see them. It's not that people with these conditions don't see color — in fact, they see it just fine. But a given color is simply shifted to a different color, so saying *color shifted* is likely a better term, and a term like *color blindness* doesn't apply.

Relying on hardware augmentation

Many kinds of human activity challenges require more than just software to address adequately. The "Considering the use of exoskeletons" section, earlier in this chapter, tells you about the various ways in which exoskeletons see use today

Using AI to Address Medical Needs

in preventing injury, augmenting natural human capabilities, or addressing specific needs (such as enabling a person with paraplegia to walk). However, many other kinds of hardware augmentation address other needs, and the vast majority require some level of AI to work properly.

Consider, for example, the use of eye-gaze systems (eyegaze.com). The early systems relied on a template mounted on top of the monitor. A person with quadriplegia could look at individual letters, and that action would be picked up by two cameras (one on each side of the monitor) and then typed into the computer. By typing commands this way, the person could perform basic tasks at the computer.

Some of the early eye-gaze systems connected to a robotic arm through the computer. The robotic arm could do extremely simple but important actions, such as help users pour a drink or scratch their nose. Modern systems actually help connect a user's brain directly to the robotic arm, making it possible to perform tasks such as eating without assistance. In addition, some newer systems are doing things like restoring a person's sense of touch (www.wired.com/story/this-brain-controlled-robotic-arm-can-twist-grasp-and-feel).

Completing Analysis in New Ways

Using AI in a manner that best suits its capabilities maximizes the potential for medical specialists to use it in a meaningful way. Data analysis is one area in which AI excels. In fact, entire websites are devoted to the role that AI plays in modern medicine, such as the one at tinyurl.com/amanphxc.

Merely taking a picture of a potential tumor site and then viewing the result might seem to be all that a specialist needs to make an accurate diagnosis. However, most techniques for acquiring the required snapshot rely on going through tissue that isn't part of the tumor site, thereby obscuring the output. In addition, a physician wants to obtain the best information possible when viewing the tumor in its smallest stages.

Using AI to help perform the diagnosis not only assists in identifying tumors when they're small and with greater accuracy but also speeds up the analysis process immensely. Time is critical when dealing with many diseases.

As impressive as the detection and speed capabilities of AI are in this area, what truly makes a difference is the capability to combine AI in various ways to perform Internet of Things (IoT) data compilations. When the AI detects a condition in a particular patient, it can automatically check the patient's records and display the relevant information onscreen with the diagnosed scans, as shown in the article at www.ncbi.nlm.nih.gov/pmc/articles/PMC10740686. Now, the doctor has every last piece of pertinent information for a patient before making a diagnosis and considering a particular path.

TIP

To see other amazing uses of AI in medicine, check out the site at tinyurl. com/275mztss.

Relying on Telepresence

In the future, you may be able to call on a doctor to help with a problem and not even visit the hospital or clinic to do it. For that matter, you may be able to call on other professionals in the same way. The use of telepresence in all sorts of fields will likely increase as the availability of professionals in specific areas decreases due to continuing specialization. The following sections discuss telepresence and describe how it relies largely on AI in some respects.

Defining telepresence

The term *telepresence* simply means to be in one place and seem as though you're in another. The *ScienceDirect* article at tinyurl.com/xs2sb6sa talks about how telepresence and augmented reality walk side by side to provide special kinds of experiences. Though augmented or virtual reality exists essentially in artificial worlds, telepresence exists in the real world. For example, using telepresence, you might be able to see the Grand Canyon more or less directly without actually being there. The thing that separates telepresence from simply using a camera is that, through the use of sensors, a person experiences telepresence through their own senses. It's almost, but not quite, the same as being there in person.

When the person is also able to interact with the other environment, perhaps through a robot-like device, many people call it *teleoperation*. A gray area exists here because it's hard to tell in many cases precisely where telepresence ends, and teleoperation begins. However, the central idea in both cases is that it feels as though you're actually there.

Considering examples of telepresence

One of the most common uses of telepresence is to reduce costs in hospitals in various ways. For example, a robot might monitor a patient in ways that monitoring equipment can't and then alert either a nurse or a doctor to changes in a patient's condition that the robot isn't designed to handle (tinyurl.com/ypzw52pt). Telepresence means being able to monitor patients from essentially anywhere, especially in their homes, making nursing home stays less likely (tinyurl.com/26tav7zv). In addition, telepresence allows a patient to visit with family when such visits wouldn't be possible for any of a number of reasons.

Telepresence is also making an appearance in factories and office buildings (www.robots4good.com.au/blog/how-telepresence-robots-will-transform-the-way-we-work-robots4good). A security guard is safer in a secure room than walking the rounds. Using a telepresence robot allows guards to patrol the premises without putting themselves at risk. In addition, it's possible to fit a robot with special vision to see things a human guard can't see.

Enforced use of telepresence will likely increase its use and provide an incentive to improve the technology. During the COVID-19 pandemic, many doctors also began to rely on telepresence to maintain contact with their patients. The National Institutes of Health (NIH) also recommended using telepresence for patient-based teaching during the pandemic, which was a problem for many people, especially the older population, as described in the article at tinyurl.com/ykvadwxb. All these pandemic-enhanced uses of telepresence will likely make the technology more common and potentially reduce its cost due to economies of scale.

TIP

The capabilities of the telepresence device determine its usefulness. The site at tinyurl.com/y7sm2ytr shows that the robotic form comes in all sorts of sizes and shapes to meet just about every need.

Understanding telepresence limitations

The problem with telepresence is that humans can quickly become too comfortable using it. For example, many people criticized a doctor who used telepresence, rather than a personal visit, to deliver devastating news to a family (see tinyurl.com/3azcb7w8). In some cases, personalized human touch and interaction is an essential component of life.

Telepresence also can't replace human presence in some situations requiring senses that these devices can't currently offer. For example, if the task requires a sense of smell, telepresence can't support the need at all. Given how often the sense of smell becomes an essential part of performing a task, even in a hospital, overreliance on telepresence can be a recipe for disaster.

TIP

The article at tinyurl.com/w8pbvx78 provides some additional insights into when telepresence may simply be a bad idea.

Devising New Surgical Techniques

Robots and AI now routinely participate in surgical procedures. In fact, some surgeries would be nearly impossible without the use of robots and AI. However, the history of using this technology isn't lengthy. The first surgical robot, Arthrobot, made its appearance in 1983. Even so, the use of these life-saving technologies has reduced errors, improved results, decreased healing time, and generally made surgery less expensive over the long run. The following sections describe the use of robots and AI in various aspects of surgery.

Making surgical suggestions

You can view the whole idea of surgical suggestions in many different ways. Here are three examples:

>> **Analyzing data and suggesting surgical approaches.** An AI might analyze all the data about a patient and provide the surgeon with suggestions about the best approaches to take based on that individual patient's record. The surgeon could decide on the approach, but it would take longer and might be subject to errors that the AI won't make. The AI doesn't grow tired or overlook things; it consistently views all the data available in the same way every time.

>> **Supplying a second opinion during surgery.** Unfortunately, even with an AI assistant surprises still happen during surgery, which is where the next level of suggestion comes into play. The patient receives the benefit of what amounts to a second opinion to handle unforeseen complications during surgery. Mind you; the device isn't actually doing anything more than making already existing research, which was created by other doctors, readily available in response to surgeon requests; no real thinking is involved.

>> **Analyzing preparatory scans.** Preparing for surgery also means analyzing all those scans that doctors insist on ordering. Speed is an advantage that AI has over a radiologist. Products such as Enlitic (www.enlitic.com), a deep learning technology, can analyze radiological scans in milliseconds — up to 10,000 times faster than a radiologist. In addition, the system is 50 percent better at classifying tumors and has a lower false-negative rate (0 percent versus 7 percent) than humans.

Assisting a surgeon

Most robotic help for surgeons today assists, rather than replaces, the surgeon. The first robot surgeon, the PUMA system, appeared in 1986. It performed an extremely delicate neurosurgical biopsy, which is a nonlaparoscopic type of surgery. *Laparoscopic* surgery is minimally invasive, with one or more small holes serving to provide access to an organ, such as a gallbladder, for removal or repair. The first robots weren't adept enough to perform this task.

By 2000, the da Vinci Surgical System provided the ability to perform robotic laparoscopic surgery using a 3D optical system. The surgeon directs the robot's movements, but the robot performs the actual surgery. The surgeon watches a high-definition display during the surgery and can see the operation better than being in the room performing the task personally. The System also uses smaller holes than a surgeon can, reducing the risk of infection.

The most important aspect of the da Vinci Surgical System, though, is that the setup augments the surgeon's native capabilities. For example, if the surgeon shakes a bit during part of the process, the system removes the shake — similarly to how antishake features work with a camera. The system also smooths out external vibrations. The system's setup enables the surgeon to perform extremely fine movements — finer than a human can natively perform, thereby making the surgery far more precise than the surgeon could accomplish alone.

TECHNICAL STUFF

The da Vinci Surgical System is a complex and extremely flexible device. The FDA has approved it for both pediatric and adult surgeries of the following types:

>> Urological surgeries

>> General laparoscopic surgeries

>> General noncardiovascular thoracoscopic surgeries

>> Thoracoscopically assisted cardiotomy procedures

The point behind including all this medical jargon is that the da Vinci Surgical System can perform many tasks without involving a surgeon directly. At some point, robot surgeons will become more autonomous, keeping humans even farther away from the patient during surgery. In the future, no one will actually enter the clean room with the patient, thereby reducing the chances of infection to nearly zero. You can read more about the system at `tinyurl.com/4h44vtyy`.

Replacing the surgeon with monitoring

In *Star Wars,* you see robotic surgeons patching up humans all the time. In fact, you might wonder whether any human doctors are available. Theoretically, robots could take over some types of surgery in the future, but the possibility is still a long way off. Robots would need to advance quite a bit from the industrial sort of applications that you find today. The robots of today are hardly autonomous and require human intervention for setups.

However, the art of surgery for robots is making advances. For example, the Smart Tissue Autonomous Robot (STAR) outperformed human surgeons when sewing a pig intestine, as described at `tinyurl.com/aezx65u3`. Doctors supervised STAR during the surgery, but the robot actually performed the task on its own, which is a huge step forward in robotic surgery.

Performing Tasks Using Automation

AI is great at automation. It never deviates from the procedure, never grows tired, and never makes mistakes as long as the initial procedure is correct. Unlike humans, AI never needs a vacation, a break, or even an 8-hour day (not that many in the medical profession have that luxury, either). Consequently, the same AI that interacts with a patient for breakfast will do so for lunch and dinner as well. So, at the outset, AI has some significant advantages if viewed solely on the basis of consistency, accuracy, and longevity (see the earlier sidebar "Bias, sympathy, and empathy" for areas in which AI falls short). The following sections discuss various ways in which AI can help with automation through better access to resources, such as data.

Working with medical records

One major way in which an AI helps in medicine is with medical records. In the past, everyone used paper records to store patient data. Each patient might also have a blackboard that medical personnel use to record information daily during a hospital stay. Various charts contain patient data, and the doctor might also have notes. Storing all these sources of information in so many different places made it hard to keep track of the patient in any significant way. Using an AI, along with a computer database, helps make information accessible, consistent, and reliable. Products such as DeepMind, a part of Google Health (health.google) enable personnel to mine the patient's information to see patterns in data that aren't obvious.

Predicting the future

Some truly amazing predictive software based on medical records includes Autonomous Health, which uses algorithms to determine the likelihood of a patient's need for readmission to the hospital after a stay. By performing this task, hospital staff can review reasons for potential readmission and address them before the patient leaves the hospital, making readmission less likely. Along with this strategy, Anju (www.anjusoftware.com) helps doctors evaluate various therapies and choose those most likely to result in a positive outcome — again reducing the risk that a patient will require readmission to the hospital.

In some respects, your genetics form a map of what will happen to you in the future. Consequently, knowing about your genetics can increase your understanding of your strengths and weaknesses, helping you to live a better life. Deep Genomics (www.deepgenomics.com) is discovering how mutations in your genetics affect you as a person. Mutations need not always produce a negative result; some mutations actually make people better, so knowing about mutations can be a positive experience, too. Check out the video at tinyurl.com/fjhs638b for more details.

Making procedures safer

Doctors need lots of data to make good decisions. However, with data being spread out all over the place, doctors who lack the ability to analyze that disparate data quickly often make imperfect decisions. To make procedures safer, a doctor needs not only access to the data but also some means of organizing and analyzing it in a manner reflecting the doctor's specialty. Oncora Medical (`www.oncora.ai`) is a product that collects and organizes medical records for radiation oncologists. As a result, these doctors can deliver the right amount of radiation to just the right locations to obtain a better result with a lower potential for unanticipated side effects.

Doctors also have trouble obtaining necessary information because the machines they use tend to be expensive and huge. An innovator named Jonathan Rothberg decided to change all that by using the Butterfly Network (`www.butterfly network.com`). Imagine an iPhone-size device that can perform both an MRI and an ultrasound. The picture on the website is nothing short of amazing.

Creating better medications

Everyone complains about the price of medications today. Yes, medications can do amazing things for people, but they cost so much that some people end up mortgaging their homes to obtain them. Part of the problem is that testing takes a lot of time. Performing a tissue analysis to observe the effects of a new drug can take up to a year. Fortunately, products such as Strateos (`strateos.com`) can greatly reduce the time required to obtain the same tissue analysis to as little as one day.

Of course, better still, would be for the drug company to have a better idea of which drugs are likely to work (and which aren't) before investing any money in research. Atomwise (`www.atomwise.com`) uses a huge database of molecular structures to perform analyses on which molecules will answer a particular need. In 2015, researchers used Atomwise to create medications that would make Ebola less likely to infect others. The analysis that would have taken human researchers months or possibly years to perform took Atomwise just one day to complete.

Drug companies also produce a huge number of drugs. The reason for this impressive productivity, besides profitability, is that every person is just a little different. A drug that performs well and produces no side effects on one person might not perform well at all for another person, and could even do harm. Turbine (`turbine.ai/`) enables drug companies to perform drug simulations so that the drug companies can locate the drugs most likely to work with a particular person's body. Turbine's current emphasis is on cancer treatments, but it's easy to see how this same approach could work in many other areas.

Some companies have yet to realize their potential, but they're likely to do so eventually. One such company is Recursion Pharmaceuticals (`www.recursion.com`), which employs automation to explore ways to solve new problems using known drugs, bioactive drugs, and pharmaceuticals that didn't previously make the grade. The company has had some success in helping to solve rare genetic diseases, and it has a goal of curing 100 diseases in the long term (obviously, an extremely high goal to reach).

Combining Robots and Medical Professionals

Semiautonomous robots with limited capabilities are starting to become integrated into society. In most cases, these robots can perform simple tasks, such as reminding people to take medications and playing simple games, without much intervention. However, when needed, a doctor or another medical professional can take control of the robot from a remote location and perform more advanced tasks by way of the robot. Using this approach means that the person obtains instant help when necessary, reducing the potential for harm to the patient and keeping costs low.

REMEMBER

These sorts of robots are in their infancy now, but expect to see them improve with time. Although these robots are tools to assist medical personnel and can't actually replace a doctor or nurse for many specialized tasks, they do provide the constant surveillance that patients need, along with a comforting presence. In addition, the robots can reduce the need to hire humans to perform common, repetitive tasks (such as dispensing pills, providing reminders, and assisting with walking) that robots can perform quite well even now.

Considering Disruptions That AI Causes for Medical Professionals

As you can see, integrating AI into medical practices is extremely valuable. However, it's not without challenges and disruptions (both positive and negative) for medical professionals themselves. Here are three to consider:

» Change in clinical roles and responsibilities: AI's ability to automate diagnostic processes and analyze vast amounts of medical data can shift the traditional roles of medical professionals. Though AI can enhance diagnostic accuracy and treatment plans, it necessitates changing how physicians and other healthcare providers approach their roles, moving toward a more collaborative model with AI systems.

» Training and adaptation: Integrating AI into healthcare requires medical professionals to acquire new skills related to AI technologies. This includes understanding how AI tools work, interpreting AI-generated insights, and integrating these into clinical decision-making. The need for ongoing education and training to keep up with rapidly evolving AI technologies can be a significant disruption.

» Patient-physician relationship: The introduction of AI into patient care can impact the patient-physician relationship. Though AI can free up time for physicians to focus more on patient interaction by automating administrative tasks, there is a concern that an overreliance on AI could depersonalize care. Ensuring that AI enhances rather than detracts from the human aspects of care is a critical challenge.

IN THIS CHAPTER

» Adapting work and school approaches to AI use

» Understanding critical thinking strategies

» Creating personalized learning opportunities

» Exploring ideas for educators

» Grasping why banning AI from schools is a bad idea

Chapter **3**

Leveraging AI in Education

When generative AI (GenAI) was introduced, students immediately began using it to do their homework. However, many chose to use it not to *help* with their homework but to do it *for* them. Educators weren't amused. A kerfuffle followed as educators and parents fretted that AI was an instrument for cheating and would rob students of their ability to hone critical thinking skills. The worriers were only partly right.

Cheaters are going to cheat, and teachers need to catch them if they can. This undertaking isn't always easy. It can be an especially vexing task when cheaters use ChatGPT or another GenAI tool because they generate text that's difficult to distinguish from human writing. However, educators are adept at catching cheaters despite their ever-changing methods. For decades, educators and teaching assistants have confiscated crib notes, barred calculator use in classes and tests, busted test ringers, checked dutifully for plagiarism, and generally outed the ne'er-do-wells and the ethically impaired. So, really, GenAI brings nothing new to the ongoing need to check for cheaters.

I urge educators and employers to focus on grading or evaluating work based on accuracy, originality, execution, and quality instead of trying to figure out whether an AI tool was used in the process.

Therefore, in this chapter, I don't spend time covering how to cheat because that will be sorted in due time. Instead, this chapter is about how educators can use GenAI to better serve their students by offering more personalized support and instruction. It's also about how GenAI can reinvent education. That's probably why (without assuming, of course) you are reading this book — to get the most out of emerging technology. The prompting techniques covered in Book 2 will help you use GenAI in both how and what you teach in the age of AI. You might also want to take a look at Book 3, Chapter 5, to see how different disciplines use GenAI to further help you understand how your students may need to use tools like ChatGPT after graduation.

Using AI Is Here to Stay

Regarding the use of AI for completing assignments, the harm is more likely to come from the use of AI detection tools in the chase for cheaters rather than from cheaters slipping a machine-generated assignment past the gatekeepers. To date, I've never seen an AI detection tool that's accurate or even consistent in labeling works as either AI- or human-made. Yet far too many educators and employers treat these tools as infallible and wield the results as the final word.

Avoiding false accusations of cheating

WARNING

Unfortunately, the people who are falsely accused by these AI detection tools typically have no recourse and can never prove their innocence. These unfortunate souls find their careers and school records irrevocably stained. The harm done by a false positive result is almost incalculable. This practice needs to come to an immediate halt.

To be clear, yes, GenAI does repeat phrases, words, and sentence structures. But so do people. There are no set writing patterns, word choices, sentence structures, or anything else that's uniquely and undeniably associated with GenAI outputs. That's why AI detection tools don't work. There's no sure "tell" to find.

Spotting AI in use by students is a worthless exercise anyway. It's now part of today's existence, for better or worse. Using AI effectively is now a core mission for educators to teach students and a fundamental tool all students must master if they're to navigate their daily lives or be employed.

Accepting the role of AI at school and work

Make no mistake, both educators and students will outlive any current generative AI tool. These early manifestations continue to morph into something more than the sum of their new features or are replaced by competing tools, such is the nature of all living and invented things. Even so, AI is reshaping the world and is firmly entrenched as an integral part of it. Whether AI's presence today is more insidious or illuminating depends entirely on how you see it and use it. For a balance to be struck or the scales to be tipped in favor of all that is good, educators must step up and teach that. You can't teach that if you keep attacking AI use in schools like it's evil incarnate.

AI will be a permanent fixture in life going forward. Of course, it may fade into the background and become the backbone of all the tools rather than function as a standalone as GenAI tools currently do. But AI will never go away. As the Borg on *Star Trek* would say, "Resistance is futile." Better to embrace it and make rules assuming that AI will be used than waste your time and your students' academic lives trying to forbid it and root it out.

REMEMBER

GenAI use requires skill in to get skill out. Yes, that's my way of saying that "garbage in, garbage out" still applies. The quality of the work speaks directly to the skill level of the person who made it, regardless of the type of tool they used. If the quality of work, the originality of thought, the uniqueness in its creativity, or a flawless execution of the task is present, then the person who made it — with or without GenAI's help — earned a grade to match.

Changing the Structure of Education

Speaking of upcoming changes in educational institutions and processes: Some major disruptions are easy to foresee. But these changes won't be the last. Ripple effects will spread across decades as both AI and educators evolve to meet the challenges and opportunities of the day.

GenAI's integration into education is poised to transform both institutional structures and teaching methods significantly. At the core of this transformation is the shift toward personalized learning. Traditionally, students progress through a standardized curriculum at the same pace, but AI allows learning to be tailored to individual needs, pacing, and level of understanding. GenAI can act as a personalized tutor, responding to each student's questions, identifying areas for improvement, and adapting content dynamically. Over time, this can lead to a shift away from age- or grade-based progression toward competency-based advancement, in which students move forward upon mastering the material, which isn't based on time spent in a classroom or memorization skills.

Using AI in tutoring, testing, and updating curriculum

Tutoring and support are also likely to change drastically. Many students currently rely on scheduled, often costly tutoring sessions, which may not always be accessible. GenAI is constantly available as long as limits in tokens or chats aren't exceeded. Provided schools make GenAI accessible to all, even students with little to no private resources can receive instant support, explanations, and feedback. This shift might lead institutions to reconsider how they allocate all resources, potentially allowing teachers to focus more on specialized lessons and support while GenAI handles foundational content review and reinforcement outside the classroom.

Traditional assessment tools might undergo an even more dramatic change. Today's reliance on standardized tests means that knowledge is evaluated periodically, which may not always reflect how much information students understand, retain, and can successfully apply now or going forward. GenAI, however, can offer immediate and ongoing feedback on a student's performance. It can also present the same information in different ways to match individual learning styles to help students grasp difficult concepts and overcome learning obstacles.

REMEMBER

If you're an educator, instead of high-stakes testing, you can move toward continuous assessment, in which students receive ongoing evaluations that may better capture their learning progress. This type of assessment can significantly reduce test-related stress and focus more on actual comprehension and critical thinking development.

The traditional curriculum, which often lags behind the latest knowledge and trends in the real world, also stands to benefit from AI. GenAI's access to a vast amount of information allows you to easily update lesson plans and incorporate the latest research. AI can help ensure that students learn content relevant to their futures, making curriculums more dynamic. This potential for fluid content creation allows you and other teachers to focus on more interactive and practical applications rather than spending time updating static content. Such an approach is better and more efficient in helping students stay aligned with current developments.

Preparing for shifts in educator roles

Your role as an educator will likely shift along with approaches to education. You'll act less as a content deliverer and more as a mentor and learning facilitator. As AI tools take over foundational teaching tasks, you'll have more time to focus on guiding critical thinking, honing intuitive intelligence, sharpening research and fact-checking skills, promoting socio-emotional learning, and cultivating creativity. This role evolution may lead to changes in hiring and training practices, with a growing emphasis on interpersonal skills and adaptability, as well as mastery in integrating AI into classroom management and lesson plans.

Gaining efficiency with AI help for administrative tasks

Administrative tasks, which currently consume significant resources in education, will also likely see gains in efficiency with AI. To be clear, GenAI tools generally can't automate anything beyond the text and images they generate. For example, ChatGPT, at its core, is a text generator, but it can manage some image work behind the scenes with the aid of other GenAI tools, such as the sister application DALL-E. I point that out only to make you aware that you'll need to use GenAI outputs in other software to fully leverage its capabilities.

For example, GenAI can help you with grading student work and tests, tracking student progress, and managing communications with students and parents. It can't complete the tasks for you, but by using GenAI alongside other automation apps, or embedded in specialized automation apps, or as the UI and orchestrator of autonomous AI agent systems, you can automate these processes. Never fear: GenAI is already embedded in most work software, so you have plenty of options available. More will appear on the market soon.

Any way you choose to use GenAI to lighten the administrative load will be instrumental in reallocating resources toward enriching educational experiences or reducing operational costs. This, coupled with AI-enabled flexibility, may give rise to more hybrid learning models, allowing students to participate in a blend of digital and physical classrooms with digital and physical instructors present in either or both environments.

Providing equal access to quality instruction

By making quality education more accessible to geographically isolated or underserved students, AI can contribute to a truly globalized education system. GenAI can act as an equalizer, providing access to quality resources and instruction regardless of location, which can lead to an expansion of international, online educational platforms and credentialing systems. Today, when several countries are experiencing aging populations and too few young people to fill jobs and drive each country's progress further, global education may go far in tapping into highly skilled and educated labor forces in countries with younger populations. Conversely, it can help older people teach and store skills and information that may otherwise be lost to time.

As AI becomes more integrated into education, institutions may transform into adaptable, personalized, and globally accessible models. Instead of rigid structures, schools may become more fluid environments that equip students with skills for an increasingly dynamic world, reshaping both the experience and the objectives of education.

Flipping the Teaching Model

As I mention in the chapter introduction, some educators, parents, and employers are concerned that students who use AI will miss out on developing critical thinking skills. This problem will likely self-correct to a degree, but it can also be prevented by flipping the teaching model.

Currently, students are taught information and then quizzed. With GenAI, the student must first ask the right question to unlock the information, an approach that reverses how critical thinking is traditionally taught and tested.

GenAI's outputs are only as good as the inputs that a teacher or a student gives the tool. To prompt the AI to deliver the answers they seek, students need to think carefully and critically about how to word their query or command. Teaching them how to think about and write prompts is an effective albeit different way to help them develop critical thinking skills.

Consider and compare the following two examples:

1. *Basic prompt:* "Generate an image of a cat."

   This prompt is straightforward, but it lacks details. The outcome could be any cat — small, large, fluffy, hairless, sitting, jumping, indoors, or outdoors. The result may not be specific to what you want.

2. *Better, strategic prompt:* "Generate an image of a fluffy, orange tabby cat with green eyes sitting on a windowsill. The cat should be looking out at a rainy cityscape in the background, with drops of rain visible on the glass. The setting is cozy, and the cat is surrounded by indoor plants and books."

   Version 2 is much more detailed and specific. By specifying the cat's appearance, the setting, and even the mood (cozy), you increase your chances of getting an image that matches your vision. This prompt demonstrates critical thinking by considering factors like context, environment, and cat's characteristics.

The strategic prompt in the second example illustrates why it's important to think critically: The more detail and clarity you provide, the more likely you are to receive output that meets your expectations. It's about guiding the outcome and ensuring the final product aligns with your vision.

This comparison illustrates why critical thinking helps you get the most out of GenAI. You really can't get far by being vague or lazy about prompting. That's why I advocate grading the quality of a student's work over whether they used tools like Word or ChatGPT. The outcome is invariably the result of their own effort with or without AI tools.

And so, you can teach critical thinking, at least in part, by teaching prompting skills. Here are some benefits of this approach:

>> **It's a win-win for students** because both critical thinking and prompting skills are in high demand by employers. These skills can also improve the quality of life by elevating students' performance in daily life problem-solving.

>> **Prompting and critical thinking will remain necessary and in high demand** for the lifetime of students and likely for generations afterward. Although writing prompts will soon be automated by AI, too, critical thinking will remain as important in commanding and overseeing AI agents as it is now in writing prompts. Consider this scenario:

1. AI like AutoGPT can write prompts, which are useful down the chain of AI agent systems wherein one AI orchestrates several specialized AI bots to work together to complete a bigger task.

2. A user must initiate the action and approve AI decisions along the way. In other words, you would have to write a prompt to get the party started, and then that AI could automate prompts to invite, orchestrate, and manage other AI agents to join in.

3. A human will still have to approve or correct AI agents' actions along the way.

REMEMBER

The evolution of AI agent systems will go a long way toward making AI benefits accessible to everyone, but autonomous AI agents won't eliminate the need for creative and critical thinking. In this age of AI, those who can wield these tools well will prosper, which makes critical thinking skills and prompt engineering excellent job skills for educators to teach — and for educators and students to learn.

Leveraging GenAI to Aid Overworked Educators

If you're an educator, you're notoriously overworked and underappreciated, often juggling a multitude of responsibilities that extend far beyond the classroom and the workday. The advent of GenAI AI tools such as ChatGPT offers a promising solution to alleviate some of this strain.

Getting help with grading assignments

GenAI can assist in grading assignments with a level of depth and analysis that you may not have the time to provide. Further, AI can deliver test scores and evaluations of other forms of student work along with detailed feedback for you and students to act on.

But this process isn't nearly as arduous as you're probably imagining. Indeed, teachers have been quietly using GenAI to grade tests and papers ever since it came out. But it's only recently that schools are beginning to encourage its use. Here's one way you can see for yourself how this process might work for you in grading papers if you were to use ChatGPT Plus to do it. (You can't grade multiple papers in a single prompt, so taking these manual steps may be too slow if you have a large class and many papers to grade.)

1. **Prepare the paper to grade for review by ChatGPT Plus.**

    Depending on whether student "papers" (that is, homework or thesis papers or whatever it is that you're grading) are in digital form or written on an actual sheet of paper, you can

    -   Take a screenshot or a picture of the paper.

    -   Upload the digital document.

REMEMBER

2. **Label and save the image or the document.**

3. **Attach the saved image to the prompt bar.**

4. **Type instruction such as "Grade this paper" or "List correct and incorrect responses on the attached image."**

    If you prompt for a list of right and wrong answers, you can calculate the grade yourself.

5. **Review and fact-check the response.**

    Essentially, make sure that you agree with the score.

6. **Repeat the process on the other student papers.**

Of course, more tools are appearing on the market every day, offering efficient ways to use GenAI for grading tasks. One example is Writable, which can assist you with grading any assignment in Word or Google Doc formats. It comes with more than a thousand prompts, assignments, and the Houghton Mifflin Harcourt curriculum built in for your use. You can edit them, too, if you want. Essaygrader. ai is another GenAI tool specializing in, you guessed it, grading essays.

I'm not endorsing any particular GenAI tool. I'm just trying to give you a sense of what's available. Keep an eye out because more options will hit the market over time.

Exploiting AI for efficient mentoring

GenAI can readily access and identify areas in which each student is struggling and offer personalized suggestions for improvement. This enables you to develop and execute tailored teaching or mentoring plans for each student, enhancing the overall learning experience and hopefully doing so without adding anything to your already full workload.

Moreover, GenAI can perform these tasks in a matter of minutes. It can compute homework, tests, and project scores quickly. This efficiency means that you and your assistants can use AI to score assignments before the end of the workday, freeing up valuable time for other important tasks or for personal pursuits in off-duty hours.

Adapting lessons and admin tasks

GenAI is also a valuable tool for developing or adapting lesson plans. You can generate comprehensive and detailed lesson plans on-demand and fit them to your own requirements as the instructor or to the needs of an individual student. Further, you can customize lesson plans to fit specific classroom needs or a change in learning environments. For example, if you're teaching a unit on the American Revolution, a GenAI tool such as ChatGPT-4o can provide a structured lesson plan complete with objectives, activities, video or audio avatar reenactment scripts, and assessment methods. If you prefer a more concise version, ChatGPT can condense the information accordingly.

Beyond classroom instruction, GenAI can assist you with various administrative tasks. From making a list of classroom supplies needed for specific lessons to completing paperwork required by school administrators, GenAI streamlines these processes, allowing you to focus more on teaching and less on bureaucratic tasks.

TIP

As an educator, you can use AI efficiently to get your private time back without compromising the quality of education you deliver.

Changing How Subjects Are Taught

GenAI is significantly transforming education now and for the future. This transformation is visible in several key areas that involve adapting learning content, including

>> **Personalized learning:** GenAI can adapt educational content to meet the needs of individual students, providing tailored explanations, exercises, and feedback based on each student's level of understanding. For example, a student struggling with algebra might receive step-by-step explanations and additional practice problems specifically designed to address their weak points.

>> **Learning style and access:** GenAI can adapt content according to educational standards set forth in VAK (Visual, Auditory, Kinesthetic) and VARK (which adds Reading/Writing) styles. Because GenAI is available 24/7, students can access help at any time, extending learning opportunities beyond traditional classroom hours.

>> **Student engagement:** GenAI enhances the learning experience by creating interactive content as well as a variety of gamification plans. Imagine a history lesson in which students can engage in a simulated conversation with a historical figure, asking questions and receiving detailed, context-rich responses. This kind of interaction makes learning more dynamic and engaging. Additionally, students benefit from instant feedback on their work, helping them quickly understand and correct mistakes and accelerating the learning process.

REMEMBER

GenAI can also assist in creating worksheets and other educational materials, which saves time and money and typically improves the quality of resources available. For instance, if you're preparing a unit on environmental science, you might use GenAI to generate quizzes and discussion prompts tailored to the specific topics covered in the unit or your field trip.

Providing safer spaces for learning

Language learning is another area in which GenAI is making a substantial impact. Students can practice conversational skills in a new language by engaging in dialogues with the AI, which provides a safe and supportive environment for practice. For example, a student learning Spanish can converse with GenAI, practicing their speaking and listening skills without the fear of judgment. The AI can also explain complex grammar rules and translate phrases, making it easier for students to grasp new languages.

The potential of GenAI is even more expansive. The development of highly sophisticated AI tutors capable of understanding and adapting to a student's unique learning style, pace, and preferences is a certainty on the near horizon. For example, an AI tutor might recognize that a student learns best through visual aids and adjust its teaching methods accordingly, using more diagrams and visual explanations.

Immersive learning environments can also become commonplace, with GenAI integrated into virtual reality (VR) and augmented reality (AR) experiences. Imagine a biology class in which students can virtually explore the human body in 3D or a history lesson in which they can walk through ancient Rome. These immersive experiences make learning more engaging and memorable. Additionally, AI-driven gamified learning platforms can incorporate elements of game design into the curriculum, motivating students through challenges and rewards.

Inclusive education stands to benefit greatly from AI advancements, too. GenAI can provide support for students with disabilities or whose learning journey was interrupted for one reason or another, causing them to fall behind. By offering alternative ways to interact with educational content, these and other obstacles can be overcome. For example, a student with a visual impairment might use text-to-speech features, whereas a student with a hearing impairment might benefit from speech-to-text capabilities.

Further, GenAI can bridge language barriers in diverse classrooms by providing the same lessons in multiple languages as needed, ensuring all students have access to the same quality of education.

Learning collaboratively

Collaborative learning is another area in which AI can make a significant impact. Global classrooms, where students from different parts of the world collaborate on projects, share perspectives, and learn from each other in real time, might become a reality. Imagine a science project in which students from different countries work together to solve a global environmental issue, facilitated by GenAI. GenAI platforms can also support peer-to-peer learning by mediating discussions, providing prompts, and ensuring conversations remain productive and on-topic.

In terms of curriculum improvement, AI can analyze vast amounts of educational data to identify gaps and suggest enhancements. This means that curricula can be continually updated based on new discoveries, societal changes, and technological advancements, keeping education current and forward-looking. For example, if data shows that students are consistently struggling with a particular concept in physics, educators can be alerted to this issue, and GenAI can provide suggestions, strategies, and lesson plans to address it.

REMEMBER

As AI becomes more integrated into education, it's crucial to address ethical considerations such as data privacy, algorithmic bias, and the digital divide. Ensuring that AI tools are used responsibly and equitably is key to maximizing their positive impact on education.

In short, you can leverage GenAI to provide a more effective, enjoyable, and accessible experience for all learners. But that requires that you take a proactive role now in plotting the path forward as an educator. Remember, GenAI does nothing until prompted to do so and then only as prompted. It's up to education leaders and futurists to decide where education is going with AI.

Supporting Special Education Needs

GenAI presents immense potential in special education by helping to tailor support for students with diverse learning needs. Specialized GenAI tools are better for these tasks than the generalized version. It's not as if you can hand any kid a tablet with ChatGPT on it and expect everything to work out somehow. As an educator, you need to design GenAI tools and chatbots to specifically work with special-needs students. You might be able to do that on your own, but you'll probably be more comfortable and successful working with AI scientists or an AI-skilled technologist to make it happen. Look for vendors to produce GenAI tools aimed at delivering services that uniquely assist with this student group.

Here are some major benefits of using GenAI in special education:

>> **Its ability to create customizable learning aids.** For instance, students with dyslexia can benefit from personalized reading exercises that adapt to their pace and learning or coping style. GenAI can generate texts with adjustable complexity, ensuring that students are neither overwhelmed nor under-challenged. Additionally, it can offer real-time assistance, such as breaking down complex sentences or providing synonyms for difficult words, thereby enhancing the student's reading experience and boosting their confidence.

>> **Its capacity to provide behavioral and emotional support.** Students with emotional and behavioral disorders often require consistent support to manage their challenges effectively. GenAI can offer a form of virtual counseling or encouragement. Assigning GenAI to such a role can provide students with strategies to cope with anxiety, stress, or frustration.

REMEMBER

GenAI can guide a student through deep-breathing exercises or help them develop a step-by-step plan to address a particular issue they're facing. However, GenAI isn't a substitute for counselors or mental health professionals.

>> **It's role as a nonjudgmental listener,** which allows students to express their thoughts and feelings freely. This aspect can be particularly therapeutic for those who might find it difficult to open up to others. Just be aware of the serious privacy concerns in sharing private and vulnerable information with any AI tool.

Furthermore, specialized GenAI tools can assist you in supporting students' progress. They can identify patterns indicating that a student is struggling so you can intervene promptly. This proactive approach ensures that students receive the support they need before their challenges become upsetting or more severe.

Delivering Data-Driven Insights for Educators

Data-driven insights have become a cornerstone of enhancing and evaluating teaching effectiveness and student outcomes. GenAI offers one approach to compiling and analyzing data. Indeed, its greatest strength is in data discovery.

REMEMBER

However, it's generally a mistake to replace all other analytics and data tools with GenAI. The smarter plan is to add GenAI to your school's tool chest rather than ditch the tools you already use. I say that because there's substantial value in using analytical tools that you're familiar with over one that introduces a rather long learning curve and sometimes questionable responses. Additionally, the performance, accuracy, and reliability of modern analytics tend to vastly outperform GenAI tools at the moment. There's really no advantage to stopping their use.

Using GenAI tools for efficiency

The role of GenAI tools in education is growing, although their impact on student performance analysis is still under examination. These tools offer several potential benefits. For instance, they can enhance efficiency in task completion, with studies indicating that students, particularly in fields like business informatics, can complete certain tasks more rapidly. Additionally, GenAI can aid students in gathering information and brainstorming ideas more effectively.

However, there are notable limitations and concerns. Research, such as a 2024 study titled "Is it harmful or helpful? Examining the causes and consequences of generative AI usage among university students" published in the *International Journal of Educational Technology in Higher Education*, has linked increased use of GenAI to declining academic performance, as evidenced by lower grade point averages.

Furthermore, the same study found that GenAI usage is associated with increased procrastination and self-reported memory loss. Another significant issue is the need for human oversight. Although GenAI can efficiently analyze text, human judgment remains crucial in interpreting results, particularly in contexts such as course evaluations.

Questionable student progress tracking

Regarding the current state of GenAI in classrooms, the concept of a specialized GenAI tool for comprehensive student progress tracking isn't yet widespread or well established. Although such systems might be in development or undergoing limited testing, they're not commonly used in educational settings. Most research to date focuses on GenAI's impact when used as a general tool rather than as a specialized tracking system. GenAI's ability to accurately track and analyze complex student interactions in real time hasn't been proven or widely implemented. Additionally, concerns about data privacy, accuracy, and the potential for AI bias in educational settings present significant challenges.

TIP

The integration of GenAI tools in education is an evolving field that requires careful consideration of both its benefits and its potential drawbacks.

Banning GenAI Stifles Education

Despite some drawbacks, banning GenAI from schools and education programs is a dire mistake. AI is here to stay, and it's reshaping the nature of work and, indeed, the human experience.

WARNING

If you're an educator who doesn't guide students through this transition into effective use of GenAI, you're doing them an injustice. Navigating and functioning in the world without AI skills will soon be as difficult as getting by without computer skills, smartphones, and internet access.

Adopting a nuanced approach to AI

The better course is to acknowledge that change really is the only constant and that it's your duty as an educator to help students master each new turn. Educators are the ones who move a society forward and enable it to adapt. Teach accordingly.

The decision to ban GenAI in educational settings can have far-reaching consequences, stifling innovation, exacerbating educational inequities, and leaving students unprepared for a future where artificial intelligence (AI) plays an increasingly pivotal role.

One of the most significant drawbacks of banning GenAI is the missed opportunities for innovation in education. GenAI has the potential to revolutionize the way students learn by providing personalized and adaptive learning experiences. For instance, through natural language processing, GenAI can offer tailored feedback on student assignments, helping students understand their mistakes and guiding them toward improvement. This immediate and personalized feedback loop can accelerate learning and comprehension, which traditional methods may not achieve as efficiently.

Additionally, GenAI can assist in creating interactive and engaging educational content, such as virtual simulations and problem-solving scenarios, which can make learning more dynamic and appealing. By banning GenAI, educational institutions may forego these innovative approaches, potentially hindering the evolution of teaching methodologies that better cater to diverse student needs.

Equity and accessibility are also at risk when GenAI is banned. In many educational systems, there's a significant disparity in resources available to students. GenAI can bridge this gap by providing consistent and high-quality educational support to all students, regardless of their socio-economic background. For example, students in underfunded schools may not have access to specialized tutoring or advanced coursework. GenAI can fill this void by offering supplementary educational materials and personalized tutoring sessions, ensuring that all students have the opportunity to succeed. Banning GenAI can widen the educational gap, further entrenching existing inequalities.

Preparing students for the future

Moreover, preparing students for the future workforce necessitates familiarity with AI technologies. As AI becomes increasingly integrated into various industries, the demand for workers who understand and can skillfully interact with

AI systems is growing. By incorporating GenAI into the educational curriculum, students gain hands-on experience with AI, developing critical skills that will be valuable in their future careers.

For instance, students can learn how to leverage AI for research, data analysis, and problem-solving, skills that are highly sought after in fields such as technology, healthcare, and finance. Without exposure to AI technologies like GenAI, students may find themselves at a disadvantage in the job market, lacking the necessary skills to thrive in an AI-driven world.

Bottom line: Banning GenAI in education can have detrimental effects, including missed opportunities for innovation, increased educational inequities, and inadequate preparation for the future workforce. Embracing AI technologies can enhance educational experiences, promote equity, and equip students with the skills they need to succeed in a rapidly evolving world. But GenAI doesn't equal or replace professional human educators. You need both educators and AI to move students to the front line of a quickly evolving and uniquely challenging future.

IN THIS CHAPTER

» **Changing SEO strategies**

» **Siri and Alexa get smarter**

» **A new breed of knowledge assistants rises**

» **Misinformation on-demand**

» **Narrowing human minds**

» **Brain impacts**

Chapter **4**

Using GenAI in the Real World

A s glitzy and even glamorous as GenAI and its outputs can be, it's the usefulness of this tool in managing everyday life that tends to prove its value. Or not. It's the changes to the routine and the mundane — the things you tend to view as constants in your personal and work life — that will be the most disrupted by GenAI and the most challenging to navigate. Life, as you know it, will change in a multitude of ways. Some will be profound, some will be barely noticeable, and others will be harmful.

In this chapter, you gain some insight into what some of these changes are likely to be. There will be more. Many more. But for now, consider these few earthshaking impacts.

Dying Keywords

ChatGPT and its competitors, such as Microsoft Copilot, Google Gemini, and Meta AI, are already reshaping how people interact with search engines and use search engine optimization (SEO) to make content and websites searchable.

Because ChatGPT and the others can provide direct, summarized, and unified answers, many will accept those outputs as answers to their search query and look no further. In other words, they'll frequently bypass traditional search engines entirely. And when they do visit a search engine, they'll often be disinclined to click on traditional search results to investigate the matter further — or to fact-check the AI's response.

This hard shift in user behavior challenges the business model of search engines, which have long relied on users clicking on links. If too few people regularly click on links in search engine results, website traffic could diminish, which would also negatively affect ad-based revenue models.

Diminishing website traffic fallout

For example, Google may suffer a drop in traditional search ad revenue if people don't click on ads in the search results or click on ads posted on partner websites. Google faces a dilemma. To summarize, Google may be impacted negatively either way. Google Search can't compete with the likes of Bing Copilot and Perplexity AI search with its instant citation of sources for its AI responses if Google doesn't provide an AI alternative. So, of course, it does provide AI summaries at the top of some search results. But in doing so, it could be hurting its own revenue streams.

ChatGPT and competitor summaries at the head of search results bring no joy to any person or organization seeking to attract online traffic to their content or website. Web traffic may slow or even dry up in the future. The SEO keywords that these people long relied upon to bring traffic will lose their appeal to searchers because generative AI chatbots don't need keywords to understand and answer your question.

The one saving grace is that AI will continue to use keywords to find and pull information off the internet and out of private databases. ChatGPT and its competitors will use other techniques, too, but the point is that search capabilities are still necessary at least for the moment.

Evolving SEO tactics

Meanwhile, SEO tactics will evolve as ranking in traditional search results becomes less critical, but machines will still use them. Content creators will need to focus on ensuring their material is easily accessible to AI applications and systems. Organized, machine-readable data (structured data), information enriched with clear context and meaning (semantic content), and indicators of credibility and trustworthiness (authoritative signals) will become increasingly important as AI tools like ChatGPT aggregate insights from a variety of sources."

This shift in user behavior on traditional search engines is likely to change how content is presented online as well. For example, consider a marketing content funnel, which is a common marketing strategy that uses targeted content to guide potential buyers from general awareness of a subject to the purchase of a specific product. This tunnel has three parts:

>> **The top of the funnel** consists of general interest content designed to attract potential customers early in the buying cycle and links to content further down the funnel.

>> **The middle of the funnel** offers content that contains more in-depth information and nurtures sales leads.

>> **The bottom of the funnel** is filled with content focused on completing the sale of a specific product or service.

REMEMBER

Top-of-the-funnel content will likely disappear as ChatGPT's narrative summaries can easily and quickly answer any requests for information on almost any topic. This has the potential of diminishing the draw of the tunnel strategy since search narratives will not point to or link to marketing content in any company's funnel.

Over-relying on AI-curated information

ChatGPT and other AI chatbots' ability to curate information may also reduce the time that you and others spend browsing individual websites. This might severely disrupt content consumption patterns and challenge businesses reliant on search-driven traffic.

Unfortunately, over-reliance on search summaries will likely add to the rise of misinformation, too. When people blindly accept AI summaries and outputs as factual, they're easily fooled. It's important to fact-check and verify generative AI outputs — ChatGPT results or otherwise — but that's not likely to happen on an appreciable scale because people tend to opt for convenience over substance.

As generative AI tools like ChatGPT continue to disrupt search results and content delivery, traditional SEO and monetization strategies will need to adapt. Bottom line: This fundamental shift in search behavior can mean that not only are keywords dying in the public's eye, but so may various types of online businesses and industries.

Moving from Information Search to Knowledge Assistants

As I note in the previous section, ChatGPT and similar AI models are driving a shift from traditional information search to the use of AI summaries as a unified search result. In so doing, these AI chatbots are also driving a swifter evolution in knowledge assistants. You're most likely familiar with earlier forms of knowledge assistants, such as Siri, Alexa, and Google Assistant. Instead of searching through links, you can ask questions and receive direct and unified answers, and that effectively transforms search into a conversation.

Now ChatGPT and similar AI chatbots are being embedded in these same knowledge assistants to supercharge their evolution. Thus, each can then provide more personalized, interactive, and contextualized responses.

Finding new purposes for knowledge assistants

But knowledge assistants are also expanding into new areas with new purposes. They can be built to help customers and employees or even serve the elite — from celebrities and CEOs to specialists in medicine, science, and space exploration. Each of these knowledge assistants has access to specialized and personalized data.

In general, knowledge assistants designed for highly specialized and customized service share a main purpose: delivering instant answers from a company's internal data sources through a conversational interface. They can comprehend queries and sift through knowledge bases, databases, and other internal repositories to provide precise answers and detailed processes. In doing so, both the work quality and the speed are greatly enhanced, which assists you in making informed decisions without having to constantly stop to manually search for information or reach out to colleagues.

WARNING

Be careful not to confuse terms while you're sorting the various generative AI tools and functions. For example, agent assist tools suggest specific actions to facilitate work done by human helpdesk and customer service agents, but knowledge assistants are AI applications that focus on supplying information — either to the human agent working at the helpdesk or in IT support or directly to the customer. Knowledge assistants facilitate access to data, while agent assist tools manage the workflow. Another difference: Knowledge assistants allow for follow-up questions, suggest related queries, offer analytics on trends and effectiveness, and identify knowledge gaps. AI agent assist tools just focus on performing specific tasks.

Noting the pros and cons of knowledge assistants

The pros of the shift to knowledge assistants include faster access to information, convenience, and the ability to get detailed, contextual responses without sifting through multiple sources. Knowledge assistants can also handle more complex queries than traditional AI assistants by combining information from different sources and from a specialized perspective.

However, cons come into this shift, too. People may become overly reliant on or even addicted to AI systems and tools like ChatGPT-enabled knowledge assistants. That could severely reduce critical thinking and independent research skills and activities. Transparency, accuracy, and bias are ongoing concerns with AI systems and tools; they may not always provide the most reliable or diverse sources of information. Additionally, the lack of direct interaction with websites may overly limit users' exposure to diverse perspectives and in-depth knowledge. In short, users may be dumbed down.

Living with Misinformation and Manipulation

Society has entered a new era of widespread false and misleading information. You need only look at the multitude of conspiracy theories zipping across the web on any given day to see that. But with GenAI, information dissemination jumps to an entirely new level, with significant implications in the spread of disinformation.

People can exploit generative AI chatbots to create convincing — but entirely fabricated — news articles, social media posts, and fake testimonials that are indistinguishable from legitimate content online. Consider these examples:

>> **Anyone can prompt ChatGPT to fabricate a news story about a political figure involved in a scandal that never occurred.** The story, replete with fabricated quotes and false evidence, can spread rapidly across social media platforms, sowing confusion and manipulating public perception. It could even tilt an election, especially if many such falsely generated stories are spewed by these chatbots in every language and in every internet nook and cranny where targeted audiences can be reached.

>> **The underlying generative AI models can be fine-tuned to mimic the writing style of specific individuals or reputable news outlets,** making the distinction between authentic and fake content increasingly difficult for the average person. Malicious actors can, for example, manipulate stock prices, influence election outcomes, and incite social unrest through a series of tweets and other social media posts and comments that appear to be from a trusted journalist, a respected business leader, or a political figure.

WARNING

The speed and scale at which GenAI chatbots can produce AI-generated disinformation poses significant challenges for social media platforms and individuals to overcome in the effort to maintain integrity in public discourse.

Manipulation tactics go beyond spreading false narratives to include strategies that create and maintain emotional and psychological impact. GenAI tools can analyze vast amounts of data to instantly identify the most effective ways to attract, engage, and manipulate specific individuals or groups. For example, GenAI tools can create polarizing or provocative material that's more likely to be shared and believed, even if it's entirely baseless. This capability can amplify existing divisions and create new ones within any given community. It can also undermine trust in news media, respectable sources, and the larger information ecosystem.

REMEMBER

The line between reality and lies becomes increasingly blurred as GenAI tools continue to progress. The potential for misuse of these technologies requires the development and use of strong and continued countermeasures. Such countermeasures can include digital literacy education, the development of sophisticated detection tools, and the implementation of strict ethical guidelines governing the use of AI in the generation and dissemination of content.

Narrowing Options

If you're relying solely on ChatGPT or similar AI tools, be aware that it can limit your exposure to diverse perspectives, narrow your understanding of an issue or topic, and limit your awareness of differing evidence, opinions, and broader sources of information. Always remember that and make a point to look for other sources of information outside of AI, or even through interactions with other AI tools that use a different underlying model than the first AI tool you used.

REMEMBER

GenAI tools offer speed and convenience, but they do so at the cost of limiting your understanding of complex issues and your ability to connect the dots in information that can lead to new breakthroughs.

Recognizing the limitations of GenAI info

Lots of dangers for you and society can be found in overreliance on GenAI tools. Not all of them are obvious. For example, algorithmic bias is often invisible to your eye and your mind; nonetheless, it might cause you to unknowingly receive a skewed or incomplete picture of any issue or situation.

Further, when AI condenses complex topics into easily digestible AI summaries, you're losing out on the depth and nuance that may deliver an entirely different meaning than you gleaned from the AI's summary. It's as if you're trying to understand quantum physics but listening only to sound bites. For example, if you want to understand geopolitical conflicts, you may think you've got a good handle on the issues when you only have a simplified AI overview that excludes the historical context or conflicting ideologies involved. Over time, continued shallow exposures to information lead to a more surface-level or childlike understanding of important and complex subjects.

Looking only for confirmation

Confirmation bias, the tendency to interpret new evidence as confirmation of your own beliefs or theories, can also be a big problem. ChatGPT and similar generative AI tools generate responses based on patterns in your interactions with them. This can result in them delivering responses that inadvertently confirm and strengthen any preexisting viewpoints you may have.

If you consistently ask for information that aligns with your own biases, GenAI models will continuously oblige. You can even write prompts that inadvertently expose your belief or opinion in some way, which can cause a model to respond in the same vein, creating an echo chamber that seemingly confirms your stance.

For example, if you aren't careful in your prompting while seeking political information, you may receive responses that mirror your views and ignore opposing arguments.

Many GenAI tools also don't routinely provide links to the original sources they use to generate a response. You can often prompt the model to provide that information for you — but even then, the list may be incorrect or even fabricated.

Exploiting varied information sources

Finally, using AI as the sole source of information limits the discovery of new information. You're more likely to find yourself covering familiar information repeatedly than you are to stumble upon new, unexpected ideas through exploring different sources. Traditional search often leads users to diverse content they weren't initially looking for, which can aid critical thinking and spur new ideas. By contrast, AI-generated responses tend to be more targeted and specific, which often eliminates any opportunity to find something new.

You can overcome this narrow perspective somewhat by prompting a GenAI tool to deliver related or associated information. That's still typically not as useful as free-thinking your way through search results, although those can limit your thinking, too. Every technological choice results in a trade-off of some sort. The more you allow technology to think for you or to assist you by hand-feeding you information, the more you limit your ability to expand your own knowledge.

Your Brain on GenAI

For better or worse, every technology affects the human brain in some way. For example, a study by McGill University in 2020 found that frequently using GPS causes a corresponding decline in hippocampal-dependent spatial memory. In essence, you don't remember the way to places, so you rely on GPS to guide you again to the same place, and then you're stuck on repeat, each time becoming more reliant on GPS to get anywhere. Similarly, reliance on autocorrect diminishes your spelling skills, overuse of calculators softens math skills, and relying on your smartphone's contact database makes it hard for you to recite anyone's phone number.

Some technologies affect the human body as well, such as the effect too much screen viewing has on the eyes and the effect that always hunching over a smartphone or other device has on posture and neck pain.

Effects of GenAI on thinking skills

It should come as no surprise then that generative AI tools also affect you and society. For example, a research paper published in *Nature* titled "Impact of Artificial Intelligence on Human Loss in Decision Making, Laziness and Safety in Education" found that AI tools rob people of decision-making skills and lead to laziness. I would add that ChatGPT and other GenAI tools reduce intellectual curiosity and critical thinking skills. What's there to be curious about or contemplate when you know that anything you might want to know at any time is there for the asking? In other words, what is the purpose of extended knowledge exploration or pursuit if ChatGPT already has all the answers for you?

One of the more alarming aspects is that GenAI is supposed to free more of your time so you can spend it on higher purposes — presumably inventing, innovating, and creating stuff. But can you, though, if using these tools also reduces your cognitive ability?

In any case, it's good to be aware of what can happen so you can temper your use of this tech or take steps to offset the impact.

REMEMBER

Cognitive atrophy is the elephant in the worry-room. Overreliance on GenAI tools to perform tasks such as writing, problem-solving, and even engaging in conversation might squash your ability to perform these tasks without assistance. That's similar to, but more dire I think, than the "Google effect," aka "digital amnesia," that the Columbia University researchers detailed in the study "Google Effects on Memory: Cognitive Consequences of Having Information at Our Fingertips." Essentially, they found that the ease of finding information online impairs your ability to remember it. In the case of GenAI tools, you could soon find yourself struggling to carry on a conversation or write an email.

Effects of AI tools on interpersonal skills

Other researchers have found that overuse of conversational AI tools can affect social behavior and interpersonal skills. Essentially, you become more comfortable chatting with the AI tool than with another human. Sherry Turkle's research at MIT went even further by suggesting that people become isolated and lose their sense of empathy when they overuse technology.

But it's also important to realize that this discussion is about a tool and not a drug or a demon. You can control how and when you use it and balance your life so that you have plenty of interactions that don't involve AI or a device. And, as I mentioned before, GenAI tools bring many benefits. I've detailed many of them in other chapters of this book.

Protecting yourself from GenAI fallout

The key is to avoid thinking of GenAI tools as smarter than you. They aren't. They're just outstandingly good at data retrieval and data repackaging. Your brain, my friend, does way more than that.

TIP

Don't rely excessively on this tech, but do use it like you would any other data repository, be that a dictionary, encyclopedias, the internet, your car's operating manual, whatever. Keep GenAI in its place and yourself in your place and venture boldly forth to make your own mark on the world. And when you do, take full credit. Generative AI tools are no more the creator of your work than a hammer is for building an architect's design.

If, however, you let GenAI take the lead — to make your decisions and do your work — then it (and not you) receives the credit, although you'll still get the blame. Don't believe me? Just wait until you copy ChatGPT's homework only to discover it was completely wrong or outright plagiarism. Trust me, the court will summon you, not ChatGPT, to account and pay for the deed.

Chapter **5**

Financial Planning and Other Money Matters

I n this chapter, you take a comprehensive snapshot of your finances and budget with the help of AI. Although much has been written about AI's use and impact on investing (including in the book *AI Investing For Dummies*), investing is really just a portion of the larger world of financial planning. Investing comes together with the other components of your financial world for you to achieve all the financial goals necessary for a good life.

Financial planning is the universe, and investing is just a primary galaxy, so to speak. If you focus on investing success but have flaws or weaknesses in other aspects of your financial situation, then you risk falling short of your ultimate goals.

What good is successful investing if you have significant problems with your career, burdensome debt, or overspending habits?

TIP

I realize that financial planning and its associated topics can easily be an entire book. But I hope that you see that virtually every aspect of your financial and business worlds can be impacted for the better when you harness AI.

Walking through the Stages of Financial Planning

Confused about where to start your financial planning? What better way to begin than to ask AI? Here's a sample prompt:

> "What is the complete financial planning process? Please provide the answer in bullet-point style with a comprehensive explanation of each item and in the person's chronological order of their life."

ChatGPT's response is in the following text (My added comments are in *italics.*):

> The financial planning process is a structured approach to managing one's finances throughout their life. It typically consists of several stages, from setting financial goals to retirement planning.
>
> Here's a chronological breakdown of the complete financial planning process with explanations for each stage:
>
> **Stage 1: Setting Financial Goals (Early Adulthood)**
>
> **1. Determine Financial Goals:** Identify short-term and long-term financial objectives, such as buying a home, paying off student loans, or saving for retirement.
>
> *Comments: Whatever your activity is, what is the result you want? The studies over the years have shown that college graduates, for example, frequently miss their retirement funding targets. Recent studies show that approximately half of Americans have less than $1,000 in savings and/or are a paycheck away from financial difficulty. Teaching financial literacy, such as determining financial goals (and sticking to them!), should be part of young adults' learning during high school and college years so there are more happy financial endings. Use AI to set goals, your action plan, and so forth.*
>
> **2. Establish a Budget:** Create a budget to track income, expenses, and savings goals. This helps you allocate resources to achieve your goals.
>
> *Comments: If you can't manage your finances (inflow and outflow of your funds), then you will have difficulty managing and growing your investments. You don't need AI for that conclusion. More about budgeting appears later in this chapter.*
>
> **Stage 2: Building Financial Foundation (Early Adulthood)**
>
> **3. Emergency Fund:** Build an emergency fund to cover unexpected expenses, typically 3–6 months' worth of living expenses.

REMEMBER

Comments: Before you start investing, address this issue. Having an emergency fund is not only a financial good; it's a psychological good. If, for example, you have $10,000 in a savings account, you will have less stress over your day-to-day finances, which can result in better financial decisions. Who will have a better time avoiding a panicky or hasty financial decision — the person with a solid emergency fund who is regularly paying their daily obligations or the person with no savings who is a paycheck away from difficulty? Use AI to learn tactics and strategies to increase your savings and establish an adequate emergency fund for your particular situation.

4. Debt Management: Manage and reduce high-interest debts, like credit card balances and student loans.

WARNING

Comments: At the time of writing, debt in all categories (consumer, corporate, government, and so on) is at or near all-time highs. Whether interest rates rise or fall, the debt load is unsustainable. Consumers should make every effort to pare this back before a financial crisis unfolds. Use AI to learn strategies and tactics to manage and ultimately reduce your overall debt (and other liabilities).

5. Insurance: Acquire appropriate insurance coverage, including health, auto, home, and life insurance, to protect against unexpected events.

Comments: Too often, investors and consumers don't prioritize insurance. Insurance is there to keep large, unforeseen expenses from blowing up your finances. Examples include the death of the main breadwinner or the disability of a significant job holder in your household. Use AI to analyze your insurance needs and then speak with an insurance pro.

Stage 3: Wealth Accumulation (Mid-Adulthood)

6. Investing: Develop an investment strategy based on risk tolerance and financial goals. Consider assets like stocks, bonds, real estate, and retirement accounts.

7. Retirement Planning: Contribute to retirement accounts, such as 401(k)s and IRAs, to ensure a comfortable retirement. Consider employer matches.

Comments: This topic is covered in Chapter 6. Obviously, the more you can set aside and keep managing for growth, the better you will be at the retirement finish line. Once there, you will focus on income generation.

8. Tax Planning: Optimize your tax situation by taking advantage of deductions, credits, and tax-efficient investments.

Comments: In the world of managing cash flow in which money flows in (income and gains) and money flows out (outgo such as debt and expenses), taxes are a major expense. The more you can reduce it, the more funds you can devote to your current and future financial needs.

Stage 4: Major Life Events (Various Life Stages)

9. Marriage and Family: Adjust financial plans for significant life changes, such as getting married, having children, or sending kids to college.

Comments: Your finances are ultimately there to support your important social goals. Strong finances tend to help bolster your marital bliss and to better your children and other dependents. Use AI to gain insights and learn strategies to support this area. Major life events such as weddings, education (covered later in this chapter), and funerals tend to be expensive, so plan accordingly and long before they become issues.

10. Estate Planning: Create a will, assign beneficiaries, and set up powers of attorney and healthcare directives to manage your assets and healthcare decisions.

Comments: Estate planning is a necessity, and it can be a complicated one. Use AI to create checklists, understand wills and trusts, and so on. More on this topic is in Chapter 6 .

Stage 5: Midlife Adjustments (Midlife)

11. Education Funding: Save for your children's education expenses by utilizing tax-advantaged accounts like 529 plans.

Comments: Yes, this is a biggie. First, decide whether a traditional college route is the right path. In recent years, the overall return on investment has greatly diminished. More and more folks are seeking college alternatives so they can decrease the massive cost while still enhancing job prospects. I discuss college planning later in this chapter.

12. Debt Reduction: Focus on paying off remaining debts and becoming more debt-free as retirement approaches.

Comments: See #4 earlier in this list for my thoughts on debt management.

Stage 6: Preparing for Retirement (Late Adulthood)

13. Social Security and Pension: Plan for the utilization of Social Security benefits and any employer pensions to supplement retirement income.

Comments: I usually tell my retirement planning students and clients to plan their retirement as if Social Security is not happening. Although I am sure that Social Security will be there for you, I am not 100 percent certain. But if you achieve financial independence without it, then getting it is gravy! Use AI to help you understand your Social Security benefits, how to file, and how soon.

14. Healthcare Costs: Consider healthcare costs in retirement and investigate Medicare and supplemental insurance options.

Comments: For retirees, would-be and current, health is both a major physical concern and a financial concern. Use AI to help you figure out health issues, Medicare, and so forth.

15. Long-Term Care: Plan for potential long-term care expenses by exploring insurance options or savings strategies.

Comments: Same issue as item #14. Explore long-term care and see whether it is a viable consideration for you. Use AI, but it's best to confer with a human specialist.

Stage 7: Retirement (Late Adulthood)

16. Asset Allocation: Adjust your investment portfolio to prioritize income and preservation of capital over growth.

Comments: Great investing issue! Specialized AI (such as robo-advisors) will help here. The main focus here at this stage of life is safety of principal through conservative, dividend-paying stocks, treasury bonds, bank CDs, and so forth.

17. Withdrawal Strategy: Develop a systematic withdrawal plan for retirement accounts to ensure your savings last through retirement.

Comments: Here, the issue highlighted is recommended minimum distributions (RMD), among others. You have grown and accrued assets all your working life for a purpose, and that has arrived. Start enjoying your money.

18. Estate Distribution: Review and update estate plans to ensure a smooth transfer of assets to heirs or charitable organizations.

Comments: This is part of your estate planning strategies. Check out Chapter 6 for more on this.

Stage 8: Legacy Planning (Late Adulthood)

19. Charitable Giving: Plan for charitable contributions and develop strategies for giving back to the community.

Comments: For those folks who have more than is needed for the tail end of their lives, charitable giving becomes a consideration to help reduce what could become a taxable estate.

20. Legacy and Estate Preservation: Explore options to minimize estate taxes and preserve wealth for future generations.

Comments: With whatever is left at the end of your life, you should have the decision to give as much of it as possible to whom you want to give it to (family, friends, charities, and so on).

The financial planning process is dynamic, and individuals may revisit these stages as their life circumstances change. Working with a certified financial planner can provide valuable guidance and ensure that financial goals are aligned with the most current strategies and investment options.

Comments: Nice summation!

TIP

OK, pilgrim, start your AI engines and get cracking on financial planning. Here are some prompts to consider:

>> "What are the legal forms of ownership? Provide an explanation and an example of each." (This is especially crucial in estate planning, which is covered in Chapter 6.)

>> "How do I file for Social Security? Please provide a step-by-step approach and then provide ten ways I can boost my benefits."

>> "What are ten ways to easily add extra income to my situation in the near future using only my laptop and/or my smartphone? Provide an explanation of each along with resources online that can help me."

Getting a Handle on Budgeting

Budgeting is all about managing financial inflow and outflow. When you budget, you know where the money is coming from, and you know where it's going — every penny (or close enough).

REMEMBER

The goal of having a budget is simple:

>> Keep increasing your inflow and keep decreasing your outflow.

>> Then save and invest the difference. Then, it's rinse and repeat until you meet your financial goals.

If your financial goals include financial independence and a comfortable lifestyle, then you know what needs to be done.

Let's ask AI about inflow. Check out the following prompt:

"Please give me five specific strategies to increase the amount of money I bring into my financial situation for the next 12 months."

ChatGPT's response is in Figure 5-1. Although I specialized in financial planning and investing education for nearly four decades, I was always an advocate for anyone (everyone!) to have a home-based business in their spare time. Fast-forward to today's world, and the variety of ways to earn extra income is greater than ever.

ChatGPT

Certainly! Here are five specific strategies to increase the amount of money you bring into your financial situation over the next 12 months:

1. **1. Diversify Income Streams:**
   * Explore opportunities to diversify your sources of income. This could involve taking on a side job, freelancing, consulting, or starting a small business. By diversifying, you reduce reliance on a single income stream and create multiple avenues for earning money.

2. **2. Enhance Skills and Marketable Qualifications:**
   * Invest in developing or enhancing skills that are in demand in the job market. This might involve taking courses, obtaining certifications, or acquiring new qualifications. Increasing your expertise can make you more valuable in your current job or open doors to higher-paying opportunities.

3. **3. Negotiate a Raise or Promotion:**
   * Evaluate your performance and contributions in your current job. If you believe you've added significant value, consider negotiating a raise or promotion. Prepare a case outlining your achievements, responsibilities, and the impact you've had on the organization. Be ready to discuss how you can contribute even more in the future.

4. **4. Create Passive Income Streams:**
   * Explore opportunities to generate passive income. This could involve investing in dividend-paying stocks, real estate, or creating and selling digital products. Passive income streams can provide a steady flow of money with less active involvement over time.

5. **5. Cut Unnecessary Expenses:**
   * Review your monthly expenses and identify areas where you can cut unnecessary costs. This might involve renegotiating bills, canceling subscription services you don't use, or finding more cost-effective alternatives for daily expenses. The money saved can be redirected towards increasing your overall financial situation.

Remember to approach these strategies with careful planning and consideration of your personal circumstances. Building additional income or cutting expenses requires effort and discipline. Combining multiple strategies can have a compounding effect, contributing to a more significant positive impact on your financial situation over the next 12 months.

FIGURE 5-1:
Increasing
your inflow.

TIP

By the way, a good way to start is by listing/selling your unwanted stuff on venues such as eBay and Amazon (and dozens of other venues). Yes, ask AI lots of questions about home business ideas, part-time gigs, and so forth.

And then you can use AI to get ideas for the outflow. Here's a sample prompt:

"Please give me five specific strategies to decrease the amount of money that is flowing out of my financial situation for the next 12 months."

ChatGPT's response is in Figure 5-2. Reducing your "outflow" should be easier than increasing your "inflow." Too many folks are buying stuff that is simply not needed. Ask yourself whether a given purchase will add psychological or material value to your situation in the coming months. My neighbor, for example, bought an RV. They were likely better off renting it as they needed it — and saving thousands of dollars. In addition, the RV is a depreciating asset that will lose value over time. What are you considering buying now that is better off delayed or done a cheaper way?

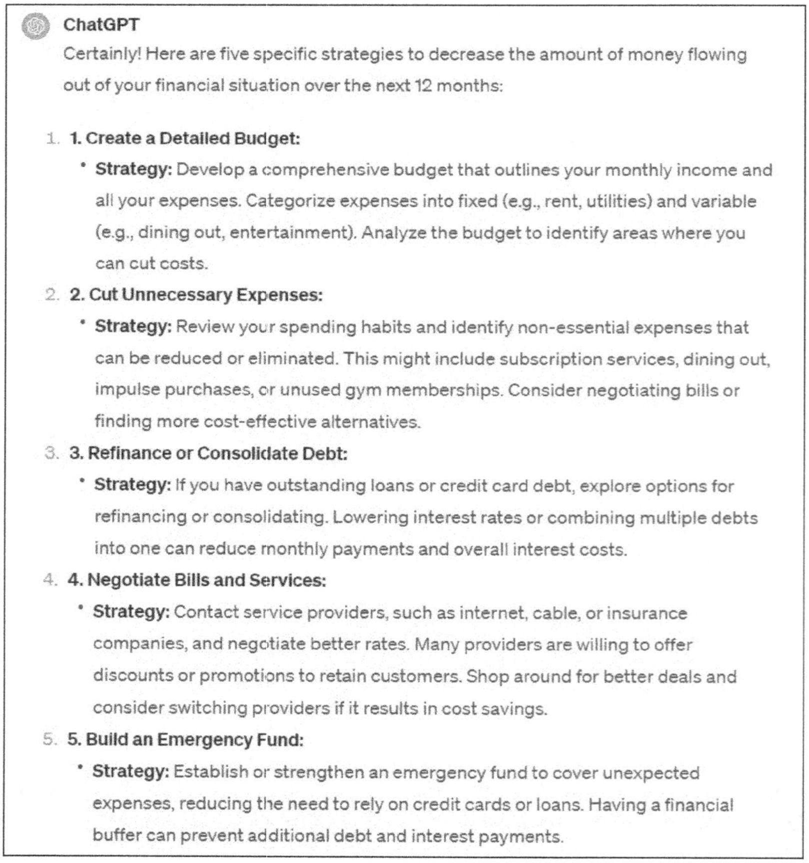

ChatGPT

Certainly! Here are five specific strategies to decrease the amount of money flowing out of your financial situation over the next 12 months:

1. **1. Create a Detailed Budget:**
   * **Strategy:** Develop a comprehensive budget that outlines your monthly income and all your expenses. Categorize expenses into fixed (e.g., rent, utilities) and variable (e.g., dining out, entertainment). Analyze the budget to identify areas where you can cut costs.

2. **2. Cut Unnecessary Expenses:**
   * **Strategy:** Review your spending habits and identify non-essential expenses that can be reduced or eliminated. This might include subscription services, dining out, impulse purchases, or unused gym memberships. Consider negotiating bills or finding more cost-effective alternatives.

3. **3. Refinance or Consolidate Debt:**
   * **Strategy:** If you have outstanding loans or credit card debt, explore options for refinancing or consolidating. Lowering interest rates or combining multiple debts into one can reduce monthly payments and overall interest costs.

4. **4. Negotiate Bills and Services:**
   * **Strategy:** Contact service providers, such as internet, cable, or insurance companies, and negotiate better rates. Many providers are willing to offer discounts or promotions to retain customers. Shop around for better deals and consider switching providers if it results in cost savings.

5. **5. Build an Emergency Fund:**
   * **Strategy:** Establish or strengthen an emergency fund to cover unexpected expenses, reducing the need to rely on credit cards or loans. Having a financial buffer can prevent additional debt and interest payments.

FIGURE 5-2: Decreasing your outflow.

Spotlighting College Expenses

The major expenses we typically deal with are usually milestones in our lives: weddings, births (and raising children), college funding, and funerals. AI can certainly give you lots of research, ideas, and so on about all of those. In this section, I focus on one of those — college.

Among that list of major expenses, college is likely #1 given that it's easy to end up spending six-figures on a four-year college education. But as you read this, the college world is facing tectonic shifts, and consumers (parents!) are spending more and more money for less and less educational value.

Obviously, if you're opting for a traditional four-year degree for your child, I wish you success. But before you take this expensive plunge, consider the alternatives since there may be greater satisfaction there for your child (and a lot less cost for you). Here's an example prompt that's food for thought:

> "Please give me ten practical alternatives to an expensive four-year traditional college degree. Please provide a good rationale for each choice."

ChatGPT's response is in Figure 5-3. I cover this as a recent phenomenon that has shown that college debt surpassed the $1 trillion mark during 2022–2023, and an extraordinary number of college graduates have taken on jobs that didn't require a college education. I speak for those who personally know many college graduates with huge college debt balances who are working as cashiers and office clerks.

TIP

Keep in mind that any huge cost you undertake (college, buying a house, and so on) should be done through the lens of "return on investment" (ROI). Whatever money you put in, you should have reasonable expectations of gaining benefit (financial or otherwise) that is ultimately greater in its totality than the total amount that was invested. Consider using AI to construct a spreadsheet to do the financial pros and cons, cost comparisons, and so forth to make an informed decision. Consider plotting that same spreadsheet with the choices/ideas in Figure 5-3.

Of course, there are still some subjects in which a traditional four-college route is still the best way to go. Examples include engineering and medical careers. Fortunately, the well of college money is still deep, and more students than ever can qualify. Here is a sample prompt on this to get you started:

> "List seven sources of grants and scholarships to help fund a traditional four-year college education for a student in liberal arts who comes from a middle-income family. Also, include a description and the relevant URL or website."

If a four-year traditional college can help you gain a lucrative job coupled with career satisfaction, then AI's help has been worth it.

ChatGPT

Certainly! Pursuing alternatives to a traditional 4-year college degree can be a practical and cost-effective way to gain valuable skills and credentials. Here are 10 alternatives, along with their rationales:

1. **Community College or Two-Year Associate's Degree:**
   * Rationale: Community colleges offer affordable tuition and provide a solid foundation for various careers or as a stepping stone to a 4-year degree.
2. **Trade or Technical School:**
   * Rationale: Technical and vocational schools focus on specific trades, such as plumbing, electrician, or medical assisting, and provide hands-on training for high-demand jobs.
3. **Apprenticeships:**
   * Rationale: Apprenticeships combine on-the-job training with classroom instruction and are an excellent way to earn while you learn in fields like construction, healthcare, and information technology.
4. **Online Courses and Certifications:**
   * Rationale: Many accredited institutions and platforms offer online courses and certifications in various subjects, allowing you to gain knowledge and skills at your own pace and often at a lower cost than traditional college.
5. **Bootcamps and Coding Schools:**
   * Rationale: Coding bootcamps provide intensive training in web development, software engineering, and data science, preparing you for high-demand tech jobs in a shorter time frame.
6. **Entrepreneurship and Business Start-up:**
   * Rationale: Starting your own business or pursuing entrepreneurial ventures can provide valuable experience and, with success, potentially lead to financial independence without a degree.
7. **Military Service:**
   * Rationale: Joining the military can offer valuable training, education benefits, and a structured career path in various fields, from aviation to healthcare.
8. **Online Freelancing or Gig Work:**
   * Rationale: Platforms like Upwork and Freelancer allow you to offer your skills and services to clients, creating income opportunities in writing, design, programming, and more.
9. **Nonprofit and Volunteer Work:**
   * Rationale: Volunteering and nonprofit work can provide valuable experience and networking opportunities in social services, community development, and other fields.
10. **Apprenticeships:**

   * Rationale: Apprenticeships combine on-the-job training with classroom instruction and are an excellent way to earn while you learn in fields like construction, healthcare, and information technology.

Each of these alternatives offers a different path to gaining skills, experience, and credentials without the high cost of a traditional 4-year college degree. Your choice should align with your career goals and personal interests while considering the financial aspects and time commitment.

FIGURE 5-3: Alternatives to four-year college degrees.

Chapter **6**

Retirement and Estate Planning

Although retirement and estate planning should be on every adult's radar screen, it is most "top of mind" for those folks past 50 (give or take a decade). Between the two, estate planning is the more complicated and daunting for many of us. In this chapter, I show you that (fortunately) AI is a powerful and welcome tool that makes both pursuits much less daunting.

Digging into Retirement Planning

Whether you're planning your retirement when you're 20 years old, 40, 55, or beyond, part one of the plan is quite simple: Spend less than you earn, invest/ save the difference, rinse, and repeat. Part two of your approach is this: Figure out your income needs at the age you are hoping/planning to retire so you can accrue enough assets to generate that needed income. The following sections can help you get started.

REMEMBER

Be sure to consult a professional as you plan your retirement.

Your starting point: A personal balance sheet

To get rolling with your retirement planning, assessing what you currently own (assets) and owe (liabilities) is obviously an essential first step. Here's a sample prompt for AI:

> "To retire, I will need a personal balance sheet. Please create an extensive personal balance sheet complete with each line item as a bullet point coupled with an explanation for each line item."

ChatGPT's response is in the following text:

> Creating a personal balance sheet is an essential step in understanding your financial health and planning for retirement. A personal balance sheet summarizes your assets, liabilities, and net worth at a specific point in time. Here's an extensive personal balance sheet with each line item as a bullet point, along with an explanation for each:
>
> **Assets:**
>
> **1. Cash and Cash Equivalents:**
>
> **Explanation:** This includes money in checking accounts, savings accounts, and any other easily accessible cash.
>
> **2. Investment Accounts:**
>
> **Explanation:** The value of your investment portfolios, including stocks, bonds, mutual funds, and brokerage accounts.
>
> **3. Retirement Accounts (e.g., 401(k), IRA):**
>
> **Explanation:** The total value of your retirement savings, which can include employer-sponsored plans and individual retirement accounts.
>
> **4. Real Estate:**
>
> **Explanation:** The estimated value of your primary residence and any other real estate properties you own.
>
> **5. Vehicles:**
>
> **Explanation:** The value of your cars, motorcycles, boats, or other vehicles you own.
>
> **6. Personal Property:**
>
> **Explanation:** The value of valuable personal possessions such as jewelry, art, antiques, and collectibles.

7. Business Ownership:

Explanation: If you own a business, the value of your ownership stake should be included here.

8. Cash Value of Life Insurance:

Explanation: If you have life insurance policies with a cash value component, include the current cash value.

9. Other Investments:

Explanation: Any other investments not mentioned above, such as real estate investment trusts (REITs) or certificates of deposit (CDs).

10. Other Assets:

Explanation: Include any miscellaneous assets like loans owed to you, prepaid expenses, or any significant assets not covered in the categories above.

Liabilities:

11. Mortgage(s):

Explanation: The outstanding balance on your mortgage(s) for your primary residence and other properties.

12. Home Equity Loans or Lines of Credit:

Explanation: Any outstanding balances on home equity loans or lines of credit secured by your home.

13. Auto Loans:

Explanation: The amount you owe on car loans or leases.

14. Credit Card Debt:

Explanation: The total balance on all your credit cards.

15. Student Loans:

Explanation: Outstanding student loan balances, if applicable.

16. Personal Loans:

Explanation: Any unsecured personal loans or debts owed to friends or family.

17. Other Loans:

Explanation: Include any other outstanding loans, such as business loans or medical debts.

18. Taxes Payable:

Explanation: Outstanding income taxes or property taxes due but not yet paid.

19. Other Liabilities:

Explanation: Include any miscellaneous liabilities not covered above.

Net Worth:

20. Net Worth (Assets – Liabilities):

Explanation: Calculate your net worth by subtracting your total liabilities from your total assets. This represents your true financial position.

A personal balance sheet provides a snapshot of your financial situation, helping you assess your progress toward retirement goals and make informed financial decisions. Regularly update your balance sheet to track changes in your wealth over time and make adjustments to your retirement plan as needed.

REMEMBER

For most folks, doing a "financial inventory" is the first and most essential step for retirement planning. All your assets (as much as possible, anyway) should be on the path to growth, and you should be reducing your liabilities. Ideally, when retirement time comes, your assets should be positioned to generate income (dividends, interest, and so on) needed for a comfortable retirement.

The "5–10 approach" and a reality check

In my retirement planning seminars and workshops, I reference something I refer to as the "5–10" approach. It refers to an assumption of "5 percent income and 10 percent growth." Whenever you're doing retirement planning, you can't avoid the fact that since you're planning for the future (and typically many years into the future), you have to make assumptions because you have no idea what the distant future looks like until you get there.

Given that, assume that you can reasonably expect to generate an income from future assets of 5 percent (when you complete reconstructing your portfolio for optimal income generation at that time). Also, assume that you could (on average) achieve 10 percent growth in your assets between today and when you're ready to shift to income mode later on at retirement time.

For example, say you will need at retirement time $25,000 of investment income (perhaps as a supplement to your future Social Security annual income). If $25,000 is 5 percent of income, then in that case, you would need at least $500,000 in investable assets to generate that amount ($25,000 is 5 percent of $500,000). That way you could have income without needing to dip into principal (in other words, start cashing in some of that $500,000 amount).

Since you'll need $500,000 at that time, you'll need a financial calculator (or AI) to figure out how to get from where you are currently (your net worth from the personal balance sheet covered earlier in this chapter) to where you need (or want) to be.

So here's the first prompt I used:

> "I have $150,000 in investments, and I want to grow it to $500,000. If it is growing annually at an average rate of 10 percent, how long will it take in years?"

After a long explanation and layout of the formula and calculation, ChatGPT ended its response with the following:

> So, it will take approximately 20.14 years for your $150,000 investment to grow to $500,000 at an annual growth rate of 10 percent. Since you can't have a fraction of a year in reality, you'd likely need to wait for 21 years to reach your goal.

The interesting thing is that when I asked that same exact question to Bing's AI-enhanced Bing Chat, it gave the answer in Figure 6-1.

> You have $\ast$ $\ast$ $150,000$ $\ast$ $\ast$ $in investments and you want to grow it to$ $500,000$ at an annual growth rate of **10%**. To calculate the number of years it will take to reach your goal, we can use the formula:
>
> $$\log_{1+r}\left(\frac{FV}{PV}\right)$$
>
> where **r** is the annual interest rate, **FV** is the future value, and **PV** is the present value.
>
> Plugging in the values, we get:
>
> $$\log_{1+0.1}\left(\frac{500000}{150000}\right)$$
>
> Using a pocket calculator, we get:
>
> $$\log_{1.1}\left(\frac{5}{3}\right) \approx 5.3596$$
>
> Therefore, it will take approximately **5.36 years** to grow your investments from $150,000 to $500,000 at an annual growth rate of 10%. Please note that this is an estimate and the actual time it takes may vary depending on market conditions.
>
> 1 of 30

FIGURE 6-1: One of several answers from AI on reaching an investment goal.

Hmmm. While ChatGPT estimated "21 years" (rounded up from 20.14 years), Bing estimated 5.36 years. Interestingly, both AI estimates were off.

Then I went to a reliable (non-AI) online financial calculator (found at www.calculator.net), and I got the answer of 12.632 years. My conclusion is that the actual answer is in the neighborhood of 12 to 14 years, given my experience with financial projections.

REMEMBER

Artificial intelligence (in spite of the name) is *not* artificial perfection! For sensitive or important calculations or issues, consult more than one source — and add a competent, experienced human to the mix, too.

But here's where folks need to be really careful in terms of AI reliability. I took the preceding example a step further and added (what I thought) was a simple additional step. Here's the revised prompt:

"I am starting today with an investment amount of $150,000, and I want it to reach $500,000 in 9 years. Assuming an annual growth rate of 10 percent during that period of time, how much should my regular monthly contribution be?"

After a long explanation and layout of the formula and calculation, ChatGPT's response caused my jaw to drop:

So, to reach $500,000 in 9 years with an average annual growth rate of 10 percent, you would need to invest approximately $36,575.38 each month during that time frame.

Say what?! $36,575.38 each month? For 108 months (9×12 months)? Wow! That's an amazing inaccuracy! Any calculator would've told you that 108 months times $36,575.38 is a whopping $3,950,141.04 (even excluding any growth at all!). Even when I kept re-asking ChatGPT and regenerating the response, I got wildly inaccurate amounts, and they all differed with each other and, more importantly, with reality.

WARNING

The bad part of this is that artificial intelligence is still not perfected, and you should not rely 100 percent on it — especially if your issue or concern is very important and accuracy is vital. Unlike horseshoes and grenades, accuracy will be a vital concern, especially if the matter is your health, your finances, or another important aspect of your life.

The good news is that those folks who are posting online content about how AI will take over the world can take a breath. AI first needs to get the math correct (among other things).

TIP

Meanwhile, do your research with multiple sources, human as well as AI.

A helpful checklist

With your personal balance sheet done, now you can roll up your sleeves and get rolling with planning. Consider a prompt like this:

"Please create a comprehensive checklist of documents and steps for retirement planning. Do it in a checklist approach complete with an explanation of each item."

ChatGPT's response is in the following text:

Retirement planning is essential to ensure financial security and a comfortable lifestyle during your retirement years. Here's a comprehensive checklist for retirement planning, complete with explanations for each item:

1. Set Retirement Goals:

Explanation: Determine your retirement age, lifestyle expectations, and financial goals. Understanding what you want will guide your planning.

2. Calculate Retirement Expenses:

Explanation: Estimate your future expenses, including housing, healthcare, daily living costs, travel, and entertainment. Be realistic and account for inflation.

3. Assess Current Financial Situation:

Explanation: Review your current assets, debts, income, and expenses to understand your financial position.

4. Create a Retirement Budget:

Explanation: Develop a budget that aligns with your retirement goals. This will help you track your spending and ensure you don't outlive your savings.

5. Determine Retirement Income Sources:

Explanation: Identify potential sources of retirement income, such as Social Security, pensions, IRAs, 401(k)s, annuities, and investment accounts.

6. Maximize Employer Retirement Contributions:

Explanation: Contribute the maximum allowable amount to employer-sponsored retirement plans like a 401(k) and take advantage of any employer-matching contributions.

7. Open and Fund an IRA:

Explanation: Consider opening an Individual Retirement Account (IRA) to supplement your employer-sponsored retirement plan. Contribute regularly to benefit from tax advantages.

8. Diversify Your Investment Portfolio:

Explanation: Spread your investments across different asset classes to manage risk and potentially increase returns. Consult a financial advisor for guidance.

9. Establish an Emergency Fund:

Explanation: Set aside three to six months' worth of living expenses in a liquid, easily accessible account to cover unexpected expenses during retirement.

10. Pay Off High-Interest Debts:

Explanation: Prioritize paying off high-interest debts, such as credit cards and personal loans, reducing financial stress in retirement.

11. Review Social Security Benefits:

Explanation: Understand your Social Security benefits, including when you can start receiving them and how your age at retirement affects the amount you receive.

12. Consider Healthcare Costs:

Explanation: Plan for healthcare expenses, including insurance premiums, deductibles, and potential long-term care needs. Explore Medicare and Medigap options.

13. Create a Withdrawal Strategy:

Explanation: Develop a plan for withdrawing money from your retirement accounts to minimize taxes and make your savings last throughout retirement.

14. Evaluate Long-Term Care Insurance:

Explanation: Consider purchasing long-term care insurance to protect your assets in case you require extended care in a nursing home or at home.

15. Update Legal Documents:

Explanation: Review and update important legal documents, such as your will, power of attorney, and healthcare proxy, to ensure they reflect your wishes.

16. Assess Life Insurance Needs:

Explanation: Determine whether you still need life insurance in retirement. It can be a valuable asset or a source of income for beneficiaries.

17. Plan for Estate Distribution:

Explanation: Outline your wishes for the distribution of your assets after your passing and consider minimizing estate taxes through estate planning strategies.

18. Explore Part-Time Work or Hobbies:

Explanation: Think about how you'd like to spend your time in retirement, whether it's through part-time work, volunteering, or pursuing hobbies and interests.

19. Review and Adjust Your Plan Regularly:

Explanation: Periodically revisit your retirement plan, especially as you get closer to retirement, to make necessary adjustments based on changing circumstances and goals.

20. Seek Professional Advice:

Explanation: Consult with a financial advisor, accountant, or retirement specialist to ensure your retirement plan is on track and aligned with your objectives.

Retirement planning is an ongoing process, and early preparation is key to achieving a secure and fulfilling retirement. Regularly monitoring and adjusting your plan as needed will help you stay on course to meet your retirement goals.

The preceding response is generally good. But let's make AI work a little harder. Keep reading!

Even more AI retirement planning prompts

TIP

Sometimes, what retirees need (current and future) are more than answers; they need to ask good questions to uncover solutions, including some they may not have considered. AI tools like ChatGPT are not only good for answers; they can help with questions, too. Consider the following prompt:

> "Please provide a list of prompts for ChatGPT that a retiree would need to know. Give each one as a question or request and provide an accompanying explanation as to why that is a good prompt."

ChatGPT responded as follows:

> Certainly, here is a list of prompts/questions that a retiree might find useful when interacting with ChatGPT. Each prompt is followed by an explanation of why it's a good question or request:
>
> **1. "How can I maximize my retirement income?"**
>
> **Explanation:** This prompt seeks advice on optimizing retirement income sources, including investments, Social Security, and pensions, to maintain financial security.
>
> **2. "What are the best investment options for retirees?"**
>
> **Explanation:** This question helps retirees explore safe and income-generating investment options suitable for their retirement portfolio.
>
> **3. "Can you explain the tax implications of my retirement withdrawals?"**
>
> **Explanation:** Understanding the tax consequences of retirement account withdrawals is crucial for financial planning. This request seeks clarification on this topic.
>
> **4. "What are some effective strategies for managing healthcare costs in retirement?"**
>
> **Explanation:** Retirees often face rising healthcare expenses. This question seeks advice on managing and budgeting for healthcare in retirement.

5. "How can I create a retirement budget that ensures I don't outlive my savings?"

Explanation: Planning a realistic budget is vital for maintaining financial stability throughout retirement. This prompt seeks guidance on creating such a budget.

6. "Tell me about long-term care insurance options and considerations for retirees."

Explanation: Long-term care insurance can be a critical component of retirement planning. This question seeks information on available options and factors to consider.

7. "What are the advantages and disadvantages of downsizing or relocating in retirement?"

Explanation: Deciding whether to downsize or relocate is a significant retirement decision. This question explores the pros and cons of these options.

8. "How can I ensure my estate is properly planned and distributed to my heirs?"

Explanation: Estate planning is essential for retirees. This prompt seeks advice on wills, trusts, and strategies to minimize estate taxes.

9. "What are some creative ways to stay mentally and physically active during retirement?"

Explanation: Staying active and engaged in retirement is essential for overall well-being. This question explores activities and strategies for doing so.

10. "Tell me about the best practices for managing my time and setting goals in retirement."

Explanation: Retirement often comes with newfound free time. This prompt seeks guidance on time management and goal setting to maintain purpose and fulfillment.

11. "Can you explain the basics of required minimum distributions (RMDs) from retirement accounts?"

Explanation: Understanding RMDs is crucial to avoid penalties and manage retirement account withdrawals effectively. This question seeks clarification on this topic.

12. "What are some strategies for leaving a financial legacy or making charitable contributions in retirement?"

Explanation: This prompt explores options for retirees who wish to leave a legacy or make charitable contributions as part of their financial plan.

13. "How can I protect myself from financial scams and fraud in retirement?"

Explanation: Retirees can be vulnerable to financial scams. This question seeks advice on protecting one's finances and identity.

14. "What are some best practices for maintaining a healthy work-life balance in retirement?"

Explanation: Achieving a satisfying work-life balance in retirement is essential. This question seeks strategies to help retirees manage this balance effectively.

15. "Can you provide tips on effective communication with family members about financial and estate matters?"

Explanation: Open communication with family members about finances and estate planning is crucial. This request seeks advice on how to approach these discussions.

These prompts cover a range of important topics for retirees, helping them navigate various aspects of retirement planning and lifestyle.

REMEMBER

In terms of a clearly laid-out action plan, AI is shining brightly. The earlier experience in this chapter regarding an overall calculation (refer to Figure 6-1) was off — something you would think that AI should be strong on. I am sure that by the time you read this, the calculating power of AI will be refined to provide better results (at least, I hope!), but in the meantime, folks planning for retirement should be using multiple tools and services (both AI and non-AI) for a more accurate picture of their future prospects.

Thinking about Estate Planning

Your retirement planning was a success! You'll be able to cover your retirement living expenses, and you'll have more than you need (sweet!). But now the issue is deciding what to do about your remaining assets (your estate). Now you need to do estate planning (ugh).

Defining "estate planning"

First, let's define it. Whaddya say, AI?

> "What is estate planning, and why should I do it? Explain it as if I am a high school student."

ChatGPT's response is in Figure 6-2. I don't know about you, but I consider the language of estate planning right up there with Aramaic and Martian. Understanding the terms and concepts is the first battle, and AI is very useful in this regard. I like the feature where I can specify a way to communicate to me because success in a pursuit begins with basic understanding.

ChatGPT

Estate planning is a crucial process that involves making decisions about how your assets and affairs will be managed, distributed, and cared for after your death or in the event of incapacity. Here are several compelling reasons why you should consider estate planning:

1. **Asset Distribution:** Estate planning allows you to specify how your assets will be distributed among your heirs, beneficiaries, or charitable organizations. Without a plan, state laws may determine the distribution, which might not align with your wishes.

2. **Probate Avoidance:** Proper estate planning can help minimize or avoid probate, a legal process that validates a will and oversees the distribution of assets. Probate can be time-consuming, expensive, and public, but certain estate planning strategies can help streamline this process.

3. **Minor Children's Guardianship:** If you have minor children, estate planning allows you to designate guardians who will take care of them in the event of your death. This ensures that your children are placed under the care of individuals you trust.

4. **Incapacity Planning:** Estate planning includes documents such as a durable power of attorney and healthcare directives, which designate someone to make financial and medical decisions on your behalf if you become incapacitated.

5. **Tax Planning:** Estate planning enables you to minimize potential estate taxes, ensuring that more of your assets go to your chosen beneficiaries rather than to taxes. This is particularly important for individuals with larger estates.

6. **Business Succession Planning:** If you own a business, estate planning can facilitate a smooth transition of ownership to your chosen successors, ensuring the continuity of the business.

7. **Medical Preferences:** Through advance healthcare directives or living wills, estate planning allows you to express your medical treatment preferences in case you are unable to communicate them yourself.

8. **Family Harmony:** Having a clear and comprehensive estate plan can help prevent disputes among family members and reduce the likelihood of conflicts regarding asset distribution or other important decisions.

9. **Charitable Giving:** Estate planning provides an opportunity to include charitable giving as part of your legacy. You can specify how you want to support charitable organizations and causes that are meaningful to you.

10. **Peace of Mind:** Knowing that you have a well-thought-out estate plan in place can provide peace of mind. It allows you to have control over your affairs and ensures that your wishes are carried out according to your intentions.

11. **Asset Protection:** Certain estate planning tools can be used to protect your assets from creditors, lawsuits, or other potential threats. This can be especially important for individuals with significant wealth.

12. **Family Business Protection:** For families with businesses, estate planning can help protect the business by establishing plans for succession and providing liquidity for tax obligations.

13. **Avoiding Intestacy Laws:** If you pass away without a will or estate plan, the laws of your state will determine how your assets are distributed, which may not align with your preferences.

In summary, estate planning is a proactive and responsible way to manage your financial and personal affairs, ensuring that your wishes are honored and that your loved ones are taken care of. It provides peace of mind and helps create a legacy that reflects your values and priorities.

FIGURE 6-2:
AI's explanation of estate planning.

With estate planning, the bulk of the work is assembling and recording all the assets (financial, real property, personal effects, and so on) and deciding on the ownership status of each item (I own this; we own that; and so forth). That's most of the physical work of assembling the estate — and AI can help at each juncture.

In the preceding exchange with ChatGPT, I asked for an answer to be at the "high school student" level. In a prior exchange, my requested level was an "eighth-grade student," so I chuckled when it started off with "Estate planning is like making a plan for your stuff . . ." The point here is to remind you that the style and grade level of ChatGPT's response is within your control.

Beginning the estate planning process

Keep in mind that estate planning is, of course, done with an experienced attorney. I don't suggest you go it alone even if you do use AI. But you should consider using it to make the process as simple and as painless as possible. Here's a prompt to start you off:

> "Please create a comprehensive checklist of documents and steps for estate planning. Do it in a checklist approach complete with an explanation of each item."

ChatGPT's response is in the following text due to length.

> Estate planning is a crucial process that involves organizing your financial and personal affairs to ensure that your assets are distributed according to your wishes after your passing. It also involves making arrangements for your healthcare and decision-making in case you become incapacitated. Below is a comprehensive checklist for estate planning, along with explanations for each item:
>
> **1. Create or Update Your Will:**
>
> **Explanation:** A will is a legal document that outlines how your assets should be distributed upon your death. It can also appoint guardians for minor children and an executor to manage your estate.
>
> **2. Establish a Trust:**
>
> **Explanation:** Trusts allow you to transfer assets to beneficiaries with specific conditions or instructions. They can help avoid probate, provide for minors or individuals with special needs, and manage assets over time.
>
> **3. Choose an Executor or Trustee:**
>
> **Explanation:** Appoint a responsible person to carry out your wishes as outlined in your will or trust. This person will be responsible for managing your estate and distributing assets.

4. Designate Beneficiaries:

Explanation: Ensure that your retirement accounts, life insurance policies, and other financial assets have designated beneficiaries. These assets pass directly to beneficiaries and bypass the probate process.

5. Create a Durable Power of Attorney (POA):

Explanation: Appoint someone to manage your financial affairs if you become incapacitated. A durable POA remains valid even if you are unable to make decisions.

6. Establish a Healthcare Power of Attorney:

Explanation: Designate someone to make medical decisions on your behalf if you are unable to do so. Discuss your healthcare preferences with your chosen agent.

7. Draft a Living Will or Advance Healthcare Directive:

Explanation: Outline your preferences for medical treatment, end-of-life care, and organ donation in case you are unable to communicate your wishes.

8. Organize Important Documents:

Explanation: Gather and store essential documents, including birth certificates, marriage certificates, deeds, titles, financial statements, and insurance policies in a secure location. Ensure your executor or trustee knows where to find them.

9. Create a Digital Estate Plan:

Explanation: Document your digital assets, such as email accounts, social media profiles, and online financial accounts. Specify how you want them managed or closed after your passing.

10. Review and Update Beneficiary Designations:

Explanation: Periodically review and update beneficiary designations on your retirement accounts, life insurance policies, and other assets to reflect changes in your life.

11. Minimize Estate Taxes:

Explanation: Explore strategies to minimize estate taxes, such as gifting assets, establishing trusts, or taking advantage of the estate tax exemption.

12. Plan for Business Succession:

Explanation: If you own a business, create a succession plan that outlines how it will be managed or transferred to family members or partners.

13. Consider Long-Term Care and Medicaid Planning:

Explanation: If applicable, plan for long-term care needs and consider Medicaid planning strategies to protect your assets.

14. Consult an Estate Planning Attorney:

Explanation: Seek professional legal advice to ensure that your estate plan complies with state and federal laws and is tailored to your specific needs and goals.

15. Communicate Your Wishes:

Explanation: Discuss your estate plan and your intentions with your family members, beneficiaries, and the individuals you've chosen to fulfill key roles to avoid confusion and conflicts.

16. Periodically Review and Update Your Estate Plan:

Explanation: Life circumstances change, so regularly review and update your estate plan to ensure it reflects your current wishes and financial situation.

17. Consider Life Insurance:

Explanation: Evaluate whether life insurance can help provide for your loved ones or cover outstanding debts and funeral expenses.

18. Plan for Funeral and Burial Arrangements:

Explanation: Document your preferences for your funeral and burial or cremation arrangements and ensure your loved ones are aware of them.

19. Secure Your Digital Assets:

Explanation: Create a list of your digital accounts, passwords, and access instructions for your executor or trustee.

20. Preserve Family Heirlooms and Sentimental Items:

Explanation: Specify how you want sentimental items and family heirlooms to be distributed among your heirs.

Estate planning is a complex process that should be done with careful consideration and the guidance of professionals like attorneys and financial advisors. It's crucial to keep your estate plan up to date to reflect your evolving circumstances and ensure that your wishes are carried out as intended.

Yes, estate planning can be complicated and involved. Fortunately, tools such as AI are there to help you in the process. Two examples of AI tools that specialize in estate planning include Appara (https://appara.ai/solutions/estate-planning) and Luminary (www.withluminary.com).

REMEMBER

As with retirement planning, use AI to drill down on each topic and discuss them with your advisor (hopefully, an experienced estate planning attorney).

6

Applying AI in Coding

Contents at a Glance

CHAPTER 1: **How Coding Benefits from AI** 519

CHAPTER 2: **AI Coding Tools** 547

CHAPTER 3: **Coding with Chatbots** 571

CHAPTER 4: **Progressing from Plan to Prototype** 601

IN THIS CHAPTER

» **Automating repetitive tasks**

» **Getting help with syntax**

» **Testing your programs**

» **Enhancing your learning with AI**

» **Pairing programming with AI**

Chapter **1**

How Coding Benefits from AI

I f you're a programmer or learning to program, generative artificial intelligence (*GenAI*) can help you be more productive, make fewer mistakes, and learn new skills and languages more quickly, as you discover in this chapter. In the process, you work with some tools to get a taste of what's available. All the topics in this chapter are described in detail in later chapters.

Although you might be able to use AI to generate working computer programs without knowing how to code, I strongly discourage you from doing this — especially if you plan to deploy anything you generate. Generative AI doesn't know how to program. If you don't know how to code either, there's a good chance that code you create with AI will have serious security problems, functionality problems, or worse.

Banishing Boring Tasks

One of the most basic and useful things you can do with the current crop of generative AI models is to use them to generate the types of code programmers lovingly refer to as boilerplate code.

TECHNICAL STUFF

The term *boilerplate* dates to the 19th century when steel plates were used as templates for making steam boilers.

Boilerplate code is the stuff that's the same or nearly the same in every file or every project. No one likes to write boilerplate code, but we have to do it because the code we want to write (the fun stuff) won't work without the boilerplate.

Spotting boring tasks

To identify tasks that can be automated with AI, think about the tasks that you do repeatedly in multiple projects. JavaScript developers might select an element in the browser window, such as a button, and attach to it an event listener to do some action when a user interacts with that element. Or they might do something more complex, such as writing the code for a database-driven application that handles creating, reading, updating, and deleting (CRUD) tasks.

For web developers and designers, a simple example of boilerplate code that can be automated is the basic structure of an HTML page. Every valid HTML page starts with a document type declaration followed by an HTML element, then a head element (including several internal elements, such as the title and meta tags), and then a body element.

Letting AI write the template

You can minimize the work required to generate a simple HTML template in many ways, such as by using a code snippet or searching the web for an example. However, if you want to create a custom boilerplate that includes some structure and gives you a good start on the design of a future website, you could simply ask your AI. For example, I gave ChatGPT the following request:

```
Please generate an HTML template with a style element that
uses flexbox to create a three column layout with a sample
top navigation bar and a footer.
```

And here is the code that ChatGPT generated:

```
<!DOCTYPE html>
<html lang="en">
<head>
    <meta charset="UTF-8">
    <meta name="viewport" content="width=device-width,
  initial-scale=1.0">
    <title>Three Column Layout</title>
```

```
<style>
    body {
        margin: 0;
        padding: 0;
        font-family: Arial, sans-serif;
    }
    .container {
        display: flex;
        flex-direction: column;
        min-height: 100vh;
    }
    header {
        background-color: #333;
        color: #fff;
        padding: 10px 0;
        text-align: center;
    }
    nav {
        background-color: #444;
        color: #fff;
        padding: 10px 0;
        text-align: center;
    }
    .main-content {
        flex: 1;
        display: flex;
        justify-content: space-between;
        padding: 20px;
    }
    .sidebar {
        flex-basis: 20%;
        background-color: #f0f0f0;
        padding: 20px;
    }
    .content {
        flex-basis: 60%;
        background-color: #fff;
        padding: 20px;
    }
    .aside {
        flex-basis: 20%;
        background-color: #f0f0f0;
        padding: 20px;
    }
```

```
        footer {
            background-color: #333;
            color: #fff;
            padding: 10px 0;
            text-align: center;
        }
    </style>
</head>
<body>
    <div class="container">
        <header>
            <h1>Top Navigation Bar</h1>
        </header>
        <nav>
            <ul>
                <li> <a href="#">Home</a> </li>
                <li> <a href="#">About</a> </li>
                <li> <a href="#">Services</a> </li>
                <li> <a href="#">Contact</a> </li>
            </ul>
        </nav>
        <div class="main-content">
            <div class="sidebar">
                <h2>Sidebar</h2>
                <p>This is the sidebar content.</p>
            </div>
            <div class="content">
                <h2>Main Content</h2>
                <p>This is the main content area.</p>
            </div>
            <div class="aside">
                <h2>Aside</h2>
                <p>This is the aside content.</p>
            </div>
        </div>
        <footer>
            <p>Footer</p>
        </footer>
    </div>
</body>
</html>
```

The resulting HTML generated by my request (also known as a *prompt*) matched fairly well with what I would have done if I'd written it by hand. Figure 1-1 shows the resulting web page when I save the generated HTML markup in a file and open it in a browser without modifying it.

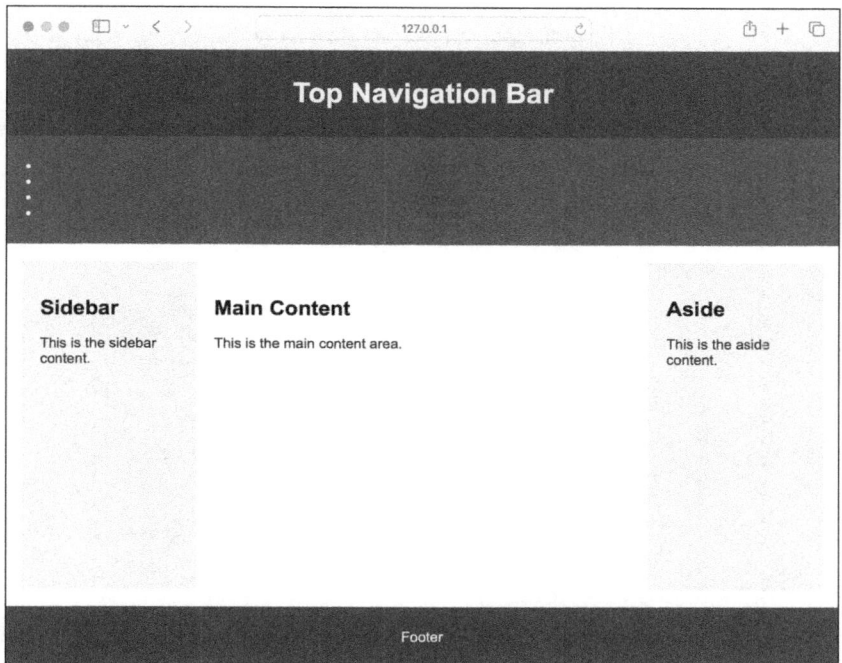

FIGURE 1-1
A ChatGPT
generated HTML
template

ChatGPT

REMEMBER

You can find all the code used in this book, including the HTML template shown in Figure 1-1, at www.dummies.com/go/codingwithaifd.

Crafting CRUD with AI

One of the most common tasks in any computer program is accessing a data source and writing functions for performing operations with the data source. The basic operations you can do with any data source are creating a record, reading a record, updating a record, and deleting a record. The collective name for the code that makes these operations possible is the wonderfully evocative acronym CRUD. Most people don't enjoy writing CRUD.

In this section, you use generative AI to reduce the amount of work it takes to generate some CRUD. To get started with this exercise, you need to have access to an interface for chatting with a generative AI model such as ChatGPT, Google Gemini, or Microsoft Copilot. If you don't have an account with any of these services yet, follow the instructions in Book 2, Chapter 4 to sign up for ChatGPT.

Then, after you have a chat window in front of you, start with a short request to the generative model to see what it will do. If the service you're using won't or can't fulfill your request, you won't have wasted much time crafting a detailed prompt. For example, when I asked Copilot to generate CRUD, it started to, but then told me to ask something else, as shown in Figure 1-2.

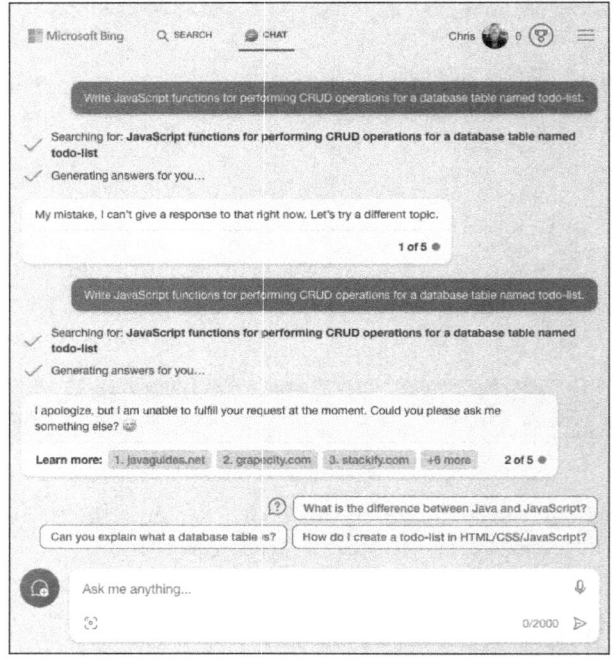

Microsoft Corporation

FIGURE 1-2:
Copilot refused to generate CRUD.

Now, determine whether the response shows any promise. If you didn't get a response, try using a different generative AI model.

Here is the beginning of the response I got to my initial prompt ("Write JavaScript functions for performing CRUD operations for a database table named todo-list.") from ChatGPT using the GPT-3.5 model:

```
// Simulated in-memory database for the todo-list
const todoListDB = [];
// Function to Create a new todo item
function createTodoItem(title, description) {
  const newItem = {
    id: todoListDB.length + 1,
    title,
    description,
    completed: false,
  };
  todoListDB.push(newItem);
  return newItem;
}
```

The response is adequate, but because I failed to provide enough information about my desired application, ChatGPT used an array as if it were a database, which is unlikely to be what is needed here.

If you get a promising response to your initial prompt, give the model additional details. For example, my next step would be to tell ChatGPT that this is a Node.js application that will be working with a MongoDB database and that it should use Mongoose.

The process of refining your instructions to a GenAI model and providing context and examples is called *prompt engineering.* Book 2, Chapter 2 covers the process of prompt engineering in detail. Figure 1-3 shows my second prompt.

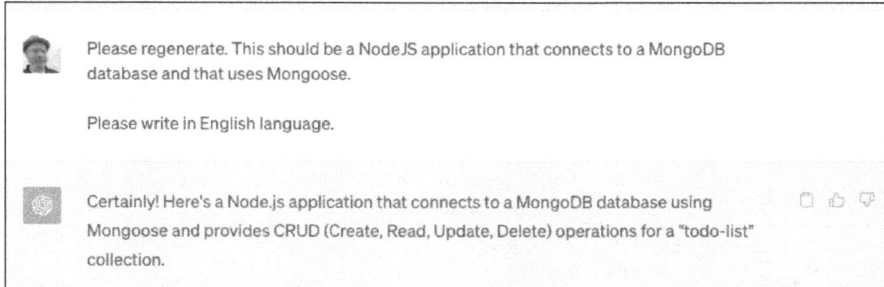

Please regenerate. This should be a NodeJS application that connects to a MongoDB database and that uses Mongoose.

Please write in English language.

Certainly! Here's a Node.js application that connects to a MongoDB database using Mongoose and provides CRUD (Create, Read, Update, Delete) operations for a "todo-list" collection.

FIGURE 1-3:
Adding context
to get a better
response.

ChatGPT

This time, ChatGPT responded with a complete Node.js application that connects to a local database and can perform CRUD operations. Listing 1-1 shows the regenerated code.

LISTING 1-1: **ChatGPT's second attempt**

```
const mongoose = require('mongoose');
// Connect to MongoDB
mongoose.connect('mongodb://localhost/todo-list', {
  useNewUrlParser: true,
  useUnifiedTopology: true,
});
// Define a TodoItem schema
const todoItemSchema = new mongoose.Schema({
  title: String,
  description: String,
  completed: Boolean,
});
// Create a TodoItem model
const TodoItem = mongoose.model('TodoItem', todoItemSchema);
// Function to Create a new todo item
async function createTodoItem(title, description) {
  const newItem = new TodoItem({
    title,
    description,
    completed: false,
  });
  try {
    await newItem.save();
    return newItem;
  } catch (error) {
    throw error;
  }
}
// Function to Read all todo items
async function getAllTodoItems() {
  try {
    const todoItems = await TodoItem.find();
    return todoItems;
  } catch (error) {
    throw error;
  }
}
// Function to Read a specific todo item by ID
async function getTodoItemById(id) {
  try {
    const todoItem = await TodoItem.findById(id);
    return todoItem || null;
  } catch (error) {
```

```
      throw error;
    }
  }
  // Function to Update a todo item by ID
  async function updateTodoItem(id, updatedData) {
    try {
      const updatedItem = await TodoItem.findByIdAndUpdate(id,
    updatedData, { new: true });
      return updatedItem;
    } catch (error) {
      throw error;
    }
  }
  // Function to Delete a todo item by ID
  async function deleteTodoItem(id) {
    try {
      const deletedItem = await TodoItem.findByIdAndRemove(id);
      return deletedItem || null;
    } catch (error) {
      throw error;
    }
  }
```

This isn't bad at all. I like that ChatGPT (mostly) used the latest JavaScript syntax, properly handled errors that may happen, and wrote good comments. I've seen human-written code that's much worse.

The real test, however, is whether the code runs. After it generated the CRUD functions, ChatGPT provided some examples of how they can be used. These examples are shown in Listing 1-2.

LISTING 1-2: **Example usage code from ChatGPT**

```
// Example usage:
(async () => {
  try {
    const newItem = await createTodoItem("Buy groceries", "Milk,
  eggs, and bread");
    console.log("Created item:", newItem);
    const allItems = await getAllTodoItems();
    console.log("All items:", allItems);
    const itemToUpdate = await getTodoItemById(newItem._id);
```

(continued)

How Coding Benefits
from AI

LISTING 1-2: *(continued)*

```
    if (itemToUpdate) {
      const updatedItem = await updateTodoItem(itemToUpdate._id, {
  completed: true });
      console.log("Updated item:", updatedItem);
    }
    const deletedItem = await deleteTodoItem(newItem._id);
    console.log("Deleted item:", deletedItem);
  } catch (error) {
    console.error("Error:", error);
  } finally {
    mongoose.disconnect();
  }
})();
```

If Node.js and MongoDB are installed on your development machine, you can try out this code by copying Listings 1-1 and 1-2 into a file and saving it with the.js extension.

Before you run the application, you need to initialize the directory containing the. js file as a Node package by entering the following in a terminal window:

```
npm init -y
```

Then install Mongoose by entering the following:

```
npm install mongoose
```

Next, run the program by entering **node** followed by the file name, like this:

```
node listing0102.js
```

Figure 1-4 shows what happened when I ran this program.

To verify that ChatGPT's code worked, I commented out the code that deletes the created record, ran the Node.js application again, and then started the Mongo shell and looked at the contents of the todo-list collection, as shown in Figure 1-5.

```
● (base) chrisminnick@chris-mac chapter01 % node listing0103.js
  Created item: {
    title: 'Buy groceries',
    description: 'Milk, eggs, and bread',
    completed: false,
    _id: new ObjectId("650c4885564f597926a10ac0"),
    __v: 0
  }
  All items: [
    {
      _id: new ObjectId("650c4885564f597926a10ac0"),
      title: 'Buy groceries',
      description: 'Milk, eggs, and bread',
      completed: false,
      __v: 0
    }
  ]
  Updated item: {
    _id: new ObjectId("650c4885564f597926a10ac0"),
    title: 'Buy groceries',
    description: 'Milk, eggs, and bread',
```

FIGURE 1-4
Running
my Node.js
application

```
test> use todo-list
switched to db todo-list
todo-list> show collections
todoitems
todo-list> db.todoitems.find()
[
  {
    _id: ObjectId("650c49f3acefaa817b939047"),
    title: 'Buy groceries',
    description: 'Milk, eggs, and bread',
    completed: true,
    __v: 0
  }
]
todo-list> █
```

FIGURE 1-5
Viewing the
collection's
contents in
MongoDB

Helping with Syntax

A large part of the work involved in computer programming is simply remember-ing or looking up the rules that define the structure of a programming language, also known as its *syntax.* Each language or code library has its own way of doing things. After you know the basics of how a programming language works (such as how to create a function, use basic operators, and write loops), you need to know what built-in functions are available in your environment (whether it's a browser or a mobile operating system) and what parameters and types of data they expect to receive. That's a lot to remember, and no programmer I've ever met can remember everything there is to remember about one programming lan-guage, much less several programming languages. With the help of GenAI tools, you can have instant access to the collected knowledge of millions of coders.

You may be asking yourself at this point, "But is it ethical for AI to harvest every-one's code like that?" This topic is hotly debated and the subject of at least one lawsuit. You can learn about legal and ethical issues having to do with GenAI in Book 1, Chapter 6, and throughout this book.

Stop remembering trivial details

When I teach programming, my students often ask me questions about syntax and application programming interfaces (APIs) rather than how something works. When I get a question about syntax, I answer the question if I can without looking it up; otherwise, I encourage students to "Google it." With time and experience, remembering syntax just starts to happen.

TIP

When writing software, one of the best skills is knowing how and where to look for answers. And most of the time, the best place is through a search engine. Because search engines employ machine learning to determine the best results to show in response to queries, we've been using AI for coding for some time now.

Hinting at code mastery

One of the oldest forms of computer-assisted coding is code completion. Microsoft introduced its implementation of code completion, IntelliSense, in Visual Studio in 1996. These types of tools work by suggesting functions and methods that partially match something you've started typing, as shown in Figure 1-6. Traditional code completion functionality doesn't employ GenAI, and its suggestions can often be frustratingly incorrect. However, if you need help with the syntax or spelling (or don't want to type the full names of functions), code completion is useful.

```
const scoreElement = document.getElementById('score');
                        getElementB…      (method) Document.getElementById(elementI…
// Set up event listener getElementsByClassName
                        getElementsByName
// Display the current q getElementsByTagName
function displayQuestion getElementsByTagNameNS
    // Clear the previous getSelection
    answerButtonsElement.innerHTML = '';
```

FIGURE 1-6:
Code completion
is often helpful.

Generative AI takes code completion to the next level by offering suggestions based on its training. When integrated into your IDE, tools such as GitHub Copilot or Amazon CodeWhisperer can suggest entire statements or functions, rather than just single function calls.

GenAI models trained on large datasets of code can offer multiple suggestions based on what other programmers have written, libraries, classes, and functions you've imported into the current file, and even other files that are open in your IDE or in your code repository.

Figure 1-7 shows a suggestion from Copilot based on the fact that I named my file validatePhoneNumber.js.

FIGURE 1-7
Copilot's suggested phone number validation function.

```
validatePhoneNumber.js 3, U ●                                                      ⟲ ☐  ...

validatePhoneNumber.js  <  2/3  >  Accept Tab  Accept Word ⌘ → ...
  1    export function validatePhoneNumber(phoneNumber) {
           const re = /^(\+98|0)?9\d{9}$/;
           return re.test(phoneNumber);
       }
```

Microsoft Corporation

WARNING

Unfortunately, in this instance, the suggested function is worse than useless to most people because it returns `true` only when provided with a phone number starting with 98, which is the country code for Iran.

However, more context can coax the model into returning a better response. When I provided a comment describing what I was trying to do, the model returned a much better suggestion, as shown in Figure 1-8. While not perfect and far too wordy, at least this suggestion gets me closer to what I'm looking for.

In Part 2, you learn much more about how to use GenAI tools to write, format, translate, and optimize your code.

```
                                            ← →              🔍 coding-with-ai                                   ☐ ☐ ☐ ☐

  EXPLORER                           ...    validatePhoneNumber.js U ●                                            ⟲ ☐ ...
  ∨ OPEN EDITORS  1 unsaved                 validatePhoneNumber.js > ⊗ validatePhoneNumber
     ●    validatePhoneNumber.js      U    1    // a function for validating that a phone number is any valid 10-digit phone number
  ∨ CODING-WITH-AI                          2    // returns true if valid, false if not
     > ■ .git                               3
       .gitignore                           4    function validatePhoneNumber(phoneNumber) {
       index.html                      U    5        // check if the phone number is a string
       README.md                       U    6        if (typeof phoneNumber !== 'string') {
       validatePhoneNumber.js          U    7            return false;
                                            8        }
                                            9
                                           10        // check if the phone number is 10 digits
                                           11        if (phoneNumber.length !== 10) {
                                           12            return false;
                                           13        }
                                           14
                                           15        // check if the phone number contains only numbers
                                           16        if (isNaN(phoneNumber)) {
                                           17            return false;
                                           18        }
                                           19
                                           20        // if all checks pass, return true
                                           21        return true;
                                           22    }
                                           23
  > OUTLINE
  > TIMELINE
  main*  CodeTogether  ⊗ 0 △ 0  ⚡ 0    AWS: AWS Builder ID  CodeWhisperer      Spaces: 2  UTF-8  LF  {} JavaScript  ✓ Prettier
```

FIGURE 1-8
GenAI models do better when given context.

Microsoft Corporation

Adapting to new syntax

Like code hint features in IDEs, GenAI can help you learn or remember the syntax for functions or methods. For example, Github Copilot will give you hints as you type; you can ignore these by continuing to type or accept them by pressing tab.

For example, I have trouble remembering the order of the arguments to pass to the `Array.reduce` method. Figure 1-9 shows a Copilot hint for starting the method.

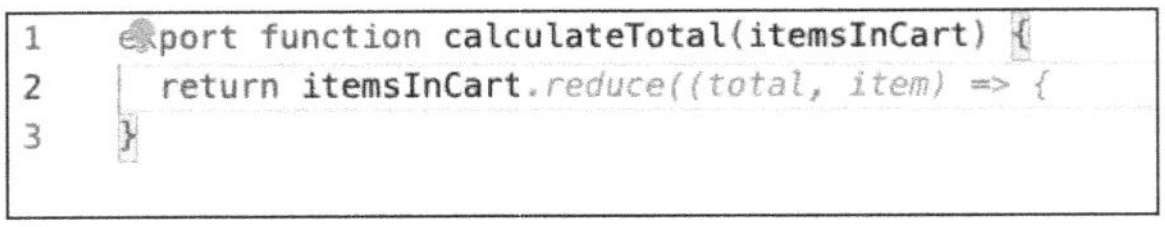

FIGURE 1-9:
Getting syntax
support from
Copilot.

```
1    export function calculateTotal(itemsInCart) {
2        return itemsInCart.reduce((total, item) => {
3    }
```

You can also use GenAI chat interfaces to learn about new syntax. However, keep in mind that the model you're using may have been trained on data that predates the existence of the function or method you're seeking help with. For example, GPT-3's training data cutoff date is September 2021, so the model has no knowledge of events or technologies developed after that date. Figure 1-10 shows what happened when I asked GPT-3 about a feature of JavaScript introduced in 2022.

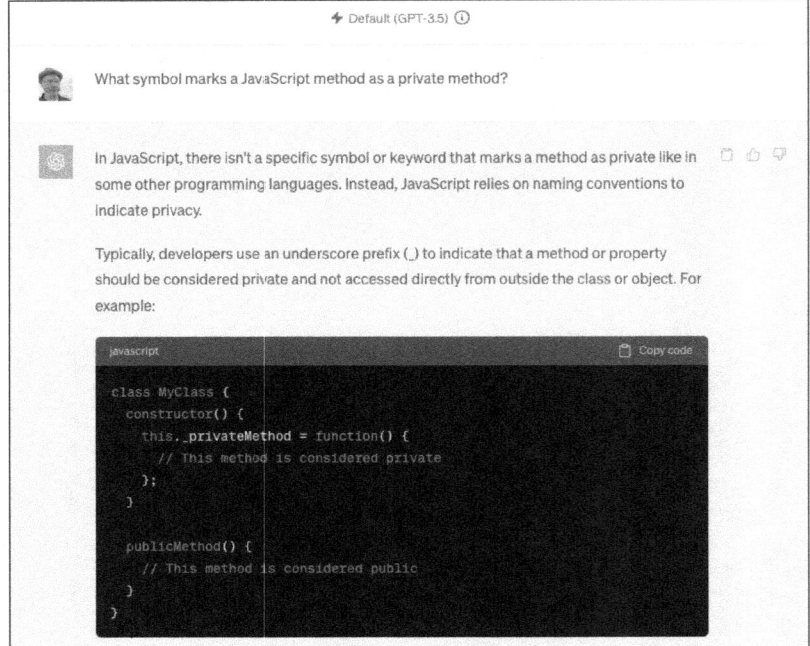

FIGURE 1-10:
GPT-3 doesn't
know about
recent additions
to JavaScript.

ChatGPT

GPT-4, on the other hand, has a more recent training data cutoff. Also, ChatGPT has the ability to search the web while using GPT-4. Figure 1-11 shows ChatGPT's response to the same question but with the model set to GPT-4.

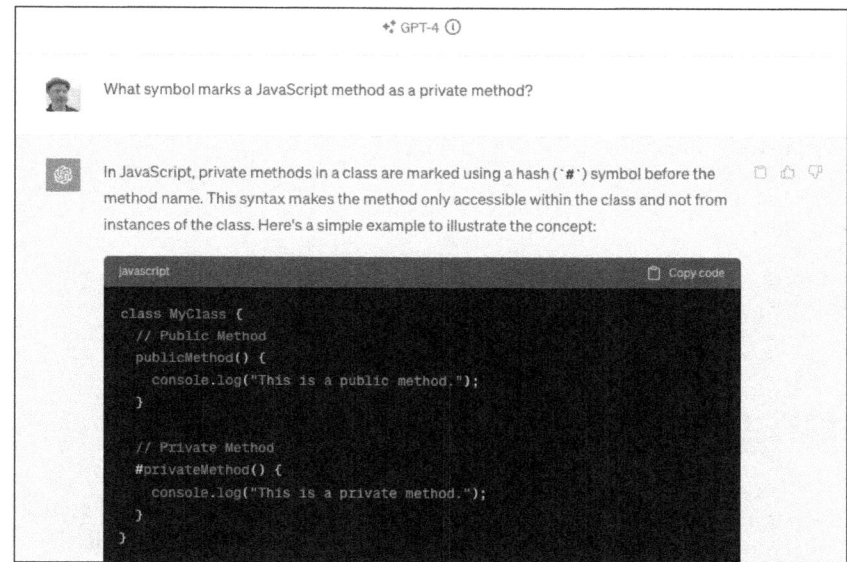

FIGURE 1-11:
GPT-4 generates
a correct answer
when asked
about new
syntax.

ChatGPT

WARNING

Also, remember that, in response to a query, a GenAI model may just invent something that sounds plausible but is incorrect. ChatGPT's tendency to make up facts and people is legendary. However, in cases in which something is as rule-based as a computer language, it usually gets the facts right. As a rule, have a certain amount of distrust of any AI-generated code. Always verify.

Figure 1-12 shows ChatGPT 3.5's response to my question about a non-existent JavaScript method.

How Coding Benefits
from AI

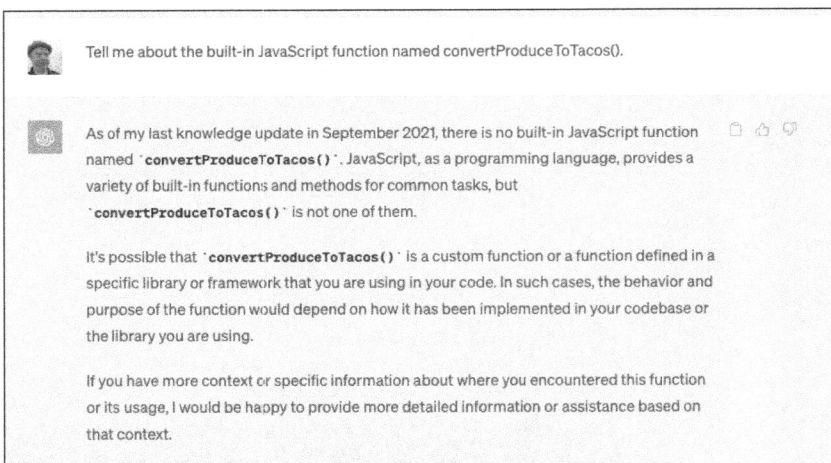

FIGURE 1-12:
ChatGPT
is usually
correct about
programming
language
syntax basics.

Linting with AI

Linters are tools that flag programming errors, bugs, and style issues. The technical name for the job that linters do is static code analysis. The *static* part of *static code analysis* refers to the fact that these tools check the code without compiling or running it. Using a linter can help you improve the quality of your code.

Since most GenAI tools are (at the time of this writing) incapable of compiling and running the code you write, anytime you prompt a machine learning model to look for errors or bad style in your code, you're using it as a linter.

Detecting bad code with static code analysis

To use an AI chatbot as a linter, you can prompt the model with your code and ask it what's wrong with it. Since GenAI models have been trained on a large quantity of working code, they're generally pretty good at finding typos, inconsistencies, and code that doesn't look right.

Simply write something like "What's wrong with this code?" and then paste in the code that's not working. Figure 1-13 shows Google Gemini's response to my question about a function with several typos and examples of bad coding style.

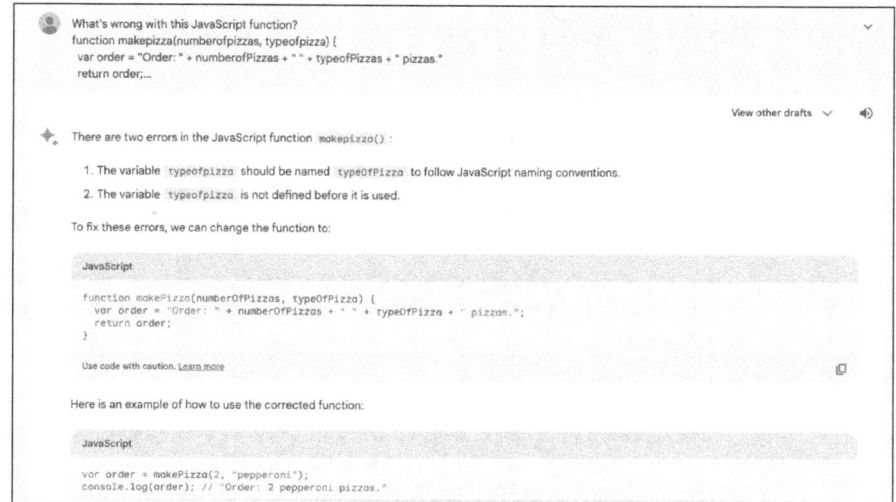

FIGURE 1-13:
Using Bard
as a linter.

Integrating AI with static code analysis

Because programming languages have strict rules, linters don't necessarily need to use AI to detect bad code. However, linting tools that make use of AI can provide functionality that's not possible with standard code linters, such as

>> Detailed natural language explanations of what's wrong with your code

>> Defining new rules using natural language

>> Fixing problematic code or refactoring problematic code or both

Many linters that aren't AI-enhanced can automatically fix certain kinds of problems with your code, and defining new rules generally isn't difficult. The potential for providing detailed descriptions as well as improving your code is promising.

Several tools add AI to existing linters. For example, eslint-ai (available at `https://github.com/iamando/eslint-ai`) is an open-source project that uses GPT-3 to enhance the errors returned by the most popular JavaScript linter, ESLint.

Using eslint-ai requires you to have an account and an API key from OpenAI, and using the tool may result in OpenAI charges. However, GitHub Copilot and other tools include features for cleaning, fixing, and improving your code as part of their standard subscriptions.

How Coding Benefits
from AI

Using AI as a Tutor

The question of whether generative AI should be used in education is hotly debated. On the one hand, AI chatbots and AI-enhanced search engines can often provide customized and accurate answers to questions that traditional search engines can't. On the other hand, it may be tempting for a new coder to rely on code generated by AI rather than on gaining experience through struggling with coding for endless hours, which is the traditional way people learn to program (or to write, or anything else for that matter). In this section, I touch on some of the pros and cons of using AI to learn to code.

Studying AI's potential in education

AI can be a useful tool for someone who is learning to code. Just as search engines, online tutorials, and coding books are used today by both new and experienced programmers, AI chatbots and coding assistants will soon be seen as normal and essential tools.

Whether you're learning from older technologies (such as books or a human instructor) or the latest GenAI model, there's no substitute for gaining experience through writing code or from interacting with more experienced programmers.

TIP

When using an AI chatbot to learn to code, ask the right questions and be skeptical of its answers.

Avoiding potential pitfalls

GenAI models and the chatbots that make use of them don't know how to code. All they do is crunch the numbers, based on their training, and tell you the next most likely word. Even with this seemingly simple functionality, large language models such as GPT-4 are often surprisingly accurate and human-sounding.

WARNING

Although efforts are underway to make GenAI models properly express themselves when they have doubts about their answers, today's models are supremely confident in their answers, even when what they say is completely wrong. Never fully trust a GenAI model. You should always test and verify any code output you get, especially before using it in a production environment.

Pairing Up with AI

Pair programming is a software development technique in which two programmers team up at one computer. In pair programming, one person acts as the driver and handles all the typing, while the other acts as the navigator. Ideally, both programmers are equally skilled and switch roles between navigator and driver as needed to take advantage of each person's strengths. However, pair programming also works well when one of the programmers is more experienced (known as expert–novice) or when both programmers are inexperienced (novice–novice).

Pair programming helps team members share knowledge and learn to work together, and it leads to fewer mistakes and better code.

Overview of pair programming styles

Depending on the skill levels of the programmers, several different variations of pair programming might be used:

>> **Driver-navigator:** This style of pair programming is the most common. In driver-navigator, the driver handles the typing while the navigator looks at the big picture and keeps an eye out for mistakes being made by the driver.

>> **Backseat navigator:** In this style, the driver still does the typing, and the navigator takes a more active role and dictates instructions, such as when to create a file or method or what to name a variable. This style works best when the navigator is a more experienced programmer.

>> **Tour guide:** In the tour guide style, the driver is the expert programmer. They handle the typing and explain to the navigator at every step what they're doing and why.

>> **Ping-pong:** The ping-pong style is designed for test-driven development as a pair. The first person writes a piece of code designed to verify that a feature works as expected (a *test*). The second programmer writes the code to make the test pass. Then the second programmer writes a new test, and the first programmer writes the code to make it work. This style usually requires two expert developers.

Understanding the pros and cons of pair programming with AI

In AI pair programming, you're the navigator who sets the direction and does the strategic thinking. You communicate the project's goal to the AI through comments and code that you write. As you type, the AI navigator suggests snippets and code blocks. With each suggestion, you have to decide whether to accept the suggestion, write your own solution, or ask your AI assistant to try again.

Following are some of the benefits of pair programming with an AI partner:

>> You (the coder) can spend less time looking up syntax and typing repetitive or boilerplate code.

>> The AI assistant is available whenever you are.

>> The AI assistant is fast.

>> The GenAI model behind the assistant is trained on many different programming languages and programming styles, potentially giving you access to solutions you might not have otherwise considered.

The cons of pair programming with AI may include the following:

>> Team members, each working individually with an AI partner, don't get the knowledge-sharing benefits of traditional pair programming.

>> AI-suggested code may not be accurate or up-to-date with the latest syntax or coding styles.

>> AI-suggested code may contain security flaws or other types of issues that a human coding partner would easily spot.

WARNING

Pair programming with AI works best for coders who know their language and have experience writing code without the use of AI. As you're coding, remember that your partner (the GenAI model) speaks confidently but doesn't know anything about programming.

AI pair programming session

In this section, you work with an AI pair programmer to develop an interactive web-based trivia game. For this exercise, you need access to GitHub Copilot.

Installing Copilot

If the Copilot extension isn't installed in your code editor, follow these steps to install it and sign up for a Copilot free trial:

1. **Open Visual Studio Code.**

If Visual Studio Code isn't installed, you can download it at https://code.visualstudio.com.

2. **Click the extensions icon in the left sidebar of Visual Studio Code and search for Copilot, as shown in Figure 1-14.**

3. **Install the Copilot extension.**

   Note that the Copilot Chat extension is installed automatically when you install Copilot.

4. **In your browser, go to** `https://github.com` **and sign in.**

   If you don't have an account, create one and then sign in. To use Copilot, you need a GitHub account.

5. **In the window that appears in Visual Studio Code after you installed Copilot, click Sign In to GitHub.**

   If the window isn't open, click the Copilot icon in the lower-right corner of Visual Studio Code.

6. **Walk through the dialog boxes that appear to give Visual Studio Code access to your GitHub account.**

   When you've linked GitHub and Visual Studio Code, Copilot displays a message saying that you don't have access to Copilot.

7. **Click the link to go to GitHub and sign up for a 30-day free trial of Copilot.**

Extensions icon

FIGURE 1-14:
Searching for the
Copilot extension.

Microsoft Corporation

TIP

You must have a Copilot subscription to use Copilot. A free trial is available at `https://github.com/features/copilot#pricing`. Educators and students have free access to Copilot through GitHub Global Campus at `https://education.github.com/`.

WARNING

Signing up for a Copilot trial requires you to enter payment information, and the trial converts to a paid subscription automatically after 30 days unless you cancel it.

After you've signed up with Copilot, the Copilot icon in the lower-right corner of Visual Studio Code is active. If you click the icon, several options appear at the top of VS Code, including Deactivate Copilot, which turns off suggestions from the model until you click the icon again and reactivate it.

Congratulations! You've signed up with Copilot and are ready to create a trivia game.

Using prompting to create a trivia game

In this section, you use Copilot to help you build a trivia game that displays one multiple-choice question at a time and then randomly picks a new question when the user selects an answer. Think about the structure of the application you want to build. What other details can you imagine will be important to make sure that Copilot offers usable selections?

In the following steps, you see how the exercise went for me. Your experience will be different:

1. **Create a file named index.html and type an HTML comment.**

   Here's the comment I wrote:

   ```
   <!-- Homepage for a trivia game about machine learning -->
   ```

   In response to this prompt, Copilot suggests a DOCTYPE declaration for an HTML5 file, which is correct.

2. **Press the tab key to accept Copilot's suggestion and then press Enter to go to the next line and evaluate the next suggestion.**

3. **Continue accepting Copilot's suggestions until it provides one you don't want.**

   Copilot suggested a basic HTML template containing a form that submits to a PHP script. This isn't what I envisioned, so I need to provide additional information for my initial prompt. I revised my prompt as follows:

```
<!--
Homepage for trivia game about Machine Learning.
This game will display one multiple-choice question at
a time, using JavaScript that gets data
from data/trivia.js.
Possible answers will be displayed with radio buttons
to their left. When a radio button is clicked, the
user will be shown a new random question.
-->
```

With the additional context, Copilot was able to create something that much more closely resembling what I envisioned:

```
<!DOCTYPE html>
<html lang="en">
<head>
    <meta charset="UTF-8">
    <title>Machine Learning Trivia</title>
    <link rel="stylesheet" href="css/style.css">
</head>
<body>
    <div class="container">
        <header>
            <h1>Machine Learning Trivia</h1>
        </header>
        <main>
            <div id="question"></div>
            <div id="answers"></div>
            <div id="score"></div>
        </main>
        <footer>
            <p>&copy; Chris Minnick</p>
        </footer>
    </div>
    <script src="js/trivia.js"></script>
</html>
```

4. Add `type="module"` to the `<script>` tag to tell Copilot that you'll be using an `import` statement inside the trivia.js file.

5. Create three folders named js, css, and data.

6. Inside the data folder, create a file named triviaQuestions.js.

7. **Write a comment at the beginning of triviaQuestions.js that describes what the file should contain.**

This is what I wrote:

```
// A module containing an array of 10 objects
// containing quiz questions and answers.
```

8. **If your prompt, like mine, didn't generate the content you expected, do the following:**

a. *Click the Chat icon in the left panel of Visual Studio code to open the Copilot Chat interface.*

You can also use ChatGPT for this step.

b. *In the Chat interface, enter the following prompt:*

```
Give me a JavaScript array containing 10 multiple-choice
    trivia questions about machine learning.
```

In response to this prompt, Copilot Chat gave me a properly formatted and appropriate array of questions and answers. The first few questions follow:

```
const triviaQuestions = [
  {
    question: "What is the name of the algorithm that is
  commonly used for supervised learning?",
    choices: ["Decision Tree", "K-Means", "Naive Bayes",
  "Random Forest"],
    answer: "Decision Tree"
  },
  {
    question: "What is the name of the algorithm that is
  commonly used for unsupervised learning?",
    choices: ["K-Means", "Decision Tree", "Naive Bayes",
  "Random Forest"],
    answer: "K-Means"
  },
  {
    question: "What is the name of the algorithm that is
  commonly used for reinforcement learning?",
    choices: ["Q-Learning", "K-Means", "Naive Bayes",
  "Random Forest"],
    answer: "Q-Learning"
  },

  ...
];
```

9. Copy the generated array and paste it into your data file.

10. You'll be importing the array into your JavaScript file, so add the `export` keyword before `const`, like this:

```
export const triviaQuestions = [
```

11. Create a new file in the js folder named trivia.js.

REMEMBER

Make sure that you keep triviaQuestions.js and index.html open while you're working on trivia.js. Copilot uses files you have open as context for the one you're working on.

12. Write a comment at the beginning of trivia.js describing what it should do.

Here's the comment I wrote:

```
/* JavaScript for the Trivia Game.
This script is loaded by the index.html file
and will display questions and possible answers
that users can select from. The game will display
a new random question when the user clicks a radio
button to choose an answer and keep track of the
user's score. */
```

13. Immediately following the comment, start a JavaScript `import` statement to import the question data.

Whether Copilot figures out what you're doing and helps you or not, the import statement should look like this:

```
import {triviaQuestions} from '../data/triviaQuestions.js';
```

14. Press Enter and accept the variables that Copilot suggests.

Eventually, Copilot will suggest a function.

TIP

Don't accept the suggested function right away. If Copilot isn't making any suggestions, try inserting a blank line. After that, look at the Copilot icon in the lower-right corner. It should start spinning, and after a few seconds you'll see a suggestion for how to start writing the code.

15. Hover your mouse pointer over the function suggestion to display the Copilot menu, which might list multiple possible suggestions, as shown in Figure 1-15.

16. If you like one of the suggestions, accept it. If not, try refining your comment to provide more information about what you want.

17. Continue this process of accepting suggestions, writing code, and using comments to provide context until you have something that might work.

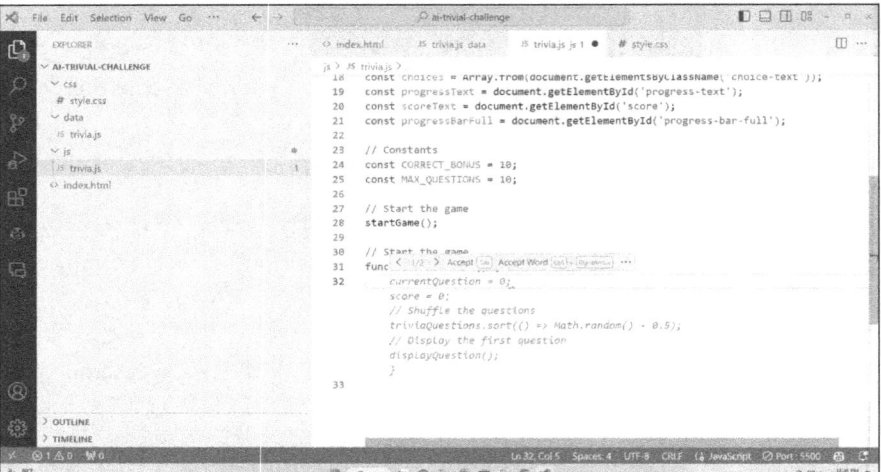

FIGURE 1-15:
Viewing the
Copilot menu
and multiple
suggestion
options.

Now it's time to preview your application:

1. **Click the extensions icon to the left of VSCode (labeled in Figure 1-14) and use the Search box to find the Live Server extension.**

2. **Click the Install button under the Live Server extension.**

   This extension opens HTML files using a development server.

3. **In Visual Studio Code's File Explorer, right-click index.html and select Open with Live Server.**

   Your application opens in your default web browser.

Figure 1-16 shows the (rough and unready) game that I created with Copilot's help. The process took me around 20 minutes on my second attempt.

If your application doesn't work, try debugging with the help of Copilot Chat.

Whether or not you ended up with a usable — or even good — application, ask yourself the following questions:

>> Was pair programming with AI easier or more difficult than pair programming with another coder?

>> Were you surprised (positively or negatively) by the suggestions offered by Copilot?

>> How would you change your approach to pair programming with AI if you were to repeat this exercise?

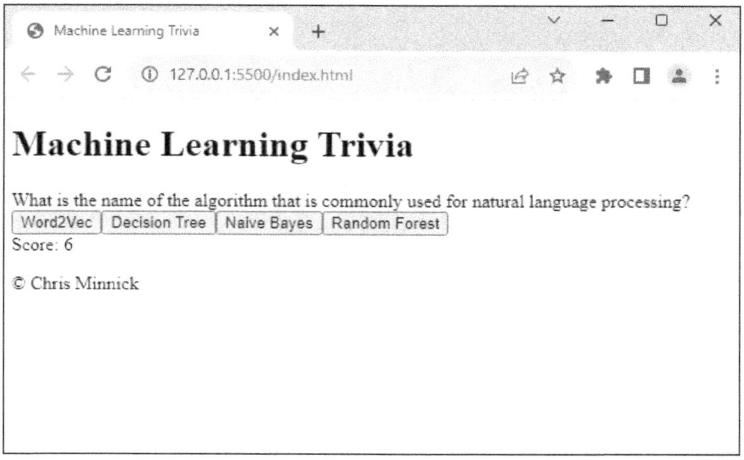

FIGURE 1-15:
A somewhat
functional
trivia game.

In Chapter 3 of this book, you learn much more about how to get better results from GenAI. In the next chapter of this book (Chapter 2), you find out about some of the tools that are available for coding with AI.

» **Flying with Copilot**

» **Coding with Tabnine**

» **Working together with Replit**

Chapter **2**

AI Coding Tools

Generative AI has made new types of tools available to coders and has enabled many legacy tools to integrate AI functionality. In this chapter, you look at three of the most popular GenAI coding tools — GitHub Copilot, Tabnine, and Replit — gaining hands-on experience setting up and using the basic features of each.

Navigating GitHub Copilot

GitHub Copilot is a cloud-based AI coding tool developed by GitHub (which is part of Microsoft) and OpenAI (the creators of the GPT-x models behind ChatGPT and many other tools). Copilot was launched in June 2021 and currently integrates with several code editors and IDEs, including Visual Studio Code, Visual Studio, Neovim, and JetBrains's IDEs.

The GenAI model behind Copilot is named OpenAI Codex. Codex is based on OpenAI's GPT-3 and is also trained on source code from millions of public GitHub repositories and other publicly available source code.

Although Copilot works best with Python, JavaScript, TypeScript, Ruby, and Go, it has been trained on source code from more than a dozen programming languages and will continue to become more fluent in additional languages over time.

Installing the Copilot plug-in

The first step in using Copilot is to install the GitHub plug-in (or extension, as it's called in VS Code). The process for installing the extension differs based on your IDE. You can find detailed installation instructions for every IDE supported by Copilot at `https://docs.github.com/en/copilot/getting-started-with-github-copilot`. In Book 6, Chapter 1, I provide details on installing and enabling the Copilot extension for VS Code.

To follow along with the examples in this chapter, you should use VS Code or GitHub's in-browser code editor, CodeSpaces (`https://github.com/codespaces`). CodeSpaces is based on VS Code and, therefore, very similar to the installable version of VS Code.

When you install the Copilot extension in VS Code, the Copilot Chat extension is installed automatically. After you install Copilot, the Copilot status icon will appear in the lower-right corner of VS Code (see Figure 2-1, top). If you're not currently logged into a GitHub account with access to Copilot, the Copilot status icon appears with an exclamation point (see Figure 2-1, bottom).

FIGURE 2-1:
The Copilot status icon in connected and disconnected mode.

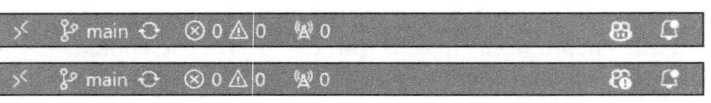

Microsoft Corporation

Although you can install the plug-in without having a Copilot account, you must have a GitHub account and either an individual subscription ($10 per month) or a business subscription ($19 per user per month) to use Copilot. A free 30-day trial is available, as well as free accounts for students and educators.

You can click the Accounts icon in VS Code to create a GitHub account, if necessary. Then log into GitHub and grant the Copilot extension access, as shown in Figure 2-2.

The Copilot extensions don't have many adjustable settings. Perhaps the most important setting you can control is whether or not Copilot is actively giving you suggestions. To disable Copilot so you can think, click the Copilot status icon. In the menu that appears at the top of the VS Code interface, select Disable Completions. (When completions are disabled, an Enable Completions link appears in the menu.)

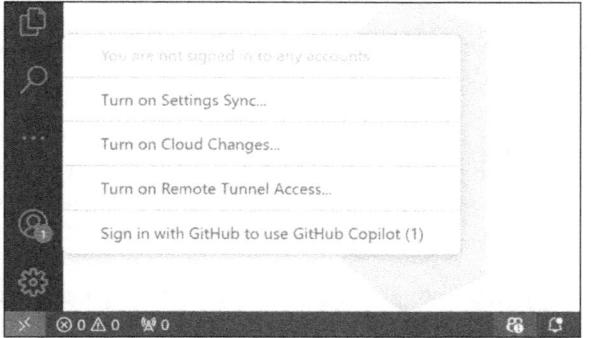

FIGURE 2-2:
Click the Accounts
icon to grant
Copilot access
to your GitHub
account.

To access other settings, click the Extensions icon in the left panel of VS Code. Then click the gear icon next to an extension and select Extension Settings from the menu that appears. Figure 2-3 shows the Extension Settings screen for the Copilot extension.

Extensions icon

FIGURE 2-3:
The Extension
Settings screen
for Copilot.

Working efficiently with Copilot

After you have installed and enabled Copilot, using it is just a matter of starting to type some code. However, just as with any GenAI tool, context is everything. The first piece of context you should provide to Copilot is the type of code you intend to write. You can do this by starting a new file with the file extension of the programming language you'll be using, such as .js for JavaScript or .py for Python.

Choose your filename carefully because it determines the types of suggestions Copilot gives you.

Copilot generates suggestions using context from the file you're currently working on and neighboring tabs — the other files open in your editor. So, if your current project contains other files that will be related to the new one you're starting, open those as well so that Copilot can glean information from them.

The goal of learning how to provide good context to Copilot is to increase its accuracy. The longer you use Copilot on a project, the more its accuracy will improve on its own. You can further improve the accuracy of suggestions through better prompting and providing better context.

According to research published by GitHub, developers accepted an average of 30 percent of Copilot's suggestions immediately. After six months of using Copilot, the average suggestion acceptance rate increased to 34 percent. Reading this book may help you to beat the average!

Following are some best practices for getting the most accurate suggestions from Copilot:

>> Specify your goal up front.

>> Break things down into small steps.

>> Give Copilot examples.

>> Open related files.

You see examples of each of these best practices next.

Specify your goal

Especially if you're starting with a blank file or an empty repository, you'll want to begin to code by describing, in detail, what you want to create. Most often, you do this by writing code comments at the beginning of the file.

A vague comment is not going to result in Copilot being helpful. Here is the initial code generated by Copilot in response to the prompt *a to-do app*:

```
// a to-do app
var todoList = {
  todos: [],
  displayTodos: function () {
```

```
    console.log('My Todos:', this.todos);
  }
};
```

Instead, try starting out with at least the amount of detail you would give to another coder:

```
/* A to-do app. Users can check a box to mark a task
complete, and completed tasks will be shown in a separate
list below the uncompleted tasks. */
var todoList = {
  todos: [],
  displayTodos: function () {
    console.log('My Todos:', this.todos);
  },
  addTodo: function (todoText) {
    this.todos.push({
      todoText: todoText,
      completed: false,
    });
    this.displayTodos();
  },
  changeTodo: function (position, todoText) {
    this.todos[position].todoText = todoText;
    this.displayTodos();
  },
  deleteTodo: function (position) {
    this.todos.splice(position, 1);
    this.displayTodos();
  },
  toggleCompleted: function (position) {
    var todo = this.todos[position];
    todo.completed = !todo.completed;
    this.displayTodos();
  },
};
```

With additional details, Copilot still didn't get it right, but at least it took into account some of the pieces of my prompt, such as that users can mark tasks as completed.

Break things down

GenAI models have a limited attention span. To improve results, give Copilot information as a series of steps, rather than as a request for a large block of code all at once. After each step, let Copilot generate some code, and then write the next step.

For example, in the following, I broke down the to-do app I want to write into areas of functionality, and I accepted the first suggestion Copilot made for each step.

```
/*
1. Create a constant called toDoItems
containing an array of objects. Each object
should have a todoText property and a completed property.
*/
const toDoItems = [
  {
    todoText: 'item1',
    completed: false,
  },
  {
    todoText: 'item2',
    completed: false,
  },
  {
    todoText: 'item3',
    completed: false,
  },
];
/*
2. Create a function that displays a list of to-do
items in an element with an id attribute set to "to-dos" in the
  browser.
*/
function displayTodos() {
  const todosUl = document.querySelector('#to-dos');
  todosUl.innerHTML = '';
  toDoItems.forEach((item) => {
    const todoLi = document.createElement('li');
    todoLi.textContent = item.todoText;
    todosUl.appendChild(todoLi);
  });
}
```

This code is much closer to what I was looking for and is a decent starting point for my app.

Give examples

If you already have an idea of what you want Copilot to generate, start by giving it an example or two. For example, if you want it to generate an array of objects, tell it what an object should look like. In the following, I refined my first step from the preceding example to specify what I'm looking for:

```
/*
1. Create an array of to-do items with the following shape:
[{todoTitle:'', todoDesc:'', date:'', completed:false}]
*/
const toDoItems = [
  {
    todoTitle: 'item1',
    todoDesc: 'item1 description',
    date: '2024-07-01',
    completed: false,
  },
  {
    todoTitle: 'item2',
    todoDesc: 'item2 description',
    date: '2024-07-02',
    completed: false,
  },
  {
    todoTitle: 'item3',
    todoDesc: 'item3 description',
    date: '2024-07-03',
    completed: false,
  },
];
```

Open related files

Copilot gets context for the file you're working on from other files you have open in your editor. If you're working on a JavaScript file that will affect an HTML page or that imports code from other JavaScript files, open those files in separate tabs.

In my to-do app example, the JavaScript will affect the display of the HTML page, so creating the HTML page and opening it in another tab will help Copilot generate more accurate JavaScript code.

Using keyboard shortcuts

Although you can successfully use Copilot by just coding as you normally would and using the tab key to accept suggestions, knowing a few more keyboard shortcuts will make your coding sessions more productive. The keyboard shortcuts you'll want to remember are shown in Table 2-1.

TABLE 2-1

Copilot Keyboard Shortcuts

Shortcut	What It Does
Tab	Accepts inline code suggestions
Esc	Dismisses inline code suggestions
Alt +] (or Option +])	Shows the next suggestion
Alt + [(or Option + [)	Shows the previous suggestion
Alt + \ (or Option + \)	Triggers a suggestion
Ctrl + Enter	Generates up to 10 suggestions in a separate pane

The Ctrl+Enter shortcut is particularly useful. When Copilot gives you a suggestion and you want to find out whether it might be able to suggest something better, press Ctrl+Enter. A new pane will open in your code editor and (after a minute or so) display up to 10 other suggestions, as shown in Figure 2-4.

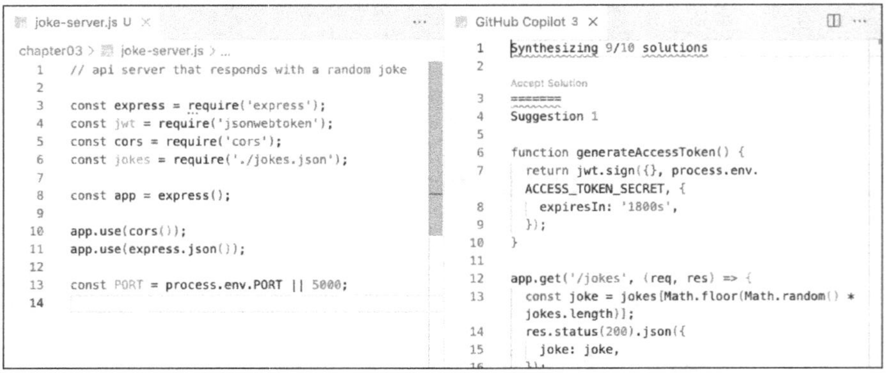

FIGURE 2-4: Getting more suggestions.

Microsoft Corporation

Exploring Tabnine

Tabnine is an AI coding assistant and the name of the company that created it. The company was formed in 2012 and released the first version of its coding assistant in 2018, making Tabnine one of the longest-established AI-powered coding tools.

Tabnine is available in three versions: starter, pro, and enterprise. The starter version offers basic code completion. The pro plan offers AI code features similar to those of Copilot: whole-line and function code completions, natural-language-to-code completions, and a chat interface. The enterprise version allows a company to locate the model in the corporate firewall and provide access to every developer in the company.

A 7-day free trial (which for me turned out to be a 14-day trial) of the pro plan is available. I show you features from both the starter plan and the pro plan in this chapter.

One of the biggest differences between Tabnine and other AI coding assistant tools is that Tabnine runs on its own model, which they've trained on publicly available open-source code with permissive licenses. So coders and organizations should be able to use Tabnine-generated code without facing legal issues regarding intellectual property violations. This added assurance has made Tabnine popular with large organizations.

TECHNICAL STUFF

You can view the entire list of repositories that Tabnine is trained on by going to `https://trust.tabnine.com/`.

WARNING

Be aware of the risk of violating the licenses of the code a model was trained on. In 2022, a class action lawsuit was filed against Microsoft (the owner of GitHub and GitHub Copilot) and OpenAI, claiming that the companies violated the open-source licenses of programmers whose code was used to train the model Copilot uses.

Tabnine takes code privacy seriously. Their privacy policy (available at `https://tabnine.com/code-privacy`) states that they never store or share any of your code. This point is important for businesses concerned that AI coding assistants may inadvertently leak their intellectual property.

Businesses that use Tabnine can create their own model, which can live on the business's premises or in the cloud. To create a private code model, Tabnine trains its public model with the client's codebase. When customers with a private model submit a query, it's sent to Tabnine's public model and the private model and picks the most relevant code suggestion from the two options returned. The private model is continuously trained from the code and decisions made by its users.

Installing Tabnine

Tabnine is available as a plug-in, or extension, for many of the most popular code editors, including VS Code, Eclipse, Android Studio, WebStorm (as well as all JetBrains code editors), and Sublime.

Follow these steps to install Tabnine:

1. **Go to** `https://www.tabnine.com` **and click the Get Tabnine link at the top of the page.**

   A page with a Search box and a list of IDEs appears, as shown in Figure 2-5.

2. **Select your IDE and follow the steps to install the extension.**

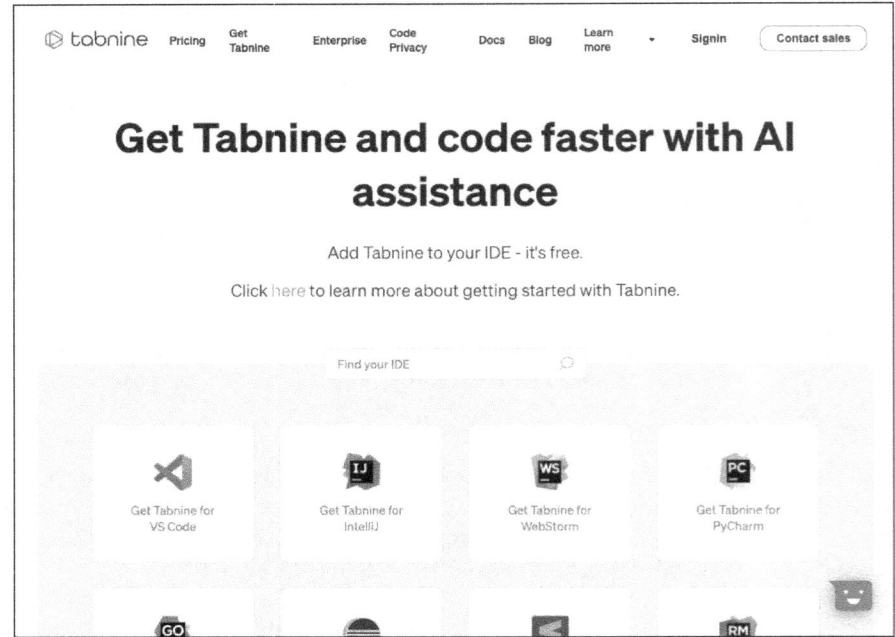

FIGURE 2-5: Choosing the IDE where you want to install the Tabnine extension.

Tabnine

Before you can use the Tabnine extension, you need to create a Tabnine account by going to `https://app.tabnine.com/signup`. After you've installed the Tabnine extension, you may need to restart your IDE.

Setting up Tabnine

After you've installed the extension and logged in, you'll see a link at the bottom of your IDE (in the case of VS Code) that says what plan you're subscribed to. Click this link to open Tabnine Hub.

Tabnine Hub is where you can adjust settings and read about the latest features. If you're using the starter plan, as I am in Figure 2-6, you'll also see links for a lot of features that you won't have access to and links to upgrade to a paid plan. The starter plan is quite capable, however, and you may want to stick with it while you learn about Tabnine's capabilities.

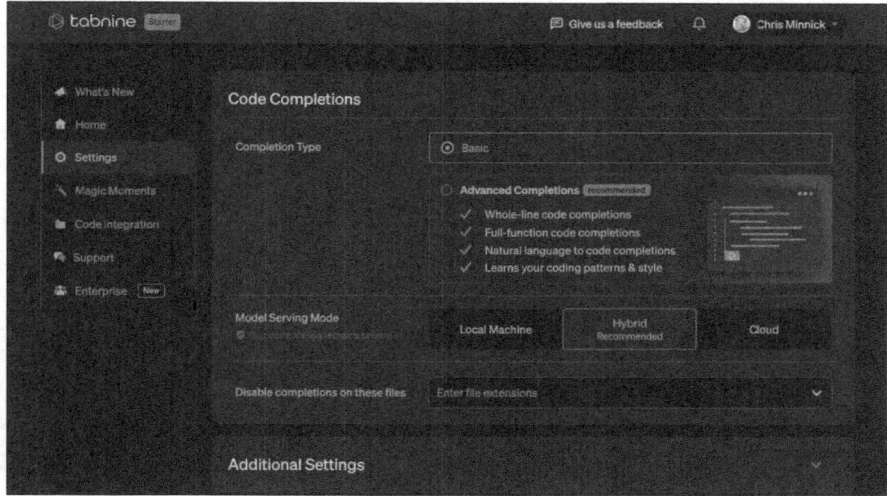

FIGURE 2-6: Tabnine Hub.

Tabnine

Tabnine allows you to choose from one of three model-serving modes: local machine, cloud, or hybrid. Which of these you choose will affect the quality of responses you get:

>> **Local machine:** When you choose the local machine mode, Tabnine stores a smaller copy of the model on your local machine and allows you to work offline without any of your code being sent to Tabnine's servers. The local model is not as powerful as the cloud model, however, and it will increase your local machine's CPU and memory usage.

>> **Cloud:** The cloud model uses Tabnine's servers, so it requires a connection to the internet. Because it processes your completions on the server, the results you get from the cloud model will be more accurate and longer.

>> **Hybrid:** The hybrid model, which is the default mode, combines the benefits of both the cloud and local machine models. You can get suggestions while offline but also take advantage of the computing power of the cloud.

None of the three models stores any of your code. The cloud modes use a technique Tabnine calls *ephemeral processing,* in which your code is processed by the model and then immediately discarded after the model returns a completion.

Understanding Tabnine's AI-driven code completion

To get started coding with Tabnine, you work in much the same way as you would if you were using Copilot. As you enter code in your editor, Tabnine makes suggestions. You accept the suggestions by pressing the tab key.

To help the local model learn about your coding style, you can rate Tabnine's suggestions. Open Tabnine Hub and click Magic Moments in the left navigation, as shown in Figure 2-7. Magic Moments is available only in the Pro version (or the free trial). On the Magic Moments screen, give a thumbs up or thumbs down to individual suggestions. Tabnine uses this feedback to help the local model learn about your coding style.

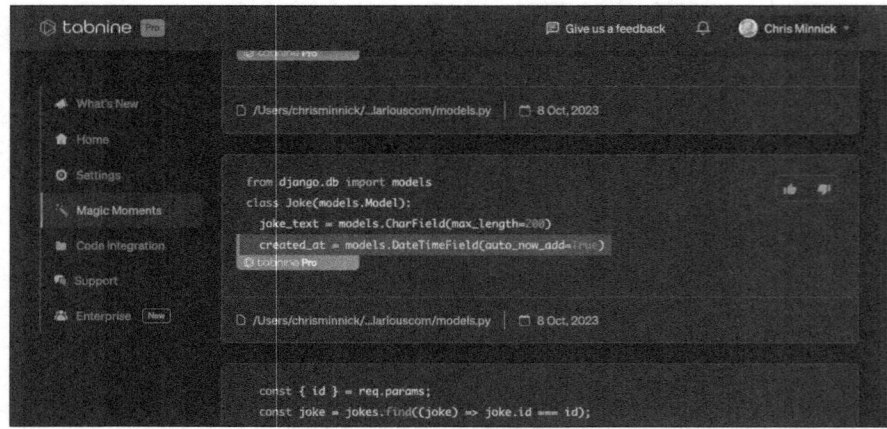

FIGURE 2-7:
Viewing previous "magic moments."

Tabnine

Like other AI code assistant tools, Tabnine requires context to be able to give good suggestions. Here are some tips for improving the suggestions you get from Tabnine:

>> Write more comments in your code than you normally would.

>> When you start working with Tabnine, act as if it's a junior developer who's new to the project. Don't assume that Tabnine can guess what you want it to do, even if it seems obvious to you.

>> Be patient. Since Tabnine learns from previous code of yours that it's seen, it may take time for the model to learn your preferences.

Reviewing Replit

Replit is a browser-based IDE with AI assistance features, collaboration features, and a large and active community of developers. Replit has support for every popular programming language and framework. Because it's an in-browser environment, using it doesn't require any setup beyond creating a free account.

TIP

After you've created a program using Replit, you can then use it for deploying the program. If you prefer to work offline or be free from the distractions of the Replit website, download and install the Replit desktop or mobile app.

To get started with Replit, go to https://replit.com and create an account using your email address, a Google account, or your GitHub account. The default home page is shown in Figure 2-8.

Although the core feature of Replit.com is the IDE, the site also has a Learn section where you can view video tutorials and interactive coding lessons.

In the Bounties section of Replit, shown in Figure 2-9, people and companies post programming jobs, and coders advertise their services, along with a price for each.

The fastest way to get started on a project in Replit is by using one of the prebuilt templates, which are available by clicking the Templates link in the left navigation bar. On the Templates page, shown in Figure 2-10, you can find a template by searching or browsing.

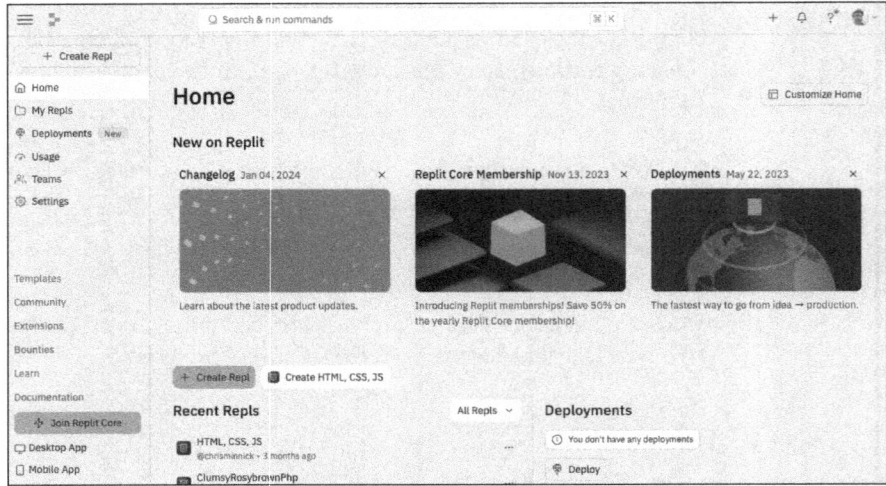

Replit, Inc.

FIGURE 2-8:
The Replit
home page.

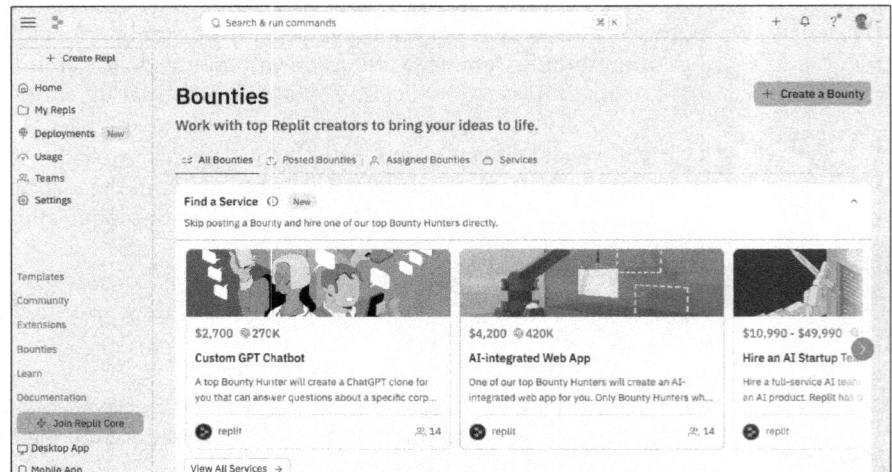

Replit, Inc.

FIGURE 2-9:
Coders can
advertise and
find gigs through
Replit Bounties.

If you prefer to start from scratch, you can create a project without using a template by clicking the Create Repl button on the home page or in the left navigation bar.

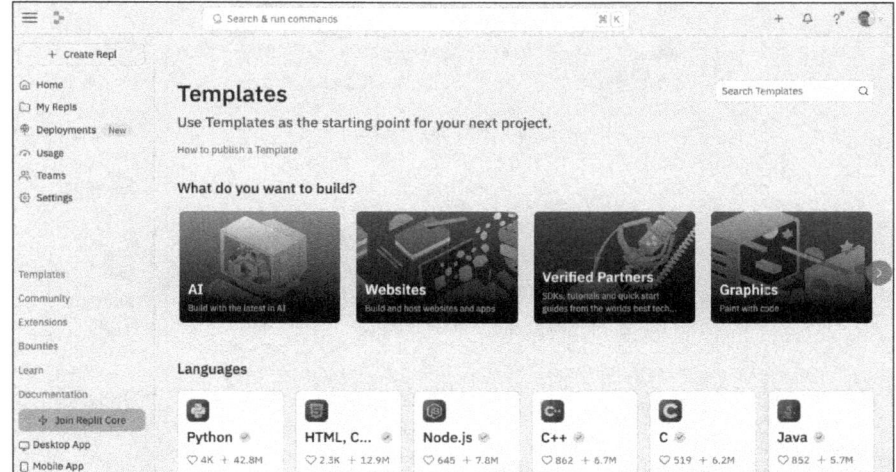

Replit, Inc.

FIGURE 2-10:
Get started
quickly with a
template.

Starting a website with Replit

It's time to experiment with Replit and its AI features. Follow these steps to build a website using HTML, CSS, and JavaScript:

1. **While logged in to Replit, click the Templates link in the left navigation.**

2. **Click the Websites link and then locate the HTML, CSS, JS template.**

   You can also find the template by using the search bar.

   When you're searching for a template and several are available, choose the most popular one by looking at the icons that indicate the number of likes and runs, as shown in Figure 2-11.

TIP

3. **Click in the box for the HTML, CSS, JS template, but don't click the Use Template option yet.**

   The template appears, as shown in Figure 2-12.

4. **Read through the description of the template and click each of the files in the left panel (index.html, script.js, and style.css) to see what they do.**

   In the case of the HTML, CSS, JS template, there's not much to see except that it displays the text *Hello World*.

5. **Click Use Template and give your website a name and description in the pop-up box that appears.**

6. **Still in the pop-up window, click Use Template again.**

   The template opens in the Replit workspace, as shown in Figure 2-13.

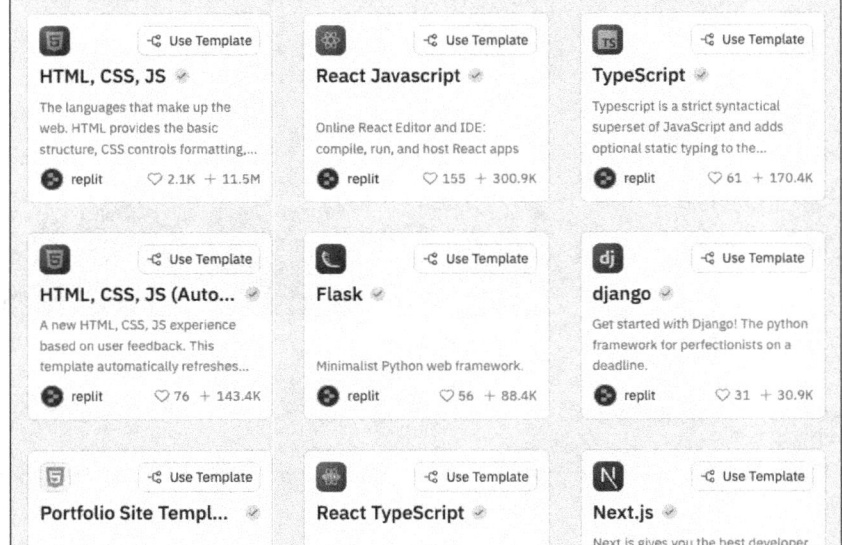

Replit, Inc.

FIGURE 2-11:
A template's popularity is often a good indicator of its quality and usefulness.

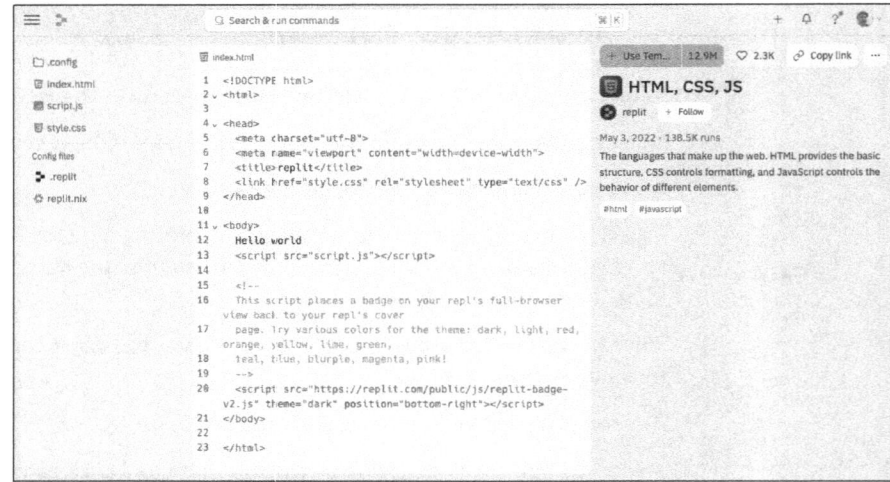

Replit, Inc.

FIGURE 2-12:
Viewing more information about a template.

Exploring the Replit workspace

The Replit workspace is an in-browser IDE that includes features for creating, debugging, and collaborating on software. The workspace is split into two areas: the sidebar area and the tabs and panes area.

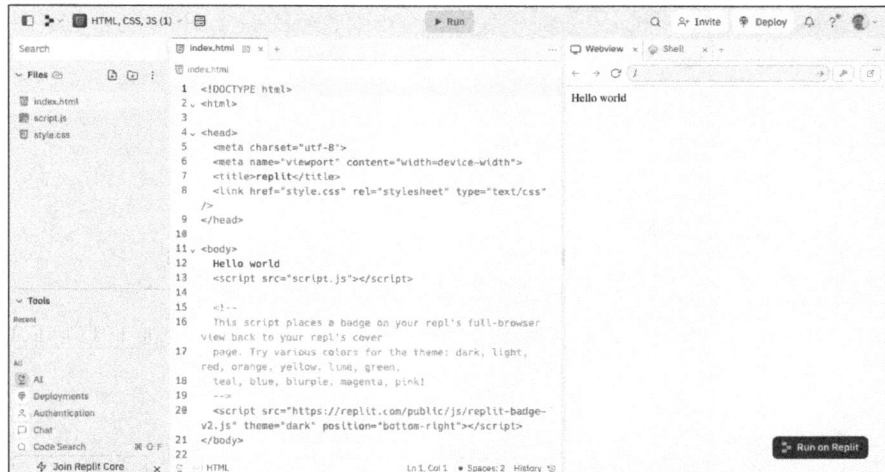

Replit, Inc.

FIGURE 2-13:
Your copy of the
template in the
Replit workspace.

The sidebar

The sidebar is the left column of the workspace. At the top of the sidebar is the file explorer. Here is where you can organize and create files and folders in your project. The file explorer works the same way as most file browsers. Clicking a file in the list opens that file for editing.

Below the file explorer are the tools, including a debugger, a command shell, a web browser (called Webview), and an AI assistant tool (which you learn about in the next section). To see all the tools, you may need to resize the Tools panel. Figure 2-14 shows all the tools that are currently part of the workspace.

Clicking a tool opens it in a new tab to the right of any open code files.

Tabs and panes

To the right of the sidebar are panes. In each pane, there may be multiple open tabs. When you first open the workspace, you'll see two panes. The first displays a code editor, and the second contains two tabs: Webview and Shell.

The Webview tool displays a live preview of your project as it appears in a web browser. The shell tool provides access to a Linux command shell.

You can rearrange tabs and panes in the workspace by clicking and dragging their headers. For example, in Figure 2-15, I moved the pane containing the Webview and Shell tabs to the bottom of the browser window.

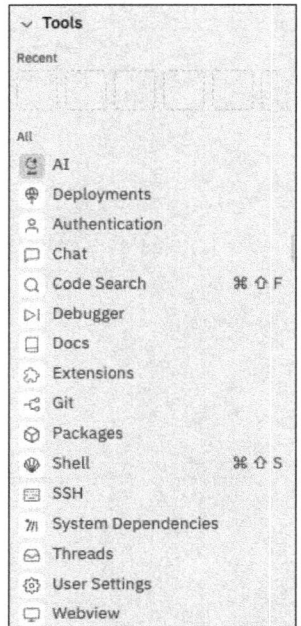

FIGURE 2-14:
Viewing the
workspace
tools panel.

Replit, Inc.

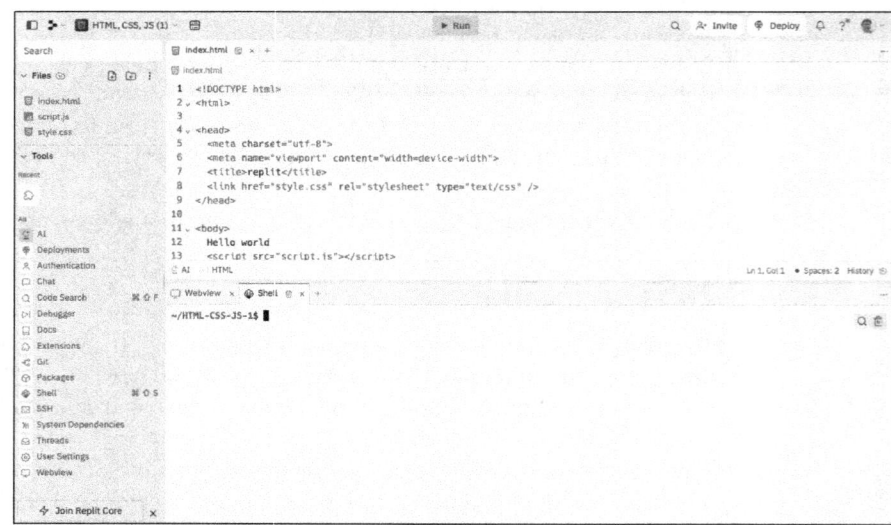

FIGURE 2-15:
Rearranging
panes.

Replit, Inc.

Pairing up with Replit AI

Replit's AI assistant is called Replit AI. With the workspace open, you'll see a link to AI in the Tools panel at the lower left of the screen (refer to Figure 2-15). Clicking the AI icon opens a new tab to the right of the code editor, as shown in Figure 2-16.

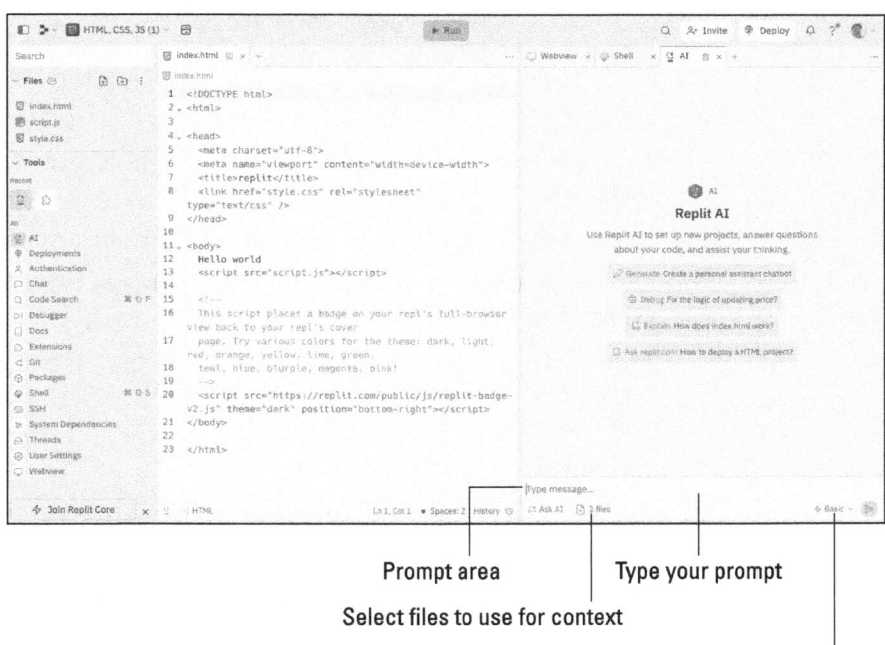

Prompt area

Type your prompt

Select files to use for context

Select the basic of advanced model

FIGURE 2-16:
The AI tab opens in the right panel.

Replit, Inc.

Replit AI is available to all Replit members. However, paid Replit members can access a more advanced version of the AI by going to `https://replit.com/cycles`, where you can also see your balance of Cycles (Replit's virtual tokens) and buy Cycles.

REMEMBER

You can earn Cycles by completing Bounties.

Replit AI has four tools: Generate, Debug, Explain, and Modify, in addition to Copilot-style code completion as you code. To access the Generate, Debug, and Explain tools, right-click in the code editor. The Modify and Explain tools, which change and explain code, respectively, are available only when you've selected code you want the AI to modify or explain.

All of the tools can be used through the Chat interface as well. At the bottom of the AI pane is the text box for prompting the model. Follow these steps to begin using Replit to build a website for a fictitious punk rock band called Grapefruit Pulp:

1. **Give AI the following prompt:**

   ```
   Act as a professional web designer. Use HTML and CSS to
       design the homepage for my punk rock band, "Grapefruit
       Pulp." Include a placeholder for a photo of the band. The
       navigation for the site should have links for Tour Dates,
       Contact Info, and a photo gallery.
   ```

   After a moment, the model returns some HTML and CSS code. My results are shown in Figure 2-17.

2. **Select everything in index.html and delete the sample template code.**

3. **Click the Insert link at the top of the HTML response to insert the generated HTML into index.html.**

   The chat interface can't interact with your files directly, so you need to copy any suggestions that you like from the chat window to your files yourself (using copy and paste or the insert link).

4. **Open style.css and delete its contents.**

5. **Use the Insert link at the top of the CSS response to insert the CSS into style.css.**

6. **Click the Run button at the top of the IDE to open your website in Replit's web view.**

   Figure 2-18 shows my site. It isn't spectacular, but it's a decent start.

Replit AI has two different models: basic and advanced. The basic model is faster but more limited. The advanced model is larger and slower but much more likely to give a better response to a vague or creative prompt. The advanced model is available only with a paid Replit account.

If you have a paid account, you can retry the prompt with the advanced model by toggling the Basic/Advanced selection at the bottom of the AI window (labeled in Figure 2-16). Or, if you're a paid member, you can use the advanced model by default by clicking the Advanced button at the top of the AI chat interface (refer to Figure 2-17).

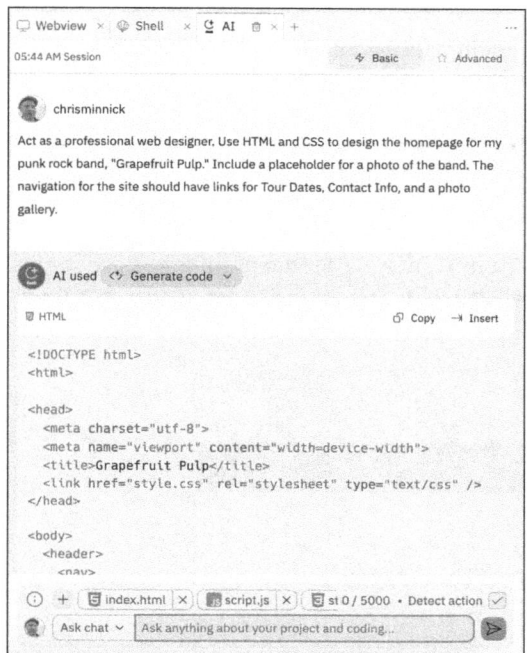

FIGURE 2-17:
Generated HTML
and CSS from
Replit AI.

Replit, Inc.

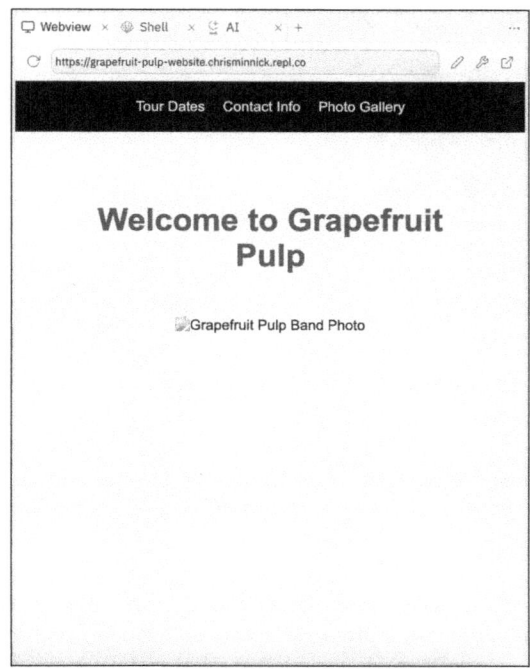

FIGURE 2-18:
The start of
my website for
Grapefruit Pulp.

Replit, Inc.

To see how good Replit AI's advanced model is with more difficult tasks, I gave it the following prompt:

```
Use SVG and CSS to draw a grapefruit wearing a leather
jacket. It should be inserted in place of the placeholder
image.
```

The result is shown in Figure 2-19. This prompt seemed to push the limits of the model's creativity, although this might be a start for an awesome logo.

FIGURE 2-19:
Replit AI's SVG
punk grapefruit.

Next, I switched to working in the photo gallery. I gave the model the prompt shown in Figure 2-20.

When I uploaded some images, the result was decent and close to what I had imagined. Figure 2-21 shows the photo gallery after I clicked a photo to open it in a lightbox.

Used correctly, coding assistant tools such as the ones you learned about in this chapter can make you a more productive coder. In the next chapter, you discover how to talk to AI chat tools to generate ideas and code.

FIGURE 2-2□:
Prompting
for a JavaScript
photo galler/.

 chrisminnick

Create a JavaScript photo gallery that will display 1 image at a time, for 15 seconds before moving to the next one. It should have buttons for moving forwards and backwards through the photos and clicking a photo will open the photo in a lightbox.

Replit, Inc.

FIGURE 2-2□:
My Repl t
AI-generate□
lightbo□.

From Yannis Papanastasopoulos

Chapter **3**

Coding with Chatbots

L
arge language models (LLMs) enable computers to understand and generate human languages with astonishing accuracy. *Chatbots* are easy-to-use interfaces to LLMs that enable conversations with a generative AI model. Using a chatbot, anyone can converse with an LLM in a way that's similar to how you would message a friend or coworker. (To learn about how machine learning and LLMs work, check out Book 2.)

Because the generative AI models that underlie AI chatbots have been trained on an enormous amount of text, it can sometimes seem like the chatbots are omniscient. However, after some time working with chatbots and sometimes getting responses that are incoherent or plainly wrong, you'll realize that they're not.

In this chapter, you learn how to use several popular AI chatbots to generate programming code. You also learn how to get better results by improving the inputs, or prompts, that you give an LLM.

Improving Your Prompts

Prompt engineering is the art and science of developing and optimizing prompts to use LLMs more effectively. By learning about prompt engineering, you'll not only become better at getting what you want out of LLMs but also gain a greater appreciation for what LLMs can and can't do.

Adjusting the temperature

The results you get from an LLM are greatly influenced by a setting called *temperature*, which directly determines how creative or factual the model will be. When set to a lower temperature, the LLM will always return the most probable responses. When set to a higher temperature, the LLM will be more creative and random.

In most language models, the temperature scale goes from 0 to 1. For ChatGPT, the default setting is 0.7. Depending on the type of response you want, you may want to set this value lower or higher.

It's possible to set the temperature to as high as 2.0 with OpenAI's models, but temperature settings above 1.0 are more likely to be gibberish.

To illustrate what a difference the temperature makes, I asked ChatGPT for a list of words that rhyme with *Python*. I didn't specify a temperature, so ChatGPT used its default value. The response is shown in Figure 3-1. It told me that Python isn't a common word in English and gave me four words that all sort of rhyme with *Python* and repeated *bison* as the fifth word — presumably because it figured that four items weren't enough for a "list of words," but it couldn't come up with anything else.

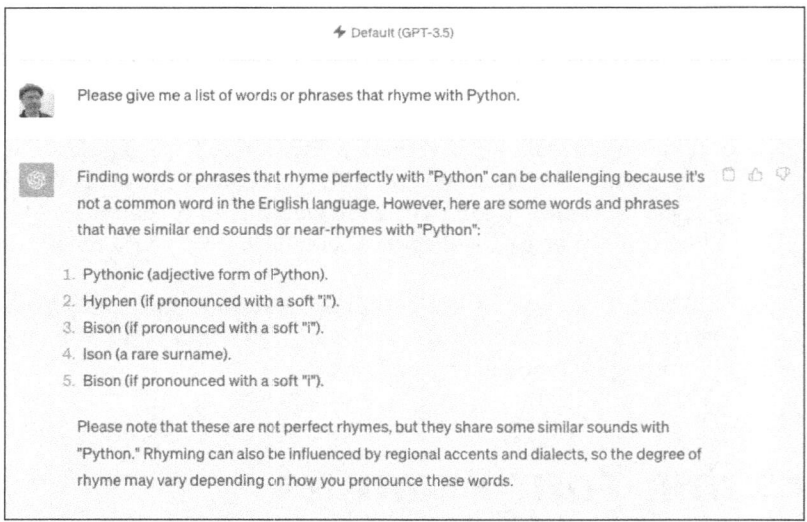

FIGURE 3-1:
Asking ChatGPT to rhyme at 0.7 temperature.

ChatGPT

Next, I asked ChatGPT the same question but told it to set the temperature to 1.0. The response is shown in Figure 3-2.

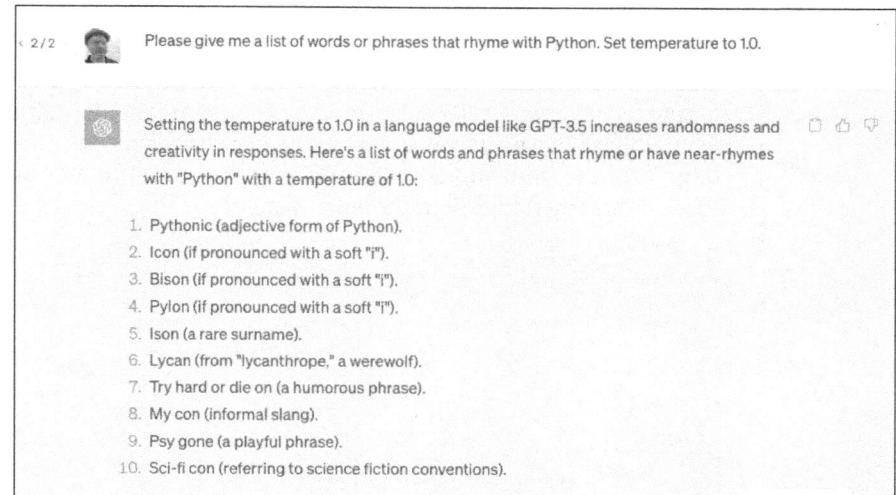

FIGURE 3-2:
Asking ChatGPT
to get more
creative.

ChatGPT

This time, it returned ten words or phrases, and eight of them were rhymes. Next, I asked ChatGPT to set the temperature to 2.0. The response is shown in Figure 3-3. It returned 19 suggestions for words that rhyme with Python, including my favorite suggestion: *Thai cuisine.*

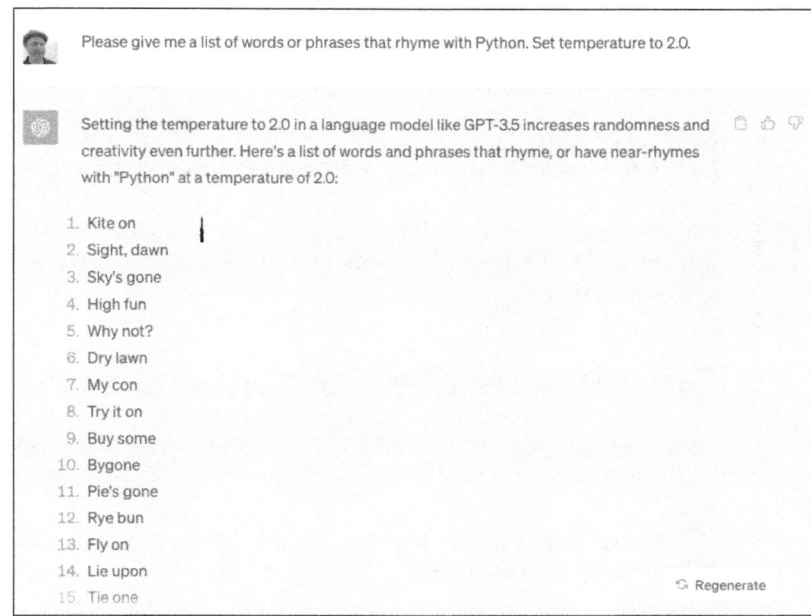

FIGURE 3-3:
Setting the
temperature to
2.0 in ChatGPT.

ChatGPT

Because ChatGPT is tuned to always generate something sensible (even when it's being creative), adjusting the temperature doesn't have as great an effect on the output as adjusting it when working with OpenAI's models directly. To illustrate what it looks like when you crank up the heat on the model, Figure 3-4 shows the output for the same prompt with the temperature set to 2.0 but doing it through the API directly rather than through ChatGPT.

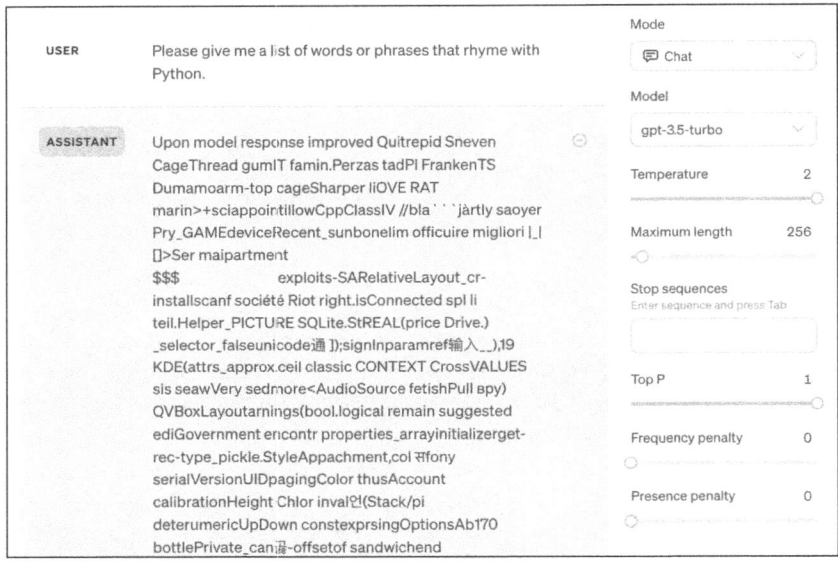

FIGURE 3-4:
What it looks like when the model gets too creative.

ChatGPT

I cover how to work with the OpenAI models through the API later in this chapter.

Some AI assistants may allow you to set the temperature even higher than 2 if you ask nicely. However, be aware that higher temperatures will almost certainly generate garbage.

WARNING

Deciphering the elements of a prompt

Prompts can be simple, such as the completion request *bread and,* or complex and multi-part. Prompts may include all or just some of the following elements:

>> **Instruction:** A task you want the model to do. For example, *Translate the following text into Spanish.*

>> **Context:** Additional information or files that the model should consider while generating the response. The files you have open in neighboring tabs while using Copilot are examples of context.

>> **Input data:** The input or question you want the AI to answer or respond to. If your instruction is to translate some text to Spanish, the input data would be the text you want translated.

>> **Output format:** The type or format in which the model should provide the output. Examples of output format are JSON data, tab-delimited data, and markdown format.

Open-ended versus closed-ended prompts

Prompts may be either open-ended or closed-ended. *Closed-ended prompts* ask for a specific and targeted response, such as

>> Write a function to validate an email address input.

>> Check this function for bugs.

>> What is the tallest building in Indianapolis?

Open-ended prompts are designed to generate expansive responses, such as

>> Write an email to my landlord telling him that I'm moving out if he doesn't fix the leak.

>> Draft an outline for an article about nutrition and school lunches.

>> Write a story about a magician squirrel in the style of Dr. Seuss.

Using different types of prompts

A chatbot will do its best to return an accurate completion for any prompt that you give it. However, you can use various types of prompts for different purposes, as you explore in this section.

Zero-shot prompting

In a *zero-shot prompt*, you don't give the model context or examples of what you're looking for, but instead rely entirely on its training. An example of a zero-shot prompt is

```
What is the capital of Maine?
```

For simple questions or tasks, many LLMs can do zero-shot prompting. As your requests become more complex, however, you'll need to move on to other forms of prompts.

TIP

As models have become larger, an increasing number of tasks can be accomplished using simple zero-shot prompts. However, if you want an LLM to do a task involving math or complex reasoning, you may have better success with one of the prompt types described in the following sections.

Few-shot prompting

In *few-shot prompting*, you start by explaining the parameters of a correct response and giving at least one example. Here's an example of a few-shot prompt to generate fake data for an API:

```
Give me 20 made-up records for customers,
in JSON format, with the following shape:
[
  {
    "Title": "Ms.",
    "GivenName": "Geneva",
    "MiddleInitial": "W",
    "Surname": "Cole",
    "StreetAddress": "3447 Reeves Street",
    "City": "Mill Center",
    "State": "WI",
    "ZipCode": 54301,
    "Birthday": "1/5/1978"
  },
```

A common technique in few-shot prompting is to provide examples of correct answers using Q&A format, as in this example:

```
Q: I drove for 30 minutes and drove 30 miles.
   How fast was I driving?
A: 60MPH
Q: I drove for 10 minutes and drove 5 miles.
   How fast was I driving?
A: 30MPH
Q: I drove for 120 minutes and drove 100 miles.
   How fast was I driving?
A:
```

The model will respond in the same format as in your examples, as shown in Figure 3-5.

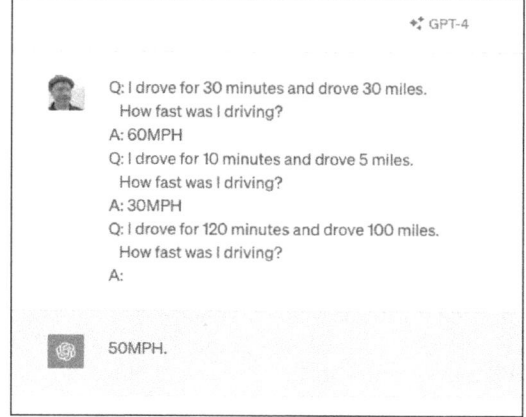

FIGURE 3-5:
Few-shot
programming
gives examples
and specifies the
expected format.

Chain-of-thought prompting

In a *chain-of-thought prompt,* a series of intermediate reasoning steps is provided to improve the model's capability to perform complex tasks. For example, you could improve the accuracy and speed of the AI's response to the few-shot prompt in the preceding section by explaining how you came up with your answers:

```
Q: I drove for 30 minutes and drove 30 miles.
   How fast was I driving?
A: If you drove 30 miles in 30 minutes, that's 1 mile
   per minute (30 miles / 30 minutes), or 60MPH
   60MPH = (30 miles / 30 minutes) * (60 minutes / 1 hour)
Q: I drove for 10 minutes and drove 5 miles.
   How fast was I driving?
A: If you drove 5 miles in 10 minutes, that's.5 miles
   per minute (5 miles / 10 minutes), or 30MPH
   30MPH = (5 miles / 10 minutes) * (60 minutes / 1 hour)
Q: I drove for 120 minutes and drove 100 miles.
   How fast was I driving?
A:
```

Once again, the model will work through the problem in a step-by-step way that more or less follows the same format as the examples you provided. According to a 2022 study from Google Research ("Chain-of-Thought Prompting Elicits

Reasoning in Large Language Models"), chain-of-thought prompting can dramatically improve an AI's capability to complete arithmetic, commonsense, and symbolic reasoning tasks accurately.

Prompting like a pro

Although prompting a language model often involves trial and error, you can improve your prompts by remembering the following tips:

>> **Keep prompts short and precise.** Rather than stuffing every bit of information the model will need into one prompt, split complicated prompts into shorter ones that build on the previous ones in the conversation.

>> **Use *continue.*** This tip is especially useful when generating large code blocks. A chat interface will limit the amount of output it gives for each prompt, so you may get only part of a function at once. Prompting with *continue* will cause the model to return additional content.

>> **Use *Act as a* or *You are a*:** Follow the phrase with a description of the ideal personality or person for a task (such as *professional software developer, experienced database administrator,* or *helpful AI assistant who responds in pirate-speak*). This phrasing can result in higher-quality output.

>> **Tell the model to follow current industry best practices.** This tip will lead to fewer usages of obsolete techniques or deprecated syntax.

>> **Provide cues.** Indicate where and how the model should provide its completion when possible. For example, when asking a model to summarize an article, you might write the following to get the model to respond with a bulleted list:

```
The key points of this article are: *.
```

>> **Label the prompt elements.** Specify the parts of your prompt that are instruction, input, context, or an output format. For example:

```
Input: text of an email.
Instruction: Write a response to this email with a list of
    action items.
Output format: Professional email with a bulleted list of
    next steps I'll take in response to the email.
Context: The sender is my boss.
```

>> **Evaluate the output and ask for improvements if needed.** Always remember that you're the expert, and never simply accept a response you're not sure about.

Chatting with Github Copilot

Copilot provides a direct interface to prompting its model through the Chat extension. The Chat extension is installed automatically when you install Copilot, and you can access it by clicking the Chat icon in the left panel of VS Code.

The first time you access Chat, you'll see some basic instructions for using it, as shown in Figure 3-6.

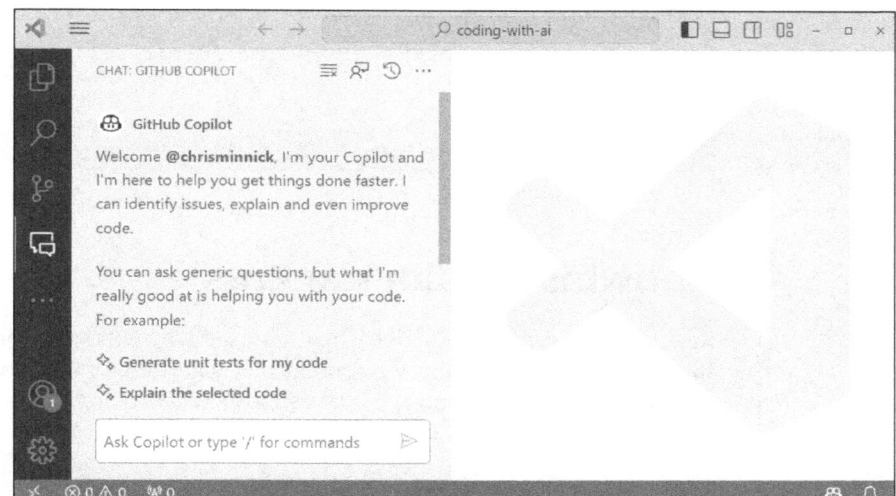

Microsoft Corporation

FIGURE 3-6:
The Copilot
Chat plug-in.

Understanding slash commands

Copilot chat has several built-in *slash commands,* which are shortcuts you can use to accomplish certain tasks or find out something. To see a list of slash commands, enter a forward slash character (/) into the chat input text box, as shown in Figure 3-7.

To get more information about the slash commands and other things you can do with Copilot Chat, type **/help** in the text box.

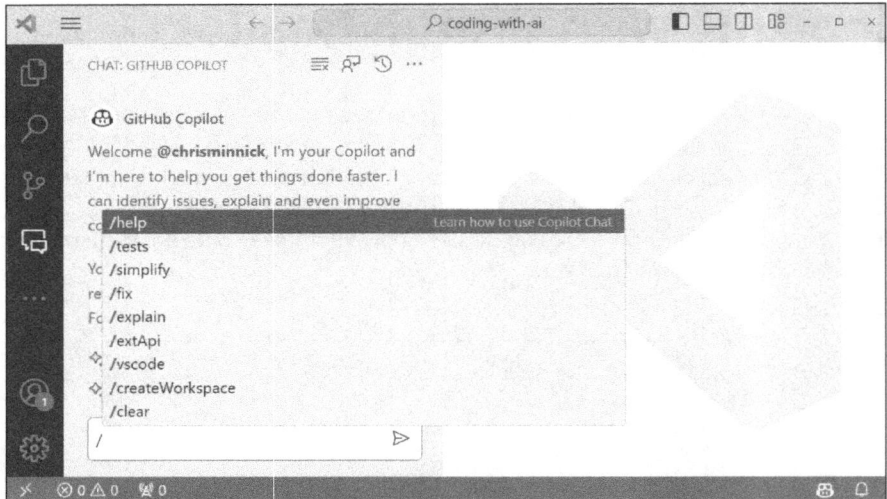

Microsoft Corporation

FIGURE 3-7:
The slash
commands
in Copilot.

Knowing Copilot's agents

Agents are a feature of Copilot when it's used with VS Code. *Agents* allow you to further specify and expand the context that you want Copilot Chat to consider in its response. You invoke an agent by using @ followed by the name of the agent in your prompt. The following agents are available:

» **@workspace:** This agent makes Copilot Chat consider all the files in your current VS Code project when generating a response.

» **@vscode:** You can use this agent to ask questions specifically about how to use VS Code.

» **@terminal:** Use this agent to ask Copilot Chat how to do something in VS Code's integrated terminal.

The @workspace agent is a powerful tool. The best use for it is when you need Copilot to think holistically about your project, rather than just about the file or files you're currently viewing.

Getting the most out of Copilot Chat

Copilot chat works best when you treat it like it's a human coder — perhaps the most talkative human coder you've ever met but one who seems to know a lot, so you'll put up with it. For example, suppose you wanted help fixing a bug in your code. Your interaction with a more knowledgeable human colleague might go something like this:

You: Hey, Linda, do you have time to help me fix something in my code?

Linda: Sure. What's the problem?

You: Do you see any potential security problems with the way I've written the signup and login endpoints in this server?

Linda: Let me see. Nope. Looks pretty standard.

You: How would you test it?

Linda: Probably with Jest and Supertest.

You: Yeah, okay. I don't know how to use those.

Linda: Read the docs.

You: Okay, thanks.

If you were to have the same conversation with Copilot Chat, your questions might be exactly the same (at least to start). Let's see how it goes. The following is my actual conversation with Copilot.

```
Me: Hey, Copilot, do you have time to help me fix something in
   my code?
Copilot Chat: Of course! I'd be happy to help. What seems to be
   the issue?
Me: Do you see any potential security problems with the way I've
   written the signup and login endpoints in this server?
Copilot Chat: I'm not sure, could you show me the code for those
   endpoints?
```

At this point, I opened the file containing the code I was referring to.

```
Me: Here they are.
Copilot Chat: I see that you're using JWTs to authenticate
   users. That's a good start. However, I don't see any
   validation on the user input. You should always validate user
   input to prevent attacks like SQL injection or cross-site
   scripting (XSS). Additionally, it's important to hash
   passwords before storing them in the database to prevent them
   from being exposed in case of a data breach.
Me: I am validating the input, and I'm hashing the password
   using bcrypt. Can you look again?
Copilot Chat: I see that you're using the bcrypt library to hash
   the password before storing it in the database, which is
   great. However, I don't see any validation on the user input.
   You should always validate user input to prevent attacks like
```

```
SQL injection or cross-site scripting (XSS). One way to do
this is by using a library like express-validator to validate
the input before processing it.
```

Here, Copilot was right. It turned out that I wasn't validating the input. Copilot also provided me with a suggested next prompt, as shown in Figure 3-8.

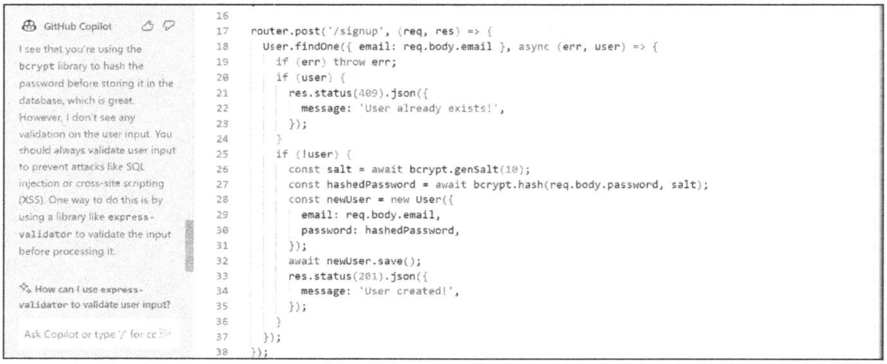

Microsoft Corporation

FIGURE 3-8: Copilot correctly identifies the problem with my code and offers to help.

I asked the follow-up question and implemented the suggested solution, but I still wasn't convinced. I asked the same question I had asked my coworker Linda:

```
Me: How would you test it?
Copilot Chat: To test the validation, you can send a POST
    request to the /signup endpoint with invalid input and check
    if the server returns the correct error response. Here's an
    example of how you can test it using supertest and jest:
```

Not only did Copilot give me basically the same answer as my coworker, but it was much more patient and even wrote a sample test for me.

Chatting with ChatGPT

ChatGPT, which I introduced earlier in the chapter, stands for Chat Generative Pre-trained Transformer. This chatbot was developed by OpenAI to serve as a friendly front-end to the OpenAI GPT models. After its release on November 30, 2022, ChatGPT quickly became the fastest-growing consumer software application in history. ChatGPT converses with users and generates remarkably human-like responses while considering context and previous prompts.

Unlike GitHub Copilot, ChatGPT isn't specifically trained to understand or generate code. Instead, it's tuned to be good at conversation. However, the enormous models it uses include programming code. Depending on the model you use with ChatGPT, it often handles prompts related to coding at least as well as Copilot.

ChatGPT is (currently) based on GPT-3.5 and GPT-4. The models have been further tuned through a process OpenAI calls reinforcement learning from human feedback (RLHF). Human trainers ranked responses from the model and created reward models to be able to converse with humans while using a safety system to avoid generating harmful content.

Because it's fine-tuned for conversation, ChatGPT can help with more creative tasks involving more than just a few lines of code. For example, I've used ChatGPT to generate sample data for an application I'm developing. I've used it also to help brainstorm ideas for new features to add to an app.

Signing up and setting up

You can sign up for a ChatGPT account by going to `https://chat.openai.com`. Click the Sign Up link to get to the screen shown in Figure 3-9.

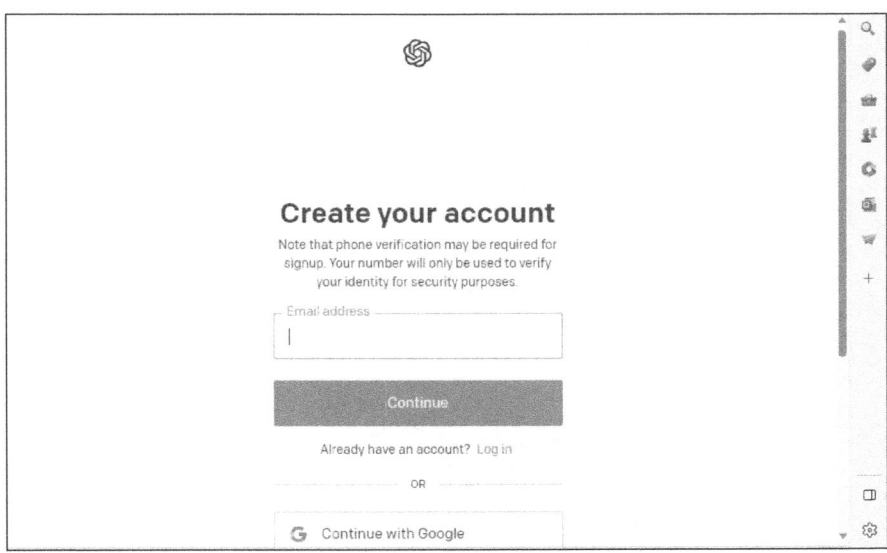

FIGURE 3-9: Signing up for a ChatGPT account.

ChatGPT

When you've finished the signup and phone number verification process, you'll see the ChatGPT user interface, as shown in Figure 3-10.

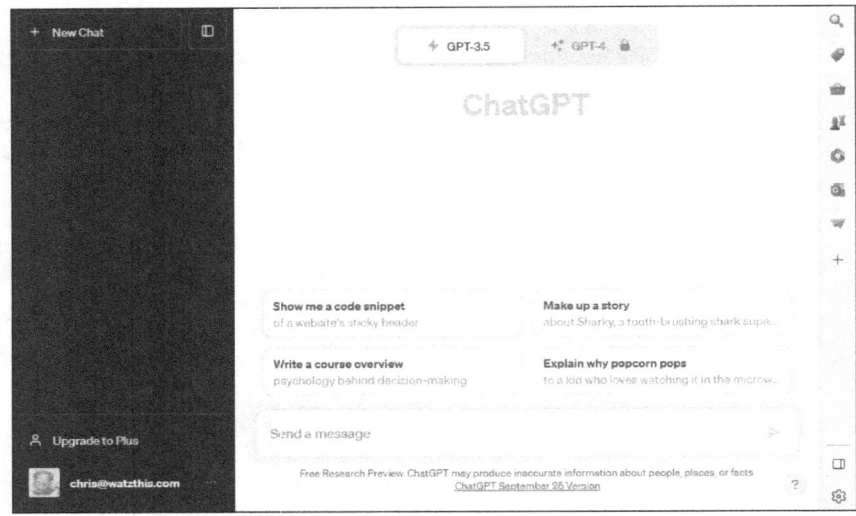

FIGURE 3-10:
The ChatGPT UI.

With a free account, you'll have access to an older language model, which is currently GPT-3.5. However, don't rush to sign up for a paid account just yet. The older model is faster than the newer one and is perfectly capable for our purposes.

Setting custom instructions

When you have a ChatGPT account, the first thing you'll want to do is to give ChatGPT some overall context about you and how you'd like the model to respond. You can do this by clicking your profile icon in the upper right of the ChatGPT interface and selecting Customize ChatGPT, as shown in Figure 3-11.

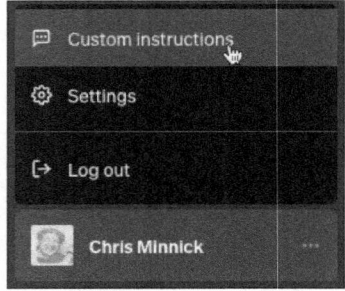

FIGURE 3-11:
Opening
the Custom
Instructions
window.

In the Custom Instructions window that opens, which is shown in Figure 3-12, you can provide up to 1,500 characters about yourself and 1,500 characters describing how you'd like ChatGPT to behave and provide answers.

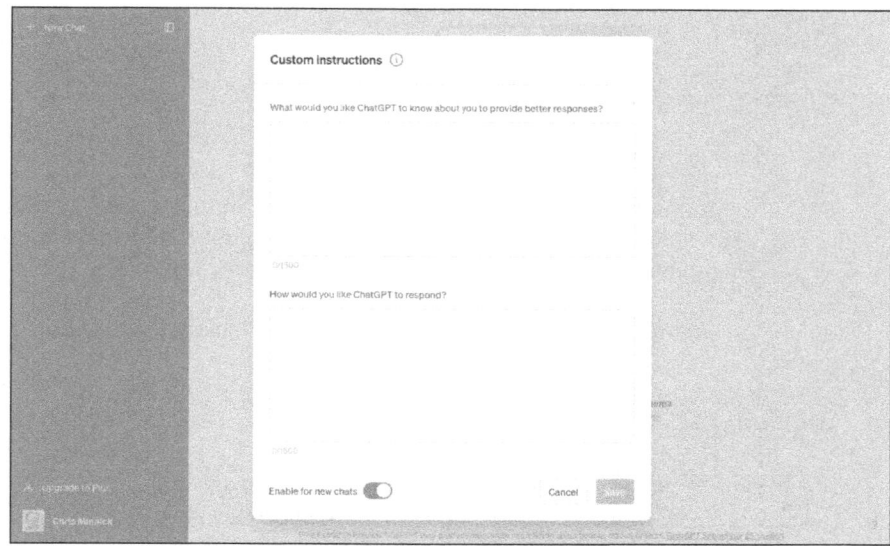

FIGURE 3-12:
The Custom
Instruction
window.

ChatGPT

REMEMBER

Earlier in this chapter, we discussed the four elements of a prompt: instruction, context, input, and output format. Here, you're providing some context and output format information.

Telling ChatGPT about you

The first box, labeled "What would you like ChatGPT to know about you to provide better responses?" is where you can provide context that will be applied to every conversation you have with ChatGPT. In the same way that you're able to have more meaningful interactions with your doctor, employee, or friends than you are with a stranger who knows nothing about you, this is the model's way of establishing some baseline understanding of what you may know already and who you are.

To see what ChatGPT suggests you include here, click the text area, and the help window shown in Figure 3-13 appears.

The tips provided are a great start. Don't worry about the structure or style of what you write. The important thing is to communicate any general information that the model should know to assist you better.

What would you like ChatGPT to know about you to provide better responses?
Thought starters
• Where are you based?
• What do you do for work?
• What are your hobbies and interests?
• What subjects can you talk about for hours?
• What are some goals you have?
0/1500
Hide tips

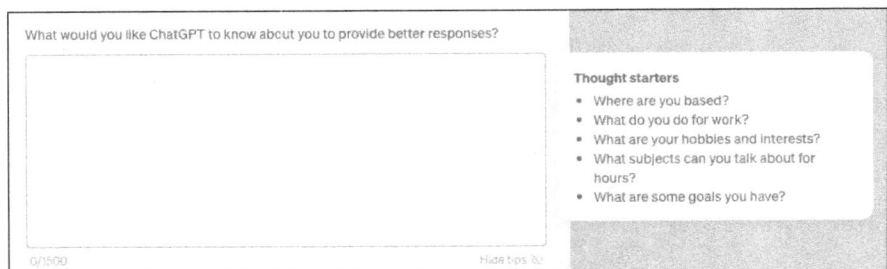

FIGURE 3-13: Viewing ChatGPT's suggestions for the context custom instructions.

ChatGPT

If you're using ChatGPT to help you with writing code, mention whether you're a student or a professional software developer, and include programming languages you know and your level of experience with each.

Figure 3-14 shows my current "about me" custom instruction.

What would you like ChatGPT to know about you to provide better responses?
I'm an experienced author, teacher, and software developer. I've written over 25 books about web and software development, including JavaScript All-in-One For Dummies and Coding with AI For Dummies. I teach classes and coding bootcamps and I specialize in teaching JavaScript frameworks (such as React).
I'm an expert at JavaScript, and intermediate with Python. I love to learn new languages, libraries, and frameworks and am always interested in learning about new tools to help me do my job better.
501/1500

FIGURE 3-14: Example text for the first custom instruction.

ChatGPT

TIP

You don't have to use all 1,500 characters for either custom instruction. However, there's no reason not to.

Telling ChatGPT your expectations

In the second text area, you can give ChatGPT some general guidelines for how you'd like it to respond to your prompts. Just as with the first text area, if you click into the text area, you'll see a pop-up window that gives you some ideas about what to include in this section, as shown in Figure 3-15.

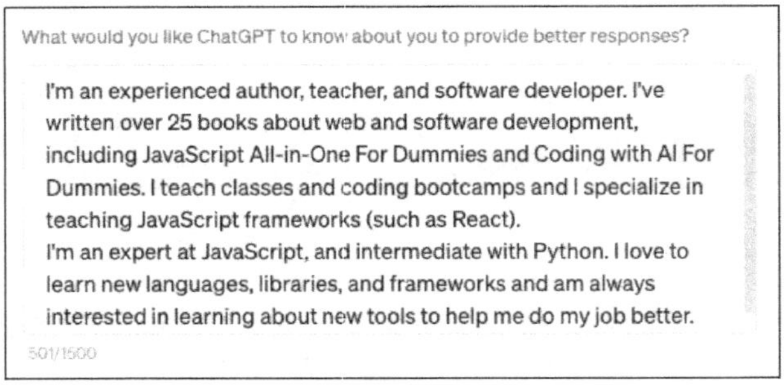

FIGURE 3-15:
Viewing
ChatGPT's
suggestions
for the output
format custom
instructions.

ChatGPT

To make ChatGPT more helpful as a coding assistant, you might want to provide the following instructions in this text area:

>> You are an experienced professional software developer.

>> Provide accurate responses to coding questions and flag uncertainties.

>> Since I'm an expert in AI, skip explanations about your limitations.

>> Examples of programming code should use the latest syntax and best practices.

>> When I ask for programming code, I always just respond with the code and no explanations unless I specifically ask you to explain it.

You can modify your custom instructions any time you want, and you should do so whenever you have a new idea for how ChatGPT might be more helpful or pleasant to work with. Here are some additional ideas for things you may want to try adding to the second custom instruction:

>> I always appreciate new ideas for ways to ask questions or form prompts that will help you be a better assistant to me.

>> I like to be complimented. Sometimes, you should offer enthusiastic praise for a prompt or idea I give you.

>> If I start my prompt with Pirate, you should respond in pirate-speak.

Below the two text input boxes is the Enable for New Chats switch, which is enabled by default. If you want to turn off your custom instructions temporarily (without deleting them), turn off this switch.

When you've finished editing your custom instructions, click the Save button.

Coding with Chatbots

TIP

New instructions will apply only to new conversations, so if you do modify your instructions and want to try them out, remember to start a new chat.

Figure 3-16 shows the beginning of a new conversation that takes into account my new custom instructions.

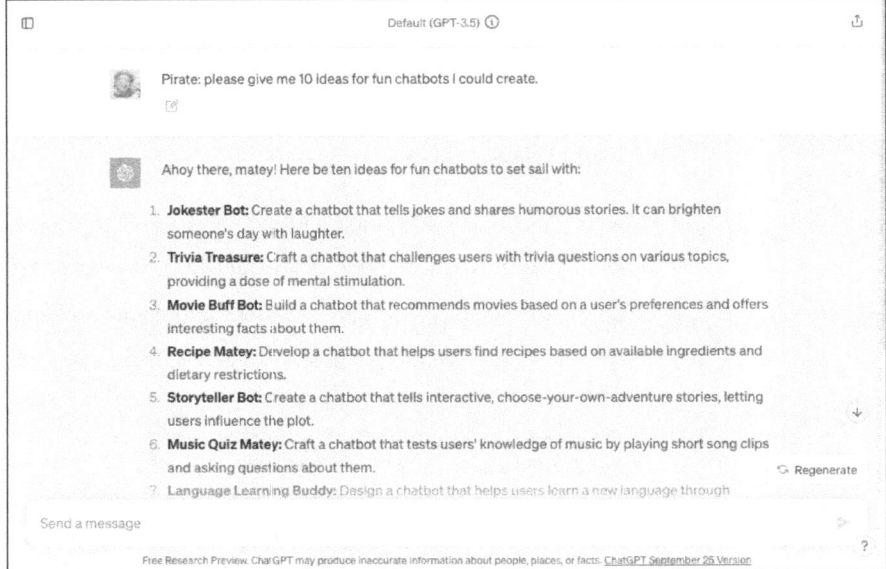

Diving into the OpenAI Platform

Now that you're an expert at using ChatGPT, it's time to dive deeper into using the OpenAI models. In this section, you learn how to access OpenAI's developer platform, get an OpenAI API key, and build an application that makes use of the OpenAI API.

You can get more direct access to the OpenAI models by accessing the OpenAI developer platform site. Follow these steps to get started:

1. Go to https://platform.openai.com in your web browser.

2. If you already have an account with OpenAI (which you do, if you've been using ChatGPT), click the Login button in the upper-right corner and log in.

   Otherwise, sign up for a new account.

3. **Click the Playground link in the left navigation strip.**

The icon for the Playground is the top one. The Playground interface opens, as shown in Figure 3-17.

Playground link

FIGURE 3-17:
The OpenAI
Playground.

ChatGPT

Checking your credits

Using the OpenAI API and the Playground requires you to set up a payment method separate from your subscription to ChatGPT and to purchase credits. You can view the current rates for using different models by going to https://openai.com/api/pricing/. Pricing is based on the number of tokens of input you send to the model and the number of tokens the model outputs. For example, the GPT-4o model currently costs $2.50 per 1,000,000 tokens of input (about 750,000 words) and $10.00 per 1,000,000 tokens of output.

WARNING

While you're experimenting with the OpenAI API, you're unlikely to accrue more than a few dollars in charges. If you build an application with the OpenAI API that becomes popular, you'll want to watch out that your costs don't get out of control.

If you just signed up for an OpenAI account, you may have been given free trial credits. To check whether you have credits in your account, go to https://platform.openai.com/account/billing/overview. If you don't have a free trial or if you have used all your free trial credits, you'll need to create a paid account, which you can do from this page as well.

After you have some credit in your account or you've set up a paid account, you're ready to use the OpenAI models in the Playground.

Messing around in the Playground

The OpenAI Playground (`https://platform.openai.com/playground`) gives you an interface for experimenting with the OpenAI API. The first time you access the Playground (refer to Figure 3-17), you'll see the Assistants interface, which provides an easy way to create an AI assistant.

To see how to customize the settings of a GPT model, you need to be in Chat mode. Select Chat from the left menu (see Figure 3-18).

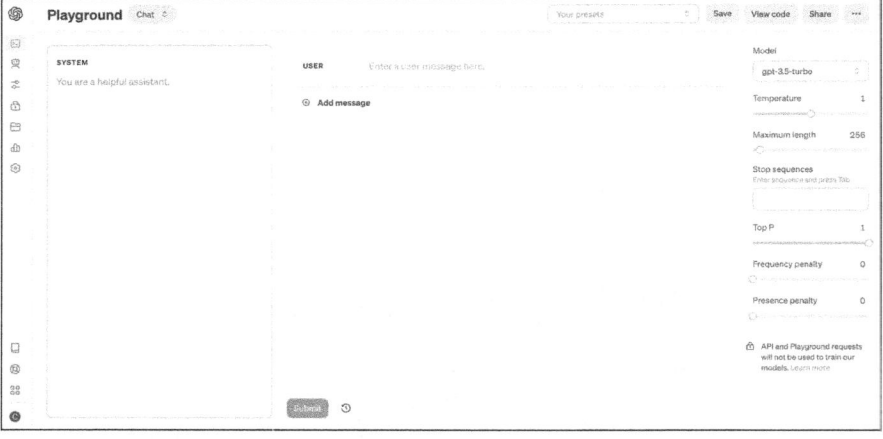

FIGURE 3-18:
Chat mode in the OpenAI Playground.

ChatGPT

Before you use Chat mode, however, you should know the following:

>> You can enter instructions or choose a preset to get completions from the model.

>> You can change the model to which your request will be sent.

>> Use good judgment when sharing completions; you're free to attribute them to yourself or your company.

>> Requests you send to the API aren't used to train the models.

>> Currently, the cutoff for the default model is April 2023.

There isn't much obvious onscreen help for using the Playground. However, if you hover your cursor over the labels for the settings on the right, you'll see information about each setting. Additional help for both the Playground and the OpenAI platform, in general, is available through the documentation and help links in the left navigation strip.

Running examples

OpenAI provides examples of prompts to try, which you can access by clicking the Your Presets drop-down menu at the top right of the page (refer to Figure 3-18) and selecting Browse Examples. The Examples page, shown in Figure 3-19, displays samples of prompts. You can also search for prompts by using the Search box and the category drop-down menu.

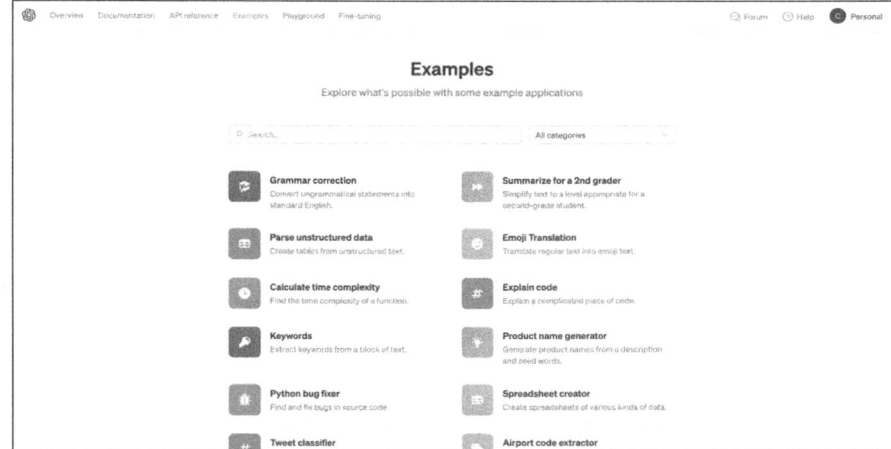

FIGURE 3-19: The OpenAI Examples page.

ChatGPT

When you click one of the example prompt descriptions, a pop-up window will appear that contains the instruction (which the Playground calls *system*) and sample input (which the Playground calls *user*), as shown in Figure 3-20. Below the sample input, you'll see sample output from the application.

After you've looked through the sample input and output, click the green Open in Playground button at the top of the pop-up window to open the prompt in the Playground. The system and user parts of the prompts will be filled out for you, and the settings on the right side of the screen will also be preset to good values for the task at hand. If you open a coding-related example, note that the temperature setting will be set very low so that the model will return the most accurate response it can. If you open an example that requires creativity, such as the Product Name Generator example, the temperature will be set to a higher level.

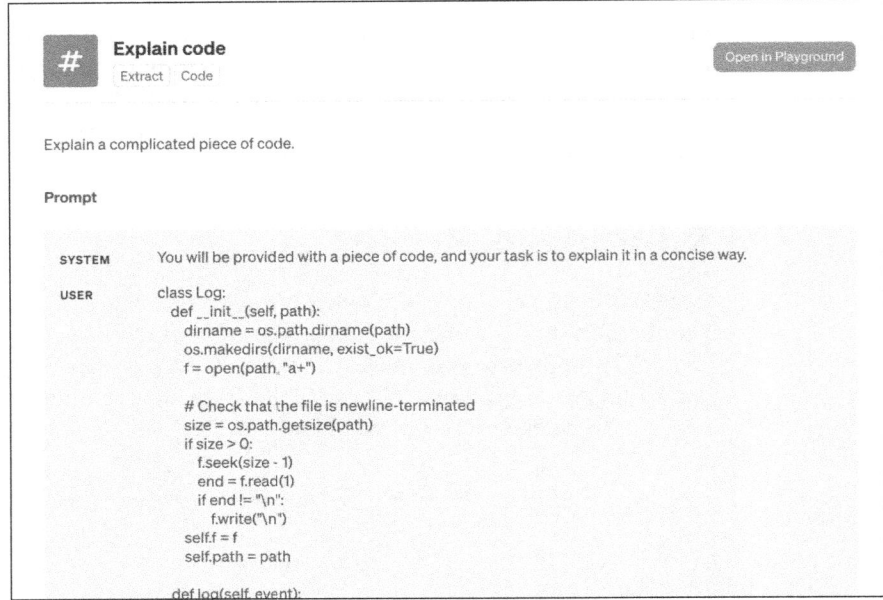

FIGURE 3-20:
Viewing one of OpenAI's example prompts.

ChatGPT

Playing the roles

OpenAI Playground's Chat mode has two large areas where you can input data to prompt the model. Within these two areas, you can enter text to play three different characters: system, user, and assistant.

The left text area is the system text area. Use this area to specify who or what you'd like the model to act like, and what the model should do with input that will be forthcoming (in the other text area). The default system message is *You are a helpful assistant.*

The text area to the right of the system input box is the user or assistant area. You can switch between the user and assistant roles by toggling the User or Assistant label in the message input field. Anything you label as user input will be given to the model after the system input. The assistant role is used by the model to respond to messages from the user role. You can also act as the assistant to give the AI model examples of what its output should look like.

Adjusting the model's settings

On the right of the Playground's Chat mode interface, choose the model you want to use. The default model is currently gpt-4o, but you can select any model that's available.

REMEMBER

Some models cost more than others to use. You can check the pricing for OpenAI's different models at `https://openai.com/api/pricing`.

Below the model selection drop-down menu, you have access to the following additional settings:

>> **Temperature** controls the randomness of responses.

>> **Maximum Length** sets the maximum number of tokens that will be used when you submit your prompt. The tokens are shared between your prompt and the model's response.

>> **Stop sequences** are combinations of characters that will cause the model to stop generating content. For example, if you want the model to return a numbered list containing ten items, you could set the stop sequence to 11, or if you want the model to return only a single line of text, you can set a carriage return as a stop sequence.

>> **Top P** is another way to control the creativity and diversity of responses. Top-P can be set to a value between 0 and 1. (The *P* in *Top P* stands for *probability.*) With a low Top P setting, the model considers only the most probable responses and will tend to generate predictable responses. The higher the Top P, the larger the pool of possible responses that the model will randomly select from when generating responses and the more diverse and creative the output will be.

>> **Frequency penalty** determines how much new tokens will be penalized based on how many times they appear in the previously generated tokens. The value of the frequency penalty can be set to a value between 0 and 2. A higher frequency penalty will cause the model to generate more unique words.

>> **Presence penalty** determines how much to penalize tokens based on their appearance in the previous text. The presence penalty can be set to a value between 0 and 2. A higher presence penalty will make the model have more diverse ideas.

TIP

When generating code, the frequency penalty and the presence penalty should both be set to 0 or a low value. You should set the frequency penalty to 0 because it's common and necessary for the same keywords (such as `def` in Python or `function` in JavaScript) to appear many times in a program. The presence penalty should be a low value to indicate that you prefer accuracy and consistency over seeing multiple ways of doing the same thing.

Getting an API key

Before you can write your own programs that make use of the OpenAI models, you have to have an API key. Follow these steps to get your key:

1. **Log in to the OpenAI Playground at** `https://platform.openai.com/playground`.

2. **Click the Gear icon in the top toolbar and then click API keys from the left menu.**

3. **Click the Create New Secret Key button and give your key a name that relates to what you're going to use it for, as shown in Figure 3-21.**

4. **Click Create Secret Key.**

   Your new API key appears.

5. **Copy your API key and save it where you won't lose it.**

   This is the only time OpenAI will show you your new secret key, so make sure not to rush through this step. However, if you do lose your secret key, it's easy enough to generate a new one.

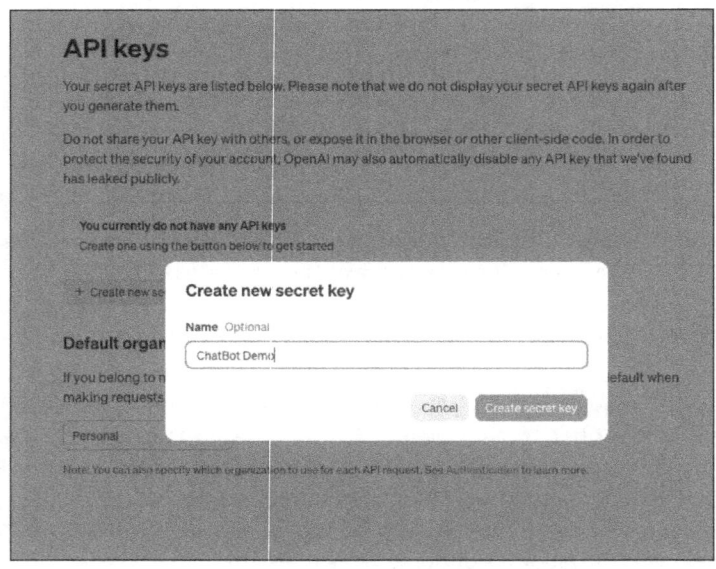

FIGURE 3-21: Naming your secret key.

ChatGPT

Don't commit any files containing your API key into your code repository.

WARNING

Developing a Chatbot with OpenAI

Let's make a chatbot! We'll be using the OpenAI API and Gradio, a Python tool for quickly creating a web interface for machine learning models. Don't worry if you've never used Gradio before (or even Python). ChatGPT will generate some code, and then I walk you through the process of running it. (Or you can try asking ChatGPT how to run it.)

Submit the following prompt (or something similar) to ChatGPT or the OpenAI Playground:

> Write a custom chatbot that uses the OpenAI API and Gradio. The chatbot should first ask the user what kind of bot they'd like to talk to (such as 'coding assistant' or 'therapist') and then present them with input and output areas.

Note that this prompt is vague. With the first prompt, my goal is just to get something that works. After I see what ChatGPT generates, I can refine my prompt or start working with the code myself.

Listing 3-1 shows the Python code that ChatGPT returned.

LISTING 3-1: **A GPT-Generated Chatbot**

```python
import openai
import gradio as gr
# Set your OpenAI API key
openai.api_key = "YOUR_OPENAI_API_KEY"
def chatbot_response(input_text):
    response = openai.Completion.create(
        engine="davinci",
        prompt=f"I'd like to talk to a {input_text}.",
        max_tokens=50  # You can adjust this for longer responses
    )
    return response.choices[0].text
# Create the Gradio interface
iface = gr.Interface(
    fn=chatbot_response,
    inputs=gr.inputs.Textbox("text", label="Enter the type of bot
  you want to talk to (e.g., 'coding assistant' or 'therapist')"),
```

(continued)

LISTING 3-1:   *(continued)*

```
        outputs="text",
        live=True,
        title="Custom Chatbot",
        description="Select the type of bot you'd like to talk to and
    start the conversation."
)
iface.launch()
```

At this point, I don't yet know whether the code will work, but I can see that it's not what I meant. But, I see a problem I'd like to fix right away: The API key is hard-coded in the file, which would result in me checking my API key into my Git repository, which I just said you should never do.

I could fix this problem myself, but I decided to let ChatGPT do it. Here's my next prompt:

> I don't want to hard code my API key into this file.
> How can I avoid doing that?

In response to this prompt, ChatGPT suggested setting an environment variable containing the API key, which wasn't what I was looking for. I responded that I wanted to have a config file for the API key, and it gave me what I was looking for and correctly instructed me to add the config file to .gitignore. Listing 3-2 shows the revised code.

LISTING 3-2:   My revised Chatbot

```
import openai
import gradio as gr
from config import OPENAI_API_KEY
# Set the API key from the configuration file
openai.api_key = OPENAI_API_KEY
def chatbot_response(input_text):
    response = openai.Completion.create(
        engine="davinci",
        prompt=f"I'd like to talk to a {input_text}.",
        max_tokens=50  # You can adjust this for longer responses
    )
    return response.choices[0].text
# Create the Gradio interface
iface = gr.Interface(
    fn=chatbot_response,
```

```
        inputs=gr.inputs.Textbox("text", label="Enter the type of bot
    you want to talk to (e.g., 'coding assistant' or 'therapist')"),
        outputs="text",
        live=True,
        title="Custom Chatbot",
        description="Select the type of bot you'd like to talk to and
    start the conversation."
)
iface.launch()
```

To test this script, copy the code into a file named chatbot_demo.py and open it in VS Code. At this point, VS Code may prompt you to install a Python interpreter if you don't already have one, or you may need to install Python on your computer (which you can do by going to `https://www.python.org/downloads/`).

Create a second file named config.py for your API key. The config.py file should look like Listing 3-3, with your API key inserted at the appropriate place, of course.

LISTING 3-3 **The config.py File**

```
OPENAI_API_KEY = "YOUR_API_KEY_HERE"
```

Before you can run the chatbot, you'll need to install Gradio and the OpenAI library. Run the following two commands in your terminal:

```
pip install openai
pip install gradio
```

When those are installed, you can run the program by typing **python chatbot_ demo.py** into your terminal.

This code technically works in that it sends the text I enter into the textbox to the OpenAI API and displays a result. But it's not what I had in mind, and the completion it returns is gibberish, as shown in Figure 3-22.

The biggest issue is that the program is sending every keystroke to the API, rather than waiting for me to finish my input and click a button. Checking my OpenAI platform account, I see that my quick test of this program cost me 3 cents. It's not much, but I suspect changing the code so it waits to send prompts all at once rather than sending one letter at a time would save me a lot of money and result in better output.

FIGURE 3-22:
My first attempt
at creating a
chatbot with
ChatGPT was
a failure.

ChatGPT

Simply changing the value of the `live` property from `True` to `False` solves this problem.

The next problem is that the model is using the GPT-3 model. I suspect the results I get will be much better if I switch to using a newer model. To fix this, I changed `model="davinci"` to `model="gpt-3.5-turbo"` and then stopped and restarted the Python program. This time, when I tried to submit my input, I got an error in the console that the endpoint didn't support chat completions.

I consulted the Python OpenAI docs and found that I needed to change `openai.Completion` to `openai.ChatCompletion` and change the parameters I was passing to the OpenAI. I tested it again, and the result is shown in Figure 3-23.

The process I went through to get a working demo involved browsing the docs in the Python OpenAI library and the Gradio library more than getting helpful tips from AI models. In the end, although I got my chatbot working, I was left feeling like it would have been much faster to code the app from scratch without the help of AI.

In the next chapter of this book, I show you a better approach to working with generative AI that is more likely to result in working code that does what it's supposed to do.

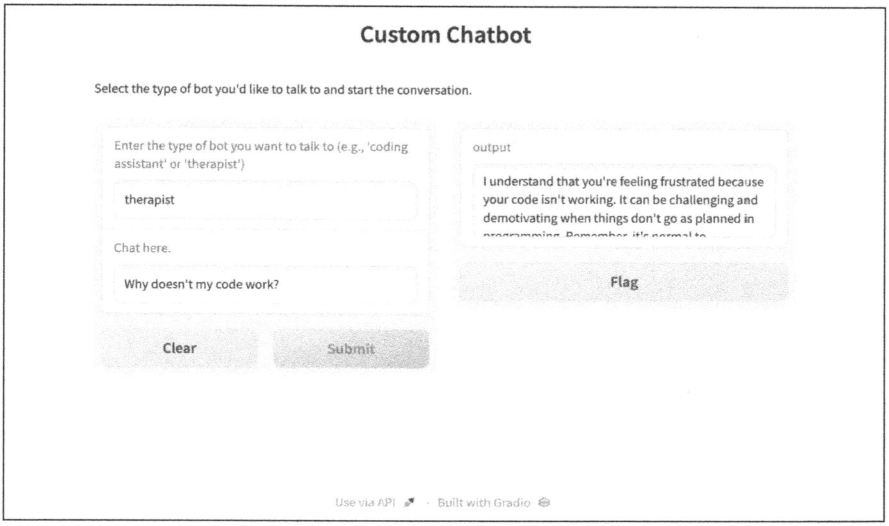

Custom Chatbot

Select the type of bot you'd like to talk to and start the conversation.

Enter the type of bot you want to talk to (e.g., 'coding assistant' or 'therapist')

therapist

Chat here.

Why doesn't my code work?

output

I understand that you're feeling frustrated because your code isn't working. It can be challenging and demotivating when things don't go as planned in programming. Remember, it's normal to

Flag

Clear   Submit

Use via API 🔗 · Built with Gradio 🟠

FIGURE 3-23:
Testing my fixes.

ChatGPT

Chapter **4**

Progressing from Plan to Prototype

Although it's possible to work with an AI coding assistant to generate working code and even entire programs, acceptable results are far from guaranteed. The quality of the results you'll get depends on several factors, including the LLM you use, the input you give the model, your own coding skills, and how clearly you've defined the project's requirements.

Chapter 3 provides an example of using AI to do something most programmers could do faster and better without AI. In this chapter, you start to learn processes and tips for getting consistent and higher-quality results.

Understanding Project Requirements

If you've ever been thrown into working on a new project that you don't fully understand, you can identify with what a coding assistant would feel like all the time — if a coding assistant could feel anything. Although coding assistants have seen a lot of code, the only way they can be helpful to you is if they have context about the particular requirements of the code you're writing.

Determining the software requirements

When starting to work with a coding assistant, think about what you need to know before working on a project. Specifically, you need to know the following:

- >> What will the software do?
- >> Who are you building the software for?
- >> Who will use the software?
- >> Where and how will the software do what it does?
- >> How will the user interact with the software?
- >> What languages and technologies will you use to build the software?
- >> What are the goals of the software?
- >> Are there any legal or regulatory standards that the software must comply with?

In the world of software development, we call the answers to these questions the *software requirements*. You can specify your project's software requirements by using a *software requirements specification (SRS)*, which is a document that describes, in detail, what the planned software will do and how it will be expected to perform. For small projects, a full SRS is usually not necessary. However, some sort of documentation of requirements is essential to any project, and figuring out the requirements for yourself is essential to being able to communicate them to another developer or to an AI coding assistant.

Software requirements can be divided into three broad categories: domain requirements, functional requirements, and non-functional requirements.

Domain requirements

Domain requirements are particular to the category, purpose, or industry in which the software will be used. It's possible for a piece of software to be functional and user-friendly without being acceptable for use because it doesn't meet domain requirements. For example, if you develop an online banking app that doesn't meet the legal and regulatory requirements that apply to online banking apps, it doesn't fulfill its requirements.

Functional requirements

Functional requirements define how the software system behaves and are generally defined using specific responses to inputs or conditions. These statements of functional requirements are called use cases or user stories.

A *use case* is a detailed description of a functional requirement. It defines, using natural language, the ways in which a user can interact with a system (such as a piece of software or a website) and how the system will respond.

The details specified in a use case include the following:

>> The goal

>> Whether the user (called the *actor* in use cases) is human or another system

>> Preconditions that must be present for the use case (for example, the user must be logged in)

>> The series of steps the system will take

>> Alternative steps (for example, what happens when the user isn't logged in)

>> What happens after the steps are complete (also known as *postconditions*)

Use cases are no longer common in modern software development due to the popularity of agile software development, in which functional requirements are specified with user stories.

User stories are generally informal one-sentence statements written from the user's point of view. They contain the who, what, and why of an outcome that the users want to accomplish with the system. User stories are often written using the following format:

> As a [persona], I [want to], [so that].

For example:

> As a user, I want to be able to reset my password if I forget it, so I can regain access to my account.

This format, however, is not required when writing user stories. It's also common, especially during the initial process of documenting functional requirements, to see less structured statements that may eventually be turned into user stories.

Whether you decide to write use cases or user stories, the following are examples of functional requirements:

>> The system must allow users to create an account.

>> The system must allow users to log in with a username and password.

>> The system must allow users to click a forgot password link to reset their password.

>> After a user signs up for an account, they'll see a login page where they can enter their username and password to log in.

>> When a user successfully signs in, they'll see the newsfeed page.

>> The newsfeed page presents the user with a list of the latest posts made by other users.

>> At the bottom of the newsfeed page, users can enter text into an input field and click a submit button to create a new post.

You don't need to capture every detail of the functional requirements for the SRS. However, stating who will be using the system, what needs to be built, and why it needs to be built will give you more clarity as you're writing code and will give your AI assistant more context.

Non-functional requirements

Non-functional requirements relate to the quality of the software system, including security, maintainability, reliability, scalability, and reusability. Prioritizing non-functional requirements often involves considering the different assumptions and constraints that apply to the project.

Assumptions are factors that are believed to be true but aren't confirmed. Following are the categories of assumptions:

>> **Technical assumptions** relate to technology, such as hardware, operating systems, and infrastructure. For example, a technical assumption may be that the user's computer will have a certain amount of RAM.

>> **Operational assumptions** have to do with user or organizational behavior and factors. For example, an operational assumption for this book is that the reader is a computer programmer (or wants to be one).

>> **Business assumptions** focus on the business context in which the project will be used, such as business policies and market conditions that may affect the design or functionality of the software.

>> **Environmental assumptions** are external factors that may affect the software, such as cultural, social, or geographical factors or availability of a stable internet connection.

Constraints restrict the options available to developers of a system. Types of constraints include the following:

>> **Interface constraints** define the limitations that the software's user interface puts on the project. If you're developing a mobile app, the size of the mobile device screens places limits on the functionality and design of the app.

>> **Performance constraints** define specific performance criteria that the software must meet. For example, you might define a percentage of uptime or a maximum time for the website to finish loading.

>> **Operating constraints** relate to existing organizational processes, policies, or practices. Examples include whether the company where the software will be deployed allows the use of certain software libraries or the organization's policies regarding the use of AI coding assistants.

>> **Life cycle constraints** have to do with maintainability, portability, and the ongoing life of the software after it's built.

>> **Economic constraints** involve the budget for building and operating the software. Finances are a major limitation of any project.

TIP

Specifying software requirements is an important part of any project, and with the emergence of AI coding assistants, a skill that every software developer should have. Many books have been written about software requirements, but the most essential one is *Software Requirements*, 3rd Edition (Microsoft Press) by Karl Wiegers and Joy Beatty.

Writing an SRS

I've decided I want to create a tic-tac-toe game. To help me and my AI coding assistant understand the project, I formulated the following prompt for ChatGPT:

```
Act as an experienced software project manager. Ask me
questions and use my responses to write a software
requirements specification for a tic-tac-toe game.
```

TECHNICAL
STUFF

I'm looking for a more creative response, so I'm using the GPT-4 model rather than the standard (at this time) GPT-3.5 model.

ChatGPT's response is shown in Figure 4-1.

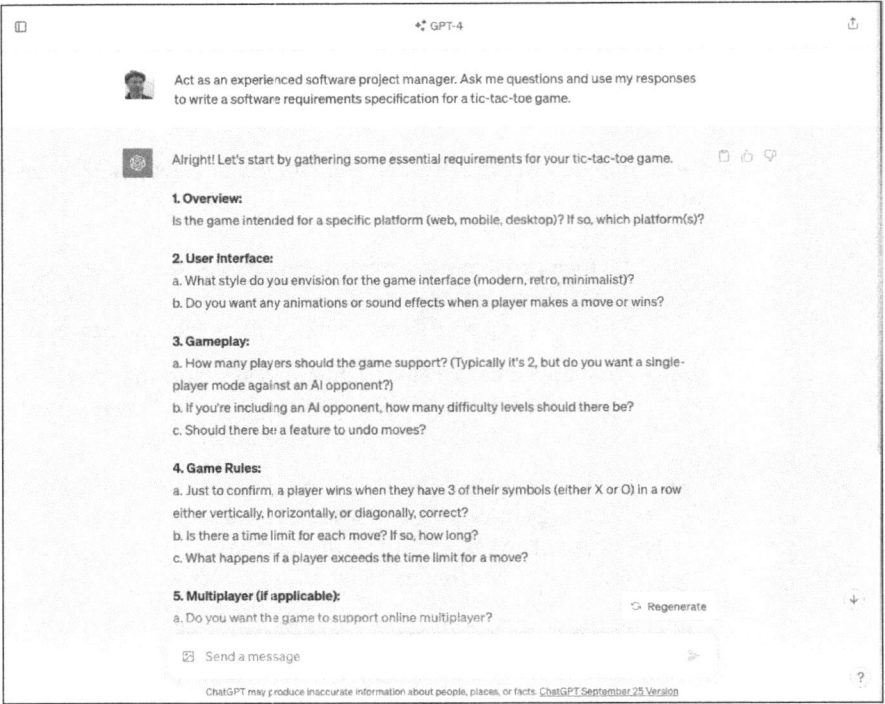

FIGURE 4-1:
Asking ChatGPT
to help write
an SRS.

My next task is to compose responses to ChatGPT's questions. Because ChatGPT has its questions as context in my current conversation, I prefaced each of my responses with the number and letter of the specific question, as shown in Figure 4-2.

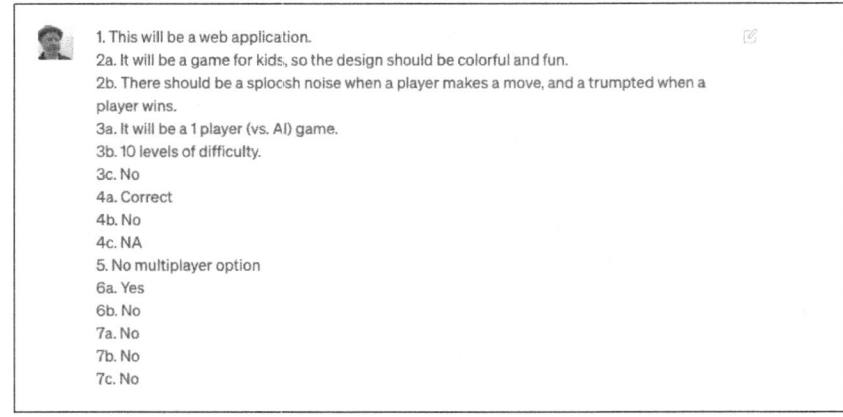

FIGURE 4-2:
My answers
to ChatGPT's
questions.

TIP

To avoid using unnecessary tokens, I entered my response to the questions in a single message by pressing Shift+Enter after each line of my response. This allows ChatGPT to get the entire response at once and avoids making the model respond to each answer individually.

After submitting my answers, ChatGPT responded with the SRS shown in Figure 4-3.

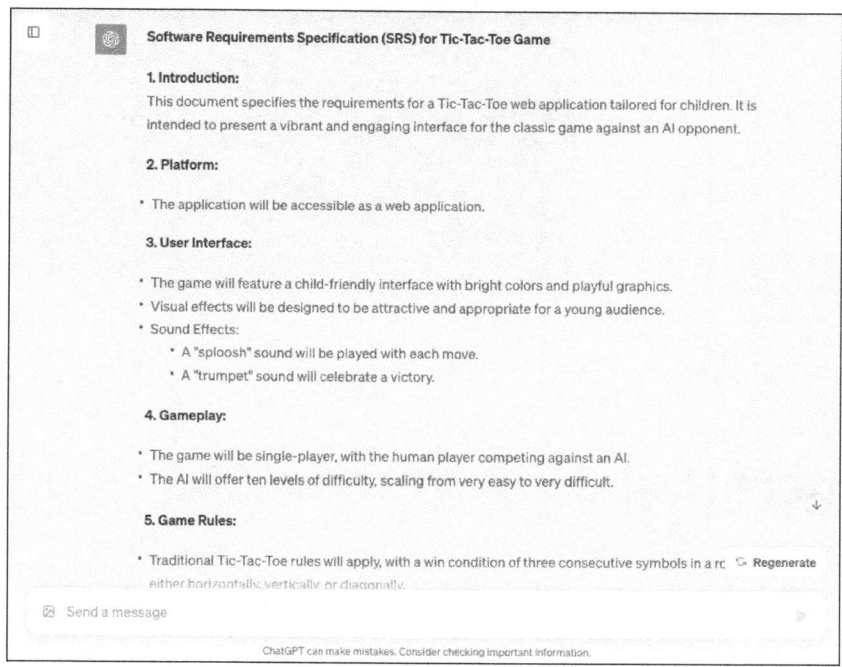

FIGURE 4-3:
A ChatGPT-generated SRS.

ChatGPT

The SRS looks good enough, but if I want to keep it in a file outside a ChatGPT window, I'll need it in a more usable format. I prompted ChatGPT to convert the SRS to Markdown syntax. (*Markdown* is a simple markup language for adding formatting to plain-text documents.) The result is shown in Figure 4-4.

I copied the markdown code and saved it in a file with the.md extension in a new Git repository for the project.

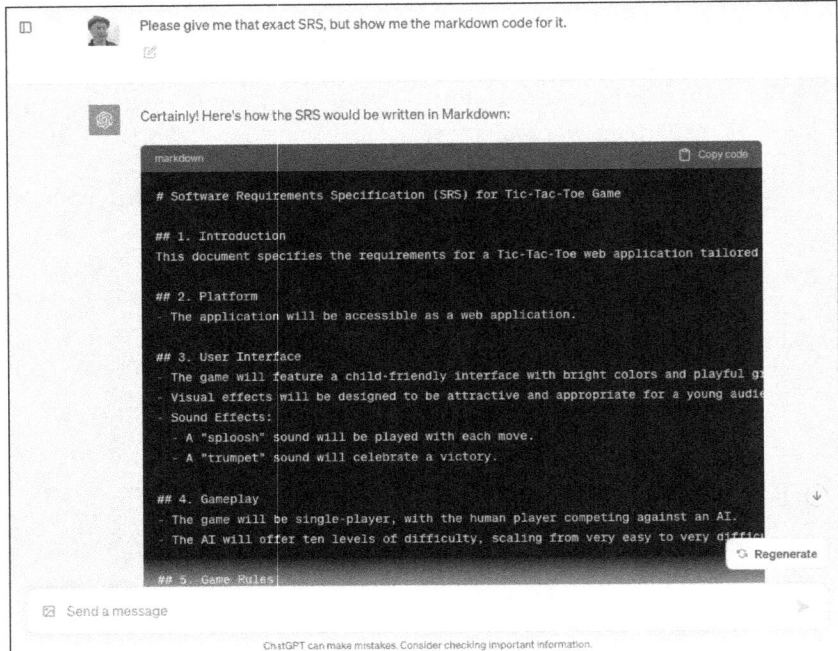

FIGURE 4-4:
Converting to
Markdown makes
documents more
usable.

ChatGPT

Generating Code from an SRS

Once you have an SRS (whether you wrote it or had your AI assistant's help), you're in a good position to begin coding. You might take a couple of different approaches. The first way is to just ask ChatGPT to code the program described in the SRS. At the very least, this will result in some ideas that you can use to begin coding it yourself.

Using a zero-shot approach

If you're feeling lucky, you can try a simple prompt asking the chatbot to generate the entire program based on the SRS. This approach is called a zero-shot prompt and is described in more detail in Chapter 3.

A zero-shot prompt is one in which you don't give examples or code and instead just rely on the data the model has been trained on.

REMEMBER

In the same conversation as the one where I asked ChatGPT to write an SRS, I entered the following prompt:

```
You are a professional software developer. Write the tic-
tac-toe game described in the above SRS.
```

After a few seconds, ChatGPT returned HTML, CSS, and JavaScript for what it described as a simplified version of the application, as shown in Figure 4-5.

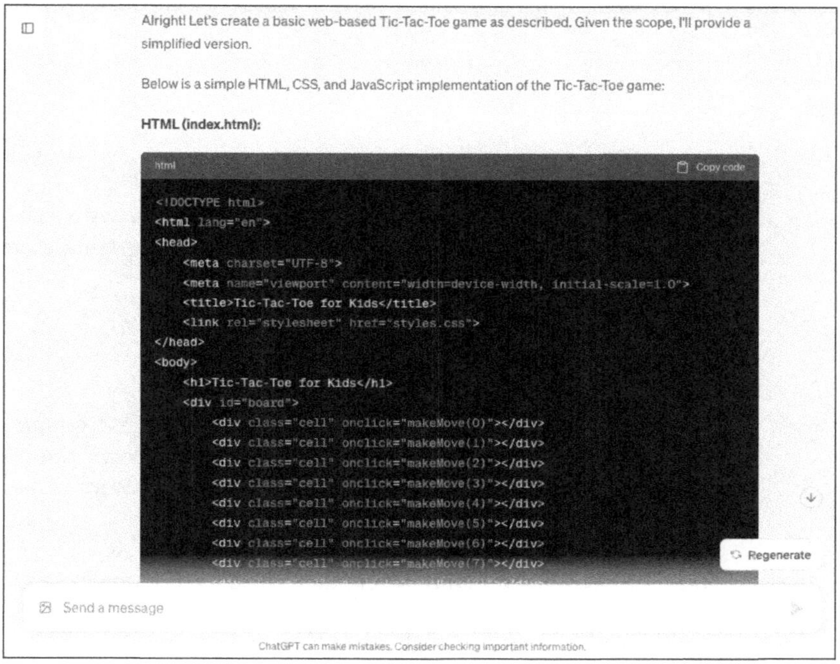

Alright! Let's create a basic web-based Tic-Tac-Toe game as described. Given the scope, I'll provide a simplified version.

Below is a simple HTML, CSS, and JavaScript implementation of the Tic-Tac-Toe game:

HTML (index.html):

```html
html                                                    Copy code
<!DOCTYPE html>
<html lang="en">
<head>
    <meta charset="UTF-8">
    <meta name="viewport" content="width=device-width, initial-scale=1.0">
    <title>Tic-Tac-Toe for Kids</title>
    <link rel="stylesheet" href="styles.css">
</head>
<body>
    <h1>Tic-Tac-Toe for Kids</h1>
    <div id="board">
        <div class="cell" onclick="makeMove(0)"></div>
        <div class="cell" onclick="makeMove(1)"></div>
        <div class="cell" onclick="makeMove(2)"></div>
        <div class="cell" onclick="makeMove(3)"></div>
        <div class="cell" onclick="makeMove(4)"></div>
        <div class="cell" onclick="makeMove(5)"></div>
        <div class="cell" onclick="makeMove(6)"></div>
        <div class="cell" onclick="makeMove(7)"></div>
```

Send a message

ChatGPT can make mistakes. Consider checking important information.

FIGURE 4-5:
The ChatGPT-
generated tic-tac-
toe game code.

ChatGPT

REMEMBER

You can find the full source code for this application on the website for *Coding with AI For Dummies* at, www.dummies.com/go/codingwithaifd, or in my GitHub repository, at https://github.com/chrisminnick/aiaio-fd.

Before examining the code, I copied it into index.html, styles.css, and script.js files in my code editor and opened the HTML file in a browser. The user interface resembles a tic-tac-toe game, and it uses what might be considered kid-friendly colors and text. Upon trying to play the game, however, I discovered that it fails to meet the most critical requirement. Take a look at Figure 4-6 and see whether you can identify the problem here.

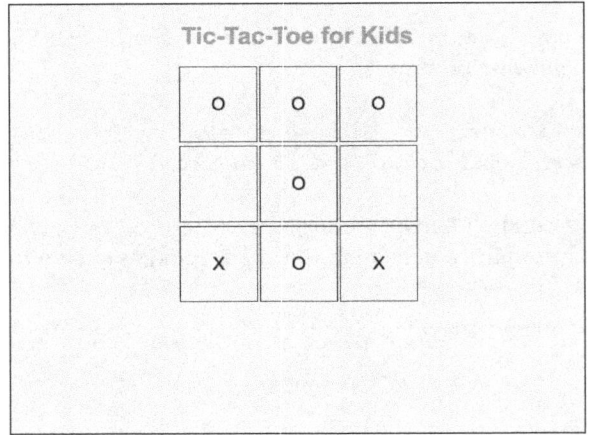

Tic-Tac-Toe for Kids

O	O	O
O		
X	O	X

FIGURE 4-6:
A frustratingly
difficult game of
tic-tac-toe.

ChatGPT

In this first attempt at a tic-tac-toe game, the AI has written a game that doesn't properly alternate between X and O, resulting in O getting more turns and, thus, always winning the game. AI cheats.

Breaking down the problem

With a request as complicated as generating software from an SRS, you're much more likely to get acceptable results by breaking down the problem into steps. However, pieces of the output from the zero-shot prompt response can be helpful in figuring out how to break apart the problem.

Since ChatGPT is tuned to be creative (it has a high default temperature), it was the perfect tool for helping with writing an SRS. However, it's not usually the best option for generating working code. For my second attempt at building a working tic-tac-toe game, I turned to GitHub Copilot.

Before asking Copilot to help with my app, I used the built-in debugger in the Chrome browser to figure out what was wrong with the code ChatGPT provided. It turns out that the function that places the user's X on the board has the following line of code to alternate the user's symbol between X and O:

```
currentPlayer = currentPlayer === 'X' ? 'O' : 'X';
```

**TECHNICAL
STUFF**

In this statement, the `currentPlayer` variable holds the symbol (X or O) that will be played on the board when the human user makes a move. The conditional (or ternary) operator in this statement checks whether the value of `currentPlayer` is X and changes it to O if it is. Otherwise (if `currentPlayer` is not equal to X) it changes its value to X. The problem, however, is that the value of `currentPlayer` is used in the program only to represent the human player. As a result, switching the value of currentPlayer to O makes the human play every other move with the AI's symbol.

After commenting out that line, I was able to play tic-tac-toe and win every time (because the computer player is just randomly picking from the available squares at this point). With a smarter opponent, the game should be a draw every time, so I decided to implement the levels of difficulty feature from the SRS.

Blending Manually Written and AI-Generated Code

When you have AI-generated code that fulfills at least some of the requirements of the software, it's time to start writing code manually. A good strategy for getting from a basic app, such as the one the AI generated in the preceding section, to something that works correctly is to start by developing the back end.

The *back end* defines the business logic and data in the app, as well as how the user interface will interact with the logic and data. In the case of an AI tic-tac-toe game, writing the back end will start with crafting the prompt that I'll use to get an AI model to play tic-tac-toe with me.

Writing the prompt

After thinking about the problem of how to make an AI tic-tac-toe player, I decided to try using the OpenAI API and the GPT-4 model. I experimented for a while with the OpenAI playground and ended up with the following system prompt:

```
You are an AI tic-tac-toe player. You are always 'O'
and I'm always 'X'.
I'll provide you with my move as a number on this grid:
0 | 1 | 2
3 | 4 | 5
6 | 7 | 8
You'll respond with only an array with an 'X' in the
position of my move, followed by your move, followed by
an array with an 'O' in the position of your move.
If one of us wins or it's a draw, tell me 'you win',
'I win', or 'draw'.
```

```
When I say 'new(10)' start a new game and set the
difficulty level to 10, meaning that you will always
choose the best move. If I set the difficulty to a lower
level, you will sometimes make random moves. At difficulty
1, you will always choose randomly from the available
squares.
```

Using this system prompt and the temperature set to 0.5 (so the model would be creative but not too creative), I was able to enter my moves and get responses that I should be able to use in my program, as shown in Figure 4-7.

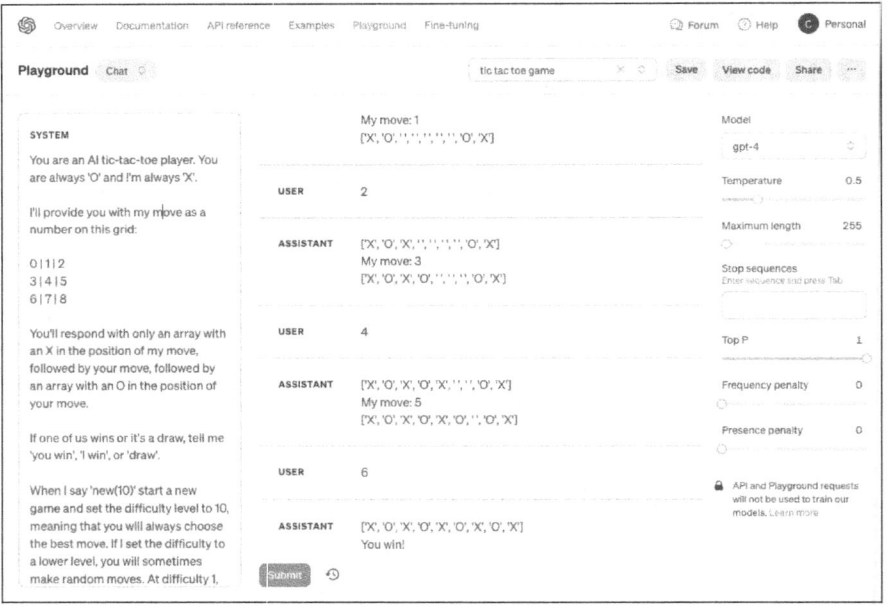

FIGURE 4-7:
An AI tic-tac-toe
bot in the OpenAI
playground.

ChatGPT

Writing the server

I decided to write a Node.js server to talk to the OpenAI API, so as not to have to store the API key in my client application. I created a new directory for my server, initialized the directory as a Node.js package (using npm init), and created a file named server.js.

To start writing server.js, I clicked the View Code button in the upper-right corner of the playground and selected Node.js as my library. The View Code window opened with the necessary code for sending the current settings and prompts to the API and getting the next completion.

I copied this code from the playground and pasted it into server.js. I also added code to import the API key from a .env file. A .env file is used in Node.js to store environment variables outside the main program. Environment variables hold information that is particular to an installation of the software (such as API keys) and shouldn't be distributed with the software (since you don't want other people using your API key). The beginning of my server is shown in Figure 4-8.

Progressing from Plan to Prototype

FIGURE 4-8:
Node.js code
to get the next
completion from
the OpenAI API.

ChatGPT

The next step was to create my own API server that gets results from OpenAI and returns them to my client application. Since writing an API server is a fairly standard task, I decided to use Github Copilot Chat to generate it.

I started with the following prompt:

```
I want to turn the code in server.js into an API server
that I can send a new message to and have it appended to
the messages array before submitting it to the OpenAI API.
The server should return the response from the OpenAI API.
```

The code generated by Copilot was a good start. The complete code is shown in Listing 4-1.

LISTING 4-1: **The First Version of the Tic-Tac-Toe Server**

```javascript
import express from 'express';
import OpenAI from 'openai';
import 'dotenv/config';
const app = express();
const openai = new OpenAI({
  apiKey: process.env.OPENAI_API_KEY,
});
app.use(express.json());
app.post('/chat', async (req, res) => {
  const { message } = req.body;
  const response = await openai.chat.completions.create({
    model: 'gpt-4',
    messages: [
      {
        role: 'system',
        content:
          "You are an AI tic-tac-toe player. You are always 'O'
          and I'm always 'X'.\n\nI'll provide you with my move
          as a number on this grid:\n\n0 | 1 | 2\n3 | 4 | 5\n6
          | 7 | 8\n\nYou'll respond with only an array with an
          'X' in the position of my move, followed by your move,
          followed by an array with an 'O' in the position of your
          move.\n\nIf one of us wins or it's a draw, tell me 'you
          win', 'I win', or 'draw'.\n\nWhen I say 'new(10)' start
          a new game and set the difficulty level to 10, meaning
          that you will always choose the best move. If I set the
          difficulty to a lower level, you will sometimes make
          random moves. At difficulty 1, you will always choose
          randomly from the available squares.",
      },
      {
        role: 'user',
        content: message,
      },
    ],
  });
  res.json({ response });
});
app.listen(3000, () => {
  console.log('Server listening on port 3000');
});
```

Submitting follow-up prompts

At the bottom of Copilot's response, it explained the code it generated and suggested a follow-up prompt:

```
How can I test the API server?
```

This was going to be my next prompt anyway, so I clicked the suggested prompt, and Copilot (correctly) suggested using curl or Postman to test it and gave instructions for using both, as shown in Figure 4-9, left.

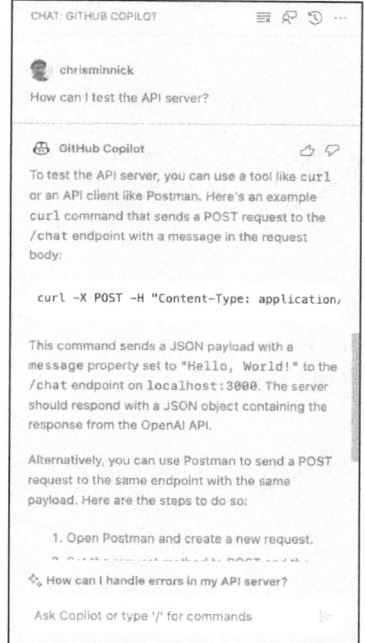
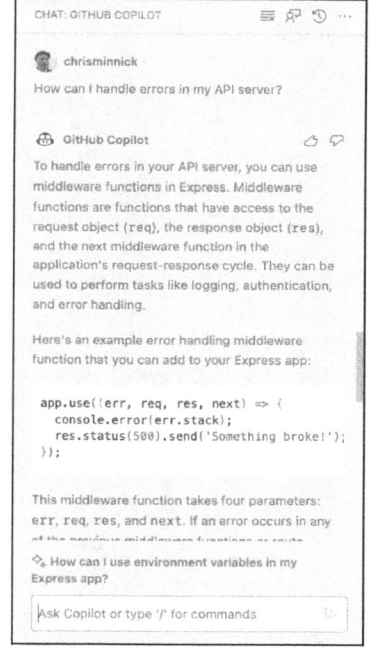

FIGURE 4-9: Suggestions for testing the API server (left) and for handling API server errors.

ChatGPT

The model also suggested another follow-up prompt, which seemed like an excellent idea to me, so I clicked that to ask for code for handling errors returned by the API server. The response to that prompt is shown in Figure 4-9, right.

Testing the server

Armed with Copilot's suggestions for testing and error handling, I had several tasks to work on before I could make the server work with the client app. First, I had to figure out whether the server works at all. From browsing the code, it looks like a standard Node.js API server that should be able to receive a message, pass it along to the OpenAI server, and return a response in JSON format.

Using the testing suggestions from Copilot, I started the server (using `node server.js`) and entered the following `curl` command into a new terminal window (all on one line):

```
curl -X POST -H "Content-Type: application/json" -d '{"message": "new(5)"}' http://localhost:3000/chat
```

This command should tell the AI tic-tac-toe game to start a new game with a difficulty level of 5. And the response I got from the server shows that was what it did:

```
"message":{"role":"assistant","content":"Understood.
We start a new game with a difficulty level of 5, which
means a mix of optimal and random moves. Your
move!"},"finish_reason":"stop"}],"usage":{"prompt_tokens":
199,"completion_tokens":29,"total_tokens":228}}}%
```

Next, I tried submitting my first move, and the AI responded appropriately. However, after a few moves, my AI opponent seemed to lose track of the game and responses were taking far too long. My first attempt at playing tic-tac-toe against the AI using my API server is shown in Figure 4-10.

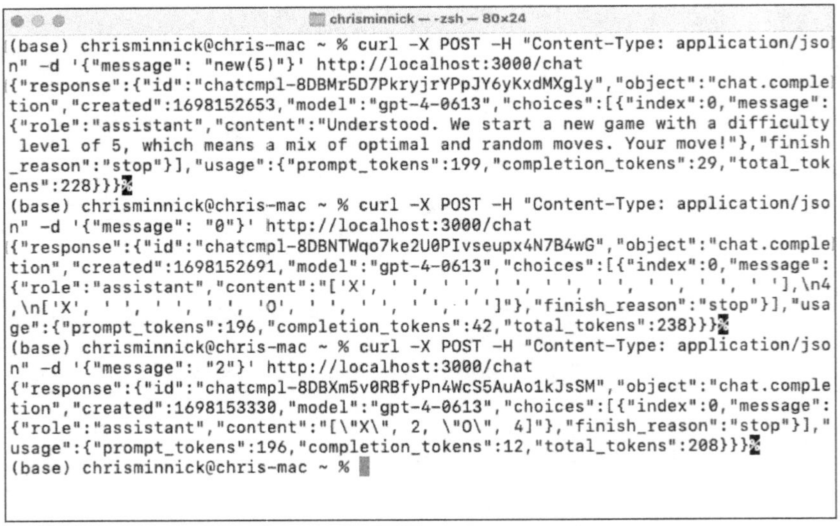

FIGURE 4-10:
My AI opponent
loses track of its
instructions.

chrisminnick — -zsh — 80×24
(base) chrisminnick@chris-mac ~ % curl -X POST -H "Content-Type: application/jso
n" -d '{"message": "new(5)"}' http://localhost:3000/chat
{"response":{"id":"chatcmpl-8DBMr5D7PkryjrYPpJY6yKxdMXgly","object":"chat.comple
tion","created":1698152653,"model":"gpt-4-0613","choices":[{"index":0,"message":
{"role":"assistant","content":"Understood. We start a new game with a difficulty
 level of 5, which means a mix of optimal and random moves. Your move!"},"finish
_reason":"stop"}],"usage":{"prompt_tokens":199,"completion_tokens":29,"total_tok
ens":228}}}
(base) chrisminnick@chris-mac ~ % curl -X POST -H "Content-Type: application/jso
n" -d '{"message": "0"}' http://localhost:3000/chat
{"response":{"id":"chatcmpl-8DBNTWqo7ke2U0PIvseupx4N7B4wG","object":"chat.comple
tion","created":1698152691,"model":"gpt-4-0613","choices":[{"index":0,"message":
{"role":"assistant","content":"['X', ' ', ' ', ' ', ' ', ' ', ' ', ' '],\n4
,\n['X', ' ', ' ', ' ', 'O', ' ', ' ', ' ',' ']"},"finish_reason":"stop"}],"usa
ge":{"prompt_tokens":196,"completion_tokens":42,"total_tokens":238}}}
(base) chrisminnick@chris-mac ~ % curl -X POST -H "Content-Type: application/jso
n" -d '{"message": "2"}' http://localhost:3000/chat
{"response":{"id":"chatcmpl-8DBXm5v0RBfyPn4WcS5AuAo1kJsSM","object":"chat.comple
tion","created":1698153330,"model":"gpt-4-0613","choices":[{"index":0,"message":
{"role":"assistant","content":"[\"X\", 2, \"O\", 4]"},"finish_reason":"stop"}],"
usage":{"prompt_tokens":196,"completion_tokens":12,"total_tokens":208}}}
(base) chrisminnick@chris-mac ~ %

Microsoft Corporation

The problem is that, although this code works, it doesn't have any way to keep track of the state of the game. Each request will only send the latest move from the client to OpenAI. Also, the AI would benefit from some examples of the response format that I'm looking for.

REMEMBER

Giving the AI examples of correct responses is called *few-shot prompting.* For details on this type of prompting, see Chapter 3.

Implementing few-shot prompting on the server

To give the AI more context, I wrote a series of messages (using the OpenAI playground) to simulate a correctly played game between the AI assistant and a human user. I then hard-coded those into the server, as shown in Figure 4-11.

```
10    messages: [
11      {
12        role: 'system',
13        content:
14          "You are an AI tic-tac-toe player. You are always 'O' and I'm always 'X'.\n\nI'll
             provide you with my move as a number on this grid:\n\n0 | 1 | 2\n3 | 4 | 5\n6 |
             7 | 8\n\nYou'll respond with only an array with an X in the position of my move,
             followed by your move, followed by an array with an O in the position of your
             move.\n\nIf one of us wins or it's a draw, tell me 'you win', 'I win', or 'draw'.
             \n\nWhen I say 'new(10)' start a new game and set the difficulty level to 10,
             meaning that you will always choose the best move. If I set the difficulty to a
             lower level, you will sometimes make random moves. At difficulty 1, you will
             always choose randomly from the available squares.",
15      },
16      {
17        role: 'user',
18        content: 'new(10)',
19      },
20      {
21        role: 'assistant',
22        content: 'new game',
23      },
24      {
25        role: 'user',
26        content: '0',
27      },
28      {
29        role: 'assistant',
30        content:
31          "['X', ' ', ' ', ' ', ' ', ' ', ' ', ' ', ' ']\nMy move: 4\n['X', ' ', ' ', ' ',
```

FIGURE 4-11:
Giving more context to the AI.

I then restarted the server and attempted to play a new game using the `curl` command. The new game started correctly, but on my first move, the AI responded that I should start a new game to continue playing, as shown in Figure 4-12.

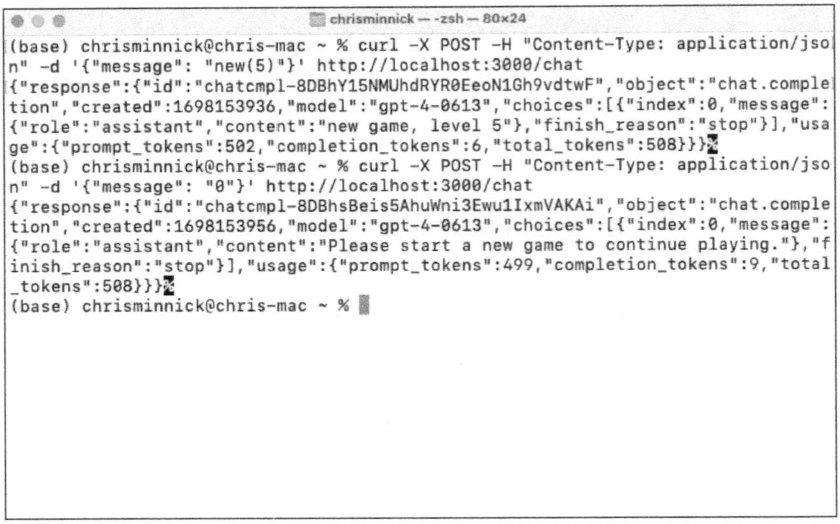

```
● ● ●                            🖥 chrisminnick — -zsh — 80×24
(base) chrisminnick@chris-mac ~ % curl -X POST -H "Content-Type: application/jso
n" -d '{"message": "new(5)"}' http://localhost:3000/chat
{"response":{"id":"chatcmpl-8DBhY15NMUhdRYR0EeoN1Gh9vdtwF","object":"chat.comple
tion","created":1698153936,"model":"gpt-4-0613","choices":[{"index":0,"message":
{"role":"assistant","content":"new game, level 5"},"finish_reason":"stop"}],"usa
ge":{"prompt_tokens":502,"completion_tokens":6,"total_tokens":508}}}
(base) chrisminnick@chris-mac ~ % curl -X POST -H "Content-Type: application/jso
n" -d '{"message": "0"}' http://localhost:3000/chat
{"response":{"id":"chatcmpl-8DBhsBeis5AhuWni3Ewu1IxmVAKAi","object":"chat.comple
tion","created":1698153956,"model":"gpt-4-0613","choices":[{"index":0,"message":
{"role":"assistant","content":"Please start a new game to continue playing."},"f
inish_reason":"stop"}],"usage":{"prompt_tokens":499,"completion_tokens":9,"total
_tokens":508}}}
(base) chrisminnick@chris-mac ~ % █
```

FIGURE 4-12:
The AI doesn't remember the last command.

Microsoft Corporation

This happened because the previous prompts in the conversation were not being sent to the server. Since the server has no way of tracking sessions between an individual user and the AI, the best place to implement session state is on the client.

Before working on the client, however, I have to set up the server to combine the prompts that are hard-coded on the server with the prompts that come from the client. I stored the system prompt and the example game in a variable and then prepended that to the messages that the client app sends to the server.

I also simplified the example game so the AI is returning only the number of the square where it wants to place a O. This change makes the client app easier to code and has the additional benefit of greatly reducing the number of tokens necessary for playing a game.

The finished server app is shown in Listing 4-2.

LISTING 4-2: My Finished API Server

```
import express from 'express';
import OpenAI from 'openai';
import 'dotenv/config';
import cors from 'cors';
const app = express();
```

```
const openai = new OpenAI({
  apiKey: process.env.OPENAI_API_KEY,
});
app.use(express.json());
app.use(cors());
app.post('/chat', async (req, res) => {
  const context = [
    {
      role: 'system',
      content:
        "You are an AI tic-tac-toe player. You are always 'O'
        and I'm always 'X'.\n\nI'll provide you with my move as
        a number on this grid:\n\n0 | 1 | 2\n3 | 4 | 5\n6 | 7 |
        8\n\nYou'll respond with only your move, which must not
        be a number that has already been played in the current
        game.\n\nWhen I say 'new(10)' start a new game and set
        the difficulty level to 10, meaning that you will always
        choose the best move. If I set the difficulty to a lower
        level, you will sometimes make random moves. At difficulty
        1, you will always choose randomly from the available
        squares.",
    },
    {
      role: 'user',
      content: 'new(10)',
    },
    {
      role: 'assistant',
      content: 'new game, level 10',
    },
    {
      role: 'user',
      content: '0',
    },
    {
      role: 'assistant',
      content: '4',
    },
    {
      role: 'user',
      content: '1',
    },
    {
```

(continued)

LISTING 4-2:   *(continued)*

```
      role: 'assistant',
      content: '2',
    },
    {
      role: 'user',
      content: '6',
    },
    {
      role: 'assistant',
      content: '8',
    },
    {
      role: 'user',
      content: '5',
    },
    {
      role: 'assistant',
      content: '3',
    },
    {
      role: 'user',
      content: '7',
    },
  ];
  const newMessage = req.body.messages;
  const messages = [...context, ...newMessage];
  const response = await openai.chat.completions.create({
    model: 'gpt-4',
    messages: messages,
    temperature: 0.5,
    max_tokens: 255,
    top_p: 1,
    frequency_penalty: 0,
    presence_penalty: 0,
  });
  res.json({ response });
});
app.listen(3000, () => {
  console.log('Server listening on port 3000');
});
```

Improving the client

To make the client application send my moves to the server and get the AI's moves back from the server, I wrote a new function named getAIMove(). This function sends the API server all the moves in the current game and gets back the AI's new move.

I also created a function named startNewGame() that takes the level of difficulty and passes the command to the server to start a new game. The complete code for the client-side script is shown in Listing 4-3.

LISTING 4-3: **The Client-Side JavaScript**

```
let board = ['', '', '', '', '', '', '', '', ''];
let currentPlayer = 'X';
let isGameOver = false;
let messageHistory = [];
function startNewGame(levelOfDifficulty) {
  board = ['', '', '', '', '', '', '', '', ''];
  currentPlayer = 'X';
  isGameOver = false;
  messageHistory = [];
  messageHistory.push({
    role: 'user',
    content: 'new(' + levelOfDifficulty + ')',
  });
  document.querySelectorAll('.cell').forEach((cell) => (cell.
   innerHTML = ''));
  const response = getAIMove(messageHistory);
  return response;
}
function makeMove(index) {
  if (board[index] === '' && !isGameOver) {
    board[index] = currentPlayer;
   document.getElementsByClassName('cell')[index].innerHTML =
  currentPlayer;
    messageHistory.push({
      role: 'user',
      content: index.toString(),
    });
    if (checkWin()) {
      alert(currentPlayer + ' Wins!');
```

(continued)

LISTING 4-3: **(continued)**

```
        isGameOver = true;
        return;
      }
      if (checkDraw()) {
        alert('Draw!');
        isGameOver = true;
        return;
      }
      aiMove(messageHistory); // Player is X, AI is O
    }
  }
  async function getAIMove(message) {
    // This function will send a message to the API server
    // The message will contain each previous move and the user's
    latest move
    // The API server will return the AI's next move
    const response = await fetch('http://localhost:3000/chat', {
      method: 'POST',
      headers: {
        'Content-Type': 'application/json',
      },
      body: JSON.stringify({
        messages: message,
      }),
    });
    const data = await response.json();
    document.getElementById('message').innerHTML =
      data.response.choices[0].message.content;
    return data.response.choices[0].message.content;
  }
  async function aiMove(messageHistory) {
    let move = await getAIMove(messageHistory);
    messageHistory.push({
      role: 'assistant',
      content: move.toString(),
    });
    board[move] = 'O';
    document.getElementsByClassName('cell')[move].innerHTML = 'O';
    if (checkWin()) {
```

```javascript
      alert('O Wins!');
      isGameOver = true;
    }
  }
}
function checkWin() {
  let winCombos = [
    [0, 1, 2],
    [3, 4, 5],
    [6, 7, 8],
    [0, 3, 6],
    [1, 4, 7],
    [2, 5, 8],
    [0, 4, 8],
    [2, 4, 6],
  ];
  for (let i = 0; i < winCombos.length; i++) {
    if (
      board[winCombos[i][0]] &&;
      board[winCombos[i][0]] === board[winCombos[i][1]] &&;
      board[winCombos[i][0]] === board[winCombos[i][2]]
    ) {
      return true;
    }
  }
  return false;
}
function checkDraw() {
  return board.every((cell) => cell !== '');
}
```

Once I finished writing the client-side script and updating the HTML page to add the Start Game button, I tested the game. After a little debugging, the game worked, and I could play tic-tac-toe with GPT-4 through my web browser.

However, after several games, it became apparent that although GPT-4 knows the rules of tic-tac-toe, it is terrible at strategy. I won every game, even when I set the level of difficulty to 10 and I played wrong, as shown in Figure 4-13.

GPT-4 model is a language model, and it's not well-equipped to handle reasoning.

REMEMBER

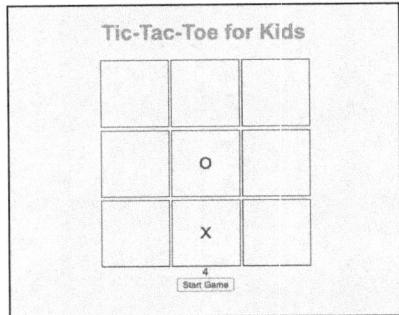
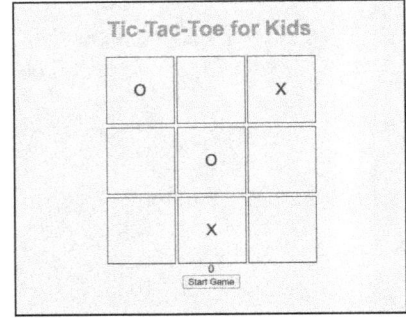
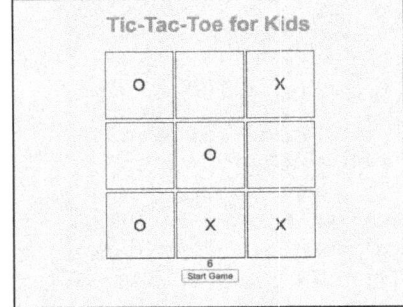
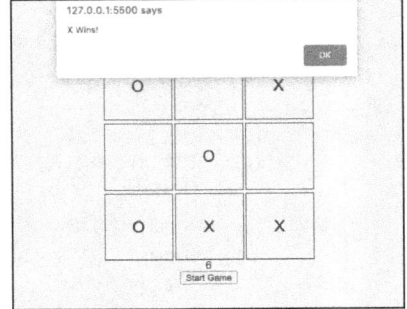

FIGURE 4-13:
GPT-4 is no good
at tic-tac-toe.

Moving logic from AI to the client

When integrating responses from an AI into an app, consider whether parts of the response from the AI can be done in your client- or server-side code. If so, you can reduce the complexity of the instructions to the AI as well as the number of interactions between your application and the AI. This will have multiple benefits, including reduced costs for AI usage, improved performance, and allowing the AI to focus on fewer tasks, which may improve its accuracy.

Because the level of difficulty simply adjusts the number of random responses, making random moves seems like a natural thing to take off the AI's plate. My idea was to handle the level of difficulty on the client side, and not even prompt the AI for random moves.

To accomplish this, I went back to the completely random tic-tac-toe move code that ChatGPT generated and modified it so that the selected level of difficulty would determine how frequently moves are generated randomly.

First, I revised the system prompt to eliminate the description of the levels of difficulty. Here's my new prompt:

```
{
    role: 'system',
    content:
        "You are an AI tic-tac-toe player. You are always
        'O' and I'm always 'X'.\n\nI'll provide you with
        my move as a number on this grid:\n\n0 | 1 | 2\n3
        | 4 | 5\n6 | 7 | 8\n\nYou'll respond with only
        your move, which must not be a number that has
        already been played in the current game.\n\nWhen I say
    'new()' start a new game.",
}
```

Then, to start writing the random move functionality, I entered the following comment at the beginning of the getAIMove() function:

```
/*
    Use the value of difficulty to decide whether to
    query the API for a move or use a random move.
    If difficulty is 10, always query the API
    If difficulty is 0, always use a random move
    If difficulty is between 0 and 10, use a random move
    (100 - difficulty x 10) percent of the time
    and use the best move (difficulty x 10) percent of the time
*/
```

The modified function I wrote with the help of Copilot is shown in Listing 4-4.

LISTING 4-4: **The new getAIMove() Function**

```
async function getAIMove(message) {
    /*
    Use the value of difficulty to decide whether to
    query the API for a move or use a random move.
    If difficulty is 10, always query the API
    If difficulty is 0, always use a random move
    If difficulty is between 0 and 10, use a random move
    (100 - difficulty x 10) percent of the time
    and use the best move (difficulty x 10) percent of the time
    */
```

(continued)

LISTING 4-4: *(continued)*

```
let random = Math.random();
if (random < difficulty / 10) {
  const response = await fetch('http://localhost:3000/chat', {
    method: 'POST',
    headers: {
      'Content-Type': 'application/json',
    },
    body: JSON.stringify({
      messages: message,
    }),
  });
  const data = await response.json();
  document.getElementById('message').innerHTML =
    data.response.choices[0].message.content;
  return data.response.choices[0].message.content;
}
let move = Math.floor(Math.random() * 8);
while (board[move] !== '') {
  move = Math.floor(Math.random() * 8);
}
document.getElementById('message').innerHTML = move.toString();
return move.toString();
}
```

With this new prompt and function, I could set the difficulty (in the script at first, and then through the use of a slider input in the HTML) and adjust the percentage of moves made by GPT-4 versus moves randomly generated in the client application.

The AI still couldn't play tic-tac-toe worth a darn, however, even with the difficulty level set to 10.

It may be possible, though better prompting, to get GPT-4 to be good at tic-tac-toe. Email me at chris@minnick.com if you figure it out!

TECHNICAL STUFF

You can find the complete code for the tic-tac-toe game on this book's website at www.dummies.com/go/codingwithaifd.

REMEMBER

Tips and Tricks for Code Generation

The results you get from a generative AI model will vary widely, based on your prompts, the context and input you provide to the model, the specific LLM you use, the temperature and other settings provided to the model, and more.

As you become more comfortable working with an AI coding assistant, you'll start to become more familiar with what it can and can't do. If you follow certain practices, however, you can get the LLM to generate good code more reliably. In this section, I tell you some of the tips and tricks that I've found to be most helpful, as well as a few practices that will end up costing you more time than it's worth to use the AI.

Don't stop coding

While AI can generate complete functions, or even working programs, it works best when you take the lead. Keep your skills up-to-date and use AI as a tool to help you write more code, rather than as a tool that will write your code for you. Not only will the AI learn from you and write better code, but you'll also be able to fully understand the code you're writing, which is essential to creating high-quality software.

Be specific

When prompting a coding assistant to generate code, or when asking a question about how to do something, be as specific as possible. When you're exploring an idea that you don't yet know how to code, it can be helpful to start with a vague prompt to generate ideas. But after you understand the problem and the domain, ask for details.

Think in steps

Complex requests are much more likely to result in unacceptable responses. Instead, break down every problem into its smallest units. Instead of saying, "How do I write an Instagram clone?" start with a plan (which you should consider writing as an SRS) and then with a small piece, such as the new user signup page.

Ask follow-up questions

If you're unsure about how a piece of generated code works or whether a response is unexpected, ask the AI assistant to clarify, explain, or try again. For example, if a function generated by the AI doesn't look quite right to you, but you don't know exactly what's wrong with it, ask the AI to provide several other ways that the function might be written. Just as you might watch several YouTube videos before finding the best solution to a problem, having your AI assistant generate options can be a great way to figure out what will work best. If you don't like the responses one AI assistant gives you, try another AI assistant. Or try feeding the code generated by one AI assistant to another one, asking it to improve the code.

Check the official documentation

Remember that coding assistants are trained on publicly available code, and the LLM behind the assistant may have a training data cutoff date. As a result, code generated by an LLM may use deprecated syntax, an older version of a library, or libraries that are no longer recommended. If a code assistant uses syntax or a library that you're not familiar with, check the official documentation to make sure you're using it correctly.

Use examples and context

Although the latest LLMs have amazing capabilities, they aren't mind readers. If you want the output from a request to be in a specific format, give the AI an example of that format. If the code you ask the AI to generate will integrate with some other function or service, provide the relevant information to the AI as context.

Prioritize security

Chatbots and coding assistants may use your input to train the underlying model. To be certain that no sensitive or personally identifying information will show up in suggestions given to other users of the LLM, always anonymize sensitive data. For example, if you ask the AI to summarize a long email, remove or change the email addresses and names from the email before submitting it as input to an LLM.

Keep learning

Working with a chatbot or a coding assistant is a great way to get answers to coding questions, but it's no substitute for staying up-to-date the same way programmers always have — by talking with other programmers, engaging in online forums on StackOverflow, Reddit, and Hacker News, watching videos, taking classes, and reading high-quality books like the one you have in front of you!

Keep your tools updated

AI coding tools are evolving quickly. Make sure that you have the latest version of whatever tools you're using. If you learn about a new tool that seems promising (through any of the sources mentioned in the preceding tip), try it out. If a new tool or IDE works better for you than the one you've been using, consider switching to it.

Be mindful of AI's limitations

As you see repeatedly in this book, LLMs aren't perfect or omniscient. They were trained on a lot of data and can make predictions based on patterns they find. If you're writing code that's unlike anything the AI has seen before, it will be of little help to you.

7

Creating Custom AI Solutions

Contents at a Glance

CHAPTER 1: **Personalizing the Customer Journey by Using AI**... 633

CHAPTER 2: **Boosting Online Business Growth with AI** 649

CHAPTER 3: **Enhancing Customer Service with Conversational AI Chatbots**........................ 665

CHAPTER 4: **Making Custom Copilots** 681

CHAPTER 5: **Expanding Copilot's Capabilities with Plugins** 705

Chapter **1**

Personalizing the Customer Journey by Using AI

M ost people enjoy getting brand emails that seem to be written specifi-cally for them. Consumers today expect that every company will deliver personalized interactions and custom recommendations based on their specific needs. Any organization that can successfully provide AI-based personal-ization can gain a competitive advantage.

This chapter explains how to deliver a personalized journey for your customers using several AI tools and techniques. We show you how to

» Determine how customers feel using sentiment analysis

» Provide what customers want by utilizing recommendation engines

» Predict what customers will do by employing predictive analytics

» Deliver information customers need with chatbots and virtual assistants

» Automate the delivery of content using marketing automation

We also look at how you can use generative AI (GenAI)) to leverage the data you get from these tools to create valuable assets for marketing, sales, and support. Book 4 has more information on using GenAI to create content and assets.

REMEMBER

Implementing AI technologies usually requires an up-front investment, but it can result in long-term cost savings, improved efficiency, and increased customer retention.

Discovering the Customer Journey

To understand how AI tools impact the customer journey, we begin by looking at the concept of the customer journey itself. The customer journey is the trip that customers take as they learn about, evaluate, and buy a product or service from your brand.

Taking the customer journey

Online practitioners know that improving the customer journey is one of the best ways to help customers choose their brand. Here are the five customer journey stages:

1. **Awareness**

   The customer recognizes their need and the possible solutions available to them. Marketing and advertising drive the awareness of the brand and its products. AI can facilitate the creation of these assets.

2. **Consideration**

   The customer researches their options and compares competitors. Content like product reviews and comparisons influence their choices. Sales content generated by AI can be used to answer questions and build credibility.

3. **Purchase**

   The customer chooses the best option and decides to buy. The transaction process should be seamless. AI can be used to provide shipping information or other details automatically.

4. **Retention**

   After purchasing, the goal is to retain the customer for additional business. This is usually done by delivering additional support, loyalty programs, and continuing great service.

5. **Advocacy**

> This is the stage at which the customer becomes so satisfied and engaged with a brand that they actively promote it to others.

TIP

Your customer journey should focus on guiding customers through each stage. Personalized interactions will move customers along the journey from initial awareness to loyal customers.

REMEMBER

Each journey stage generates volumes of behavioral data about how your customers make decisions. AI analyzes that data and provides key insights that help you create a winning journey for your brand.

Examining touch points

The customer journey typically involves many interactions with a brand, known as *touch points.* So, what are touch points? Touch points are the interactions that happen between the customer and the company throughout their relationship. The customer will experience a multitude of touch points when engaging with your brand. They include such things as:

>> Visiting your website for the first time

>> Receiving email offers from you

>> Seeing your ads on social media

>> Making brick-and-mortar store visits

>> Participating in tech support calls

>> Getting text messages about company events

REMEMBER

Each touch point represents an opportunity to delight customers, meet their needs, and deliver a great experience that guides them to a purchase.

Introducing AI Personalization

Personalizing the customer journey requires a combination of insights (driven by data analysis) and human touch points (like sales calls) to deliver a seamless experience. To provide effective personalization, you need to:

>> **Analyze customer data and insights.** AI tools produce customer profiles and uncover preferences and behaviors that provide the raw material to understand customer motivations.

>> **Blend AI and a human touch.** AI can process data to automate and scale personalization, but having people oversee the output is crucial to delivering content with a human touch.

>> **Use an omnichannel approach.** Connecting customer data across all touch points is essential so customers recognize your brand wherever they see it.

TIP

One example of blending AI and a human touch is an AI technology known as Einstein, which is part of the Salesforce customer relationship management (CRM) platform. Einstein creates an autogenerated personalized email for every sales conversation, making the salesperson more productive and providing the customer with a personalized follow-up email.

Delivering personalized content

Delivering consistent messages on all channels ensures that customers receive relevant information based on their preferences and interests. So, how does AI accomplish this? By doing the following:

>> Identifying patterns and segments from customer data to define personas

>> Determining which types of content each customer is likely to interact with

>> Continuously testing different content to maximize personalization effectiveness

>> Creating and delivering custom experiences automatically without any human involvement

REMEMBER

Continuous monitoring and optimization of AI systems are crucial for maintaining relevance as customer preferences change.

TIP

AI extracts insights from customer data that would be virtually impossible for humans to accomplish manually. This allows the delivery of results in real time at an almost unlimited scale.

Personalizing the journey with AI

As the customer proceeds through the journey, personalized content needs to reach them at each phase. Here are some examples of how AI-driven personalization is delivered throughout the customer journey stages, as introduced in the section "Taking the customer journey" earlier in the chapter:

>> **Awareness:** Visitors see display ads, social media posts, and website content reflecting their interests based on their browsing history.

>> **Consideration:** Product recommendations and comparison tools display customized options that consumers will prefer.

>> **Purchase:** Email and web content emphasize benefits and features that matter most to each customer.

>> **Retention:** Existing customers get personalized promotions, restock reminders, and cross-sell suggestions over time.

>> **Advocacy:** Loyal customers are offered personalized rewards and incentives and are encouraged to share their experiences with the product.

By continually optimizing experiences around a customer's choices, AI-powered personalization guides customers to a purchase.

REMEMBER

Some customers are sensitive to what they consider to be too much personalization. Be aware that some people may see personalization that constantly hits their inbox as intrusive.

Benefitting from AI Tools for the Customer Journey

Using AI tools to create and enhance the customer journey helps marketers, sales, and support teams deliver a great customer experience. Here are several benefits to consider:

>> **An enhanced customer experience:** AI can analyze large amounts of data to personalize the customer journey to deliver a more relevant customer experience.

>> **Better (business) decision-making:** AI provides valuable insights through predictive analytics or sentiment analysis, enabling businesses to make better decisions about pricing, product development, or marketing campaigns.

>> **Improved sales performance:** By using AI-powered tools, staff can understand customer needs to make more informed and targeted sales pitches.

>> **Real-time customer support:** With AI-powered chatbots or virtual assistants, businesses can provide support 24/7, improving response times and overall satisfaction.

>> **A competitive advantage:** Businesses that effectively leverage AI in their sales and support processes gain a competitive edge by serving customers content that matters to them. Of course, sometimes, human intervention is essential to close a sale or fix a problem.

>> **Reduced churn:** By showing customers you understand their desires and needs, you strengthen their loyalty and encourage them to remain customers.

Churn is a marketing term that refers to customers who quit using a product or service within a designated period.

REMEMBER

>> **Increased efficiency:** AI tools automate repetitive tasks such as data entry, which lets support teams focus on more important activities.

Determining How Customers Feel

Customers' feelings about a brand affect their buying decisions. Unfortunately, emotions are difficult to measure objectively in text and spoken language. This is where sentiment analysis is a valuable tool. By analyzing customer content across the customer journey, sentiment analysis uncovers the attitudes and feelings hidden inside volumes of customer data.

Sentiment analysis can determine customer emotions by analyzing their feedback or social media interactions. By understanding customer sentiment, you can send the right content at the right time, improving the customer experience.

TIP

Understanding sentiment analysis

Sentiment analysis is a technique that uses AI to find out whether content has a positive, negative, or neutral sentiment. For example, "I really like this product" would be considered a positive sentiment, "They have the worst service ever" is obviously negative, and "They delivered the package on time" would probably be considered neutral.

Sentiment analysis lets you discover patterns and trends about how customers feel. It analyzes the tone and mood of customers at different points along the journey and alerts you to potential problems. Using sentiment analysis techniques enables staff to pinpoint problems along the customer journey and fix them.

TIP

Here are some ways you can apply sentiment analysis:

>> **Eliminate pain points.** You can identify and fix the significant pain points to keep them from further frustrating customers.

>> **Discover problems when you make changes.** You can monitor sentiment changes following a product, service, or campaign modification.

>> **Spot major issues.** You can alert support teams to a customer problem so that they can fix it before it becomes a major issue.

Sentiment analysis applications help staff find and solve the problems that will deliver the greatest customer satisfaction.

Evaluating emotions across the customer journey

Organizations use sentiment analysis to gain insights across the customer journey. Here are some examples of how you can use it at each stage:

>> **Awareness:** You can analyze blog and video comments and other touch-point responses to understand the beginning opinions of the brand.

>> **Consideration:** You can look at customer inquiries, event feedback, and other interactions to see how their feelings change.

>> **Purchase:** To measure satisfaction after buying, you can categorize the sentiment from tech support comments, service calls, and conversations.

>> **Retention:** You can continuously analyze social media, reviews, customer support calls, and other channels to monitor ongoing attitudes.

>> **Advocacy:** You can find out which topics are most positively discussed in your community and use that information for your advocacy programs.

Creating assets using sentiment analysis data

In the past, sentiment analysis data was not widely available to organizations. The data was trapped inside social media platforms or on websites. Only a few staff or consultants would see comments, and not at scale. Now, you can use sentiment analysis data to create assets with GenAI.

Here are some examples of things you can create:

>> **Product development:** Use GenAI to create prototypes or feature lists based on positive or negative sentiments about your existing products.

>> **Crisis management:** If you receive serious negative alerts, use the data to help generate public relations (PR) responses or action plans.

>> **Employee engagement:** Use sentiment data from employee surveys to create internal training programs or motivational content.

REMEMBER

Data analysis shows what customers *do*, whereas sentiment analysis shows how they *feel.* By incorporating sentiment analysis, companies can create a brand that stands out.

Providing What Customers Want

Most consumers are overwhelmed by the choices they have online. Whether they're shopping or just browsing, they have endless options. For this reason, recommendation engines have become an essential AI tool. By providing custom suggestions, recommendation engines help customers find the most relevant products and services for their needs.

Understanding recommendation engines

Recommendation engines enable marketers to provide targeted, high-value suggestions that evolve with the customer's needs. As customers change, the engine continuously revises its suggestions based on the latest data. This level of personalization helps drive engagement, conversions, satisfaction, and loyalty across the entire customer life cycle.

Recommendation engines use algorithms to analyze customer data to predict customer preferences. They look at things like

>> **Purchase history:** What the customer bought before because this data can show future interest.

>> **Browsing history:** What the customer has viewed but not bought.

>> **Item attributes:** The customer's current preferences. They examine things like brand, price, and category.

>> **Ratings:** Explicit feedback the customer has provided on items, which signals the customer's likes and dislikes.

>> **Demographics:** Traits such as customer age, location, and more.

TIP

Customer recommendations can appear on product pages, emails, home pages, or any other touch point along the customer journey. They're typically displayed as the top personalized picks for the specific item the customer is considering.

Improving the customer journey with recommendations

Recommendation engines can influence several stages of the customer journey. Here are some examples of how recommendation engines can impact your customers:

>> **Awareness:** Recommendation engines help surface products that match a customer's needs but which the customer is unaware of. This presents relevant options early in the journey.

>> **Consideration:** Recommendation engines can provide educational materials, reviews, tutorials, and comparisons to help customers evaluate choices. This builds credibility during the research phase.

>> **Purchase:** Recommendation engines can suggest alternatives that meet the customer's criteria based on items viewed, reminding the customer of preferences they may have forgotten.

>> **Retention:** Recommendation engines can influence existing customers by recommending new releases, products the customer is running out of, and complementary items. This can help reduce churn.

>> **Advocacy:** Recommendation engines can recommend special offers or loyalty programs that are exclusive to customers who are in the advocacy stage. This rewards customers for their loyalty and encourages further advocacy.

Creating assets with recommendation engine data

Recommending products and services helps introduce your customers to things that were previously unknown to them. Here are some examples of using recommendation engine data to create assets with GenAI:

>> **Personalized content:** Use the data to create tailored articles, emails, or social media posts.

>> **Customer segmentation:** Use the data to create customer profiles that you can use for targeted marketing campaigns.

>> **Content curation:** Use the data to curate content reading lists or education courses customized to customer preferences.

Predicting What Customers Will Do

Companies have access to more customer data than ever, from website clicks to social media activity. Although this data is valuable, making sense of it is tricky. This is where predictive analytics comes in. It analyzes large amounts of customer data to predict preferences, behavior, and needs.

Utilizing predictive analytics

Predictive analytics makes predictions based on what customers have done in the past. Companies can use it to analyze the customer journey and predict what customers will do next. For example, it can predict that customers who buy a product after viewing that product's video several times have a higher customer lifetime value (CLV).

REMEMBER

CLV refers to the amount a customer will spend during their entire relationship with a company.

After the data is analyzed, predictive analytics tools create models to determine what will happen next. This is where your company can find great value. For example, here are some questions you'll be able to answer with authority:

>> Which types of content will specific customer segments be most interested in?

>> How likely will customers churn in the next three months based on their engagement level?

>> Given their average conversion value, how much should be spent on re-targeting ads to a specific audience segment?

Optimizing the customer journey

Knowing what customers may do next is valuable when analyzing the customer journey. Here are some examples of how predictive analytics can impact the customer journey:

>> **Awareness:** Predictive analytics can find potential customers based on demographic and behavioral data. This helps marketers more effectively target their awareness campaigns.

>> **Consideration:** By analyzing past interactions and purchase history, predictive analytics can personalize content to engage prospects.

>> **Purchase:** Predictive analytics can predict the likelihood that a prospect will make a purchase, allowing marketers to increase their focus on customers who are more likely to purchase.

>> **Retention:** Predictive analytics can identify patterns that signal potential customer churn, which alerts staff to take proactive measures to retain these customers.

>> **Advocacy:** By analyzing customer satisfaction and engagement metrics, predictive analytics can identify potential brand advocates, helping to increase word-of-mouth marketing.

Creating assets with predictive analytics data

You can use GenAI to develop the insights from predictive analytics into assets that take advantage of new opportunities and challenges. Here are some examples of assets that you can create using GenAI:

>> **Ad campaigns:** Leverage predictive analytics data to discover high-value keywords or customer segments. GenAI can then create ad variations that are more likely to result in a purchase.

>> **Churn prevention:** You can predict which customers will likely churn and use GenAI to create retention-focused content like special offers or educational materials.

>> **Simulations:** Predictive analytics can foresee the development of potential business problems. GenAI can create content that prepares you for these scenarios by suggesting training modules or videos. For example, a retail chain might use predictive analytics to identify a potential future dip in customer satisfaction. GenAI might respond by creating targeted training modules and videos for staff, focusing on enhancing customer service skills to address this issue preemptively.

TIP

Predictive analytics delivers great value to organizations by anticipating customer needs and proactively serving them up. It removes the guesswork staff must make when deciding what content to provide.

Delivering Information Customers Need

Providing real-time answers to customer questions is imperative for brands. But scaling this personal support without AI tools would be virtually impossible. Enter chatbots and virtual assistants. These AI-powered tools automate conversations to give customers the information they need anytime, anywhere. By providing real-time assistance, they enhance the user experience, save money, and solve problems quickly.

REMEMBER

You've already engaged with a virtual assistant if you've used Apple's Siri, Amazon Alexa, or Google Assistant. They make daily tasks like setting alarms or checking the weather fun and easy.

Utilizing chatbots and virtual assistants

Chatbots are software designed to understand questions and provide text or voice-based replies that mimic human conversation. (Virtual assistants add more advanced features like voice recognition and integration with your organization's backend systems.)

TIP

Chatbot capabilities can run the gamut. They can provide simple canned responses or advanced ones using machine learning to handle more complex interactions. You can easily choose one that is suited to your needs.

In addition, the chat feature should tell the customer whether they're dealing with a chatbot or a human. It's important for the company to make that clear.

Self-service along the customer journey

Chatbots and virtual assistants reshape the customer journey by offering conversational self-service. Here are some examples of how to deploy them along the customer journey:

>> **Awareness:** Chatbots and virtual assistants can pop up on websites to introduce the brand and answer common questions for prospects who are merely browsing.

>> **Consideration:** Chatbots and virtual assistants can provide personalized product guidance and recommendations to assist with evaluation.

>> **Purchase:** Chatbots and virtual assistants can process transaction details, track orders, and explain returns to increase conversions.

>> **Retention:** Chatbots and virtual assistants can follow up post-purchase to answer customer questions, upsell other products, and build relationships.

>> **Advocacy:** Chatbots and virtual assistants can prompt customers to share referral codes with their network, offering both the customer and their friend special discounts or rewards.

Creating assets using chatbots

Chatbots can generate insights into customer needs, behavior, and sentiment by capturing and analyzing conversational data. You can use that data to create assets using GenAI. Here are some examples:

>> **Case studies:** Use the data you get from customer support chatbots to identify success stories and use GenAI to draft case studies.

>> **Social media posts:** Use the data from chatbot interactions to generate social media content such as common questions or insights.

>> **Email campaigns:** Use AI to create personalized email content based on the questions and opinions expressed in the chat.

Chatbots engage visitors and support customers without any human intervention. They're valuable because, in many cases, they reduce problems and increase satisfaction throughout the customer journey by providing 24/7 assistance. Just be aware that they don't always have the desired effect.

Automating the Delivery of Content

Customers expect to receive relevant real-time information when interacting with brands. But manually distributing content to audiences would require unlimited time and effort. This is where AI marketing automation platforms become essential. By organizing content delivery, automation enables marketers to give customers timely, personalized content on a scale.

TIP

According to Gartner, the research and advisory firm, automating customer messages will help large companies be more productive. Gartner predicts that in the next couple of years, 30 percent of outbound messages from large organizations will be AI-created (https://tinyurl.com/3666hdtp).

Viewing AI marketing automation

AI marketing automation software uses rules and workflows to automate marketing tasks. Automation platforms can assemble and distribute content tailored to each customer based on their behaviors and preferences. This creates targeted experiences that build the customer relationship.

Observing data-driven personalization

Modern automation platforms can analyze customer data and turn it into actionable insights. Here's how they do this:

>> **Customer profiles:** Data is collected from multiple channels to build unified customer profiles.

>> **Audience segmentation:** Segmentation is based on attributes like demographics, behaviors, and preferences.

>> **Mapping:** Journey mapping is used to understand typical pathways users take.

>> **Rules:** Trigger-based rules deploy content to customers when specified criteria are met.

Automating across the customer journey

Automated content delivery streamlines critical phases of the journey. Here's how it maps to the different stages:

>> **Awareness:** Automated emails send new prospects customized introductory information when they sign up.

>> **Consideration:** Behavior-triggered content recommends relevant resources to help with product evaluation.

>> **Purchase:** Web personalization automatically shows special offers and messaging to those poised to buy.

>> **Retention:** Existing customers receive automated cross-sell offers and restock reminders.

>> **Advocacy:** Automated surveys collect customer opinions. You can then automatically share these opinions as testimonials (with the customers' permission).

Creating assets and delivering them with marketing automation

Marketing automation allows you to automatically deliver valuable content to customers at the right time to spur engagement. Here are some examples of assets that you can create and automatically send at just the right time:

>> **Triggered notifications:** Send automated notifications or reminders when a user takes a specific action like abandoning a shopping cart.

>> **Personalized emails:** Automatically use subscriber data to segment audiences and customize email content, offers, and messaging.

>> **Automated workflows:** Set up a sequence of emails, offers, and content that guides users through your conversion funnel.

REMEMBER

As automation capabilities evolve, marketers can spend less time on manual efforts and more time on strategy. This lets technology handle the complexity of orchestrating seamless customer experiences at scale.

Chapter **2**

Boosting Online Business Growth with AI

Would you like to hire a free business strategy consultant who can help your company gain a competitive edge? Luckily, you have several good choices. AI apps can act as your digital consultant. They can help you research your competitors and make customized plans for your company's needs.

This chapter explores several ways AI apps can help boost your company's online business growth:

» Outsmarting your competitors

» Enhancing brand building

» Maximizing your conversions

» Scaling paid advertising return on investment (ROI)

» Tracking key performance indicators (KPIs) with AI

» Innovating new offerings

Outsmarting Your Competitors

AI tools are becoming increasingly popular because they can effectively identify market trends and consumer behavior better than traditional methods. They let you "see around corners" and hopefully outthink the competition.

Adopting AI tools helps you gain an advantage that is difficult for other businesses to equal without using their own AI tools. By implementing AI tools customized to your specific business goals, you can future-proof your strategy and boost growth.

TIP

Many business leaders have started to embrace AI tools, specifically GenAI. According to the 2023 KPMG AI Survey, 74 percent of business leaders put AI as the top emerging technology that will impact their business over the next year and a half.

AI can analyze your competitors' digital strategies by looking at such things as the keywords they use for search engine optimization (SEO), where their web traffic comes from, their ad spending, and their customers' social media engagement. Analyzing these elements helps you find their weaknesses and blind spots to exploit them. In the following sections, we look at each of these in turn.

Analyzing competitor keywords

To begin, you can use AI tools to analyze your top competitors' websites. You should identify the keywords they rank for in search engines and their keyword gaps (that is, search terms they don't target). In fact, identifying keyword gaps is one of the most valuable features of AI-powered keyword analysis. These gaps are search terms that your competitors aren't targeting but that are relevant to your business. Discovering them is important because it helps you find untapped opportunities in the marketplace.

REMEMBER

Keywords are the words and phrases that potential customers type into search engines. You can drive traffic to your website by ranking for the right keywords and increasing conversions. When selecting an AI tool for keyword analysis, consider factors like ease of use, data accuracy, and cost. Tools to consider include the following:

>> **Semrush** (www.semrush.com): Semrush, as shown in Figure 2-1, allows you to evaluate your competitors' various SEO metrics, including the authority score, referring domains, backlinks, and search traffic.

>> **Ahrefs** (https://ahrefs.com/keywords-explorer): The Ahrefs Keywords Explorer, shown in Figure 2-2, lets you discover a competitor's top-ranking keywords. You can sort by search volume and difficulty to uncover the best opportunities.

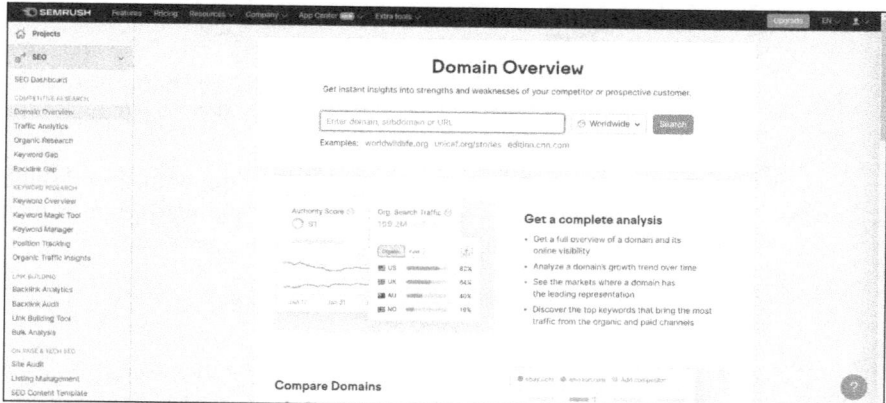

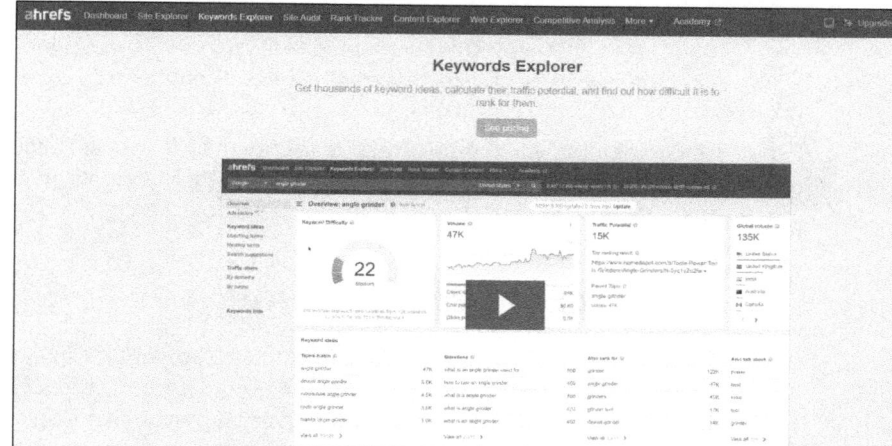

FIGURE 2-2:
The Ahrefs
Keywords
Explorer

Discovering traffic sources

Do you know where your competitors' traffic is coming from? You should. Understanding where their traffic comes from is critical for crafting your own marketing strategy. It can help you identify where you should be focusing your resources.

AI tools can analyze competitors' website traffic sources by looking at such things as

>> **Organic searches:** Look at the keywords driving traffic to your competitors' sites. Are there any you haven't targeted yet?

>> **Social media engagement:** Analyze which platforms are the most effective for your competitors and the type of content that gets the most engagement. This provides you with clues about what your audience wants.

>> **Paid ads:** Identify the keywords and platforms where your competitors invest in paid advertising. This can tell you where they are seeing the highest ROI. This is a great way to know what to invest in without having to experiment.

The preceding information lets you find your competitors' seldom-used channels (for example, less well-known social media platforms or niche forums). Then, you can optimize your marketing strategy accordingly.

Some tools to consider include the following:

>> **Similarweb (**www.similarweb.com**):** This AI-powered market platform analyzes a website's traffic sources and channels. It breaks down things like referrals, search, social, and paid traffic.

>> **BuzzSumo (**https://buzzsumo.com/use-cases/competitor-intelligence**):** This content tool analyzes your competitors' KPIs. You see metrics such as likes, shares, and comments.

TIP

Understanding your competitors' traffic sources is not just about keeping tabs on them. It's about refining your own strategy. By leveraging AI tools, you discover insights that were once only found by expert marketers.

Monitoring ad spending

Use AI tracking tools to determine how much competitors spend on search, social, display, and other online ads. This helps you determine the level of paid marketing you need to spend to stay ahead. Make sure to adjust your ad budgets to gain the edge.

Here are some tools to try:

>> **SpyFu (**www.spyfu.com**):** SpyFu tracks competitors' paid search ad keywords, ad copies, and their estimated monthly spending on Google, Bing, and YouTube.

>> **Moz (**https://moz.com/competitive-research**):** Moz has a suite of SEO tools to assist with keyword research, rank tracking, and backlink analysis. Of particular interest in competitive intelligence is their free SEO Competitive Analysis Tool. You can use it to analyze your competitors' domains to get a wealth of information.

TIP

To learn more about AI in advertising, see the "Scaling Paid Advertising ROI" section, later in this chapter.

Analyzing social media performance

AI can track competitors' social media followers, engagement, hashtags, mentions, and influencer partnerships. You can use these insights to shape a more effective social media approach for your company. Consider trying these tools:

» **Brandwatch** (www.brandwatch.com): Brandwatch is a social listening platform that tracks competitors' followers, engagement, sentiment, and influencers.

» **Talkwalker** (www.talkwalker.com): The Talkwalker platform tracks social performance, customer feedback, sentiment, and trends.

Enhancing Brand Building

Another way to boost online business growth is to enhance the branding that resonates with your audience. You can use AI tools to do things like refine your visual identity, simplify your messaging, and clarify your tone of voice. The key is to utilize AI's creative capabilities while staying true to your brand identity. In the following sections, we look at these ways to leverage AI to make your branding more compelling.

Refining visual brand identities

Visual assets like logos, fonts, color palettes, and imagery must reflect your brand DNA. AI tools can help you refine your branded visuals by allowing you to analyze elements in ways you couldn't before. These include

» **Automating design generation:** AI tools can generate several design options based on your defined parameters. This lets you perform A/B testing to accelerate the design process and ensure that the final design is data driven (see the "Creating Ad Copy" section later in this chapter for A/B testing).

» **Choosing colors:** AI tools can analyze customer interactions and preferences to suggest color schemes that resonate with your target audience. For example, you could analyze sales data to see if specific product colors sell better than others for different customer segments.

» **Making font choices:** AI apps can analyze text elements in real time to suggest popular fonts across different platforms. This can enhance the user experience. Of course, humans need to make the final decision.

- **Image recognition and tagging:** AI apps can automatically tag and categorize images. This process makes it easier for brands to manage their visual assets. This is crucial for e-commerce platforms where thousands of product images must be sorted and displayed. Doing this manually would take a great deal of time and be prone to human error.

- **Analytics and insights:** AI tools can provide insights by tracking how users interact with your creative elements. Then, this data can be used to make decisions that refine your brand's identity.

TIP

To learn how AI tools can impact visual content, check out Book 4, Chapter 3.

Crafting strong brand messaging

Consistent messaging is crucial for brand building. This is an area in which AI can be especially helpful. AI can optimize your messaging for impact by utilizing its natural language capabilities. Here are a few ways it can assist you:

- **Sentiment analysis:** Sentiment analysis provides insights into how your messaging resonates. It analyzes social media conversations and website comments to identify positive and negative associations, emotions, and perceptions related to a brand. (For more about using sentiment analysis, see Chapter 1 of this book.)

- **Content generation:** AI can generate slogans and taglines and copy alternatives that convey the right positioning.

- **Contextual targeting:** Understanding audience demographics and interests allows AI apps to customize messaging to be more relevant.

- **Competitive analysis:** By monitoring your competitors' messaging and performing a comparative analysis, AI tools can help create significant differentiation between you and your competitors.

REMEMBER

Great brands live in the minds of their customers. As a brand, you can't control what your customers think, but you can learn how you impact them based on what they tell you.

Defining brand voice and tone

Your brand's voice includes your vocabulary, style, and overall personality. It serves as the foundation for building all your customer relationships. You can use AI tools to enhance your branding foster engagement and loyalty. These tools allow you to continuously learn from your customer data to test and refine your brand voice across many touchpoints rapidly. Here are a few ways AI tools support defining your brand voice and tone:

>> **Analyzing language patterns:** It's necessary to identify the vocabulary, sentence structures, and idioms that make up your brand's voice. You can codify what makes your brand's voice unique by identifying these elements and applying them.

>> **Evaluating values and target audience:** It is essential to understand who your brand is and who it's speaking to. AI tools can evaluate your brand values to identify appropriate voice and tone aspects like formal/informal, emotional/rational, and authoritative/conversational.

>> **Competitive analysis:** This step is often overlooked. Knowing how your brand's voice stacks up against competitors can provide insights into areas for differentiation and improvement. You can more confidently create your messaging when you understand how your brand is understood by your customers.

TIP

Using AI, data-driven iterations let you quickly prototype and test your brand assets to increase their impact without making decisions blindly.

Maximizing Conversions

Effective online professionals strive to do all they can to maximize conversions regardless of their position in the organization. AI tools let you optimize every element of your digital presence to get those conversions and sales. They allow you to deliver the right content to the right person at the right time (often referred to as the "holy grail of marketing"). This results in visitors who engage, buy, and promote your brand as advocates.

You can do things to maximize conversions with AI, including segmenting your audience and personalizing content. We look at these in the following sections.

Understanding the segmentation of audiences

One of the key things AI tools permit you to do when analyzing your audience is divide customers into different segments based on their behavior and preferences. This lets you develop targeted marketing strategies for each segment. This is of enormous value to you as a marketer or salesperson.

Here are some of the benefits you get from AI audience segmentation:

- **Targeting:** AI algorithms can analyze large data sets to identify customer behavior patterns, enabling you to create more accurate segmentation.

- **Adapting in real time:** AI models can adapt to changes in customer behavior. This ensures that the segments are always up to date.

- **Optimizing resources:** You can allocate your marketing resources more effectively by knowing which segments will likely convert.

- **Personalizing experiences:** Personalizing the content you send to customers can significantly boost conversions.

- **Predicting behavior:** AI apps can forecast the future behavior of each segment, allowing you to proactively create effective marketing strategies. (See Chapter 1 for more about predictive analytics.)

- **Enhancing ROI:** Better targeting and allocation of resources lead to higher conversion rates, which improves your ROI.

- **Automating insights:** AI can automatically generate insights about each of your audience segments, making it easier for you to make data-driven decisions.

TIP

To utilize segmentation, consider collaborating with influencers or industry experts with a strong following in the specific segments of your target audience. This will give you a better chance to accelerate sales.

If you want to check out some AI tools that segment your audiences, you can consider some customer data platform (CDP) tools like the following:

- **Klaviyo** (www.klaviyo.com)**:** Klaviyo is a marketing platform that analyzes customer data like purchases and browsing history to create customized audience segments to send emails and texts.

- **Segment Personas** (https://segment.com/customer-data-platform/)**:** Segment Personas is a feature within the Segment CDP, shown in Figure 2-3. It creates segments across channels using data from different sources like your website, mobile app, or customer relationship management (CRM) system.

REMEMBER

A CDP is software that helps businesses understand their customers by creating a complete customer profile from their customer data. You can then use this profile to create personalized, targeted marketing campaigns that meet customers' needs and preferences.

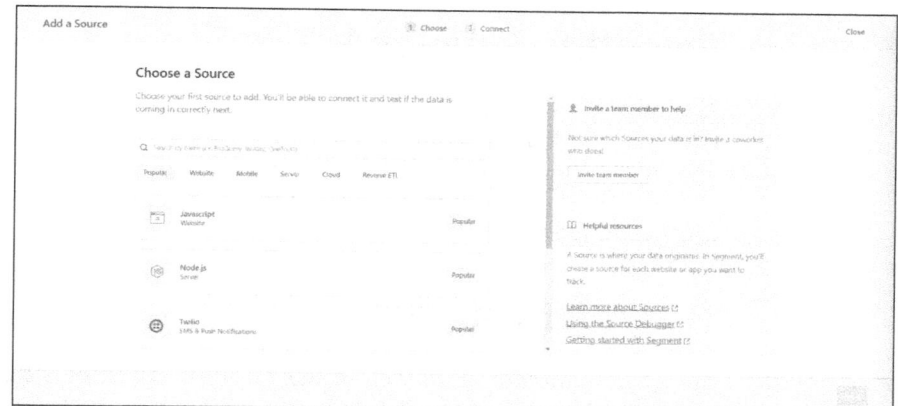

FIGURE 2-3:
Segment
Personas collects
your data across
different sources
you select.

Personalizing content

We cover AI personalization and its impact on the customer journey in Chapter 1. In this section, we look at two ways it relates to optimizing your sales funnel by personalizing user experiences:

» **Lead scoring:** Lead scoring with AI helps you learn which potential customers are most likely to buy by analyzing current and historical data to see what customers did before they made a purchase. It then uses that information to give scores to new potential customers.

» **Content testing and optimization:** AI tools test multiple content variations, like images, headlines, and copy, to determine which performs best. They also continuously optimize based on new visitor data. By using this real-time data, you're always getting the best optimization.

Scaling Paid Advertising ROI

Paid advertising is a standard way for brands to drive qualified traffic and sales. AI tools have helped to simplify the creation and management of paid advertising campaigns by conducting in-depth optimization. This would be impossible for staff to do manually.

AI tools are currently very beneficial in producing ads. They automate the process by selecting the most effective keywords, optimizing bids, and creating ad copy that is likely to convert. This analysis not only saves time but also improves the ROI of your advertising campaigns. In the following sections, we look at each process in turn.

Selecting keywords

AI combs through large amounts of search query data to identify high-performing keywords. It can also predict emerging keyword trends, which allows you to find new opportunities (hopefully before your competitors do). This level of automation and optimization leads to more targeted campaigns, which can drive higher conversion rates.

Optimizing bids

One great feature of AI ad tools is that they can adjust bids based on real-time metrics and market conditions. This ensures that you get the most value for your advertising dollar. This means that bid optimization is no longer a static, one-time selection.

TIP

AI ad tools continuously analyze metrics (like click-through and conversion rates) and changes in competitor bids. This real-time analysis lets the AI adjust bids to maximize ROI, which ensures you're not overspending.

Creating ad copy

GenAI can produce multiple variations of ad copy, which can then be A/B tested to identify the most effective messaging. It can create multiple variations of ad copy in seconds, each tailored to different segments of your audience. This enables A/B testing, which allows you to quickly identify which messages resonate most with your target market. The AI can also adapt the copy based on real-time performance data to ensure that your advertising continues to be relevant.

Personalizing and testing

AI can also personalize ad campaigns to individual user profiles and perform continuous testing to optimize performance. AI can segment your audience based on factors like browsing behavior, past purchases, and demographic information. This enables highly personalized ad campaigns that speak directly to the individual's needs and preferences. Additionally, AI can perform continuous multivariate testing on these personalized campaigns, refining them to achieve peak performance over time.

TECHNICAL STUFF

Multivariate testing is a method that tests variations of several elements on a web page or application at the same time to determine which combination performs the best. Unlike A/B testing, which compares two versions of a single element, multivariate testing evaluates multiple elements and their variations at the same time.

USING AI FOR ADS?

Are you looking for a way to begin using AI ad tools? If so, consider trying this AI-powered framework to optimize your paid ad performance:

- **Segment your audience:** Leverage AI tools to analyze your customer data and build predictive models to identify your high-value segments. Then, create your ads by starting with high-priority targets.

- **Craft high-converting ads:** Use GenAI copywriting tools to create engaging ad copy and relevant images for each audience. This drives engagement and clicks.

- **Personalize at scale:** After users click through, you should continue personalizing the experience. AI can customize each user's copy and creatives based on their profile and behavior.

- **Optimize campaigns:** Continue using GenAI to extract the maximum value from paid ads across channels like Facebook, Instagram, and Google Ads.

Some tools you might consider trying include

- **AdCreative.ai** (www.adcreative.ai): AdCreative.ai is an AI tool that optimizes digital advertising creatives. It provides insights into ad performance and provides competitor tracking.

- **ADYOUNEED** (www.adyouneed.com): ADYOUNEED is a multi-platform advertising tool that simplifies and optimizes digital ad creation and management. It supports platforms including Google Ads, Meta Ads (Facebook and Instagram), and LinkedIn.

REMEMBER

Constantly optimizing your ads using AI will drive higher-quality traffic and maximize the ROI on your ad budget. This will help you maintain an ongoing scalable engine for online business growth.

Considering the pros and cons

One of the great benefits of using AI in advertising is that it can analyze real-time data to redistribute budget across various campaigns. This ensures that resources are allocated to the most effective channels, maximizing ROI. Additional benefits include the following:

- **>> Cost efficiency:** By automating budget adjustments, businesses can reduce the need for manual oversight, thereby saving time and reducing operational costs.

>> **Data-driven decision-making:** AI provides actionable insights based on data analytics, which allows you to make more informed decisions. This is particularly useful for identifying trends and making quick adjustments to capitalize on them.

>> **Risk mitigation:** AI can predict the performance of different advertising channels and suggest budget adjustments to mitigate risks associated with overspending on underperforming campaigns.

On the negative side, some people have criticized using AI tools in advertising. They believe using AI for budget adjustments could lead to unfair or unethical advertising practices. Here are some of the concerns:

>> **Data privacy:** AI algorithms require access to substantial amounts of data for effective decision-making. This raises concerns about how this data is stored, who has access to it, and how it's used. It could potentially infringe on consumer privacy.

>> **Transparency and accountability:** The use of AI in advertising often operates in a "black box." This makes it difficult for people to understand how decisions are made. This lack of transparency can be a significant issue when it comes to ethical advertising practices.

>> **Regulatory compliance:** Different industries and regions have specific regulations regarding data privacy and ethical advertising. Using AI tools that are not compliant can result in legal repercussions.

>> **Unethical branding:** Unethical use of AI can harm a brand's reputation, causing a loss of consumer trust and revenue.

So, what can you do to avoid risk?

>> **Vet AI tools.** Before adopting any AI tool for advertising, be sure it complies with industry standards and regulations. These standards include the General Data Protection Regulation (GDPR) and the California Consumer Privacy Act (CCPA). For a complete listing of standards and regulations, check out the Interactive Advertising Bureau (IAB) at www.iab.com.

>> **Choose transparency.** Pick AI solutions that offer some level of transparency in their decision-making algorithms. Transparent AI solutions are clear, responsible, and ethical. Choosing transparent solutions helps you meet legal standards and gain the trust of your users.

>> **Monitor continuously.** Regularly audit the AI's decisions to ensure they align with ethical standards and are free of bias. To do this, first define your own ethical standards and identify potential biases. Look at decision-making data to spot any unfair patterns or issues, and make sure to include people with diverse perspectives to catch biases that may not be obvious.

Tracking Key Performance Indicators with AI

KPIs are business metrics that help organizations monitor their performance against objectives. Tracking KPIs has always been an important method for businesses to keep their eye on what's important. KPIs help businesses analyze their growth. Thanks to the use of AI tools, monitoring KPIs has come a long way.

Traditionally, KPIs have been tracked manually. Marketers had to rely on manual processes to collect and analyze data, which was time-consuming and produced errors. Today, AI tools automatically handle data collection and analysis.

Here are some other ways KPI tracking was inadequate:

» **Limitations:** Due to technological limitations, KPIs could focus on only easily quantifiable metrics like sales volume. Marketers couldn't get the understanding of customer behavior that is available today.

» **Siloed data:** Audience segmentation wasn't available in the way AI handles it today. Different departments held different parts of the information, making it almost impossible to get a unified view of marketing performance across different channels and campaigns.

» **Delayed reporting:** Insights from historical data were compiled into reports with a lag time. This lag thwarted the ability to make timely decisions.

Here's how AI tools can significantly enhance the process of KPI tracking to grow your business:

» **Real-time monitoring:** AI apps can continuously collect and analyze data, providing real-time updates on various KPIs. This allows your business to make timely adjustments to your strategies instead of waiting for end-of-month reports. This is a significant improvement because it lets you make changes as soon as they're warranted.

TIP

Traditional KPI tracking often focuses on single metrics like sales revenue or customer satisfaction. AI can analyze many metrics at once, which enables a more holistic view of your business's performance.

» **Benchmarking:** AI can compare your KPIs against industry benchmarks or competitor data to better understand your total performance. This data helps you set more realistic targets.

>> **Customizing:** AI tools allow for the customization of KPI dashboards, enabling you to focus on metrics specific to your goals and industry. This gives you a clearer picture of the threats and risks you face.

>> **Detecting anomalies:** AI algorithms can identify anomalies or outliers in KPI data that could indicate underlying issues. Early detection of these anomalies lets you take immediate action. This could be troubleshooting a problem or capitalizing on an unforeseen positive trend.

Innovating New Offers

Most online businesses try to discover their customers' unmet needs and develop new product concepts and features. Launching innovative new products and services is critical for companies that want to remain competitive. But the risks of innovation are high, and coming up with fresh ideas is always a challenge.

This is where leveraging AI tools is valuable. AI helps businesses identify opportunities for new offerings. This section looks at trend forecasting, generating creative concepts, and refining your innovations related to innovating your products.

Trend forecasting

Being able to see around corners is a very valuable skill. AI-generated reports help anticipate future events by analyzing historical data and current markets. AI predictive analytics can help you capitalize on market trends and provide insights about events that could negatively impact your business. This predictive capability readies companies for challenges and opportunities they may not see coming.

REMEMBER

Your analysis will only be as good as the quality of your data. The insights will be misleading or unreliable if you have error-prone or inaccurate data. For instance, AI tools can analyze several years of sales data to predict future products that may be popular. But if your sales data is flawed, your analysis will be, too.

WARNING

AI tools can tell you what is happening, but they can't tell you why it's happening. For that, you still need to apply your business and industry knowledge. For example, an AI tool could alert you to a big increase in social media mentions, but it (and you) won't know if this is due to a successful marketing campaign, a viral news story, or some other factor.

Generating creative concepts

You can conceptualize new products or services with the insights you've collected from your AI tools. You can input an idea, and AI can help produce detailed concepts to evaluate. This content speeds up the ideation process and provides faster decision-making.

Refining your innovation

When you have a promising idea, AI tools can help you refine it into a workable concept. GenAI tools can write business plans, create relevant marketing copy, and even produce pitch decks to help launch your innovation.

REMEMBER

You can continually ideate, develop, and launch new offerings by developing an AI pipeline. Integrating AI into your innovation strategies will help you deliver unique, relevant products that will hopefully make your competitors have to play catch-up.

Chapter **3**

Enhancing Customer Service with Conversational AI Chatbots

The use of AI chatbots represents a major shift away from conventional customer service to a more effective approach. Previously, customer support relied solely on interactions between customers and staff. Now, using AI chatbots, companies can automate tasks, reduce costs, and provide round-the-clock support. In this chapter, we look at conversational AI (CAI) chatbots, which are the next iteration of traditional chatbots.

These advanced CAI chatbots can handle a wide range of customer service tasks. In some cases, they've already shown that they can outperform staff when it comes to consistency and availability. This chapter looks at the transformational role of CAI chatbots for customer service and the impact they can have on your business and customer satisfaction.

Finding Out about Conversational AI Chatbots

Customer service chatbots are AI-powered programs that handle conversations with customers across communication channels. They can answer questions, provide information, and help with tasks like taking orders or assisting with account issues.

Understanding the process

Traditional rules-based chatbots provided limited responses and no ability to learn from customer interactions. CAI chatbots use natural language processing (NLP) and machine learning (ML) to meet customer needs.

It's useful to understand the capabilities that enable CAI chatbots to deliver automated services. They can

>> Understand the context of the response to respond appropriately during a customer interaction

>> Process personalized data like order history to provide customized responses

>> Escalate issues that involve human emotions or very nuanced language to human agents

>> Integrate across backend systems (like servers or databases) to efficiently serve customers

Here's how a chatbot technically "responds" to a customer question:

1. The customer submits a query to the chatbot. It could be text, voice, or another input method.

2. The query is captured and preprocessed by the CAI system. The CAI system analyzes the request to identify the user's intent, which involves processing NLP techniques to understand the meaning.

3. The chatbot matches the customer intent to predefined categories in the chatbot's knowledge base. This information helps the chatbot understand the context of the request.

4. That information is used to generate a response that addresses the customer's query. The response can be text, images, audio, or a combination of these formats, depending on what the company chooses.

5. The generated response is delivered back to the customer.

Defining the differences between conversational AI chatbots and ChatGPT

To understand chatbots further, we need to understand the differences between CAI chatbots and ChatGPT. Unfortunately, some people incorrectly label chatbots as ChatGPT. When it comes to customer service, this can be confusing and misleading. CAI chatbots and ChatGPT both use AI, but they differ in their capabilities and use cases — especially when it comes to handling conversations.

Developers designed CAI chatbots for use cases like customer service or sales support. You can integrate them into things like apps or messaging platforms (for example, Facebook Messenger) to answer questions or help with transactions. They focus on mimicking human-like conversation using AI. They combine NLP and ML to create a more natural interaction.

Although you can combine CAI chatbots with GenAI capabilities from tools such as ChatGPT and Microsoft Copilot, the two technologies are not the same thing. CAI chatbots are developed to predictably respond to questions about a limited number of topics. GenAI chatbots are multipurpose tools designed to generate original content that's similar to content it was trained on. See Chapter 4 of this book to find out how to use Microsoft Copilot Studio to create a CAI that uses capabilities from Microsoft Copilot.

REMEMBER

CAI chatbots are customizable for the specific needs of a business or application. You can integrate them with backend systems and databases to provide responses based on real-time data. For example, CAI chatbots can retrieve corporate data like purchase history to answer questions about shipping dates.

Visualizing the differences

Visualizing the differences between CAI chatbots and ChatGPT can be helpful in understanding them. Table 3-1 details the clear distinctions.

TABLE 3-1   Conversational AI Chatbots versus ChatGPT

Feature	Conversational AI Chatbots	ChatGPT (Advanced AI)
Operation	AI-driven, typically using a mix of rules and ML techniques	Utilizes deep learning (GPT architecture)
Conversation handling	Capable of handling a variety of interactions with some level of contextual understanding	Capable of handling a broader range of topics, more contextually relevant
Flexibility	More flexible than traditional chatbots; can adapt to different conversation styles	Highly adaptable, generates responses based on volumes of training data
Learning capability	Some ability to learn from interactions, but is limited	Doesn't learn in real-time; relies on pretraining data
Context understanding	Better at handling off-script conversations than traditional chatbots but has limitations	Better at understanding context but not adept at highly complex dialogues
Human-like interaction	More adept at mimicking human conversation than traditional chatbots	Highly capable of mimicking human-like conversation styles

REMEMBER

CAI chatbots blend rule-based approaches with AI elements. This provides improved quality over traditional chatbots but is not at the level of sophistication of ChatGPT.

Benefitting from Conversational AI Chatbots for Customer Service

CAI chatbots provide immediate responses. This quick response leads to higher customer satisfaction and a better overall service experience. You can get several other benefits by deploying CAI chatbots:

» **The ability to provide 24/7 support:** CAI chatbots are operational all day, every day. This constant availability ensures that customer support is accessible at any time, serving customers in different time zones and schedules.

» **Cost efficiency:** By handling routine inquiries and tasks, CAI chatbots can make large customer service teams unnecessary. This leads to savings in operational costs over time.

» **Scalability:** CAI chatbots can manage a high volume of queries at one time without compromising the quality of the service. This scalability is helpful for businesses experiencing growth or seasonal spikes in customer inquiries.

>> **Task automation:** By automating repetitive tasks, CAI chatbots free up human agents to focus on higher-priority customer issues. This division of labor increases overall efficiency in customer service operations.

>> **Improved data collection:** CAI chatbots are effective in gathering customer data during interactions. You can use this information to improve future marketing strategies and service offerings to make them more in tune with customer needs.

>> **Reduced wait times:** CAI chatbots significantly cut down the time customers spend waiting for responses. This efficiency is key to maintaining customer satisfaction and reducing the frustration associated with long wait times.

>> **Help for internal staff:** Although chatbots assist customers, they're also valuable to internal staff. Having chatbots deal with internal duties provides the following advantages:

- **Reduction in burnout:** By taking over the handling of routine inquiries, chatbots can help prevent agent burnout. Agents can stay focused on delivering better service instead of jumping back and forth from issue to issue.

- **Improved efficiency:** With chatbots handling the usual questions, agents can use their time to handle tasks that require judgment. This leads to a more efficient workflow and helps to improve their performance.

- **Reduced ticket volume:** By resolving basic issues using automation, the use of chatbots reduces the number of tickets that agents need to handle.

CONVERSATIONAL AI CHATBOTS VERSUS TRADITIONAL AUTOMATED RESPONSE SYSTEMS

Customer service has taken a great leap forward with the introduction of CAI chatbots. Previously, traditional automated response systems couldn't deliver a satisfying customer experience. CAI chatbots offer a more seamless experience because of their ability to understand natural language dialogue instead of looking for specific words.

Traditional response systems were rigid and frustrating to use, especially if the customers asked questions that were outside programmed responses. Here are three key differences that demonstrate the value of CAI chatbots over traditional systems:

- **Learning and adaptability:** CAI chatbots utilize ML and NLP to learn from interactions, adapt to new queries, and improve over time. They understand and respond

(continued)

(continued)

to a range of natural language inputs. Traditional response systems typically worked based on preprogrammed rules and set responses. They couldn't learn from or adapt based on past interactions and were limited to expected questions.

- **Conversational capabilities:** CAI chatbots are designed to simulate human conversations and understand context. Traditional automated response systems were limited to basic, menu-driven interactions (like phone tree systems). They couldn't handle open-ended conversations.

- **Personalization:** CAI chatbots can provide personalized responses based on customer data and past interactions. When using traditional response systems, personalization was limited, and these systems typically couldn't store or process specific information beyond each session.

The advances that CAI chatbots provide are a great improvement over the old way. The difference in customer experience is recognized and welcomed by customers.

Constructing Conversational AI Chatbots

When it comes to implementing chatbots for customer service, several key points should shape your development. Here are several considerations to use to guide your chatbot development:

>> **Finding the right use cases for your chatbot:** It is crucial to identify the specific areas in which chatbots can add value to customer service. It could be handling frequently asked questions (FAQs), providing product recommendations, or providing order tracking. Make sure the use case aligns with customer needs.

>> **Defining the chatbot's purpose:** Before building a chatbot, you need to define its purpose. This involves determining what tasks it will do, the questions it can answer, and the tone it should use.

REMEMBER

Setting a chatbot tone that matches your brand is important. Creating a tone that feels natural to the brand will make your customers feel comfortable using it.

>> **Focusing on customer-centric design:** Always keep the customer at the forefront when you're designing your chatbot. Make sure you know their pain points and preferences.

>> **Making data-driven decisions:** Leverage data and analytics to improve your chatbot's performance. Monitor customer interactions and use feedback to identify areas for improvement.

Measuring the Return on Investment of Conversational AI Chatbots

One question frequently asked by management regarding chatbots is about the return on investment (ROI) from implementing them. Understanding how to measure the ROI of CAI chatbots is key to justifying their use. In the next sections, we look at some important measures you can take and let you know the results you should look for.

REMEMBER

Before calculating ROI, it's important to set a baseline for comparison. This helps evaluate the direct impact of chatbots on business operations and your customers' experiences. You should also continuously monitor relevant metrics to assess the ongoing effects on your business.

Improving customer service efficiency

To do: Compare the efficiency and costs between human agents and CAI chatbots in handling customer inquiries.

Expected outcome: Look for a reduction in average handling time and an increase in queries resolved without human intervention. However, for the full picture, consider the complexity of queries that chatbots can handle and their evolving capabilities.

Reducing operational costs

To do: Analyze the reduction in staffing, training, and overhead expenses. Include costs related to integrating the chatbot into existing systems and the required updating of its knowledge base.

Expected outcome: There may be a reduction in the need for a large customer service team.

REMEMBER

Before making staff adjustments, remember to factor in initial setup costs and ongoing maintenance for your CAI chatbot.

Boosting sales conversion rates

To do: Track the sales conversions initiated by chatbot interactions. Consider the design, interaction quality, and integration of the chatbot into the sales process.

Expected outcome: CAI chatbots can typically upsell or cross-sell, which directly contributes to the bottom line. Be aware that the effectiveness can vary by industry and application.

Enhancing lead generation

To do: Assess the chatbot's effectiveness in generating and qualifying leads. Look at the quality of leads and the efficiency of the qualification process.

Expected outcome: Successful lead generation by chatbots is a value-add to sales teams.

REMEMBER

The integration of chatbots into the overall sales strategy is the key to this success. You need to have your sales team on board, working in conjunction with the technology.

Tracking engagement metrics

To do: Examine interaction patterns, including interaction frequency, duration, and repeat usage. Measure engagement subjectively and consistently.

Expected outcome: You should expect increased engagement and customer satisfaction levels, but methods of measurement should be carefully considered.

TIP

Use customer feedback on chatbot interactions to get more insights about customer sentiment. You can capture this information without having to quiz customers directly, which is a great advantage.

Increasing resolution rate

To do: Calculate the percentage of queries completely resolved by the chatbot. Consider the chatbot's capability to escalate complex issues to human agents.

Expected outcome: You should get an increase in resolution rates and customer satisfaction levels. Just remember to consider the complexity of resolved questions.

Ensuring accuracy

To do: Monitor the accuracy and misunderstanding rates of chatbot responses — factor in the chatbot's learning and adaptation capabilities over time.

TRAVELING ON AMTRAK WITH CONVERSATIONAL AI

Betting on AI to solve business problems turned out to be a great investment for Amtrak, the largest train passenger provider in the United States. According to a 2023 LinkedIn article written by Ethel Emmons (www.linkedin.com/pulse/how-ai-chatbot-transforming-customer-service-amtrak-ethel-emmons), Amtrak made impressive gains using a CAI chatbot for customer service.

- **Problem:** Amtrak experienced a 47.4 percent decrease in passengers in 2020 due to the pandemic (with a slight recovery in 2022), but the numbers were still well below peak ridership.

- **Solution:** Amtrak invested in an AI-backed chatbot, "Next IT," evolving from its initial "Julie" system created in 2012. The AI chatbot offered personalized, 24/7 customer support, improving customer satisfaction and engagement. This new AI chat platform handles more than five million queries annually, ranging from travel bookings to general inquiries, significantly improving customer service efficiency.

- **Results:** The AI system reported a 50 percent annual increase in usage, contributing to a 30 percent increase in revenue compared to other booking methods. Amtrak saved approximately $1 million annually in customer service expenses, with an 800 percent ROI.

This demonstrates how even traditional companies can realize significant gains using AI.

Expected outcome: High accuracy rates will mean better ROI. The CAI chatbot's ability to learn and improve from interactions is a factor in long-term ROI.

Integrating Conversational AI Chatbots into Existing Systems

The key to integrating AI chatbots into existing company systems is balancing automation with human oversight. To successfully integrate chatbots, here are a few steps to take:

>> **Assess conversational workflows.** Take a close look at your current conversational processes between your customers and agents. Identify areas where chatbots can automate certain steps to streamline the workflow.

>> **Ensure data integration.** Determine how the chatbot will integrate with your existing data sources. Plan which data the chatbot will need to access to serve customers, such as account information or order history.

>> **Develop NLP components.** Create intents, entities, and dialogs to enhance the chatbot's natural language capabilities. Use existing support content, such as FAQs and documentation, to speed up the development process.

REMEMBER

Developers teach chatbots to understand language by building three main parts:

- **Intents:** What the customer is trying to do (for example, book a flight).

- **Entities:** The details about what the customer wants. These are variables that the user needs to fill in to help the chatbot understand and get details from the user's message.

- **Dialogs:** Possible conversations around each intent. These are different ways that customers may state their requests.

This allows the chatbot to understand the requests, collect the details, and respond to customer questions.

>> **Evaluate channel options.** Consider which channels are most appropriate for your chatbot, such as website, text message, or social media direct messages (DMs). Integrate the primary channels that your customers commonly use first.

>> **Plan for scalability.** Expect that conversation volume will increase over time. Make sure that your chatbot is designed to handle increased usage, especially on your popular channels.

>> **Prioritize maintainability.** Regular content and feature updates are necessary, so your chatbots must be easy to update and improve.

>> **Address security concerns.** Consider security, compliance, and data privacy requirements. Understand the policies that need to be followed because chatbots have access to customer data.

TIP

Consider enabling human handoff workflows for conversations the AI can't handle well. Combining AI and human support can ensure round-the-clock coverage.

Personalizing Customer Interactions

CAI chatbots are designed to deliver personalized experiences — light years away from the generic, script-based responses that were previously available. These chatbots improve customer support by providing highly personalized assistance.

For example, if you had a specific issue in the past, the CAI chatbot can recall those details, making the resolution process more efficient. Each interaction with the chatbot then becomes a building block that creates a more personalized customer experience.

TIP

CAI chatbots can enhance the customer journey by "remembering" preferences and past interactions. This allows for quicker transactions and support and improves the customer experience. (For more about the customer journey, check out Chapter 1 in this book.)

Improving the shopping experience

When it comes to online shopping, CAI chatbots have transformed the experience by making shopping more personalized. They can

» Personalize shopping advice based on browsing history

» Offer product recommendations customized to individual customer preferences

» Assist with the checkout processes, making it more likely that customers won't abandon their shopping carts before making a purchase

Ensuring ethical personalization

The ability of chatbots to remember past interactions and preferences raises privacy concerns. You must design and operate them in compliance with data protection regulations and with respect for customer privacy.

TIP

For more information about using AI responsibly and ethically, turn to Book 1, Chapter 6.

Using Chatbots with Human and AI Collaboration

Choosing between live agents and chatbots for customer service is a major decision. It's tempting to choose a pure human agent system or a chatbot-only model for all your customer-facing interactions. But it's important to understand that both options have their limitations, so you may want to consider a hybrid model.

TIP

A hybrid model combines the efficiency of chatbots with the personal attention of live agents. It's effective because it adapts to the specific needs of each customer. Some people may want quick, automated responses, while others want human interaction.

Understanding the hybrid model

In a hybrid system, the opening interaction is typically handled by a chatbot. CAI chatbots answer FAQs and perform basic tasks. Chatbots are very efficient, but they're not yet capable of handling very complex questions. This is where the live agent steps in, and the user is informed that they've been sent to a human.

Over time, as live agents interact with the system, they contribute to the chatbot's "learning." This is done using ML, in which the chatbot gradually improves its responses and decision-making capabilities by analyzing new data. The more the chatbot is used, the smarter it becomes, eventually leading to higher performance output.

Collaborating with agents and chatbots

Agents can monitor chatbot conversations in real time. This can prove useful because it's not just about human interaction but also about learning and improving the chatbot. If the chatbot struggles or a customer shows signs of frustration, the agent can take over. This transition should be natural, with the chatbot programmed to understand signs of customer unhappiness and suggest escalating to a live agent.

TIP

Are you wondering whether a hybrid customer service system raises questions about staff availability for a 24/7 operation? You don't have to have round-the-clock staffing by live agents. You have the option of using chatbots exclusively for non-business hours. If your business is global, you can shift to staff members who are working at different hours from different locations. Also, if a chatbot encounters a question it can't handle and no agents are available, it can let the customer know about the next available time for live support and offer to schedule a callback or email response.

Considering Best Practices

Although using advanced chatbots for customer service is relatively new, there are several best practices you can follow:

>> **Simplify design.** Plan for clear interactions in your chatbot. Use simple language instead of jargon to avoid confusing your customers. The key is to provide easy communication.

>> **Incorporate visuals.** Where appropriate within a conversation, integrate visual elements like images, graphics, and buttons. You can use these visuals to explain a point further or facilitate customer input. It's more appealing than heavy blocks of text alone.

REMEMBER

Make sure visual aspects meaningfully supplement the information. Everything you display should improve the clarity of the conversation.

>> **Gather feedback.** Provide customers with an easy mechanism to offer feedback, such as a simple thumbs up/down or number rating. This gives you the ability to constantly track satisfaction. It also helps you identify issues and add popular features.

>> **Create a personality.** Give your chatbot a personality that reflects your brand's voice. Use humor (carefully) to make interactions more fun. Make your chatbot feel like an extension of your brand voice. Make sure to keep the personality consistent across features so the conversations don't feel robotic.

>> **Stay up to date with trends.** Your chatbot content can't remain the same over time. Things like language and priorities are constantly changing. You need to update phrasing or even web slang to stay current. You want to demonstrate that you understand your customers and speak their language.

>> **Identify escalation triggers.** Determine pain points or topics in customer issues early on that provide signals for automated or customer-driven escalation to live agents as needed. You should create these triggers based on such things as contextual cues, perceived lack of confidence in the chatbot responses, or direct requests for agents. The goal is to maximize how often the chatbot can resolve the customer's needs without getting human help by using triggers.

TIP

Escalation triggers are rules that transfer a customer from the CAI chatbot to a human agent when additional help is needed. This happens if the customer asks for an agent or if the chatbot doesn't understand a question. The triggers detect when the AI chatbot reaches its limits in helping someone. All chatbots have some gaps in their abilities. The triggers bridge the human/AI capabilities.

>> **Conduct A/B testing.** Continuously perform A/B testing to perfect the chatbot's responses and flow. This lets you improve the answers by testing strategies and using the most successful ones. Continuous experimentation using A/B testing of conversation components provides the feedback you need to optimize performance.

Reviewing Options for Creating Chatbots

Not every business has the in-house technical expertise or resources necessary to implement CAI chatbots. This may be because you have a lack of specialized knowledge in AI or limited access to the tools. You also have maintenance and updates to keep up with. If you're in this position, you can

- **Use a no-code chatbot platform.** If your team doesn't have coding knowledge, you may want to consider a no-code platform. These platforms typically have drag-and-drop interfaces and prebuilt templates. They're limited in the ways you can customize them, but if you want to try this option, here are tools to consider:

  - **Manychat** (`https://manychat.com`): Manychat, shown in Figure 3-1, has customizable templates to build bots without coding skills.

  - **Chatfuel** (`https://chatfuel.com`): Chatfuel is easy to customize to create bots for messaging apps visually.

  - **Microsoft Copilot Studio** (`www.microsoft.com/en-us/microsoft-copilot/microsoft-copilot-studio`): Copilot Studio enables you to build custom AI agents (see Chapter 4) and custom Copilot plugins (see Chapter 5).

- **Outsource chatbot development.** You can hire agencies or freelancers for chatbot design. This gives you access to expert skills if you don't have technical staff. It also enables you to get a chatbot customized to your exact needs. Of course, this would typically cost more than no-code solutions.

- **Utilize a prebuilt chatbot.** You may want to use customizable chatbot templates made for specific industries or functions. This saves time and gets you started. The chatbot should meet your needs right out of the box, but it may not integrate easily with your other internal systems.

- **Adopt chatbot plugins or integrations.** You may try integrating chatbot plugins into existing website platforms or your customer relationship management (CRM) system. This helps streamline operations and integrate with workflows. You should also be aware that this makes you reliant on third-party program updates.

- **Utilize chatbots with limited functionality.** You can implement chatbots for specific tasks like answering FAQs or handling customer inquiries. This simplifies development and management and is faster to build. However, you may find it difficult to expand its scope in the future.

- **Explore managed chatbot services.** If you want to focus on things like content creation and branding, consider outsourcing the technical management of your chatbots. This would allow you to have your builds and updates managed for you. The caveat is that you're then dependent on a vendor's limitations and timeline. If you want to try this option, here are some tools that manage backend operations:

- **LivePerson** (`www.liveperson.com`): LivePerson, is a CAI platform that combines chatbots and human agents.

- **Chatbotly** (`https://chatbotly.co`): Chatbotly, shown in Figure 3-2, is a managed chatbot creation and hosting platform that handles the building, deploying, and updating of bots.

TIP

Start with a chatbot pilot or trial. Beginning on a small scale allows you to experiment and reduce risks.

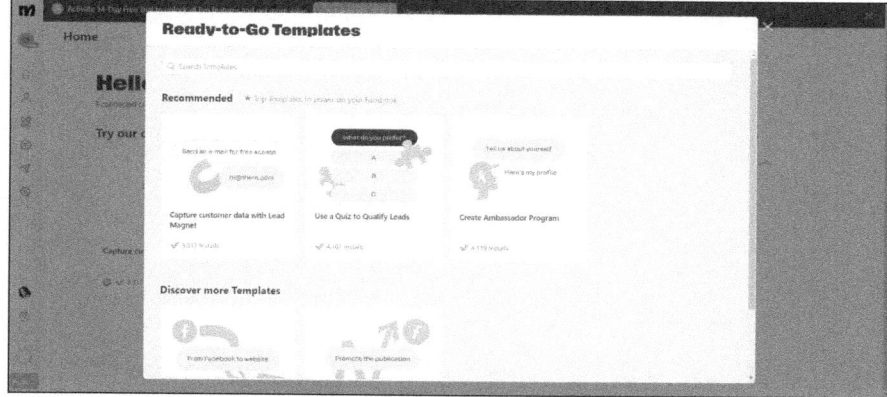

FIGURE 3-1
Manychat has many templates to choose from

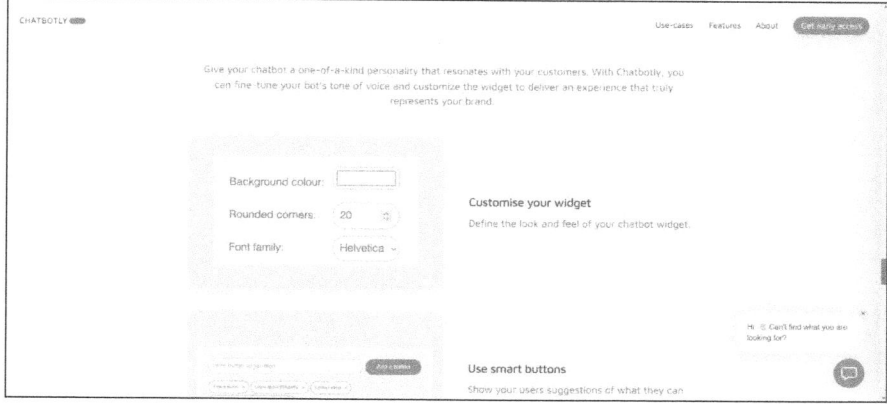

FIGURE 3-2
Chatbotly manages chatbot creation and hosting

Chapter **4**

Making Custom Copilots

Throughout this book, you've seen and explored many ways that generative AI (GenAI) has been integrated into different applications and types of devices. Thus far, I've only touched on a small subset of everything GenAI chatbots are capable of. My favorite feature of the latest GenAI chatbots is the ability to create customized chatbots to handle specific tasks by referencing documents or knowledge sources that you provide.

Microsoft Copilot Studio is a tool that enables you to create your own *copilots* (also known as Copilot agents). As you find out in this chapter, Copilot Studio is a powerful tool that's also easy to use.

Building Your Own Copilot Agent with Copilot Studio

Microsoft Copilot Studio lets you create your own Copilot agents or Copilot plugins and then publish them to be used in Microsoft 365 Copilot.

To try out Copilot Studio, go to `www.microsoft.com/en-us/microsoft-copilot/microsoft-copilot-studio` in your browser. You'll see a screen similar to the one shown in Figure 4-1.

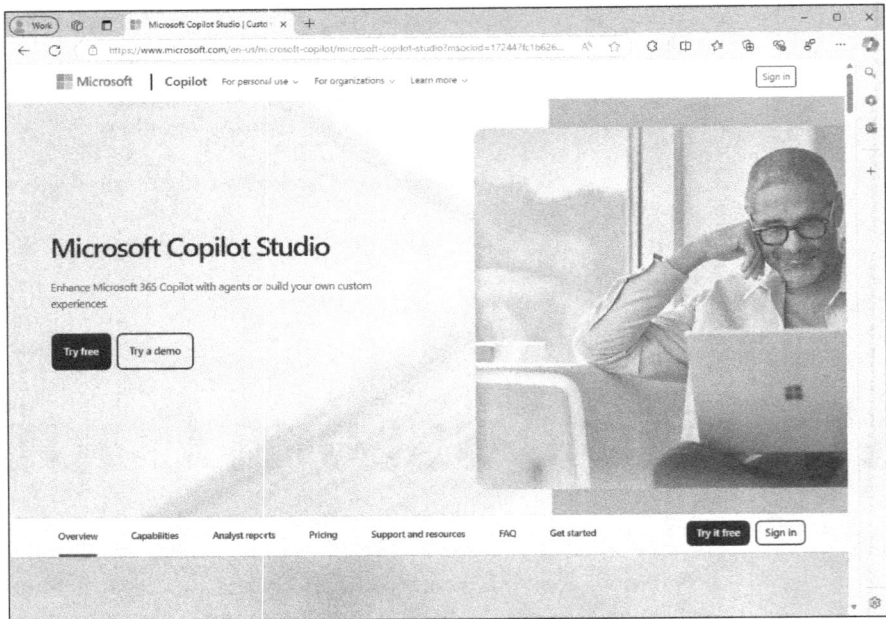

FIGURE 4-1:
The Copilot
Studio
homepage.

Click the Try a Demo button. This will take you to the Copilot Studio demo site at `https://copilotstudio.microsoft.com/tryit`, where you can enter any website address and create a Copilot agent that can answer questions specifically about that website.

When you first open the Copilot Studio demonstration, a popup window will appear, as shown in Figure 4-2, and ask you for the URL of your website.

If you don't have your own website, you can enter any other website you like here. I entered my website address (`www.chrisminnick.com`).

After you enter a website address, your agent will be created, and it will greet you as the *virtual assistant* for the website you entered, as shown in Figure 4-3.

TECHNICAL STUFF

Behind the scenes, Copilot Studio prefaces the conversations in this window with an instruction to use search results from Bing for the website address you entered to answer questions.

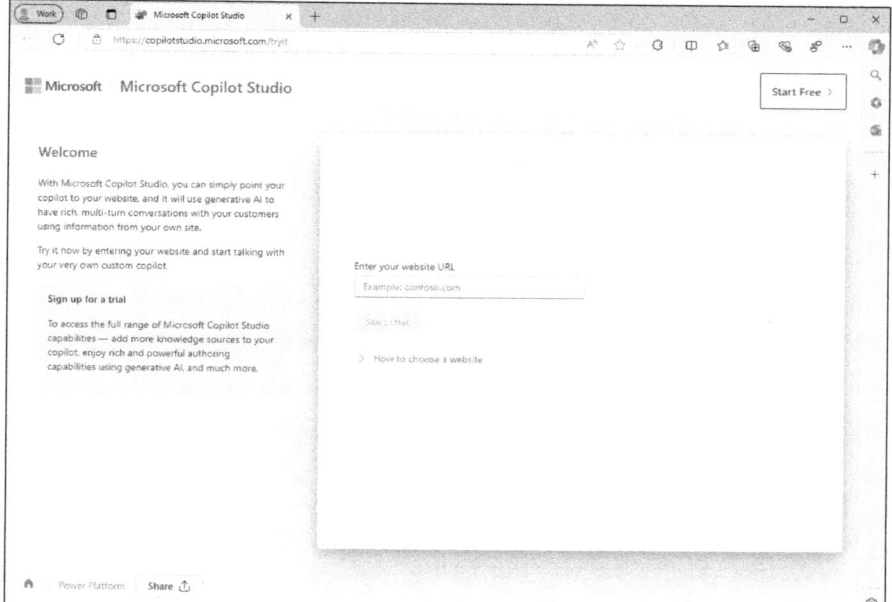

FIGURE 4-2:
Getting started
with the Copilot
Studio demo.

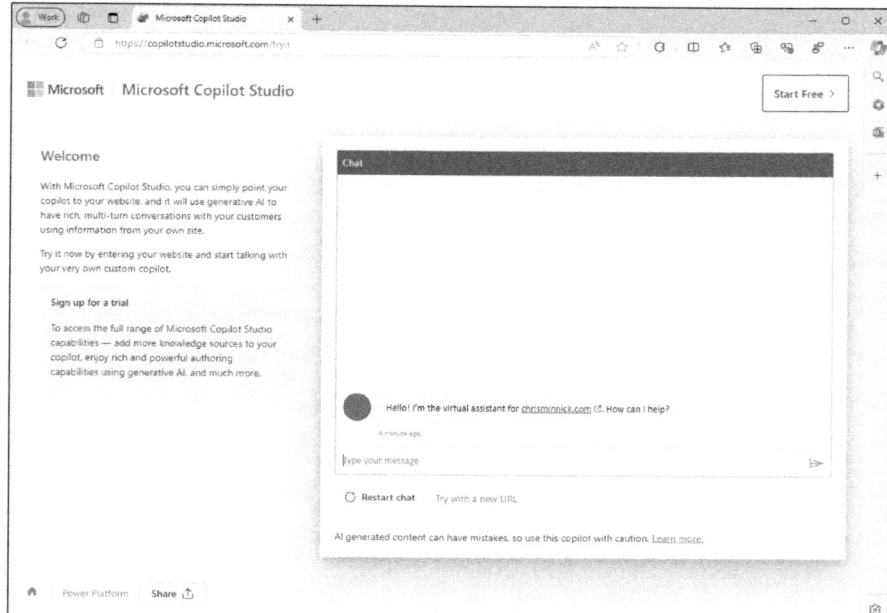

FIGURE 4-3:
Meet your virtual
assistant.

Making Custom
Copilots

In my tests of this demo, my virtual assistant for chrisminnick.com was able to reliably return correct information from my website along with references for the exact pages where it got the information. Figure 4-4 shows a typical response.

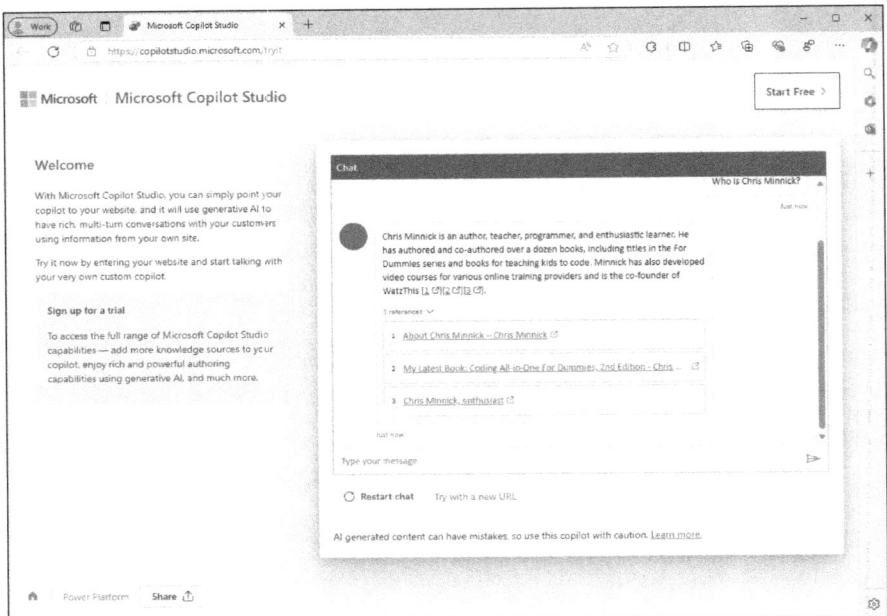

FIGURE 4-4:
A response
from the
chrisminnick.
com virtual
assistant.

You've likely seen this type of AI customer service agent before. Check out Chapter 3 in this book to find out more about how and why businesses create Conversational AI (CAI) chatbots. Now that you know how easy it is to create one of these agents, you can try out some more complex projects. Click the Start Free button in the upper-right corner of the demo screen.

If you're logged into a Microsoft account with access to Copilot Studio, you'll be asked if you want to use Copilot Studio with that account. Otherwise, you'll be asked to log in or create a new account.

After you've logged in to your Microsoft account, you'll be taken to Copilot Studio, where you'll see a Welcome slideshow, as shown in Figure 4-5.

When you close the welcome message, you'll see the Copilot Studio homepage, which will look similar to the screenshot in Figure 4-6.

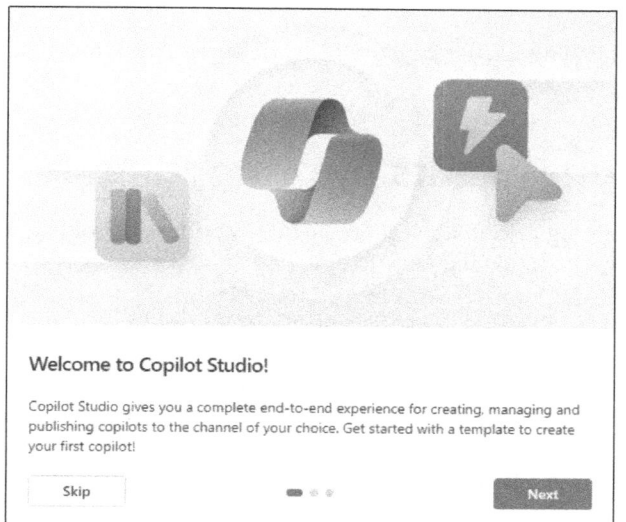

FIGURE 4-5:
The Copilot
Studio welcome
slideshow.

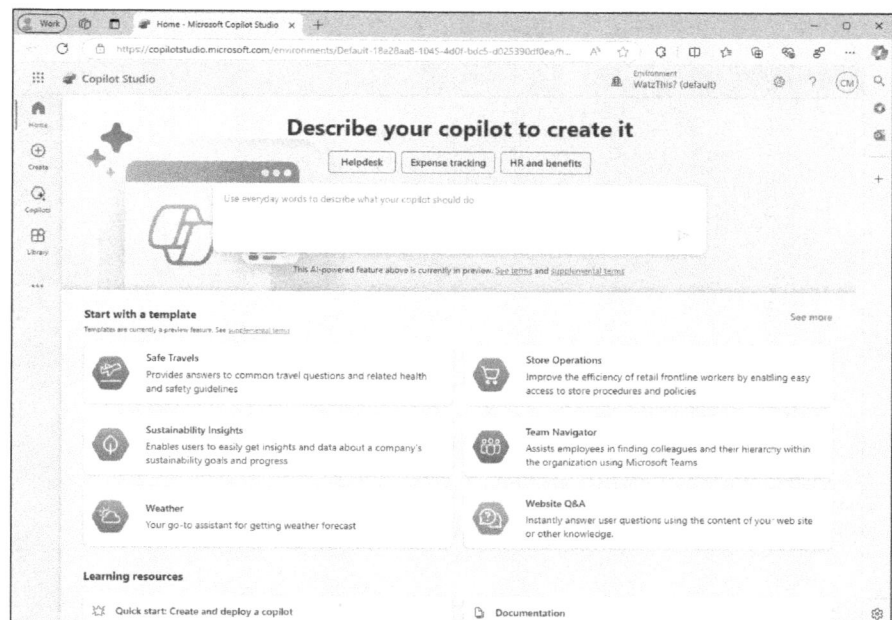

FIGURE 4-6:
The Copilot
Studio
homepage.

You can create Copilot agents in one of two ways:

>> Entering a description of the agent into the text input box in the top third of Copilot Studio

>> Starting with a template

In the following sections, you will learn about these tools and the capabilities of each.

Creating agents by prompting

The prompting area in Copilot Studio doesn't offer a lot of help with how to use it other than the following instruction:

Use everyday words to describe what your copilot should do.

After thinking about it for a moment, I decided to start with something seemingly simple (for an AI agent, anyway). I gave Copilot Studio the following prompt:

A helpful assistant that references `Wikipedia.org` when answering questions.

After submitting the prompt, a conversation window opens, as shown in Figure 4-7, and Copilot asks follow-up questions about the agent you want to create.

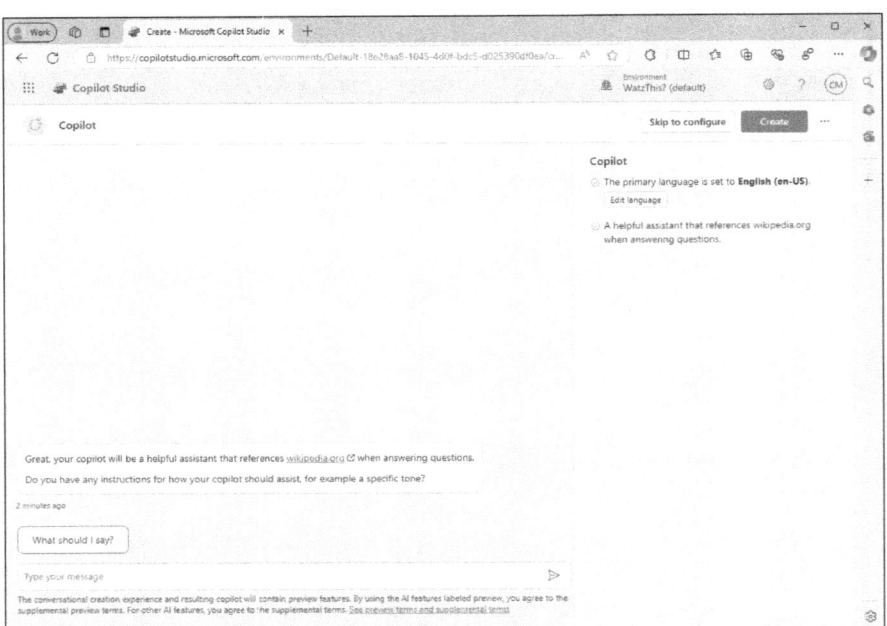

FIGURE 4-7:
Chatting with the agent creator.

The follow-up questions it asks are all useful things to think about when you create an agent using the more manual process later on, including

>> Do you have any instructions for how your copilot should assist, for example a specific tone?

>> Where should the copilot find important information? Provide any publicly accessible websites that your copilot will need.

>> Are there any topics or tasks this copilot shouldn't help with or talk about?

After you've answered the follow-up questions, you'll see the instructions that Copilot generated from your guidance and a button labeled I'm Done, as shown in Figure 4-8.

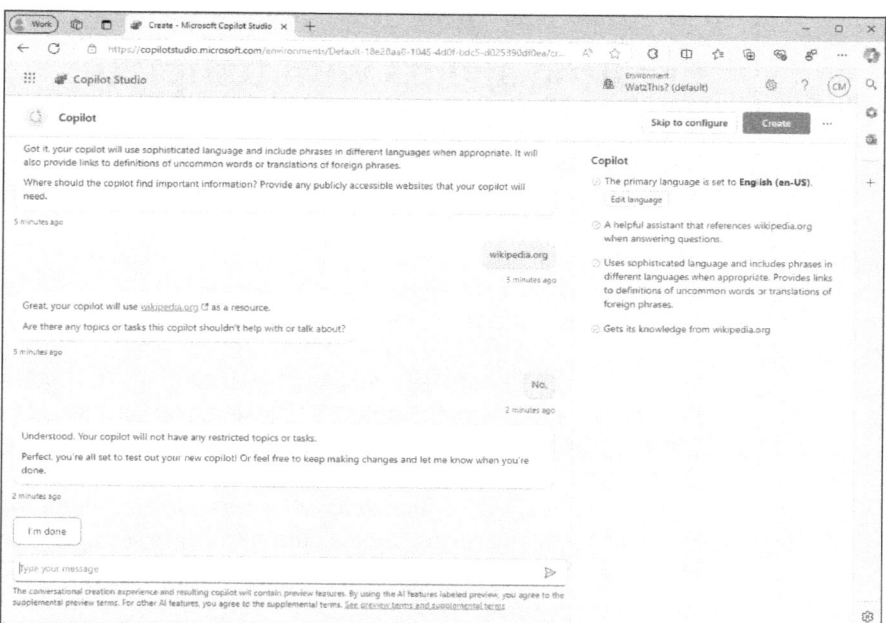

FIGURE 4-8:
Completing the AI-assisted agent creation process.

If you're ready, click the I'm Done button to enter a conversation with the agent you've created. In my first test of the AI agent-creation process, I also had to click the Create button in the upper-right corner of the screen to complete the AI-assisted portion of the agent-creation process.

The next screen you'll see is shown in Figure 4-9.

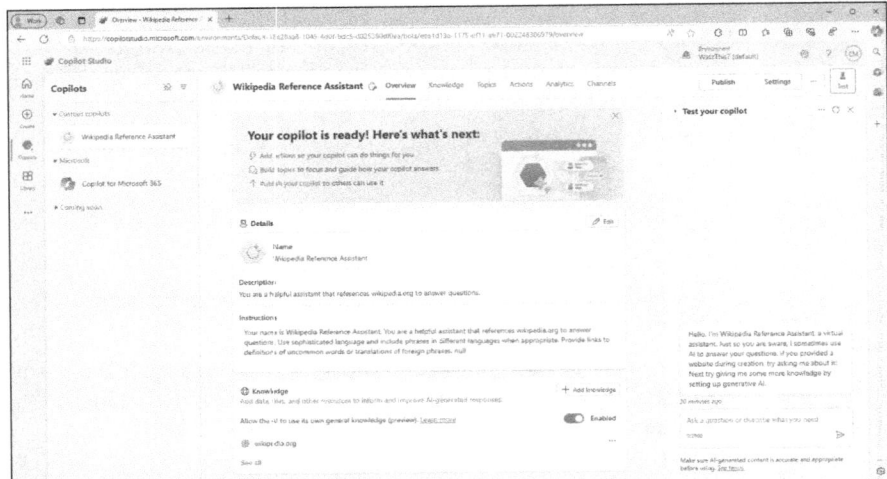

FIGURE 4-9:
The agent editor.

Creating agents with templates

In addition to using the prompting method to create Copilot agents, you can also start with one of the pre-built templates. Ten templates are currently available, and another six are listed as Coming Soon on Copilot Studio's Create page.

To see the available templates, click the Create icon on the left side of Copilot Studio and scroll down to the section labeled Start with a Template. You'll see the options shown in Figure 4-10 (and hopefully additional ones, too!).

You can select any of the templates by clicking on it. A screen appears with a link to the template instructions and the template settings. Figure 4-11 shows the Website Q&A Copilot template instructions.

You can customize the name, description, instructions, or knowledge for the agent on this page; then click the Create button to create the agent. You'll then be taken to the Copilot Agent Editor interface.

From this point on, working with an agent started from a template is the same as working with any other agent. You can modify the agent's various settings, test it out, view the agent's analytics, and publish it when you're ready to share it with your selected channels. The next section explains how to do all this and more with your agent.

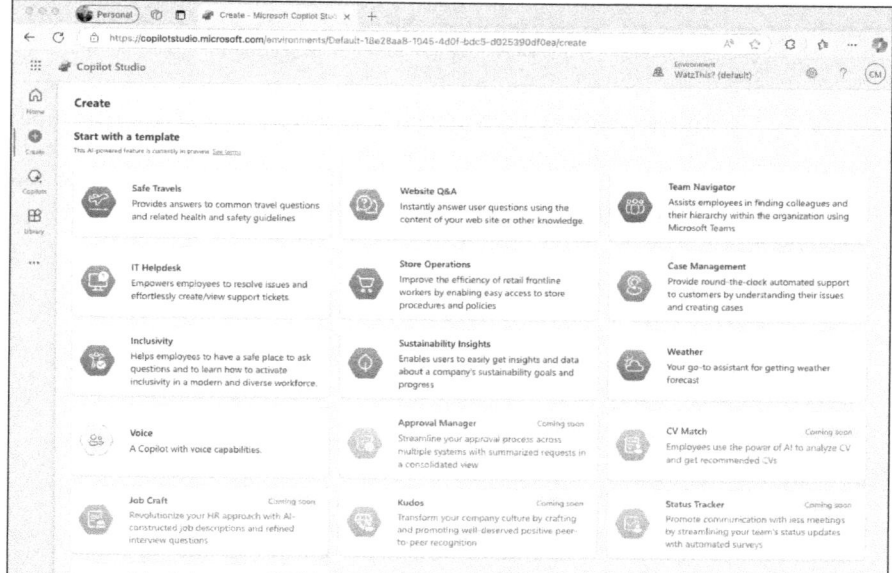

FIGURE 4-10:
The available agent templates

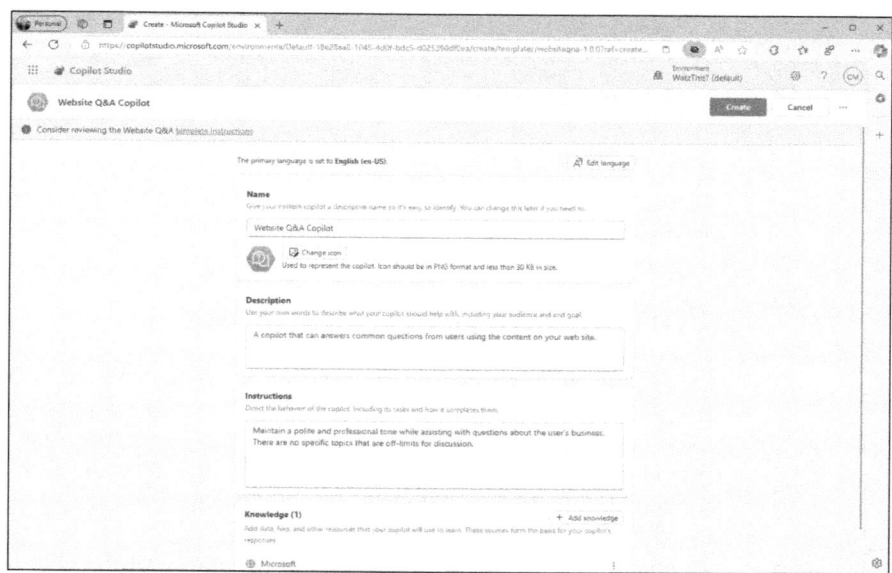

FIGURE 4-11:
The Website Q&A template settings.

Testing and Editing Your Agent

The first thing you should do is to try out your new agent. Type a request into the Test Your Copilot sidebar and see what you think of the response. By default, your agent will likely be pretty dry and boring — just the facts. Figure 4-12 shows my first conversation with my Wikipedia agent.

If this factual and dry approach is what you want, that's excellent. But, for my agent, I want to make it a bit more fun. To accomplish this, I need to adjust some settings.

Configuring generative AI

By default, your agent is configured to be strict about what particular phrases trigger its actions. It will use generative AI as little as possible and will instead stick to using quotes and precise interpretations from the knowledge sources you provide. If you enable generative AI, your agent will be able to respond to requests without requiring an exact phrase and will be more creative.

To enable generative AI, click the Settings button in the upper-right corner and then click the Generative AI option on the left. You'll see a screen where you can read about the difference between the Classic mode and the Generative mode. You can select how strict the content moderation should be for your agent. In the case of this agent, I want it to be as creative as possible, so I enabled Generative mode and set content moderation to low strictness.

After you've made your selections and clicked the Save button, you can close the Settings. You'll be returned to the Copilot Agent Editor.

Using the Copilot Agent Editor

The Copilot Agent Editor is where you can adjust everything that makes your agent act the way it does. At the top of the interface is a row of tabs that allow you to customize different aspects of your AI agent. The first tab, Overview, displays a condensed version of the information from the other five tabs. These additional tabs are

>> Knowledge

>> Topics

>> Actions

>> Analytics

>> Channels

The Knowledge tab

On this screen, shown in Figure 4-13, you can view a list of the knowledge sources your agent has access to. You can also add knowledge sources.

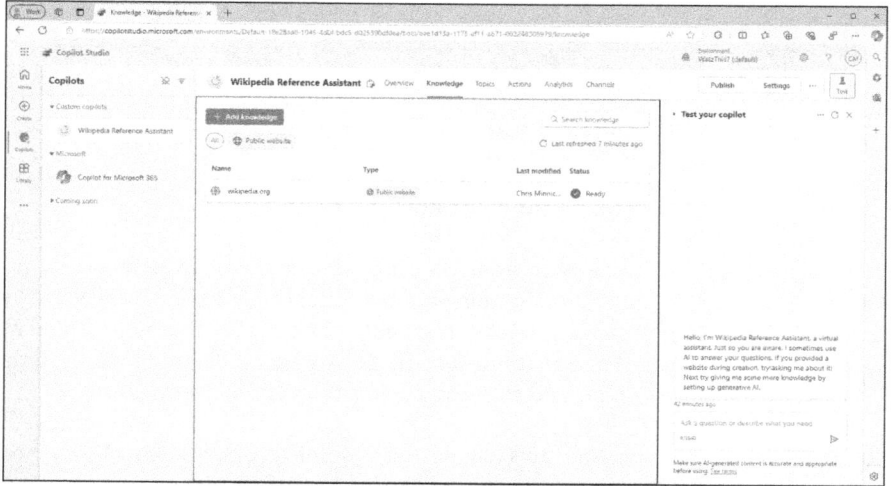

FIGURE 4-13:
Viewing and editing your agent's knowledge.

Thus far, you've only added public websites as knowledge sources. By clicking the Add Knowledge button, you can give your agent access to data in specific files, data in SharePoint and OneDrive, data in enterprise databases, and much more. There's also a Custom Connector option where you write your own connector for a data source that isn't already covered by one of the other connectors.

Some of the connectors that are available by clicking the Add Knowledge button are shown in Figure 4-14.

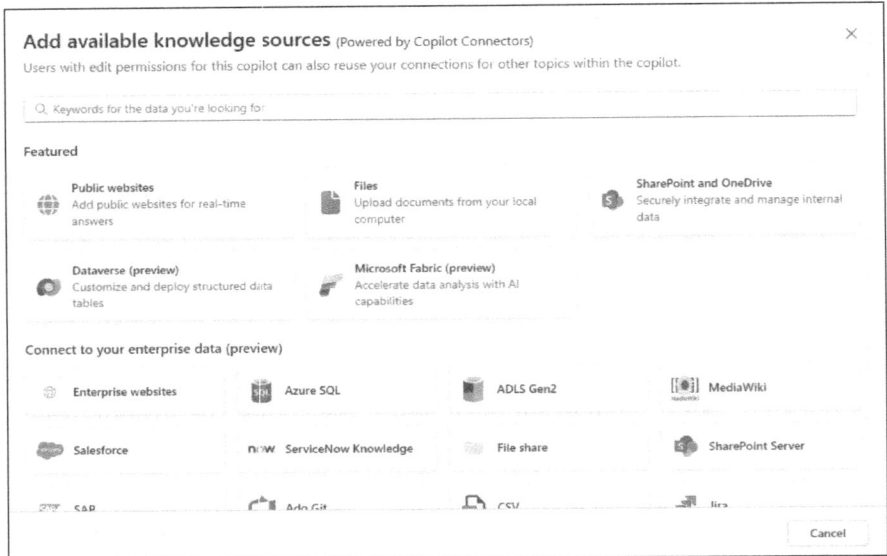

The Topics tab

The Topics tab, shown in Figure 4-15, is where you can configure the custom and system topics for your agent.

Topics are ways that the Copilot agent will respond when it detects a specific trigger. Topics are split into two categories: custom topics and system topics. Custom topics are topics that you've created (or that your AI agent creator assistant created) and that are specific to this agent. System topics are things that are built into Copilot and that you can customize for your agent.

If you switch to viewing the system topics, you can hover over each one to see what it does. For example, the On Error system topic triggers when the agent detects an error. If you want your agent to reply in some particular way when an error occurs, you can customize its response by clicking on the On Error system topic.

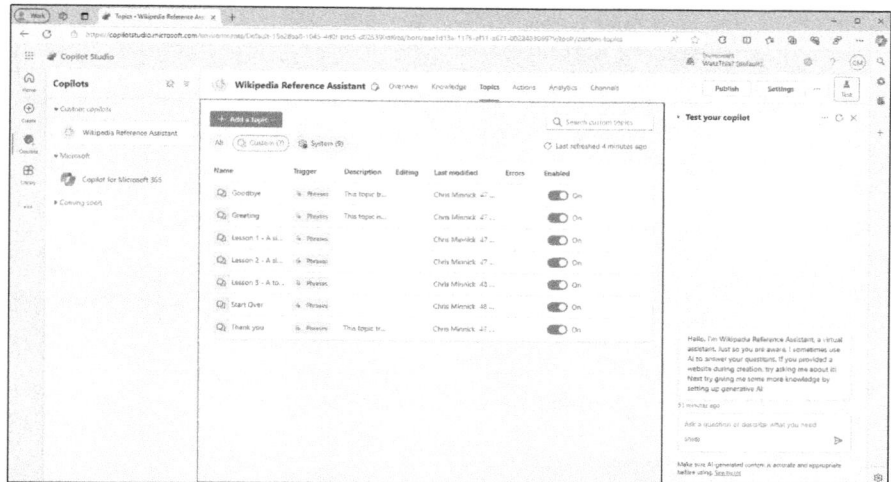

FIGURE 4-15:
The Topics tab.

When you edit a topic, you'll see a flow chart view of what the topic does, as shown in Figure 4-16.

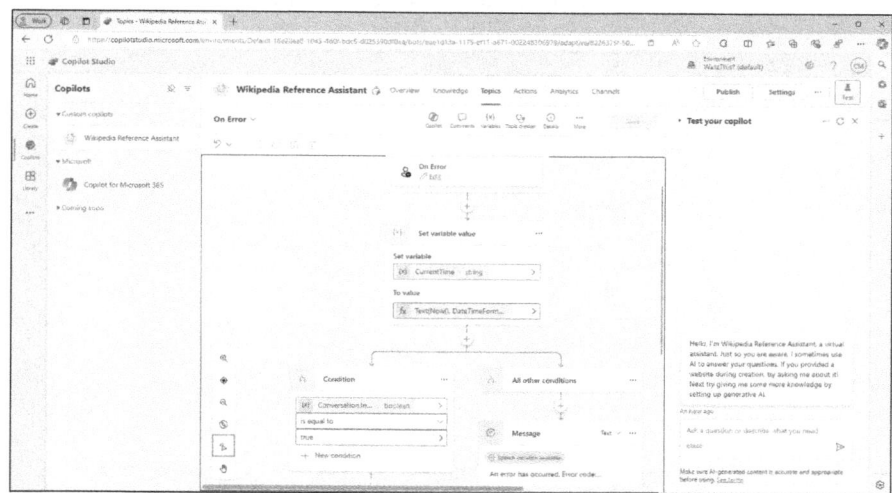

FIGURE 4-16:
Editing a topic.

Every topic starts with a trigger. The *trigger* is the phrase or event that causes the topic to be activated. After the trigger, topics may involve multiple conditions, messages, actions, and more.

CREATE A TOPIC

The best way to understand what's possible with topics is to create a new one. As with creating entire agents, you can create new topics through prompting. Follow these steps:

1. **Click the Add a Topic button in the Topics tab.**

   A submenu will appear, as shown in Figure 4-17, where you can choose whether to create the topic from scratch or by entering a description.

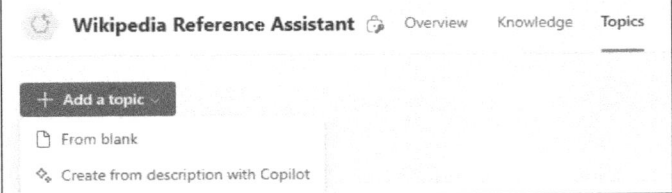

FIGURE 4-17: Choosing how to add the topic.

2. **Select Create from Description with Copilot.**

   The window shown in Figure 4-18 will open.

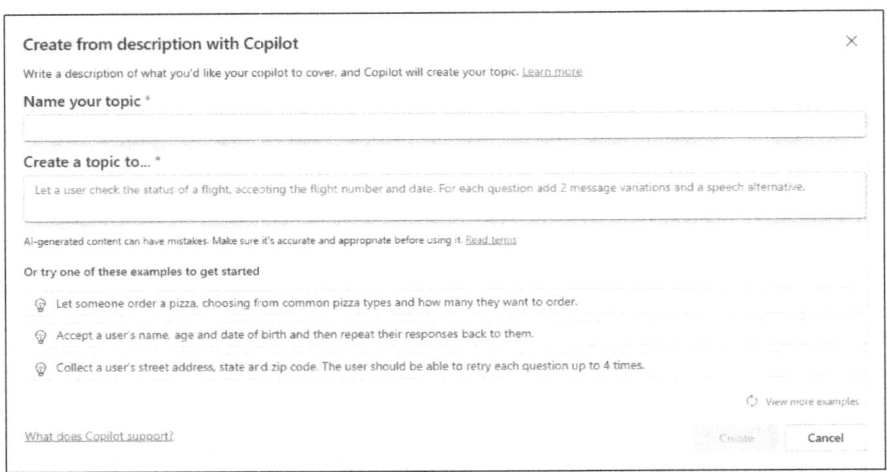

FIGURE 4-18: Describing your topic.

3. **View the examples on this page and select one by clicking on it or enter your own custom description.**

4. **Give your new action a name and click the Create button.**

Your new action will be created, and you'll see the topic editor, where you can see what Copilot added and make changes or additions to it. Figure 4-19 shows the user data collection action that I created.

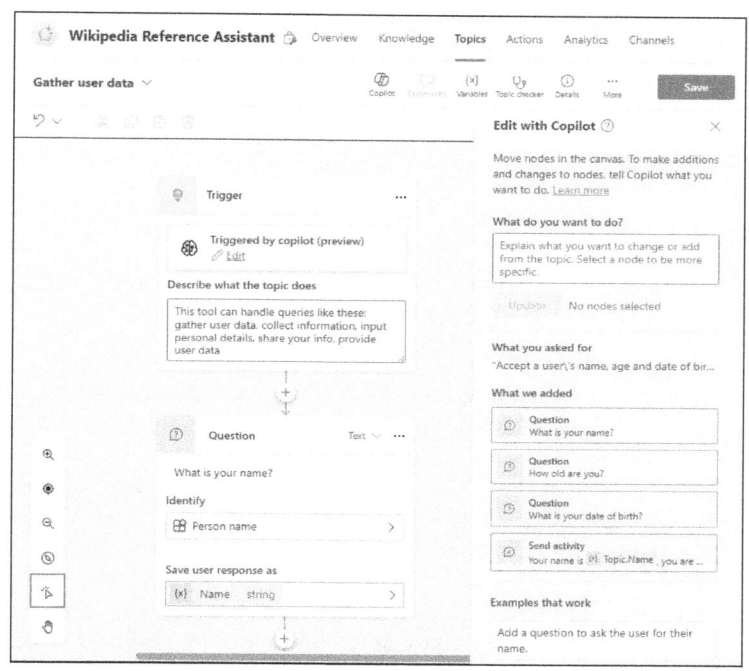

FIGURE 4-19:
Editing a new
action.

When you're happy with your new action, click the Save button and try it out!

TEST A TOPIC

To test your new topic, first look at the trigger specified by the new topic you just created. In the case of my topic, it uses Copilot to detect whether the user has asked to share their personal details.

If your new topic is working, you should be able to type a prompt into the Test Your Copilot pane in Copilot Studio, and Copilot will activate the topic.

Before you try that, however, you should activate the conversation map. The *conversation map* is a tool that shows you what's happening in your test conversation and why.

To activate the conversation map, click the map icon at the top of the test chat window, as shown in Figure 4-20.

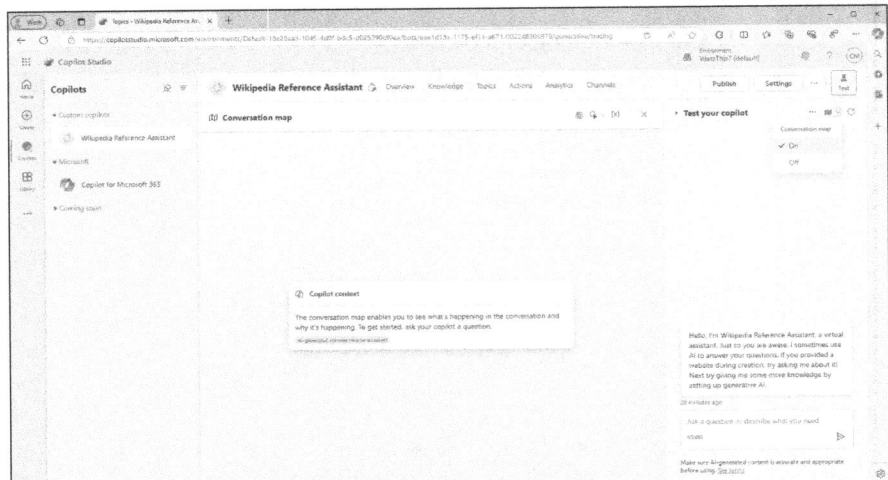

FIGURE 4-20:
Opening the
conversation map.

When you enable the conversation map, a new window will open in the center area of Copilot Studio, and wait for something to happen in the conversation.

Find the icon at the top of the Conversation map called Track Between Topics and enable it. This icon looks like a speech bubble. Now, it's time to test your agent. Enter a question or other prompt into the test chat window.

Try experimenting with the conversation map's other options and see whether you can trigger other topics. Some prompts you might try include

>> Thank you!

>> Start a new conversation.

>> Hello!

>> I want to talk to a person.

Figure 4-21 shows what happens when I prompt my agent with a request to talk to a real person.

The Actions tab

The Actions tab of the Copilot editor is where you can view, create, and edit specific tasks that you want your Copilot agent to do. Actions can be invoked from within topics, or they can be selected and run by Copilot automatically if you have Generative mode turned on for the agent.

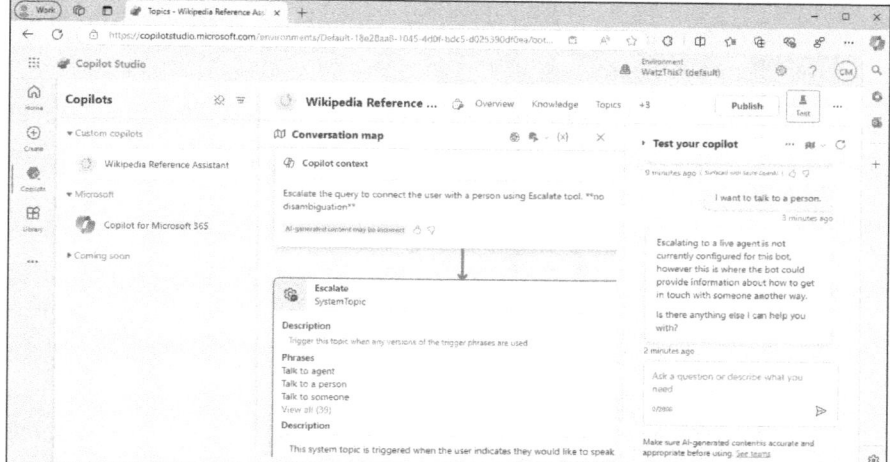

FIGURE 4-21:
Asking to talk
with a person.

REMEMBER

Actions are the things your copilot can do. Topics may consist of triggers, messages, variables, conditions, and actions that are put together into a flow.

Follow these steps to add a weather action to your Copilot agent:

1. **Click the Add an Action button in the Actions tab.**

The window shown in Figure 4-22 will appear. This window allows you to search for existing actions that you have access to or to create or import a new action.

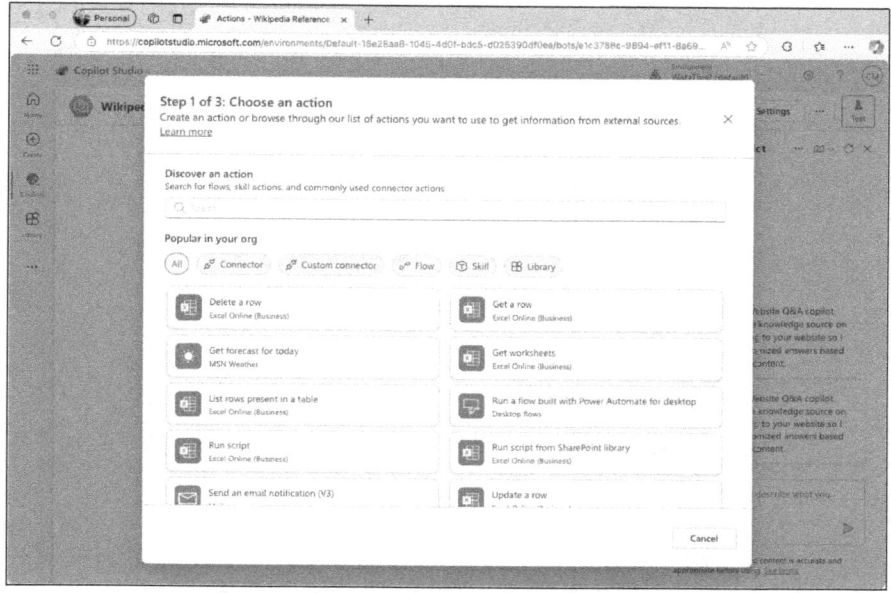

FIGURE 4-22:
Choose or create
an action.

2. **Find the action named Get Forecast for Today and click on it to start configuring it.**

3. **Choose the User Authentication option in the Connector settings.**

4. **Modify the Action Name, Display Name, or Description if you like. See Figure 4-23.**

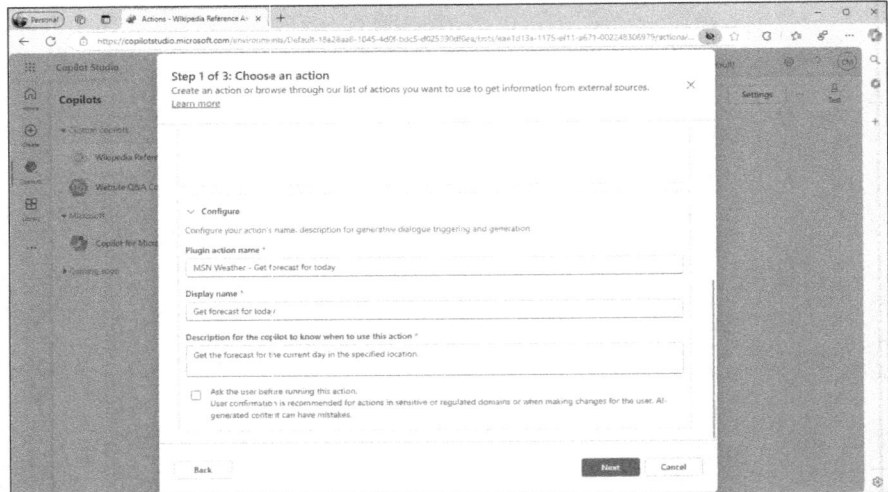

5. **Click Next to view the inputs and outputs for the action, as shown in Figure 4-24.**

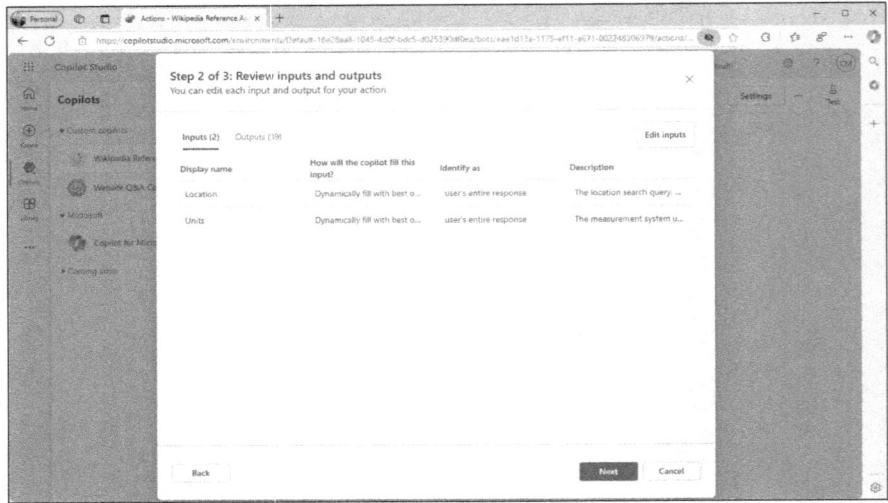

6. **Click Next to view the Review and Finish screen.**

You shouldn't need to change anything here.

7. **Click Finish.**

After a moment, your action will be saved and will appear on the Actions page.

Try out your action by entering something like "What's the weather forecast for Portland, OR?" When I tried this, the action was triggered by Copilot and asked me to specify whether I wanted to use the Imperial or Metric measurement system. After I answered that, my copilot notified me that it needed additional permission to run the action, as shown in Figure 4-25.

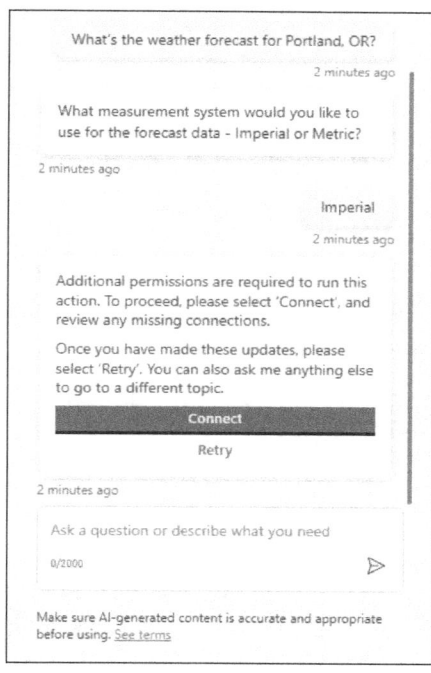

FIGURE 4-25: Copilot needs more permission.

I clicked the Connect button, and a new tab opened in my browser where I could click through a couple of steps to connect the MSN Weather action.

After connecting the action, I went back to the window with my test conversation and retried my prompt.

My copilot didn't respond, but when I switched to the conversation map, I saw that the results did come back from the MSN action, as you can see in Figure 4-26.

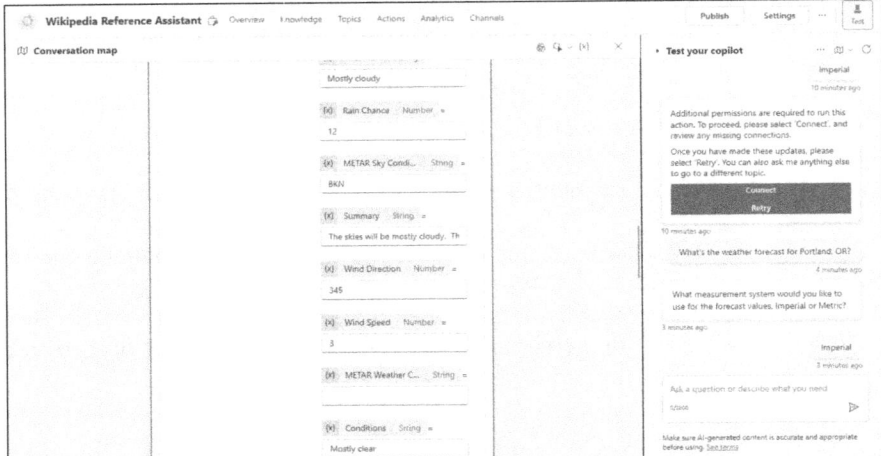

FIGURE 4-26:
Viewing the result
of an action.

To cause Copilot to report the weather back to you, click the action to open it for editing; then click the Outputs tab and check the box shown in Figure 4-27, which is labeled Respond to the User After Running this Action.

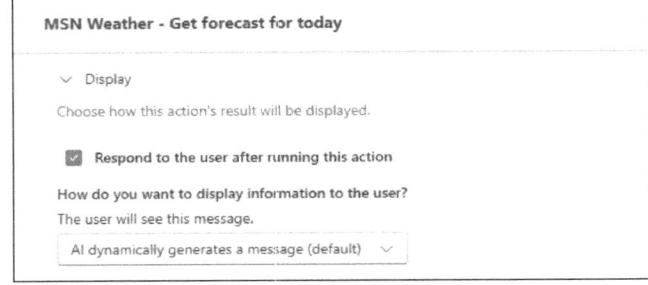

FIGURE 4-27:
Enabling your
copilot to
respond to
the user.

Try your prompt again now, and it should respond with an AI-generated forecast using the data from the MSN Weather connector, as shown in Figure 4-28.

The Analytics tab

The next tab in the Copilot Agent Editor is the Analytics tab. When you go to this tab, you see various graphs displaying information about how your agent is being used, as shown in Figure 4-29.

The available data from this screen is particularly important if you've created a customer service agent. Some of the data that's available includes

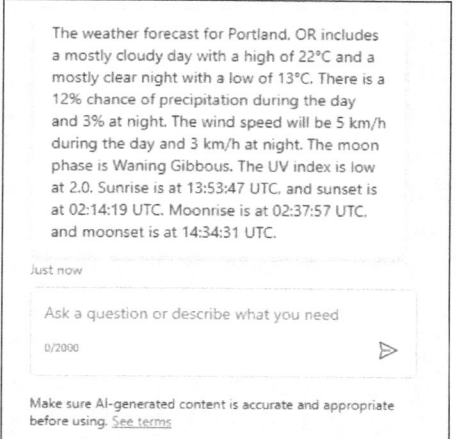

The weather forecast for Portland, OR includes a mostly cloudy day with a high of 22°C and a mostly clear night with a low of 13°C. There is a 12% chance of precipitation during the day and 3% at night. The wind speed will be 5 km/h during the day and 3 km/h at night. The moon phase is Waning Gibbous. The UV index is low at 2.0. Sunrise is at 13:53:47 UTC, and sunset is at 02:14:19 UTC. Moonrise is at 02:37:57 UTC, and moonset is at 14:34:31 UTC.

Just now

Ask a question or describe what you need

0/2000

Make sure AI-generated content is accurate and appropriate before using. See terms

FIGURE 4-28:
Getting the weather forecast.

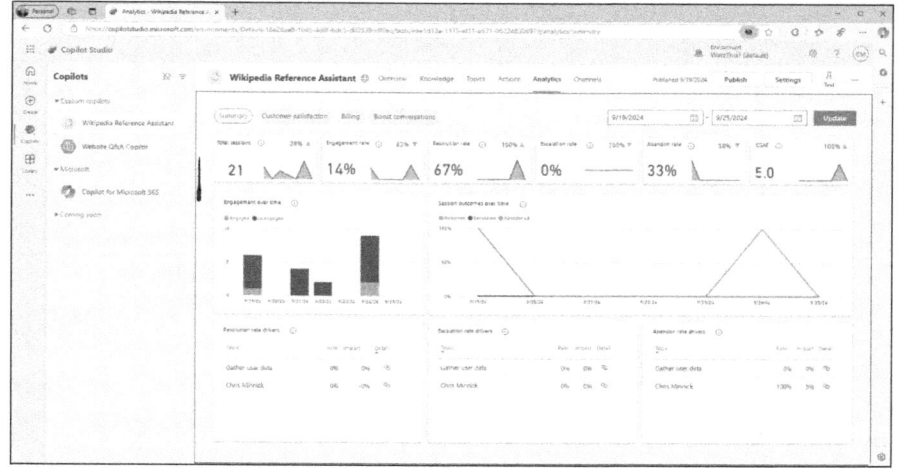

FIGURE 4-29:
The agent's analytics interface.

>> **Total sessions.** This is the number of conversations that your agent has engaged in during the period of the report.

>> **Engagement rate.** This is the percentage of conversations in which the user entered a prompt that triggered a topic to run.

>> **Resolution rate.** This is the number of conversations in which the user reaches the "end of conversation" topic. Resolution is typically when the user is asked to respond to a survey.

>> **Abandon rate.** This is the percentage of time that an engaged user (someone who enters a prompt that triggers a topic) leaves the conversation without getting to a resolution.

A well-designed and effective agent will have a high resolution rate and a low abandon rate. By monitoring your agent's stats over time, you can find out whether it's doing its job and make adjustments as necessary.

The Channels tab

The last tab is the Channels tab, which is shown in Figure 4-30.

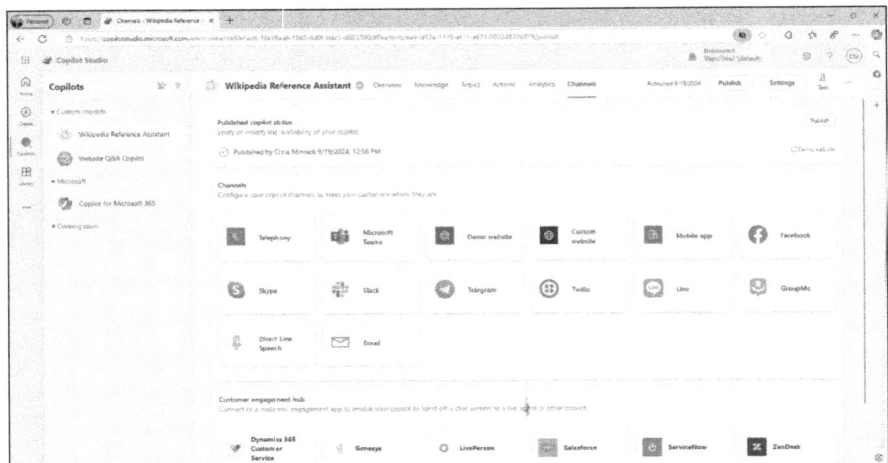

FIGURE 4-30:
The Channels tab.

Channels are places where your Copilot agent will be available once it's published. The channels that are currently available are

>> **Telephony.** Allows your agent to handle phone calls

>> **Microsoft Teams.** Makes your agent available to users in your organization from within Teams

>> **Custom Website.** Embeds your agent in a website

>> **Custom Mobile App.** Adds your agent to a mobile app

>> **Facebook.** Allows users to interact with your agent through Facebook messenger

>> **Skype.** Makes your agent available to users via Skype

>> **Slack.** Allows people to interact with your agent through Slack

>> **Telegram.** Connects your agent to the Telegram messaging app

>> **Twilio.** Connects your agent to Twilio, giving it the ability to communicate via text messages

- **>> Line.** Connects an agent to the Line app, which is a free voice and video calling app

- **>> GroupMe.** Connects with Microsoft's GroupMe group messaging app

- **>> Direct Line Speech.** Connects with text-to-speech and speech-to-text capabilities

- **>> Email.** Allows your agent to interact with users via email

When you click on any of the available channels, a popup window will open that contains instructions and any links necessary to enable that channel. For example, Figure 4-31 shows the code that can be used to embed my Wikipedia assistant agent into a website.

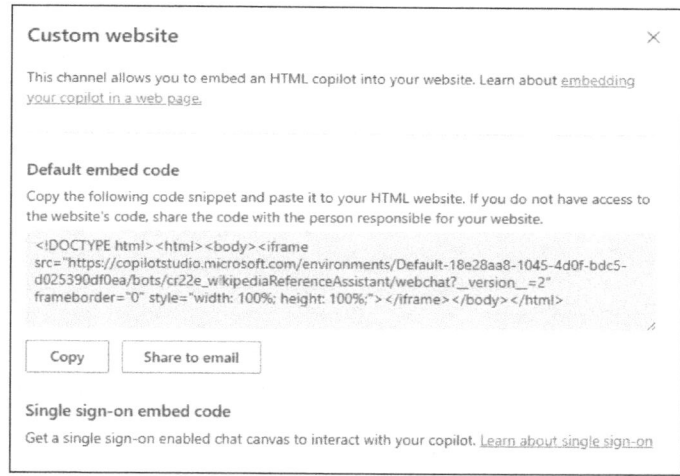

FIGURE 4-31: How to embed the agent in a website.

Before you can use your new agent in your selected channels, you have to publish it. You learn how to publish an agent in the next section.

Publishing Your Agent

When you've finished your agent and are ready to deploy it and test it in the real world, you can publish it. To publish your agent, click the Publish button in the upper-right corner. A popup will display asking you to confirm that you want to make your agent available in the connected channels. When you answer Yes, your agent will be published!

Figure 4-32 shows my Wikipedia Reference Bot embedded in a page on my website at www.chrisminnick.com/wikibot.

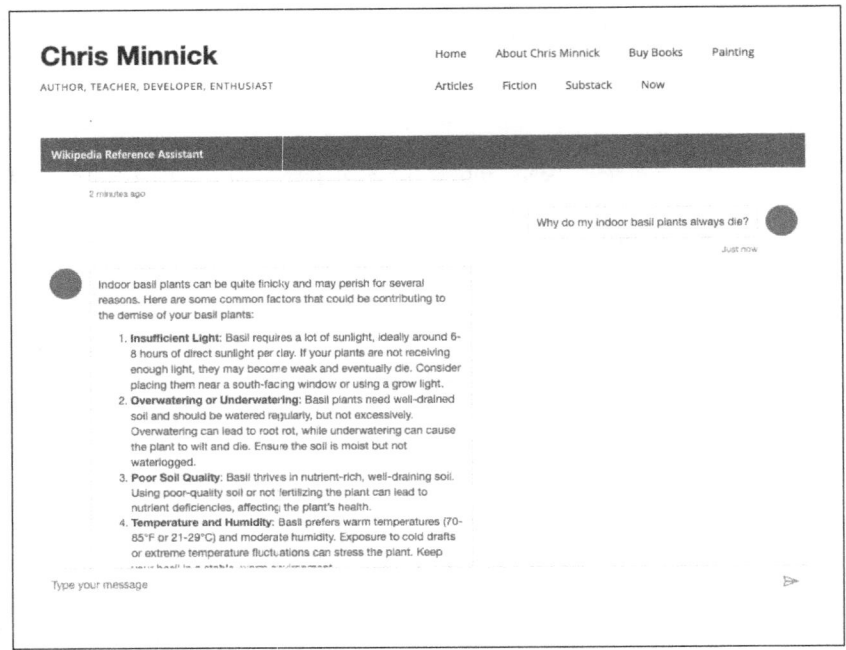

Exploring Copilot's more advanced features, such as Copilot Studio and custom Copilots, opens up infinite possibilities for how people and companies can use generative AI. With Copilot Studio, you can now have your own AI assistant, with access to your own selected data sources.

In the next chapter, you learn how to use — and even create — Copilot plugins.

Chapter **5**

Expanding Copilot's Capabilities with Plugins

I n Chapter 4, you learn about creating custom copilots, called *agents*, using Copilot Studio. Custom agents are the way to go when you're building a product that uses Copilot and you want to fully customize it, or when you want anyone to be able to use your agent, regardless of whether they have a Microsoft Copilot 365 license.

The other option for giving Copilot new capabilities is to use (or even create!) plugins. In this chapter, you learn about what plugins are, find out how to create them, and see many different examples of them.

Using Plugins Wisely

Plugins are programs that can be added to a Copilot chat window to give Copilot new capabilities. The main difference between plugins and custom agents is that plugins work within (or "on top of") Microsoft 365 Copilot. Agents, on the other hand, are independent from Microsoft 365 Copilot.

Copilot can use plugins when it deems it necessary or beneficial. Just as a carpenter who has a variety of specialized tools and knows how to use them can do more types of work, Copilot with plugins can handle different types of problems than just Copilot by itself.

In fact, you've already seen some examples of plugins in Copilot. For example, the Web Content plugin gives Copilot the ability to access results from Microsoft Bing, and the Kayak plugin gives Copilot the ability to find flight information and link to the Kayak results.

Understanding orchestration

On a more technical level, a big difference between Copilot plugins and custom agents is that plugins use Copilot's orchestration layer.

The *orchestration layer* is the AI decision-maker that intercepts every prompt you submit to Copilot and decides on the best plugin to handle it. For example, you might submit a request such as the following to Copilot:

Use the web to find more information about how to build Copilot plugins.

Copilot doesn't have a specific rule built into it that looks for every phrase a person might submit that is a request to search the web. Instead, Copilot's orchestration layer uses its understanding of the meaning of the prompt to decide that using the Web Content plugin is the best way to handle the request.

When you create a custom agent, as you can learn about in Chapter 4 of this book, you must specify a trigger that will cause one of the custom or system actions to run.

Just as my dog looks at me with a confused face when I ask him if he'd like to go for a stroll, rather than if he wants to go for a walk, a Copilot agent that's only triggered by the phrase "check my balance" won't react to the phrase "How much money do I have?".

Although it's not enabled by default, you can enable Copilot's AI orchestration within custom agents by enabling Generative AI for an agent. You can learn more about enabling Generative AI in a custom agent in Chapter 4.

Knowing the limitations of LLMs

Large language models (LLMs), such as the one Copilot uses, are fantastic at understanding language and responding. This is what they're made to do. What they're less good at, however, is answering questions that require up-to-date information.

The reason for this is that every LLM has a *knowledge cutoff date*. A knowledge cutoff date is the most recent creation date of the information that was used to train that LLM. Because it takes a long time (and a lot of effort and energy) to train an LLM, the cutoff date may be months or even years behind the current date.

By itself, Copilot doesn't know anything about anything that's happened since its knowledge cutoff date. You can determine the current knowledge cutoff date simply by asking Copilot.

At the time of this writing, when I asked Copilot for its knowledge cutoff date, it told me October 2023, as shown in Figure 5-1.

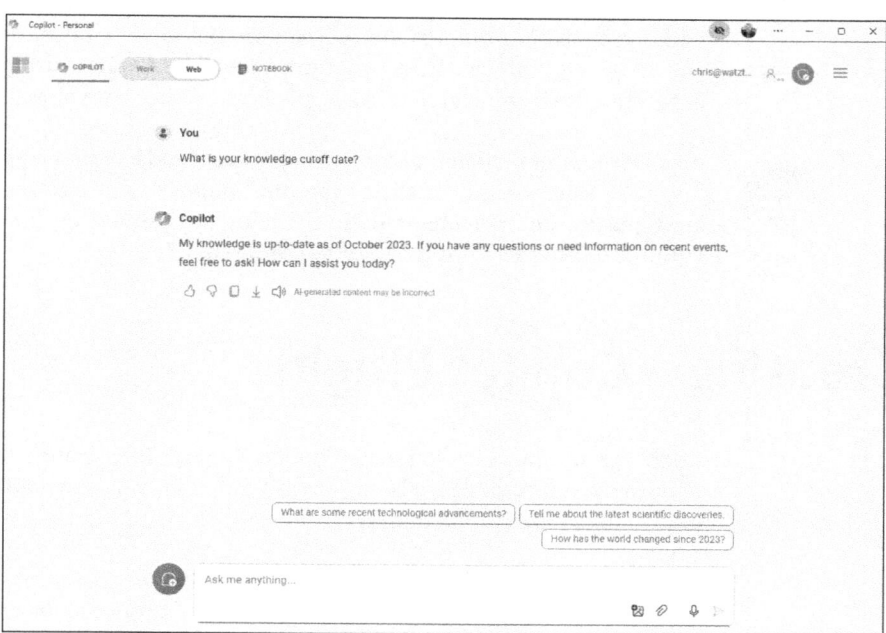

FIGURE 5-1:
Asking Copilot for its cutoff date.

Enhancing functionality with plugins

If you don't enable the Search plugin (in the personal version of Copilot) or the Web Content plugin (in the work/education version), Copilot won't be able to answer questions about events that have happened after its knowledge cutoff date. With the Web Content or Search plugin enabled, however, Copilot can perform Bing searches to find up-to-date information.

When I asked Copilot 365 (without the Web Content plugin) to tell me who won the Super Bowl in 2024, it couldn't tell me. When I asked who won the Super Bowl in 2022, it was able to respond (and it was correct).

With the Web Content plugin enabled, Copilot was able to give me full and accurate answers, along with details, for both years.

The Search plugin is the most flexible and important of the Copilot plugins. Other plugins serve more specific purposes, as you learn in the section of this chapter called "Seeing Examples of Plugins."

Two types of plugins

You find two basic types of plugins: Teams Message Extensions and API plugins. Teams Message Extensions are plugins for Microsoft Teams that are only available within Teams. API plugins are the plugins that you can use in Microsoft Copilot 365 Chat. API plugins access programs outside of Copilot (using their application programming interface) to retrieve and even change data in the external program.

An *application programming interface* (API) is a standardized way that programmers make the functionality of their program available to other programs. These APIs are typically well documented, and Copilot can use API documentation to figure out how to interact with the external program.

Creating a Copilot Plugin

There are several ways to create Copilot plugins. These range from methods that require some knowledge of how to write computer code to a method you've already seen — by using Copilot Studio.

In Chapter 4, you learn how to create Copilot agents. Agents are standalone copilots that have triggers, connectors, topics, and actions. Agents may or may not use Generative AI to decide how to respond to prompts.

In this section, you learn how to create a custom action that you can enable and use in any Microsoft 365 Copilot Chat.

You can read more about triggers, connectors, topics, and actions in Chapter 4.

You'll create your first plugin by creating what Microsoft calls a Custom Connector action. You must have a work or school Copilot account and be granted sufficient permission by the account administrators to be able to create plugins.

Follow these steps:

1. **Go to Copilot Studio in your browser** (https://copilotstudio.microsoft.com) **and log in.**

2. **Click the Library icon on the left toolbar.**

3. **Click Add an Item on the Library screen.**

4. **Click New Action in the Extend Copilot for Microsoft 365 window.**

   The popup window shown in Figure 5-2 will appear.

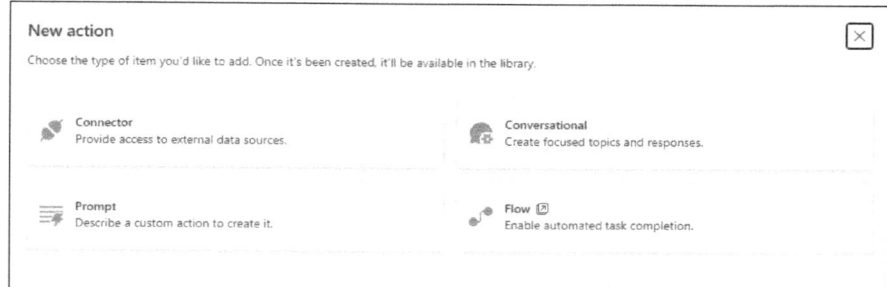

FIGURE 5-2:
Select your
action type.

5. **Click the Connector button in the popup window.**

   You'll see a long list of connectors. Take your time browsing through this list to see how many of the connectors are for websites and services you use. Many of the connectors require authentication and a lot of set up, but this exercise chooses one that you'll be able to use very quickly.

6. **Search for the Library of Congress connector and click on it.**

   The next screen, shown in Figure 5-3, shows a description of the custom connector and asks you to select a solution. A solution is a group of actions. For example, Copilot in Excel is a solution that includes actions for things like creating rows, deleting rows, summarizing data, and so forth.

7. **For the Action Name, enter** Search the LOC for Books. **You can leave the description as it is for now.**

   The Action Name and Description are what Copilot uses to decide whether to trigger the plugin, so you should pay extra attention to these. You may need to tweak them later after you've tested your plugin.

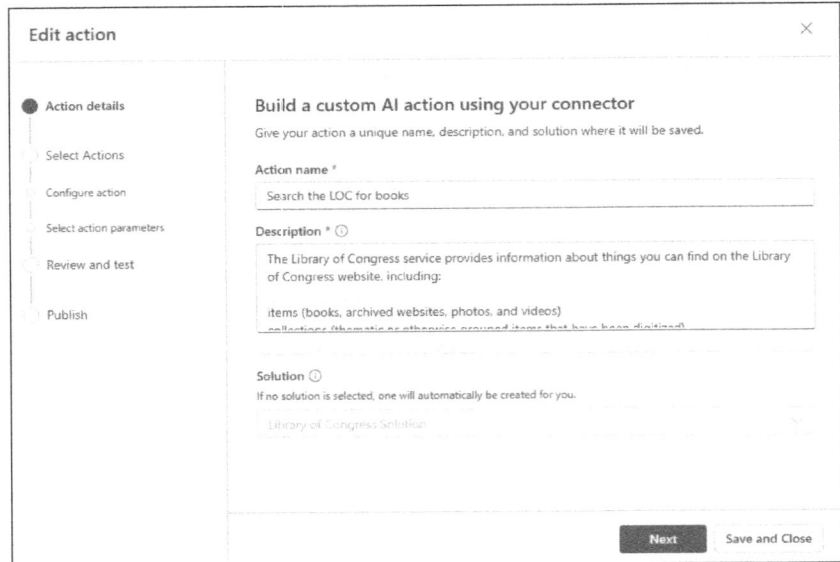

Edit action

Action details

Select Actions

Configure action

Select action parameters

Review and test

Publish

Build a custom AI action using your connector

Give your action a unique name, description, and solution where it will be saved.

Action name *

Search the LOC for books

Description * ⓘ

The Library of Congress service provides information about things you can find on the Library of Congress website, including:

items (books, archived websites, photos, and videos)

Solution ⓘ

If no solution is selected, one will automatically be created for you.

Library of Congress Solution

Next   Save and Close

8. **Still on the Action Details screen, leave the Solution blank, since this is the first action you're creating using the Library of Congress connector.**

9. **Click the Next button.**

10. **Choose the action named Search by Format for Items on the next screen, then click Next.**

11. **The next screen shows the inputs and outputs for the action. You don't need to change anything on this screen. Just click Next.**

    Your new custom action will be saved (which may take a minute or so), and you may need to click the Next button again when it finishes saving.

    If you now see the screen shown in Figure 5-4, you've successfully created a connector action! There are just a couple more steps before you publish it as a plugin.

12. **Click the New Connection link.**

    A connection will make the action available in Microsoft 365 Copilot.

13. **Click the Create button on the preview window that pops up.**

14. **Select the new connection you created from the drop-down menu then click the Test Action button.**

    Copilot Studio will get the plugin ready to be tested in Copilot. When it's ready, you'll see a link named Open to Test.

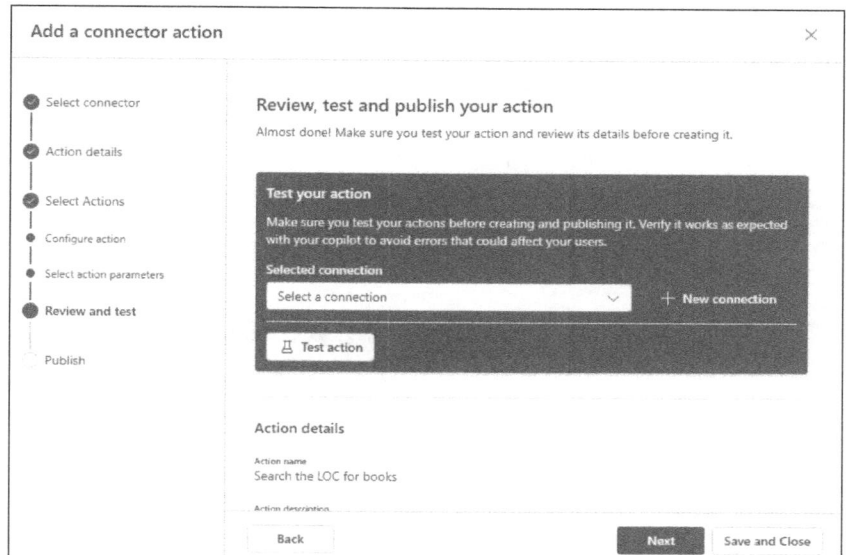

FIGURE 5-4:
Your first action is
saved and almost
ready to test.

15. **Click the Open to Test link.**

Copilot will launch Copilot.

16. **Click the Manage Copilot Extensions (or Plugins) in Copilot and look for your test plugin.**

Its name will start with "Test," as shown in Figure 5-5.

17. **Make sure the test plugin is enabled, and then test your custom plugin by entering something like** Search the Library of Congress for items about cheese.

TIP

In my experiments with this plugin, asking for "items" in the prompt seemed to work better than asking for "books." This may be due to the words that are used in the connector's description.

If everything works, you can return to Copilot Studio and click the Next button to publish your connector action.

TIP

Many factors influence whether a Copilot plugin works as you expect it to. If you don't get the results you're expecting, try changing the plugin's description, try out a different action from the same plugin to see if that one works, change the prompt you're testing with, or just wait an hour and try again to see if the problem is outside of your control.

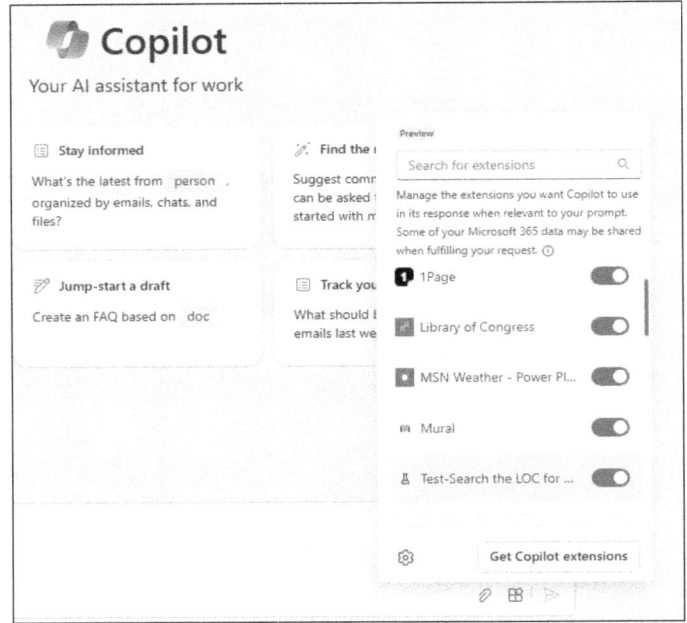

FIGURE 5-5:
Your test plugin is
now installed.

When you enable the connector action, it will be available to you whenever you use Microsoft 365 Copilot in Teams. You can also share your plugin with other people in your organization.

**TECHNICAL
STUFF**

Want to make your plugin available to anyone in the world? At the time of this writing, there isn't a process in Copilot Studio for doing that. However, it may be possible in the future. Because of the possibility of security or privacy concerns, publishing plugins for the world to find and install will likely require additional testing and approval.

Seeing Examples of Plugins

In the personal version of Microsoft Copilot 365, you can select up to three plugins to enable at a time from the list of plugins that appears when you open the Plugins sidebar, as shown in Figure 5-6.

In the work or educational version of Copilot, the account administrator can enable additional plugins using the integrated apps settings in the Microsoft 365 Admin Center, as shown in Figure 5-7, or you can create plugins for your own use, as you read about in this chapter.

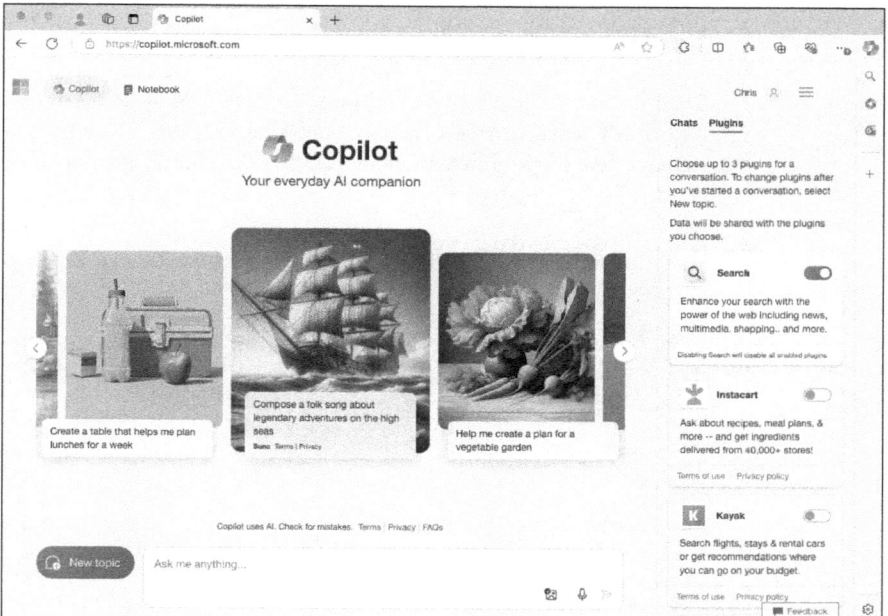

FIGURE 5-6:
The Plugins
sidebar.

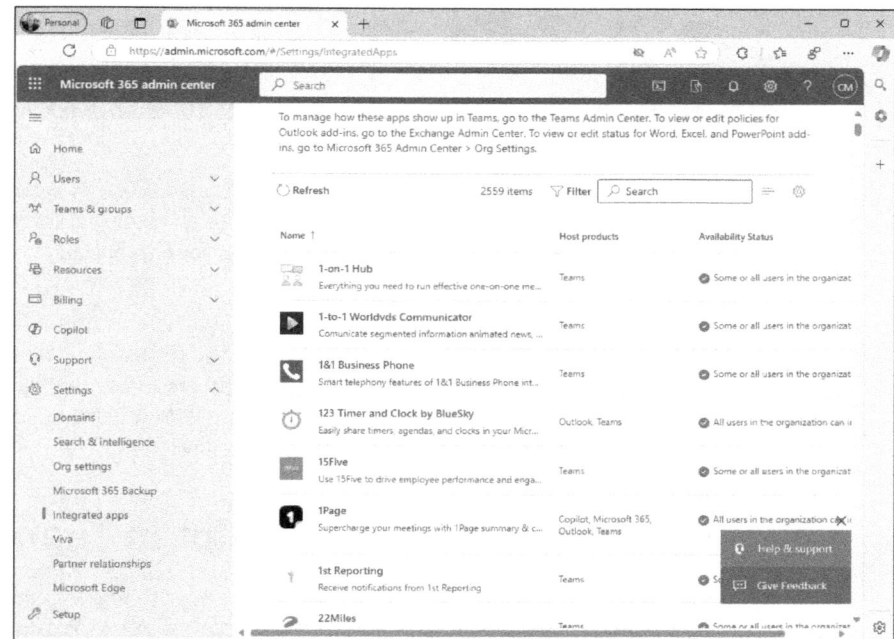

FIGURE 5-7:
The integrated
apps settings in
Microsoft 365.

CHAPTER 5 **Expanding Copilot's Capabilities with Plugins** 713

Where can plugins be used?

The big picture of plugins is still developing, and figuring out where plugins work and don't work can be confusing. In this section, I attempt to make a comprehensive list of the places where plugins do and do not work (at the time of this writing):

>> Copilot in Microsoft Office applications (for macOS and Windows) can't use plugins.

>> With the free version of Copilot (at https://copilot.microsoft.com) you can enable up to three plugins selected from a short list of API plugins (refer to Figure 5-6).

>> Subscribers to Copilot Pro can use the same group of plugins as free users of the free version.

>> Subscribers to Microsoft 365 Copilot can't use the plugins that are available to free users or Copilot Pro users.

>> On Windows PCs, Microsoft 365 Copilot subscribers can enable the Web Content plugin when they're using the Work chat at https://copilot.microsoft.com.

>> In Microsoft 365 apps, subscribers to Microsoft 365 Copilot can enable the Web Content plugin, which gives Copilot access to Bing.

>> If you create your own Copilot agents, which you learn about in Chapter 4 of this book, those agents can't use plugins.

>> Microsoft 365 Copilot Chat in Teams has access to custom agents created by people in your organization, and you can use an extensive list of extensions as well as custom plugins that you or others in your organization create.

Is your head spinning from trying to figure out where and when plugins work? Mine, too. I expect this will get smoother in the future, but for now, the best way to experiment with the widest variety of plugins is to use the free version of Copilot at https://copilot.microsoft.com along with a work or school subscription to Microsoft 365 Copilot Chat in Teams (aka BizChat).

Popular plugins for Copilot in Teams

Message extensions in Microsoft Teams are a way to allow Teams users to interact with other apps by clicking a button or typing in the Teams search bar. With a Microsoft 365 Copilot subscription, message extensions can be used as Copilot plugins.

When Copilot is enabled in Teams, not only can human users of Teams use these enabled message extensions, but Copilot can, too!

The possibilities for things that can be done with this capability are enormous. In this section, you learn about some of the more popular Copilot extensions that you can enable in Teams. But I only have space to touch on a few out of the hundreds of message extensions that have been created.

You can explore available Copilot extensions in Teams by clicking the Manage Extensions icon in the prompt input area of the Copilot chat in Teams.

In the menu that opens when you click the Manage Extensions button, you'll see a button labeled Get Copilot Extensions, as shown in Figure 5-8.

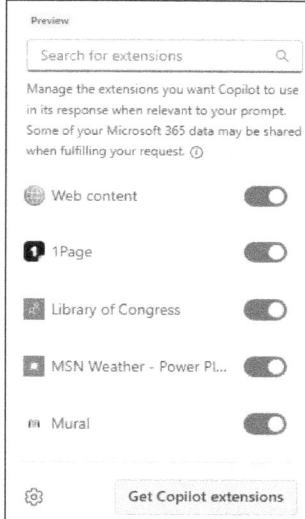

FIGURE 5-3: Get Copilot extensions.

Clicking this button opens the Teams app store, where you can explore all the available apps for Teams. Since we're only exploring Copilot Extensions at this point, I recommend you click the Filter link in the upper-right corner of the screen and narrow down the choices, as shown in Figure 5-9.

A few of the more popular Copilot Extensions in Teams include

>> **Mural.** Mural is a visual collaboration tool that allows teams to work together in a digital whiteboard environment. The Mural Copilot Extension allows you to ask Copilot questions about projects you're working on in Mural, ask for template recommendations, and search your projects.

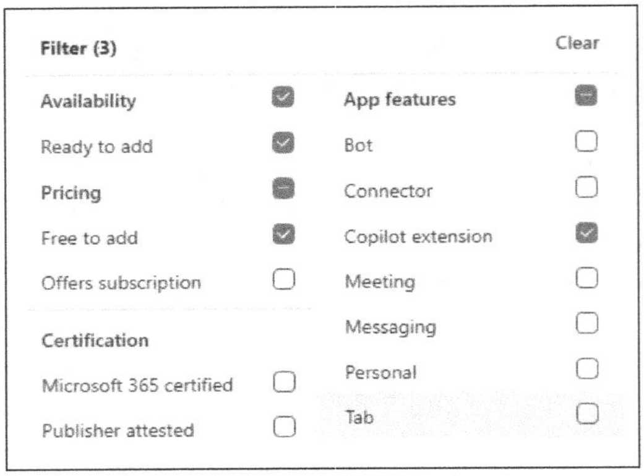

FIGURE 5-9:
Filtering the
apps.

>> **Dropbox.** Dropbox is a popular cloud file storage and sharing app. With the Dropbox extension enabled, you can share, upload, search, and preview files in Dropbox from within Teams and ask Copilot about files you've stored in Dropbox.

>> **Monday.com.** Monday.com is a project management tool. When you install the Monday.com extension, you gain the ability to use many of Monday.com's features from within Teams and to ask Copilot questions about your projects.

Considering the Future of Plugins

Plugins give Copilot access to data outside of the data it was trained on. The idea is simple, but the potential for changing how you work is impressive. Of course, there's always a downside, and plugins can be fickle and unpredictable. The key to using plugins at this early stage of development is to be patient, understand what they can and can't do, and know when the job you want to do would be better accomplished using a traditional tool such as a search engine.

Index

A

A* search, 54
ad campaigns, 644
Adams, Douglas (author), 42
Adidas, 339
ADKAR model, 324–325
Adobe Firefly, 43, 345
Adobe Photoshop, 379
Adobe Sensei, 375
Adobe Target, 376
adversarial games, 54–55
Agilisium, 165
Ahrefs, 414, 417, 650–651
AI chaining, 397
AI Dungeon, 401
AI effect, 48
AI for Good, 114
AI Governance Alliance, 113
AI Partnership for Defense, 113
AI-complete problem, 50
Airbus, 339
AIVA, 378
Alan Turing Internet Scrapbook
    (website), 14
Alexa, 77
algorithms, 28–30, 29–30, 47–58
alpha-beta pruning, 55
AlphaGo, 54, 62–63
AlphaGo Zero, 63
Amper Music, 378
Amtrak, 673
analogizers, 20
Anju, 460
Anthropic, 163
API plug-ins, 708
application programming
    interface (APIs), 167, 708
application-specific integrated
    circuits (ASICs), 73, 75
ARIA (AI Research Assistant), 384
Artbreeder, 379
Arthrobot, 457
artificial general intelligence
    (AGI), 138
artificial intelligence (AI)
  adoption of
    benefits of, 319
    models for, 322–327
    organizational culture
      aligning with, 319–320
    overcoming resistance to,
      327–332
    overview, 317–318
    roadmap for, 320–322
    stakeholders, 318–319
  categories, 17–18
  computing system for, 22–23
  defining
    by discerning intelligence,
      10–13
    four ways, 13–16
    overview, 1, 9–10, 82
  history of, 18
  hype and overestimation,
    avoiding, 20–22
  for ideation and planning
    hallucinations and, 339–342
    overview, 335–336
    real-world examples,
      338–339
    steps for idea generation,
      342–345
    tools for idea generation,
      345–347
    Wharton study, 336–338
  overview, 1
  strong vs. weak, 17
  uses of, 19–20
artificial neural networks
    (ANNs), 82
assumptions, 604–605
Atlantic Council's GeoTech
    Center, 112
Atomwise, 461
attention, 194
AudioCraft, 144
Author's Guild v. Google case,
    33–34
Authors.ai, 401
Autodesk, 375
automated data collection, 33
automation, 19
autonomous AI agents, 169
Autonomous Health, 460
autonomous learning
    systems, 47
AWS (Amazon Web
    Services), 165

B

back end, 611
backset navigator pair
    programming style, 537
backward chaining, 61
Barkeley, Edmund Callis
    (writer), 1
Bayes, Thomas, 91
Bayesians, 20
Beatty, Joy, 605
BenchSci, 384
BERT, 95
BertViz tool, 93–95
best-first search, 53–54
biased data, 40, 43–44

big data, 26, 27
Bilal, Mushtaq, 384
Bing Chat, 191
bio-inspired sensors, 77
blind search, 53
BMW, 378
bodily-kinesthetic intelligence, 11
boilerplate codes, 523–529
Bombe machine, 68
books, writing with GenAI, 399–401
botnets, 45, 45–46
brain imaging, 15
Brainwave, 75
branch nodes, 50
Brandwatch, 653
breadcrumb navigation, 410
breadth-first search (BFS), 53
Bridges, William, 326
Bridges Transition Model, 326
Brightedge, 417
business communications, 390–391
Butterfly Network, 461
BuzzStream, 414
BuzzSumo, 417, 652

C

caching, 69
Canva, 379
Capterra, 351
Caption Health, 458
case studies, 645
Catanzaro, Bryan, 71
chain-of-thought prompting, 577–579
CharacTour, 401
charts, 258–261
ChatBot, 128
Chatbotly, 679
chatbots. *See also* conversational AI chatbots

coding with
    ChatGPT, 582–588
    GitHub Copilot, 578–582
    OpenAI platform, 588–599
creating assets using, 644–645
delivering info to customer using, 644–645
Chatfuel, 678
ChatGPT. *See also* OpenAI
    account versions of, 176
    chatting with, 582–588
    vs. conversational AI chatbots, 667–668
    email assistance with, 351
    GPT minis, selecting, 184–185
    GPT model, selecting, 182–183
    integrating with other software, 167–168
    managing chat history on, 219
    memory
        adding information to, 214–216
        guidelines on limits of, 217–218
        manipulating, 216–219
        testing, 218–219
    overview, 128, 175, 582–583
    prompts
        chained, 212–214
        image inputs in, 208–214
        pictures as inputs, 209
        random brilliant thoughts as inputs, 209–212
    pros and cons of, 187
    rendering outputs to final forms, 185–186
    setting custom instructions
        overview, 584–588
        telling GPT about yourself, 585–586
        telling GPT your expectations, 586–588
    setting up individual account with, 176–178, 583–584
    signing up for, 583–584

text outputs in, 144
    for translation, 422
    user interface, 178–182
    vs. Wharton MBA students, 336–338
ChatGPT 4o (omni), 145
checkers (game), 55
Chen, Tianshi, 72
chess, 62
churn, 638, 644
citations, 394–396
Claude, 405
Clearscope, 417
Clippy (Office Assistant), 193
cloud AI tools, 168
CNET, 408–409
Coca-Cola, 339, 373
coding with AI
    benefits of, 519–545
    blending manually written and AI-generated code
        few-shot prompting on server, 617–620
        follow-up prompts, 615
        improving client, 621–624
        moving logic from AI to client, 624–626
        testing server, 615–617
        writing prompt, 611–612
        writing server, 612–614
    chatbots for, 571–599
    code learning, 536
    generating boilerplate codes
        crafting CRUD with AI, 523–529
        letting AI write template, 520–523
        overview, 519–520
        spotting task to automate, 520
    generating code from SRS, 608–610
    linting, 534–535
    pair programming, 537–545

project requirements, 601–608

static code analysis, 534–535

syntax assistance, 529–533

tips and tricks for code generation, 627–629

tools for, 547–569

Cohere, 164

college expenses, 499–500

COMPAS software, 44

complex analysis, 19

concept drift, 221

conflict resolution, 61

Connected Papers, 390

connectionists, 20

constraints, 605

containers, 165

content generation, 20

ContextMinds, 346

conversational AI chatbots. *See also* chatbots

vs. automated response systems, 669–670

benefits of, 668–669

best practices, 676–677

capabilities of, 666–667

vs. ChatGPT, 667–668

constructing, 670

hybrid model, 675–676

integrating into existing systems, 673–674

options for creating, 678–679

overview, 665–666

personalizing customer interactions with, 674–675

ROI on, 671–673

convolutional neural networks (CNNs), 91

Copilot. *See* GitHub Copilot; Microsoft Copilot

Copilot agents. *See also* Microsoft Copilot

building with Copilot Studio, 681–685

creating by prompting, 686–688

overview, 681

plug-ins, 705–716

publishing, 703–704

templates for, 688–689

testing and editing, 690–703

Copy.ai, 377

CoSchedule, 378

creative assets

enhancing

adding and modifying content, 372

audio, 371–372

images, 371

videos, 372

illustrations, 364–365

overview, 363–364

tools and techniques for, 373–377

visual assets, 365–370, 379–380

creative intelligence, 12

creative thinking, 116–117

CRUD (creating, reading, updating, deleting), 523–529

CUDA, 71

customer data platform (CPD), 656

customer journey

AI tools for, 637–638

chatbots and virtual assistants, 644–645

content delivery, 646–647

overview, 633–634

personalization of, 635–637

predictive analytics, 642–644

recommendation engines, 640–642

sentimental analysis, 638–640

stages of, 634–635

touch points, 635

customer service, 19

D

da Vinci Surgical System, 458

DALL-E 2, 143

DALL-E 3, 379

data

acquisition of, 41–43

algorithms and, 28–30

analysis of, 47, 250

automated data collection, 33

big, 26, 27

cleaning, 248–249

converting to table, 241–242

drift, 221

ethical collection of, 33

finding, 26–30

formatting, 245–246

human input, 31–33

inference, avoiding, 34

from internet, 27–28

labeled, 90

manicuring, 35–37

misalignments, 36–37

missing, 35–36

mistruths in

bias, 40

commission, 38

frame of reference, 41

omission, 38–39

overview, 37–38

perspective, 39–40

opening and cleaning, 257

overview, 25–26

record, 35

reliable, 31

security of

biased data, 43–44

botnets and, 45–46

data-source corruption, 44–45

overview, 43

separating useful data from other, 37

data (continued)
  sorting, 247–248
  sources of, 30,
    corruption of, 44–45
    free data, 240–241
    overview, 30
  structured, 26, 240
  types, changing, 246–247
  unstructured, 26, 239
  visualizing, 256–261
data analytics, 237
Data.gov, 240
Datahub.io, 241
dataset, 35
decision trees, 90
Deep Dream Generator, 379
Deep Genomics, 460
deep learning, 29–30, 82
deep learning processors (DLPs), 71–74
DeepMind, 54, 62, 163–164
Defense Advanced Research Projects Agency (DARPA), 74
demand models, 86
DENDRAL, 59–60
density, 69
depth-first search (DFS), 53
Descript, 376
DianNoa chips, 72
digital assistants, 48
digital rights management (DRM), 67
digital watermarks, 103–104
DIRECT model, 326–327
Dirichlet, Peter Gustav Lejeune, 91
display adapter, 70
DistilBERT, 95
domain requirements, 602
driver-navigator pair programming style, 537
Dropbox, 716

E
economic constraints, 605
education, AI in
  AI detection tools and, 466
  aiding overworked educators, 472–474
  changing how subjects are taught, 474
  collaborative learning, 475–476
  drawbacks of banning, 478–480
  flipping of teaching model, 470–471
  nuanced approach in, 479
  overview, 465–466
  preparing students for future, 479–480
  role in school and work, 467
  safer spaces for learning, 474–475
  shift in educator roles due to, 468–470
  special education, 476–477
  student progress tracking, 478
  use in tutoring, testing, and updating curriculum, 468
  using GenAI tools for efficiency, 477–478
Electra, 95
emails
  AI as assistant for writing, 350–352
  campaigns, 645
  emailing with Copilot, 352–361
  overview, 349
  prompts for, 352
  using GenAI with discernment, 362
EmailTree, 351
embedded systems, 168
Emmons, Ethel, 673
emojis, 437–438
emoticons, 437–438

emotional intelligence (EQ), 114
engagement metrics, 672
engineering models, 86
Enlitic, 457
environmental sensors, 77
ephemeral processing, 558
Epic Systems, 308
estate planning, 511–515
evolutionaries, 20
exoskeletons, 451–452
expert systems, 59–62
eye-gaze systems, 454

F
feature writing, 397–398
Federal Drug Administration (FDA), 448
few-shot prompting, 576–577, 617–618
field programmable gate arrays (FPGAs), 75
financial models, 86
financial planning, stages of, 492–496
first-order logic, 60
forward chaining, 61
frame interpolation, 372
frame-of-reference mistruth, 41
fraud detection, 19
functional requirements, 603–604
fuzzy logic, 61

G
Gardner, Howard (psychologist), 11
Gartner, 646
Gemini, 145
General AI, 138
generative adversarial networks (GANs), 335

generative AI (GenAI). *See also*
   artificial intelligence (AI)
vs. artificial general
   intelligence, 138
autonomous AI agents, 169
big secret to working with,
   136–138
content originality/excellence
   applying journalistic ethics,
      106–109
   joining the responsible AI
      movement, 110–114
   maintaining quality
      standards, 105–106
   overview, 101–102
   strategies for, 102–103
defined, 134
effects of
   on interpersonal skills, 489
   overview, 488
   protecting yourself from, 490
   on thinking skills, 489
in finance, 310–311
in healthcare
   applications, 309–310
   identifying useful use
      cases, 307
in human resources, 295–296
integration with other
   software, 167–168
in IT operations, 312–313
in journalism
   checking chat history, 307
   exploring politics and current
      issues, 303
   organizing notes, 304–306
   overview, 302
   pitching stories, 304–306
   preparing interview
      questions, 306
   prompting for facts, figures,
      and summaries, 303–304
   translations, 306

keeping up with
   advancements on
   adopting an agile mindset,
      172–173
   community engagement, 171
   educational resources,
      171–172
   ethical considerations, 173
   by following leaders, 170–171
   investing in architecture, 173
   research papers, 171
   by upskilling, 172
key players in, 162–166
in legal
   drafting and editing legal
      documents, 298–300
   drafting client responses or
      legal arguments, 301–302
   overview, 297
   researching for legal
      precedents and
      statutes, 301
limitations of
   accuracy issues, 98–99
   lack of common sense, 98
   language models are wordy,
      97–98
   limited knowledge, 98
   mathematics, 96–97
   overview, 139
   potential for bias, 99
in marketing
   analyzing customer data,
      294–295
   creating general to detailed
      content, 294
   overview, 293
models, 95–96, 143–145
myths vs. reality, 147–148
new businesses based on,
   313–315
overview, 82, 133–134
parameters, 96, 134–135

practical applications of
   problem-solving with creative
      projects, 234–236
   visual assistant, 231–232
   writing assistant, 225–231
practical uses of, 145–147
prompts, 140–142
real-world use of
   confirmation bias and,
      487–488
   as knowledge assistants,
      484–485
   limitations of information
      from AI, 487
   misinformation and
      manipulation, 485–486
   overview, 481
   search engine optimization,
      482–484
   using varied information
      sources, 488
services and solutions,
   166–167
vs. virtual assistants,
   135–136
as visual assistant
   generating visual content,
      232–233
   graphic design and visual
      arts, 232
   visual creativity, 234
as writing assistant
   drafting content, 227–230
   enhancing creativity in
      writing, 230–231
   generating ideas, 226–227
   overview, 225–226
generative pre-trained
   transformers (GPTs), 183
defined, 182
latest release, 183
model options, 182–183
Genpact, 165

GitHub Copilot
  agents, 580
  best practices, 549–553
  chatting with, 579–582
  installing, 547–548
  keyboard shortcuts, 554
  vs. Microsoft Copilot, 190
  overview, 547
  slash commands in,
    579–580
GitHub Global Campus, 540
Global Index on Responsible
  AI, 112
Global Partnership on Artificial
  Intelligence (GPAI), 113, 114
Go (game), 62
Google
  algorithms, 29–30
  AutoDraw, 345
  Books, 34
  Brain, 71
  dataset search (website), 240
  DeepMind, 54, 62, 163–
    164, 460
  Health, 460
  mT5, 422
  overview, 165
  Tensor, 72
  Trends, 412, 417
  Workspace, 352
GPT-2, 95
GPT-3, 95
GPT-4, 95, 405, 413
Gradio, 595
Grammarly, 352, 390, 401
Graphcore, 75
graphics processing units
  (GPUs), 67–71
graphs
  creating, 258–259
  defined, 50
  nodes, 51–52
  traversing, 52–53
greedy search, 54

H

hallucinations
  causes of, 339–340
  described, 138, 338
  non-traditional storytelling
    from, 340–341
  testing and experimentation
    with, 341
  unexpected ideas and
    concepts from, 340
hardware
  deep learning processors,
    71–74
  GPUs, 67–71
  Harvard architecture, 67
  increasing capabilities of
    ASICs, 75
    FPGAs, 75
    interactions with
      environment, 78–79
    neuromorphic computing,
      75–76
    overview, 74–75
    quantum processors, 76
    sensors, 76–78
  specialized processing
    environment, 74
  standard, 65–67
  von Neumann architecture, 66
Harnad's Total Turing Test, 14
Harvard architecture, 67
Hauppauge 4860, 70
headers, adding context to,
  242–245
heatmapping, 416
Hemingway, 390
Herr, Hugh, 79
heuristic search, 53–54,
  55–58
heuristics, 49
hidden Markov models
  (HMMs), 91
hill climbing, 57
Hintze, Arend, 17

*Hitchhiker's Guide to the Galaxy,
  The* (Adams), 42
Huawei, 72
HubSpot, 352
Hugging Face, 95, 163, 422
HuggingChat, 144
human acts, 14
human interaction, AI-enhanced
  in communication
    automating language
      translation, 438–439
    emojis and emoticons,
      437–438
    incorporating body language,
      439–450
    overview, 436–437
  exchanging ideas
    by augmenting
      communication, 440–441
    by creating connections, 440
    by defining trends, 441
  in human sensory perception
    augmentation, 443–444
    shift in data spectrum, 443
    multimedia use, 441–442
    overview, 435–436
human process, 16
human thoughts, 15
Humbly, Clive
  (mathematician), 237
hype, sources of, 21–22
HyperWrite, 346

I

IBM TrueNorth chip, 75–76
IEEE Global Initiative on Ethics of
  Autonomous and Intelligent
  Systems, 114
Imagen, 143
Imitation Game (movie), 68
Imitation Game (test), 1
inference engine, 60
information retrieval AI, 137
informed (heuristic) search, 53

InnovateTech, 331–332
Intel 80860 chip, 70
Intel Loihi chip, 75–76
intelligence
  discerning, 10–11
  mental activities list for, 10
  process of, 10–11
  types of, 11–13
intelligence augmentation
  (IA), 444
Intellisense, 530
interface constraints, 605
International Electrotechnical
  Commission (IEC), 113
International Organization for
  Standardization (ISO), 113
internet of things (IoT), 27
intrapersonal/interpersonal
  intelligence, 12
introspection, 15
Iris.ai, 383
iterative prompting, 151

J

Jasper, 128, 346, 376, 377, 413
Jintronix, 449
Job Access With Speech
  (JAWS), 453
job security
  becoming an early adopter,
    128–129
    using AI for thought
      leadership, 129
  career transitions
    adapting to new realities,
      125–126
    shifting professional
      landscapes, 126–127
    steering clear of pitfalls,
      127–128
  skills inventory and gap
    analysis, 120–121
  tasks that AI can't replace
    creative and strategic
      thinking, 115–117

emotional intelligence and
  human interaction, 116
jobs of the future, 118
new roles that use AI, 119
overview, 115
translating current skills into
  AI-proof roles
  AI-resilient career journey,
    124–125
  overview, 121
  role evolution and
    adaptation, 123–124
  skill transferability analysis,
    122–123
  upskilling for AI-proof jobs,
    119–121
Jukebox, 144

K

Kaggle, 240
key performance indicators
  (KPIs), 661–662
keyword analysis, 650–651
KFC, 424
Klaviyo, 656
knowledge assistants, 484–485
Krizhevsky, Alex, 71
K'Watch, 447

L

labeled data, 90
Laird, Philip Johnson
  (researcher), 15
large language models (LLMs)
  defined, 134
  multilingual, 421–422
  parameters, 134
  temperature, 220
  weights, 220–221
latency, 69
latent Dirichlet allocation
  (LDA), 91
lead generation, 672

leaf nodes, 50
Let's Enhance, 376
life cycle constraints, 605
limited memory, 17
linguistic intelligence, 12
Link Explorer, 415
linters, 534
LivePerson, 679
local search, 55–58
localization and translation
  AI tools for, 424–426
  applying AI'S capabilities in,
    423–424
  core strategies in
    cultural adaptation tools, 427
    enhancing efficiency, 428
    leveraging machine learning,
      426–427
    quality control, 428–429
  cultural context, 420–421
  multilingual large language
    models for, 421–422
  overview, 419–420
  real-time, 429–432
logical-mathematical
  intelligence, 13
logistic regression, 90
long-form content
  academic papers, 382–388
  books, 399–401
  citations and references,
    394–396
  feature writing, 397–398
  long-form articles, 396–399
  overview, 381
  research designs and outlines,
    391–394
  white papers and reports,
    388–391
long-tail keywords, 410
Lovelace test 2.0, 14
low-order polynomial time,
  53–54
Lumen5, 377, 380

M

machine efficiency, 20

machine learning
cloud-based, 168
defined, 82
fairness, 62–63
models, 86
overview, 43–44

Machines Who Think (McCorduck), 48

Magisto, 377

Mailbutler, 352

Mailshake, 414

Majestic, 414

Manychat, 678

Marcus test, 14

MarketMuse, 413, 417

Markov, Andrey, 91

Mass General Brigham, 308

master algorithm, 20

Mattel, 338–339

McCorduck, Pamela (author), 48

medicine, AI in
bias/sympathy/empathy and, 450
devising new surgical techniques, 457–459
diagnosis, 454–455
disruptions for medical professionals, 462–463
exoskeletons, 451–452
games for therapy, 449
hardware augmentation, 453–454
overview, 445–446
portable patient monitoring, 445–449
semiautonomous robots, 462
software-based solutions, 453
for special needs, 452–453
for task automation
creating better medications, 461–462

medical records, 460
overview, 459–460
predictive software, 460
safer procedures, 461
telepresence, 455–457

memory speed, 69

Meta, 422

metadata, 104

microservices architecture, 168

Microsoft
Azure AI, 166
Brainwave, 75
collaboration with Epic Systems, 308
Tay chatbot, 99
Turing Multilingual Language Model, 422

Microsoft 365 Copilot, 194–195, 352

Microsoft Copilot
core functionalities and benefits, 192
eligibility criteria, 196
emailing with
drafting emails, 356–358
email coaching, 359–360
overview, 352–353
reply suggestions, 359
summarizing email threads, 353–355
summarizing long emails, 355

Excel, using in
automating data analysis, 250–253
creating formulas, 253–256
limitations of, 261
preparing data, 241–249
visualizing data, 256–261
working data, 239–241

features, 192
vs. GitHub Copilot versus, 191
history, 189–191
how it works, 193–194

installing on code editor, 538–540
integration with Microsoft 365 apps, 194–195
key differentiators from other assistants, 192–193
meeting management with, 361
overview, 145, 187, 190, 191

PowerPoint, interacting in
built-in actions, 264–265
built-in prompts, 273–276
defining and refining topics, 265–266
designing slides with Designer, 271
evaluating generated content, 269
evaluating generated design, 269–270
evaluating generated presentation, 268
evaluating use of images, 270
organizing presentations, 277
personalizing ideas, 267–268
practicing with Copilot feedback, 277–279
redesigning slides, 272

prompting and interacting with, 201–202
signing up for, 195–201
subscription plans and pricing, 196–198

Teams, using in
accessing post-meeting summaries, 288–290
limitations of, 290–291
preparing for meetings, 283–286
real-time meeting assistance, 286–288
setting up meetings, 283–286

Microsoft Copilot Studio
Agent Editor, 691–703
configuring generative AI, 690

demo, 682–684

home page, 682, 685

overview, 678

virtual assistant, 682–684

Microsoft Teams, 714–716

Midjourney, 143, 164, 380

minimum intelligent signal test, 14

min-max approximation, 54

Moderna, 308

Monday.com, 716

Moov monitor, 446, 447

Moz, 413, 415, 552

Moz Pro, 417

multithreading, 70

Mural, 715

MYCIN, 59–60. *See also* expert systems

N

naïve Bayes classifiers, 90

National AI Initiative (NAII), 113

natural language, 102

naturalistic intelligence, 13

natural-language generation (NLG), 87

natural-language processing (NLP), 87–91, 134, 427

natural-language understanding (NLU), 87

neural machine translation (NMT), 427

neural networks, 82–86

neural processing units (NPUs), 72

Neural Radiance Fields (NeRFs), 144

Neurala Inc., 74

neuromorphic computing, 75–76

neurons, 82

Ng, Andrew, 71

NightCafe Studio, 380

nodes, 50–51

non-functional requirements, 604–605

NP-complete problems, 49–50

numerical vectors, 93

Nvidia, 71, 166

NVIDIA A100 GPU, 71

O

OECD, 114

Oncora Medical, 461

online business growth with AI

analyzing competitors' strategies

ad spending, 652

keywords, 650–651

social media performance, 653

traffic sources, 651–652

enhancing brand building, 653–655

generating creative concepts, 663

maximizing conversions

by audience segmentation, 655–657

by personalizing content, 657

refining innovation, 663

scaling paid advertising ROI, 657–660

tracking key performance indicators, 661–662

trend forecasting, 662

OpenAI

API

accessing, 588–589

adjusting model's settings, 592–593

API key, 593

Chat mode, 590–591

checking credits, 589–590

developing chatbots, 595–599

playing roles, 592

running examples, 591–592

ChatGPT 4o (omni), 134

Codex, 144, 189–190

GPT-2, 95

GPT-3, 95, 134, 189

GPT-4, 95, 422

overview, 163

operation, 48

Optimizely, 413

output stitching, 397

overestimation, 22

overfitting, 87, 221

P

paid advertising, 652, 657–660

pair programming. *See also* coding with AI

installing Copilot for, 538–540

pros and cons of, 537–538

styles, 537

using prompts to create trivia game, 540–545

PaLM 2, 144

parameters, GenAI, 134–135

Partnership on AI (PAI), 114

pathfinding algorithm, 58

peaks, 57

performance constraints, 605

Perplexity AI, 406

personally identifiable information, 34

physical augmentation, 444

Pictory, 346

ping-pong pair programming style, 537

plateaus, 57

policy network, 63

portable patient monitoring, 446–449

"The Portrait of Edmond de Belamy," 335

predictive analytics, 642–644

prefeteching, 69

Primo.ai, 72

processor caching, 69

professional documents, 389–390

Project Music GenAI Control, 144

Prometheus, 194

prompt, 571

prompts and prompting
 adding data to prompts, 208–214
 adjusting temperature, 572–573
 avoiding pitfalls, 158–160
 creating effective, 154–155
 for domain-specific applications, 154–155
 elements of prompts, 574–576
 for email, 352
 guiding GenAI responses with, 152–153
 iterative prompting, 151
 Microsoft Copilot, 201–202
 open-ender *vs.* closed-ended, 575
 outputs, 203–207
 overview, 140–142, 149–150, 192
 prompt chaining, 151, 212–214
 for providing models with supplemental data, 157–158
 tips and tricks, 156–157, 578
 types of, 575–578

Prosci, 322

ProWritingAid, 390, 401

psychological testing, 15

PUMA system, 458

Python, 597

Q

quantum bits (qubits), 76

quantum processors, 76

quantum sensors, 77

QuickMail, 352

R

Ragno, Marco (researcher), 15

random access memory (RAM), 69

RankBrain, 39

rational acts, 16

rational process, 16

rational thoughts, 16

reactive machines, 17

recommendation engines, 640–642

recurrent neural networks (RNNs), 91, 92

Recursion Pharmaceuticals, 462

references, 394–396

reinforcement learning, 63

Replit, 559–569

research and academic writing
 academic publication process, 387–388
 overview, 382–383
 pitfalls or AI limitations, 386–387
 refining outputs, 384–386
 tools for, 383–384

research projects, 391–394

Research Rabbit, 383

resolution rate, 672

Resoomer, 390

Responsible AI Institute, 113

responsible AI movement, 110–115

retirement planning, 501–511

retrieval-augmented generation, 137, 206

reverse Turing test, 14

rich snippets, 410

Riffusion, 346

Rivest, Ronald, 54

RoBERTa, 95

robot soccer, 17

robotic legs, 79

robotic monitoring system, 31

Roomba, 55

root nodes, 50

Runway, 346, 376, 377, 380

S

safety systems, 20

sales conversions, 671–672

Salesforce's Einstein, 413

Samsung, 72

Sanebox, 352

sanitization technique, 34

scheduling, 19

schema markups, 409–410

scientific models, 86

SciWriter, 384

Scrivener, 390

search engine optimization (SEO)
 AI tools for, 416–417
 enhancing user experience with AI, 409–410
 maximizing
  content optimization, 413–414
  keyword and metadata search, 411–412
  link building, 414–415
  predictive SEO, 415–416
 search generative experiences, 404–405
 success strategies in the AI era, 406–408
 use of GenAI in, 482–484

search generative experiences, 404–405

Segment Personas, 656–657

self-attention, 92–93

self-awareness, 17

self-improving systems, 47

Semantic Scholar, 383

Semrush, 412, 415, 417, 650–651

sensor fusion, 77

sensors, 76–78

sentimental analysis, 638–640

Shortliffe, Edward, 59
Similarweb, 652
simulated annealing, 57
simulated neural networks (SNNs), 82
simulations, 644
singularity, 20–22
skill transferability analysis, 122–123
skills inventory and gap analysis, 120–121
Slack, 168
slash (/) commands, 579–580
social media posts, 645
software development kits (SDKs), 168
software libraries, 168
Software Requirements (Wiegers/ Beatty), 605
Sondergaard, Peter, 237
spiking neural networks (SNNs), 76
SpyFu, 417, 652
Stability AI, 163
Stable Diffusion, 143, 144, 347, 376, 380
state spaces, 50
state-space search, 50
strategic thinking, 117
Strateos, 461
structured data, 26, 240
StyleGAN 3, 143
sub-word tokenization, 93
supervised learning, 90
Surfer SEO, 417
symbologists, 20
SyNAPSE, 74
Synthesia, 128–129, 144, 347, 377
system downtime, 313

T

T5, 95
Tableau, 390

Tabnine, 555–559
taboo search, 57
Talkwalker, 653
Tardiest, Christian, 335
Tay chatbot, 99
Teams Message Extensions plug-ins, 708
telepresence, 455–457
temperature setting, 220
tensor processing unit (TPU), 72–74
TensorFlow, 72–73
tetrachromats, 77
theory of mind, 17
TheWordsmith.ai, 376
Tiger Analytics, 165
TikTok's Creative Assistant, 345–346
tokens, 93–95
touch points, 635
tour guide pair programming style, 537
transformer models, 91–95
trees, 50–51
Turbine, 461
Turing, Alan, 1, 68
Turing test, 1, 14, 15
Twiddle algorithm, 57

U

Ulrich, Karl (professor), 337
underfitting, 221
uninformed (blind search), 53
University of Kansas Life Span Institute, 308
unstructured data, 26, 239
unsupervised learning, 90
USAID's Digital Strategy, 113
user experience (UX), 409–410

V

value network, 63
VanceAI, 380

Versace, Massimiliano, 74
vertexes, 51
VidMob, 376
virtual assistants, 135–136, 644–645
Vischeck, 453
visual assets, 379–380
Visual Studio Code, 538–540
visual-spatial intelligence, 13
von Neumann architecture, 66–67
von Neumann bottleneck, 66, 69–70
von Neumann, John, 66

W

Watson, 27
wearable monitors, 447
Weichman, Gordon, 68
weight, 51
Where's Waldo? illustrations, 364–365
white papers, 388–391
Wiegers, Karl, 605
Winograd schema challenge, 14
Wondershare EdrawMind, 347
word tokenization, 93
Writer, 347, 376, 377, 413

X

XLNET, 95

Y

YAMM, 352
Yewno Discover, 390

Z

Zapier, 128
zero-shot prompting, 575–576, 608–610
Zotero, 383–384

About the Authors

Chris Minnick is a seasoned computer programmer, author, and technical instructor with more than 25 years of experience. Specializing in AI education, Chris teaches professionals globally about generative AI, prompt engineering, and how to integrate AI into their work.

Jeffrey Allan is the director of Nazareth University's Institute for Responsible Technology, where he serves as a leading voice for the advancement of responsible AI and its application across business and society.

Pam Baker is a veteran analyst, freelance journalist, and author.

Stephanie Diamond is an author and marketing management professional with more than 25 years of experience building profits in more than 75 different industries.

Sheryl Lindsell-Roberts is a business communications expert, author of 25+ books, and founder of Sheryl Lindsell-Roberts & Associates.

Luca Massaron is a data scientist and marketing research director with more than a decade of experience in multivariate statistical analysis, machine learning, and customer insights.

Paul Mladjenovic was a Certified Financial Planner (CFP) from 1985 to 2021 and is a national speaker, educator, author, and financial coach. Since 1981, he has specialized in investing, financial planning, and home business issues.

John Paul Mueller was a freelance author and technical editor. He had writing in his blood, having produced 119 books and more than 600 articles to date.

Shiv Singh, with more than 25 years of accumulating expertise in marketing and business, has been instrumental in elevating major brands through innovative marketing strategies, customer engagement mechanisms, and data-driven results.

Daniel Stanton, also known as Mr. Supply Chain, is an accomplished supply chain project manager with extensive experience across various industries and sectors.

Dedication

Dedicated to Patrick A. Minnick, mechanical engineer, master woodworker, and tinkerer. If he were here, he'd disassemble his laptop to figure out how generative AI works — and he'd be successful, too!

Author's Acknowledgments

Thank you to my editors for this project, Leah Michael (development editor) and Kelly Henthorne (copyeditor). Big projects like this wouldn't be possible without your amazing skills and attention. Thank you to everyone at Wiley who worked on this book and is mentioned below. Thank you also to my agent, Carole Jelen, and to Steve Hayes at Wiley for making this book happen.

Publisher's Acknowledgments

Executive Editor: Steve Hayes

Project Manager and Development Editor: Leah Michael

Copy Editor: Kelly Dobbs Henthorne

Production Editor: Tamilmani Varadharaj

Cover Image: © Miha Creative/Shutterstock

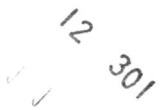